Medieval Muslim Mirrors for Princes

The 'mirror for princes' genre of literature offers advice to a ruler, or ruler-to-be, concerning the exercise of royal power and the well-being of the body politic. This anthology presents selections from the 'mirror literature' produced in the Islamic Early Middle Period (roughly the tenth to twelfth centuries CE), newly translated from the original Arabic and Persian, as well as a previously translated Turkish example. In these texts, authors advise on a host of political issues which remain compelling to our contemporary world: political legitimacy and the ruler's responsibilities, the limits of the ruler's power and the limits of the subjects' duty of obedience, the maintenance of social stability, causes of unrest, licit and illicit uses of force, the functions of governmental offices and the status and rights of diverse social groups. *Medieval Muslim Mirrors for Princes* is a unique introduction to this important body of literature, showing how these texts reflect and respond to the circumstances and conditions of their era, and of ours.

LOUISE MARLOW is Professor of Religion at Wellesley College. She is the author of *Counsel for Kings: Wisdom and Politics in Tenth-Century Iran* (2016) and *Hierarchy and Egalitarianism in Islamic Thought* (1997). She is the editor of *The Rhetoric of Biography: Narrating Lives in Persianate Societies* (2011), *Dreaming across Boundaries: The Interpretation of Dreams in Islamic Lands* (2008) and, with Beatrice Gruendler, *Writers and Rulers: Perspectives on Their Relationships from Abbasid to Safavid Times* (2004).

CAMBRIDGE TEXTS IN THE HISTORY OF POLITICAL THOUGHT

General editor
QUENTIN SKINNER
Queen Mary University of London

Editorial board
MICHAEL COOK
Princeton University
HANNAH DAWSON
King's College London
ADOM GETACHEW
University of Chicago
EMMA HUNTER
University of Edinburgh
GABRIEL PAQUETTE
University of Oregon
ANDREW SARTORI
New York University
HILDE DE WEERDT
Leiden University

Cambridge Texts in the History of Political Thought is firmly established as the major student series of texts in political theory. It aims to make available all the most important texts in the history of political thought, from ancient Greece to the twentieth century, from throughout the world and from every political tradition. All the familiar classic texts are included, but the series seeks at the same time to enlarge the conventional canon through a global scope and by incorporating an extensive range of less well-known works, many of them never before available in a modern English edition, and to present the history of political thought in a comparative, international context. Where possible, the texts are published in complete and unabridged form, and translations are specially commissioned for the series. However, where appropriate, especially for non-western texts, abridged or tightly focused and thematic collections are offered instead. Each volume contains a critical introduction together with chronologies, biographical sketches, a guide to further reading and any necessary glossaries and textual apparatus. Overall, the series aims to provide the reader with an outline of the entire evolution of international political thought.

For a list of titles published in the series, please see end of book

Medieval Muslim Mirrors for Princes

An Anthology of Arabic, Persian and Turkish Political Advice

LOUISE MARLOW
Wellesley College

CAMBRIDGE
UNIVERSITY PRESS

CAMBRIDGE
UNIVERSITY PRESS

University Printing House, Cambridge CB2 8BS, United Kingdom

One Liberty Plaza, 20th Floor, New York, NY 10006, USA

477 Williamstown Road, Port Melbourne, VIC 3207, Australia

314–321, 3rd Floor, Plot 3, Splendor Forum, Jasola District Centre,
New Delhi – 110025, India

103 Penang Road, #05–06/07, Visioncrest Commercial, Singapore 238467

Cambridge University Press is part of the University of Cambridge.

It furthers the University's mission by disseminating knowledge in the pursuit of education, learning, and research at the highest international levels of excellence.

www.cambridge.org
Information on this title: www.cambridge.org/9781108425650
DOI: 10.1017/9781108348645

First published 2023

A catalogue record for this publication is available from the British Library.

ISBN 978-1-108-42565-0 Hardback
ISBN 978-1-108-44292-3 Paperback

Sylvia and Christopher
in loving memory

Contents

List of Figures and Maps *page* xi
Preface and Acknowledgements xiii
Conventions xv
List of Abbreviations xvii

PART I INTRODUCTION 1

1 The Arabic, Persian and Turkish Mirror Literatures 3
1.1 Development 6
1.2 The Early or Formative Period (Eighth and Ninth Centuries) 7
1.3 The Early Middle Period (Tenth to Twelfth Centuries) 10
1.4 The Later Middle Period (Thirteenth to Fifteenth Centuries) 12
1.5 The Early Modern Period (Sixteenth and Early Seventeenth Centuries) 16
1.6 Reception 18

2 Contexts 24
2.1 The Early Middle Period 25
2.2 The Polities of the Tenth and Eleventh Centuries 33

3 Texts and Authors 47
3.1 Pseudo-Aristotle, *Kitāb al-Siyāsa fī tadbīr al-riyāsa* (*Sirr al-asrār*) (Arabic) 47
3.2 Pseudo-Māwardī, *Naṣīḥat al-mulūk* (Arabic) 51

3.3 Al-Thaʿālibī, *Ādāb al-mulūk* (Arabic) 54
3.4 Yūsuf Khāṣṣ Ḥājib, *Kutadgu bilig* (Karakhanid Turkish) 56
3.5 Kaykāʾūs b. Iskandar, *Qābūsnāmeh* (*Andarznāmeh*) (Persian) 59
3.6 Al-Māwardī, *Tashīl al-naẓar wa-taʿjīl al-ẓafar fī akhlāq al-malik wa-siyāsat al-mulk* (Arabic) 61
3.7 Niẓām al-Mulk, *Siyar al-mulūk* (Persian) 63
3.8 Ghazālī, Pseudo-Ghazālī, *Naṣīḥat al-mulūk* (Persian) 66
3.9 Al-Ṭurṭūshī, *Sirāj al-mulūk* (Arabic) 70

4 Editions and Translations 76
4.1 Pseudo-Aristotle, *Kitāb al-Siyāsa fī tadbīr al-riyāsa* (*Sirr al-asrār*) (Text 9) 77
4.2 Pseudo-Māwardī, *Naṣīḥat al-mulūk* (Text 1) 77
4.3 Al-Thaʿālibī, *Ādāb al-mulūk* (Texts 2 and 16) 78
4.4 Yūsuf Khāṣṣ Ḥājib, *Kutadgu bilig* (Text 6) 78
4.5 ʿUnṣur al-Maʿālī Kaykāʾūs b. Iskandar, *Qābūsnāmeh* (Text 8) 78
4.6 Al-Māwardī, *Tashīl al-naẓar wa-taʿjīl al-ẓafar fī akhlāq al-malik wa-siyāsat al-mulk* (Texts 3, 7, 10 and 13) 79
4.7 Niẓām al-Mulk, *Siyar al-mulūk* (Texts 11, 14 and 17) 79
4.8 Al-Ghazālī, *Naṣīḥat al-mulūk* (Text 4) 80
4.9 Al-Ṭurṭūshī, *Sirāj al-mulūk* (Texts 5, 12, 15 and 18) 81

PART II TEXTS 83

5 The Nature of Sovereignty 85
Text 1 Pseudo-Māwardī, *Naṣīḥat al-mulūk*. Chapter Two: On the Privileges of Kings in the Magnificence of Their Stations; and the Habits That They Are Obliged to Adopt in Their Cultivation of Virtue and Avoidance of Vice 86
Text 2 Al-Thaʿālibī, *Ādāb al-mulūk*. Chapter One: In Explication of the Exalted Status of Kings; the People's Inescapable Need for Kings, and Their Duty to Obey, Exalt and Glorify Them 109
Text 3 Al-Māwardī, *Tashīl al-naẓar wa-taʿjīl al-ẓafar*. Opening to Part II 130

Text 4 Ghazālī, Pseudo-Ghazālī, *Naṣīḥat al-mulūk*. Part II, Chapter One: On the Justice, Governance and Conduct of Kings 136
Text 5 Al-Ṭurṭūshī, *Sirāj al-mulūk*. Chapter Nine: Explication of the Position of the Ruler (*Sulṭān*) in Relation to the Subjects 139

6 The King's Person and Character 143
Text 6 Yūsuf Khāṣṣ Ḥājib, *Kutadgu bilig*. The Qualifications of a Prince 144
Text 7 Al-Māwardī, *Tashīl al-naẓar wa-taʿjīl al-ẓafar*. Part I, Chapter One 155
Text 8 Kaykāʾūs b. Iskandar, *Qābūsnāmeh*. Chapter Twenty-Eight: On Making Friends; Chapter Twenty-Nine: Regarding Enemies 167

7 Foundations of Royal Authority and Principles of Governance 180
Text 9 Pseudo-Aristotle, *Sirr al-asrār*. Third Discourse: On the Form of Justice 181
Text 10 Al-Māwardī, *Tashīl al-naẓar wa-taʿjīl al-ẓafar*. Part II, Section 186
Text 11 Niẓām al-Mulk, *Siyar al-mulūk*. Chapter Three: On the King's Sitting for the Redress of Grievances and the Practice of Fine Conduct 190
Text 12 Al-Ṭurṭūshī, *Sirāj al-mulūk*. Chapter Eleven: On Knowing the Qualities That Constitute the Pillars of the Ruler's Power, without Which It Has No Stability 203

8 The Practice of Good Governance 216
Text 13 Al-Māwardī, *Tashīl al-naẓar wa-taʿjīl al-ẓafar*. Part II, Section 217
Text 14 Niẓām al-Mulk, *Siyar al-mulūk*. Chapter Four: On the Conditions and the Continual Monitoring of Tax-Collectors and Viziers 234
Text 15 Al-Ṭurṭūshī, *Sirāj al-mulūk*. Chapter Twenty-Seven: On Consultation and Counsel 247

9 Problems in the Kingdom and Their Remedies 259
Text 16 Al-Thaʿālibī, *Ādāb al-mulūk*. Chapter Seven: On the Calamities That Befall Kings 259
Text 17 Niẓām al-Mulk, *Siyar al-mulūk*. Chapter Forty: On the King's Forgiveness of God's Creatures, May He Be Exalted and Glorified; and the Restoration to Their Proper Order of All Practices and Customs That Have Lost Their Order and Foundation 282
Text 18 Al-Ṭurṭūshī, *Sirāj al-mulūk*. Chapter Six: The Sultan Is a Debtor, Not a Creditor, in Relation to His Subjects, and He Stands to Lose, Not to Profit 309

Appendix: Index of Qurʾanic References and Quotations 313

Glossary 316

Bibliography 320

Index 357

Figures and Maps

Figures

1 Pages from a manuscript of al-Shayzarī's *al-Manhaj al-maslūk fī siyāsat al-mulūk* (also known under the title *al-Nahj al-maslūk fī siyāsat al-mulūk*), copied in 1115/1703–4; Garrett Collection, no. 138 HQ, ff. 4r, 9r (Islamic Manuscripts Collection, Manuscripts Division, Department of Special Collections, Princeton University Library) (see Hitti et al., *Descriptive Catalog of the Garrett Collection*, 256–7, no. 781). Photographs: Courtesy of Princeton University Library. *page* 20

2 Page from the manuscript *Kitap üs-siyase fi tedbir ir-riyase*, written in Ottoman Turkish and dated Muḥarram 1231 (December 1815); New Series no. 1669, f. 84v (Islamic Manuscripts Collection, Manuscripts Division, Department of Special Collections, Princeton University Library). Photograph: Courtesy of Princeton University Library. 50

3 A 'circle of justice' from a manuscript (perhaps copied in the fourteenth century) of the pseudo-Aristotelian *Kitāb al-Siyāsa fī tadbīr al-riyāsa* or *Sirr al-asrār*; MS Laud Or. 210, f. 90r (The Bodleian Libraries, University of Oxford). Photograph: Bodleian Libraries Imaging Services, The Bodleian Libraries, University of Oxford. 184

4 The two sides of a dinar issued during the reign of Sultan Maḥmūd of Ghazna, struck at Ghazna in 414/1023–4, and inscribed with the names of the Abbasid caliph al-Qādir bi-llāh

(obverse) and Yamīn al-Dawla wa-Amīn al-Milla Abū l-Qāsim [Maḥmūd] (reverse) (Ashmolean Museum, Islamic Coin HCR14556). Image © Ashmolean Museum, University of Oxford. 306

Maps

1 Western Asia and the Mediterranean in the tenth to twelfth centuries. Credit: Redrawn based on a map originally produced by Dani Henry. 2

Preface and Acknowledgements

This book consists of two parts. Part I comprises an introduction to the mirror-for-princes literature – that is, the literature of political advice – produced in Arabic, Persian and Turkish in a roughly two-century-long period. Part II offers translations of selections from nine mirrors composed or in circulation during this period.

It is a pleasure to thank Michael Cook for his kind invitation to propose this volume for inclusion in the series *Cambridge Texts in the History of Political Thought*, and Hugh Kennedy and Deborah Tor for their generous support of the project. I am grateful to the National Endowment for the Humanities, which provided support for the research that led to this book, and to Wellesley College, for approving my application for a sabbatical leave, during which I completed the major part of the project.

It is a further pleasure to thank the Israel Institute for Advanced Study (IIAS) for their graciousness in accommodating me as a remote member during the spring of 2021, and in particular Uriel Simonsohn and Luke Yarbrough, who invited me to participate in the IIAS's research group 'Cultural Brokerage in Pre-modern Islam'. The opportunity proved enriching for my studies of the mirror-for-princes literature; in particular, I profited from numerous stimulating discussions with my fellow core members, Michal Biran, Eugenio Garosi, Jessica Goldberg, Maria Mavroudi and Gregor Schwarb.

I am very grateful to Wellesley College's Dani Henry, who kindly created Map 1, which appears at the beginning of Part I. For their photographic services and permission to publish the images that appear in Figures 1–4, I wish to thank the Department of Special Collections at Princeton University Library (Figures 1 and 2); the Imaging Services

Department at the Bodleian Libraries, University of Oxford (Figure 3); and the Ashmolean Museum's Picture Library (Figure 4). Edinburgh University Press kindly granted permission for the reproduction in revised form of previously published materials (see Text 1). The earlier versions appeared in L. Marlow, *Counsel for Kings: Wisdom and Politics in Tenth-Century Iran: The Naṣīḥat al-mulūk of Pseudo-Māwardī* (Edinburgh: Edinburgh University Press, 2016) (© L. Marlow, 2016); reproduced with permission of Edinburgh University Press Limited through PLSclear. Text 6 is republished, with permission of the University of Chicago Press, from Robert Dankoff, *Wisdom of Royal Glory (Kutadgu bilig)* (© 1983 by The University of Chicago); permission conveyed through Copyright Clearance Center, Inc.

I am pleased, furthermore, to thank Angie Batson and Jamie Jesanis of the Interlibrary Loan Department at Wellesley College; their assistance in obtaining materials has been invaluable, particularly given the conditions imposed by the COVID-19 pandemic, during which I wrote most of this book. For their patience, their many forms of assistance and their consistent encouragement, I am deeply grateful to Elizabeth Friend-Smith, Atifa Jiwa and Elliot Beck, all of Cambridge University Press. Finally, I have benefited beyond measure from the practical assistance, patient forbearance and loving support of my husband and son, and I owe them, in this endeavour as in so many others, an incalculable debt of gratitude. I dedicate this book to the memory of my parents, whose house full of books and lifelong love of learning shaped and inspired me, and whose quiet striving towards fairness and compassion in the world did much to form my engagement with the subject of this book.

Conventions

As a rule, my transliterations from Arabic and Persian follow the standard scholarly system (used, for example, in the *Encyclopaedia of Islam Three*), with a small number of minor modifications. The most notable adjustments apply to transliteration from Persian, for which I use *ż* (instead of *ḍ*) for the letter *ḍād* (as in Abū l-Fażl), *v* (instead of *w*) for the letter *wāw* (as in Urmavī) and *-eh* (instead of *-a*) for final *hāʾ* (as in *Shāhnāmeh*).

Names of places and dynasties appear in their anglicised forms (Mecca, Damascus, Cairo; Abbasid, Ottoman, Safavid), and without diacritics. The only exceptions are for relatively little-known historical place names (al-Ḥīra, Mārib, al-Baḥrayn – the latter not to be confused with the modern Bahrain) and dynasties (Shaddādids, Banū ʿAbbād), which I have rendered in full transliteration. For Turkish names and terms, I have, in most cases, used modern Turkish spelling. Commonly used names of offices (caliph, amir, vizier, qadi) are rendered in their anglicised forms, and capitalised when applied to specific individuals or used as titles (Caliph al-Maʾmūn, Sultan Maḥmūd, the Khaqan of Samarqand). Other terms in common use in English (hadith, madrasa, sharia) appear without diacritics and in Roman script; less common terms (*tafsīr*, *khānaqāh*, *fiqh*) appear in transliteration and in italics.

I have provided translations of several but not all of the titles of compositions mentioned in this book. In deciding whether or not to translate a title, I have aimed to facilitate rather than obscure the book's accessibility. Where I have provided translations, they appear at the first mention of the composition; I have tended not to translate titles when they appear only in the notes. In references to primary texts, I use the =

sign in order to indicate equivalent sections of source texts and their translations; for example, Niẓām al-Mulk, *Siyar al-mulūk*, 4 = Darke, *Book of Government*, 2.

Like many pre-modern texts, the selections included in this volume include certain formulaic phrases, which appear after each mention of God, the Prophet, members of the Prophet's family, members of the early Muslim community and other esteemed persons. These formulae are essential elements in the original texts, and in many cases I have opted to include them; I have not done so in an entirely consistent manner, however, since to do so would sometimes involve substantial repetition, and it would add significantly to the length of the English versions.

Dates

In most cases, I have provided dates according to the *hijrī* calendar (indicated first) and the Gregorian calendar (indicated second). In the few cases where only one date appears, it represents the Gregorian calendar unless indicated otherwise. In temporal references of a general kind, such as 'fourteenth century' or 'mid-tenth century', these indicators apply to the Gregorian calendar. Names of months of the Islamic *hijrī* calendar appear in transliteration (Muḥarram, Shawwāl).

Abbreviations

Abbès, *De l'Éthique du prince*	Makram Abbès, *Al-Māwardī. De l'Éthique du prince et du gouvernement de l'état*. Traduit de l'arabe et précédé d'un *Essai sur les arts de gouverner en Islam* (Paris: Les Belles Lettres, 2015).
EI²	*Encyclopaedia of Islam, Second Edition*, ed. P. Bearman, Th. Bianquis, C. E. Bosworth, E. van Donzel, W. P. Heinrichs (Leiden: Brill, 1960–2007) (https://referenceworks-brillonline-com.ezproxy.wellesley.edu/entries/encyclopaedia-of-islam-2).
EI Three	*Encyclopaedia of Islam, Three*, ed. Kate Fleet, Gudrun Krämer, Denis Matringe, John Nawas, Everett Rowson (Leiden: Brill, 2007–) (https://referenceworks-brillonline-com.ezproxy.wellesley.edu/entries/encyclopaedia-of-islam-3).
EIr	*Encyclopaedia Iranica*, ed. Ehsan Yarshater, Elton Daniel (London and Boston: Routledge and Kegan Paul, 1985–). *Encyclopaedia Iranica Online* © Trustees of Columbia University in the City of New York (https://referenceworks.brillonline.com/entries/encyclopaedia-iranica-online/).

EQ	*Encyclopaedia of the Qur'ān*, ed. Jane Dammen McAuliffe, 6 vols. (Leiden and Boston: E. J. Brill, 2001–6).
GAL	Carl Brockelmann, *Geschichte der arabischen Litteratur*, 2 vols. (first edition, Weimar: E. Felber, 1898–1902; second edition, Leiden: E. J. Brill, 1943–9).
GAL SI, SII, SIII	Carl Brockelmann, *Geschichte der arabischen Litteratur [Supplementbände]*, 3 vols. (Leiden: E. J. Brill, 1937–42).
Lisān al-ʿarab	Ibn Manẓūr, Muḥammad b. Mukarram, *Lisān al-ʿarab* (Cairo: Dār al-Maʿārif, 1981).
Mach-Yahuda, *Catalogue of Arabic Manuscripts*	Rudolf Mach, *Catalogue of Arabic Manuscripts (Yahuda Section) in the Garrett Collection, Princeton University Library* (Princeton: Princeton University Press, 1977).
PEIPT	*The Princeton Encyclopedia of Islamic Political Thought*, ed. Gerhard Böwering (Princeton and Oxford: Princeton University Press, 2013).
Sirr al-asrār	Pseudo-Aristotle, *Kitāb al-Siyāsa fī tadbīr al-riyāsa al-maʿrūf bi-Sirr al-asrār*, ed. ʿAbd al-Raḥmān Badawī, in *al-Uṣūl al-yūnāniyya lil-naẓariyyāt al-siyāsiyya fī l-Islām* (Cairo: Dār al-Kutub al-Miṣriyya, 1954), 67–171.
Steele/Ali, *Secretum secretorum*	*Secretum secretorum* cum glossis et notulis, ed. Robert Steele; including the translation from the Arabic [by Ismail Ali], ed. A. S. Fulton, in *Opera hactenus inedita Rogeri Baconi*, Fasc. V (Oxford: Oxford University Press, 1920), 176–266.

Part I Introduction

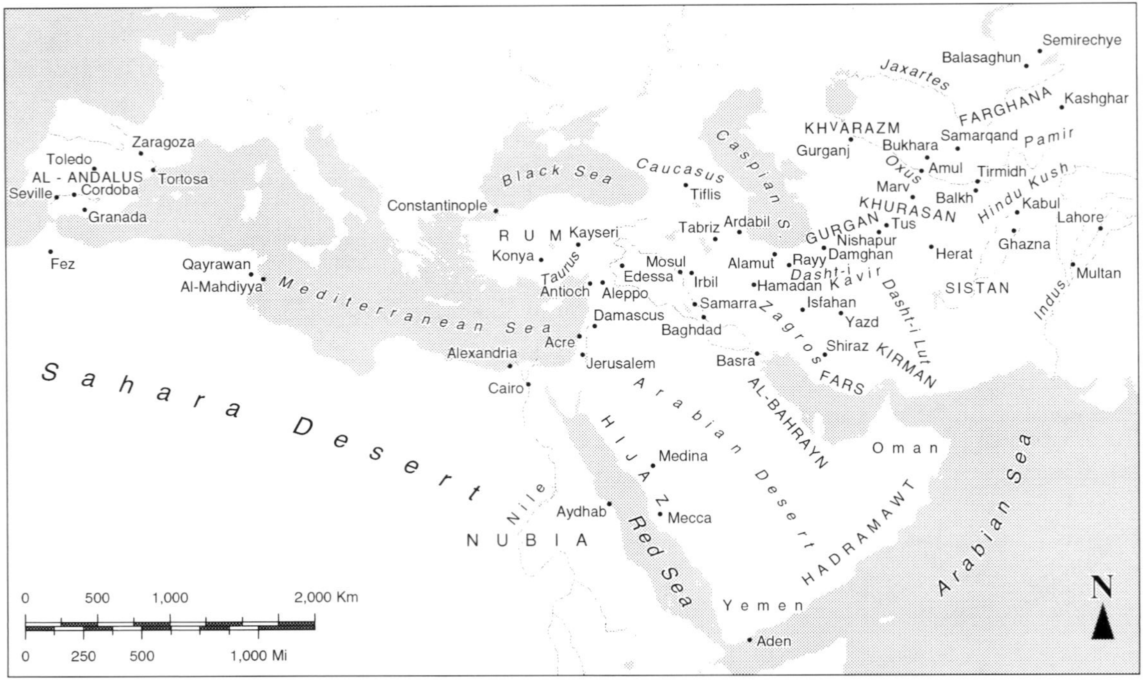

Map 1 Western Asia and the Mediterranean in the tenth to twelfth centuries.
Credit: Redrawn based on a map originally produced by Dani Henry

1

The Arabic, Persian and Turkish Mirror Literatures[1]

A 'mirror for princes' – the term derives from the Latin *speculum principis* – is a text that offers advice to a ruler, or ruler-to-be, concerning the exercise of royal power and the well-being of the body politic.[2] Attested in numerous agrarian societies, the genre flourished for over a millennium in the pre- and early modern Muslim and Christian spheres, where mirrors constituted an important vehicle for the articulation of political thought. The affinities among the mirror literatures produced in Muslim and Christian settings, and to a degree over an even wider canvas, are striking: they suggest a political culture in many respects familiar in the courtly circles of medieval Muslim and Christian rulers alike. The passage of mirrors among the lingua francas of Arabic, Latin and Greek, and into regional and vernacular languages, is perhaps as much indicative as it is causative of this affinity.[3]

[1] This volume, it must be acknowledged, is heavily weighted towards mirrors in Arabic and Persian; among nine examples, only one is in Turkish. The reasons for this uneven treatment lie in the anthology's concentration on the Early Middle Period (see below), when many more mirror-writers wrote in Arabic and Persian than in Turkish, and in the limits of the author's expertise.

[2] From *speculum principis* and similar Latin compounds (*speculum regis*, *speculum regale*), analogous terms in the vernacular European languages (*mirror for princes*, *miroir des princes*, *Fürstenspiegel*) evolved (on the metaphorical use of the term 'mirror' in late antiquity and the Latin West, see Bradley, 'Backgrounds of the Title Speculum'; Jónsson, *Le miroir*; Eberhardt, *Via Regia*, 400, 496–8). The term did not appear before the twelfth century, although the 'genre' is very much older; see Hadot, 'Fürstenspiegel'; Blum, *Byzantinische Fürstenspiegel*, 1–18.

[3] See further Yavari, *Advice for the Sultan*, esp. 7–44; Yavari, 'Political Regard'; Darling, 'Mirrors for Princes in Europe and the Middle East'; Dvornik, *Early Christian and Byzantine Political Philosophy*, II: 659–850; van Berkel, 'People of the Pen'; and, for a broader comparative study, al-Azmeh, *Muslim Kingship*.

This volume introduces a portion of the extensive body of mirror literature produced in pre-modern Muslim contexts. Also termed 'advice' or 'advisory' literature,[4] the Arabic, Persian and Turkish mirrors treat a host of political issues, including the sources and signs of political legitimacy, rulers' responsibilities towards the populations under their governance, the ruler's power and its limits, the people's duty of obedience and its limits, justice and law, the maintenance of social stability, causes of unrest, licit and illicit uses of force, the functions of governmental offices and the status and rights of diverse social groups – issues that remain of compelling importance in the contemporary world.

The contexts in which the pre-modern authors wrote, however, differed radically from the circumstances facing writers and governments in post-industrial societies. Commonly addressed (directly or indirectly) to the person of the ruler, who occupied the central position in the court, the pre-modern mirror literature circulated among many groups who participated in the courtly milieu; indeed, it was frequently viziers, administrators, secretaries, men of letters, men of learning – persons tied to the court and recipients of royal patronage – who composed mirrors.[5] While mirrors characteristically discuss many of these groups, they attend first to the royal person: it was axiomatic that the well-being of the polity depended on the welfare, physical and spiritual, of the ruler; accordingly, the upbringing and education of the prince, and the good health, rectitude, dutiful religious observance and pleasing personal habits of the king were matters of the foremost political significance. Often devoting separate treatments to the king's self-governance, his governance of the persons in his inner circle and his governance of the population at large, mirror-writers effectively (and sometimes explicitly) distinguished the distinct fields of ethics, economics and politics – the

[4] Although the image of the mirror was not entirely absent from the Arabic, Persian and Turkish advisory literatures (see Cheikh-Moussa, 'De la "communauté de salut" à la "populace"', 499–500), it did not develop into a generic marker, for which designations such as 'book of advice' and 'counsel for kings' came into common use; for the development of generic markers, see below, and n. 8.

[5] I use the term 'court' to describe a temporary grouping of people, such as the persons mentioned, rather than a stable physical space (von der Höh, Jaspert and Oesterle, 'Courts, Brokerage and Brokers', 11–12). Almost as important as kings in dispensing patronage were viziers, who, like kings, were sometimes recipients of mirrors (see below, n. 60). In general contexts, I use the terms 'ruler', 'king' and 'monarch' more or less interchangeably; in specific contexts, I use various terms, such as caliph, sultan, amir and king, according to the office or title of the individual in question. Especially in earlier centuries, the Arabic term *sulṭān*, later used as a title, connotes 'power' in the abstract sense; see Tor, 'Sultan'.

Aristotelian divisions of practical philosophy, assimilated into philosophical discourse in the medieval Muslim and Christian spheres.[6]

If the 'mirror for princes' constitutes a 'genre', its identifying features tend to be functional rather than formal: the term has been applied to compositions ranging from brief sententiae to collections of stories to long epic poems.[7] In Arabic, Persian and Turkish contexts, the raison d'être of the mirror literature lies in its overt advisory function. The phrases *naṣīḥat al-mulūk* (Arabic), 'counsel for kings', as well as *andarz-nāmeh* (Persian), *pandnāmeh* (Persian) and *nasihatname* (Turkish), 'book of advice', came to be used to describe the genre and to identify compositions that belonged to it. (Other generic terms, with slightly differing connotations, included *akhlāq al-mulūk*, 'the dispositions of kings'; *ādāb al-mulūk*, 'the aphorisms of, or regulations for, kings'; and *siyar al-mulūk*, 'rules or regulations concerning the conduct of kings'.)[8] As one of the few acknowledged vehicles of communication between a subject and his sovereign, the mirror provided a versatile mechanism through which writers sought not only to advise but also to accomplish a host of other, unstated purposes: intervening in dynastic and factional politics; advancing a protégé; gaining access to personal networks; professional advancement; competing for patronage, remuneration or employment. To accomplish these varied ends, authors adapted the medium of the mirror to suit their interests and circumstances. Almost always, mirror-writers demonstrated their familiarity with the vast cultural repertoire known as *adab*, a term which connoted a body of edifying and

[6] Behind my references to the king's 'inner circle' and 'the population at large' are the Arabic terms (also used in Persian and Turkish) *khāṣṣ* and *ʿāmm*, 'special' or 'privileged' and 'common'; in social terms, the former applied to individuals with personal ties, principally of loyalty and obligation, to the ruler, while the latter designated persons only in indirect relationship with the ruler, a group that might include a variety of urban constituencies and the general tax-paying population. Several groups among the *khāṣṣa* (the collective term for persons with *khāṣṣ* status) functioned as intermediaries between the ruler and the general population; see further Mottahedeh, *Loyalty and Leadership*, esp. 40–96; Paul, '*Khidma*'; Paul, *Herrscher, Gemeinwesen, Vermittler*; Peacock, *Great Seljuk Empire*, 158–63; Cheikh-Moussa, 'Du discours autorisé', 171–5. See further below, Chapter 5, n. 54. The three-fold modes of royal governance also appear in Carolingian mirrors; see Nelson, 'Kingship and Empire', 219–20.

[7] For a broad interpretation of the topic (with emphasis on antiquity and the Middle Ages), see Hadot, 'Fürstenspiegel'; see further Hunger, *Die hochsprachliche profane Literatur der Byzantiner*, 157–65; and Jónsson, 'La situation du *Speculum regale*', 394–7 (where a more restricted definition is proposed).

[8] See further Zakharia, 'Al-Ghazâlî, conseilleur du prince', 212–16; Gilliot, '*In consilium tuum deduces me*', 483; see also Cheikh-Moussa, 'Du discours autorisé'.

entertaining (Arabic) literature, as well as manners, appropriate comportment and moral propriety.[9] But the mirror-form was almost infinitely flexible.[10] It is not unusual to find medical, astrological, philosophical, religious, theological or legal materials in a mirror, and the relationship between advisory and historiographical writing is particularly close: mirror-writers used historical examples to teach, and historians narrated the past with a view to its lessons for the present.[11]

1.1 Development

From approximately the eighth century to the eighteenth, first the Arabic language, then Persian and Turkish, provided the linguistic media for extensive literatures of political advice. Certain features, while not *de rigueur*, became prevalent, and it is possible to identify broad phases in literary development, as well as different strands of intellectual approach. It is possible, for example, to differentiate between continuous epistles composed for specific occasions, chiefly concerned with particular areas of political life, and broadly conceived, book-length compositions subdivided into thematic chapters – even though some of the materials in the latter are likely to appear in the former. It is possible also to distinguish, among the varied types of advisory literature, compositions grounded principally in literary culture (*adab*); treatises presented within a primarily juristic or a primarily philosophical and ethical conceptual framework (works of *aḥkām* and *akhlāq* respectively); and exhortations of a homiletic type (*naṣīḥa*, pl. *naṣāʾiḥ*; *mawʿiẓa*, pl. *mawāʿiẓ*).[12] Some of

9 In a useful comparison, Tarif Khalidi has likened *adab* to *paideia* (*Arabic Historical Thought*, 83). For general treatments, see Hämeen-Anttila, 'Adab (a)'; Enderwitz, 'Adab (b)'; Toorawa, *Ibn Abī Ṭāhir Ṭayfūr and Arabic Writerly Culture*, 1–6; Toorawa, 'Defining *Adab* by (Re)defining the *Adīb*', 286–308; for a consideration of interconnections between the concepts of *adab* and *siyāsa* (governance), see Makdisi, *Ibn ʿAqil: Religion and Culture in Classical Islam*, 159. For the plural form *ādāb*, see Sadan, '*Ādāb* – règles de conduite et *ādāb* – dictons, maximes'.

10 The same quality is evident in the European mirror literatures; see, for example, Barrau, 'Ceci n'est pas un miroir', 90 (with reference to the *Policraticus* of John of Salisbury (*c.* 1120–80)).

11 See further Waldman, *Toward a Theory of Historical Narrative*; Meisami, 'History as Literature'; Meisami, 'Exemplary Lives, Exemplary Deaths'; Meisami, *Persian Historiography*.

12 See Toelle and Zakharia, *À la découverte de la littérature arabe*, 160; and above, at n. 8. In her pioneering studies of mirrors, A. K. S. Lambton restricted the use of the term 'mirror for princes' to compositions in the 'literary' (*adab*) mode ('Islamic Mirrors for Princes', 419; *State and Government*, xvii).

these distinctions emerge over time, and accordingly it is useful to consider the development of the Arabic, Persian and Turkish mirror literatures in terms of four loose historical periods, to which I shall refer as the Early or Formative Period, the Earlier Middle Period, the Later Middle Period and the Early Modern Period.[13]

1.2 The Early or Formative Period (Eighth and Ninth Centuries)

The Early or Formative Period witnessed the first post-conquest compositions of instructive prose in Arabic. It also encompasses the recording in writing of sixth- and early seventh-century Arabic literature, and the great wave of translations of Middle Persian, Greek, Syriac and Sanskrit writings into Arabic. Beginning towards the end of the Umayyad period, usually with caliphal patronage, a wealth of material was translated from these languages. Particularly significant for the formation of a mirror literature in Arabic were narrative cycles, such as *Kalīla wa-Dimna* and *Bilawhar wa-Būdhāsaf*; accounts of the kings of the past and collections of royal pronouncements, such as the 'Testament of Ardashīr' (*'Ahd Ardashīr*); prescriptive accounts of manners, including stipulations for appropriate conduct at court (Middle Persian *ēwēn*, Ar. *ā'īn*); epistles, such as the 'Letter to Julian (the Apostate)' of Themistius (d. *c.* 388) and the 'Letter of Tansar'; and treatises in the fields of ethics, economics and political philosophy, such as Aristotle's *Nicomachean Ethics*, the *Oikonomicos* of Bryson (on household management), and Plato's *Republic*.[14] A voluminous repertoire of wisdom literature, in the form of edifying aphorisms and instructive maxims, entered Arabic from a variety of sources.[15] The pseudo-Aristotelian text known as *Kitāb al-Siyāsa*

[13] This sequence of periods is adapted from Hodgson's outline of a High Caliphal Period (692–945), an Earlier Islamic Middle Period (945–1258), a Late Middle Period (1258–1503) and the Period of the Gunpowder Empires (1503–1789) (*Venture of Islam*, I: 96). In its entirety, Hodgson's Middle Period covers roughly half a millennium, 1000–1500; the texts presented in this anthology date from the earlier rather than the later phase of this extended period. Cf. Hodgson, *Venture of Islam*, II: 6–7; see also Berkey, *Formation of Islam*, 179–83.

[14] On the translation movement and some of its principal products, see Gutas, *Greek Thought, Arabic Culture*; Gutas, *Greek Wisdom Literature in Arabic Translation*; de Blois, *Burzoy's Voyage to India*; Boyce, *Letter of Tansar*; Dvornik, *Early Christian and Byzantine Political Philosophy*, II: 666–9; Zakeri, *Persian Wisdom in Arabic Garb*; Zakeri, 'Muḥammad b. Khalaf b. al-Marzbān'; Forster, 'Buddha in Disguise'.

[15] Gutas, 'Classical Arabic Wisdom Literature'; Shaked, 'From Iran to Islam'; Zakeri, *Persian Wisdom in Arabic Garb*; Daiber, 'Das *Kitāb al-Ādāb al-kabīr*'.

fī tadbīr al-riyāsa ('Book of Governance: On the Strategies of Rule') or *Sirr al-asrār*, 'Secret of Secrets' (*Secretum secretorum*), a collection that includes a cycle of correspondence purportedly exchanged between Aristotle and Alexander the Great, derives in large part from materials rendered into Arabic during this Early Period.[16] The vicissitudes of textual transmission only rarely allow for the comparison of an Arabic 'translation' with its predecessor(s) in another language. Perhaps more importantly, the Arabic texts created through this process constituted an early Arabic mirror literature, as well as providing materials for inclusion and development in contemporaneous advisory writings in Arabic, and later in Persian and Turkish. In this period, the distinction between a 'translation' and an 'original', or 'new', composition in Arabic is not always easy to determine; the prevalence, acknowledged or unacknowledged, of transposed materials in Arabic writing rendered the categories far from mutually exclusive.[17]

At least as important as the textual inheritance provided by the translations was the cultural inheritance that shaped the thought and writing of many of the earliest mirror-writers in Arabic. Among the most remarkable individuals in this respect is Ibn al-Muqaffaʿ (d. *c.* 139–40/756–7), who both translated from Middle Persian and wrote new compositions, on political subjects, in Arabic prose.[18] Even centuries after the seventh-century incorporation of Iran into the Muslim caliphate, memories of the Sasanian and Zoroastrian past persisted, shaping writings in Arabic and Persian alike.[19] These memories were communicated at least as much through oral channels as through written records. As late as the latter part of the eleventh century, Niẓām al-Mulk states that, in composing his *Siyar*

[16] See Grignaschi, 'Les "Rasāʾil ʾAristāṭālīsa ʾilā-l-Iskandar"'; Grignaschi, 'Le roman épistolaire classique'. It is not self-evident from which language(s) the text was translated; see van Bladel, 'Iranian Characteristics and Forged Greek Attributions'; and further below, section 3.1.

[17] For discussion and examples, see Shaked, 'Andarz and Andarz Literature'; Shaked, 'From Iran to Islam'; Safa, 'Andarz Literature in New Persian'; Zakeri, *Persian Wisdom in Arabic Garb*; Zakeri, 'Ādāb al-falāsifa'; Zakeri, ''Alī ibn ʿUbaida al-Raiḥānī'; Yavari, *The Future of Iran's Past*; de Fouchécour, *Moralia*, 6 and *passim*; Yousefi, 'Islam without Fuqahāʾ'.

[18] See Kristó-Nagy, *La pensée d'Ibn al-Muqaffaʿ*; Kristó-Nagy, 'Marriage after Rape'; Shaked, 'From Iran to Islam'; Hamori, 'Prudence, Virtue and Self-Respect in Ibn al-Muqaffaʿ'; Lowry, 'The First Islamic Legal Theory'.

[19] See Savant, *New Muslims of Post-Conquest Iran*, esp. 90–129; Yavari, *Advice for the Sultan*, *passim*; Sattarzade, 'Persian Institutions', 72–4 and *passim*.

al-mulūk ('The Conduct of Kings'), he drew on materials that he had 'seen, learnt, read and heard'.[20]

In the Early Period, the 'new' Arabic literature of political advice comprised two principal literary vehicles, the epistle (*risāla*, also *kitāb*) and the 'testament' (*waṣiyya*, *ʿahd*), the latter an ancient Arabic genre in which a father, often shortly before his death, offered counsel to his son and heir or to his children. These compositions, initially, concentrated on particular topics intended for specific occasions; they gradually grew in scope and, incorporating the device of internal classification (*taṣnīf*), came to presage the general, subdivided book-length mirror that would become customary in the Early Middle Period. Examples include the epistles, addressed to specific individuals, of ʿAbd al-Ḥamīd al-Kātib (*c.* 69–132/688–750); and the *Kitāb al-Ṣaḥāba* or *Risāla fī l-ṣaḥāba* ('Epistle concerning the Ruler's Companions') of Ibn al-Muqaffaʿ, who also composed an important advisory manual, *al-Ādāb al-kabīr*.[21] These compositions circulated at the caliphal court and in the circles of the caliph's secretaries.[22] They were soon followed by the *Kitāb al-Kharāj* ('Concerning the Land-Tax') of the chief judge Abū Yūsuf Yaʿqūb b. Ibrāhīm al-Kūfī (113–82/731–98) and the 'Testament' of Ṭāhir b. al-Ḥusayn Dhū l-Yamīnayn (159–207/776–822) – the former composed in response to questions posed to the jurist-author by the caliph Hārūn al-Rashīd (r. 170–93/786–809), the latter written at the appointment of the ruler-author's son to a provincial governorship – and both already encompassing a number of topics.[23] Other ninth-century contributions to the

[20] *Siyar al-mulūk*, 4 = Darke, *Book of Government*, 2 (Darke translates, 'drawing upon what I have found out, seen, experienced and learned from masters'); the passage is cited in Sattarzade, 'Persian Institutions', 6.

[21] On these genres, see Arazi and Ben-Shammay, 'Risāla'; Latham, 'Beginnings of Arabic Prose', 154–64; Harmsen, *Die Wasiya als literarisches Genre*. On ʿAbd al-Ḥamīd, see al-Qadi, 'ʿAbd al-Hamid al-Katib'; al-Qāḍī, 'Early Islamic State Letters'; Latham, 'Beginnings of Arabic Prose', 164–79; and on the mixed sources, including Greek, Persian and Arabian materials, that contributed to his vocabulary, al-Qāḍī, 'Myriad Sources', 232–53. On Ibn al-Muqaffaʿ, see Latham, 'Ibn al-Muqaffaʿ and Early ʿAbbasid Prose'; Cooperson, 'ʿAbd Allah Ibn al-Muqaffaʿ'; Kristó-Nagy, 'Reason, Religion and Power in Ibn al-Muqaffaʿ'. See also the translations of Schönig (*Das Sendschreiben des ʿAbdalḥamīd b. Yaḥyā*) and Pellat (*Ibn al-Muqaffaʿ (mort vers 140/757), 'conseilleur' du calife*).

[22] Schoeler, 'Relationship of Literacy and Memory', 123; cf. Schoeler, *The Genesis of Literature in Islam*.

[23] For English translations, see Ben Shemesh, *Abū Yūsuf's Kitāb al-Kharāj*; and Bosworth, 'An Early Arabic Mirror for Princes'; for the latter, see further below, Chapter 2, n. 4, Chapter 8, n. 47.

Arabic literature of political advice include compositions inseparable from the formation of the corpus and culture of *adab*: the *Kitāb al-Sulṭān* ('On the Subject of Power: A Book') in the anthology *'Uyūn al-akhbār* of Ibn Qutayba (213–76/828–89) and the mid-ninth-century collection *Kitāb al-Tāj fī akhlāq al-mulūk* ('Book of the Crown: On the Characteristics of Kings'), both dedicated to al-Fatḥ b. Khāqān (d. 247/861–2), a courtier and diplomat to the caliph al-Mutawakkil (r. 232–47/847–61).[24] These compositions, in which topics are treated sequentially within a single structure, consist substantially of quoted materials, some of them drawn from translated sources.

1.3 The Early Middle Period (Tenth to Twelfth Centuries)

The Early Middle Period saw the appearance of book-length mirrors, authored compositions subdivided into thematic chapters that collectively treated a broad and flexible range of topics related to kingship and the service of kings.[25]

An unmistakable feature of the mirror literatures – Arabic, Persian and Turkish – of this period is the prominence in their production of celebrated individuals, sometimes themselves participants in the exercise of power, or exceptionally well situated to intervene in the politics of their times. Often writing in the later stages of their lives, when their authority was well established, the chief judge al-Māwardī (364–450/974–1058), the admired scholar Ghazālī (450–505/1058–1111), the vizier Niẓām al-Mulk (408–485/1018–92), the amir Kaykā'ūs b. Iskandar (r. 441–*c.* 480/1049–*c.* 1087), the esteemed jurist al-Ṭurṭūshī (*c.* 451–520 or 525/1059–1126 or

[24] Ibn Qutayba's *Kitāb al-Sulṭān* was followed in the early tenth century by an identically titled opening chapter in the anthology *al-'Iqd al-farīd* of Ibn 'Abd Rabbih (246–328/860–940). The *Kitāb al-Tāj fī akhlāq al-mulūk*, which also circulated under the rubric *Akhlāq al-mulūk*, is the work not of al-Jāḥiẓ (d. 255/868), as traditionally accepted, but of Muḥammad b. al-Ḥārith al-Taghlibī (or al-Tha'labī) (d. 250/864) (Schoeler, 'Verfasser und Titel'). As Michael Bonner points out, al-Fatḥ b. Khāqān, for all his prominence, seems not to have held any formal government position (Bonner, 'Waning of Empire', 308).

[25] On the development of the mirror literatures, see Richter, *Studien zur Geschichte der älteren arabischen Fürstenspiegel*; Lambton, 'Islamic Mirrors for Princes'; Bosworth, 'Naṣīḥat al-mulūk'; Marlow, 'Advice and Advice Literature'. Probably the earliest example of the Carolingian mirror literature is the *Via Regia*, composed in or before the year 814 (Eberhardt (*Via Regia*, 195–212, 262–3) concludes that Smaragd wrote in 810).

1131) and the popular preacher Ibn al-Jawzī (510–97/1126–1200 or 1201) – all of whom wrote mirrors in this period – needed no introduction to their recipients, who in some cases commissioned their compositions. Notably, despite the (in some circles) controversial nature of association with rulers, the mirror-writers of the Early Middle Period include a number of eminent religious scholars (*ʿulamāʾ*, sing. *ʿālim*), some of them renowned, moreover, for their dispositions towards social withdrawal and personal austerity. Al-Māwardī was called upon on several occasions to serve as an ambassador, and he composed a number of advisory texts, including (in all likelihood) mirrors for members of the Buyid dynasty.[26] Ghazālī, even after his decision to leave his prestigious post in Baghdad for a life of seclusion in his native province of Khurasan, composed mirrors for both caliphs and sultans.[27] Later in the twelfth century, Ibn al-Jawzī, the celebrated polymath, historian, jurisconsult and preacher, dedicated a mirror to the caliph al-Mustaḍīʾ (r. 566–75/1170–80), and Taqī al-Dīn Abū l-Ḥasan ʿAlī b. Abī Bakr al-Harawī (d. 611/1215) offered counsel to an Ayyubid ruler.[28]

The predominance in the Early Middle Period's extant mirror literature of writings by or attributed to well-known figures suggests the importance of illustrious authorship in securing a text's dissemination and preservation. Although less eminent persons, such as mid-level bureaucrats and local scholars, also composed mirrors in the period – the author of an Arabic *Siyāsat al-mulūk* ('The Governance of Kings'), for instance, was probably a minor official involved in the financial administration under the early Buyids – relatively few examples of this kind have survived.[29] Attributing a text to a celebrated author occurred frequently in medieval societies, and it is not surprising, therefore, that the authorship of several of the period's mirrors has been called into question. The present volume – setting aside the pseudo-Aristotelian 'Secret of Secrets' – includes extracts from three

[26] Al-Sayyid, 'al-Māwardī: al-rajul wa-l-ʿaṣr'; Abbès, *De l'Éthique du prince*, 173–209.

[27] Griffel, *Al-Ghazālī's Philosophical Theology*, 49–59; Garden, *The First Islamic Reviver*, 17–29, 127–30, 138–42; Safi, *Politics of Knowledge*, 105–24; El-Azhari, *Queens, Eunuchs and Concubines*, 288.

[28] Ibn al-Jawzī's mirror is entitled *al-Miṣbāḥ al-muḍīʾ fī khilāfat al-Mustaḍīʾ*. Al-Harawī, who composed his mirror at some point between 588/1192 and his death in 611/1215, may have intended it for al-Malik al-Ẓāhir Ghāzī (r. 582–613/1186–1216, in Aleppo); see Sourdel-Thomine, 'Les conseils du Šayḫ al-Harawī à un prince ayyūbide', 205–6, 206, n. 3. The homiletic mode of these compositions remained prominent in thirteenth-century Syria; see Peacock, 'Politics, Religion and the Occult'; and see below, n. 34.

[29] For the Buyid example, see Sadan, 'Une nouvelle source'; Sadan, 'A New Source of the Būyid Period'; Sadan and Silverstein, 'Ornate Manuals or Practical *Adab*?'.

mirrors whose authorship has been disputed; if these texts are indeed pseudepigraphic, it seems highly likely that their attributions – to al-Māwardī in the case of the Arabic *Naṣīḥat al-mulūk*, to Niẓām al-Mulk in the case of *Siyar al-mulūk* and to Ghazālī in the case of the Persian *Naṣīḥat al-mulūk*, part II – ensured their survival.

For all the individuality of the mirrors of the Early Middle Period, certain themes and certain literary features recur, and these would remain emblematic of mirror-writing in later centuries. A striking, even defining hallmark of the mirror literature, in continuity with the advisory writings of the Formative Period, is the high profile given to ancient and distant figures: Aristotle (384–322 BCE) and Alexander (356–323 BCE), and the Sasanian monarchs Ardashīr I (r. 226–41) and Khusraw I Anūshīrvān (r. 531–79) appear with particular regularity. Mirror-writers, like other authors, also referred to groups (*al-ʿarab*, *al-ʿajam*, *al-furs*, *al-hind*, *al-yūnān*, *al-rūm*), whose designations conveyed diverse ethnic, territorial and linguistic associations.[30] The mirror-writers' tendency to pile up a variety of authorities in connection with specific points was intended to display the universality – and hence unassailability – of their arguments. Furthermore, the ubiquitous references to earlier peoples and dominions permitted authors to occlude their criticisms of contemporary political conditions by presenting these criticisms as the observations of highly esteemed others, identified with distant locations and situated in the remote past.[31]

1.4 The Later Middle Period (Thirteenth to Fifteenth Centuries)

The surviving manuscripts from the Later Middle Period suggest a mass production of mirrors in Arabic and Persian. With large numbers of extant examples, it is possible to identify certain types or models, which, evident from the beginning of the thirteenth century, were available to authors to adapt and combine according to their interests and circumstances.

The earliest model, which remained in continuous popularity, developed in conjunction with *adab*, of which it constituted a branch (indeed,

[30] A notable example is the *gnomologium* entitled *Jāvīdān khirad* (Persian) or *al-Ḥikma al-khālida* (Arabic) ('Perennial Wisdom'), of the great writer, historian and ethicist Abū ʿAlī Miskawayh (d. 421/1030).

[31] Cf. Yavari, *Advice for the Sultan*, 45–60, 90; Ferster, *Fictions of Advice*, 2–3, 8.

this type might be described under the heading *adab* (or *ādāb*, pl.) *al-mulūk*). Seeking not only to impart advice but also to impress and delight, authors of this kind of mirror, providing models for literary as well as moral emulation, combined an eclectic abundance of Qurʾanic quotations and Prophetic hadith (authenticated reports of the Prophet Muḥammad's sayings and actions), narratives concerning caliphs, kings, sultans and viziers, utterances of sages and respected authorities of the pre- and early Islamic periods, wise and witty proverbs and, often of their own composition, verses of poetry. Writing in Persian, an early thirteenth-century author described his mirror as a gift of speech (*sukhan*), in which he included verses in Persian and Arabic; his ten-chapter book addresses virtue and its actualisation in conduct, or *akhlāq* and *ādāb*.[32] Perhaps a variant of this model combines set numbers of texts of a kind, often bilingual and classified into generic groups, and selected for their relevance to kings; the selection might include Prophetic hadith, proverbs, utterances of ʿAlī b. Abī Ṭālib (d. 40/661) – cousin and son-in-law of the Prophet, fourth caliph and First Imam of the Shia – and sayings of sages or early Islamic authorities.[33]

Another model, in continuity with the writings of Ghazālī, is primarily homiletic, and might be considered under the heading *naṣīḥa*, 'counsel', or *mawʿiẓa*, 'exhortation' or 'admonition'. Based substantially on Qur'anic verses and Prophetic hadith, such works, notably popular in Syria in the twelfth and thirteenth centuries, remind the ruler of the contingency of his power and the great burden of responsibility that God has placed upon him. The advisory writings of Ibn al-Jawzī and his grandson Sibṭ Ibn al-Jawzī (581 or 582–654/1185 or 1186–1256) provide

32 Niẓām al-Dīn Yaḥyā b. Ṣāʿid, *Ḥadāʾiq al-siyar*, dedicated to the Seljuk sultan of Rum ʿAlāʾ al-Dīn Kayqubād (r. *c*. 617–34/1220–37); see the author's introduction (1–12); for *akhlāq*, see especially the first chapter (13–38), and for *ādāb*, the ninth and tenth chapters (123–49). See further de Fouchécour, 'Ḥadāyeq al-siyar'; Peacock, 'Advice for the Sultans of Rum', 286–9.

33 The *Barīd al-saʿāda* (609–10/1212–13) of the secretary Muḥammad-i Ghāzī Malaṭyavī, written for the Seljuk sultan of Rum ʿIzz al-Dīn Kaykāʾūs I b. Kaykhusraw (r. 607–16/1210–19), consists of forty Prophetic hadith, twenty sayings from sages (ten are from ʿAlī b. Abī Ṭālib) and twenty Arabic proverbs. Probably dating from roughly the same period is the collection *Khiradnamā-ye jān-afrūz* (or *Khiradnāmeh*) of Abū l-Faẓl Yūsuf b. ʿAlī Mustawfī; this collection consists of 100 entries, each of which comprises a wise person's saying, a maxim from ʿAlī and a selection of verses from the *Shāhnāmeh* of Firdawsī. See de Fouchécour, *Moralia*, 129–30.

examples of this kind.[34] Overlapping with and perhaps a variant of this set of mirrors are texts that, again in continuity with Ghazālī, single out virtues strongly associated with Sufi teachings, such as repentance, renunciation, patience, constant mindfulness of and trust in God. In a period when the many inflections of Sufism, including local and transregional Sufi movements, became increasingly prominent across vast areas, these compositions emerged clearly in the thirteenth century, in the moral writings of the poet Saʿdī (d. 691/1291 or 694/1294),[35] and in the mirrors of leading Sufi practitioners, such as Najm al-Dīn Dāya Rāzī (573–654/1177–1256), who wrote in Anatolia, and ʿAlī al-Hamadānī (714–86/1314–85), who probably wrote in Kashmir.[36]

Another model, grounded in the science of moral dispositions (*ʿilm al-akhlāq*) or ethics, takes as its foundation the three divisions of practical philosophy: ethics, economics and politics. Probably the most important 'mirror' in this group is the Persian *Akhlāq-i Nāṣirī* ('Nasirean Ethics') of Naṣīr al-Dīn Ṭūsī (597–672/1201–74),[37] which provided a prestigious model for numerous later writings, such as the *Akhlāq-i Jalālī* of

[34] Meisami drew attention to the homiletic strand of mirror-writing in *The Sea of Precious Virtues*, her translation of the anonymous Persian *Baḥr al-favāʾid* (*c.* 554–8/1159–62), also composed in Syria (Meisami, *Sea of Precious Virtues*, vii). The works of Sibṭ Ibn al-Jawzī include the Arabic *Kanz al-mulūk fī kayfiyyat al-sulūk* and *Kitāb al-Jalīs al-ṣāliḥ wa-l-anīs al-nāṣiḥ* (613/1216), written in Damascus for al-Malik al-Ashraf Muẓaffar al-Dīn (r. 626–35/1229–37).

[35] Notably the *Būstān* (655/1257) and *Gulistān* (656/1258), written for the Atabeg Muẓaffar al-Dīn Abū Bakr b. Saʿd-i Zangī (r. 628–58/1231–60) and his son Saʿd II b. Abī Bakr (r. 658/1260) respectively.

[36] Both authors were members of the Kubravī order. Najm al-Dīn, shortly after his arrival in Kayseri in 618/1221, composed his Persian *Mirṣād al-ʿibād min al-mabdaʾ ilā l-maʿād* as a gift for followers of the Sufi path. He completed a second recension of the work in Sivas in 620/1223, and he dedicated this version to the Seljuk sultan of Rum ʿAlāʾ al-Dīn Kayqubād (r. *c.* 617–34/1220–37). He produced a third, heavily revised recension for the Mengücekid ruler of Erzincan, Dāʾūd b. Bahrāmshāh (see Peacock, 'Advice for the Sultans of Rum', 293). ʿAlī Hamadānī, author of the Persian *Dhakhīrat al-mulūk*, composed it at the behest of a group of rulers and eminent persons who solicited such a work as a 'useful reminder' (*Dhakhīrat al-mulūk*, 2).

[37] Ṭūsī, who initially composed the work in 633/1235 for the Ismaili ruler (*muḥtasham*) Nāṣir al-Dīn ʿAbd al-Raḥīm b. Abī Manṣūr (r. 621–55/1224–57), wrote a new preface after joining the inner circle of the Mongol Il-Khan Hülegü (r. 654–63/1256–65), who had destroyed the Ismaili settlements in Quhistan and Alamut. A number of scholars differentiate between the distinctive discourse of *akhlāq* and the mirror-for-princes literature; acknowledging this distinctiveness, I include the former in this discussion nevertheless: presented as political advice, often addressed and dedicated to named rulers, and incorporating more or less substantial materials from the repertoire of *adab*, treatments of *akhlāq* overlap in function as well as content with other modes of mirror-writing.

Muḥammad b. Asad Davānī (830–908/1427–1503) and the *Akhlāq-i Muḥsinī* of Ḥusayn-i Vāʿiẓ Kāshifī (d. 910/1504–5).[38] The second part of the Persian *Laṭāʾif al-ḥikma* ('Fine Points of Wisdom') (655/1257) of the chief judge Sirāj al-Dīn Maḥmūd b. Abī Bakr Urmavī (594–682/1198–1283) also conforms to this model.[39] The ethical sections in treatises of this kind invoke the four cardinal virtues (wisdom, courage, temperance and justice) based on Plato's divisions of the soul, and the Aristotelian definition of virtue as the mean between the two extremes of excess and deficiency (*ifrāṭ* and *tafrīṭ*); each virtue, including the many subordinate virtues derived from each of the four cardinal virtues, is portrayed as the point of balance between two vices. The titles under which the treatises in this group circulated indicate the convention of naming the treatise after the figure to whom it was dedicated – a practice that would persist in Ottoman and Mughal contexts.

These models did not imply rigid forms. Instead, they indicated the range of established advisory discourses, and mirror-writers commonly combined characteristics of all of these types.

In addition to many of the examples cited in the preceding section, and in contrast to the extant literature of the Early Middle Period, numerous mirrors of the Later Middle Period (several of which survive in single manuscripts) appear to have been the compositions of little-known authors. In these cases it seems likely that the mirror facilitated, or was intended to facilitate, the establishment of ties between the previously unconnected author-adviser and his named recipient. This pattern of mirror-writing – in which the mirror functioned rather like a letter of introduction – became widespread in the Later Middle Period; in societies in which, for various voluntary and involuntary reasons, many people were highly mobile, writers often composed their mirrors upon arrival in a new milieu in which they hoped to be

[38] Muḥammad b. Asad Davānī (830–908/1427–1503) dedicated his *Lavāmiʿ al-ishrāq fī makārim al-akhlāq*, better known as the *Akhlāq-i Jalālī* (*c.* 880/1475), to the Aqquyunlu ruler Uzun Ḥasan (r. 857–82/1453–78) and his son Sulṭān-Khalīl. Ḥusayn-i Vāʿiẓ Kāshifī (d. 910/1504–5), a contemporary of Davānī, composed his *Akhlāq-i Muḥsinī* (completed in 907/1501–2) for the use of Abū l-Muḥsin, the son of the Timurid sultan Ḥusayn Bayqara (r. 875–912/1470–1506). See Woods, *The Aqquyunlu*, 103, 105, 233–4; and Subtelny, 'A Late Medieval Persian Summa on Ethics'.

[39] Composed in Konya and dedicated to the Seljuk sultan of Rum ʿIzz al-Dīn Kaykāʾūs II (r. 644–55/1246–57); the title *Laṭāʾif al-ḥikma al-ʿIzziyya* appears towards the end of the author's text (Urmavī, *Laṭāʾif al-ḥikma*, 289). The first part of this text is devoted to *ḥikmat-i naẓarī*, speculative or theoretical philosophy, and the second to *ḥikmat-i ʿamalī*, practical philosophy.

able to settle.[40] These writers required the mediation of other individuals to convey their mirror-books to their recipients at the court. (It is possible, of course, that some mirrors operated in this fashion in earlier periods, and that the impression given by the manuscript record is to some extent an accident of preservation.)

1.5 The Early Modern Period (Sixteenth and Early Seventeenth Centuries)

The Early Modern Period saw the continuing composition of mirrors, especially in the courts of the Ottoman and Mughal emperors, who inherited, continued and developed earlier patterns of mirror-writing. The educated Ottoman élites, within and beyond the imperial court, as well as in provincial Ottoman settings, created a considerable demand for advice literature in Arabic, Persian and, conspicuously, Turkish.

Turkish, now a fully established companion to the literary languages of Arabic and Persian, became the vehicle for the distinctive *nasihatname*, a generic name sometimes applied to a new type of advisory composition concerned with political reform. In the sixteenth century, the vizier Lutfi Paşa (d. *c.* 970/1562–3), author of the *Asafname* ('Book of Asaf'), and Kınalızade Ali Çelebi (916–79/1510–1572), author of the *Ahlak-i Ala'i* (972/1564), made substantial use of the earlier mirror literatures, which they adapted and expanded.[41] Still in continuity with the models of the past but at the same time introducing new elements of directness and specificity, the historian and bureaucrat Mustafa Âli (948–1008/1541–1600), in the later sixteenth century, adopted a strikingly critical approach;[42] several seventeenth-century Ottoman writers echoed and even amplified Âli's concerns.[43]

[40] See Marlow, 'The Way of Viziers'.

[41] Lutfi Paşa's discussion of the principles of government was informed by his extensive practical experience; his title invokes Asaf, Solomon's vizier (see Coulon, 'Magie et politique'). Kınalızade's reworking of the *Akhlāq-i Jalālī* of Davānī referred to a diverse group of earlier authorities. See Aksan, 'Ottoman Political Writing'; Howard, 'Ottoman Historiography'; Ferguson, *The Proper Order of Things*, 255–63.

[42] On Âli's *Nushat üs-selâtin* (989/1581), dedicated to Sultan Murad III (r. 982–1003/1574–95), see Fleischer, *Bureaucrat and Intellectual*, 95–9; Tietze, *Muṣṭafā ʿĀlī's Counsel for Sultans of 1581*. Âli also prepared a Turkish adaptation of the *Kitāb al-Tāj fī akhlāq al-mulūk* (Fleischer, *Bureaucrat and Intellectual*, 166).

[43] These writers include the anonymous author of the *Kitāb-ı Müstetab*, Koçi Beğ, Kâtib Çelebi and Na'ima (Fleischer, *Bureaucrat and Intellectual*; Murphey, 'The Veliyyuddin *Telhis*'; Ferguson, *The Proper Order of Things*, 235–76).

The increased demand among Turkish readers also occasioned the translation, often with the sponsorship of sultans and viziers, of earlier mirrors, including the *Qābūsnāmeh* ('Book of Qābūs') of Kaykā'ūs, Ghazālī's *Naṣīḥat al-mulūk*, the *Sirāj al-mulūk* ('Lamp of Kings') of al-Ṭurṭūshī and the *Mirṣād al-ʿibād* ('Path of God's Bondsmen') of Najm al-Dīn Dāya.[44]

The Mughal emperors similarly provided extensive patronage for both the composition and translation of works of advice. Like several of their Ottoman counterparts, a number of Mughal mirror-writers adopted the rubric of *akhlāq*, perhaps in part because the emphasis in that intellectual tradition on social harmony among interdependent groups disregarded differences of religious affiliation.[45] Examples include the *Akhlāq-i Ḥakīmī* (987–8/1579–80) of Ḥasan ʿAlī Munshī Khāqānī and the *Akhlāq-i Jahāngīrī* (1029–31/1620–2) of Qadi Nūr Allāh Khāqānī.[46] Like these compositions, the *Mawʿiẓeh-yi Jahāngīrī* (1021/1612–13) of Muḥammad Bāqir Najm al-Thānī (d. 1047/1637) reflects continuity with earlier models of mirror-writing, adapted for the author's circumstances.[47]

The Later Middle and Early Modern Periods also saw the translation of Arabic mirrors, in particular, and to a lesser degree Persian mirrors, into Hebrew, Latin and a variety of European vernacular languages. The case of *Secretum secretorum* is only the best known of several examples.[48] In another case, it seems that Francisco de Gurmendi (fl. 1607–21) – a royal secretary, who had learnt not only Arabic but also Persian, from which language he translated diplomatic correspondence from the Safavid court – used and incorporated al-Ṭurṭūshī's *Sirāj al-mulūk*, as well as, probably, Miskawayh's collection of wisdom *al-Ḥikma al-khālida* (*Jāvīdān khirad*) and Ghazālī's *Naṣīḥat al-mulūk*, in his writings. Gurmendi dedicated his manual for kingship *Doctrina phísica y moral*

[44] See, for the translations into Turkish of the *Qābūsnāmeh*, de Bruijn, 'Kaykāvus', and de Fouchécour, *Moralia*, 179–222; of Ghazālī's *Naṣīḥat al-mulūk*, Bagley, 'Introduction', xvi–xxiv; of *Sirāj al-mulūk*, Fierro, 'Al-Ṭurṭūshī', 394–5, and Yılmaz, *Caliphate Redefined*, 60, 83; of *Mirṣād al-ʿibād*, Algar, 'Introduction', 14–16, 20.

[45] Alam, *Languages of Political Islam*, 11–15.

[46] The former was composed for the Mughal prince and governor of Kabul Muḥammad Ḥakīm Mīrzā, and the latter for the emperor Jahāngīr (r. 1014–37/1605–27), to whom several other mirrors were also dedicated (Alvi, *Advice on the Art of Governance*, 9–11; Dānishpazhūh, 'Chand athar-i fārsī dar akhlāq', 275–7).

[47] Alvi, *Advice on the Art of Governance*, 11–34 (for Alvi's translation and edition of this text, see 37–207).

[48] See Williams, *The Secret of Secrets*, 31–141; Forster, *Das Geheimnis der Geheimnisse*, 113–247; and below, section 3.1.

de príncipes (1615) and a translation entitled *Libro de las calidades del rey* – both reportedly dependent on translations from Arabic manuscripts – to Francisco de Sandoval y Rojas, the future Duke of Lerma (1553–1625) and tutor of the future Philip IV.[49]

1.6 Reception

The royal ideals that formed part of courtly political culture included the expectation that kings should listen to and heed sound advice. They should also, for similarly instructive and edificatory purposes, study and emulate the conduct of the wise and just kings of the past.[50] These ideals created an auspicious environment for the presentation of mirrors, and their practical enactment, carefully controlled, constituted a significant element in the image of royal legitimacy.[51] It is likely that mirrors were read aloud in courtly gatherings (*majālis*, sing. *majlis*), where authors might rehearse the deeds of past rulers and reaffirm royal ideals, and, in the case of the more homiletic examples, that their lecture accompanied religious observances held on Fridays or during the month of Ramaḍān.[52] For the king, seeking to learn from the examples of his royal predecessors, emulating the great monarchs of the past and heeding the moral reminders of the learned and virtuous contributed to his reputation and remembrance in the present world and to his salvation in the next. A good many rulers, at various points in their reigns, took these injunctions very much to heart: for example, the Seljuk sultan of Rum ʿAlāʾ al-Dīn Kayqubād (r. *c.* 617–34/1220–37), the recipient of two advice works in Persian and one in Arabic, consciously modelled himself on the virtuous kings of the past.[53]

In their courtly settings, mirrors also carried a presentational value. Intended for formal delivery to the court and storage in the royal library, many mirrors took the guise of gifts, a function sometimes signalled in

[49] Gilbert, *In Good Faith*, 224–7.

[50] For examples of this ubiquitous injunction, see Ghazālī, *Naṣīḥat al-mulūk*, 112, 127–8 = Bagley, *Ghazālī's Book of Counsel for Kings*, 63, 74.

[51] See further al-Azmeh, *Muslim Kingship*, 54–61; Sperl, 'Islamic Kingship and Arabic Panegyric Poetry', 32; Ali, *Arabic Literary Salons*, 33–74; Zaman, *Religion and Politics under the Early ʿAbbāsids*, 81.

[52] Authors of mirrors urge this custom upon their royal audiences (Ghazālī, *Naṣīḥat al-mulūk*, 4 = Bagley, *Ghazālī's Book of Counsel for Kings*, 5) and praise rulers who practised it (for instance, Urmavī, *Laṭāʾif al-ḥikma*, 288, with reference to the Ayyubid ruler al-Malik al-Kāmil (r. 615–35/1218–38)).

[53] Peacock, 'Advice for the Sultans of Rum', 283.

their titles (notably *Tuḥfa*, 'Gift').[54] A common topos in the mirror-writer's preface describes his fruitless searching for a fitting present to give to the sovereign whose exalted status leaves him in need of nothing; the author's mirror signals his trust, nevertheless, that by dint of his royal magnanimity, the king will not despise his servant's only possible offering, namely a gift of wisdom and counsel. Tokens of an asymmetrical exchange, mirrors sometimes included sections or chapters devoted to the topic of gift-giving, and they also discussed the importance of gifts in diplomatic relations. Niẓām al-Dīn Yaḥyā b. Ṣāʿid, in a mirror for the above-mentioned Seljuk sultan ʿAlāʾ al-Dīn Kayqubād, cites the aphorisms, 'The giving of charitable donations (sing. *ṣadaqa*) defends against the afflictions of the next world, and the giving of gifts (sing. *hadiyya*) averts the misfortunes of this world' and 'Nothing is more effective in abating the wrath of kings and in pleasing them than gifts'.[55]

In keeping with this presentational function, the book of advice occasionally took the form of a precious artefact: the collection of cautionary animal fables *Kalīla wa-Dimna* and the pseudo-Aristotelian *Sirr al-asrār*, for example, sometimes included illustrations.[56] While the use of pictorial images is uncommon, the text's appearance was nevertheless important. To enhance their visual appeal as well as to display their logic, some mirrors take the form of 'trees', their points represented through an interconnected system of roots, trunk, branches and twigs (*tashjīr*).[57] Whether intended for audiences within or outside the court, mirrors often reflect the care of their designers and calligraphers: the use of different scripts and different colours of ink for the various voices in the texts and the various elements in the pages' composition provided visual interest and at the same time facilitated the reader's navigation of the text (Fig. 1).[58]

[54] See, for instance, M. T. Dānishpazhūh's edition of an anonymous fourteenth-century *Tuḥfeh dar akhlāq va-siyāsat*; cf. Marlow, 'Teaching Wisdom'. For a Byzantine parallel, see Arabatzis, 'Nicephoros Blemmydes's *Imperial Statue*', 100–1.

[55] Niẓām al-Dīn, *Ḥadāyiq al-siyar*, 145; cited in 'Gift Giving', *EIr*.

[56] See O'Kane, *Early Persian Painting*; Luyster, 'Kalīla wa-Dimna Illustrations'; Ben Azzouna, *Aux origines du classicisme*, 102, n. 101, 127, 184; *Islamic Calligraphy* (Catalogue, Sam Fogg Rare Books and Manuscripts), no. 25.

[57] Examples include the *Sulūk al-mālik fī tadbīr al-mamālik*, also known as the *Akhlāq al-mushajjara* (655/1256) of Ibn Abī l-Rabīʿ (this Arabic work is usually assumed to have been dedicated to the caliph al-Mustaʿṣim (r. 640–56/1242–58)); and the *Jawāmiʿ al-ʿulūm* of Ibn Farīghūn (see the facsimile edition of Fuat Sezgin, *Compendium of Sciences: Jawāmiʿ al-ʿulūm by Ibn Farīʿūn*).

[58] See Fig. 1, which represents two pages from a manuscript of al-Shayzarī's mirror *al-Manhaj al-maslūk fī siyāsat al-mulūk*, copied in 1115/1703–4 (Islamic Manuscripts

(a)

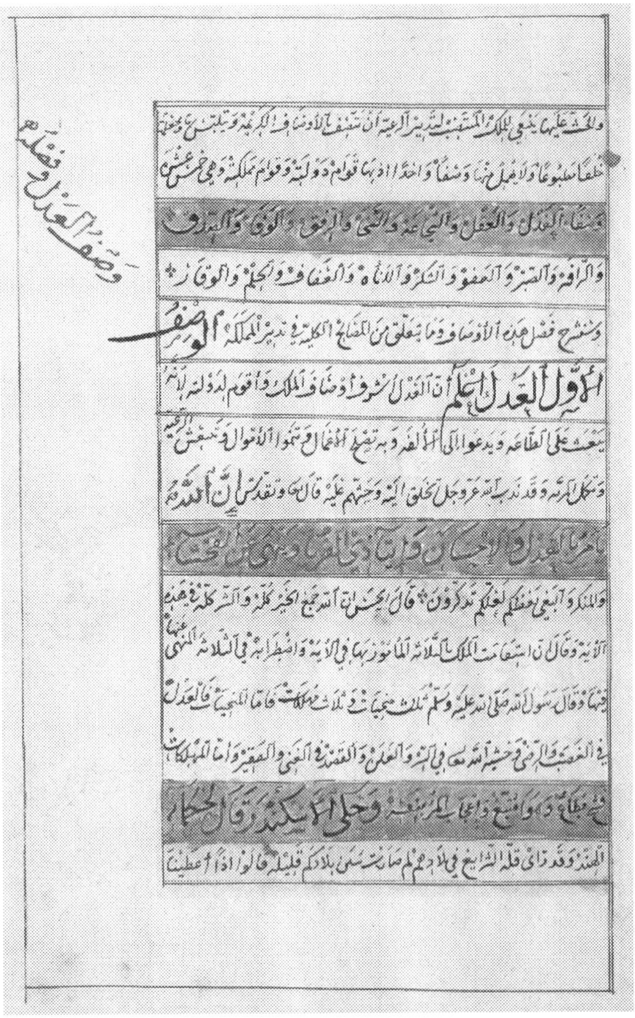

Figure 1 Two non-consecutive folios from a copy (dated 1115/1703–4) of al-Shayzarī, *al-Manhaj* [*sic*] *al-maslūk fī siyāsat al-mulūk*, Islamic Manuscripts Collection, Manuscripts Division, Department of Special Collections, Princeton University Library; Garrett Collection 138 HQ. The pages show entries for two (the first and the fifth) of fifteen royal qualities that al-Shayzarī identified as essential to the stability and endurance of the realm. Fig. 1a: MS 138 HQ, f. 4r, includes the point in the text where al-Shayzarī enumerates these fifteen indispensable royal qualities and begins his treatment of the first, justice (*ʿadl*). Fig. 1b: MS 138 HQ, f. 9r, includes the point in the text where al-Shayzarī discusses the fifth necessary quality, kindness (*rifq*). The different sections and voices in the text are reflected in the design of the pages. On f. 4r (Fig. 1a), the third line, set off by its gold background, presents al-Shayzarī's list of the fifteen necessary qualities; the fifth to sixth lines, using larger black lettering, introduce the first, justice, which is also

(b)

Figure 1 (cont.)

marked in the margin ('the quality of justice and its excellence'); the ninth line, set off in red lettering against a gold background, is a Qur'anic passage (16:90); and the penultimate line, against a gold background, introduces a narrative concerning Alexander. On f. 9r (Fig. 1b), the second line, using red ink and against a gold background, introduces the fifth quality, kindness (*rifq*). The formula following the invocation of the Prophet continues into the margin of the text at line 5, and accordingly highlights Prophetic speech. The lower marginal annotation, in which red ink appears against a gold background, signals a passage concerning Anūshīrvān, and the corresponding line within the frame, in the same palate, represents the beginning of this passage.
Photographs: Courtesy of Princeton University Library

Despite the centrality of the king in the mirror literature, mirrors concerned the entire courtly population, and many examples found a wide reception beyond the court as well.[59] Not uncommonly, viziers played almost as important a role in providing patronage as their sovereigns, a standing reflected in the large numbers of mirrors addressed to them.[60] A fair number of mirrors declare their importance to a general audience: one manuscript of the Arabic translation of Ghazālī's *Naṣīḥat al-mulūk* carries the label *Kitāb Naṣīḥat al-mulūk wa-kull ghanī wa-ṣuʿlūk* ('Book of Counsel for Kings and Every Rich Man and Beggar'), and extended 'titles' such as *Kitāb al-Adab wa-l-sulwān fī naṣāʾiḥ al-salāṭīn wa-l-mulūk wa-l-quḍāt wa-l-wuzarāʾ wa-l-wulāt wa-l-umarāʾ* ('Book of Etiquette and Solace: Counsels for Sultans, Kings, Judges, Viziers, Governors and Military Commanders') are not unusual.[61] In thirteenth-century Damascus, the Ashrafiyya Library, which catered not only to its resident scholars and students but also to external visitors, held copies of several of the items selected for inclusion in this volume.[62] Marginal annotations similarly reflect the engagement of readers with the mirror literature.[63] The manuscript record leaves little doubt that mirrors enjoyed a broad audience, especially in the seventeenth and eighteenth centuries, when in certain cities not only growing rates of literacy but also the increased affordability of books extended their availability to new, middle-level sections of society. Collections of wise sayings were

Collection, Manuscripts Division, Department of Special Collections, Princeton University Library; Garrett Collection, MS no. 138 HQ, ff. 4r, 9r).

59 The mirror literatures of medieval Christian Europe display the same feature; see, for example, Stone, 'Kings Are Different'.

60 Examples include the *Qawānīn al-wizāra* of al-Māwardī; a *Tuḥfat al-wuzarāʾ* by or attributed to al-Thaʿālibī (see Orfali, 'Works of Abū Manṣūr al-Thaʿālibī', 298–9, no. 36); the *Dustūr al-vizāra* of Maḥmūd b. Muḥammad b. al-Ḥusayn al-Iṣfahānī; the *Minhāj al-wuzarāʾ* of Aḥmad al-Iṣfahbadhī; see also van Gelder, 'Mirror for Princes or Vizor for Viziers'.

61 The manuscripts are MS Laud Or. 210, Bodleian Libraries, University of Oxford (see Bagley, 'Introduction', xxiii), and MS Garrett no. 4150Y, ff. 33r-46r, Islamic Manuscripts Collection, Manuscripts Division, Department of Special Collections, Princeton University Library (see Mach-Yahuda, *Catalogue of Arabic Manuscripts*, 409, no. 4753). Especially in its first recension, the *Mirṣād al-ʿibād*, mentioned above, provides another example of a mirror intended for a broad audience (see further Peacock, 'Advice for the Sultans of Rum', 290).

62 Hirschler, *Medieval Damascus: Plurality and Diversity in an Arabic Library*, 38, and entry nos. 1337 (Ghazālī, *Naṣīḥat al-mulūk*); 559, 1571 (al-Ṭurṭūshī, *Sirāj al-mulūk*); 554 (*al-Siyāsa = Kitāb al-Siyāsa fī tadbīr al-riyāsa*); 1266a (al-Māwardī, *Tashīl al-naẓar wa-taʿjīl al-ẓafar*); see also nos. 67, 1286a, 558.

63 Peacock, 'Advice for the Sultans of Rum', 295–300.

perennially in demand, and numerous variously edificatory pieces survive in miscellanies. An early seventeenth-century text of eclectic contents entitled *al-Tuḥfa al-saniyya fī siyāsat al-raʿiyya* ('The Splendid Gift: On the Governance of the Subjects') offers discussion of five pillars of sovereignty, ten requirements of royal justice, philosophers' testaments addressed to kings, the transmitted counsel of various authorities, a chapter composed of Prophetic texts drawn from the prolific scholar and historian Jalāl al-Dīn al-Suyūṭī (849–911/1445–1505), a chapter devoted to citations from sages, a sequence of narratives, an epilogue and, finally, added twelve days later, a supplement explicating pertinent expressions (*alfāẓ*).[64]

[64] By Muḥammad b. Muḥammad al-Burrī al-Mālikī, *al-Tuḥfa al-saniyya* survives in the author's autograph copy (dated Rabīʿ II 1026/April 1617) (Islamic Manuscripts Collection, Manuscripts Division, Department of Special Collections, Princeton University Library, Garrett no. 4150Y; see Mach-Yahuda, *Catalogue of Arabic Manuscripts*, 408–9, no. 4747).

2

Contexts

The examples of political advice contained in this anthology, written across terrain that stretched from Egypt to Central Asia, date from the first half of the tenth century to the first half of the twelfth century, a period that corresponds roughly to Hodgson's Islamic Early Middle Period (*c.* 945–1250).[1] Several factors contributed to the texts' selection. Firstly, limiting the examples to texts composed in the Early Middle Period highlights the writers' perceptions of and responses to the times in which they lived – a relatively contained period which nevertheless saw significant change. Secondly, it was during this period, as noted in Chapter 1, that the single-authored, thematically subdivided (*muṣannaf*) mirror-book emerged, and, since no prevailing set of expectations had yet become established, the mirrors of the Early Middle Period are often compositions of striking interest and individuality. Thirdly, the period's mirrors include several of the most celebrated examples of the entire Arabic, Persian and Turkish corpora of political advice.

The first section of this chapter (2.1) offers a general thematic summary of the period. It refers incidentally to periods of dynastic rule to be treated directly in section 2.2. This second section provides a roughly chronological account, in order to locate the specific settings in which the anthology's selected mirrors were produced and to convey the interconnections among their authors.

[1] See Hodgson, *Venture of Islam*, II: 6–7; and Chapter 1, n. 13.

2.1 The Early Middle Period

The Early Middle Period begins with the political disintegration of the territories that had made up the eighth- and ninth-century caliphate and ends with a political re-integration of a new and quite different character. In social, cultural and religious terms, it marks a transition from a long period of striking variety – in the words of one scholar, 'exuberant hybridity' – towards a period of greater homogeneity, through the generation of new forms that would prove remarkably durable.[2]

The tenth century witnessed a relocation of power and economic vitality from Baghdad and Iraq to regional settings, where a commonwealth of polities, under the rule of Muslim dynastic families, rose, flourished and fell, largely independently of the Abbasid caliphs. At the base of this regional redistribution of power lay a series of economic factors, including the collapse of the earlier Abbasid fiscal system, the reduced productivity of Iraq and the subsequent loss of revenue accruing to the caliphate.[3] The reduction of caliphal power had begun in the previous century, when the Abbasid governors Ṭāhir (I) b. al-Ḥusayn (159–207/776–822) and Aḥmad b. Ṭūlūn (220–70/835–84) had succeeded in passing on their powerful offices to their heirs, initiating the dynasties of, respectively, the Tahirids (205–78/821–91) in Khurasan and the Tulunids (254–92/868–905) in Egypt.[4] Even in Iraq, the Abbasids lost control to their Turkish military commanders, who regularly installed and deposed caliphs according to their interests.[5] The general rise of regional polities in the tenth century completed the caliphs' loss of effective power.

As the power of the caliphs diminished, the caliphal office gradually attained new kinds of significance. It came to represent a powerful symbolic link with the early Muslim community; the caliphs' endorsement of the new dynastic rulers provided the latter with a prized token of legitimacy; and in the first half of the eleventh century, beginning with

[2] Chamberlain, 'Military Patronage States'; the quotation is from p. 135.

[3] Kennedy, 'The Late ʿAbbāsid Pattern', 360–93.

[4] Ṭāhir (I) b. al-Ḥusayn, governor of Khurasan from 205–7/821–2, was also the author of a widely disseminated advisory Testament (see above, and Chapter 1, n. 23). Aḥmad b. Ṭūlūn became governor of Egypt from 257/871. On the Tahirids, see Bonner, 'Waning of Empire', 313–22; Kaabi, *Les Ṭāhirides*, 173–312; Daniel, 'Islamic East', 490–3. On the Tulunids, see Bonner, 'Waning of Empire', 319–22; Brett, 'Egypt', 559–60.

[5] Bonner, 'Waning of Empire', 305–13; Van Steenbergen, *History of the Islamic World*, 150–6; Kennedy, *The Prophet and the Age of the Caliphates*, 158–87; Gordon, *Breaking of a Thousand Swords*, esp. 75–140.

the caliph al-Qādir (r. 381–422/991–1031), the Abbasids emerged as leaders of, specifically, a newly self-conscious Sunni Muslim community. Under propitious conditions, this new status facilitated a brief resumption of significant caliphal political and military power in the early twelfth century.[6]

From North Africa to Transoxiana and present-day Afghanistan, the provinces formerly under caliphal governance, now separate political entities, remained interlinked by ties of religion, language, trade and pilgrimage.[7] In many regions, conversion, though highly uneven, with marked differences from town to town and between urban and rural locations, had produced Muslim majorities, and most major cities now possessed prominent local Muslim families.[8] The Arabic language had become, and remained, an administrative, commercial, scholarly and literary lingua franca within and beyond the area of the former caliphal domains. But the Early Middle Period also saw the development of distinctive, regionally defined cultural patterns, including the rise of the New Persian language and its transregional spread, from modern-day Pakistan and Afghanistan to Anatolia.[9] The mirrors selected for inclusion in this anthology reflect the period's regional diversity and the immense cultural achievement that its disparate political formations fostered.

The period's regional polities depended on their ability to command military force. To establish and maintain their power they relied upon either professional armies composed largely of military slaves, the support of tribal populations who had affiliated themselves with the dynastic family, or a combination of the two; each of these models tended to produce a different pattern of state formation.[10] Reliance on

[6] In the later Seljuk period, the sultans' power decreased, and the political and military power of the caliphs increased; see Tor, 'Political Revival of the Abbasid Caliphate'; Hanne, *Putting the Caliph in His Place*, 141–80 and *passim*.

[7] Kennedy, 'The Late ʿAbbāsid Pattern', 361.

[8] Bulliet, *Patricians of Nishapur*, 85–8; Bulliet, 'Conversion to Islam'.

[9] Eventually the language would become deeply established across South Asia as well; see Spooner and Hanaway, 'Introduction: Persian as *Koine*'; Alam and Subrahmanyam, *Writing the Mughal World*, esp. 311–38; de Weese, 'Persian and Turkic from Kazan to Tobolsk'.

[10] Kennedy, 'The Late ʿAbbāsid Pattern', 362–4. My occasional use of the term 'state' to refer to the various polities of the period implies their capacity to exert only a fairly minimal degree of control over their subject populations. In the Early Middle Period, rulers' contacts with the vast majority of their subjects, always indirect (see Chapter 1, n. 6), entailed principally taxation and sporadic levies of troops. The obligations of the

professional armies, composed chiefly of soldiers initially acquired as slaves and trained for military service, required a system of governance capable of producing an abundant and steady stream of revenue, both for the constant acquisition and training of slaves and for the payment of their salaries. Tribal forces presented no need for systematic arrangements of this kind, but nor were they amenable to the restrictions or impositions, such as taxation, that a state, once established, was likely to demand. The Samanids and Ghaznavids, like the Abbasids, depended heavily on the use of slave soldiers (*ghilmān*, sing. *ghulām*, or *mamālīk*, sing. *mamlūk*). Neither the Buyids nor the Fatimids, who owed their early successes to the support of Daylami and Kutama ('Berber') populations respectively, began with this dependency, but both developed into states in which military slavery figured increasingly substantially.[11] The Karakhanids, by contrast, seem never to have used the mechanism of military slavery; they relied instead on their fellow tribesmen, with whom they maintained close relations.[12] In the most striking example of the period, the Seljuks owed their rise to power to their successful leadership of various nomadic Turkish groups (chiefly Oghuz, some of whom became known as Türkmen).[13] In the Seljuk case, it seems that the nomads, rather than receiving payment for their services, supported themselves by means of their herds and the booty captured in battles and raids; their leaders probably received presents, rather than salaries, from the ruling house.[14] The Türkmen groups remained important in the maintenance and extension of Seljuk power, even as, probably from about 447/1055, the Seljuk dynasty, like many earlier polities, eventually

ruling power towards the subject population included the provision of security against external invasion and internal threats, and the upholding of justice. The redress of grievances (*maẓālim*), an important demonstration of royal justice, permitted subjects limited forms of direct contact with the ruler or, more commonly, the ruler's representatives (for examples, see Lev, *Administration of Justice*, 202–28); see further Nielsen, 'Maẓālim'; van Berkel, 'Politics of Access'; and Chapter 7, n. 24.

11 Donohue, *The Buwayhid Dynasty*, 192–210; Brett, 'Egypt', 576–7; Van Steenbergen, *History of the Islamic World*, 161–3; Tor, 'Mamluks in the Military'.

12 Bosworth, 'Steppe Peoples', 29.

13 The term Türkmen, which appears as early as the tenth century as a designation for Oghuz who had become Muslim, continued to be used for the Seljuks' nomadic subjects. See Peacock, *Great Seljuk Empire*, 22–5, 27–8; Bosworth, 'Steppe Peoples', 34; Safi, *Politics of Knowledge*, 12–13. The name Oghuz is Turkish; its form in Arabic and Persian is Ghuzz. Similarly, *türkmen* is the Turkish form of the word; the Persian form is *turkamān* (sing.), *turkamānān* (pl.).

14 Amitai, 'Armies and Their Economic Basis', 542.

resorted, in addition, to professional armies composed of diverse contingents of slave troops.[15]

The rise of Turkish Muslim rulers in the states established in the former caliphal domains and the migrations of Turkic peoples into Iran and Western Asia were among the most striking and enduring transformations of the Early Middle Period. In the case of the Ghaznavids, it was military slavery that created their opportunity to seize power; their founding rulers began as *ghilmān* and proceeded, in the first example of the pattern, to initiate a dynasty of their own. The Seljuks, by contrast, already constituted a leading family when they and their nomadic followers irrupted into the easternmost fringes of Muslim settlement. Their military strength, grounded in the groups of Oghuz nomads who had joined them, permitted their gradual expansion across Iran. When, having reached western Iran, the Seljuks made that area into the centre of their empire, numbers of their Türkmen followers continued their quest for pasturage into the north and west. These migrations effected permanent demographic, environmental and economic changes in Iran, Azerbaijan, the southern Caucasus and Anatolia, with the spread of pastoralism and the eventual settlement of Turkish (and Muslim) populations in these regions.[16]

As important as the increased presence of nomads in parts of Iran, Iraq and the north-west were developments in practices of land tenure, taxation and agriculture. A characteristic feature of the period was the spread and increasing scope of the *iqṭāʿ*, a term applied to a great variety of fiscal and land-holding arrangements, all of which involved an initial grant, made by the governing authority, of rights to collect taxes in a given area of land.[17] The system, never uniform, evolved continuously during (and after) the Early Middle Period. Its gradual expansion reflected governmental difficulties in meeting the high costs of salaries

[15] See Chamberlain, 'Military Patronage States', 143–4. The composition and training of the army received the attention of Niẓām al-Mulk; see *Siyar al-mulūk*, 136–9 = Darke, *Book of Government*, 99–102 (and see further below, n. 64).

[16] Peacock, *Early Seljūq History*, 1–6, 128–63; Bosworth, 'Steppe Peoples', 23; Amitai, 'Armies and Their Economic Basis', 545–6; Peacock, *Great Seljuk Empire*, 20–71.

[17] On the *iqṭāʿ*, see Lambton, 'Eqṭāʿ'; Cahen, 'L'évolution de l'iqtaʿ'. The term was sometimes applied to the land-grant itself. On the emergence of *iqṭāʿ*, see also Gordon, 'The Turkish Officers of Samarra'. For the Buyid period, see Mottahedeh, 'Note on the "*Tasbīb*"'; Cahen, 'L'évolution de l'iqtaʿ', 38–42; Bonner, 'Waning of Empire', 352–4; for the Seljuk period, see Lambton, 'Eqṭāʿ'; Safi, *Politics of Knowledge*, 87–90; Peacock, *Great Seljuk Empire*, 189–215 and *passim*.

for military personnel: the *iqṭāʿ* effectively allowed the grantee to collect his salary directly and released the government from the obligation to provide monetary payments. A widespread result of the system was military involvement in the management of agricultural land. In the Buyid period, the terms of the grant usually included an explicit limit on its duration and the denial of all rights of jurisdiction over the territory's tax-paying population. In practice and over time, and especially in the Seljuk period, the grantees' effective powers over the land and its population grew so much that, especially in the case of large grants, the division between the *muqṭaʿ* (assignee), on the one hand, and the local governor, on the other, became indistinct; both individuals functioned as deputies to the ruler.[18] If in some cases the arrangements worked to encourage investment in the land and its development, in other cases they exposed the population to hardship and abuse. A large part of the mirror-writers' overriding concern with justice was economic in nature: a sound economy, in which the producers of wealth were secure enough to be able to provide dependable labour, was essential to the support of the state – not only in financial terms, through the generation of revenue, but also in political terms, through the maintenance of social stability. Agriculture, the major economic base of the state, was always vulnerable to anomalous natural and climatic conditions and to political events; to offset this unpredictability, the mirror-writers urged their ruler-recipients to oversee the maintenance of irrigation structures and to promote investment in the land's productivity.

In another lasting change of the Early Middle Period, the era's new political configurations coincided with and to some degree stimulated the development of firmer delineations of sectarian differences. This process included the articulation of contrasting expressions of Shiʿi Islam. The Buyids and Fatimids, most notably, promoted the development of distinctive intellectual and ritual markers to distinguish themselves as much from one another as from non-Shiʿi polities and populations.[19] The Buyids, who had taken the Abbasid capital of Baghdad in 334/945, sponsored, with the Shia of Baghdad, the development of Twelver Shiʿi intellectual and cultural forms. Rather than seeking to displace the caliphs, they strived to achieve an accommodation with them; indeed, like most of the period's rulers, they coveted the caliphs' formal

[18] Peacock, *Great Seljuk Empire*, 191.
[19] Lev, 'The Fāṭimid Caliphate and the Ayyūbids', 205–6.

endorsement of their power.[20] By contrast, the Fatimids, who were Ismaili Shiʿis, explicitly rejected the Abbasid caliphate; they themselves claimed to have inherited the office of the imamate in a direct line of descent from ʿAlī, the First Imam, through Ismāʿīl, oldest son of Jaʿfar al-Ṣādiq (d. 148/765), the Sixth Imam.[21]

The eleventh century, partly in response to the defining of Shiʿism, witnessed a trend towards a consolidation of Sunnism.[22] This process, though neither uniform nor co-ordinated, found expression in all branches of the religious sciences; some of the mirror-writers represented in this collection contributed to the project.[23] The caliph al-Qādir (r. 381–422/991–1031) promulgated a creed, which his successor al-Qāʾim (r. 422–67/1031–75) affirmed; specifically Sunni rituals developed as well.[24] Gradually, the categories of Sunni and Shiʿi acquired

[20] The Buyids, who styled themselves *amīr*, *malik* and sometimes *shāhānshāh* ('king of kings', an ancient Iranian title), assumed titles such as Muʿizz al-Dawla ('magnifier of the state') and ʿAḍud al-Dawla ('support of the state'); ending in the formula *al-Dawla*, these titles suggested a role within rather than above or outside the state, implicitly, in this case, the caliphal state. On Buyid titulature, see Madelung, 'The Assumption of the Title Shāhānshāh'; Treadwell, '*Shāhānshāh* and *al-Malik al-Muʾayyad*'; Richter-Bernburg, '*Amīr-Malik-Shāhānshāh*' (see further below, at n. 45). For a striking enactment of Abbasid-Buyid relations, see the encounter between ʿAḍud al-Dawla, seeking additional caliphal recognition, and Caliph al-Ṭāʾiʿ (r. 363–81/974–91) in the year 367/977 (Ibn al-Jawzī, *al-Muntaẓam*, XIV: 252–3; translated and discussed in al-Azmeh, *Secularism in the Arab World*, 36–7).

[21] When Ismāʿīl predeceased his father, the universally revered Jaʿfar al-Ṣādiq, most of the latter's followers transferred their allegiance to his surviving son Mūsā, but some, who would become known as Ismailis, continued to follow a line through Ismāʿīl's son Muḥammad; see Daftary, *The Ismāʿīlīs: Their History and Doctrines*, 87–98. The term 'imamate' (Ar. *imāma*) was used widely in theological and juristic discourses to denote legitimate leadership of the Muslim community, but it developed different connotations among different groups, who identified it with different individuals and lineages. In the Shiʿi tradition, after ʿAlī, who became the Fourth Caliph and was, for the Shia, the First Imam, the imamate and the historical caliphate diverged. The Fatimids' adoption of the title 'caliph' in addition to 'imam' marked their repudiation of Abbasid claims to legitimate authority.

[22] Berkey, *Formation of Islam*, 189–202; Ephrat, 'The Seljuqs and the Public Sphere'; Peacock, *Great Seljuk Empire*, 246–72; Bulliet, *View from the Edge*, 115–27, 145–68, esp. 146–8; Van Renterghem, 'Controlling and Developing Baghdad', 120–3.

[23] Al-Māwardī, for example, composed *al-Iqnāʿ*, representing the Shāfiʿī perspective, in response to Caliph al-Qādir's request for juridical manuals from each of the four Sunni schools of law (*madhāhib*).

[24] See Makdisi, *Ibn ʿAqil: Religion and Culture in Classical Islam*, 8–12; Hanne, *Putting the Caliph in His Place*, 70–2, 112–13 and *passim*. The boundaries articulated in the creed rejected not only Shiʿism but also, in at least as pronounced a fashion, the broad rationalist movement of Muʿtazilism (on which see Vasalou, *Moral Agents and Their Deserts*). Affinities with Muʿtazilī reasoning appear in the work of Pseudo-Māwardī and

clearer and, as Jonathan Berkey has pointed out, more homogeneous forms.[25] The process proceeded alongside Ismaili challenges, which persisted, albeit highly unevenly, through most of the Early Middle Period. In the later ninth century, a network of Ismaili missionaries (*duʿāt*, sing. *dāʿī*) – agents charged with *daʿwa*, the call for allegiance – had become active in several areas, including Iraq, Syria, Fars and Khurasan, in which last province their most notable converts included the Samanid amir Naṣr II b. Aḥmad (r. 301–31/914–43).[26] By far the greatest Ismaili political accomplishment, however, was the formation of the Fatimid empire, which, following the Fatimids' expansion from Tunisia into Egypt in 358/969, began sending its own missionaries throughout Western Asia and Iran.[27] In these circumstances, the Buyids' competitors, notably the Ghaznavids and the Seljuks, found it expedient to accentuate their Sunni affiliations and to portray themselves as defenders of the Abbasid caliphs against Buyids and Fatimids alike. In fact, following the Seljuks' replacement of the Buyids in Baghdad in 447/1055, the new dynasty proved unyielding in its treatment of the Abbasids, who resisted the demotion that the Seljuks visited upon them; the Seljuks' actions, moreover, did not reflect the implacable hostility towards Shiʿis that their rhetoric might have implied.[28] Nevertheless, the Ghaznavids' and Seljuks' expressions of obeisance to the Abbasids enhanced the prestige of the latter, who now presented themselves as leaders of a specifically Sunni Muslim population. As Hugh Kennedy has observed, by the death of the caliph al-Qādir, the Abbasid caliph commanded no troops and controlled no land beyond the gates of his palace, but he had established his moral and religious authority for the Sunni community.[29]

to a degree, if indirectly, al-Māwardī himself (on the former, see Anṣārī, 'Yek andīsheh-nāmeh'; on the latter, see Melchert, 'Māwardī, Abū Yaʿlá, and the Sunni Revival', 46–7; Cook, *Commanding Right*, 344; Marlow, *Counsel for Kings*, I: 14, 248, n. 76).

[25] Berkey, *Formation of Islam*, 189.

[26] See Daftary, *The Ismāʿīlīs: Their History and Doctrines*, 98–126; Bonner, 'Waning of Empire', 324–32; Crone and Treadwell, 'A New Text on Ismailism'; and below, Chapter 9, Text 16.

[27] See Daftary, *The Ismāʿīlīs: Their History and Doctrines*, 137–237; Walker, 'The Ismaili Daʿwa in the Reign of . . . al-Ḥākim'. On the Fatimids, see below, section 2.2.

[28] Van Renterghem, 'Controlling and Developing Baghdad', 118–20; Hanne, *Putting the Caliph in His Place*, 102–41; Safi, *Politics of Knowledge*, 1–42, esp. 35–42; Peacock, *Great Seljuk Empire*, 124–55; Tor, 'Tale of Two Murders'; Tor, 'Political Revival'; and see below, n. 65.

[29] Kennedy, 'The Late ʿAbbāsid Pattern', 393.

The visible successes of non-Sunni movements and communities constituted only one factor in the consolidating trends in Sunni identity. In the eleventh century, numerous cities from Baghdad to Herat suffered from internal conflicts often expressed in terms of sectarian or factional difference. A particularly common line of fracture appeared between adherents of the Ḥanafī and Shāfiʿī (and in Baghdad, the Ḥanbalī) schools of (Sunni) law. These factional conflicts were neither new nor invariable, but they seem to have augmented in intensity with the coming of the Seljuks, who (with perhaps unanticipated results) intervened in carefully balanced local configurations of power and status.[30] A notable feature of the period, the founding of madrasas – part-residential institutions of higher learning, especially associated with the teaching of law according to the established legal schools (*madhāhib*, sing. *madhhab*) – may on occasion have exacerbated tensions, even as it perhaps also, in some cases, contributed to a re-centring of Sunni Islam.[31] The creation of madrasas, and of the *khānaqāh*s, likewise combining residential, instructional and ritual facilities, that developed for Sufi communities, provided new opportunities for patronage and a new stimulus to mobility; not only merchants, but also students, scholars, Sufis, scientists, philosophers, men of letters and poets spent years of their lives far away from their homelands, and broader sections of the population strived to undertake the pilgrimage to Mecca (*ḥajj*), often travelling great distances, if they were able to do so.[32]

This volume's selections chart different moments and reflect different perspectives in this period of transition and change. The following

[30] See Berkey, *Formation of Islam*, 217–18; Ephrat, *A Learned Society in a Period of Transition*, 85–93; Bulliet, *Patricians of Nishapur*, 61–74; Bulliet, 'Local Politics of Eastern Iran' (treating also Ghaznavid strategies intended to win the support of local factions); Bulliet, *View from the Edge*, 122–4; Durand-Guédy, *Iranian Elites and Turkish Rulers*, 197–204, 230–55; Safi, *Politics of Knowledge*, 25–35, 53–6, 93–5; Peacock, *Great Seljuk Empire*, 37–8, 202, 249–50, 268–72, 311–14.

[31] Safi, *Politics of Knowledge*, 90–7; Mottahedeh, 'Transmission of Knowledge', 66, 71; Berkey, *Formation of Islam*, 196–8; Chamberlain, *Knowledge and Social Practice*, 69–90; Van Renterghem, 'Controlling and Developing Baghdad', 121–3. The concept of a 'recentering' of Sunnism (as opposed to a 'revival') is Bulliet's (*View from the Edge*, 145–68, 177–8 and *passim*).

[32] On the madrasa as an instrument of patronage, see Peacock, *Great Seljuk Empire*, 211–15, 266–7; Safi, *Politics of Knowledge*, 90–7; Bulliet, *Patricians of Nishapur*, 70–4; Chamberlain, 'Military Patronage States', 145; Durand-Guédy, *Iranian Elites and Turkish Rulers*, 123–9. On the *khānaqāh*, see also Safi, *Politics of Knowledge*, 97–100; Berkey, *Transmission of Knowledge*, 56–60; Van Steenbergen, *History of the Islamic World*, 196–200.

section offers an account of the specific regions and polities that saw the production of the mirrors presented in Part II.

2.2 The Polities of the Tenth and Eleventh Centuries

The Samanids

Setting aside the authorless *Sirr al-asrār*, the earliest of this volume's mirrors is probably the *Naṣīḥat al-mulūk* of Pseudo-Māwardī. It seems likely that Pseudo-Māwardī wrote in the Samanid domains, possibly during the reign of the amir Naṣr II b. Aḥmad (r. 301–31/914–43), who, as previously mentioned, embraced towards the end of his reign the teachings of the Ismaili *daʿwa*. The Samanids (204–395/819–1005), a dynastic family of Iranian background, began their rise to power when the caliph al-Maʾmūn (r. 198–218/813–33) initiated the appointment of four Samanid brothers to the governorships of locations to the east and south of the Oxus River: Samarqand, Farghana, Shash (modern-day Tashkent) and Herat.[33] The family established its rule throughout Transoxiana. Following their defeat of the Saffarids (247–393/861–1003) at Balkh in 287/900, the Samanids also acquired the province of Khurasan.[34] The caliph al-Muʿtaḍid (r. 279–89/892–902) promptly appointed the victorious Samanid amir Ismāʿīl b. Aḥmad (r. 279–95/892–907) governor of the two provinces, Transoxiana and Khurasan. Through the conventional markers of *khuṭba* and *sikka* – respectively, the oration delivered in conjunction with the Friday noon-time congregational prayer and the coinage – the Samanids maintained a minimal acknowledgement of Abbasid authority, but their liminal position (they retained their capital in the city of Bukhara) ensured their autonomy.[35]

[33] See Treadwell, 'Political History', I: 64–103; Daniel, 'Islamic East', 498–505; Bonner, 'Waning of Empire', 344–6.

[34] On the Saffarids, whose relative absence from this discussion reflects only the seeming lack of advisory literature addressed to them, see Bosworth, *History of the Saffarids*; Tor, 'Historical Representations of Yaʿqūb b. al-Layth'; Daniel, 'Islamic East', 493–8. The Saffarids appear as largely negative examples in *Siyar al-mulūk* and elsewhere; see Chapter 7, Text 11.

[35] Acknowledgement of the ruling authority was a traditional element in the *khuṭba*; see Qutbuddin, '*Khuṭba*: The Evolution of Early Arabic Oration', 190–4. The inclusion of the caliph's name in the *sikka*, coinage, constituted a formal acknowledgement of and subservience to the caliph of the time (see Heidemann, 'Numismatics', 648–9, 660). See further below, Chapter 6, n. 48, and for a Ghaznavid example, see Figure 4.

The early Samanids' proximity to the frontier enabled them to benefit from lucrative transregional trade and from campaigning in the Inner Asian steppe; warfare against non-Muslim populations brought them large numbers of slaves and strengthened their claims to legitimacy.[36] At times the Samanids campaigned in the Caspian regions, where they established their suzerainty and negotiated alliances with local dynasties such as the Ziyarids (*c.* 319–483/931–1090), who, founded by the brothers Mardāvīj b. Ziyār (r. 319–23/931–5) and Vushmgīr, ruled in Gurgan and Tabaristan.[37] The Ziyarid amir Kaykāʾūs, whose mirror, known as the *Qābūsnāmeh*, takes its name from the author's grandfather, the amir Qābūs b. Vushmgīr (r. 366–71/977–81 and 388–403/998–1012 or 1013), was among the last of the Ziyarid rulers.[38]

In the latter half of the tenth century, the Samanids faced the rising power of the Buyids, with whom they competed over territory in central and northern Iran. Among the most notable initiatives of the Samanids and their governors was the promotion of the literary medium of New Persian, that is, the Persian language, now including a large vocabulary of Arabic loanwords, written in the Arabic script. The Samanids also sponsored an extensive project of translations from Arabic into Persian.[39]

The Karakhanids

The confessional frontier shifted when the Karakhanids (382–609/992–1212), a Turkish confederation within which members of the ruling family held different cities and regions, converted to Islam in roughly the mid-tenth century. It was to the Karakhanids and the Ghaznavids that the Samanids fell at the end of the century. Ḥasan Bughra Khan occupied Bukhara in 382/992; when in 389/999 another member of the Karakhanid family, the Ilig Naṣr b. ʿAlī of Özkend, took Bukhara, he

[36] Bonner, 'Waning of Empire', 344.

[37] On the Ziyarids, see Bosworth, 'Chronology of the Ziyārids'; Madelung, 'Minor Dynasties of Northern Iran', 212–16 and *passim*.

[38] At one point in 369/979, Qābūs was evicted by the Buyids, who proceeded to rule his territories directly, while he took refuge with the Samanids. In 388/998 Qābūs returned, on good terms with the Samanids' successors, the Ghaznavids, with whom the Ziyarids also intermarried. Qābūs excelled in the literary arts, demonstrating his skill in Arabic and, to a lesser extent, Persian; his grandson Kaykāʾūs, author of the *Qābūsnāmeh*, wrote his mirror in Persian (see below, section 3.5 and Chapter 3, n. 45).

[39] Daniel, 'Islamic East', 502–3; Meisami, *Persian Historiography*, 15–37; Zadeh, *The Vernacular Qurʾan*, 302–30.

divided the Samanid domains with the Ghaznavid sultan Maḥmūd (r. 388–421/998–1030).[40] Out of the loose confederation of the Karakhanids, two lines, an eastern and a western branch, eventually emerged. From roughly the early to mid-eleventh century, the eastern 'Ḥasanid' branch consolidated its power in the original Karakhanid territories of Semirechye, Farghana and Kashgharia, while the western branch controlled the formerly Samanid territories of Transoxiana. The two branches developed somewhat different cultural styles: the western Karakhanids, in Transoxiana, continued the cultural patterns – specifically the use of Persian – of their Samanid predecessors; the eastern branch fostered the use of Turkish, both as an official and a literary language. A prime example of this early Karakhanid Turkish literature is the mirror for princes *Kutadgu bilig* ('Wisdom of Royal Glory'), which its author Yūsuf Khāṣṣ Ḥājib, writing in the religious and cultural centre of Kashghar, dedicated to Khan Ḥasan b. Sulaymān (r. 467–96/1075–1103).[41]

Like the Ghaznavids, the Karakhanids sought the recognition and endorsement of the Abbasid caliphs: in their coinage, the western Karakhanids, following an established model, styled themselves *mawlā amīr al-muʾminīn*, 'Client of the Commander of the Faithful'.[42] At various times, the western and eastern branches of the Karakhanids became vassals of the Seljuks.[43]

The Buyids

Hailing from Daylam, along the south-western shore of the Caspian Sea, the Buyids (320–454/932–1062) created a large though decentralised polity in Iraq (334–447/945–1055) and western and central Iran. Initially mercenary soldiers in the employ of various rulers, including, latterly,

[40] The terms *ilig* and *khan* were distinct ranks in the ruling hierarchy of the dynasty, the former subordinate to the latter (Bosworth, 'Ilek-k͟hāns or Ḳarak͟hānids').

[41] On the Karakhanids' 'distinctly Turco-Islamic culture', see Golden, 'Turks and Iranians: An Historical Sketch', 28; see also Paul, 'Karakhanids'.

[42] This honorific title, attested as early as the reign of Caliph al-Manṣūr (r. 136–58/754–75), did not necessarily imply any formal relationship with the caliph (Wensinck and Crone, 'Mawlā'; Crone, *Slaves on Horses*, 75). It was in common use in the Early Middle Period: Kaykāʾūs refers to himself by this epithet (*Qābūsnāmeh*, 3), and in 426/1035 the Seljuks described themselves as *mawālī amīr al-muʾminīn*; see Bosworth, 'Steppe Peoples', 41; Safi, *Politics of Knowledge*, 5; Van Steenbergen, *History of the Islamic World*, 180.

[43] Bosworth, 'Steppe Peoples', 53–4.

Mardāvīj b. Ziyār, members of the Buyid family eventually took control of the territories that their services had helped Mardāvīj to attain.[44] Three Buyid brothers succeeded in gaining caliphal recognition: the eldest, ʿAlī, invested with the title ʿImād al-Dawla, ruled in Fars; Ḥasan, with the title Rukn al-Dawla (d. 366/976), ruled in the Jibal; and Aḥmad, with the title Muʿizz al-Dawla, ruled in Kirman and Khuzistan.[45] In 334/945 Aḥmad entered Baghdad and established there the Buyid dominion that would endure until the last Buyids fell to the Seljuks in 447/1055. When ʿAlī, ʿImād al-Dawla, ruler of Fars, died in 338/949 without heir, Ḥasan's son ʿAḍud al-Dawla (324–72/936–83) took control of the province and became the leading member of the dynastic family. The various territories within the Buyid domains were, as in the case of ʿAḍud al-Dawla's reign, sometimes united under a single Buyid ruler and sometimes separate. Like the Samanids, the Buyids at times compelled the allegiance of dynasties in the Caspian region, such as the Ziyarids, who, after about 400/1011–12, became vassals of the Ghaznavids and then the Seljuks.

The linkage under Buyid rule of Iraq and western Iran played a significant role in the continued nearly exclusive use of Arabic as the language of administration and literary culture in these areas, even as Persian had developed extensively in the eastern regions over the course of the previous century. Indeed, the Buyid era saw great accomplishments in Arabic letters, as exemplified not least in the *oeuvres* of the Buyids' viziers (most notably, al-Ṣāḥib Ibn ʿAbbād, d. 385/995), as well as the prose writings of the historian, philosopher and ethicist Miskawayh (d. 421/1030).[46]

At the beginning of the Buyids' rule, borders between Sunni and Shiʿi understandings of Islam, and within the Shia, were often indistinct, but, as mentioned in section 2.1, the Buyids, once they had attained

[44] On the Buyids, see Nagel, 'Buyids'; Kennedy, 'Late ʿAbbāsid Pattern', 364–70; Mottahedeh, *Loyalty and Leadership*; Busse, *Chalif und Grosskönig*; Donohue, *The Buwayhid Dynasty*.

[45] Titulature played an important part in rulers' self-presentation and claims to rule. For the Samanids' and Buyids' adoption of the titles *malik*, 'king', and *shāhānshāh*, 'king of kings', see Madelung, 'The Assumption of the Title Shāhānshāh'; Treadwell, '*Shāhānshāh* and *al-Malik al-Muʾayyad*'; Richter-Bernburg, '*Amīr-Malik-Shāhānshāh*'; Busse, *Chalif und Grosskönig*, 159–84; and above, n. 20.

[46] On al-Ṣāḥib Ibn ʿAbbād, see Pomerantz, 'Political Biography'. Miskawayh was employed as a secretary and librarian under several Buyid viziers and eventually under the amir ʿAḍud al-Dawla.

ascendancy in Baghdad, fostered a blossoming of the religious sciences among the Twelver Shia and promoted the establishment of distinctively Shiʿi festivals. Seeking at the same time to establish a constructive co-existence with the Abbasid caliphs, the Buyids depended on intermediaries, whom they found among the notable Shia families of Baghdad, such as the Sharīfs al-Raḍī (d. 406/1015) and al-Murtaḍā (355–436/967–1044), theologians and littérateurs, and certain Sunni intellectuals, such as the chief judge al-Māwardī, who associated with and seems to have composed mirrors for Abbasid and Buyid figures alike. The Buyids faced competition in the earlier part of their rule from the Samanids, and later, more significantly, from the Ghaznavids, who, seeking to use their Sunnism to their advantage, carried out a destructive occupation of Rayy in 420/1029.[47] In 447/1055, the Seljuks took control of Baghdad and completed the fall of the Buyid dominion.

The Ghaznavids

The Ghaznavids rose to power in present-day Afghanistan in the second half of the tenth century.[48] A Turkish dynasty, the Ghaznavids were named not for an eponymous ancestor but for the city of Ghazna, captured first by the former Samanid general Alptigin and next, in about 366/977, by a slave soldier in Alptigin's employ, Sebüktigin (d. 387/997). In the last days of the Samanids, Sebüktigin led his army into Khurasan. Ghazna became the capital of Sebüktigin's son Maḥmūd (r. 388–421/998–1030), who, after the fall of the Samanids, inherited almost all of Khurasan and Afghanistan.[49] In this period, the Ghaznavids amassed enormous wealth on the basis of, on the one hand, the abundant tax revenues of Khurasan and, on the other, the extraordinarily rich plunder seized in the course of Maḥmūd's numerous campaigns against non-Muslim communities in Afghanistan and Hindustan (northern India). Permanent annexation seems unlikely to have constituted a major objective of these early expeditions into South Asia.[50] Nevertheless, Maḥmūd continued to extend the

[47] The Ghaznavid assault against Rayy singled out Shiʿis, Muʿtazilīs and their institutions, notably libraries; see Bosworth, *Ghaznavids*, 53, 200.

[48] On the Ghaznavids, see Bosworth, *Ghaznavids*; Inaba, 'Ghaznavids'; Kennedy, 'Late ʿAbbāsid Pattern', 370–80.

[49] See above, at n. 40.

[50] Lahore, however, became an important centre in the early Ghaznavid state; as early as the reign of Maḥmūd, the Ghaznavid mint in Lahore issued bilingual Arabic-Sanskrit coins.

Ghaznavid territories; notably, in 408/1017, he took direct control of Kh^{v}arazm, the province previously under the rule of his late brother-in -law, the Kh^{v}ārazmshāh al-Maʾmūn II b. Maʾmūn I (r. 399–407 or 408/1009–17), recipient of the *Ādāb al-mulūk* of al-Thaʿālibī. The Maʾmūnid Kh^{v}ārazmshāhs (385–408/995–1017), a short-lived line of rulers bearing this ancient title, had seized power in Kh^{v}varazm in 385/995 and made their capital in Gurganj (Ar. al-Jurjaniyya), on the left bank of the Oxus. Maḥmūd's seizure of Kh^{v}arazm brought the Ghaznavids into immediate proximity with the Oghuz nomads of the surrounding steppes.

The Ghaznavids in many respects perpetuated the administrative and cultural models of their Samanid predecessors. In a symbolic demonstration of royal prestige, they gathered an assembly of intellectual luminaries at their court.[51] After Maḥmūd took control of Kh^{v}arazm, he brought back to Ghazna the scientist Abū Rayḥān al-Bīrūnī (d. after 442/1050) and al-Thaʿālibī, both of whom wrote almost exclusively in Arabic. The Ghaznavids also sponsored literary composition, in poetry and prose, in the Persian language. The most notable product of this initiative was the great epic, the *Shāhnāmeh* of Firdawsī (d. 410/1019 or 416/1025), who had begun the poem under the Samanids but completed it in around 400/1010, during the reign of Maḥmūd. Many of the mirror-writers included in this volume invoke the Samanids and the Ghaznavids, singly and by implication collectively, in positive contexts; writers of the Seljuk period, such as Niẓām al-Mulk, himself shaped in the service of the Ghaznavids, hark back to these predecessors as models of sound government. The Iranian kings of the *Shāhnāmeh* also appear, selectively, in the mirror literature, as exemplars of both wise and occasionally foolish royal conduct.

The Seljuks

Much of the reign of Masʿūd (r. 421–32/1030–41), Maḥmūd's son and successor, was spent in protracted struggles against the rising Seljuks, a nomadic Turkish dynastic family, who, led by the brothers Tughril Beg

The city became the Ghaznavid capital in the dynasty's last days before falling in 581/1185–6. After the fall of Khurasan to the Seljuks, the later Ghaznavids retained their territories in Afghanistan and extended their rule over parts of Hindustan (see Bosworth, *Ghaznavids*, 76–8; Bosworth, *The Later Ghaznavids*, 64, 76–7; Inaba, 'Ghaznavids').

51 Al-Thaʿālibī discusses this aspect of kingship in Text 2.

(r. 431–55/1040–63) and Chaghri Beg (d. 452/1060), grandsons of the dynasty's eponym Seljuk, and their uncle Mūsā Yabghu,[52] crossed the Oxus to enter Khurasan, Ghaznavid territory, in 426/1035. The Seljuks, who had become Muslim probably in the late tenth century, had lent their military services to various regional rulers, including the later Samanids and certain Karakhanids. In 429/1038, having heard that Nishapur had opened its gates to Tughril (Marv had surrendered to Chaghri Beg the previous year), Masʿūd marched into Khurasan; during his occupation of Nishapur, Tughril had the *khuṭba* read in his own name (perhaps in addition to that of the caliph) and adopted, in formal usage, the sweeping title *al-sulṭān al-muʿaẓẓam* ('Supreme Ruler').[53] At Dandanqan two years later, in 431/1040, Masʿūd suffered a complete defeat, which resulted in the Ghaznavids' permanent loss of their western territories.[54] Chaghri remained in Khurasan, where he consolidated his power and competed with the Ghaznavids for control of territories further east. Tughril, meanwhile, continued the Seljuks' westward expansion across Iran. His campaigns in the Caspian regions included the invasion of the Ziyarids' territories in 433/1041–2, after which date the latter dynasty became Seljuk tributaries. In 447/1055, Tughril entered Baghdad and deposed the Buyid al-Malik al-Raḥīm Khusraw Fīrūz (r. 440–7/1048–55). Significantly later, in 449/1058, the caliph al-Qāʾim bestowed honorific titles and robes of honour on Tughril and contracted a marriage with

[52] Mūsā Yabghu (Bayghu) b. Seljuk. Yabghu, an ancient Turkish title, denoted varying ranks at different times in its long usage (see Bosworth, 'Yabghu'). For broad treatments of the Seljuks, see Peacock, *Early Seljūq History*; Peacock, *Great Seljuk Empire*; Durand-Guédy, 'New Trends in the Political History of Iran'.

[53] On Seljuk titles, including their use of the expansive term *sulṭān*, see Peacock, *Great Seljuk Empire*, 135–7, 138; Safi, *Politics of Knowledge*, 9–10, 26; Van Steenbergen, *History of the Islamic World*, 179–80. Sanjar ruled as *malik* over the eastern provinces (from 490/1097 to 511/1118), and as supreme ruler (*al-sulṭān al-muʿaẓẓam*) when in 511/1118 he attained rule over the Seljuks' western domains as well. Use of the title *al-sulṭān al-muʿaẓẓam* was not unprecedented; certain Buyid rulers and the later Ghaznavids had employed it (Nagel, 'Buyids'; Bosworth, 'Amīr'; Bosworth, *The Later Ghaznavids*, 47, 55–6). According to one report, al-Māwardī refused to countenance such titles, and his abstention caused a rift between him and Jalāl al-Dawla (Ibn al-Jawzī, *al-Muntaẓam*, XV: 264–5, *sub anno* 429). The honorific title *aqḍā l-quḍāt*, 'the most decisive of the judges', awarded in the same year 429 by the caliph al-Qāʾim to al-Māwardī, already Chief Judge (*qāḍī l-quḍāt*), was also a matter of controversy: see Melchert, 'Māwardī, Abū Yaʿlá, and the Sunni Revival', 44.

[54] Following this defeat, Masʿūd, retreating to India, was deposed, and in 432/1041 killed. Notwithstanding the scale of the Ghaznavid defeat at Dandanqan, the Ghaznavids and Seljuks remained deeply intertwined for at least the next two decades (Inaba, 'Ghaznavids').

a daughter of Chaghri.[55] With these developments Tughril became supreme ruler over the former Buyid lands in western and southern Iran. With his capital in Marv, Chaghri ruled over Khurasan and Khʷarazm until his death in 452/1060, whereupon Tughril assumed control of his brother's territories as well. The Seljuks had now brought together a territorial expanse that recalled the domains of the Sasanian Empire.[56]

After defeating a number of challenges to his accession, Alp Arslan (r. 455–65/1063–72), a son of Chaghri Beg (Tughril had died without issue), followed Tughril in his rule of both the western and the eastern portions of the Seljuk Empire. All subsequent rulers of the 'Great Seljuk' line, in Iran and Iraq, sprang from Alp Arslan.[57] The Seljuk Empire reached its height during the reigns of Alp Arslan and his son Malikshāh (r. 465–85/1073–92), a thirty-year period inseparably associated with the tenure in office of the vizier Niẓām al-Mulk. Niẓām al-Mulk's effective governance of the Seljuk Empire during this period led the historian Ibn al-Athīr (555–630/1160–1233) to coin the phrase *al-dawla al-Niẓāmiyya*, 'the Niẓāmian turn in power', a term which evokes the extensive network of personal, familial and professional connections that the vizier established across the empire.[58] Indeed, the vizier has been likened to a shadow ruler, and his family to a shadow ruling family, on which the Seljuks of the period depended to maintain their power and the unity of their territories.[59]

In some respects, the Seljuk era displayed a continuity of earlier patterns. From their nomadic beginnings, the Seljuks gradually moved towards an imperial, territorially based model of sovereignty, and they adopted and extended certain political forms that they had initially encountered in Khurasan.[60] Having taken the cities of that province, Tughril retained his Ghaznavid predecessors' administrative structures and staff. As the boundaries of the state moved, Khurasanians were charged with the administration

[55] On the tense relations between the Seljuks and the Abbasids, see Peacock, *Great Seljuk Empire*, 124–55; Safi, *Politics of Knowledge*, 1–41; Van Renterghem, 'Controlling and Developing Baghdad'; Tor, 'Political Revival of the Abbasid Caliphate'.

[56] The similarity is noted in Chamberlain, 'Military Patronage States', 139.

[57] The term 'Great Seljuk' is commonly applied to the line of Seljuk sultans who ruled over the central territories of Iraq and western Iran, especially if they also ruled eastern Iran; it distinguishes this line of rulers from the regional Seljuk polities of Kirman and Rum (Anatolia) and the various city-based polities that developed in northern Iraq and Syria.

[58] Ibn al-Athīr, *al-Kāmil*, VIII: 365 (*sub anno* 456); see further Peacock, *Great Seljuk Empire*, 68; Safi, *Politics of Knowledge*, 47.

[59] Chamberlain, 'Military Patronage States', 143.

[60] Chamberlain, 'Military Patronage States', 135.

of the new territories, including the city of Isfahan, which Tughril's grandson Malikshāh (r. 465–85/1073–92), who was born there, would adopt as the Seljuk capital.[61] Particularly under the leadership of Niẓām al-Mulk, himself a native of Khurasan, numbers of families from Khurasan resettled in western Iran and Iraq.[62] These families contributed to the extension of the administrative and intellectual cultures of Khurasan to the western parts of the empire. The advent of the madrasa and *khānaqāh* would transform the cities of the western provinces as they had those of Khurasan. It was also under the Seljuks that Persian, as a leading literary and administrative language, spread from eastern to western Iran. The present volume's two mirror-writers who wrote for Seljuk rulers, Niẓām al-Mulk and Ghazālī, both hailed from the Khurasanian city of Tus. Both men spent long periods of their lives in western Iran and Iraq; famously, Niẓām al-Mulk founded his Niẓāmiyya madrasa (completed in 459/1067) in Baghdad and, in 484/1091, appointed Ghazālī to lead it.

Alp Arslan's constant military activity was directed chiefly against the Christian powers to the north and west, where, in the 450s/1060s, he led or organised sporadic campaigns against Armenia, Georgia and the Byzantine Empire. These campaigns, punctuated by periods of truce, allowed Alp Arslan's Türkmen troops, who comprised the majority of his army, to continue their pursuit of pasturage. As the Türkmen forces moved largely into Azerbaijan, the southern Caucasus and eastern Anatolia, they remained within reach of the Seljuk dynasty, who continued to depend on their support, but beyond the control of the Seljuk administration, with its interests in revenue collection, and in matters of agriculture and trade. David Durand-Guédy has suggested that, possibly to facilitate the Seljuks' continued relations with the Türkmen groups, the Seljuk court, a tented encampment, was located sometimes just outside the city walls, but sometimes, especially in summer, in far-away pastures, in closer proximity to the nomads.[63] Like many earlier dynasties, the Seljuks also began to acquire slave soldiers, to whose training Niẓām al-Mulk devoted a chapter in his book of advice.[64]

61 Durand-Guédy, *Iranian Elites and Turkish Rulers*, 106–9, 230–55.

62 Bulliet, *View from the Edge*, 145–68; Durand-Guédy, *Iranian Elites and Turkish Rulers*, 112–29, 230–55; Durand-Guédy, 'An Emblematic Family of Seljuk Iran'.

63 Durand-Guédy, 'Ruling from the Outside'; Durand-Guédy, 'Where Did the Saljūqs Live?'; Hillenbrand, 'Aspects of the Court of the Great Seljuqs', 23.

64 Amitai, 'Armies and Their Economic Basis', 543–4; *Siyar al-mulūk*, 141–3 = Darke, *Book of Government*, 106–8, and see above, n. 15.

The Seljuks' campaigns in the north and west hastened Turkish expansion into Anatolia, particularly after Alp Arslan's defeat of the Byzantine army at Manzikert (Malazgird) in 463/1071 and the capture of the emperor Romanus IV Diogenes. Alp Arslan's great victory resulted more from chance than from design, since his intention had been to advance through Syria and into Egypt in order to confront and defeat the Fatimids.[65] Although Alp Arslan did not immediately press his advantage and promptly released Romanus, the Battle of Manzikert had the effect of reducing still further the Byzantines' capacity to resist continuing Turkish attacks.[66]

The Fatimids

The Fatimid dynasty established its rule first in North Africa, from 297/909, and subsequently in Egypt (358–567/969–1171). Claiming descent from ʿAlī and the Prophet's daughter Fāṭima, the Fatimids gained the allegiance of a significant portion of the Ismaili movement. In North Africa, they established the rule of a caliph-imam who assumed the name ʿAbdallāh al-Mahdī (r. 297–322/909–34). Attempts during al-Mahdī's reign to conquer Egypt met with failure, but during the reign of the caliph-imam al-Muʿizz li-Dīn Allāh (r. 341–65/953–75), the Fatimids succeeded in extending their rule to the east. The victorious general initiated construction of a new palace city, to be called al-Qāhira (Cairo), which rapidly replaced the earlier al-Mahdiyya, located on the Tunisian coast, as the centre of the Fatimid state. The holy cities of Mecca and Medina acknowledged Fatimid suzerainty, and the Fatimids eventually extended their empire into Yemen, although their control over positions in Palestine and Syria, and even North Africa, proved difficult to sustain. Nor did the several scattered Ismaili communities necessarily accept the Fatimids' claims to the imamate; most notably, the Qarmaṭiyya, followers of Ḥamdān Qarmaṭ in Iraq and eastern Arabia (al-Baḥrayn), withheld their allegiance and continued to reject Fatimid authority.

For a period of nearly twenty-two years, the administration of the Fatimid state fell largely to the Fatimids' first-named vizier, Yaʿqūb Ibn

[65] Despite their rhetorical claims to defence of the Sunni caliphs against a generalised Ismaili threat, the Seljuks took relatively little action against Ismaili communities; see Tor, 'Tale of Two Murders', 280; Hillenbrand, 'Power Struggle between the Saljuqs and the Ismaʿilis of Alamūt'.

[66] Mallett, 'Alp Arslan'.

Killis (318–80/930–91), who had been born Jewish in Baghdad and converted to Islam in Egypt. While the Fatimids did not attempt in a sustained way to impose Ismaili Islam on their subject populations, they did, with certain exceptions, reduce the differences in status among the various confessional constituencies, Muslim, Christian and Jewish, in their domains.[67] In the later eleventh century, facing chronic instability, the Fatimids enlisted the aid of their governor in Acre, the Armenian *mamlūk* Badr al-Jamālī (d. 487/1094), who entered Cairo with his corps of largely Muslim Armenian troops in 466/1074 and rapidly attained immense power. His appointment ushered in a succession of 'military viziers', and Heinz Halm has described his office as a de facto sultanate, akin to the sultanate of the Seljuks in their relations with the Abbasids.[68] In 477/1084, Badr's son al-Afḍal assumed the post of vizier; in a demonstration of his power, the latter arranged marriages between members of his family and the Fatimid dynasty. Al-Afḍal was killed in 515/1121 and replaced as vizier by Ibn al-Baṭāʾiḥī, recipient of al-Ṭurṭūshī's *Sirāj al-mulūk*, which the author had intended for al-Afḍal but completed only after the latter's assassination.

By the early twelfth century, the Fatimids faced the new challenge of the Crusades. By 504/1110, the Fatimids had lost Jerusalem (492/1099) and almost all of the Mediterranean coastal towns, except for Tyre and Ascalon (lost to the Crusaders in 518/1124 and 548/1153 respectively). Faced in 564/1168 with the threat of a Frankish invasion of Egypt, the Fatimids, having rejected the earlier appeal of Nūr al-Dīn Maḥmūd b. Zangī (d. 569/1174) of Aleppo to join forces in the waging of *jihād* against the Franks, appealed to Nūr al-Dīn for support. The threat receded, but in 564/1169, the Fatimid caliph-imam al-ʿĀḍid appointed Nūr al-Dīn's Kurdish commander Ṣalāḥ al-Dīn Yūsuf b. Ayyūb (532–89/1138–93) to the vizierate. Ṣalāḥ al-Dīn, the last of the Fatimid viziers, adopted a markedly pro-Sunni policy, and, calling in 567/1171 for the reading of the *khuṭba* in the name of the Abbasid caliph, al-Mustaḍīʾ (r. 566–75/1170–80), he asserted Abbasid suzerainty over Egypt and the

[67] Brett, 'Egypt', 571. Among the most notable exceptions, the caliph-imam al-Ḥākim bi-Amr Allāh (r. 386–411/996–1021) imposed the sharia upon Muslims and enforced restrictive and discriminatory measures against Christians and Jews. He also ordered the destruction of churches, including, in 400/1009, the Church of the Holy Sepulchre in Jerusalem (Brett, 'Egypt', 575).

[68] Halm, 'Fatimids'. Badr held the title *wazīr al-sayf wa-l-qalam* ('vizier of the sword and the pen'), and his private troops were numbered at over 7,000 (Dadoyan, 'Badr al-Jamālī').

establishment of Sunnism.[69] After over two centuries, the Fatimid state collapsed, and Ṣalāḥ al-Dīn (Saladin) became the founder of the Ayyubid dynasty, which lies beyond the scope of this collection.

Throughout the Early Middle Period, the capacity of rulers to establish or maintain a centralised hold on power was limited.[70] In many cases, a senior member of the dynastic family appointed male relatives to provincial territories, where they often ruled with little interference from the head of the family. The establishment of rule in a given lineage often faced repeated challenges from contenders in lateral lines of descent. In the case of the Seljuks – more a confederation, or collection of powerful households, than a unified polity – the apportionment of territories was also supported by the law and custom of the steppe.[71] As previously noted, Alp Arslan, after the deaths of his father Chaghri in 452/1060 and his uncle Tughril in 455/1062, assumed rule of the empire in its entirety, but the political unity of the Seljuk Empire remained tenuous. After the death of Malikshāh, the Seljuk dominions were effectively divided, as they had been in the period of Tughril and Chaghri, into a western part (*maghrib*) and an eastern part (*mashriq*). Sanjar, a son of Malikshāh, ruled for many years (490–511/1097–1118) as *malik* in Khurasan and the east; following the death of his brother Muḥammad b. Malikshāh in 511/1118, he emerged as the supreme ruler (*al-sulṭān al-muʿaẓẓam*) over the Seljuks' western domains as well, and ruled, largely from Marv, until his death in 552/1157. Branches of the Seljuk family ruled in Kirman and Anatolia, and members of the Seljuk family or the *atabeg*s, guardian-tutors, of young Seljuk princes established subordinate dynasties of their own in principalities across Syria and Iraq.[72]

In situating the mirror literature within medieval Muslim political thought, scholars have not hesitated to describe it as 'secular'.[73]

69 See Van Steenbergen, *History of the Islamic World*, 213–20.

70 Daniel, 'The Islamic East', 466; Paul, *Herrscher, Gemeinwesen, Vermittler*, esp. 237–60.

71 Peacock, *Great Seljuk Empire*, 128–31; Chamberlain, 'Military Patronage States', 142. The autonomy of these appanages is reflected in the considerable numismatic variation among the Seljuk rulers, each of whom appears to have had the right of *sikka* (Bosworth, 'Steppe Peoples', 43, 49).

72 See Peacock, *Great Seljuk Empire*, 72–123; El-Azhari, *Queens, Eunuchs and Concubines*, 301–39. The previously mentioned Nūr al-Dīn of Aleppo and the Zangid dynasty to which he belonged held the title of *atabeg*.

73 Crone, *Medieval Islamic Political Thought*, 246–7, 150 and *passim*; Yavari, *Advice for the Sultan*, esp. 7–44, 81–94; Yavari, 'Political Regard', *passim*; Dakhlia, 'Les Miroirs des princes islamiques'; see also Dahlén, 'Kingship and Religion in a Mediaeval

Certainly, authors of mirrors acknowledge two categories, sovereignty or temporal power (*mulk* (Ar.), *pādshāhī* (Persian)) and religion (*dīn*). From the Formative Period onwards, authors of mirrors almost invariably invoke Ardashīr's pronouncement:

> Know that religion and sovereignty are (like) twin brothers: neither endures without its partner. For religion is the foundation of sovereignty, and sovereignty in its turn becomes the guardian of religion. Sovereignty depends on its foundation, and religion depends on its guardian. For whatever lacks a guardian vanishes, and whatever has no foundation crumbles.[74]

The axiom affirms the necessity and interdependence of the two spheres, and at the same time it assumes their separation. The Sasanian background, explicit in the maxim's attribution to the founder of the dynasty, enhanced rather than detracted from its prestige in its Arabic and later Persian and Turkish settings; the formulation appears in the writings of (Sunni) religious scholars and jurists almost as unfailingly as in the compositions of secretaries and administrators. The duality of 'sultanate' and 'caliphate', prominent in the Seljuk period, similarly evoked an interdependence of the two entities, each with distinct functions. Al-Māwardī's distinction between two kinds of governorship, the 'amirate by appointment' (*imārat al-istikfāʾ*) and the 'amirate by seizure' (*imārat al-istīlāʾ*), acknowledged a plurality of sources of power; Ghazālī identified the necessity of *shawka*, military force, separable from but a potential partner to the imamate.[75] For the Sunni Muslim jurists, concepts of separate but potentially co-operative spheres, one representing military power and the other connoting a historically and religiously legitimated authority, contributed to the shifting meanings of the

Fürstenspiegel'. For a thorough, comparative treatment of secularism in Christian and Muslim contexts, see al-Azmeh, *Secularism in the Arab World*, 7–83.

[74] *ʿAhd Ardashīr*, 53, 97; cited, in the texts represented in this anthology, in Pseudo-Māwardī, *Naṣīḥat al-mulūk*, 108; al-Māwardī, *Tashīl al-naẓar wa-taʿjīl al-ẓafar*, 201–2; Ghazālī, *Naṣīḥat al-mulūk*, part II: 106 = Bagley, *Ghazālī's Book of Counsel for Kings*, 59; Niẓām al-Mulk, *Siyar al-mulūk*, 80 = Darke, *Book of Government*, 60; al-Ṭurṭūshī, *Sirāj al-mulūk*, I: 252. See further below, Chapter 5, Text 3, n. 125.

[75] The two Shāfiʿī scholars, with others, developed these ideas principally in their juristic writings. See al-Māwardī, *al-Aḥkām al-sulṭāniyya*, 31–6 = Wahba, *Ordinances of Government*, 32–7; Ghazālī, *al-Mustaẓhirī*, 169–225 (see esp. 182–4, a discussion of courage (*najda*), necessary in the imam but attainable through acquisition rather than innate); Hillenbrand, 'Islamic Orthodoxy or Realpolitik?'; Crone, *Medieval Islamic Political Thought*, 219–55.

caliphal office.[76] In the mirror literature, the importance of religion lay primarily in its social and political functions: right religion promoted social cohesion, and, through its support for the principles of justice and moderation and its repudiation of abuses of power, upheld stability and order; whereas heterodoxy, deemed to undermine these principles, was equated with division, conflict and unrest, and portrayed as a disguise for sedition.

[76] See above, at n. 6.

3

Texts and Authors

With the exception of *Sirr al-asrār*, the texts selected for this anthology emanated from specific, roughly datable environments, as indicated in general terms in Chapter 2. An introduction to the texts, in approximate order of their appearance or composition, appears in the following pages.

3.1 Pseudo-Aristotle, *Kitāb al-Siyāsa fī tadbīr al-riyāsa* (*Sirr al-asrār*) (Arabic)

The most widely disseminated of the mirrors presented in this collection is the text known in Arabic as *Kitāb al-Siyāsa fī tadbīr al-riyāsa* or *Sirr al-asrār* and in Latin as *Secretum secretorum*.[1] This text, presented in the form of correspondence between Aristotle and Alexander, consists largely of Aristotle's advice, reportedly submitted in writing when the philosopher's age and infirmity prevented him from joining his young sovereign on military campaigns. Some Aristotelian pseudepigrapha circulated in Syriac and Arabic at an early date, before the full development of the large-scale movement of translation from Greek, Middle Persian and Sanskrit into Arabic.[2] The text of *Sirr al-asrār* is composite; it comprises several pieces,

[1] The text circulated under several 'titles'; for examples, see Manzalaoui, 'The Pseudo-Aristotelian *Kitāb Sirr al-asrār*', 147; and Hirschler, *Medieval Damascus: Plurality and Diversity in an Arabic Library*, Catalogue nos. 509, 1237c.

[2] The provenance of the texts that would eventually comprise the Arabic *Sirr al-asrār* remains uncertain. Neither a Greek nor a Syriac version has come to light, although parts of the *Sirr al-asrār* have been shown to be consistent with Hellenistic and classical Greek antecedents (Manzalaoui, 'The Pseudo-Aristotelian *Kitāb Sirr al-asrār*', 201–2; further documented in Williams, *The Secret of Secrets*, 23–6), and a significant portion of the text suggests a Persianised context (Manzalaoui, 'The Pseudo-Aristotelian *Kitāb Sirr*

some of which also circulated as independent compositions. Among *Sirr al-asrār*'s most substantial components is the epistolary cycle known as *Kitāb fī l-Siyāsa al-ʿāmmiyya*, a collection of epistles purportedly exchanged between Alexander and Aristotle, and perhaps transmitted into Arabic in the first half of the eighth century.[3] Over the next two centuries, the *Sirr al-asrār* increased in size and in scope.[4] The Arabic record, with the translations into Latin made from it, reflects the development of two major recensions, a 'Short Form' (in seven or eight chapters) and a 'Long Form' (in ten chapters).[5]

From Arabic the *Sirr al-asrār* was translated into Hebrew (and thence into Russian), and into Latin, from which language numerous translations into vernacular European languages were made.[6] The translation into Latin by John of Seville (Johannes Hispalensis) in the early twelfth century was based on the Short Form version in circulation in Iberia at that time. A little over a century later, in about 1230, a cleric named Philip, visiting the city of Antioch with the Bishop of Tripoli, found a full (Long Form) Arabic manuscript of the *Sirr al-asrār*, which, at the Bishop's request, Philip translated into Latin. By the early fourteenth century, this text was known to both scholarly and lay readers throughout the Latin West.[7] The

al-asrār', 161; Grignaschi, 'Remarques sur la formation et l'interprétation du *Sirr al-ʾasrār*'; Grignaschi, 'La "Siyâsatu-l-ʿâmmiyya" et l'influence iranienne'; Van Bladel, 'Iranian Characteristics and Forged Greek Attributions'; Marsham, *Rituals of Islamic Monarchy*, 161–2). See also Grignaschi, 'L'origine et les métamorphoses du Sirr alʾasrār'; Williams, *The Secret of Secrets*, 17, 29.

3 Following the studies of Mario Grignaschi, it is commonly agreed that Sālim Abū l-ʿAlāʾ, secretary to the Umayyad caliph Hishām (r. 105–25/724–43), played a central role in the collection's early formation and transmission (Grignaschi, 'Les "Rasāʾil ʾArisṭāṭālīsa ʾilā-l-Iskandar" de Sālim Abū-l-ʿAlāʾ'). See further Cottrell, 'An Early Mirror for Princes and Manual for Secretaries'.

4 Manzalaoui's positing of a long 'process of accretion' from numerous antecedents and backgrounds seems apt (Manzalaoui, 'The Pseudo-Aristotelian *Kitāb Sirr al-asrār*', 193).

5 The designations are Manzalaoui's ('The Pseudo-Aristotelian *Kitāb Sirr al-asrār*', 148). From the perspective of European reception of the text, Steele had referred to the 'Western Arabic Form' and the 'Eastern Arabic Form', in a distinction corresponding to Manzalaoui's Short and Long Forms respectively; see his 'Introduction', in *Secretum secretorum cum glossis et notulis*, xiii–xv. On the dating and versions of the Arabic text, see Forster, *Das Geheimnis der Geheimnisse*, 11–30.

6 Grignaschi, 'La diffusion du "Secretum secretorum" (Sirr-al-ʾasrār) dans l'Europe occidentale'; Ryan and Schmitt, *Pseudo-Aristotle*, The Secret of Secrets.

7 Schmitt, 'Pseudo-Aristotle in the Latin Middle Ages', 5; Forster, *Das Geheimnis der Geheimnisse*, 1. On Philip's translation, see Williams, *The Secret of Secrets*, 7–30, 60–108; Forster, *Das Geheimnis der Geheimnisse*, 120–9. On John's translation, see Williams, *The Secret of Secrets*, 31–59; Forster, *Das Geheimnis der Geheimnisse*, 114–20; Figueiras, 'La traduction castillane de l'*Epistola Aristotelis ad Alexandrum de dieta servanda* de Jean de Séville'.

philosopher Roger Bacon, whose interest lay less in the book's political contents than in the sections dedicated to the occult sciences, prepared an annotated edition of the text in about 1275.[8] In medieval Christian and Muslim contexts, *Sirr al-asrār* and other pseudo-Aristotelian works circulated at least as widely as, if not more widely than, 'genuine' Aristotelian works.[9]

Numerous translations into languages in use in Muslim communities also appeared. The manuscript record reflects not only the geographical and intercultural spread but also the longevity of the text's interest. A nineteenth-century copy of a Turkish translation, made apparently from Arabic, appears with illuminated chapter headings written mostly in Persian (Fig. 2).[10] In its many versions, *Sirr al-asrār* forms an important link among the mirror literatures in Arabic, Hebrew and Latin, and it both reflected and contributed to a shared foundational political culture among Muslims, Jews and Christians across pre-modern Eurasia.

The subjects treated in *Sirr al-asrār* vary from one redaction to another. In all its forms, the collection deals with matters considered relevant to rulership, such as the functions and treatment of viziers, secretaries, ambassadors, governors and generals, as well as, especially in the Long Form versions, medicine, physiognomy, talismans and hygiene. The text reflects the correspondences among the human body, the body politic and the cosmos; it offers counsel concerning the king's comportment, according to the seasons, his physical health, parts of the body, remedies for the ills that result from an imbalance of the humours, medical and pharmacological prescriptions, and matters of military strategy. The physical and bodily and the psychological and moral dimensions of the king's person are presented as interconnected.[11] A significant portion of the text is aphoristic: often introduced with the vocative direct address, 'O Alexander!', the aphorisms sometimes announce a theme on which the text elaborates.

Considerable interest lies in the medical and magical sections included in certain recensions; the very title 'Secret of Secrets' evokes esoteric

8 See Grignaschi, 'Remarques sur la formation et l'interprétation du *Sirr al-'asrār*', esp. 9.

9 Grignaschi, 'La diffusion du "Secretum secretorum" (Sirr-al-'asrār) dans l'Europe occidentale'; Schmitt, 'Francesco Storella'; Gutas, 'Arabic Lives of Aristotle' (with an important discussion of the meaning in this context of 'authenticity').

10 See Fig. 2. For an example of the 'circle of justice' in an Arabic manuscript, see Fig. 3.

11 Manzalaoui, 'The Pseudo-Aristotelian *Kitāb Sirr al-asrār*', 194; Forster, *Das Geheimnis der Geheimnisse*, 108–11.

Figure 2 A page from an early nineteenth-century copy (dated 1231/1815) of a Turkish translation of the Pseudo-Aristotelian *Kitāb al-Siyāsa fī tadbīr al-riyāsa* (*Kitap üs-siyase fi tedbir ir-riyase*, Islamic Manuscripts Collection, Manuscripts Division, Department of Special Collections, Princeton University Library, New Series, no. 1669). This page (f. 84v) shows the pseudo-Aristotelian 'circle of justice' in diagrammatic form, and beneath it, in red ink, the title of the following section and the invocation, 'O Alexander!', both in Persian; the writing then returns to black ink and Turkish.
Photograph: Courtesy of Princeton University Library

connotations. It is quite striking that a frequent point of difference among the manuscripts is the inclusion or exclusion, and the location, of the esoteric materials, including the sections devoted to physiognomy and onomancy, which sometimes stand alone.[12] In Spain, the text's initial (twelfth-century) interest lay in its medical contents; it was only in the mid-thirteenth century that the text gained an audience as a political treatise.[13] In its Arabic forms, *Sirr al-asrār* quite often appears in miscellanies that contain other mirrors for princes, or other works related to medicine or esoterica.[14] The text's lasting and widespread popularity; the ubiquitous appearances of Aristotle and Alexander in Arabic, Persian and Turkish mirrors; the high frequency of citations (variously attributed) of the text's contents; and the text's adoption as a model justify its inclusion in the present anthology.[15] Among the mirror-writers considered in the present volume, Pseudo-Māwardī cites Aristotle's counsel to Alexander more often than he does any other (non-scriptural) authority, and it is evident from *Sirāj al-mulūk* that al-Ṭurṭūshī either knew *Sirr al-asrār* in its Long Form or had access to a common source.[16]

3.2 Pseudo-Māwardī, *Naṣīḥat al-mulūk* (Arabic)

One of the earliest extant book-length mirrors in Arabic is the *Naṣīḥat al-mulūk* attributed to the eminent Shāfiʿī jurist, judge, caliphal envoy and adviser al-Māwardī (364–450/974–1058). Like the ascriptions of many medieval compositions, the attribution of this mirror to al-Māwardī is open to question.[17] The present author takes the text to have originated in tenth-century eastern Iran, although a later reworking, perhaps in the

[12] For a list of Arabic manuscripts, see Manzalaoui, 'The Pseudo-Aristotelian *Kitāb Sirr al-asrār*', 148–56.

[13] Bizzarri, 'Le *Secretum secretorum* en Espagne', 187–213.

[14] Examples include The Bodleian Libraries, University of Oxford, MS Laud Or. 210; Royal Asiatic Society, MS Arabic 57.

[15] See further Forster, *Das Geheimnis der Geheimnisse*, 30–48.

[16] Manzalaoui, 'The Pseudo-Aristotelian *Kitāb Sirr al-asrār*', 158–9; Forster, *Das Geheimnis der Geheimnisse*, 20–1 and n. 98.

[17] Scholarly opinion on the subject is mixed. Scholars who consider the work among al-Māwardī's writings include Kh. M. Khiḍr and M. J. al-Ḥadīthī, who published editions of the text in 1983 and 1986 respectively; Mikhail, *Politics and Revelation*, 64–8; al-Sayyid, 'Tamhīd', 70–1, and 'al-Māwardī: al-rajul wa-l-ʿaṣr', 102; Bosworth, 'Naṣīḥat al-mulūk'; Toelle and Zakharia, *À la découverte de la littérature arabe*, 161. Scholars who have concluded that al-Māwardī did not write the book include Fuʾād ʿAbd al-Munʿim Aḥmad, *al-Māwardī wa-Kitāb Naṣīḥat al-mulūk*, and 'Muqaddimat al-dirāsa wa-l-taḥqīq'; Anṣārī, 'Yek andīsheh-nāmeh'; Leder, 'Aspekte arabischer und persischer

time of al-Māwardī, is entirely possible. If the pseudepigraphical status of the text is granted, the identity of its author remains unknown (hence the epithet Pseudo-Māwardī), although Hassan Ansari has presented a detailed and plausible case for the authorship of Abū l-Ḥasan ʿAlī b. Muḥammad al-Ḥashshāʾī al-Balkhī, a student of the Muʿtazilite theologian Abū l-Qāsim ʿAbdallāh al-Kaʿbī al-Balkhī (d. 319/931), the principal theologian of the Baghdadi school of Muʿtazilite theology in early tenth-century Khurasan.[18] *Naṣīḥat al-mulūk* reflects a distinct intellectual milieu in which local traditions of rationalism (specifically the Muʿtazilī theology associated with al-Kaʿbī and the philosophy of the Kindian tradition), an affiliation with the Ḥanafī legal school, a strong emphasis on scripture, and a fluency in the repertoire of Arabic letters combine.[19]

Composed of ten chapters and an epilogue, *Naṣīḥat al-mulūk* is an interdisciplinary work: it draws on scriptural, theological, philosophical, juristic, literary and poetic corpora and is exceptionally dense and diverse in the range of authorities that it invokes. A large number of Pseudo-Aristotelian passages appear, and authorities identified as 'Indian', including references to and citations from the Buddha, are unusually plentiful. The mirror's ten chapters cover the acceptance of counsel; the status of kings and the qualities they should adopt; causes of corruption in the kingdom; exhortations; the king's self-governance; the king's governance of his inner circle (*al-khāṣṣa*); the king's governance of the people at large (*al-ʿāmma*); collecting and dispensing wealth; managing enemies; and matters of controversy. The three central chapters, devoted to the three governances (of the royal self, the king's inner public and his outer public), correspond, although Pseudo-Māwardī does not identify them in this manner, to the Aristotelian triad of ethics, politics and economics. In his appeal to the king to govern himself, Pseudo-Māwardī urges the cultivation of divine qualities, such as generosity and forbearance, the acquisition of the divinely enjoined qualities, such

Fürstenspiegel', 31, n. 39; Crone, *Medieval Islamic Political Thought*, 439; Marlow, *Counsel for Kings*, I: 9–17; Abbès, *De l'Éthique du prince*, 202–3.

[18] Anṣārī, 'Yek andīsheh-nāmeh'.

[19] Anṣārī, 'Yek andīsheh-nāmeh'; Marlow, 'Abū Zayd al-Balkhī'; Marlow, 'Kings and Sages'. For an interesting comparison, see Kaya, '*Kalām* and *Falsafa* Integrated for Divine Unity' (I am grateful to the author of this study for bringing the commonalities to my attention).

as patient endurance and prudential resolve, and the following of the divine commandments.[20]

Much of the Arabic *Naṣīḥat al-mulūk* resembles a treatise; like al-Māwardī's works, its arguments could be charted in a sequence of points and sub-points. Pseudo-Māwardī makes copious use of axiomatic, poetic and narrative exempla, and he advises contemplation of history, but at least as prominent in his mirror is the use of logic and rational argument. In this respect *Naṣīḥat al-mulūk* might be compared with the very much later *De regimine principum* (*c.* 1277–80) of Giles of Rome (1247–1316), which, unlike the mirrors of his European contemporaries and predecessors, presents a logical and systematic sequence of arguments, a demonstration of the principles which underpin the good governance of kings and kingdoms.[21]

Naṣīḥat al-mulūk also bears comparison with *Kitāb al-Tāj fī akhlāq al-mulūk*, since identical passages appear in both texts (it is likely that the two authors drew on a common source).[22] Like al-Taghlibī, author of *Kitāb al-Tāj*, Pseudo-Māwardī portrays kingship in exceptional terms: the king occupies a unique position in the cosmic order, standing immediately after prophets in a hierarchical sequence; his power requires him to mediate between the divine and the human realms through scrupulous observance of the divine law and care for the subjects whose welfare is vouchsafed to him. Just as his earthly lot surpasses that of all other human beings, his responsibilities, and the punishment that awaits failure, exceed those of the subjects under his governance.

Pseudo-Māwardī's mirror also displays affinities with the works of the philosopher al-ʿĀmirī (d. 381/992), who lived in Khurasan, where he developed the philosophical tradition of Abū Yūsuf Yaʿqūb al-Kindī (*c.* 183–256/800–70).[23] Both writers emphasise the importance of rational enquiry into matters of religion. For example, they discuss

[20] See especially Pseudo-Māwardī's fifth chapter (*Naṣīḥat al-mulūk al-mansūb ilā Abī l-Ḥasan al-Māwardī*, 143–202). Following the divine pattern and the divinely enjoined model also constitutes a recurrent theme in Byzantine and Carolingian political discourses; see Dvornik, *Early Christian and Byzantine Political Philosophy*, II: 680, 686, 693, 719; Arabatzis, 'Nicephoros Blemmydes's *Imperial Statue*', 99; Eberhardt, *Via Regia*, 559–69.

[21] Kempshall, 'The Rhetoric of Giles of Rome's *De regimine principum*', esp. 166–75.

[22] On this text and its authorship, see Chapter 1, n. 24.

[23] See Adamson, 'Kindian Tradition'; Rowson, *A Muslim Philosopher on the Soul and Its Fate*; Heck, 'Crisis of Knowledge'.

the duty of *jihād* in philosophical rather than merely legal terms.[24] Furthermore, both writers place an emphasis on the importance of religious practice, that is to say, the acknowledgement of the external (*ẓāhir*) aspects of religion (in Paul Heck's felicitous phrasing, 'visible Islam as agent of the sociopolitical good'), against contemporaries who subordinated external aspects to interior (*bāṭin*) dimensions and, by extension, figurative interpretations.[25] This internally focused exegetical orientation appeared in a number of contexts, but was a particularly prominent feature of Ismaili Shiʿism, which, as noted in Chapter 2, had gained in the early tenth century the allegiance of several notable individuals, including prominent figures at the Samanid court. Indeed, several features of *Naṣīḥat al-mulūk* suggest its first composition towards the end of the reign of the amir Naṣr II b. Aḥmad (r. 301–31/914–43), who at that time embraced Ismaili Islam – possibly to the alarm of observers such as Pseudo-Māwardī, who equated heterodoxy with political instability.[26] Pseudo-Māwardī's successors al-Thaʿālibī and Niẓām al-Mulk, formed in the same region and heirs to the same sense of the lessons of the region's history, would recapitulate this perspective in their eleventh-century mirrors and would detail the case of Naṣr II in order to support their arguments.[27]

3.3 Al-Thaʿālibī, *Ādāb al-mulūk* (Arabic)

The prodigious philologist and littérateur Abū Manṣūr Muḥammad al-Thaʿālibī (350–429/961–1038), a native of Nishapur in Khurasan, began his career in the days of the last Samanids. He spent his entire life at venues in the east. At various times, he resided in the north-eastern Caspian province of Gurgan (Ar. Jurjan), where he dedicated several

[24] Al-ʿĀmirī, *al-Iʿlām bi-manāqib al-Islām*, 124, 147–9, 156; cited in Heck, '*Jihad* Revisited', 104–6, nn. 12, 13.

[25] See Marlow, *Counsel for Kings*, I: 52, 204–6 and *passim*; Heck, 'Crisis of Knowledge'; the quoted passage appears on p. 117.

[26] Anṣārī proposed this dating in 'Yek andīsheh-nāmeh'; see also Marlow, *Counsel for Kings*, I: 25–60.

[27] Al-Thaʿālibī, *Ādāb al-mulūk*, 169–72 (see below, Chapter 9, Text 16); Crone and Treadwell, 'A New Text on Ismailism'; Niẓām al-Mulk, *Siyar al-mulūk*, 287–96 = Darke, *Book of Government*, 212–18. It is perhaps worth noting that whereas the efforts of the Seljuks against the Ismailis were sporadic and unsystematic (see Chapter 2, n. 65), the Khurasanian families imported into Seljuk Isfahan undertook in the early twelfth century a sustained campaign against the Ismailis in that city and its environs (Durand-Guédy, *Iranian Elites and Turkish Rulers*, 182–97).

works to the Ziyarid amir Shams al-Maʿālī Qābūs b. Vushmgīr, a ruler widely admired for his literary talents and whose name would become attached to the mirror of his grandson Kaykāʾūs.[28] In the early eleventh century, al-Thaʿālibī moved to Khᵛarazm, where he joined the court at Gurganj and dedicated several works, including his mirror *Ādāb al-mulūk*, to the Khᵛārazmshāh, Amir Abū l-ʿAbbās Maʾmūn b. Maʾmūn (r. 390–407/1000–16). Maʾmūn and his vizier participated vigorously in the region's literary culture, and the Maʾmūnid court was remarkable for its assembly of eminent men of letters, philosophers and scientists, including al-Bīrūnī and Ibn Sīnā (Avicenna) (d. 428/1037). Al-Thaʿālibī devotes special attention to royal patronage of the arts and sciences in his portrayal of the benefits of kingship. After Maḥmūd's invasion of Khᵛarazm in 408/1017 and his extinction of the line of Maʾmūnid Khᵛārazmshāhs (385–408/995–1017), al-Thaʿālibī, like some other eminent individuals, was obliged to abandon the Maʾmūnid court and move to Ghazna.[29] Eventually, he returned to teach in Nishapur, where he died at an advanced age.[30]

Ādāb al-mulūk, like the Arabic *Naṣīḥat al-mulūk*, consists of ten chapters. Al-Thaʿālibī's chapters cover the need for kings and the duty of obedience to them; kingship and the manners of kings; the sayings and counsels of kings, especially caliphs; governance; the customs of kings; viziers, judges, secretaries, doctors, musicians and other persons in attendance at the court; warfare and the army; the conduct of kings towards different categories of people; and the service of kings. With a strong emphasis on the divine mandate upholding kingship and the exceptional nature of the royal office, the mirror reflects al-Thaʿālibī's lifelong experience in the courts of the north-east. A great many of his examples are drawn from this regional environment, and he evinced a particular admiration for the Samanids.[31] His mirror displays a preference for recent and specific examples over the distant and generic references that became increasingly dominant in mirrors of the subsequent centuries. As Julia Bray has demonstrated, a strong 'aristocratic principle' runs through the mirror; this principle appears in, for example, al-Thaʿālibī's attachment to the charisma of noble, and above all royal, birth, and in his recommendations regarding the drinking of wine, an

[28] See Chapter 2, n. 38, and section 3.5. [29] See section 2.2 and Text 2.
[30] For al-Thaʿālibī's life and works, see Rowson, 'al-Thaʿālibī'; Orfali, 'Works of Abū Manṣūr al-Thaʿālibī' and *The Anthologist's Art*, esp. 34–96, 97–138.
[31] See Bray, 'Al-Thaʿalibi's *Adab al-muluk*'.

aspect of courtly culture that he takes for granted.[32] The work also displays al-Thaʿālibī's expert knowledge of figures of speech, which, in addition to the thematic categories of his chapters, he uses to organise his materials.

3.4 Yūsuf Khāṣṣ Ḥājib, *Kutadgu bilig* (Karakhanid Turkish)

The second half of the eleventh century saw the appearance, for the first time, of mirrors in Turkish and Persian in addition to Arabic. These Turkish and Persian mirrors, indeed, figured conspicuously in the literary development of the two languages. The language of the *Kutadgu bilig*, written in Kashghar in 462/1069–70, is Karakhanid Turkish. The author, Yūsuf Khāṣṣ Ḥājib, whose title Khāṣṣ Ḥājib (Privy Chamberlain) reflects his promotion to that rank in recognition of his work, dedicated his mirror to the Karakhanid prince of Kashghar, Tavghach Bughra Khan (Ḥasan b. Sulaymān, r. 467–96/1074–1102).

Kutadgu bilig is a didactic and allegorical poem. It takes the form of a set of dialogues situated within a frame-tale. The dialogues involve four protagonists: Rising Sun, who represents the king and justice; Full Moon, who represents the king's vizier and fortune; Highly Praised, who represents a sage and intellect; and Wide Awake, who represents an ascetic and humankind's last end.[33] The poem falls into two parts. In the first part, after extensive preliminary sections, the king Rising Sun longs for a good vizier and, upon being introduced to the virtuous young man Full Moon, appoints him vizier; Full Moon's son Highly Praised becomes the king's counsellor; and the country prospers as a result of royal justice. In the second part, Highly Praised and his 'brother' Wide Awake engage in a debate concerning the merits of royal service and communal engagement, on the one hand, and seclusion, on the other;

[32] Bray, 'Al-Thaʿalibi's *Adab al-muluk*', 37, with reference to al-Thaʿālibī, *Ādāb al-mulūk*, 200–1. The consumption of wine is similarly taken for granted in the mirrors of Kaykāʾūs (*Qābūsnāmeh*, 67–70) and Niẓām al-Mulk (*Siyar al-mulūk*, 119, 161–2 = Darke, *Book of Government*, 88, 118–19). Yūsuf Khāṣṣ Ḥājib assumes that royal culture customarily entails the pleasures of wine-drinking and hunting, even as he counsels against them (Text 6). In his collection *Khāṣṣ al-khāṣṣ*, al-Thaʿālibī describes wine, shared among friends, as 'the alchemy of intimate companionship and the key to gladdening the soul' (71).

[33] Dankoff, *Wisdom of Royal Glory*, 3.

Wide Awake, who initially declines the king's summons, is eventually persuaded to counsel the king, but dies shortly afterwards.

The topics covered in *Kutadgu bilig* are numerous, and in their wide remit they recall the encyclopaedic quality of the nearly contemporaneous *Qābūsnāmeh* of Kaykāʾūs.[34] They include the qualities and responsibilities of the prince, vizier, commander, chamberlain, gatekeeper, envoy, secretary, treasurer, cook and cupbearer; the proper manner of serving the prince; how to associate with nobles and commoners, descendants of the Prophet, scholars, physicians, diviners, dream interpreters, astrologers, poets, cultivators, merchants, stockbreeders, craftsmen, the poor; choosing a wife, bringing up children and managing a household; how to deal with servants, and how to behave in attending and hosting feasts. As these topics illustrate, *Kutadgu bilig*, like other mirrors of the Early Middle Period, seems to address not only the ruler to whom it is dedicated, but the entire courtly audience, and possibly an audience beyond the court as well.

Yūsuf, who acknowledged the challenges of writing in Turkish, observes that advisory compositions are represented in 'every town and city, every court and palace'. The 'nobles of this eastern realm', he writes, refer to the genre as 'Adornment of Princes', while in Iran it is called *shāhnāmeh* ('book of kings'), and in Turan *kutadgu bilig* – a passage that suggests the use of the phrase *kutadgu bilig*, like *shāhnāmeh* or *naṣīḥat al-mulūk*, as a generic designation.[35]

Beyond the question of language, *Kutadgu bilig* reflects a thoroughly mixed cultural environment, a product of the Karakhanids' liminal situation, their proximity to the steppe and their long contacts with the Samanids and Ghaznavids. The mirror contains many allusions to Qurʾanic and Prophetic texts. It also reflects a milieu steeped in the discourses of contemporary Sufism: narratives concerning individual Sufis and reports of their utterances appear frequently, and the themes of contemplation and action – for example, the relative merits of withdrawal and austerity, on the one hand, and participation in community

[34] See section 3.5.

[35] Dankoff, *Wisdom of Royal Glory*, 253, 259, 260. Yūsuf's discussion would seem to reflect the reception of the *shāhnāmeh* genre as a mode of advisory discourse, a reception explored at length, with specific reference to the *Shāhnāmeh* of Firdawsī, in Nasrin Askari's *Medieval Reception of the* Shāhnāmeh. The juxtaposition of Iran and Turan, vaguely defined territorial and political entities, suggests the geographical imagination and language of Firdawsī's *Shāhnāmeh*; see further below, at n. 38.

and governance, on the other – occupy a substantial part of the text.[36] In addition, *Kutadgu bilig* evokes the Karakhanids' long familiarity with Iranian culture and with Persian, with which language Yūsuf's Turkish is deeply inflected. On the world-conqueror's need for virtue, mind and wisdom in order to rule, Yūsuf writes, 'The Iranians have written all this down in books.'[37] The mirror includes the Persian poetic form, the quatrain, and it is written in *mutaqārib*, the metre of Firdawsī's *Shāhnāmeh*;[38] furthermore, the idea of the fickleness of fortune, a dominant theme in the *Shāhnāmeh*, emerges prominently in parts of *Kutadgu bilig*. Robert Dankoff regards the citations ascribed to almost all of Yūsuf's Turkish authorities, most identified only in general terms ('the Khan of the Turks', 'the Beg of Begs'), as well as the Turkish proverbs and quatrains ascribed to anonymous poets, as the work of Yūsuf himself.[39] A connection with *Bilawhar wa-Būdhāsaf*, transmitted in Uighur, Parthian and Persian and translated into Arabic from Middle Persian, is possible;[40] but in general, Dankoff sees little influence of Buddhism in *Kutadgu bilig*.[41]

The title *Kutadgu bilig* denotes 'The Wisdom that Conduces to Royal Glory or Fortune'.[42] Yūsuf's concentration on the attribute of wisdom, indispensable to the king's success, imparts a reflective quality to his mirror. He differentiates between wisdom and intellect, the former acquired and the latter innate; in this respect his vision resembles al-Māwardī's, with its distinction between acquired and innate types of intellect or reason.[43]

The extent to which Yūsuf's allegorical mirror circulated is difficult to assess. Although it did not, apparently, become a model for later Turkish mirrors, it is possible that it contributed to later poetic allegories, also

36 Dankoff, *Wisdom of Royal Glory*, 16–22.

37 Dankoff, *Wisdom of Royal Glory*, 48. See further Aneer, 'Kingship Ideology and Muslim Identity'.

38 Dankoff, *Wisdom of Royal Glory*, 8.

39 Dankoff, *Wisdom of Royal Glory*, 10.

40 See Asmussen, 'Barlaam and Iosaph'; Forster, 'Buddha in Disguise'.

41 Dankoff, *Wisdom of Royal Glory*, 13–15.

42 Dankoff, *Wisdom of Royal Glory*, 1. On *bilig*, see Chapter 6, Text 6. Aneer perceives a parallel between the Turkish *kut* and the Persian *farr*, as well as other analogies ('Kingship Ideology and Muslim Identity', 46). Denoting the nimbus or aura of kingship or, loosely, royal charisma, the concept of *farr* appears in the mirrors of Pseudo-Ghazālī and Niẓām al-Mulk (see Chapter 5, Text 4 and n. 133; *Siyar al-mulūk*, 81 (*farr-i ilāhī*); and see below, at n. 65).

43 Dankoff, *Wisdom of Royal Glory*, 12–13; see further Chapter 6, Text 7 and n. 19.

written in *mutaqārib*, such as the *Manṭiq-i ṭayr* ('Conference of the Birds') of Farīd al-Dīn ʿAṭṭār (d. *c*. 618/1221).[44]

3.5 Kaykāʾūs b. Iskandar, *Qābūsnāmeh* (*Andarznāmeh*) (Persian)

The *Qābūsnāmeh* ('Book of Qābūs') is one of the earliest surviving examples of Persian mirror literature. It is the composition of the penultimate ruler of the Ziyarid dynasty, ʿUnṣur al-Maʿālī Kaykāʾūs b. Iskandar b. Qābūs b. Vushmgīr (b. *c*. 412/1021–2, r. 441–*c*. 480/1049–*c*. 1087), who composed it for the benefit of his son, Gīlānshāh, the last known member of the dynasty.[45] According to the generally received text of the *Qābūsnāmeh*, Kaykāʾūs, who had come to the throne in 441/1049, began his book in 475/1082–3, when he was sixty-three years old.[46] In his personal and highly distinctive mirror, Kaykāʾūs drew on decades of experience spent in power or in the vicinity of the powerful. Before his accession, he had spent eight years as a boon-companion at the Ghaznavid court of Mawdūd b. Masʿūd (r. 433–40/1041–50), and had married a Ghaznavid princess, who became the mother of Gīlānshāh.[47] Kaykāʾūs also spent a period of time in the far north-west, at the court of the Shaddādid ruler Abū l-Aswār Shāwur I b. Faḍl (Faḍlūn) I, who ruled in Dvin (Armenia) from 413/1022 and from 441/1049 in Ganja (in the province of Arrān, now in Azerbaijan).[48] During his residence at the Ghaznavid and Shaddādid courts, Kaykāʾūs participated in campaigns at, respectively, the frontiers with Hindustan and Rum.[49] As a member of a regional dynastic family frequently in unequal alliance with or

[44] Dankoff, *Wisdom of Royal Glory*, 9.

[45] Sometimes referred to under the generic titles *Andarznāmeh*, *Pandnāmeh* or *Naṣīḥat al-mulūk*, Kaykāʾūs's mirror, for reasons that remain obscure, is commonly known as the *Qābūsnāmeh*, apparently an evocation of the author's grandfather, the ruthless ruler, learned patron and littérateur (in Arabic) Shams al-Maʿālī Qābūs (d. 403/1012–13) (see Chapter 2, n. 38). See de Fouchécour, *Moralia*, 179–223; de Bruijn, 'Kaykāvus b. Eskandar'.

[46] *Qābūsnāmeh*, 263. It has been suggested that the date indicated in the manuscript as 475 should perhaps be read as 457 (Badavī, *Baḥth dar-bāreh-yi Qābūsnāmeh*, 88–99; Badawī, 'Tamhīd', 27–8; cf. Yūsufī, 'Muqaddimeh', 16–17); most scholars, however, take the date of composition to be 475 (Bosworth, 'Chronology', 32–3; de Fouchécour, *Moralia*, 179 and n. 9).

[47] *Qābūsnāmeh*, 234. [48] *Qābūsnāmeh*, 41–3, cf. 198–9.

[49] *Qābūsnāmeh*, 41. The Shaddādids were a dynasty of Kurdish origin. They ruled from about 950 to 1200, first in Dvin and Ganja and later in Ani (Peacock, 'Shaddadids'; Madelung, 'Minor Dynasties of Northern Iran', 239–43).

vassalage to powerful neighbours, notably the Samanids, Buyids, Ghaznavids and Seljuks, Kaykāʾūs was acutely aware of the fragility and contingency of power, and wrote to prepare his son for any number of potential eventualities; his own experience had entailed many years of activity in capacities other than those of prince or ruler.

The *Qābūsnāmeh* consists of forty-four chapters devoted to a great variety of topics. In case Gīlānshāh were to be prevented from acceding to power, Kaykāʾūs (as implied in the previous paragraph) offered advice regarding not only the royal office but also numerous other professions. The book's chapters fall roughly into three main groups. The first seven chapters cover broad religious and moral topics: knowledge of God, the prophets, gratitude and obedience, relations with parents, the cultivation of accomplishments and speech. The eighth chapter, which marks a transition between the first and second sections, consists of fifty-eight maxims reportedly inscribed on the wall of Anūshīrvān's tomb. The ninth to thirtieth chapters address the rules of social behaviour; beginning with the theme of old age and youth, Kaykāʾūs discusses the etiquette of eating, wine-drinking, hospitality; jesting, backgammon and chess; love, pleasure, bathing, sleep and rest, hunting, polo, warfare, the acquisition of wealth, the safeguarding of trusts; the purchase of slaves, houses, estates and horses; marriage, the bringing up of children, choosing friends and being wary of enemies, punishment and forgiveness. The thirty-first to forty-third chapters that make up the third major section treat the professional lives of the student, jurist and teacher, the conduct of commerce, the sciences of medicine, astronomy and geometry, the conduct of the poet and musician, royal service, the careers of the boon-companion, secretary, vizier and commander of the army, and the practice of agriculture and craftsmanship. The last chapter, which marks the culmination of Kaykāʾūs's mirror, is devoted to *javānmardī*, 'chivalry', a supreme quality that ensures a good reputation in this life and a favourable reward in the next.[50]

In the course of these forty-four chapters, Kaykāʾūs relates some fifty narratives. Rather like al-Thaʿālibī's narratives in *Ādāb al-mulūk*, a significant number of the accounts related in the *Qābūsnāmeh* concern contemporary or near-contemporary figures. Several accounts are autobiographical or concern members of Kaykāʾūs's family; some involve

[50] See de Fouchécour, *Moralia*, 179–222. On *javānmardī*, see Zakeri, 'Javānmardi'; and Chapter 6, Text 8.

members of the Samanid, Buyid and Ghaznavid dynasties. While a fair number of Kaykāʾūs's narratives feature well-known or notable persons, others involve unknown or obscure individuals.[51] Kaykāʾūs employs maxims and verses of poetry, many of his own composition; he also makes striking use of metaphor.[52] Widely admired for its elegance, simplicity and clarity, the *Qābūsnāmeh*, as the manuscript record attests, enjoyed a long popularity in the Persian-speaking world. It was translated into pre-Ottoman Turkish as well as, on several occasions, into Ottoman Turkish; it contributed to the developing Turkish *nasihatname*.[53] In its earliest translation into a European language – the German *Buch des Kabus* of Heinrich Friedrich von Diez, published in 1811 – the *Qābūsnāmeh* came to the attention of Goethe, who made appreciative use of it in his *Westöstlicher Divan*.[54]

3.6 Al-Māwardī, *Tashīl al-naẓar wa-taʿjīl al-ẓafar fī akhlāq al-malik wa-siyāsat al-mulk* (Arabic)

The polymath Abū l-Ḥasan ʿAlī b. Muḥammad al-Māwardī (364–450/974–1058) wrote several works of political and moral advice, as well as other treatments of political subjects. On account of his well-known and widely cited treatise *al-Aḥkām al-sulṭāniyya* ('Political Ordinances') and his advisory and diplomatic activities on behalf of the Abbasid caliphs, al-Māwardī is often regarded as a leading defender of the caliphate against the encroachments of non-caliphal powers, specifically the Buyids. This perception tends to obscure the independence that al-Māwardī displayed in both his actions and his writings.[55] He wrote mirrors for the benefit of various rulers, several unnamed, but almost certainly including members of the Buyid family, to whom he conveyed embassies in 423/1032 and 429/1037. His authorship of certain books ascribed to him, as already mentioned, is open to question, but a probable list of his relevant writings includes, in order of their

[51] Cf. Badavī, *Baḥth dar-bāreh-yi Qābūsnāmeh*, 130–60; de Fouchécour, *Moralia*, 182.

[52] Amirsoleimani, 'Of This World and the Next'. In one place, Kaykāʾūs includes a quatrain in the Ṭabarī dialect, followed by a translation into Darī Persian 'so that it should be comprehensible to everyone' (*Qābūsnāmeh*, 98–9).

[53] See Birnbaum, *The 'Book of Advice' by King Kay-Kāʾūs ibn Iskandar*; Yūsufī, '*Muqaddimeh*', 21; Bosworth, 'Kay Kāʾūs'; de Bruijn, 'Kaykāvus b. Eskandar'; Aksan, 'Ottoman Political Writing', 53–69; Howard, 'Ottoman Historiography and the Literature of "Decline"', 52–77.

[54] *Goethes Westöstlicher Divan*, 153–263.

[55] Abbès, *De l'Éthique du prince*, 207.

composition, the mirror *Durar al-sulūk fī siyāsat al-mulūk* ('Pearls of Conduct in the Governance of Kings'), dedicated to the Buyid amir Bahā' al-Dawla (r. 379–403/989–1012), composed at the end of the tenth century or the very early eleventh;[56] *Adab al-dunyā wa-l-dīn* ('Manners for the Lower World and Eternity'), composed between 410/1020 and 421/1030; the present mirror, *Tashīl al-naẓar wa-taʿjīl al-ẓafar fī akhlāq al-malik wa-siyāsat al-mulk* ('The Facilitating of Reflection and Hastening of Success: On the King's Moral Dispositions and the Governance of the Realm'), an expanded version of *Durar al-sulūk*, written between 423/1032 and 431/1040 and addressed to an unnamed ruler, possibly Jalāl al-Dawla (r. *c.* 418–35/1027–44), son of Bahā' al-Dawla; the *Qawānīn al-wizāra wa-siyāsat al-mulk* ('Principles of the Vizierate and the Governance of the Realm'), addressed to an unnamed vizier; and *al-Aḥkām al-sulṭāniyya*, composed late in al-Māwardī's career, probably after 435/1043, the date of al-Māwardī's mission to the Seljuk sultan Tughril Bey.[57] Whereas al-Māwardī discusses the qualifications and functions of the *imām* in *al-Aḥkām al-sulṭāniyya*, in *Tashīl al-naẓar* he discusses the qualities and duties of the *malik* – an indication that he wrote the latter for the benefit of a ruler other than the caliph.

Al-Māwardī's ethical and advisory texts, among which strong resemblances are apparent, display his versatility and range; he was steeped in *adab* no less than in *fiqh* and *tafsīr*.[58] Indeed, he compiled a collection of proverbs entitled *al-Amthāl wa-l-ḥikam* ('Proverbs and Maxims'), the contents of which recur in many of his writings. Al-Māwardī characteristically draws on a wide range of authorities and examples, including Qur'anic verses and hadith, verses of Arabic poetry, the 'Testament of Ardashīr', materials ascribed to figures of the Iranian cultural tradition, the sayings of caliphs and secretaries, Plato, Aristotle and other figures associated with Greek antiquity, kings and philosophers identified as

[56] The attribution of this mirror has been questioned; for arguments in favour of al-Māwardī's authorship, see Aḥmad, 'Muqaddimat al-dirāsa wa-l-taḥqīq', 35–40; and Abbès, *De l'Éthique du prince*, 203–9.

[57] This chronology follows the order proposed in Abbès, *De l'Éthique du prince*, 208–9. See also al-Sayyid, 'Tamhīd', 82 (with the composition of *Tashīl al-naẓar* dated to approximately 432/1040–1) and 'al-Māwardī: al-rajul wa-l-ʿaṣr', 95–6. On the relationship between *Durar al-sulūk* and *Tashīl al-naẓar*, see Abbès, *De l'Éthique du prince*, 203–6. On the probable late dating of *al-Aḥkām al-sulṭāniyya*, see also Melchert, 'Māwardī, Abū Yaʿlá, and the Sunni Revival'; Laoust, 'La pensée et l'action politiques d'al-Māwardī', 15.

[58] See Arkoun, 'L'éthique musulmane d'après Māwardī'; Abbès, *De l'Éthique du prince*, 137–64.

Indian. Occasionally, in making a point, he has recourse to his own experience.[59]

The two descriptive components of al-Māwardī's title *Tashīl al-naẓar wa-taʿjīl al-ẓafar fī akhlāq al-malik wa-siyāsat al-mulk* point to the two parts of which his mirror is composed. The first part, dedicated to *akhlāq al-malik*, 'the king's moral dispositions', details the ethical qualities (*akhlāq*) that the ruler should cultivate. The second part, dedicated to *siyāsat al-mulk*, 'governance of the realm', treats the governance (*siyāsa*) that he should pursue. Echoing a foundational precept of practical philosophy, al-Māwardī presents rulership in the context of the differences among people and the resulting necessity of co-operation. He discusses virtues, including the motivation for acquiring them; the beginning of virtues, he writes, is reason, and the result of them, justice; each virtue represents the mean between two vices. The principles of sovereignty rest on two matters, governance and its foundation – the former consisting of cultivation of the lands, protection of the subjects, management of the army, and the valuation of assets, the latter consisting of religion, power and wealth.[60] The text reflects the diffusion of philosophical concepts across an interdisciplinary range of intellectual and literary fields, well beyond the circles of the individuals identified as *falāsifa*, that is, philosophers, or specialists in the Arabic tradition of *falsafa*.[61]

3.7 Niẓām al-Mulk, *Siyar al-mulūk* (Persian)

Without doubt the most politically effective of the authors whose mirrors are under consideration, Niẓām al-Mulk (d. 485/1092), vizier to the Seljuk rulers Alp Arslan (r. 455–65/1063–72) and Malikshāh (r. 465–85/1072–92), wrote his celebrated *Siyar al-mulūk* for and at the behest of Sultan Malikshāh, during whose youth he had been appointed *atabeg*.[62] Over the thirty years of Alp Arslan's and Malikshāh's reigns, during

59 Examples appear in *Adab al-dunyā wa-l-dīn*, 81–2, 242; see also Chapter 8, Text 13.

60 *Tashīl al-naẓar*, 203–23; see Chapter 7, Text 10, and Chapter 8, Text 13, which follow sequentially.

61 See Arkoun, 'L'éthique musulmane', 257–65; and in a more general sense, Rowson, 'The Philosopher as Littérateur'.

62 On the life and career of Niẓām al-Mulk, see Yavari, 'Neẓām-al-Molk'; Safi, *Politics of Knowledge*, 43–81. The present author follows the majority of scholars in treating *Siyar al-mulūk* as the work of Niẓām al-Mulk. The question of authorship has, however, been raised repeatedly; see Simidchieva, '*Siyāsat-nāme* Revisited'; and for an alternative proposal, see Khismatulin, 'To Forge a Book in the Medieval Ages' and 'The Art of Medieval Counterfeiting'. For a persuasive affirmation of Niẓām al-Mulk's authorship, see Yavari, 'Siar al-molūk' and *Advice for the Sultan*, 149–50, n. 3.

which the Seljuk Empire reached its height, Niẓām al-Mulk, at the centre of a vast network of individuals linked to him through familial, professional and personal ties, governed the empire in conjunction with the Seljuk dynasty. Informed by Niẓām al-Mulk's extensive experience in administration, which began under the Ghaznavids, *Siyar al-mulūk* offers advice on specific matters of governance and the management of the court.[63]

Siyar al-mulūk consists of fifty thematic chapters, divided into two contrasting sections composed some five years apart. According to Niẓām al-Mulk's preface, Malikshāh solicited, in 479/1086, a treatise on governance, and approved of Niẓām al-Mulk's submission of thirty-nine chapters. In 484/1091, the vizier reportedly composed an additional eleven chapters, but this expanded version of *Siyar al-mulūk* was never presented to Malikshāh. Perhaps presciently – he was assassinated the following year – Niẓām al-Mulk entrusted the manuscript to a librarian, and left instructions that the full text should be copied and submitted to the sultan in the event of his death; this plan was obviated, however, by the death of Malikshāh barely a month after the death of his vizier. While the earlier parts of the work are highly affirmative of Malikshāh's rulership, the later chapters offer a markedly critical perspective on certain practices of the Seljuk court and identify several systemic problems in the Seljuk state.[64]

Several characteristics of *Siyar al-mulūk* echo al-Thaʿālibī's *Ādāb al-mulūk* and Pseudo-Māwardī's *Naṣīḥat al-mulūk*. In a development of the earlier authors' emphasis on the exceptional nature of kingship, underpinned by divine mandate, Niẓām al-Mulk portrays sovereignty as the result of divine appointment, symbolised by the 'divine aura' (or effulgence) (*farr-i ilāhī*).[65] He stipulates the ruler's duty to govern in accordance with justice, and the subjects' duty of obedience. Like his predecessors, Niẓām al-Mulk declares the ruler responsible for the upholding of religion and the suppression of heterodoxy and rebellion, topics that particularly preoccupied this group of authors. Ostensibly to illustrate his stated points, Niẓām al-Mulk devotes a substantial part of his mirror to unusually long narratives, drawn from a traditional Iranian repertoire and from early Islamic history; like al-Thaʿālibī and Kaykāʾūs,

[63] Noting this quality, Lambton eschewed the designation 'mirror' and described *Siyar al-mulūk* instead as an administrative handbook ('Mirrors for Princes', 420; and 'Dilemma of Government', 55–6).

[64] Yavari, 'Siar al-molūk'. [65] *Siyar al-mulūk*, 81; see above, n. 42.

he also relates episodes from recent history. He adapts and shapes these narratives to maximise their rhetorical and didactic effect.[66]

Notwithstanding his position at the apex of the imperial administration (the *dīvān*), Niẓām al-Mulk devotes considerable attention to matters pertaining to royal comportment and the optimal running of the court (*dargāh*). The Seljuk court, as noted above, took the form of a tented encampment, located 'wherever the sultan happened to be'.[67] This feature of *Siyar al-mulūk* perhaps reflects the division of activities between the administrative system, over which Niẓām al-Mulk presided, and the (itinerant) court, which was the sphere and instrument of the sultan; it seems significant that Niẓām al-Mulk urges the prevention of courtly interference in matters of administration.[68] In the second, darker part of the book, Niẓām al-Mulk warns the ruler against the invariably seditious designs of the heterodox, the susceptibility of the heedless to manipulation and the ignorant or malevolent interventions of women. These seemingly general condemnations were directed at particular contemporaneous situations, in which the constraints of the mirror-writer-vizier's position prevented him from identifying specific individuals. Niẓām al-Mulk's disparagement of religious diversity, for example, is belied by his support for intermarriage between his children and members of Shiʿi families, and by his visits, with Malikshāh, to Shiʿi shrines; similarly, the apparently pervasive misogyny that characterises his chapter 'On those who wear the veil' (*ahl-i sitr*) is thoroughly subverted by the many positive portrayals of women which appear elsewhere in the book.[69]

As David Durand-Guédy has persuasively argued, Niẓām al-Mulk's attack on the Ismailis also reflects a proximate context. In his later years, the Ismaili community in Isfahan, the Seljuk capital and seat of the vizier's personal power, grew significantly in size and importance, and

[66] Simidchieva, 'Kingship and Legitimacy'; Yavari, *Advice for the Sultan*, 95–142, *passim*; Yavari, 'Mirrors for Princes or a Hall of Mirrors?'; Yavari, 'Polysemous Texts and Reductionist Readings'.

[67] Hillenbrand, 'Aspects of the Court of the Great Seljuqs', 23; see also Peacock, *Great Seljuk Empire*, 166–72; Durand-Guédy, 'Location of Rule', 'Ruling from the Outside' and 'Where Did the Saljūqs Live?'.

[68] Bosworth, 'Political and Dynastic History', 76–7.

[69] Cf. Yavari, *The Future of Iran's Past*, 105–25; Safi, *Politics of Knowledge*, 71–4; Peacock, *Great Seljuk Empire*, 67, 258–66. The direct discussion of women appears in chapter 42 (*Siyar al-mulūk*, 242–52 = Darke, *Book of Government*, 185–92); but see also Chapter 9, Text 17.

this increase in stature presented a challenge to the dominance of the Khurasani families brought to the city by Niẓām al-Mulk.[70] In an effort to discredit his political opponents, Niẓām al-Mulk, in *Siyar al-mulūk*, implied links between these individuals and the increasingly powerful Ismailis.[71] Following the deaths of Niẓām al-Mulk and Malikshāh, civil war broke out from 485–500/1092–1107, and Isfahan became a major site in the struggle over the succession. In 500/1107, the city's Khurasani families, supporters of the victorious Sultan Muḥammad b. Malikshāh (r. 498–511/1105–18) and opponents of the Ismailis, seized the opportunity to reclaim their prevailing position in administrative affairs and among the local élites; it was at this time that the librarian to whom Niẓām al-Mulk had entrusted his expanded manuscript, with its fiercely critical treatments of heterodox groups, above all Ismailis, released the full text of *Siyar al-mulūk*.[72]

3.8 Ghazālī, Pseudo-Ghazālī, *Naṣīḥat al-mulūk* (Persian)

Abū Ḥāmid al-Ghazālī (450–505/1058–1111), who during his lifetime enjoyed the status of the foremost Sunni intellectual of the age, was heavily involved in the politics of his time.[73] In 484/1091, Niẓām al-Mulk appointed Ghazālī to teach in the prestigious madrasa that bore the vizier's name, the Niẓāmiyya, in Baghdad. Ghazālī taught at the Niẓāmiyya in Baghdad until 488/1095, when a personal crisis, probably compounded by pragmatic considerations, compelled him to resign from his post.[74] He then left Baghdad and, after some years of itinerancy, eventually returned to his native Khurasan, where he spent the last decade or so of his life (493–505/1100–11); during this period he returned for some time to teaching (at the Niẓāmiyya in Nishapur), and he produced some of his most significant works. He lived through the thirty-year zenith of the Seljuks' power but also the violent conflict that erupted after Malikshāh's death.

[70] See section 2.2, at nn. 61, 62.

[71] Durand-Guédy, *Iranian Elites and Turkish Rulers*, 142–52.

[72] Durand-Guédy, *Iranian Elites and Turkish Rulers*, 188–90.

[73] Griffel, *Al-Ghazālī's Philosophical Theology*, 49–59; Garden, *The First Islamic Reviver*, 17–29, 125–42; Safi, *Politics of Knowledge*, 105–24.

[74] For a discussion of the various factors likely to have prompted Ghazālī's clandestine departure, see Safi, *Politics of Knowledge*, 107–10.

Ghazālī maintained close relations not only with the Abbasid caliphs but also with the most powerful figures of his time, namely the Seljuk sultans, Niẓām al-Mulk and Niẓām al-Mulk's son Fakhr al-Mulk (d. 500/1006). Ghazālī treated power and authority in several of his writings, and he composed advisory texts, usually with a strongly ethical and homiletic focus, for caliphs, sultans and the general public. An important political thinker, he not infrequently embedded treatments of political leadership and integrated political advice into compositions principally dedicated to other purposes.[75] As al-Māwardī had done, Ghazālī acknowledged the separate and distinct functions of the imamate (for Ghazālī, represented by the Abbasid caliphate) and sultanate; both necessary, the former connoted legitimate and legitimising authority, while the latter provided coercive power (*shawka*), which was essential for the maintenance of order and stability; the co-operation of these two entities, Ghazālī sometimes implies, supported their effective confrontation of the common threat of Ismaili claims. As long as they paid allegiance to the imamate, the sultans were legitimate and should be obeyed.[76] In Ghazālī's lifetime, the process whereby the Abbasid caliphs became the symbols of legitimate leadership of the Sunni Muslim community and represented the community's historical and relational link with the Prophet was already quite far advanced.[77]

One of Ghazālī's earlier mirrors is the short chapter, headed 'On governing and exercising authority', that appears in *Kīmiyā-yi saʿādat* ('The Alchemy of Felicity'), Ghazālī's Persian abridgement of his magnum opus, the Arabic *Iḥyāʾ ʿulūm al-dīn* ('Revivification of the Religious Sciences').[78] In its structure, contents and tone, the chapter prefigures part I of Ghazālī's Persian *Naṣīḥat al-mulūk*. Ghazālī urges the ruler (*vālī*) – a general term that avoids identification with a particular figure or even a particular office – to remember that life is transient,

[75] The polemical *Kitāb Faḍāʾiḥ al-Bāṭiniyya wa-faḍāʾil al-Mustaẓhiriyya* (*c*. 488/1095), known as *Kitāb al-Mustaẓhirī*, composed at the behest of the Abbasid caliph al-Mustaẓhir (r. 487–512/1094–1118), provides an example of this phenomenon (see Hillenbrand, 'Islamic Orthodoxy or Realpolitik?'; Figueroa, 'Algunos aspectos del pensamiento político de Al-Ghazālī'; Garden, *The First Islamic Reviver*, 18, 25–9; Safi, *Politics of Knowledge*, 110–24).

[76] See Campanini, 'In Defence of Sunnism'.

[77] See section 2.1.

[78] *Kīmiyā-yi saʿādat* contains a number of sections absent from its Arabic counterpart. The mirror appears as a substitute for a chapter that in the *Iḥyāʾ* deals with the life and morals of the Prophet. Hillenbrand notes that the mirror retains a strong emphasis on the Prophet's ethical example (Hillenbrand, 'Islamic Orthodoxy or Realpolitik?', 90–1; Hillenbrand, 'A Little-Known Mirror'; see also de Fouchécour, *Moralia*, 223–51).

a remembrance that will prompt him to govern justly.[79] He highlights the central principle of justice, and the importance of association and consultation with religious scholars; he draws attention to the exemplary value of the ruler's actions, and points out the proportionally greater magnitude of the reward or punishment in store for rulers than for their subjects. He presents the ruler with ten instructions, rooted in the principles of the faith, the proper source of government; collectively, these injunctions emphasise the necessity of justice, the perils of injustice and the necessity of consultation with scholars.[80]

As the preceding discussion implies, no disagreement surrounds Ghazālī's authorship of part I of *Naṣīḥat al-mulūk*. The authorship of part II, however, is the subject of considerable controversy.[81] The two-part Persian mirror in question circulated under various 'titles';[82] as in the case of the text's Arabic namesake, the use of the phrase *naṣīḥat al-mulūk* probably arises from the genre to which the book was assimilated. The opening lines of part I indicate that Ghazālī composed it for a Seljuk ruler, taken to be either Sultan Muḥammad b. Malikshāh (r. 498–511/1105–18) or his brother Sanjar, during the period of the latter's rule in Khurasan (490–552/1097–1157); in any event, Ghazālī wrote the mirror late in his life (*c.* 503–5/1109–11), considerably after his return to his native Khurasan.[83] The text postdates, then, the outbreak of prolonged civil strife that followed the deaths in quick succession of Niẓām al-Mulk and Malikshāh, and the collapse of the empire's political unity; it was written, moreover, during the period of the Ismaili *daʿwa*'s most conspicuous activity

[79] Ghazālī's uses of the terms *imām* and *sulṭān* are sometimes ambiguous; see Hillenbrand, 'Islamic Orthodoxy or Realpolitik?', 90; Durand-Guédy, *Iranian Elites and Turkish Rulers*, 210; Peacock, *Great Seljuk Empire*, 192. On Ibn al-Muqaffaʿ's use, much earlier, of the term *wālī*, see Hamori, 'Prudence, Virtue and Self-Respect', 163 and n. 6.

[80] Hillenbrand, 'A Little-Known Mirror'.

[81] Against Ghazālī's authorship of part II, see Crone, 'Did al-Ghazālī Write a Mirror for Princes?' and Hillenbrand, 'Islamic Orthodoxy or Realpolitik?', 91–2; for a contrasting reading, see Safi, *Politics of Knowledge*, 115–21; for a nuanced assessment of the various factors, see Garden, *The First Islamic Reviver*, 166, 213–14, n. 88.

[82] For an example, see Gottheil, 'A Supposed Work of al-Ghazālī'.

[83] Sanjar ruled throughout the Seljuk dominions from 511–52/1118–57, but his rule in Khurasan began as early as 490/1097, in other words during Ghazālī's lifetime. That Ghazālī addressed his text to Muḥammad b. Malikshāh is specified in the Arabic translation, which combines parts I and II; the Persian original does not name the person who requested the work, but the invocation of *malik-i mashriq* ('King of the East') suggests a reference to Sanjar during his rule in Khurasan.

within the Seljuk territories.[84] The extract presented in this volume belongs to part II, and, on the strength of the significant arguments against Ghazālī's authorship, it is treated as a Pseudo-Ghazālian text. Importantly, however, the assumption of Ghazālī's authorship of the entire text has informed the reception of *Naṣīḥat al-mulūk*, its two parts having been conjoined from an early date, at least since its later twelfth-century translation into Arabic.[85]

Part I of *Naṣīḥat al-mulūk* constitutes an expanded version of the short mirror in *Kīmiyā-yi sa'ādat*.[86] It details the ten roots and ten branches of the tree of faith (*īmān*), the roots consisting of the conviction of the heart (*i'tiqād-i dil*) and the branches comprising bodily actions (*kirdār-i tan*); and the two springs that water the tree of faith. The text portrays sovereignty as a divine gift, for which the ruler will be held accountable at the Last Day. Supporting his points with Qur'anic verses, Prophetic hadith and authorities of the early Islamic period, such as the caliphs 'Umar I b. al-Khaṭṭāb (r. 13–23/634–44), 'Umar II b. 'Abd al-'Azīz (r. 99–101/717–20) and Hārūn al-Rashīd (r. 170–93/786–809), Ghazālī also makes use of narratives, especially towards the end of the text, where he adduces a sequence of five cautionary stories to convey the gravity of the ruler's duties. The effect of the stories is to impress upon the audience the transience of worldly enjoyments and their futility in the face of the inexorable judgement to come.[87]

Part II consists of seven thematic chapters dedicated to, in order, the justice, governance and conduct of kings (the first and longest chapter, from which the extract in the current volume is taken); the vizierate and the conduct of viziers; secretaries and their art; kings'

[84] On the fragmentation of the Seljuk Empire following these deaths, see Van Steenbergen, *History of the Islamic World*, 188–92. On Ismaili activities and Seljuk responses, see Daftary, *The Ismā'īlīs: Their History and Doctrines*, 301–46 and *passim*; Hillenbrand, 'The Power Struggle between the Saljuqs and the Isma'ilis of Alamūt'.

[85] Toelle and Zakharia, *À la découverte de la littérature arabe*, 161. The two parts of the work seem to have been combined at an early date, since it was the full two-part text that Ṣafī l-Dīn Abū l-Ḥasan 'Alī Ibn Mubārak al-Irbilī, member of an eminent family of Shāfi'ī scholars and literary specialists, translated into Arabic, probably in the third quarter of the twelfth century (see Ibn Khallikān, *Wafayāt al-a'yān*, IV: 151 (appended to the entry concerning the translator's nephew, Sharaf al-Dīn Ibn al-Mustawfī (564–637/1169–1239); see also Ḥājjī Khalīfa, *Kashf al-ẓunūn*, I: 337, II: 1958). The Arabic translation usually circulates under the title *al-Tibr al-masbūk fī naṣīḥat al-mulūk*.

[86] Hillenbrand, 'A Little-Known Mirror for Princes', 597, 600.

[87] See Chraïbi, 'L'homme qui ne travaille qu'un seul jour par semaine', esp. 291–2, and 'Île flottante et oeuf de *rukh*', 93.

high aspiration; philosophy and philosophers; the nobility of wisdom and the wise; and the characteristics, good and bad, of women. Its chapters consist mostly of examples that in a usually implicit manner illustrate a proposition.[88] Whereas part I addresses the ruler directly, part II presupposes a general audience, and significant parts are concerned with advice for persons who serve the ruler in various capacities.[89] It exhibits a perspective reminiscent of that of Pseudo-Māwardī and especially Niẓām al-Mulk, in which the king occupies a preferential position in the divine order: God has singled out and distinguished two groups of men, prophets and kings; prophets indicate the path to God, while kings protect people from one another and are responsible for the well-being of humankind; the ruler, who is God's shadow on earth, has received the 'divine aura' (*farr-i īzadī*), by which his legitimate, divinely bestowed sovereignty is symbolised.[90] The author employs an eclectic set of references, evoking Muslim and non-Muslim authorities, including several figures from the Iranian traditional repertoire.[91]

3.9 Al-Ṭurṭūshī, *Sirāj al-mulūk* (Arabic)

Abū Bakr Muḥammad b. al-Walīd al-Andalusī al-Mālikī, Ibn Abī Randaqa (*c.* 451–520/1059–1126 or –525/1131), known as al-Ṭurṭūshī after his birth in the prosperous commercial town of Tortosa (Ar. Ṭurṭūsha) on the Spanish Mediterranean coast, became the leading Mālikī Sunni jurist of the early twelfth century.[92] At the time of his birth, Iberia, no longer politically unified, was divided into numerous independent principalities (*ṭawāʾif*, sing. *ṭāʾifa*) of varying sizes and strengths.[93] In 452/1060, during al-Ṭurṭūshī's infancy, Tortosa, lying along the northern Iberian frontier, fell under the control of the stronger *ṭāʾifa* of the Banū Hūd in nearby

[88] Zakharia, 'Al-Ghazâlî, conseilleur du prince', 218.

[89] Bauden and Ghersetti, 'L'art de servir', 295–6; Bauden and Ghersetti, 'Comment servir', 246.

[90] *Naṣīḥat al-mulūk*, 81; see above, nn. 42, 65.

[91] Hillenbrand, 'A Little-Known Mirror for Princes', 593; Zakharia, 'Al-Ghazâlî, conseilleur du prince', 222.

[92] On the date of his death (in Alexandria), see Fierro, *Abū Bakr al-Ṭurṭūšī (m. 520/1126): Kitāb al-Ḥawādiṯ wa-l-Bidaʿ*, 24–5; and for al-Ṭurṭūshī's life and works, 17–107.

[93] These principalities were known as 'parts' or 'parties' (*ṭawāʾif*, sing. *ṭāʾifa*); their rulers were known collectively as *mulūk al-ṭawāʾif* (Arabic), or *reyes de taifas* (Spanish).

Saragossa (Ar. Saraqusṭa, modern Spanish Zaragoza).[94] Al-Ṭurṭūshī studied first in Saragossa and subsequently in Seville.[95] In 476/1084, he left his native al-Andalus to continue his studies, and to teach, in several of the major cities of Western Asia. In Baghdad, he inevitably moved in circles close to Niẓām al-Mulk, whom he perhaps met; he praised the vizier at length in *Sirāj al-mulūk*.[96] He particularly admired Niẓām al-Mulk's founding of educational and religious facilities, notably the Niẓāmiyya, and, though a Mālikī, he attended the classes of several eminent Shāfiʿī jurisconsults.[97] In Syria, al-Ṭurṭūshī visited Jerusalem, and perhaps met Abū Ḥāmid al-Ghazālī, towards whose teachings and example he evinced some ambivalence: in some of his writings, he cited Ghazālī in positive contexts, but on other occasions he expressed strong disagreement.[98] In a manner somewhat reminiscent of Ghazālī, al-Ṭurṭūshī, for a period of time, retired from public life, and withdrew to Lebanon to devote himself to meditation and austerity. Finally, in 490/1096–7, he moved to Egypt. After visiting Cairo, he returned to Alexandria, where he settled permanently, dedicated himself to the teaching of jurisprudence (*fiqh*) and hadith and provided instruction to numerous students from Spain and the Maghrib.[99]

Like Ghazālī, al-Ṭurṭūshī, by virtue of the prominence of his position and the authority attached to his judgement, became involved in the public affairs of his time. He was particularly drawn into the politics of his native al-Andalus, where during his lifetime the Almoravids (482–541/1089–1147) gradually took control of the *ṭawāʾif* still in existence in 483/1090 and brought political unification to Iberia, which, moreover, was now joined with the Maghrib.[100] Saragossa fell to the Almoravids in

[94] Viguera-Molins, 'Al-Andalus and the Maghrib', 27; Fierro, 'Al-Ṭurṭūshī', 24. Tortosa remained under the rule of a branch of the Banū Hūd until it fell to the Almoravids, probably early in the twelfth century.

[95] Fierro, *Abū Bakr al-Ṭurṭūšī (m. 520/1126): Kitāb al-Ḥawādiṯ wa-l-Bidaʿ*, 28–9.

[96] *Sirāj al-mulūk*, II: 513–18.

[97] Fierro, *Abū Bakr al-Ṭurṭūšī (m. 520/1126): Kitāb al-Ḥawādiṯ wa-l-Bidaʿ*, 34–9.

[98] Fierro, *Abū Bakr al-Ṭurṭūšī (m. 520/1126): Kitāb al-Ḥawādiṯ wa-l-Bidaʿ*, 40–1, 107 and *passim*; Laoust, 'La suivie de Gazālī', 154; Garden, *The First Islamic Reviver*, 143–68, esp. 154–5. Pointing to the numerous stories and sayings, including examples drawn from Persian and Indian sources, contained in *Sirāj al-mulūk*, Goldziher and Brockelmann both conjectured that al-Ṭurṭūshī perhaps deliberately sought to outdo Ghazālī's *al-Tibr al-masbūk* (Goldziher, *Streitschrift*, 100–1; *GAL SI*, 830).

[99] In Alexandria, al-Ṭurṭūshī effectively established Egypt's first attested madrasa (Mulder, 'Mausoleum of Imam al-Shafiʿi', 26).

[100] Viguera-Molins, 'Al-Andalus and the Maghrib', 28.

503/1110, as did Tortosa at an unknown date in the early twelfth century. Abū Bakr Muḥammad b. ʿAbdallāh Ibn al-ʿArabī (468–543/1076–1148), a member of the Ibn al-ʿArabī family of Seville and a student of al-Ṭurṭūshī's, solicited the support of al-Ṭurṭūshī, Ghazālī and the Abbasid caliph al-Mustaẓhir (r. 487–512/1094–1118) for Abū Yaʿqūb Yūsuf Ibn Tāshufīn (r. 453–500/1061–1106), effectively the first Almoravid ruler in al-Andalus.[101] The caliph sanctioned the requested regnal titles; Ghazālī, possibly with a view to his own future security in the years following the death of his patron Niẓām al-Mulk, wrote a *fatwā* in generous support of Ibn Tāshufīn; al-Ṭurṭūshī produced a more reserved and critical communication, in which he offered advice and exhortation, and emphasised the duties of justice and *jihād*.[102] Abū Bakr went on to become qadi of his native Seville.[103] Another student of al-Ṭurṭūshī, the jurist and reformer Muḥammad b. ʿAbdallāh Ibn Tūmart (d. 524/1130), would become the founder of the Almohad movement, which from 524/1130 to 668/1269 would replace the Almoravids in North Africa and al-Andalus.

Although he produced several writings in various branches of the religious sciences, al-Ṭurṭūshī's mirror for princes, *Sirāj al-mulūk*, is by far his best-known work.[104] Initially intended for the Fatimid military vizier al-Afḍal, who had summoned the author against his will from Alexandria to Cairo, the mirror remained incomplete at the time of al-Afḍal's assassination in 515/1122. Upon completing the book in 516/1122, al-Ṭurṭūshī dedicated it to al-Afḍal's successor, Abū ʿAbdallāh Muḥammad b. Abī Shujāʿ Fātik al-Baṭāʾiḥī (d. 522/1128), known as al-Maʾmūn Ibn al-Baṭāʾiḥī, who served as vizier to the Fatimid caliph al-Āmir (r. 495–524/1101–30) from 515/1122 until 519/1125, when he was arrested and imprisoned, and was finally executed in 522/1128.[105]

101 The Ibn al-ʿArabī family, especially the scholar Abū Muḥammad ʿAbdallāh b. ʿUmar Ibn al-ʿArabī (d. 493/1099, in Alexandria), had enjoyed extensive ties with the Banū ʿAbbād Ṭāʾifa of Seville (414–84/1023–91). Father and son left al-Andalus for the eastern Mediterranean as, in 482/1090, Yūsuf Ibn Tāshufīn, having completed his conquest of North Africa, and with the consent of the local *fuqahāʾ*, confronted the *ṭāʾifa* rulers (Soravia, 'ʿAbbādids').

102 For a comparison of Ghazālī's and al-Ṭurṭūshī's responses to Ibn Tāshufīn, see Viguera, 'Las cartas de al-Gazālī y al-Ṭurṭūšī'; Fletcher, 'Ibn Tūmart's Teachers', 309–11.

103 De Felipe, 'Berber Leadership and Genealogical Legitimacy', 58, 67, n. 17; Mediano, 'L'amour, la justice et la crainte', 96–7.

104 For al-Ṭurṭūshī's oeuvre, see Fierro, *Abū Bakr al-Ṭurṭūšī (m. 520/1126): Kitāb al-Ḥawādiṯ wa-l-Bidaʿ*, 54–76; for *Sirāj al-mulūk*, 68–73.

105 See Chapter 2, at nn. 68–9.

Comprising sixty-four chapters, *Sirāj al-mulūk* is, at first glance, a monumental work of synthesis, in which al-Ṭurṭūshī employs with consummate skill the full resources of the Arabic literary repertoire. The mirror is replete with instructive narratives, exemplary maxims and moral pronouncements, and includes certain references that reflect al-Ṭurṭūshī's specifically Iberian heritage.[106] Beyond its synthetic dimension, *Sirāj al-mulūk*, in its arrangement, reflects al-Ṭurṭūshī's insistence on fundamental royal attributes and responsibilities, rather than specific governmental practices, in the interests of political stability and just government.[107] Like most mirrors, the work seems intended for the edification of readers of all kinds, and not rulers alone.

A dimension of *Sirāj al-mulūk* which reflects its responsiveness to contemporaneous conditions is the unusual attention it pays to non-Muslims, including the position of non-Muslim communities in the Muslim-governed polity. The Khurasanian writers, as noted in the preceding pages, frequently displayed a high level of concern regarding heterodox groups within the Muslim fold. Although al-Ṭurṭūshī ended his days in the Fatimid domain, by this time the Fatimids had lost much of their former strength and the challenge of Ismaili Islam seemed less pressing, in cities along the western, eastern and southern shores of the Mediterranean, than the advances of European Christian forces. Al-Ṭurṭūshī was well aware of these advances, both in al-Andalus and in the eastern Mediterranean. In al-Andalus, Toledo fell to Alfonso VI, King of Castile and León (r. 1065–1109), in 478/1085; Tortosa would fall to Ramon Berenguer IV of Barcelona in 543/1148. The Fatimids, as previously noted, suffered numerous losses to the Crusaders in the eastern Mediterranean, from Jerusalem in 492/1099 to Tyre in 518/1124 and Ascalon in 548/1153. The Fatimids' resistance, when it materialised, proved ineffective, and they suffered a severe defeat in 517/1123, a mere year after al-Ṭurṭūshī's completion of his *Sirāj al-mulūk*; later, the Franks went on to invade Egypt between 560/1164 and 565/1169.[108] As al-Ṭurṭūshī wrote, the Fatimids' territorial losses were mounting, and al-Ṭurṭūshī's adopted domicile in Alexandria lay increasingly close to the frontier.[109]

106 Fierro, *Abū Bakr al-Ṭurṭūšī (m. 520/1126): Kitāb al-Ḥawādiṯ wa-l-Bida'*, 72–3.
107 See Mediano, 'L'amour, la justice et la crainte', 95–7.
108 Lev, 'The Fāṭimid Caliphate', 218; see also section 2.2.
109 As noted by Fierro, *Abū Bakr al-Ṭurṭūšī (m. 520/1126): Kitāb al-Ḥawādiṯ wa-l-Bida'*, 46.

A newcomer to Fatimid territory, a Mālikī Sunni and at the height of his career, al-Ṭurṭūshī was in a position to adopt an implicitly critical stance in formulating his advice. Against the backdrop of the cumulative military reversals in the western and eastern Mediterranean, al-Ṭurṭūshī emphasised the need for a robust defence as well as internal reform, including an enforcement of restrictions against indigenous Christian and Jewish populations. Most unusually, and possibly driven in part by the prominence of Armenians at the highest levels of authority in the Fatimid state, al-Ṭurṭūshī included a full version of the 'Pact of ʿUmar', a purported record of the conditions imposed on and assented to by the Christians of Syria after their surrender to the caliph ʿUmar b. al-Khaṭṭāb.[110] He also devoted a chapter of *Sirāj al-mulūk* to principles of warfare.[111] Al-Ṭurṭūshī's negative attitude towards Christian militarism did not, however, preclude positive treatments of other Christian figures and themes, such as miracle stories.[112]

Partly due to the scope of its contents, partly owing to al-Ṭurṭūshī's reputation and partly due to the balanced, fluent and comprehensive quality of the text, *Sirāj al-mulūk* rapidly became immensely popular; the large number of extant manuscripts attests to its appeal and dissemination.[113] The text was well known to al-Ṭurṭūshī's fellow Mālikī, the North African historian, philosopher and proto-sociologist Ibn Khaldūn (d. 808/1406), who, though he found it inadequate, discussed it at some length and made extensive use of it in his *Muqaddima* ('Introduction' [to his History *Kitāb al-ʿIbar*, 'Book of Instructive Accounts']).[114] *Sirāj al-mulūk*, which was translated into Turkish in 1584, also attained an appreciative audience among Ottoman readers.[115]

110 See Fierro, *Abū Bakr al-Ṭurṭūšī (m. 520/1126): Kitāb al-Ḥawādiṯ wa-l-Bidaʿ*, 38 (section 4.5.6), 73, 75; Fierro, 'Al-Ṭurṭūshī', 387–96; Mallett, 'Two Writings of al-Ṭurṭūshī'.

111 Included in this sixty-first chapter of *Sirāj al-mulūk* (II: 694–6) is an account of the battle of Manzikert (though the place is not named), apparently the earliest in the Islamic sources and based on recent reports and memories; see Hillenbrand, *Turkish Myth and Muslim Symbol*, 27–30.

112 Hämeen-Anttila, 'Jesus and His Disciples', 111–12, nn. 17, 19.

113 Fierro, *Abū Bakr al-Ṭurṭūšī (m. 520/1126): Kitāb al-Ḥawādiṯ wa-l-Bidaʿ*, 68; for holdings in pre-modern libraries, see, for example, Hirschler, *Medieval Damascus: Plurality and Diversity in an Arabic Library*, 222 no. 559 (three copies); and Haarmann, 'The Library of a Fourteenth-Century Jerusalem Scholar', 332.

114 Rosenthal, *Ibn Khaldûn: The Muqaddimah: An Introduction to History*, I: 83, 316–17, II: 87; cf. Irwin, *Ibn Khaldun: An Intellectual Biography*, 58–9, 67.

115 Fierro, 'Al-Ṭurṭūshī', 394–5; Yılmaz, *Caliphate Redefined*, 60, 83.

It was widely cited amongst writers of Ottoman political literature, and the historian and bibliographer Ḥājjī Khalīfa (1017–67/1609–57) wrote, 'Hardly a ruler heard it but that he asked to have it copied, and no vizier but that he made it his companion; by thorough study of it, the wise man could dispense with conferring with sages, and the king with consulting his viziers.'[116] A translation into Persian appeared in the early seventeenth century.[117]

[116] *Kashf al-ẓunūn*, II: 984.
[117] Fierro, *Abū Bakr al-Ṭurṭūšī (m. 520/1126): Kitāb al-Ḥawādiṯ wa-l-Bidaʿ*, 68.

4

Editions and Translations

With the exception of the extract from *Kutadgu bilig*, all of the translations that appear in Part II are the author's. Partly for the sake of consistency, I have opted to produce new translations even where excellent English versions already exist. Although in many cases several decades have passed since their production, these earlier translations remain extremely valuable, not least because they provide complete English versions of the source texts. Particularly for the benefit of readers who wish to explore the texts in their entirety, I have indicated, for each of the extracts that appears in Part II, the corresponding sections in previously published translations into English, French and Spanish. I have referred to several of these translations in preparing my own, and in several instances I have drawn attention to the earlier translators' interpretations in the footnotes.

In producing my translations, I have aimed for a balance of accuracy and straightforwardness. I have attempted to convey some of the freshness of the originals, the contemporary resonance of which is sometimes arresting. The writers, whose intellect and clarity of thought remain striking a millennium later, evoke for us a coherent vision of a better politics – a politics guided by certain convictions: the interconnectedness and interdependence of multiple constituencies, the indispensability of care for the whole, the imperative to live within the means available and in harmony with the natural environment; and aspiring to certain aims: the preservation of peace, the promotion of universal prosperity and the maintenance of acknowledged standards of fairness.

I have prepared my translations from published editions of the Arabic and Persian texts, with occasional reference to manuscripts. Details of the editions and several existing translations appear in the following paragraphs.

4.1 Pseudo-Aristotle, *Kitāb al-Siyāsa fī tadbīr al-riyāsa* (*Sirr al-asrār*) (Text 9)

As the basis for my translation, I have used the Arabic edition included in *al-Uṣūl al-yūnāniyya lil-naẓariyyāt al-siyāsiyya fī l-Islām*, ed. ʿAbd al-Raḥmān Badawī (Cairo: Dār al-Kutub al-Miṣriyya, 1954). The text of *Kitāb al-Siyāsa fī tadbīr al-riyāsa al-maʿrūf bi-Sirr al-asrār* covers pp. 67–171 in this collection. An English translation of *Sirr al-asrār* is available in *Opera hactenus inedita Rogeri Baconi*, Fasc. V, *Secretum secretorum cum glossis et notulis – Tractatus brevis et utilis ad declarandum quedam obscure dicta Fratris Rogeri*, edited by Robert Steele (Oxford: Clarendon, 1909). In this book, as its title indicates, Steele presented an edition of Roger Bacon's recension of the Latin version, under the name *Secretum secretorum*. Steele also included an English translation of the Arabic text. The translator, Ismail Ali, completed the project under Steele's supervision; A. S. Fulton, of the British Museum, edited the text.[1] Ali's translation covers pp. 176–266 of Steele's edition.

4.2 Pseudo-Māwardī, *Naṣīḥat al-mulūk* (Text 1)

The Arabic text is available in three published editions. They are, in order of their dates of publication, *Naṣīḥat al-mulūk*, edited by Khiḍr Muḥammad Khiḍr (Kuwait: Maktabat al-Falāḥ, 1983); *Kitāb Naṣīḥat al-mulūk*, edited by Muḥammad Jāsim al-Ḥadīthī (Baghdad: Dār al-Shuʾūn al-Thaqafiyya al-ʿĀmma, 1986); and *Naṣīḥat al-mulūk al-mansūb ilā Abī l-Ḥasan al-Māwardī*, edited by Fuʾād ʿAbd al-Munʿim Aḥmad (Alexandria: Muʾassasat Shabāb al-Jāmiʿa, 1988). For my translation I have made use, principally, of Aḥmad's 1988 edition, to which references in the notes apply, unless noted otherwise. A translation of the Arabic text into Turkish is available in Mustafa Sarıbıyık, *Siyaset Senati* (Istanbul: Sosyal Bilimler Enstitüsü, 1996). As far as I am aware, no complete translation into English has yet appeared. Versions of certain passages translated in Text 1 appeared in the present author's *Counsel for Kings* (Louise Marlow, *Counsel for Kings: Wisdom and Politics in Tenth-Century Iran: The Naṣīḥat al-mulūk of Pseudo-Māwardī* (Edinburgh: Edinburgh University Press, 2016), I: 59, 97–8, 114, 115, 117, 118–19,

[1] As Manzalaoui observed ('The Pseudo-Aristotelian *Kitāb Sirr al-asrār*', 147), Steele mentions Ismail Ali's name only in passing; it does not appear on the title page of his edition (Steele, 'Introduction', vii).

119–20, 122–4) (© L. Marlow, 2016); reproduced with permission of Edinburgh University Press Limited through PLSclear.

4.3 Al-Thaʿālibī, *Ādāb al-mulūk* (Texts 2 and 16)

I have prepared my translation from the edition of Jalāl al-ʿAṭiyya (Beirut: Dār al-Gharb al-Islāmī, 1990). Prior to the appearance of this edition, Tevfik Rüştü Topuzoğlu had produced an unpublished edition of the text, as well as an excellent translation into English, in his PhD dissertation, completed at the University of Manchester, in 1974. In 2015, a published version of Topuzoğlu's edition and translation appeared, in two volumes: *Abū Manṣūr ʿAbd al-Malik b. Muḥammad b. Ismāʿīl ath-Thaʿālibī: Kitāb Ādāb al-Mulūk al-Khwārazm-shāhī*, Vol. I: A Critical Edition with Introduction and Translation; Vol. II: The Arabic Text, Edited and Translated by Tevfik Rüştü Topuzoğlu (Ankara: Türk Tarih Kurumu, 2015). In my references to Topuzoğlu's translation, I have included references to both the 1974 dissertation and the 2015 published version, between which I have found few differences.

4.4 Yūsuf Khāṣṣ Ḥājib, *Kutadgu bilig* (Text 6)

The Turkish text is available in the edition of Reşid Rahmeti Arat, *Kutadgu Bilig* (Istanbul: Millî Eğitim Basımevi, 1947). The translation that appears in Text 6 is that of Robert Dankoff, who translated the entire work in *Wisdom of Royal Glory (Kutadgu Bilig): A Turko-Islamic Mirror for Princes* (Chicago: University of Chicago Press, 1983). The section entitled 'The Qualifications of a Prince' is republished with permission of the University of Chicago Press from Robert Dankoff, *Wisdom of Royal Glory (Kutadgu bilig)*, © 1983 by The University of Chicago; permission conveyed through Copyright Clearance Center, Inc.

4.5 ʿUnṣur al-Maʿālī Kaykāʾūs b. Iskandar, *Qābūsnāmeh* (Text 8)

In preparing my translations from the *Qābūsnāmeh*, I have used the edition of Ghulām-Ḥusayn Yūsufī (Tehran: Shirkat-i Intishārāt-i ʿIlmī va-Farhangī, 1989). A complete translation into English is available in Reuben Levy, *A Mirror for Princes: The Qābūs Nāma* (London: Cresset

Press, 1951), and I have noted the corresponding page numbers from Levy's translation for the chapters translated in Text 8. I have not seen the earlier English translation of P. B. Vachha, which was published in Bombay, 1916. The *Qābūsnāmeh* has been translated into several other languages as well; in addition to the series of translations made into Turkish during the Ottoman period, it was rendered into German (H. R. von Diez, *Buch des Kabus, oder, Lehren des persischen Königs Kjekjawus für seinen Sohn Ghilan Schach: ein Werk für alle Zeitalter aus dem Türkisch-Persisch-Arabischen übersetzt und durch Abhandlungen und Anmerkungen erläutert* (Berlin: In Commission der Nicolaischen Buchhandlung, 1811)), French (A. Querry, *Le Cabous name, ou, Livre de Cabous de Cabous Onsor el-Moali* (Paris: E. Leroux, 1886)), Russian (E. E. Bertel, *Kabus-name* (Moscow: Izd-vo Akademii nauk SSSR, 1953, 1958)) and Arabic (Muḥammad Ṣādiq Nashʾat and Amīn ʿAbd al-Majīd Badawī, *Kitāb al-Naṣīḥa al-maʿrūf bi-sm Qābūsnāmeh* (Cairo: Maktabat al-Anjalū al-Miṣriyya, 1958)).

4.6 Al-Māwardī, *Tashīl al-naẓar wa-taʿjīl al-ẓafar fī akhlāq al-malik wa-siyāsat al-mulk* (Texts 3, 7, 10 and 13)

For this text, I have prepared my translations from the edition of Riḍwān al-Sayyid, *Tashīl al-naẓar wa-taʿjīl al-ẓafar fī akhlāq al-malik wa-siyāsat al-mulk* (Beirut: Dār al-ʿUlūm al-ʿArabiyya, 1987). To my knowledge, no full-length English translation of this mirror has yet appeared. The reader is referred, however, to the fine translation into French of Makram Abbès, which, along with an excellent study and analysis, appears in his *Al-Māwardī. De l'Éthique du prince et du gouvernement de l'état* (Paris: Les Belles Lettres, 2015). The notes that accompany my translations refer the reader to the corresponding pages in Abbès's translation.

4.7 Niẓām al-Mulk, *Siyar al-mulūk* (Texts 11, 14 and 17)

I have prepared my translation from the edition of Hubert Darke (*Siyar al-mulūk (Siyāsatnāmeh)*, edited by H. S. G. Darke (Tehran: Bungāh-i Tarjameh va-Nashr-i Kitāb, 1962)). The earlier edition and the accompanying translation into French of Charles Schefer (*Siasset Namèh. Traité de gouvernement, composé pour le sultan Melik-Châh par le vizir Nizam oul-Moulk* (Paris: E. Leroux, 1891–7, 1893)) also remain in use, particularly in the updated edition of Murtażā Mudarrisī Chahārdahī (Tehran: Kitābfurūshī Ṭahūrī, 1955), to which I have also referred. Two years before his edition appeared in 1962, Darke produced a full-length translation into English (*The Book of Government or Rules for Kings* (London: Routledge and Kegan Paul, 1960)). After the subsequent appearance of an older and critically important manuscript of the Persian text (dated 673/1274 and known as the Nakhjivānī MS), Darke used it to revise his translation; this revised version appeared in 1978. Darke's edition and his revised translation are very widely used and, despite the decades since their publication, they remain exceptionally valuable. In 1960, the translation into German of Karl Emil Schabinger appeared (*Nizāmulmulk, Reichskanzler der Saldschuqen 1063–1092 n. Chr. – Siyāsatnāma, Gedanken und Geschichten* (Freiburg: Karl Alber, 1960)), and a translation into Italian (Maurizio Pistoso, *L'arte della politica (lo specchio del principe nella Persia dell'XI secolo) (Siyāsatnāma)* (Milan: Luni, 1999)) appeared in 1999.

4.8 Al-Ghazālī, *Naṣīḥat al-mulūk* (Text 4)

As the basis of my translation, I have used the edition of Jalāl al-Dīn Humā'ī (*Naṣīḥat al-mulūk* (Tehran: Kitābkhāneh-yi Millī, 1972)). I have also made occasional use of the twelfth-century Arabic translation, published under the title *al-Tibr al-masbūk fī naṣīḥat al-mulūk*.[2] The Arabic version formed the basis for several Ottoman translation-adaptations into Turkish.[3] The full-length English translation of F. R. C. Bagley, *Ghazālī's Book of Counsel for Kings* (London: Oxford University Press, 1964), remains extremely valuable; it includes, furthermore, an informative and useful introduction (pp. ix–lxxiv). I have indicated the corresponding pages in Bagley's translation whenever I have cited the Persian *Naṣīḥat al-mulūk*. Also available is the French translation of Hassan Boutaleb, *Le miroir du prince et le conseil aux rois* (Beirut: Dar Albouraq, 2014).

[2] *Al-Tibr al-masbūk fī naṣīḥat al-mulūk*, ed. Muḥammad Aḥmad Damaj (Beirut: Mu'assasat 'Izz al-Dīn lil-Ṭibā'a wa-l-Nashr, 1996). The reader is also referred to the edition, published under the same title, of Aḥmad Shams al-Dīn (Beirut: Dār al-Kutub al-'Ilmiyya, 1988). The Arabic translation passed through two recensions; see Meier, 'al-Ġazzālī, Abū Ḥāmid Muḥammad'. On the various titles under which the Arabic text survives, see Damaj, 'al-Muqaddima', 9.

[3] Meier, 'al-Ġazzālī, Abū Ḥāmid Muḥammad', 404–5.

4.9 Al-Ṭurṭūshī, *Sirāj al-mulūk* (Texts 5, 12, 15 and 18)

I have used the Arabic edition of Muḥammad Fatḥī Abū Bakr (Cairo: Dār al-Miṣriyya al-Lubnāniyya, 1994). As previously noted, the Arabic text was translated into Turkish and Persian.[4] I have consulted the full-length, two-volume translation into Spanish of Maximiliano A. Alarcón, *Lámpara de los príncipes* (Madrid: Instituto de Valencia de Don Juan, 1930–1) and indicated the corresponding page numbers in my notes.

[4] Fierro, *Abū Bakr al-Ṭurṭūšī (m. 520/1126): Kitāb al-Ḥawādiṯ wa-l-Bidaʿ*, 68, no. 24; Fierro, 'Al-Ṭurṭūshī', 394–5; and see above, section 3.9.

Part II Texts

While the mirror's flexibility allowed treatment of a wide variety of topics, certain themes recur across the Arabic, Persian and Turkish sources. These themes include the ruler's need to cultivate personal virtue, as an example for his subjects and as the foundation for his sound governance; the exceptional nature of the king's position, in which the singular bounties that he enjoys are counterbalanced by unparalleled responsibilities; the interdependence of the various elements of the polity and the centrality of justice in the maintenance of harmony among these constituencies; the king's overriding duty to guarantee justice in his realm; the ruler's responsibility for the security and prosperity of his subjects, whom God has entrusted to his care; the king's need to uphold the law and to abide by it; the importance of royal association with and deference towards the learned and the wise; the indispensability of consultation and the heeding of honest counsel; the need for royal self-control, particularly in the case of anger, and the avoidance of meting out punishments in haste; and the importance of studying the ways of past kings. Force may suffice for a ruler to seize power; but to maintain it, he must earn his subjects' love. These themes recur in this anthology's selected texts, which are grouped, loosely, under five rubrics: the nature of sovereignty; the king's person and character; foundations of royal authority and principles of governance; the practice of good governance; and problems in the kingdom and their remedies. In order to convey a sense of the interests, approach, logic and frame of reference of each author, I have, in most cases, selected full chapters or complete sections from the source texts, and I have translated them in their entirety.

5

The Nature of Sovereignty

The ancient association of kingship with sacrality remained a foundational component in the political cultures of late antique western Asia. Notwithstanding a permanent current of resistance to earthly sovereigns' claims to sacerdotal authority, symbolic linkages of the divine realm with human embodiments of monarchy evolved continuously and appeared in ever new forms in the iconography, ceremonial, artistic production and intellectual discourses that surrounded power.[1] Panegyric poets and secretary-counsellors at the early Muslim courts drew on a large, mixed repertoire of ideas and images, inherited in turn by the mirror-writers featured in the present anthology. The formula 'The ruler is God's shadow on earth', ubiquitous in the Arabic, Persian and Turkish mirror literatures, provides an example of a perennial yet versatile expression of the relationship between divine and earthly power. The notion of the divine mandate – the proposition that the king ruled by virtue of divine choice and with divine support – constitutes a prominent theme, even as several authors insisted on the ruler's accountability to divine judgement. As the texts included in this chapter will show, the mirror-authors brought a range of perspectives to the idea of the connection between divine power and human royalty; even when they invoke a common repertoire of formulae and metaphors, the writers employ them to create different meanings.

[1] Al-Azmeh, *Muslim Kingship*, esp. 3–61; cf. Marsham, *Rituals of Islamic Monarchy*. For parallels in Carolingian political thought, including mirrors for princes, see Nelson, 'Kingship and Empire', esp. 243; Anton, *Fürstenspiegel und Herrscherethos*, 357–83.

Text 1 Pseudo-Māwardī, *Naṣīḥat al-mulūk*. Chapter Two[2]

Translator's Introduction

This text constitutes Chapter Two of Pseudo-Māwardī's *Naṣīḥat al-mulūk*. In this chapter, Pseudo-Māwardī presents kingship in the context of an integrated political, social, moral and religious framework. He places emphasis on kings' exceptionalism, a theme that he develops in two directions. On the one hand, the king enjoys exceptional powers and exceptional benefits; on the other hand, he shoulders exceptional responsibility. Rather than using his powers and benefits for the sake of personal advantage or gratification, the king must treat them as a divinely given trust and employ them for the good of his subjects; he shall be held fully accountable for every aspect of his governance, and judged accordingly, in his lifetime by his subjects, after his death amongst his successors and for all eternity according to divine judgement. Throughout his carefully sequenced analysis, Pseudo-Māwardī emphasises themes of balance and reciprocity: for every favour that the king enjoys, he faces a corresponding duty; for every right that God has granted him, he incurs an obligation and owes a debt. From its opening declarations of royal greatness, this chapter acquires an increasingly critical tone as Pseudo-Māwardī turns to the topic of kings who fail in these duties and obligations; demands of conscience, he implies, limit the subjects' duty of obedience to such rulers. In presenting these ideas, Pseudo-Māwardī grounds his arguments in both divine revelation and human reason. Far from being at odds with one another, the revealed truth and rational understanding fully support one another. Pseudo-Māwardī accordingly invokes the authority of the Qurʾan and the

[2] Translation prepared from *Naṣīḥat al-mulūk al-mansūb ilā Abī l-Ḥasan al-Māwardī*, ed. Fuʾād ʿAbd al-Munʿim Aḥmad (Alexandria: Muʾassasat Shabāb al-Jāmiʿa, 1988), 61–83; with reference to al-Māwardī, *Kitāb Naṣīḥat al-mulūk*, ed. Muḥammad Jāsim al-Ḥadīthī (Baghdad: Dār al-Shuʾūn al-Thaqāfiyya al-ʿĀmma, 1986), 69–107, and al-Māwardī, *Naṣīḥat al-mulūk*, ed. Khiḍr Muḥammad Khiḍr (Kuwait: Maktabat al-Falāḥ, 1983), 53–65. Unless otherwise noted, references to the Arabic *Naṣīḥat al-mulūk* apply to the edition of Fuʾād ʿAbd al-Munʿim Aḥmad. Earlier translations of certain passages appear in L. Marlow, *Counsel for Kings: Wisdom and Politics in Tenth-Century Iran: The Naṣīḥat al-mulūk of Pseudo-Māwardī* (Edinburgh: Edinburgh University Press, 2016), I: 59, 97–8, 114, 115, 117, 118–19, 119–20, 122–4 (© L. Marlow, 2016), reproduced (with modification) with permission of Edinburgh University Press Limited through PLSclear.

Prophetic *sunna*, as well as exemplars of human wisdom, such as Aristotle, the Buddha, sagacious kings of the Indian and Iranian pasts, figures of the early Islamic period and poets of the pre-Islamic and Islamic eras. Explorations of the semantic fields associated with various Arabic words and roots provide Pseudo-Māwardī's analysis with structure and method. For example, concepts related to the root *f-ḍ-l* constitute a recurrent thematic cluster in his exposition: with its connotations of, on the one hand, priority, privilege and precedence, and on the other hand, moral excellence and virtue, *f-ḍ-l* promotes Pseudo-Māwardī's urging of the king to realise both aspects of the concept; he frequently contrasts the root with terms related to the root *s-kh-r*, connoting subordination and subjugation. In another prominent example, Pseudo-Māwardī employs the twin concepts of *niʿma*, favour or benefit, and *shukr*, gratitude, in order to evoke the reciprocal obligations of benefactor and beneficiary.

Translation

*On the Privileges (*Faḍāʾil*) of Kings in the Magnificence of Their Stations; and the Habits That They Are Obliged to Adopt in Their Cultivation of Virtue and Avoidance of Vice*

God, may He be exalted and glorified, has given precedence (*tafḍīl*) to humankind over the other animals. He has favoured (*tafḍīl*) animals over plants and minerals, and to humankind He has subjugated (*taskhīr*) everything that is in the world: every type of being and every species that He has created, whether in the sky, on land, or between the two abodes. Among people of rational intelligence (*ahl al-ʿuqūl*), this observation raises no grounds for doubt, contention, controversy or argument, since the matter is universally attested and generally observed, and rationally minded people (*al-ʿuqalāʾ*) are in agreement about it. Furthermore, God has said, 'He has subordinated (*sakhkhara*) to you that which is in the heavens and that which is in the earth, all of it, from Him' (45: 13);[3] 'He has subordinated (*sakhkhara*) to you the sun and the moon, they being persistent; and He has subordinated (*sakhkhara*) to you

[3] The verse that precedes Q 45: 13 combines the concept of subordination with the reciprocal principles of favour (*f-ḍ-l*) and gratitude (*sh-k-r*), which feature prominently in Pseudo-Māwardī's exposition in this passage. Familiarity with this preceding verse, which reads, 'It is God Who has subordinated the sea for you, so that the ships may course upon it by His command, and that you might seek His favour (*faḍl*), perchance you may be

the night and the day. He has given to you of everything that you have asked Him for, and if you were to count the bounty (*niʿma*) of God you could not reckon it' (14: 33, 34); and 'We have ennobled the Children of Adam; We have carried them on the land and the sea, We have sustained them with good things, and We have preferred them greatly (*faḍḍalnāhum ... tafḍīlan*) over many of those whom We have created' (17: 71).

Moreover, God has privileged (*faḍḍala*) kings (*mulūk*) over the categories of humanity (*ṭabaqāt al-bashar*) in the same way that He has given preference to humanity over the other kinds and species of creation. This preferment of kings takes several forms, and it is borne out in manifest signs and evidentiary proofs, which, grounded in both intellect and divine revelation, are amenable to observation and knowledge (*li ... dalāʾil mawjūda wa-shawāhid fī l-ʿaql wa-l-samʿ jamīʿan ḥāḍira maʿlūma*).

Among these signs of God's privileging of kings is the fact that He has ennobled them by calling them by the epithet that He used to describe Himself, for He has called them 'kings' and He has called Himself a 'king'. Of Himself He has said, 'King of the Day of Judgement (*malik yawm al-dīn*)' (1: 4); and 'For God is exalted, the True King (*al-malik al-ḥaqq*)' (23: 116; 20: 114). In describing the kings of humankind, He has said, 'And God has sent to you Saul as a king' (2: 247), and 'When He made prophets among you and made you kings' (5: 20). Commending the concept (*maʿnā*) by which a human being might merit the appellation 'king', and choosing that epithet of praise for Himself, He has said: 'Who possesses sovereignty (*mulk*) on this day? It belongs to God, the One, the All-Powerful' (40: 16); 'Say, O God, Owner of Sovereignty (*mālik al-mulk*), You bestow kingship (*mulk*) on whom You will, and You take kingship away from whom You will' (3: 26); 'David slew Goliath, and God gave him sovereignty and wisdom (*al-mulk wa-l-ḥikma*)' (2: 251); 'And We brought them a great kingdom (*mulkan ʿaẓīman*)' (4: 54). God has granted the king the use of this epithet (*ṣifa*) in the same way that He granted to these earlier kings the use of the name (*ism*) that He was pleased to apply to Himself, by which He praised Himself to His creation, and which He then bestowed upon them. He clarified their precedence (*faḍl*) in this regard when He said, 'We have apportioned (*qasamnā*) among them their livelihood in the life of this world, and We

thankful (*tashkurūn*)' (Q 45: 12), is likely to have informed the audience's reception of Pseudo-Māwardī's discussion.

have raised some of them above others in degrees (*rafaʿnā baʿḍahum fawqa baʿḍin darajātin*), so that some of them may take others in subordination (*sukhriyyan*)' (43: 32). No one subject to this expression (*fī ḥukmi hādhā l-lafẓ*) enjoys greater privilege (*laysa aḥad … awlā bi-l-faḍl*), a more abundant apportionment (*ajzal qisman*), or a higher degree (*arfaʿ darajatan*) than kings, since humanity is subjected to them, bound to toil in their service (*khidma*) and to act in accordance with their command and prohibition (*fī amrihim wa-nahyihim*).

Another indication of God's preferment of kings is the fact that God Almighty has made kings His deputies (*khulafāʾ*) in His lands, His trustees (*umanāʾ*) over His servants, the executors of His ordinances in His creation and of His statutes (*ḥudūd*) amongst His creatures. In this regard it has been said: 'The *sulṭān* is the shadow of God on earth',[4] because it is one of His rightful claims that His example should be emulated in the earth, and His customs kept alive amongst the earth's inhabitants. In addition, He has made kings the cultivators of His lands. He has called them shepherds (*ruʿāt*, pl. of *rāʿin*) to His servants, likening them to the shepherds who care for livestock and cattle, and comparing their relationship to their subjects to that between the shepherd and his flock.[5] In this sense the philosophers (*al-ḥukamāʾ*) have called kings 'trainers' [of animals] (*sāsa*, pl. of *sāʾis*), for their position in relation to those under their governance resembles the position of the trainer (*sāʾis*) in relation to the cattle and riding animals that he trains: since their

[4] The term *sulṭān* refers to power in the abstract and, in later centuries, to its human embodiment in the form of an individual ruler (see above, Chapter 1, n. 5). It appears sometimes in the first, general sense, sometimes in the second, specific sense, and sometimes in contexts that admit both understandings. Since both meanings apply in the case of the formulation adduced in this instance, I have on this occasion opted to leave the term untranslated. Not infrequently, this much-cited formulation is identified as a Prophetic utterance, and the image of the ruler as God's shadow, offering shade and shelter to the earth's oppressed, is ubiquitous; see below, n. 84. Pseudo-Māwardī discusses the meaning of *sulṭān* in the discussion that follows; see below.

[5] This passage calls to mind the frequently cited Prophetic hadith *allā kullukum rāʿin wa-kullukum masʾūl ʿalā raʿiyyatihi*, 'Indeed, each of you is a shepherd, and each of you is responsible for his flock' (al-Bukhārī, *Ṣaḥīḥ*, IV: 526, *Kitāb al-Aḥkām*, ch. 1, no. 7138; Muslim, *Ṣaḥīḥ*, XII: 294–6, *Kitāb al-Imāra*, ch. 5, 20; al-Maydānī, *Majmaʿ al-amthāl*, II: 448). The image of the ruler as a shepherd is an ancient one, which reappeared in ever new contexts; see Darling, '"The Vicegerent of God, from Him We Expect Rain"'; Al-Azmeh, *Times of History*, 275; Arabatzis, 'Nicephoros Blemmydes's *Imperial Statue*', 112; El-Hibri, *Parable and Politics*, 6, 14; Rubin, 'Prophets and Caliphs', 94; Van Ess, 'Political Ideas in Early Islamic Religious Thought', 160; Crone, *Medieval Islamic Political Thought*, 159. See further below, n. 57.

condition is deficient, he takes responsibility for their concerns, and he knows what is for their good (*maṣāliḥ*, pl. of *maṣlaḥa*) and what for their harm (*mafāsid*). The philosophers have called the activities that are particular to kings 'training' (*siyāsa*) (that is, 'governance').[6]

Similarly the past communities of bygone days (*al-umam al-māḍiya fī l-ayyām al-khāliya*), and the Arabs especially, used to call kings 'lords of the earth' (*arbāb al-arḍ*, pl. of *rabb al-arḍ*) – 'lords' in both an absolute and a restricted sense, since they used to regard them with awe, with the hopeful expectation that they would execute God's ordinances, carry out His statutory penalties, uphold His precepts (*farāʾiḍ*) and precedents (*sunan*), and oversee the subjects' interests (*maṣāliḥ*) and needs, and that which would harm and benefit them – so that these 'lords of the earth' would represent, in the visible realm (*fī l-shāhid*), the Lord, blessed and glorious, the perception and beholding of Whom lie beyond the realm of possibility.[7]

It was by this name that the poet al-Nābigha addressed al-Nuʿmān b. al-Mundhir (r. *c.* 580–602), when he said:

> You will find an excuse or a favourable outcome for a man
> Who bows to his lord as if in submission to the Lord of Creation;[8]

[6] Pseudo-Māwardī describes the derivation of the term *siyāsa*, customarily used for 'governance', from the terminology associated with the training or driving of animals. In keeping with this metaphor, many authors define effective government in terms of the king's adept combination of reward and punishment, the instilling in his subjects of hope and fear (*al-raghba wa-l-rahba*); the *Sirr al-asrār*, for example, stipulates the necessity of four qualities, religion (*diyāna*), love (*maḥabba*), hope (*raghba*) and fear (*rahba*), in order to secure the subjects' obedience (*Sirr al-asrār*, in Badawī, *al-Uṣūl al-yūnāniyya*, 80 = Steele/Ali, *Secretum secretorum*, 187); see further below, Chapter 7, n. 51. In this first instance of the term's appearance, I have made the reference to the training or driving of animals explicit; I shall in most other contexts translate *siyāsa* as 'governance'. Especially in its Persian usages, the term frequently carries strong connotations of discipline and punishment; see below, Chapter 8, n. 34.

[7] Al-Thaʿālibī also mentions the use of the term *arbāb*, 'lords', 'in the time of the (pre-Islamic) Khusrows'; al-Thaʿālibī, *Ādāb al-mulūk*, 38 (see Text 2, at n. 77).

[8] The renowned *jāhilī* (pre-Islamic) poet al-Nābigha al-Dhubyānī composed poetry for the Ghassanids and the Lakhmids (*c.* 300–602), Arab dynasties whose lands in the northern regions of Arabia bordered on Byzantine and Sasanian territories. For the last Lakhmid king, al-Nuʿmān III b. al-Mundhir (r. *c.* 580–602), al-Nābigha composed, among other pieces, three 'apologetic' poems (*iʿtidhāriyyāt*), including the *qaṣīda ʿayniyya*, which Pseudo-Māwardī cites in the present instance. The line quoted in Pseudo-Māwardī's text appears only in certain recensions of al-Nābigha's collected poems, notably in the recension of the philologist and lexicographer Ibn al-Sikkīt (d. 244/858) (*Dīwān al-Nābigha al-Dhubyānī*, 237, notes to line 29 of Poem II, pp. 30–9). On al-Nābigha and his apologies, see Stetkevych, *Poetics of Islamic Legitimacy*, 1–47; Arazi, 'al-Nābigha al-Dhubyānī'; van Gelder, 'Apology'.

And ʿAdī b. Zayd (d. *c.* 600) spoke these words:

> Consider the Lord of Khawarnaq, as he looked down one day –
> Contemplation leads to right guidance.[9]

On account of the glorious condition of kings, the lexicographers (*ahl al-lugha*) have called the king a 'chief' (*raʾs*), since they liken his position in relation to his subjects to the position of the head (*raʾs*) in relation to the body: all the limbs are subordinate (*musakhkhara*) to the head and prepared to support it. Furthermore, the body cannot endure, nor even stand upright, without the head; it is the part of the body in which the senses meet, and without which the animal could not survive, there being no difference between the living animal and the dead, or the world of minerals, other than on account of the senses. The head is the source of the intellect and moral discrimination (*maʿdan al-ʿaql wa-l-tamyīz*), with which God has favoured (*faḍḍala*) human beings over other animals.

On this subject, the poet, in his praise of Ḥumayd b. ʿAbd al-Ḥamīd [al-Ṭūsī, d. 210/825], said:

> Men are a body: the Imam of Guidance
> Is the head, and you are the eye in the head.[10]

9 ʿAdī b. Zayd (al-ʿIbādī) (d. *c.* 600), a renowned Arab Christian poet, spent part of his career at the Sasanian capital of Ctesiphon, and part of it at the Lakhmid capital of al-Ḥīra, where al-Nuʿmān III eventually had him executed (see Seidensticker, 'ʿAdī b. Zayd'). The verse that Pseudo-Māwardī cites alludes to the Lakhmid ruler as *rabb al-khawarnaq*, after the lavish palace that the dynasty, under Nuʿmān I (d. after 418), had had constructed in the vicinity of al-Ḥīra for his Sasanian overlord, Bahrām V (r. 420–38). The poem to which the verse belongs, said to have been composed during the poet's imprisonment, invokes the themes of life's brevity and the fleeting nature of royal power. The poem appears in Ibn Qutayba, *al-Shiʿr wa-l-shuʿarāʾ*, 225–6 (variant); al-Ṭurṭūshī, *Sirāj al-mulūk*, I: 34; Yāqūt, *Muʿjam al-buldān*, II: 402 (s.v. 'Khawarnaq', 401–3). See further El Tayib, 'Pre-Islamic Poetry', 91–2; Meisami, 'Places in the Past', esp. 65–70. Meisami translates the line in question, 'And remember the Lord of Khawarnaq: one day he looked down from on high – and in right guidance (*hudā*) is contemplation and clear wisdom' (p. 69).

10 Writers attributed this verse to two different poets. One was the poet ʿAlī b. Jabala al-ʿAkawwak (160–213/776–828), celebrated for his panegyrics, of which the most notable were addressed to the military commanders Abū Dulaf al-ʿIjlī (d. 225/840 or 226/841) and (as in this instance) Ḥumayd b. ʿAbd al-Ḥamīd (see Weipert, 'al-ʿAkawwak, ʿAlī b. Jabala'); this attribution appears in Ibn Qutayba, *al-Shiʿr wa-l-shuʿarāʾ*, 864, no. 1633; al-Thaʿālibī, *al-Iʿjāz wa-l-ījāz*, 165, no. 69. Elsewhere, the verse is attributed to the poet Manṣūr al-Namarī (d. *c.* 193/809); see al-Rāghib al-Iṣfahānī, *Muḥāḍarāt al-udabāʾ*, I: 159. The term 'imam of guidance' (*imām al-hudā*) refers here to the caliph al-Maʾmūn (r. 198–218/813–33) (Cooperson, *Classical Arabic Biography*, 27, 34–5, 67–8), whose caliphate Ḥumayd b. ʿAbd al-Ḥamīd had supported effectively against the challenge of al-Maʾmūn's uncle Ibrāhīm b. al-Mahdī (162–224/779–839). On the meanings and

Another said:

> If the head is sound and held firmly upright, then
> Every foundation will stand erect on a basis of justice.[11]

A virtuous Indian king said in a testamentary charge (*ʿahd*) to his son:

> Know, my son, that this, my testament (*waṣiyya*) and charge (*ʿahd*) to you, offers you an analogy. Imagine a man, alive and standing upright: the man's head is you, O ruler (*ayyuhā l-wālī*); his heart is your vizier, his hands are your officials (*aʿwān*),[12] his legs your subjects. The spirit (*rūḥ*) that supports you is your justice (*ʿadāla*), so protect this man as you would protect yourself, and seek the well-being (*istaṣliḥ*) of his limbs as you seek the well-being of the limbs of your body.[13]

applications of the term *imām* (pl. *aʾimmat*) *al-hudā*, see Crone and Hinds, *God's Caliph*, 34, 40, 51, 80 n. 139, 85, 90–1, 100.

[11] Like the English word 'upright', the terms *istaqāma* (v. to rise or stand upright; to be right, sound, honest) and *ʿadl* (n. straightness, justice) carry physical and moral connotations; the metaphor depends on both dimensions.

[12] The term *aʿwān* (sing. *ʿawn*), when used in the plural, connotes a group of individuals who assist and support the ruler; while imprecise, the term usually refers to the king's higher-ranking officials, auxiliaries or functionaries. Ibn al-Muqaffaʿ wrote, 'He who attempts to manage affairs requires six things to do so: sound judgement (*raʾy*), good fortune (*tawfīq*), opportunity (*furṣa*), supporters (or leading officials) (*aʿwān*), a knowledge of good and appropriate behaviour (*adab*) and exertion (*ijtihād*). These things form pairs: judgement and *adab* form a pair, since *adab* cannot be made perfect without judgement, nor can judgement reach completion without *adab*; supporters (*aʿwān*) and opportunity form a pair, supporters being of no avail without opportunity, nor opportunity without the availability of supporters; and good fortune and exertion form a pair, for exertion is the cause of good fortune, and through good fortune, exertion leads to success (*najāḥ*)' (*al-Adab al-ṣaghīr*, in *Āthār Ibn al-Muqaffaʿ*, 335–6; on the text's attribution to Ibn al-Muqaffaʿ, see Zakeri, 'ʿAlī Ibn ʿUbaida ar-Raiḥānī', but also Kristó-Nagy, 'Authenticity'). Ibn Abī Dharr, in a section dedicated to the indispensability of *aʿwān* to the king, cites two authorities: first, Aristotle, who asserts that the ruler faces responsibilities of two kinds: the large, which he cannot delegate to anyone else, and the small, which he is compelled to delegate to competent people whose access to him should be facilitated, to whose reports he should pay attention, and whose performance should be assessed, and rewarded or reprimanded; and secondly, Anūshīrvān, who affirms the king's dependence on *aʿwān* in order to keep his affairs in order, and details twenty-one individuals whom he should appoint to leading positions; this statement provides a transition to the topic that follows, namely the selection of officials (*al-Saʿāda wa-l-isʿād*, 439). Usage makes clear that under certain circumstances, the *aʿwān* are liable to transfer their assistance and support to other potentates; see below, n. 41.

[13] Cf. al-Thaʿālibī, *Ghurar al-siyar*, 483–4 (Ardashīr); al-Ṭurṭūshī, *Sirāj al-mulūk*, where the analogy appears without the mention of a source (see below, Text 5, at nn. 141–2). Compare Maróth, *Correspondence*, 13; Ibn Abī Dharr, *al-Saʿāda wa-l-isʿād*, 193–4 (attributed to Aristotle); *ʿAhd Ardashīr*, 100–1 ('Scattered Sayings', no. 23).

An indication of the king's magnificent stature is that he has been called, in the terminology of religion and lexicography (*fī l-dīn wa-l-lugha*), *sulṭān*. The word *sulṭān*, in linguistic terms, denotes a proof (*ḥujja*); God, may He be exalted and glorified, has said, 'Or have you a clear proof (*sulṭānun mubīnun*)? Then produce your writing, if you are truthful' (37: 156, 157); and [in Solomon's speech, when he gathered the birds and found that the hoopoe was absent] 'I shall punish him most severely, or I shall slaughter him, unless he brings me a clear proof (*bi-sulṭānin mubīnin*)' (27: 21). Accordingly, God, the Blessed and Exalted, has made kings, if they are just, a proof (*ḥujja*) over His creation. Similarly, the Imamiyya [also known as the 'Twelver' Shia] apply the words related from the Prophet – 'The earth shall never be devoid of a proof (*ḥujja*)'[14] – to the immaculate imam (*al-imām al-maʿṣūm*), whom they supplicate and to whose remembrance they are devoted. And on account of kings' magnificent state, the Muslims have applied to the most glorious authority in Islam (*al-sulṭān al-ajall fī l-Islām*) the term *imām*, for he is among the figures whose example must be followed, whose action must be emulated and whose command must be carried out.

It is to these lofty concepts (*hādhihi l-maʿānī al-jalīla*) that the noble names specifically applied to kings point. In this book of ours, we have chosen, among all these names, to designate the ruler by the term 'king' (*malik*), since it is the clearest and most familiar, widely used and straightforward name.

Part of the glory of the royal condition and a mark of kings' privileges (*faḍāʾil*) over their subjects and over the various categories of people (*ṭabaqāt al-nās*) lies in the fact that, although everyone subject to the king's authority is similar to him in form (*ṣūra*) and resembles him in nature (*khilqa*), and although the king is not burdened with the acquisition or purchase of his subjects, his subjects' station in relation to him is, in many respects, like that of his possessions (*maḥall al-mamlūkīn*).[15] Pertinent to this point are the words of God, may He be glorified and exalted, in the story of Sheba: 'I found a woman ruling them

[14] The hadith appears in al-Kulaynī, *al-Uṣūl min al-Kāfī*, I: 40, § 178, nos. 447, 451, 452, 453 (in the last of these attestations, ʿAlī states, 'The earth is never devoid of a proof, and by God, I am that proof'); see also Abū Nuʿaym al-Iṣfahānī, *Ḥilyat al-awliyāʾ*, I: 80 (*lā takhlū al-arḍ min qāʾim lillāh bi-ḥujjatihi liʾallā tabṭula ḥujaj Allāh wa-bayyinātuhu*). On the Twelver Shia, see section 2.1.

[15] The word *mamlūk* is also used to denote an enslaved person (see section 2.1, at nn. 10–11). I have translated it as 'possession' in this context, because of the lexicographical nature of Pseudo-Māwardī's exposition.

(*tamlikuhum*), and she has been given (a generous portion) of all things, and she has a great throne' (Q 27: 23). For 'to rule' is derived etymologically from 'property' (*milk*), and not from 'sovereignty' (*mulk*). Furthermore, the subjects can be divided into two sections: those whose station in relation to the king is that of a raw material (*mādda*), and those whose station in relation to him is that of a tool (*āla*). The king uses the latter to fashion the former according to whatever he wants, desires, wishes and envisages. In this manner, he will produce the form (*ṣūra*) that results from his labour, according to the measure of his skill in the craft and his ability to accomplish his purpose (*gharaḍ*) and intention (*niyya*).

God has stipulated, for everyone, the obligations of prompt obedience to the just ruler (*al-imām al-ʿādil*) and the virtuous king, as well as sincere support and respect for his exalted position, and refraining from opposing him, as long as he obeys God and adheres to His precepts (*farāʾiḍ*) and statutes (*ḥudūd*). For He has said, 'O you who believe! Obey God, obey the Messenger, and those in authority among you' (Q 4: 59). The Prophet (upon whom be peace) said, 'Obey the imam, even if he is an Ethiopian slave, as long as he obeys God among you.'[16] He also said, 'He who strives to subdue a *sulṭān* will himself be subdued by God.'[17]

These are a few of the many ways by which God has elucidated the excellences (*faḍāʾil*) of kings, their high status, their exalted ranks, their magnificent stations, their elevated degrees, the glory of God's favours (*niʿam Allāh*) and the many varieties of His benefits (*funūn ayādīhi*) to them.

It is therefore incumbent in every kind of situation that no one should be more thankful towards God, nor more attentive in upholding the execution of His precepts and commands, nor more assiduous in the protection and care of those whose welfare has been entrusted to him, than kings – since this behaviour constitutes the contractual part (*al-maʿhūd*) of kings' actions in relation to the bondsmen and servants over

[16] Al-Bukhārī, *Ṣaḥīḥ*, IV: 527, *Kitāb al-Aḥkām*, ch. 4, no. 7142; Muslim, *Ṣaḥīḥ*, XII: 312–13, *Kitāb al-Imāra*, ch. 8, 36–7; Ibn Māja, *Sunan*, 955, *Kitāb al-Jihād*, ch. 39, no. 2861; al-Dārimī, *Musnad*, 28, *al-Muqaddima*, ch. 16, no. 96. See also al-Rāghib al-Iṣfahānī, *Muḥāḍarāt al-udabāʾ*, I: 157 (cited, as in the present example, after Q 4: 59). On this hadith, see Crone, '"Even an Ethiopian Slave"'.

[17] Al-Tirmidhī, *al-Jāmiʿ al-kabīr*, IV: 81, *Abwāb al-fitan*, ch. 47, no. 2224 (*man ahāna sulṭāna llāhi fī l-arḍ ahānahu Allāh*).

whose affairs God has given them control (*al-maʿhūd min afʿālihim bi-man mallakahum Allāhu umūrahum min ʿabīdihim wa-khadamihim*).

Kings should also be especially thankful because, if they remember God's bounties (*niʿam Allāh*) towards even the weakest of His creatures and His kindness (*iḥsān*) to the least of His bondsmen, they will not find, in the kindness that creatures display one to another, any favour that approaches it in worth, nor any favour comparable in value. When kings make gifts to people, they are giving them the wealth of others as a trust (*wadīʿatan*) or granting them a share in authority (*sulṭān*) over others as a loan (*ʿāriyatan*), the goods being placed only temporarily in their hands. Indeed, kings' gifts to people decline quickly and disappear rapidly. Sometimes, these gifts cause harm to their recipients, and bring them no benefit; sometimes they occasion the recipients' perdition in religion and the lower world, at their end and their beginning. Moreover, kings are satisfied with their subordinates only as long as the grounds for their favours towards them continue to increase and the bases for their benefits to them become ever more apparent. They require their subordinates to become ever more grateful and ever quicker in their obedience to them; their subordinates, they hold, should undergo ever greater ordeals on their behalf; they should become ever more punctilious in the fulfilment of their kings' rightful claims (*ḥuqūq*), and in observing kings' commands and prohibitions. At the same time it is the view of kings that anyone who is remiss in a matter, anyone who seeks to modify or exchange a benefit or who displays ingratitude for it (*man qaṣṣara fī shayʾin minhu aw ghayyara aw baddala aw kafara niʿmatan*) and anyone who belittles a favour (*ghamaṭa ṣanīʿatan*) deserves their opprobrium and merits deprivation, punishment and abandonment. This response applies especially in the case of anyone who persists in such behaviour, and anyone who commits disobedience in an open fashion. This is a scale (*mīzān*) by means of which the intelligent person should weigh a good deal of that which occurs between himself and his Creator; and it is a model (*mithāl*) that he should emulate.

Since these matters proceed in the visible realm (*fī l-shāhid*) in the manner that we have mentioned, and since kings' treatment of the people beneath them follows the path that we have clarified, it follows necessarily that kings should fear the consequences of ingratitude (*kufrān*) and the recompense of disobedience (*ʿiṣyān*). If kings are mindful of the bounties that God has afforded them – the benefits that He has shown to them in exalting their status and magnifying their authority, His delegating to them the governance (*siyāsa*) of His servants and the cultivation of His lands, His assigning to them of lasting dominion and endless felicity – if, indeed, kings are mindful of God's general bounties (*ʿāmmat niʿamihi*), the number of which cannot be counted, and of His specific bounties (*khāṣṣat[u]hā*), the greatness of which cannot be described – then, it is incumbent upon kings that they should fear the consequences of ingratitude.

It is furthermore essential that the person who desires increase (*ziyāda*) in the favour he receives, who expects his shortcomings to be met with disregard (*ihmāl*) and the grant of a reprieve (*mudda*), and who aspires to divinely blessed success (*ḥusn al-tawfīq*) and support (*maʿūna*) in this world as well as a fine reward in the world to come, should persevere and strive in rendering gratitude and obedience, and shun ingratitude and disobedience; for the recompense of thankfulness is kindness and increase (*al-iḥsān wa-l-mazīd*), while the recompense of ingratitude is punishment, rejection (*tankīr*), abandonment and reproach. This understanding impresses itself upon persons who know God (*hādhā alladhī yalzamu l-ʿārifīn bi-llāh*), and it is indispensable for persons who are brought close to Him and who are mindful of His blessings (*ʿalā l-muqarrabīn bihi wa-l-dhākirīn li-ālāʾihi*), and persons who confess the truth of His Book and His Verses, for God has said: 'If you are grateful, I shall give you more, and if you are ungrateful, then My punishment is severe' (14: 7); 'God does not change a people's state until they change that which is in themselves' (13: 11); 'We exchanged for their two gardens two gardens bearing bitter fruit (*ukul khamṭ*), the tamarisk and a small amount of the lote-tree (*sidr*). In this way We recompensed them [the people of Sheba] for their ingratitude. Do We punish any other than the ungrateful?' (34: 16, 17).[18]

Next, and in addition to the imperatives that we have already mentioned, kings are subject to obligations of a different kind. The king should be the most assiduous of people in rejecting meanness and repudiating baseness. He must remain far removed from anything that compromises his honour, corrupts manly virtue, entails the ruination of the kingdom, perpetuates disparaging talk and offends the dignity of the

[18] Q 34: 16 evokes, in sequence, the domesticated landscape endowed with two luxurious gardens and irrigation systems, and the flood that caused the rupture of the dam of al-ʿArim *c.* 542 in the Yemeni city of Mārib. The Qurʾanic text presents the flood and its destructive consequences as punishment for the ingratitude of the people of Sheba, who had enjoyed such abundance (see Khoury, 'al-ʿArim'; Gonzalez, 'Sheba', 586).

royal office and the high standing of his position. He should choose the noblest and finest practices (*sunan*) and carry out the worthiest and most esteemed actions. In order to attain the level of conduct that befits his rank and corresponds to his high station, he will find it necessary to perform in ways that he will often find distressing and unpleasant, and he will need to set aside many of the pleasures that he enjoys. Ardashīr said:

> Know that there are two developments that will bring your turn in power (*dawla*) to an end: the first of the two is the triumph of a nation that opposes you; the other is the corruption of your conduct (*adab*).[19]

It is likewise incumbent upon the resolute king and the just ruler (*sā'is*) that he should be no more assertive in his efforts to improve the behaviour (*adab*) and to eradicate the corrupting and harmful appetites of anyone else – whether among his subjects, in the midst of his kingdom or among the entirety of his retainers – than in his efforts towards himself. For he who is incapable of governing his own self (*siyāsat nafsihi*) and of rectifying his own moral characteristics (*akhlāq*) will naturally find himself still less capable of rectifying anyone else's character.[20] A human being has no power over his carnal self (*nafs*) unless he is capable of subordinating his nature (*ṭab'*) to the dominion of his reason, and his passion to his judgement. Reason must rule over nature, so that the individual will choose the directions of his intellect over the inclinations of his nature, and so that he will give preference to the indications of his judgement over the desires of his passion. Then he must confront his bad points with his good characteristics, and his blameworthy traits with his praiseworthy qualities, so that he is able to accustom himself to virtuous manners, discipline himself through praiseworthy practice and acquire qualities that befit his high station, as well as actions becoming to his stature. This course of self-training should not prove onerous to him, when considered in the light of his aspiration to virtue now and in the future, and his aim to prepare for a heavenly reward and to perpetuate his good memory. For it is fixed in people's intellects and firmly established

[19] *'Ahd Ardashīr*, 58, no. 8. The felicitous rendering of *dawla* as a 'turn in power' is Mottahedeh's; see *Loyalty and Leadership*, 132, 185–9.

[20] This proposition is ubiquitous in the ethical and edificatory literatures; see, for example, al-Māwardī, *Adab al-dunyā wa-l-dīn*, 148; al-Māwardī, *Tashīl al-naẓar*, 135; al-Rāghib al-Iṣfahānī, *Muḥāḍarāt al-udabā'*, I: 18–19; al-Mubashshir b. Fātik, *Mukhtār al-ḥikam*, 140 (Plato), 279 (Luqmān), 20, 26 (Hermes).

in their souls that the most noble things cannot be attained other than by swallowing what is distasteful. The furthest reaches of the virtues cannot be reached other than by bearing severe hardships. God has said: 'You shall never attain to piety until you spend of what you love' (3: 92); and He has said: 'God has bought from the believers their lives and their possessions, because the Garden shall be theirs' (9: 111). The Prophet, upon him be peace, said: 'Heaven welcomes suffered deprivations, and Hell welcomes indulged appetites.'[21] ʿAmr b. ʿUbayd (80–144/699–761) said:

> I have trained my lower self (*nafs*) so strictly that were I to will it to abstain from water, it would abstain from it.[22]

It happened that the Commander of the Faithful al-Maʾmūn (r. 198–218/813–33) succumbed to his strong appetite for edible clay (*ṭīn*), and he ate a great deal of it. The physicians gathered and tried every possible remedy and employed every strategy to treat him, yet he would not desist. One day Thumāma b. Ashras (d. 213/828–9) entered the caliph's presence and saw the physicians gathered round him, consulting with one another over his case and deliberating together about his treatment. Thumāma said: 'O Commander of the Faithful, show some of the resolve proper to the office of the caliphate!' Al-Maʾmūn said to the physicians, 'Get up, for I have had treatment enough.' And he never returned to the habit again.[23]

Nothing dominates the speech of persons deficient in intellect and resolve more than excessive, passionate love. One person in the grip of

[21] Muslim, *Ṣaḥīḥ*, XVII: 241, *Kitāb al-Janna*, ch. 1, no. 2822; al-Tirmidhī, *al-Jāmiʿ al-kabīr*, IV: 319, *Abwāb ṣifat al-janna*, ch. 21, no. 2559; al-Dārimī, *Musnad*, 408, *Kitāb al-Riqāq*, ch. 117, no. 2877; also cited in al-Tawḥīdī, *al-Baṣāʾir wa-l-dhakhāʾir*, VII: 269 (no. 768).

[22] See also al-Zamakhsharī, *Rabīʿ al-abrār*, II: 522. ʿAmr b. ʿUbayd, a specialist in Prophetic hadith, was a member of the circle of al-Ḥasan al-Baṣrī (d. 110/728) (see below, n. 92); after his teacher's death, ʿAmr played a major role in the formation of the Muʿtazilite school of theology (which Pseudo-Māwardī appears to have followed). Renowned for his renunciation and piety, ʿAmr enjoyed a close association with Caliph al-Manṣūr; numerous narratives record his austere, admonishing counsel to the caliph (Mourad, 'ʿAmr b. ʿUbayd').

[23] See also Naṣīr al-Dīn Ṭūsī (597–672/1201–74), *Akhlāq-i Nāṣirī*, 301 (the Persian term for edible clay is *gil*); and al-Rāghib al-Iṣfahānī, *Muḥāḍarāt al-udabāʾ*, II: 624 (a different attestation of al-Maʾmūn's predilection for eating clay). The hadith literature documents a range of negative responses to the eating of clay; see al-Sakhāwī, *al-Maqāṣid al-ḥasana*, 146–7, no. 159; Vajda and Scarcia Amoretti, 'De la condemnation de la géophagie dans la tradition musulmane'. On Thumāma, see van Ess, 'Thumāma b. Ashras'.

excessive passion talked of it a good deal and described it at length. He said:

> Love is like an animal's back, and you are its rider:
> Once you take up the reins, it will turn (according to your will).

Another said:

> When fit, this heart has loved with restraint.
> Do not count what is sound to be a sin.
> A remnant fit for godliness remains in me yet –
> Were it not so, I should resemble a man avid for pleasure and my heart would yield to abandon.

Another said:

> By my life, in passionate love, I have followed my intentions
> Into old age, even when it has proven difficult:
> I have at times approached the beloved, and been told, such is passion!
> And I have at times kept my distance, and been told, this is a poor show of ardour!
> I would have surrendered to passion, were I not
> At war with myself over actions that are not permissible.

Another said, in the sense of the first verse:

> The loftiest of matters may become contaminated
> If deposited in the bellies of snakes.[24]

And another said:

> Peoples, even if they are noble, will never attain glory
> Unless – even though they might be great – they are humbled
> And abased; then you shall see beings resplendent:
> The forgiveness not of the abject, but of the forbearing.[25]

[24] The poet is Abū ʿAmr Kulthūm b. ʿAmr al-ʿAttābī; see Ibn Qutayba, *ʿUyūn al-akhbār*, I: 231–2 (variant); Ibn Qutayba, *al-Shiʿr wa-l-shuʿarāʾ*, 234–6; al-Jāḥiẓ, *al-Bayān wa-l-tabyīn*, III: 354; al-Jāḥiẓ, *Kitāb al-Ḥayawān*, IV: 266 (variant); al-Jahshiyārī, *Kitāb al-Wuzarāʾ wa-l-kuttāb*, 262; al-Thaʿālibī, *al-Iʿjāz wa-l-ījāz*, 165, no. 46; al-Thaʿālibī, *al-Tamthīl wa-l-muḥāḍara*, 61.

[25] Usually ascribed to Ibrāhīm b. al-ʿAbbās al-Ṣūlī. See Ibn Qutayba, *ʿUyūn al-akhbār*, I: 287 (attributed indefinitely to *baʿḍ al-shuʿarāʾ*); al-Māwardī, *Adab al-dunyā wa-l-dīn*, 245; al-Tawḥīdī, *al-Baṣāʾir wa-l-dhakhāʾir*, IX: 202, no. 681 (attributed to al-Naẓẓām, d. 220/835 or later); al-Rāghib al-Iṣfahānī, *Muḥāḍarāt al-udabāʾ*, I: 222; al-Ṭurṭūshī, *Sirāj al-mulūk*, I: 339; al-Ibshīhī, *al-Mustaṭraf*, I: 419.

A king said:

Those who seek glory risk calamity![26]

In commemorating the great efforts of al-Muʿtaṣim (r. 218–27/833–42) in his campaigns against the Byzantines and the caliph's endurance of hardship in his conquest of Amorium [in 223/383], the poet Abū Tammām (188–231/804–46) declaimed:

Caliph of God, may God reward your exertions
On behalf of religion, Islam and earned merit (*ḥasab*)!
You have beheld the greater repose; and you have perceived
That it is to be reached only by a bridge of toil.[27]

As these transmitted accounts, reported signs and well-known, widely disseminated verses make clear, the virtues can be attained only by struggling against nature, and by inducing the body and the carnal soul to eradicate sinful appetites and passions that undermine laudable intentions or religious precepts. Most reprehensible actions that human beings relinquish and abandon only with great difficulty arise from needs, appetites and the formation of bad habits, which engender the corruption of the self and the neglect of one's own nature. A person who wishes to move from reprehensible to praiseworthy conduct, and from distasteful to commendable actions, will find that he possesses the capacity and the power to do so. A person who accustoms himself to behaving well will find that it comes easily to him; he who grows accustomed to bad conduct, however, will find it difficult to relinquish.

In praise of the Barmakids,[28] al-ʿAṭawī produced these excellent verses:

The noble Barmakids have made habitual practice
Of benevolent action, and the people, moreover, have become accustomed to it.
When they plant, they water; when they build,
They do not undermine the foundation of their construction.

[26] For the ascription of this line to Aktham b. Ṣayfī, see al-Ḥadīthī, *Kitāb Naṣīḥat al-mulūk*, 92–3, n. 154.

[27] Al-Khaṭīb al-Tabrīzī, *Sharḥ Dīwān Abī Tammām*, I: 32–49; lines 67–8 appear on pp. 48–9. On this famous poem, and for translations of the entire text, see Stetkevych, 'The ʿAbbasid Poet Interprets History'; Bray, 'Al-Muʿtaṣim's "Bridge of Toil"'. I have benefited from the analysis and translations provided by both of these scholars.

[28] The Barmakids, who hailed from Balkh, were a family of highly influential viziers and administrators in the service of the first five Abbasid caliphs, until Hārūn al-Rashīd abruptly removed them from power in 187/803. This poem provides an example of the Barmakids' reputation for unparalleled generosity, for which they became proverbial in Arabic and Persian writings (see further van Bladel, 'Barmakids').

And when they offer their support to a human being
They provide for his permanent comfort.[29]

Another said:

I have grown accustomed to the brush of adversity, to the point that
I am entirely familiar with it.
Time has delivered me to patient endurance.
An abundance of troubles has expanded my heart's capacity for
endurance.
Nevertheless, sometimes it leaves my breast constricted.[30]

The Arabs used to say:

Goodness is a habit, and wickedness is obstinacy.[31]

They have also said:

Habit prevails through moral instruction (*adab*).[32]

Several philosophers have said:

Habit is a fifth nature.[33]

29 The poet is, presumably, Muḥammad b. ʿAbd al-Raḥmān al-ʿAṭawī (or al-ʿAṭwī) (d. 250/864); see Ibn Khallikān, *Wafayāt al-aʿyān*, V: 95 (in the entry for al-Wazīr Ibn al-Zayyāt, no. 696).

30 The poet is sometimes identified as Abū l-ʿAtāhiya (the verses appear in *Dīwān Abī l-ʿAtāhiya*, 200). See also Ibn Qutayba, *ʿUyūn al-akhbār*, III: 190 (where the verses are ascribed indefinitely to *baʿḍ al-muḥaddithīn*); al-ʿAskarī, *Jamharat al-amthāl*, I: 151; al-Ṭurṭūshī, *Sirāj al-mulūk*, I: 411.

31 Appears as a Prophetic saying in Ibn Māja, *Sunan*, 80, *al-Muqaddima*, ch. 17, no. 221 (with Muʿāwiya recorded as the immediate transmitter). See also al-Thaʿālibī, *al-Tamthīl wa-l-muḥāḍara*, 29 (a Prophetic maxim); Ibn Qutayba, *ʿUyūn al-akhbār*, III: 157 (introduced with the general formula *fī l-ḥadīth*); al-Maydānī, *Majmaʿ al-amthāl*, I: 247; also cited in al-Tawḥīdī, *al-Baṣāʾir wa-l-dhakhāʾir*, VII: 228, no. 671 (a Prophetic utterance).

32 Reading *adab* for *arab* with Muḥammad Jāsim al-Ḥadīthī (*Kitāb Naṣīḥat al-mulūk*, 96) and Khiḍr Muḥammad Khiḍr (*Naṣīḥat al-mulūk*, 59). See al-Jāḥiẓ, *al-Maʿāsh wa-l-maʿād*, in *Rasāʾil al-Jāḥiẓ*, I: 112; Ibn ʿAbd Rabbihi, *al-ʿIqd al-farīd*, III: 15 (attributed to Aktham b. Ṣayfī and Buzurgmihr). The root *a-d-b* connotes, in this instance, training, education or inculcation in the body of knowledge and the associated humane values of *adab* (see above, Chapter 1, n. 9).

33 Al-Thaʿālibī, *al-Tamthīl wa-l-muḥāḍara*, 121; al-Murādī, *al-Ishāra*, 85; al-Ibshīhī, *al-Mustaṭraf*, I: 70. Perhaps more commonly, habit is identified with second nature; see Ibn Qutayba, *ʿUyūn al-akhbār*, III: 157; al-Rāghib al-Iṣfahānī, *Muḥāḍarāt al-udabāʾ*, I: 276 (*al-ḥukamāʾ taqūlu: al-ʿāda ṭabīʿa thāniya*); al-Tawḥīdī, *al-Imtāʿ*, II: 217 (*qīla: al-ʿāda hiya al-ṭabīʿa al-thāniya*); Ibn Abī l-Ḥadīd, *Sharḥ Nahj al-balāgha*, XX: 422, no. 455 (*al-ʿāda ṭabīʿa thāniya ghāliba*).

Since the matter is as we have explained, choosing and adopting praiseworthy characteristics is more appropriate for the king than for anyone else. For the king cannot reach the true potential of his royal glory (*jalāla*), nor will he understand the priority of his station, unless he abandons many of the appetites of the carnal self and the pleasures of the body. At the same time, he must acquire virtues. Accordingly, he should choose gratitude over ingratitude; religiosity over shamelessness; knowledge over ignorance; reason over folly (*ḥumq*); courage over cowardice; generosity over miserliness; patience over impatience; praise over blame; forbearance over heedlessness; composure over frivolity; truthfulness over falsehood; humility over pride; justice over tyranny; rectitude over error; resolve over impetuosity; and so on. He should make these choices because every reprehensible characteristic bears a reprehensible fruit, and every praiseworthy quality produces a praiseworthy consequence.

It is incumbent upon the person who loves goodness that he should do nothing but good, and upon him who despises wickedness that he should avoid wickedness. Moreover, any ruler who has committed shameful acts, and any king who has engaged in blameworthy activities, resembles, in his sovereignty, an ostentatious fabrication – a fraudulent imitation of a king. It befits the virtuous king to elevate himself above such baseness and to eschew such vice. The king should not be content, for his portion of royal glory (*jalāla*), that he should be, on the one hand, called by the good and noble name of 'king', yet at the same time notorious for wicked and odious actions. If he does behave in this way, he will resemble a person with an overabundance of things that do not properly belong to him, or a person wearing clothing to which he is not entitled. There is nothing more pertinent in this sense than the words of the poet:

> If they mount the steps (of the pulpit), let them speak and act well;
> There can be no good speech that is not verified by action.[34]

We have heard that ʿAbd al-Malik b. Marwān (r. 65–86/685–705) was delivering an oration (*khuṭba*) one day in Mecca. When he came to the moment for the exhortation (*ʿiẓa*), a man from the Ṣūḥān rose and said,

[34] Muḥammad Jāsim al-Ḥadīthī has identified the poet as ʿAbdallāh b. al-Zubayr al-Asadī (*Kitāb Naṣīḥat al-mulūk*, 97–8, n. 167); see Abū l-Faraj al-Iṣfahānī, *al-Aghānī*, XII: 217–62. Al-Asadī died in the reign of ʿAbd al-Malik b. Marwān (r. 65–86/685–705); this chronology perhaps provides an associative link with the narrative account that follows. For the interpretation of the opening words, *idhā rakibū l-aʿwād*, see Fuʾād ʿAbd al-Munʿim Aḥmad (*Naṣīḥat al-mulūk al-mansūb ilā … al-Māwardī*, 76, n. 64) and Khiḍr Muḥammad Khiḍr (*Naṣīḥat al-mulūk*, 60, n. 2).

'Wait! You Umayyads are giving commands, and not following them; you are issuing prohibitions to others and not abiding by them yourselves. Should we follow your conduct, as indicated by your persons, or should we obey your command, as delivered by your tongues? If you say, "Follow our behaviour", then where, how, by what proof, and who among God's allies follows the oppressive, unjust conduct of persons who by turn consume the wealth that belongs to God and make God's servants into slaves? If you say, "Obey our command, and accept our advice", then I ask, how can the person who deceives himself counsel others? How can obedience to a ruler not firmly rooted in justice be compulsory? If you say, "Accept wisdom, regardless of where you find it, and welcome exhortation, regardless of where you hear it", then on what grounds should we entrust you with the reins of our affairs, and why should we give you the right of judgement over our lives and possessions? Do you not know that amongst us are persons who are more eloquent in the arts of exhortation, and more knowledgeable in the skilful uses of language than you? You should leave these matters to them. Otherwise, release the cord and abandon the path; then, those whom you have driven away throughout the lands and those whom you have transported to every valley will hasten to return. If, on the other hand, these things remain in your hands, as time passes and the situation reaches a point of extremity, then, for every person who now stands, there will come a day beyond which he shall not pass, and after that, a book that will be read to him: "[What kind of book is this] that leaves neither a small thing nor a great thing without counting it" (Q 18: 49); "Those who have behaved unjustly shall come to know through what sort of reversal they shall be overturned" (26: 227).'[35]

According to the 'Book of . . . Kings',[36]

[35] This account appears also in al-Nuwayrī, *Nihāyat al-arab*, VII: 249–50. Numerous parallels, in which a scrupulous person confronts the hypocrisy of a caliph or caliphal governor, exist; see, for example, al-Ṭabarī, *Taʾrīkh*, VIII: 89–90, 358–59; al-Ṭurṭūshī, *Sirāj al-mulūk*, I: 127–28; Cooperson, *Classical Arabic Biography*, 40–64; Cook, *Commanding Right and Forbidding Wrong*, 50–67.

[36] The title of this text has not survived the process of transmission. From its placement in Pseudo-Māwardī's chapter it seems likely that the title derived from the Arabic version of a Middle Persian or Sanskrit text. Each of the text's three editors has proposed a different conjecture: Khiḍr Muḥammad Khiḍr reads *Shahāmat al-mulūk*, 'The Perspicacity of Kings' (*Naṣīḥat al-mulūk*, 61); Muḥammad Jāsim al-Ḥadīthī proposes *Āʾīn-nāmat al-mulūk*, 'The Book of Protocols for Kings' (*Kitāb Naṣīḥat al-mulūk*, 99, n. 171); Fuʾād ʿAbd al-Munʿim Aḥmad suggests *Siyāsat al-mulūk*, 'The Governance of Kings' (*Naṣīḥat al-mulūk al-mansūb ilā . . . al-Māwardī*, 77, n. 74).

> Let your action be better than your words, for fine words alone may provide inducement, whereas fine action aims directly at the desired objective.

We have read in the Testament of an Indian king to one of his sons:

> Your judgement will not appear in a good light if you speak well, but to the exclusion of action; for you will reach your listeners without your action attesting to the truth of your speech, or your public exterior (*ʿalāniya*) verifying your innermost thought (*sirr*).[37]

The Indian leader who is called the Buddha said:

> With fine words but no action, a thousand men will never achieve in a single man the improvement that a single man, by way of good action, will achieve in a thousand men.[38]

The Commander of the Faithful ʿAlī, may God be pleased with him, sought refuge in God from flattering tongues, inquisitive hearts and contradictory actions.

It was in this sense, more or less, that King Shāpūr b. Ardashīr (= Shāpūr I, r. 239 or 240–70 or 273) commenced his excellent and worthy testament. In a section addressed to his son, he said:

> To proceed: You have been entrusted with a responsibility so great that no other worldly matter surpasses it, and you have reached a degree of importance beyond which no person can pass. Therefore, raise yourself, through excellent qualities, to the level that befits the magnificent position that you have attained, and, in modesty, devote yourself to justice. In this way, you will retain your current standard of opulent living, and earn its culmination in a state of well-being that has no end and is never overturned. If you abandon your current path (and undertake this path of virtue), you will win a fine and lasting reputation for yourself; for you are heir to and will be remembered for your

[37] The passage forms part of the text usually identified as 'Aristotle's Testament' (*Waṣiyyat Arisṭāṭālīs*), which, although it circulated as a free-standing text (see al-Mubashshir b. Fātik, *Mukhtār al-ḥikam*, 224), was also incorporated into the epistolary cycle that included the *Kitāb al-Siyāsa fī tadbīr al-riyāsa* or *Sirr al-asrār*, held to be Aristotle's written counsels to his pupil Alexander (see section 3.1). (On the seeming identity of Pseudo-Māwardī's 'Indian testament' with the *Waṣiyyat Arisṭāṭālīs*, see Marlow, 'Kings and Sages'.) I have amended the citation in accordance with the slight variant in published versions of the *Waṣiyyat Arisṭāṭālīs*; see Maróth, *Correspondence*, 13; Miskawayh, *Jāvīdān khirad*, 220; al-Mubashshir b. Fātik, *Mukhtār al-ḥikam*, 187.

[38] See also al-ʿĀmirī, *al-Iʿlām bi-manāqib al-Islām*, 152 (where the citation appears without attribution).

> conduct, and when you depart from this world, you are bound for whatever reward or punishment you have prepared for yourself.

In a wise Indian king's testament to his son, we have found these words:

> O my son, I have appointed you to a position of momentous importance, and I have bound you to its responsibilities. Take this responsibility upon yourself and accept it. If this position should hasten the satisfaction of a desire, take no delight in it; for that is the most harmful thing to be attained through your high position, a mere augmentation of what already afflicts you. If in these matters you find that your desire resists you, then hold it in the utmost suspicion and redouble your efforts to gain mastery over it. If God grants you victory over your desire and defends you from its harm, take greater joy in that victory than in the defeat of your enemies; for the superiority of relinquishing your desires for God's sake to the pleasure and joy that you experience from their indulgence is like the superiority of God's reward for the people of Paradise to people's allotments in their earthly lives.[39]

ʿAmr b. ʿUbayd gave concise expression to this idea in his words to Abū Jaʿfar al-Manṣūr (r. 136–58/754–75):

> God would not be pleased if any of the people should be positioned above you; you, therefore, should not be satisfied that anyone might be more thankful to Him than you are.[40]

It is among the king's duties to ensure that the excellence and nobility of his actions, qualities, intellect and integrity should complement the shortcomings of his subjects. The king is called upon to care for his subjects and summoned to protect them solely for the purposes of their care and protection: to remedy their hardship and treat their want, to avert the deficiencies of the deficient, to cover the shame of the shamed, to support the infirm, to defend his subjects' womenfolk, to bring justice to the oppressed against their oppressors and to urge them to follow the laws of their religion and the precepts, statutes and ordinances of their religious community.

[39] Maróth, *Correspondence*, 12; al-Mubashshir b. Fātik, *Mukhtār al-ḥikam*, 186 (see above, n. 37).

[40] Al-Ḥuṣrī, *Zahr al-ādāb*, I: 103. See also Ibn Qutayba, *ʿUyūn al-akhbār*, I: 106; al-Jāḥiẓ, *al-Bayān wa-l-tabyīn*, II: 100 (in both of these cases, the speaker is identified as the eighth-century littérateur and orator Shabīb b. Shayba, and his caliphal interlocutor is al-Mahdī (r. 158–69/775–85)).

Given this verity, what is the position of the ruler (*sā'is*) who is deficient and ignorant, tyrannical and unjust, or shameless and dissolute? As for the ruler among whose subjects are individuals who combine more good qualities, and who benefit from the fortification of more excellent characteristics, than he does – how, other than by force, repression, compulsion and coercion, could the virtuous, religiously observant, upright and reflective person submit to such a ruler? This person will look forward to the ruler's loss of power and disappearance, since these events promise the end of the tribulations that the ruler has visited upon him and the cessation of the king's tyranny. In these circumstances, the ruler's most excellent subjects will become his enemies, and the most virtuous people of his dominion will transfer their allegiance from him.[41] The most fitting outcome in the case of a king of this kind is his swift eclipse and imminent fall from power.

King Ardashīr said in his Testament:

> Know that if you give priority to combat against hostile nations over combatting the bad conduct (*sū' al-adab*) issuing from your subjects' lower souls (*anfus ra'iyyatikum*), then you will have failed in your duty to protect; in fact, you will have demonstrated neglect. How, moreover, is the enemy to be resisted with a people whose hearts are at odds, and susceptible to the fomenting of mutual hostility?[42]

In another section, he said:

> Know that the king should not be miserly (because miserliness is the seed of covetousness; nor should he lie), because no one has the capacity to coerce him; nor should he succumb to anger, because anger and power lead to intemperance and regret; nor should he indulge in amusement or foolery, because jesting and folly are forms of idleness; nor should he be idle, since idleness is the condition of the rabble (*sūqa*); nor should he envy, except for the kings of nations that are well managed (*'alā ḥusn al-tadbīr*); nor should he fear, for fear is the condition of the indigent; nor should he govern in an overbearing manner, lest he become deprived.[43]

[41] Literally, 'they will become supporters against him' (*kāna . . . a'wānan 'alayhi*); see above, n. 12.

[42] *'Ahd Ardashīr*, 60, with a slightly different wording.

[43] *'Ahd Ardashīr*, 69 (from which the words that appear in parentheses have been added).

The philosopher Aristotle said:

> He who lacks the capacity to put himself to rights should never rebuke anyone whom he finds lacking in rectitude.[44]

One day Asqaf of Najrān appeared before Muṣʿab b. al-Zubayr (d. 72/691), and he began talking to him about something. Muṣʿab flew into a rage. He took a stick and struck Asqaf's face with such force that he caused him to bleed. Asqaf said to him, 'If the amir wills, I shall tell him the words that God sent down on the tongue of Jesus; but don't get angry.' Muṣʿab said, 'Speak!' Asqaf continued, 'We find in the Gospels that it is not appropriate for the imam to be foolish, given that judgements are being sought from him, nor for him to be unjust, given that justice is being sought from him.'[45]

Aristotle, in his counsel to Alexander, wrote to him:

> It is incumbent upon the king that he should distinguish himself with the best of attributes, because he represents the standard to whom people refer, and the goal towards which they direct their paths.[46]

In the king, the scope of the slightest defect is far from small; in the same way, the scope of the least and most recently acquired of the king's virtues is great. In this vein the poet has said:

> The sheep cannot survive without a shepherd, who assumes responsibility for her care.
> What, then, of the people, if they lack a ruler (*wālin*)?
> If their affairs are tied to tails (followers) rather than heads (captains),
> They are in a state of dire neglect.[47]

[44] Although the text reads 'Alexander', it is usually Aristotle who is referred to as 'the philosopher', with Alexander often in the position of his pupil. The maxim's sentiment, moreover, is similar to ideas expressed in the *Waṣiyyat Arisṭāṭālīs*; cf. Maróth, *Correspondence*, 13; Miskawayh, *Jāvīdān khirad*, 219–20.

[45] The text's reference to the Torah is likely to represent a scribal error; I have followed the reports in al-Rāghib al-Iṣfahānī (*Muḥāḍarāt al-udabāʾ*, I: 169), al-Zamakhsharī (*Rabīʿ al-abrār*, IV: 224) and Ibn al-Ḥaddād (*al-Jawhar al-nafīs*, 85), which invoke not the Torah but the Injīl (Gospels). Najrān, in northern Yemen, became the major centre of Christianity in southern Arabia and a site of pilgrimage in the sixth century; Asqaf, a Christian leader, also composed poetry (al-Jāḥiẓ, *al-Bayān wa-l-tabyīn*, III: 342–3; al-Jāḥiẓ, *al-Ḥayawān*, III: 88). Muṣʿab b. al-Zubayr was the brother of ʿAbdallāh Ibn al-Zubayr, who challenged the Umayyads' claim to the caliphate and ruled from Mecca for almost a decade; Muṣʿab, who held the post of governor of Iraq, had a reputation for many virtues, as well as for occasional flights of anger.

[46] Cf. *Sirr al-asrār*, 77.

[47] Attributed to ʿUbayd Allāh b. ʿAbdallāh b. Ṭāhir, whose father, ʿAbdallāh b. Ṭāhir (182–230/798–844), governor of Khurasan, was celebrated for his poetry. For the verse and its

Another poet said:

> The people cannot rectify disorder unless they have a leader;
> And they have no leader, if it is the ignorant among them who prevail.[48]

Similarly, one of the poets said of a king when he saw him enfeebled and failing:

> Tyrants sleep, oblivious to matters of honour
> Until a power that never sleeps awakens them:
> Behold their ignominy in the largesse that they have bestowed
> And their improvement with the cessation of their favours.[49]

Another said:

> If the chief of the assemblies (*ṣadr al-majālis*) is not a lord (*sayyid*)
> There is no good in the person presiding over the assemblies.
> How many a time have I heard the words, 'Why is it that I see you walking?'
> And I have said in reply, 'Because you are the person riding.'[50]

Al-Aʿmash (Sulaymān b. Mihrān) (d. 147 or 148/764–5) reported that Shaqīq b. Salama had said to him, 'O Sulaymān, by God, these people possess neither one of two praiseworthy things: neither the godliness of the people of Islam, nor the forbearance of the people of the Jāhiliyya.'[51] How, then, can learned scholars and wise philosophers display respect

attribution, see al-Māwardī, *Tashīl al-naẓar*, 233; cf. al-Thaʿālibī, *Ādāb al-mulūk*, 69, § 144; al-Thaʿālibī, *Ghurar al-siyar*, 483 (Ardashīr).

48 Al-Afwah al-Awdī, *Dīwān al-Afwah al-Awdī*, 66, line 8; cited in Ibn Qutayba, *al-Shiʿr wa-l-shuʿarāʾ*, 223; Ibn ʿAbd Rabbihi, *al-ʿIqd al-farīd*, I: 11; al-Thaʿālibī, *al-Tamthīl wa-l-muḥāḍara*, 43–4; al-Māwardī, *al-Aḥkām al-sulṭāniyya*, 5; al-Māwardī, *al-Amthāl wa-l-ḥikam*, 33, 60–239; Usāma b. Munqidh, *Lubāb al-ādāb*, 40; al-Shayzarī, *al-Nahj al-maslūk*, 66.

49 *Dīwān Maḥmūd al-Warrāq*, 277, no. 244. The first word of the text in the *Dīwān* reads *khanāzīr*, as in Aḥmad's edition (*Naṣīḥat al-mulūk al-mansūb ilā … al-Māwardī*, 82); al-Ḥadīthī's edition, followed here, reads *jabābir* (*Kitāb Naṣīḥat al-mulūk*, 106). The first verse recalls the maxim *al-nāsu yanāmu fa-idhā mātū ntabahū*, usually included among the maxims of ʿAlī (*Miʾa kalima*, in Qutbuddin, *Treasury of Virtues*, 222, 223; al-Thaʿālibī, *al-Iʿjāz wa-l-ījāz*, 35, no. 17; al-Sakhāwī, *al-Maqāṣid al-ḥasana*, 691, no. 1240), but occasionally ascribed to the Prophet (al-Thaʿālibī, *al-Iʿjāz wa-l-ījāz*, 25, no. 2).

50 Attributed to Ḥusayn Ibn Khālawayh (d. 370 or 371/980) (al-Thaʿālibī, *Yatīmat al-dahr*, I. 137); for discussion of this possibly later inclusion, see Marlow, *Counsel for Kings*, I: 59–60.

51 See al-Zamakhsharī, *Rabīʿ al-abrār*, IV: 214. The term *jāhiliyya*, associated with lack of knowledge and sometimes wilful ignorance, referred to the period before the Qurʾanic revelation in Arabia; on the formation and meanings of the paradigm, see Drory, 'Abbasid Construction of the Jahiliyya', and Webb, '*Al-Jāhiliyya*: Uncertain Times of Uncertain Meanings'. Al-Aʿmash was a major transmitter of Prophetic hadith in Kufa; he is reported to have made extensive use of traditions allegedly transmitted by the *muʿammar*

for a ruler whose position among them fits this description, except in dire circumstances and under duress?

We have now completed our treatment of this topic. We have referred to pertinent texts and included reports from the Book of God and the exemplary practice (*sunna*) of His Prophet; in addition, we have adduced the evidentiary proofs of the rationalists and the sayings of the philosophers. We hereby mark the end of this chapter.

Text 2
Al-Thaʿālibī, *Ādāb al-mulūk*. Chapter One[52]

Translator's Introduction

This extract from the *Ādāb al-mulūk* of al-Thaʿālibī, who lived his entire life in the east and wrote perhaps a century after Pseudo-Māwardī, is the first chapter in his ten-chapter mirror. Al-Thaʿālibī echoes many of the themes of the previous extract, and he illustrates them with an eclectic set of authorities, including many relatively recent, regional historical examples. Like Pseudo-Māwardī, he emphasises the exceptionalism of kings and their uniquely privileged position in the world. Despite the prominent place given to a discussion of groups who were excessive in their veneration of kings, it is difficult to miss al-Thaʿālibī's sense of the unique status, and perhaps qualities, of the king's person (it should be remembered that he dedicated his mirror to his royal patron). In comparison with Pseudo-Māwardī, al-Thaʿālibī pays less attention to kings' ultimate accountability to the Creator, and more attention to their appropriate treatment by their underlings in this world; the theme of reciprocity between rulers and subjects is considerably less pronounced. The implicit criticism evident in the latter sections of Text 1 is also absent, and the duty of obedience is affirmed without qualification. Another point of contrast

(exceptionally long-lived) Abū Wāʾil Shaqīq b. Salama, who, despite the long life ascribed to him, was perhaps a historical figure (Juynboll, 'al-Aʿmash').

[52] Translation prepared from al-Thaʿālibī, *Ādāb al-mulūk*, ed. Jalīl al-ʿAṭiyya (Beirut: Dār al-Gharb al-Islāmī, 1990), 33–48. For the corresponding section in Topuzoğlu's translation, see T. R. Topuzoğlu, 'Kitāb Ādāb al-Mulūk al-Khwārazm-shāhī of Abū Manṣūr ʿAbd al-Malik b. Muḥammad b. Ismāʿīl ath-Thaʿālibī' (PhD diss., University of Manchester, 1974), I: 6–21, and T. R. Topuzoğlu, *Kitāb Ādāb al-Mulūk al-Khwārazm-shāhī* (Ankara: Türk Tarih Kurumu, 2015), I: 9–22.

lies in the two authors' uses of scriptural authority. Whereas Pseudo-Māwardī integrates Qurʾanic citations into a continuous argument and employs Qurʾanic language to advance the logic of his exposition, al-Thaʿālibī arranges his direct Qurʾanic citations in a separate section of his chapter; in this way, he displays his customary attentiveness to the distinctiveness of different classifications of literary expression and marks the special status of Qurʾanic language; elsewhere, he integrates echoes of Qurʾanic phrases, unmarked, into his prose.[53] His references to religious deviation anticipate a later, extended discussion of heterodoxy (see below, Text 16).

Translation

Chapter One: In Explication of the Exalted Status of Kings; the People's Inescapable Need for Kings; and Their Duty to Obey, Exalt and Glorify Them

God, may His name be exalted, has magnified the standing and status of kings. He has elevated their ranks, glorified their importance, empowered them on His earth and ennobled them with His authority. He has granted them power (*qabūl*) and majesty (*mahāba*), and endowed them with might (*ʿizza*) and splendour (*ubbaha*); for He knows that kings are necessary for the well-being (*ṣalāḥ*) of His servants, and that kings' governance and protection in matters of religion and worldly affairs, and the afterlife, are indispensable to commoners (*al-ʿāmma*) and the privileged (*al-khāṣṣa*) alike.[54] He has granted His rule (*tamlīk*) over humankind to kings, and His extension of power to them stems from His consummate wisdom (*al-ḥikma al-bāligha*) and His abundant favours

[53] Al-Thaʿālibī's often unacknowledged Qurʾanic references and allusions are examples of *iqtibās*, a rhetorical device for which al-Thaʿālibī was well known; indeed, he wrote a treatise on the subject (Orfali, 'The Works of Abū Manṣūr al-Thaʿālibī', 285, no. 9).

[54] The ubiquitous binary *khāṣṣ* (special, private, privileged) and *ʿāmm* (common, public, general), often applied to categories of people, carries a variety of more particularised meanings as it appears in different contexts. The term *khāṣṣ*, for example, was adopted at an early date to designate private crown lands, and the term's association with the ruler soon led to its being extended to cover various forms of royal property, as well as individuals closely connected to the ruler's person; in this last sense, Julia Bray has referred to *khāṣṣ* and *ʿāmm* as the ruler's inner and outer publics respectively ('Ibn al-Muʿtazz and Politics', 143). Other settings suggest different interpretations; in the context of twelfth- and thirteenth-century Syria, Daniella Talmon-Heller has referred to the *khāṣṣ* and *ʿāmm* as, respectively, the educated élite and the unlettered classes (*Islamic Piety in Medieval Syria*, 1). See further above, Chapter 1, n. 6.

(*niʿam[uhu] al-sābigha*).[55] He has made obedience to kings similar to the obligatory religious precepts (*farāʾiḍ*): the person who abides by them receives his reward, and the person who transgresses them is subject to divine punishment. The binding precepts, the mandatory duties, the acknowledged stipulations of obedience and the adopted markers of rectitude include honouring the person whom God has honoured, glorifying the person whom He has ennobled, following the person whom He has endowed with authority and submitting to the person whom He has entrusted with rule and might. The subjects (*raʿiyya*) need a ruler (*al-rāʿī*) in the way that the body needs a head, and the superiority of the ruler to the subjects resembles the superiority of the trainer (*sāʾis*) to the animal in his charge, or of the horseman (*fāris*) to his mount.[56] Were it not for kings, the people would devour one another, just as, were it not for the shepherd, wild beasts would ravage the flock.[57]

ʿAbdallāh Ibn al-Muʿtazz (247–96/861–908) articulated this idea in superb fashion in one of his 'Short Aphorisms':

> A people who have no ruler are as corrupt as a body with no soul![58]

[55] The phrase contains echoes of the Qurʾanic phrases *ḥikma bāligha* (Q54: 5), 'consummate wisdom', and *wa-asbagha ʿalaykum niʿamahu ẓāhiratan wa-bāṭinatan* (Q31: 20), 'He has laden you with His favours, without and within'.

[56] See above, n. 6. With Topuzoğlu, I have omitted the apparently redundant phrase *fī faḍl al-farāʾid* from the translation (*Ādāb al-mulūk*, 33 = Topuzoğlu, 'Kitāb Ādāb al-Mulūk' (1974), 7 = Topuzoğlu, *Kitāb Ādāb al-Mulūk* (2015), 9).

[57] The likening of the ruler to the shepherd and his subjects to the flock is ubiquitous (see above, n. 5). ʿAlī b. Abī Ṭālib is credited with the maxim, 'If the shepherd is a wolf, who will care for the sheep?' (Ibn Abī l-Ḥadīd, *Sharḥ Nahj al-balāgha*, XX: 420, no. 418 (*idhā kāna al-rāʿī dhiʾban, fa-l-shātu man yaḥfaẓuhā*)).

[58] Ibn al-Muʿtazz was a gifted poet and stylist and a highly regarded literary critic; at the same time, he was a prominent member of the Abbasid caliphal house (see Lewin, 'Ibn al-Muʿtazz'). On his 'Short Aphorisms' (*fuṣūl qiṣār*), cited several times in *Ādāb al-mulūk* and elsewhere in the writings of al-Thaʿālibī, see Bray, 'Ibn al-Muʿtazz and Politics' (the translation of the citation in al-Thaʿālibī's text in Bray's, at p. 134). Bray has argued convincingly that Ibn al-Muʿtazz, whose contribution to Arabic literary tradition has long been recognised, was not, as he has sometimes been perceived, first and foremost a man of letters who preferred artistic pursuits to worldly affairs; on the contrary, he may have seen his aphorisms as an expression of his princely birthright of wisdom, displayed as evidence of his fitness to rule. This politically assertive dimension of the 'Short Aphorisms' seems highlighted in al-Thaʿālibī's foregrounding of them in his mirror (Bray, 'Ibn al-Muʿtazz and Politics', 133–43; the maxim in question also appears in al-Thaʿālibī, *al-Tamthīl wa-l-muḥāḍara*, 97), as also in the collections of his contemporaries al-Ābī (d. 421/1030) and al-Ḥuṣrī (*c.* 420–88/1029–95) (the aphorism cited in the text appears in al-Ḥuṣrī, *Zahr al-ādāb*, II: 674). As later examples will show, several of these 'Short Aphorisms' also appear with attributions to ʿAlī b. Abī Ṭālib, a process evident in the collection of al-Ābī and continued with Ibn Abī l-Ḥadīd (586–655/1190–1257). (In al-Thaʿālibī's *al-Ẓarāʾif*

I have said many times, and I should be pleased to have it recounted from me, that, while kings' positions are high, their orders carried out and their ways of living conducive to contentment, their burdens are many, their troubles onerous and their tribulations great. Anyone who reflects intelligently upon the affairs of kings will not reckon the abundant resources available to them to be excessive. Kings are, after all, obliged to protect their subjects: to defend them from unexpected disasters, and to bear their burdens, which exceed twice over the amount that kings receive for their material welfare. Nor should the common people belittle their lot in life, since it is owing to the king's wakefulness that they are able to sleep; because of the king's exertions in guarding over their womenfolk and protecting their dwellings, the subjects find peaceful repose.[59] The wealth that the king accumulates supplies provisions to be used to defend the subjects against the onslaught of their enemies, or to confront the adversities that afflict them. In effect, then, the king and his subjects are partners, and they should avoid mutual hostility and envy.

The caliph Hārūn al-Rashīd (r. 170–93/786–809) provides an excellent example of this situation. One night, during one of his campaigns, he was caught in heavy snow, and it caused him considerable suffering. One of his companions said to him, 'Consider, O Commander of the Faithful: we are enduring the hardship (*jahd*), exertion (*naṣab*) and discomfort (*waʿthāʾ*) of this campaign, while the subjects enjoy the benefits of peace, rest and sleep.' He said, 'Be quiet. It is for them to sleep and for us to keep vigil: the shepherd must keep his flock and suffer for them.'[60]

In an ode that he composed for al-Rashīd, Abū Muḥammad [ʿAbdallāh b. ʿAyyūb] al-Taymī (d. 209/824) said:

At your anger, swords and lances stood erect
As you rose up in support of Islam.
The subjects slept in the shelter of your justice
While you remained sleepless, keeping vigil over the sleepers' oblivion.[61]

wa-l-laṭāʾif, the same aphorism appears, attributed to Ibn al-Muqaffaʿ; *al-Ẓarāʾif wa-l-laṭāʾif*, 73.)

59 Reading *ḥarīm* for *ḥurriyya* (freedom) (seemingly with Topuzoğlu, who translates 'their personal and family security' (Topuzoğlu, 'Kitāb Ādāb al-Mulūk' (1974), 7 = Topuzoğlu, *Kitāb Ādāb al-Mulūk* (2015), 10).

60 The translation of the last line is Bray's (Bray, 'Al-Thaʿalibi's *Adab al-mulūk*', 42). For this narrative, see also Pseudo-Māwardī, *Naṣīḥat al-mulūk al-mansūb ilā . . . al-Māwardī*, 258, and Ibn al-Ḥaddād, *al-Jawhar al-nafīs*, 69–70.

61 See also Pseudo-Māwardī, *Naṣīḥat al-mulūk al-mansūb ilā . . . al-Māwardī*, 258–9 (attributed to al-Taymī); Ibn al-Ḥaddād, *al-Jawhar al-nafīs*, 70 (with an indefinite attribution to

What I have said is a matter of complete agreement among people endowed with rational intellect. Furthermore, people endowed with perception have witnessed that when a person honours the Shadow of God on His earth, the Steward entrusted with His rightful claims and the Hand extended over His creatures; when he heeds him, obeys him, supports him and takes his side – that person receives praise, both in the present and the future, and he secures for himself a pleasant life. Whoever, on the other hand, turns aside from the king's command and deviates from obedience to him awaits a prescription of humiliation and misery. He shall burn in the heat of the sword before he suffers the heat of the Fire; he shall obtain the loss of both worlds, and that, indeed, is a patent loss (*al-khusrān al-mubīn*).[62]

On the Qurʾan's Pronouncements concerning Kings

God linked the obedience due to kings with obedience to the Prophet when He, the Almighty, said:

> Obey God, obey the Messenger and those among you who are in authority (Q 4: 59).

He mentioned His favour in appointing them as deputies (*istikhlāf*) when He said:

> It is He who has appointed you as deputies (*khalāʾif*) of the earth, and He has raised some of you over others in degrees (Q 6: 166).

In the story of Moses (upon him be peace), He said:

> O my people! Remember God's favour to you, how He placed prophets among you, made you kings and gave you what He had not given to any other of His creatures (Q 5: 20).

When He sent Moses and his brother to the most tyrannical and deviant of kings, He said:

> Go, both of you, to Pharaoh. For he has transgressed; speak to him in gentle words (*qawlan līnan*), that perhaps he may heed or fear (Q 20: 43–4).

'a poet' (*baʿḍ al-shuʿarāʾ*)); and, with reference to ʿUmar b. al-Khaṭṭāb instead of Hārūn al-Rashīd, Muḥammad b. ʿAbd al-Malik al-Hamadhānī, *Takmilat Taʾrīkh al-Ṭabarī*, 189 (attributed to 'the poet' (*al-shāʿir*)). On al-Taymī, see al-Ziriklī, *al-Aʿlām*, IV: 73.

62 An echo of the Qurʾanic *dhālika huwa al-khusrānu l-mubīn*, 'This is indeed a palpable loss' (Q 22: 11, 39: 15).

When he was reading this verse, Yaḥyā b. Muʿādh [al-Rāzī, d. 257 or 258/871–2] said:

> My God, since this is the kindness that You show towards the one who claims divinity, what then awaits the person who confesses his servitude to You?[63]

The Almighty Speaker said:

> Say: O God, Possessor of Sovereignty! You give sovereignty (*mulk*) to whom You will, and You withdraw sovereignty from whom You will. You exalt whom You will, and You abase whom You will (Q 3: 26).

With these words, God has indicated that the transfer of sovereignty from one nation (*umma*) to another and its departure from one family (*usra*) to another proceed in accordance with the purpose of the Most Wise (glorified be His praise). By these means He wills the optimal (*al-aṣlaḥ*) and selects the most suitable. His establishing of sovereignty in one dynasty and His removal of it from another are matters that God enacts according to His wisdom, and by means of which He supports the best interests (*maṣāliḥ*) of His creation.[64]

On People's Veneration of Kings since Time Immemorial; and the Excessive Lengths to Which Some People Have Gone in Glorifying Kings, to the Point of Taking Them as Gods apart from (the One) God

Cases of excessive exaltation and glorification of kings have been recounted in both the pre-Islamic period (the Jāhiliyya) and Islamic times. Since people saw kings determining the lives of their subjects and condemning them to death, raising them up and casting them low,

[63] A Central Asian Sufi who lived in Balkh and then in Nishapur, Yaḥyā b. Muʿādh was associated with the Karrāmiyya, an ascetic religious-theological movement that attracted numerous followers, especially among the urban and rural lower classes, in the eastern regions from the ninth to the eleventh centuries; Yaḥyā was known for his love poems to God. See Abū Nuʿaym al-Iṣfahānī, *Ḥilyat al-awliyāʾ*, X: 51–70 (no. 463); al-Qushayrī, *al-Risāla*, I: 101–2.

[64] Al-Thaʿālibī's assertion that changes in power are, on account of the divine will that underlies them, necessarily in the best interests of humankind evokes the doctrine of 'the optimal' (*al-aṣlaḥ*), associated with certain members of the Muʿtazila as an extension of the theological emphasis on divine justice. In al-Thaʿālibī's presentation, the doctrine of 'the optimal' is equated with God's wisdom; this understanding of divine action passed well beyond the circles of the Muʿtazila and rationalist theology.

appointing them to authority and dismissing them from office, giving to and withholding from them, they became fascinated by them. Like the unruly crowd and the people intent on deceiving them, the people took to treating their kings as gods and lords, whom they worshipped in the same manner that God the Creator, the Sustainer, the One, the Mighty is worshipped.[65] More than one ignorant king was gratified by this treatment. For instance, the king who argued with Abraham about his Lord said, 'I give life and cause death' (Q 2: 258);[66] and Pharaoh said, 'I am your mighty lord' (Q 79: 24).

A certain rabble (*qawm*)[67] made up of infidel philosophers, dissolute types given to free thinking[68] and religious innovations, and the devils of the human species have sought to make this pernicious claim attractive to people. In some of their formal treatises and other written fragments, they have alleged that the spirit of the Creator, may He be praised, has alighted in the person of the king, who should be worshipped until the spirit passes from him and takes up residence in someone else. Some of these people say that none of the earthly kings is without a certain piece of the Creator's spirit. This piece, they claim, settles in each king, and, according to whether it is small or great, increasing or decreasing, it determines the eminence of each king's power and the magnificence of his stature (God is exalted infinitely above the claims of these transgressors). In a similar fashion, they have claimed that a part of His beauty and His light lodges in the handsome slave-boy and the pretty slave-girl; it remains indwelling in them until the boy grows a beard and the girl reaches maturity, at which time it passes from them. I have heard that a certain band (*qawm*) of Sufis believe this vile teaching (*madhhab*) and

65 Al-Thaʿālibī's language is reminiscent of Pseudo-Māwardī's brief treatment of the phrase *rabb al-arḍ* (see Text 1, at n. 7).

66 The full verse reads: 'Think of the one who argued with Abraham about his Lord, because God had given him sovereignty (*mulk*). When Abraham said: "It is my Lord who gives life and causes death," he answered: "I give life and cause death." Abraham said: "God causes the sun to rise in the east; do you, then, cause it to come up from the west." Thereupon the disbeliever was left speechless. God does not guide the people who oppress (*wa-llāhu lā yahdī l-qawma l-ẓālimīna*).'

67 In al-Thaʿālibī's usage, the term *qawm*, 'group', 'people', elsewhere relatively neutral in its connotations, frequently appears in negative contexts with distinctly derogatory overtones (see the previous note for a Qurʾanic example; several further examples occur below).

68 Following Bray's rendering of *ahl al-ahwāʾ*, 'free thinkers' ('Al-Thaʿalibi's *Adab al-mulūk*', 41–2); see below, Chapter 9, n. 42.

subscribe to this absurd doctrine. They are called the Ḥulūliyya (people who believe in the doctrine of divine indwelling, *ḥulūl*).[69]

On this subject, Ibn Nubāta al-Saʿdī has said, in a lyric (*ghazal*):

> My soul (*nafs*) is your ransom: for you resemble the full moon
> over a branch,
> And my eyes feast hungrily at the sight.
> As I behold this vision and reflect on it,
> I am compelled to give credence to the Ḥulūliyya's doctrine of
> forms (*ṣuwar*).[70]

Concerning the permissibility of indwelling, Abū ʿAlī Muḥammad b. al-Ḥasan al-Ḥātimī (d. 388/998), in a drifting conversation, has said:

> I have a beloved: Were I to be asked for what I yearned
> It would be nothing other than to be with him, even unto death.
> How I long to take up dwelling in every single body
> So that I could see him through the glances of myriad eyes![71]

Al-Muqannaʿ ('The Veiled One', d. 163/779–80 or 166/782–3), may God curse him, was so audacious in this path of the Ḥulūliyya (Proponents of Indwelling) that he claimed divinity and called upon people to worship him. In his proselytising, he used to say that God Almighty had created Adam and instilled Himself into his form. When He brought Adam's earthly life to an end, He transposed Himself into the form of Noah. From then on, He began to move into the forms of the prophets and kings, the last of whom was Abū Muslim (d. 137/755).[72] When this last was killed, God transferred Himself into Hāshim – by which name he meant himself. In Transoxiana, a large group of misguided people followed al-Muqannaʿ. His power

[69] A departure from the frequently used translation 'incarnation', the term 'indwelling', a more nuanced rendering of *ḥulūl*, is Crone's; see her *Nativist Prophets*, 221–32.

[70] Ibn Nubāta was a Baghdadi poet; see al-Thaʿālibī, *Yatīmat al-dahr*, II: 447–66, no. 135; the poem appears at p. 449.

[71] Abū ʿAlī Muḥammad b. al-Ḥasan al-Ḥātimī (d. 388/998), a literary critic and philologist, spent a period of time in Aleppo at the court of Sayf al-Dawla (r. 333–56/944–67) and died in Baghdad. See al-Thaʿālibī, *Yatīmat al-dahr*, III: 120–4; the verse appears at p. 120. See further Bonebakker, 'al-Ḥātimī'.

[72] Abū Muslim was the main organiser and chief commander of the revolution which overthrew the Umayyads and would bring the Abbasids to power; the movement began in Khurasan, where long after his execution at the hands of Caliph al-Manṣūr, Abū Muslim inspired dissenting groups, some of whom, as al-Muqannaʿ's self-presentation reflects, held him in veneration, considering him a vessel of divine spirit, a medium between the divine and human realms (cf. Crone, *Nativist Prophets*, 42–5, 86–91, 329 and *passim*).

(*shawka*) was growing in strength and the force of his sedition was mounting, until, in the reign of al-Mahdī (r. 158–69/775–85), God Almighty destroyed him, averted his wickedness and put an end to his command. To this day, a remnant of his followers, called the Wearers of White (al-Mubayyiḍa), remains in Transoxiana. They are obliged to pay the land-tax and other exactions to their governors (*wulāt*).[73]

A pack (*qawm*) of the Rāwandiyya developed an obsession with Abū Jaʿfar al-Manṣūr (r. 136–58/754–75).[74] One day, as he left his tent, the caliph saw a clutch (*qawm*) of them prostrating before him and calling upon him in prayer, as if they were petitioning God Almighty. He rebuked them and called upon them to repent, but they would neither repent nor desist. As a consequence, al-Manṣūr ordered that they be put to death. Some were killed, some escaped and recanted, only to rise against him in a sudden revolt. These individuals drew swords against al-Manṣūr's supporters, but fate turned against them, their wicked trickery ensnared them and their affair came to an end.[75]

Something similar happened to the Commander of the Faithful ʿAlī, may peace be upon him. A crowd (*qawm*) who took their partisanship for him to an extreme (*al-ghulāt fī l-tashayyuʿ*) fell into unbelief. They said to him: 'You are our god, and the object of our worship.' When he censured them, they refused to restrain themselves, but rather insisted in their waywardness. ʿAlī then ordered his client (*mawlā*) Qanbar to burn them. On this subject, ʿAlī, peace be upon him, said:

> When I saw that it was a reprehensible matter
> I kindled the fire and called for Qanbar.[76]

73 The revolt of al-Muqannaʿ lasted fourteen years, during which time he and his followers, known as the Wearers of White (Mubayyiḍa or Sipīdjāmagān), controlled large parts of Transoxiana. Especially strong in rural areas, the movement also took the city of Samarqand, where al-Muqannaʿ minted coins, an action that signified an explicit challenge to the existing political authorities (on al-Muqannaʿ and the Mubayyiḍa, see Crone, *Nativist Prophets*, 106–43).

74 Named after ʿAbdallāh al-Rāwandī, who probably hailed from Balkh, the Rāwandiyya, extreme devotees of the early Abbasids, developed in Khurasan out of the revolutionary movement of Abū Muslim; see Crone, *Nativist Prophets*, 86–91.

75 Al-Thaʿālibī's phrase *ḥāqa l-makru l-sayyiʾu bi-him* recalls the Qurʾanic *wa-lā yaḥīqu l-makru l-sayyiʾu illā bi-ahlihi*, 'wicked trickery ensnares only the people who devise it' (Q 35: 43).

76 See Halm, 'Ġolāt'. Qanbar b. Ḥamdān was ʿAlī's servant; he was with ʿAlī at the Battle of Ṣiffīn in 37/657, and reportedly carried out ʿAlī's legal penalties. Tahera Qutbuddin translates, 'When I saw it was evil // I kindled the fire and called to Qanbar' (*Treasury of Virtues*, 210–11).

In the time of the Khusraws, people used to call kings 'lords' (*arbāb*), and they took it upon themselves to worship them. They did not dare to wear the clothes that the king wore, ride the same animals that he rode or consume the food and drink that he consumed. Moreover, they relinquished to him every precious thing that fell into their hands.[77]

It is part of the etiquette (*ādāb*) appropriate to the servants of kings that they should follow the example of the Sasanian era in their privileging of kings in everything that is suitable for them and fitting for them. ʿAmr b. Masʿada (d. 217/832) alluded to this point in his words to al-Maʾmūn, who once saw ʿAmr riding a particularly fine horse. The caliph looked at the horse with approval and admiration. Observing this response, ʿAmr conducted the horse into the caliph's presence. He addressed al-Maʾmūn with these verses:

O Imam – to whom, since he is rightly counted an imam, no one comes close;
For he surpasses the rest of the people, just as plentitude surpasses deficiency –
We have dispatched a certain steed, the likeness of which lies beyond desire:
The horse's face is like the morning, the rest of his body dark as the night.
That which befits the master (*mawlā*) is forbidden (*ḥarām*) to the servant.[78]

On Kings' Occasioning the Production of Useful Work in the Sciences and Fine Accomplishments in the Arts and Crafts (*Thamarāt al-ʿUlūm wa-l-Ādāb wa-Laṭāʾif al-Ṣināʿāt*)

One of the finest and most enduring of kings' achievements lies in the service they accept from philosophers throughout the lands, scholars across the realm and masters of the crafts. These individuals present kings with the results of their thinking; they seek proximity to kings by offering them the fruits of their intellects, and they devote meticulous attention to the works that they produce and compose in their royal patrons' names. This phenomenon constitutes a mark of the kingdom's good fortune; it indicates the link to felicity that kings provide, the people's pinning of their hopes upon

[77] See also al-Thaʿālibī, *Thimār al-qulūb*, 179; for a discussion of this passage, see Savant, *The New Muslims*, 133.

[78] ʿAmr b. Masʿada, renowned for his epistolary skill and a relative of the celebrated secretary and poet Ibrāhīm b. al-ʿAbbās al-Ṣūlī (d. 243/857), served as secretary to al-Maʾmūn, and in various financial posts. See al-Ḥuṣrī, *Zahr al-ādāb*, II: 836–8; al-Thaʿālibī, *Thimār al-qulūb*, 179 (an abbreviated allusion); Ibn Khallikān, *Wafayāt al-aʿyān*, III: 475–8 (no. 507); Yāqūt, *Muʿjam al-udabāʾ*, V: 2129–31, no. 874 (the verses appear on p. 2131); al-Ziriklī, *al-Aʿyān*, V: 86; Sourdel, 'ʿAmr b. Masʿada'.

them and their directing of their aspirations towards them. Scarcely any fine accomplishment, any rare philosophical work or remarkable feat of architecture would have seen the light of day had it not been intended for a king and produced in the hope of pleasing a king. Had it not been for the excellent kings of the past, many of the sciences would have been lost and many brilliant philosophies (*ḥikam*) deemed worthless.[79]

Kings have enabled men of learning to devote themselves solely to their work. They have bestowed upon them sufficient means that these scholars could pursue their investigations with untroubled souls, their faculties unencumbered with worry and their minds unpreoccupied. As a consequence, these individuals have been able to produce tools and implements, as well as musical instruments, capable of providing repose for the soul, rest after toil and, through the dispelling of cares, healing joy. They have constructed various amenities and fashioned several beneficial devices, including a variety of wind, stringed and percussion instruments.[80] They have developed the sciences of medicine, arithmetic, geometry, astronomy and music, and they have invented instruments of war, such as mangonels, machines for use in siege warfare, devices for the throwing of naphtha and countless other items.

The words that Alexander's mother spoke in her prayers on his behalf are pertinent in this connection:

> May God sustain you with good fortune that brings you the service of men of intelligence, rather than with an intellect used in the service of the possessors of fortunes.

With the advent of the reign of the Arabs, the rulers of Islam[81] became the occasions for exquisite writing, surpassing eloquence, widely disseminated poems and splendid, remarkable books. Were it not for them – and

[79] The term *ḥikma*, used several times in this section, carries several connotations: wisdom, philosophy, medicine; it also denotes a concise articulation of wisdom, in other words, a maxim (pl. *ḥikam*). The same range of meanings applies to the noun *ḥakīm* (pl. *ḥukamāʾ*), which might be rendered 'sage', 'philosopher' or 'physician' (or an individual who combines all three of these qualities). This semantic spectrum is often used to evoke the intellectual heritage of the ancient and late antique world and its continuing development in Islamic times, in contradistinction to the specifically Islamic religious sciences grounded in scriptural sources, such as Qurʾanic studies and exegesis, the collection of Prophetic hadith, the legal sciences and theological and metaphysical discourse.

[80] The text is somewhat unclear at this point; see Topuzoğlu, 'Kitāb Ādāb al-Mulūk' (1974), 13 = Topuzoğlu, *Kitāb Ādāb al-Mulūk*, 16.

[81] Reading with Topuzoğlu and Bray *al-ʿarab* for *al-maghrib* (Topuzoğlu, 'Kitāb Ādāb al-Mulūk' (1974), 14 = Topuzoğlu, *Kitāb Ādāb al-Mulūk* (2015), 16; Bray, 'Al-Thaʿalibi's *Adab al-mulūk*', 41).

the municipal governors (*ruʾasāʾ*) allied with them and the officials appointed to oversee their provinces (*al-mutaṣarrifūn ʿalā aʿmālihim*) – the ideas of writers and poets would have died, the intellectual faculties of scholars and philosophers would have languished untapped and the tongues of orators and men of eloquence would have been tied. Such is the favour (*faḍl*) of God that He gives to whom He will.[82]

Happiness lies in proximity to the person who witnesses divine favour.

On the Excellence of Royal Power[83] and of Kings: Reports Transmitted from the Prophet, May Peace Be upon Him, and the Pious Forebears

The Prophet, may peace be upon him, said: 'The *sulṭān* is the shadow of God on His earth. He who obeys him has obeyed me, and he who disobeys him has disobeyed me.'[84] He also said, 'A summons from the *sulṭān* is not to be rejected.'[85]

[82] The phrase *dhālika faḍlu llāhi yuʾtīhi man yashāʾu* is another example of al-Thaʿālibī's use of Qurʾanic language (Q 5: 54; 57: 21; 62: 4).

[83] On the term *sulṭān*, see above, n. 4.

[84] In this passage, al-Thaʿālibī has combined two reports, both of which he takes to be Prophetic. The first part, *al-sulṭān ẓill Allāh fī l-arḍ*, entered political discourse in several ways; often appearing with the continuation *yaʾwī ilayhi kullu maẓlūm*, 'and in him every oppressed person takes refuge', it is sometimes considered to be a Prophetic utterance (see, for example, al-Thaʿālibī, *al-Ẓarāʾif wa-l-laṭāʾif*, 72; al-Tawḥīdī, *al-Baṣāʾir wa-l-dhakhāʾir*, VII: 284, no. 832; al-Māwardī, *Adab al-dunyā wa-l-dīn*, 137; al-Ṭurṭūshī, *Sirāj al-mulūk*, I: 183; al-ʿAjlūnī, *Kashf al-khafāʾ*, I: 403, no. 1485 (with variants); see also Usāma b. Munqidh, *Lubāb al-albāb*, 34 (*al-wālī al-ʿādil al-mutawāḍiʿ ẓill Allāh ʿazza wa-jalla fī arḍihi*, with different continuation); al-Sakhāwī, *al-Maqāṣid al-ḥasana*, 181, no. 207, and al-ʿAjlūnī, *Kashf al-khafāʾ*, I: 192, no. 645 (*innamā al-sulṭān ẓill Allāh wa-rumḥuhu fī l-arḍ*)). (Pseudo-Māwardī does not take the formulation to be Prophetic; see above, at n. 4; nor does al-Thaʿālibī attribute it in *al-Tamthīl wa-l-muḥāḍara*, 95.) The second part of al-Thaʿālibī's citation is attested in the major Sunni collections of Prophetic hadith: Muslim, *Ṣaḥīḥ*, XII: 308–9, *Kitāb al-Imāra*, ch. 8, 32, 33; al-Bukhārī, *Ṣaḥīḥ*, IV: 526, *Kitāb al-Aḥkām*, ch. 1, no. 7137 (*man aṭāʿanī fa-qad aṭāʿa llāha wa-man ʿaṣānī fa-qad ʿaṣā llāha wa-man aṭāʿa amīrī fa-qad aṭāʿanī wa-man ʿaṣā amīrī fa-qad ʿaṣānī*). The maxim appears as a Prophetic utterance in al-Maydānī, *Majmaʿ al-amthāl*, II: 448, and a similar two-part quotation appears in al-Nuwayrī, *Nihāyat al-arab*, VI: 9, 10. Al-Rāghib al-Iṣfahānī records the utterance of Ibn ʿAbbās, 'Authority is God's glory on earth (*al-sulṭān ʿizz Allāh fī l-arḍ*); anyone who deems it light will suffer misfortune, and he shall have nobody to blame but himself' (*Muḥāḍarāt al-udabāʾ*, I: 186); see also al-Zamakhsharī's account, in which Ḥasan relates the hadith to al-Ḥajjāj (*Rabīʿ al-abrār*, IV: 213). Fakhr al-Dīn al-Rāzī bases the imperative of the royal cultivation of virtue on the assumption that the king is the shadow of God and deputy of the Prophet (*Jāmiʿ al-ʿulūm*, 486).

[85] Compare the variant, ascribed to *baʿḍ al-udabāʾ*, in al-Māwardī, *Adab al-dunyā wa-l-dīn*, 137.

The Prophet, upon him be peace, said: 'On the Day when only His shadow can provide shelter, God will shelter the just imam with His shadow.' He was also pleased to say of Anūshīrvān the Just (= Khusraw I, 'The Immortal Souled', r. 531–79): 'I was born in the time of the Just King.'[86]

ʿUthmān b. ʿAffān (r. 23–35/644–55) used to say:

> God restrains the people through the ruler's power more than He restrains them through the Qurʾan.[87]

Ḥudhayfa b. al-Yamān (d. 36/656) said:

> If a group (*qawm*) strives to debase God's *sulṭān*, not only will God debase them in this world; they will also suffer ignominy in the afterlife.[88]

ʿAbdallāh b. Masʿūd (d. *c*. 32–3/652–4)[89] used to say:

> The people have an inescapable need for a restraint.[90]

One of the pious forebears said:

> Anyone who reviles a *sulṭān* will find that on the Day of Resurrection, God will clothe him with a garment of fire. You

86 Al-Thaʿālibī cites this report in several places (see, for instance, *Thimār al-qulūb*, 179; *Yatīmat al-dahr*, IV: 504); see also al-Sakhāwī, *al-Maqāṣid al-ḥasana*, 707–8, no. 1271; and al-ʿAjlūnī, *Kashf al-khafāʾ*, I: 257, no. 913 (*buʿithtu fī zaman al-malik al-ʿādil*). Al-Thaʿālibī endows Anūshīrvān with a unique position among the Sasanian kings. This exceptional status is also reflected in the report that ʿAlī questioned a prominent Persian leader as to whom his people held to be the most praiseworthy of their kings, and received the answer that whereas Ardashīr had the virtue of precedence in the kingdom, the most praiseworthy in conduct was Anūshīrvān, on account of his forbearance (*ḥilm*) and equanimity (*anāt*), qualities that ʿAlī held to result in high aspiration (Ghazālī, *Naṣīḥat al-mulūk*, part II, 98–9 = Bagley, *Ghazālī's Book of Counsel for Kings*, 55; Usāma b. Munqidh, *Lubāb al-ādāb*, 38).

87 Ascribed to ʿUthmān in al-Thaʿālibī, *al-Iʿjāz wa-l-ījāz*, 34, no. 3; al-Thaʿālibī, *al-Tamthīl wa-l-muḥāḍara*, 30; al-Thaʿālibī, *al-Ẓarāʾif wa-l-laṭāʾif*, 72; al-Ḥuṣrī, *Zahr al-ādāb*, I: 37; al-Zamakhsharī, *Rabīʿ al-abrār*, IV: 236; regarded as Prophetic in al-Māwardī (*Adab al-dunyā wa-l-dīn*, 137) and al-Ṭurṭūshī (*Sirāj al-mulūk*, I: 252); without attribution in al-ʿĀmirī, *al-Iʿlām bi-manāqib al-Islām*, 158.

88 The context suggests that for al-Thaʿālibī, in this instance, God's *sulṭān* implied the divinely appointed ruler. Ibn Qutayba, *ʿUyūn al-akhbār*, I: 23 (a slight variant, similarly attributed to the Companion of the Prophet Ḥudhayfa b. al-Yamān). See also Pseudo-Māwardī, *Naṣīḥat al-mulūk al-mansūb ilā … al-Māwardī*, 81, above, at n. 17; and on *sulṭān*, see above, n. 4, and Chapter 1, n. 5.

89 An eminent Companion of the Prophet from Mecca, highly regarded as an authority on the Qurʾan and its interpretation, considered to be one of the ten Companions of the Prophet to whom Paradise was promised (Anthony, 'Ibn Masʿūd, ʿAbdallāh').

90 Al-Thaʿālibī, *al-Ẓarāʾif wa-l-laṭāʾif*, 73.

(subjects) are responsible for the burdens imposed upon you; they (rulers) are responsible for the burdens imposed upon them (*innamā ʿalaykum mā ḥummiltum wa-ʿalayhim mā ḥummilū*). Their duty is justice; your duty is to listen and obey.[91]

A man said to al-Ḥasan al-Baṣrī (21–110/642–728), 'O Abū Saʿīd: What do you have to say about royal power?' He answered: 'What should I say regarding a group of people (*qawm*) charged with responsibility for our affairs in five respects, namely the Friday prayer, the broad community, booty, the frontiers and the statutory penalties? Religion cannot be upheld without them, and even if they are unjust and oppressive, God accomplishes more good through them than He makes corrupt.'[92]

The prophet Daniel, upon him be peace, once walked alongside a king for a stretch of some four miles. Someone said to him, 'Why are you walking with this king, even though you are a prophet?' He replied, 'I am doing it in the hope that I may speak to him with words by which God will, through him, protect the people and benefit them.'

Al-Fuḍayl b. ʿIyāḍ (d. 187/803) used to say: 'If I were granted a prayer that was certain to be answered, I would transfer it to the ruler.' He was asked, 'Why would you place him before yourself?' He said, 'The prayer that I would offer on my own account would benefit me alone; whereas if he were to have it, the lands in their entirety would enjoy new life through his justice and reform.'[93]

[91] An echo of Q 24: 54: 'Say: Obey God and obey the Messenger. If you turn away, then he is responsible only for the burden that he bears, and you are responsible for the burdens that you bear (*fa-innamā ʿalayhi mā ḥummila wa-ʿalaykum mā ḥummiltum*). If you obey him, you will be rightly guided. The Messenger's duty is only the clear expression of the message.' See further below, Text 3, at n. 118. The report is also reminiscent of the utterance, 'If the imam is just, then his is the reward and your responsibility is gratitude; if the imam is unjust, then his is the burden of moral responsibility and your responsibility is patience' (Ibn ʿAbd Rabbihi, *al-ʿIqd al-farīd*, I: 10, from ʿAbdallāh b. ʿUmar).

[92] Al-Thaʿālibī, *al-Ẓarāʾif wa-l-laṭāʾif*, 73. Al-Ḥasan al-Baṣrī was among the most celebrated figures of the generation known as the 'successors' (*tābiʿūn*) to the Companions of the Prophet. Probably born in Medina but closely associated with Basra, Ḥasan was an acclaimed exegete and reciter of the Qurʾan and widely renowned for his piety, sincerity and integrity. His teachings contributed to the formation of several theological, renunciatory and mystical traditions; see Mourad, 'al-Ḥasan al-Baṣrī'.

[93] See al-Thaʿālibī, *al-Ẓarāʾif wa-l-laṭāʾif*, 72; al-Rāghib al-Iṣfahānī, *Muḥāḍarāt al-udabāʾ*, I: 162; Niẓām al-Mulk, *Siyar al-mulūk*, 66 = Darke, *Book of Government*, 49; al-Zamakhsharī, *Rabīʿ al-abrār*, IV: 223; al-Nuwayrī, *Nihāyat al-arab*, VI: 37 (for al-Faḍl read al-Fuḍayl). A leading renunciant (*zāhid*) and transmitter of hadith, al-Fuḍayl was born in Khurasan or Transoxiana, but moved to Iraq, and eventually to Mecca, where he lived until his death. He features in numerous narratives, in which he exemplifies the path of renunciation and often admonishes the holders of worldly power; cf. Ghazālī, *Naṣīḥat*

On Obedience to Royal Power

It has been reported (*fī l-khabar*) that whoever abandons obedience and separates himself from the community will die as if he had died during the Age of Ignorance.[94]

I have read in the reports of Anūshīrvān the Just that he once observed Buzurgmihr giving instruction to a member of the royal retinue. The king asked Buzurgmihr, 'What advice did you give him?' He said:

> I told him, obey your benefactor (*walī niʿmatika*) in whatever he commands you to do and forbids you to do, in the same way that you obey Him who created you and has sustained you. For obedience to the person whom Almighty God has placed in power over His creation is linked to obedience to Him: obedience to God ensures divine mercy, and obedience to the king ensures worldly benefit.

Anūshīrvān responded: 'This realm will enjoy unceasing protection as long as people like you remain in it.'[95]

Abū Bakr b. ʿAyyāsh (d. 193/808) used to say:

> The only way for the common people to approach kings is through obedience, for servants only through service, and for the king's inner circle (*biṭāna*) only through attentiveness.[96]

How excellent and concise are the words of Abarwīz (= Khusraw II Parvīz [r. 590–628]):

> Obey the person above you, so that those below you will obey you.[97]

al-mulūk, part II, 153 = Bagley, *Ghazālī's Book of Counsel for Kings*, 92; see also al-Qushayrī, *al-Risāla*, I: 62–4; and Tor, 'al-Fuḍayl b. ʿIyāḍ'.

94 Literally, he 'will die a *jāhilī* death', that is, a demise akin to the deaths of persons who died during the period that preceded the Islamic era and who lacked knowledge of the final and perfect divine revelation brought by the Prophet Muḥammad (see further above, n. 51). The report is recorded as Prophetic: Muslim, *Ṣaḥīḥ*, XII: 330–3, *Kitāb al-Imāra*, ch. 13, nos. 53–6. See also Ibn ʿAbd Rabbihi, *al-ʿIqd al-farīd*, I: 11.

95 The semi-legendary figure of Buzurgmihr frequently appears in the role of sagacious counsellor and resolute minister to Khusraw I Anūshīrvān (r. 531–79), the paradigmatically just monarch of the pre-Islamic Iranian past (see Khaleghi-Motlagh, 'Bozorgmehr-e Boḵtagān').

96 Ibn Khallikān, *Wafayāt al-aʿyān*, II: 353–4 (no. 254).

97 Ibn Ḥamdūn, *al-Tadhkira al-Ḥamdūniyya*, I: 306; al-Thaʿālibī, *al-Tamthīl wa-l-muḥāḍara*, 99; al-Thaʿālibī, *al-Iʿjāz wa-l-ījāz*, 68, no. 53; al-Thaʿālibī, *Ghurar al-siyar*, 690; Usāma b. Munqidh (citing an anonymous testament), *Lubāb al-ādāb*, 36.

I have said in my book *al-Mubhij*:

> He who obeys the *sulṭān* has obeyed the Merciful; he who disobeys the *sulṭān* has obeyed Satan.[98]

I have said there further:

> When you extend your hand in pledging allegiance (*mubāya'a*), confirm your loyalty by following in obedience.[99]

Notable Examples of Courteous and Gracious Manners (*Laṭā'if wa-Ẓarā'if min al-Ādāb*) Displayed in the Company of the Most Illustrious Kings

One day, as Yazīd b. Shajara [al-Rahāwī] (d. 58/678) was walking at (Caliph) Mu'āwiya's side and Mu'āwiya (r. 41–60/661–80) was talking to him, a loose stone struck Yazīd's face and drew blood. The blood began to flow down over his clothes, yet he did not wipe it away. Mu'āwiya said to him: 'May your father belong to God! Can't you see what has happened to you?' He replied, 'What is that, O Commander of the Faithful?' The latter responded, 'That's blood from your face that's running down over your clothes.' He said: 'If I took no joy in your reception of me, nor in the honour of conversing with you, I should be compelled to release my slaves; the delight of these two things so distracted me that I was unaware of this injury until you alerted me to it.' Mu'āwiya was delighted and increased his stipend.[100]

A similar incident, involving [Abū] Bakr al-Hudhalī, has also been recounted. One day, when al-Hudhalī was in the company of (Caliph) Abū l-'Abbās al-Saffāḥ (r. 132–6/749–54) and the latter was speaking to him, a violent gust of wind arose. It upset a dish on a terrace, and blew it down from the roof to the courtyard where Abū l-'Abbās al-Saffāḥ was sitting with his assembly. Those who were present were frightened and alarmed at this disturbance, but al-Hudhalī did not move, and his eyes remained fixed on the eyes of Abū l-'Abbās. The caliph said to him: 'How remarkable you are, Hudhalī! We were all alarmed; but you were not even startled!' Al-Hudhalī said: 'O Commander of the Faithful, in your

98 Echoes the concepts and language referred to above, n. 84.

99 The second element of the first of this pair of maxims, as well as the second maxim, appear in succession in al-Tha'ālibī's *Kitāb al-Mubhij*, 42, nos. 165, 166.

100 *Kitāb al-Tāj*, 55–7 = Pellat, *Le livre de la couronne*, 85–6; al-Bayhaqī, *al-Maḥāsin wa-l-masāwī*, 464. On Yazīd, see al-Ziriklī, *al-A'yān*, VIII: 184.

generosity you have granted me the privilege of a positive reception; my heart is completely absorbed in it and my thoughts entirely taken up with it. Were the fertile lands to be turned upside down over the dusty skies, I should not have felt it.' Abū l-ʿAbbās said, 'I have lived to understand your true worth, and I shall raise your standing.'[101]

Among the several celebrated accounts concerning [Abū ʿAlī Aḥmad] al-Ṣaghānī (d. 344/955) is the report that one day, while he was in the presence of (al-Amīr) al-Saʿīd Naṣr b. Aḥmad (r. 301–31/914–43) and conversing with him, a scorpion bit Abū ʿAlī's thigh. The creature had crawled into his trousers, and it did not stop stinging him until it had depleted its entire store of venom. Abū ʿAlī paid no attention to it, nor was he disturbed by it. When he returned to his house and removed his clothing, the tally of the bites he had suffered amounted to seventeen. This news reached al-Saʿīd, who was distressed to hear of Abū ʿAlī's ordeal. Afterwards, the king said to him: 'O Abū ʿAlī, I feel troubled about what happened to you. Why didn't you stand up and get rid of that pest?' Abū ʿAlī replied, 'If I couldn't endure the annoyance of a scorpion when I am in the king's presence, then how, if I were not in his presence, would I endure the fires of the battlefield and the blows of swords?'[102]

I heard Abū Naṣr Sahl b. al-Marzubān say:[103]

> I have read in the *Accounts of the Viziers* (*Akhbār al-wuzarāʾ*) of [Abū ʿAbdallāh] Ibn ʿAbdūs [al-Jahshiyārī] (d. 331/942) of an occasion when al-Maʾmūn was discussing some matter with certain members

[101] *Kitāb al-Tāj*, 58–9 = Pellat, *Le livre de la couronne*, 86–7; al-Masʿūdī, *Murūj al-dhahab*, III: 265–6. Al-Hudhalī's name appears sometimes as Bakr and sometimes as Abū Bakr. Compare al-Rāghib al-Iṣfahānī, *Muḥāḍarāt al-udabāʾ*, I: 186, for a similar account involving the theologian Abū l-Qāsim al-Kaʿbī and the (Samanid) amir of Khurasan.

[102] The Chaghānids (Ar. Ṣaghānids), a local dynasty in Chaghaniyan on the right bank of the upper Oxus, became vassals to the Samanids and probably the early Ghaznavids. Abū ʿAlī, a highly effective commander and indispensable source of military support to the Samanids, held the governorship of Khurasan during the reign of the Samanid amir Naṣr b. Aḥmad. See Bosworth, 'Āl-e Moḥtāj'. Compare ʿAbd al-Malik's unsuccessful ruse to rid himself of al-Ḥajjāj's presence by depositing scorpions in his trousers (al-Rāghib al-Iṣfahānī, *Muḥāḍarāt al-udabāʾ*, I: 186).

[103] On Abū Naṣr Sahl b. al-Marzubān, see al-Thaʿālibī, *Yatīmat al-dahr*, IV: 452–5. Al-Thaʿālibī was personally acquainted with this man of letters (453), with whom Abū l-Faḍl al-Hamadhānī (Badīʿ al-Zamān, 358–98/959–1008), who also spent much of his life in the cities of eastern Iran, engaged in correspondence (al-Ḥuṣrī, *Zahr al-ādāb*, I: 379, II: 828–30, 918–19).

> of his retinue.[104] These people argued about the matter and raised their voices. When they had departed, al-Faḍl b. Sahl (d. 202/817–18) ordered that they should receive a beating.[105] Al-Maʾmūn asked him what crime they had committed, and al-Faḍl said: 'In their comportment they have not heeded God's instruction (*lam yataʾaddabū bi-adab Allāh*). He stipulated: "O you who believe! Do not raise your voices above the voice of the Prophet, and do not speak to him at the top of your voices, as you do in speaking to one another" (Q49: 2); yet these people raised their voices above yours.'

Anūshīrvān used to say:

> If other people's voices are raised over the voice of the king, the latter might as well be deposed. Similarly, if he says 'no' in a matter and receives the answer 'yes', or if he says 'yes' and is told 'no', he might as well be killed.

In a similar case, it has been related that a young man, a member of the Hashimite family, entered the presence of al-Manṣūr while the latter was eating his lunch. Al-Manṣūr invited the young man to join him in the meal, but the Hashimite declined. When the latter left, al-Rabīʿ [b. Yūnus] (111–69/730–86)[106] diverted him into one of the passages and ordered that he receive a beating of a hundred lashes. The young man was carried, badly beaten, back to his house. The next day, his family gathered and went to al-Manṣūr to complain about al-Rabīʿ. They informed al-Manṣūr that al-Rabīʿ had inflicted a beating upon their young man. Al-Manṣūr said that al-Rabīʿ was not likely to have done such a thing without some cause, and so he summoned him, and said, 'Rabīʿ! Why did you beat my nephew when I had not ordered you to do so?' Al-Rabīʿ said: 'I did it, O Commander of the Faithful, because when you invited him to your table, he refused to answer in the affirmative. He did not know that an invitation to join the king's table is a matter of

[104] The surviving and published version of al-Jahshiyārī's *Kitāb al-Wuzarāʾ wa-l-kuttāb* comes to an end at the beginning of al-Maʾmūn's caliphate; the account related in al-Thaʿālibī's text does not appear in the extant part of the work.

[105] Al-Faḍl, who first served as mentor to ʿAbdallāh al-Maʾmūn, served also, after al-Maʾmūn's caliphal investiture, as his counsellor, secretary, governor general in the east, and head of his civil and military administration (Yücesoy, 'al-Faḍl b. Sahl').

[106] See also al-Bayhaqī, *al-Maḥāsin wa-l-masāwī*, 159, where the Hashimite is identified as Muḥammad b. ʿĪsā b. ʿAlī. On al-Rabīʿ, the powerful chamberlain and later vizier of al-Manṣūr, see Kennedy, *The Prophet and the Age of the Caliphates*, 138–40.

honour, not a matter of hunger. I found it desirable to teach him this lesson so that he should not repeat an action of this kind.'[107]

> I have heard Abū Jaʿfar Muḥammad b. Mūsā al-ʿAlawī al-Mūsawī al-Ṭūsī say:
>
> The custom of distributing gifts (*rasm al-nithārāt*) as a means of gaining access to kings and other important and prominent figures (*al-kubarāʾ wa-l-ruʾasāʾ*) is modelled on the exemplary practice (*adab*) of God Almighty with regard to His Prophet, upon him be peace, when He said: 'O you who believe, if you speak privately with the Prophet, give alms (*ṣadaqa*) before your conference' (Q58: 12). It seems today as if anyone who strives to gain access to the king or the municipal governor (*raʾīs*) by one means or another approaches him and places some kind of offering before him. He makes this charitable donation as a gesture of his gratitude to God for finding the king in good health in his person and thriving in his condition. The donor asks the king to regard the offering according to his judgement, and to use it for charitable purposes or in some other manner. Were he to undertake this act of giving in direct response to poverty, his behaviour might raise doubts, for 'the heart is ever divided as to the sincerity or insincerity (of a person's intentions)'.[108]

In the *Book of Viziers* of Ibn ʿAbdūs [al-Jahshiyārī], it is related that Muḥammad b. ʿAbd al-Malik [Ibn al-Zayyāt] (d. 233/847),[109] vizier of al-Muʿtaṣim (r. 218–27/833–42) and al-Wāthiq (r. 227–32/842–7), was reading a document one day before al-Wāthiq, so that the caliph could attest to his approval of it. When he had reached the point that mentioned

[107] *Kitāb al-Tāj*, 12 = Pellat, *Le livre de la couronne*, 40; Ibn ʿAbd Rabbihi, *al-ʿIqd al-farīd*, II: 291.

[108] The translation of the final phrase in this passage is Bray's ('Al-Thaʿalibi's *Adab al-mulūk*', 45, n. 19); Bray points out that the phrase has the ring of a proverb, of the kind that al-Thaʿālibī often uses to mark the conclusion of a section. The custom of largesse is well attested for the Ghaznavid and later periods of Iranian history (see 'Nithār'; Matthee, 'Gift Giving', 609–14). On Abū Jaʿfar al-Mūsawī, a contemporary of al-Thaʿālibī's and a fellow littérateur, see al-Thaʿālibī, *Laṭāʾif al-maʿārif*, 198 = Bosworth, *Book of Curious and Entertaining Information*, 134; and al-Thaʿālibī, *Yatīmat al-dahr*, IV, *passim*.

[109] A member of a family of merchants who held official positions at court, Ibn al-Zayyāt was a secretary and man of letters. Appointed to the vizierate by Caliph al-Muʿtaṣim in about 221/833, Ibn al-Zayyāt retained the position during the reign of al-Wāthiq and held it briefly at the beginning of the reign of al-Mutawakkil, who dismissed him in 233/847. With the Chief Judge Aḥmad Ibn Abī Duʾād (see following note), Ibn al-Zayyāt contributed significantly to the direction of the empire in the second quarter of the ninth century. See Ibn Khallikān, *Wafayāt al-aʿyān*, V: 94–101, no. 696; D. Sourdel, 'Ibn al-Zayyāt'; al-Ziriklī, *al-Aʿyān*, VI: 248.

the caliph's soundness in mind and body, and the concomitant lawfulness of his commands for or against a person, Abū l-Walīd [Muḥammad] b. Aḥmad Ibn Abī Du'ād (d. 239/854)[110] said, 'Is it proper that the caliph be spoken of in this manner?' Muḥammad replied, 'What's the cause of your objection? Is there anything else that could be written in these kinds of documents?' Abū l-Walīd said, 'There should be a difference between the caliph and the common people in everything.' Al-Wāthiq turned to him and said, 'How then should it be written?' Abū l-Walīd replied that a better formulation would read: 'According to the health of his body, the loftiness of his judgement and the divinely given success of his Lord.' Muḥammad was embarrassed, and al-Wāthiq ordered that Abū l-Walīd receive a hundred thousand dinars.[111]

It is related from 'Ubayd Allāh b. Sulaymān [b. Wahb] (226–88/840–901), concerning a document written on behalf of al-Mu'taḍid (r. 289–95/902–8), that this caliph also disliked this kind of phrasing, and that he had it replaced with the formula 'in the health of his body and the accuracy of his judgement'.[112]

When Muḥammad b. 'Abd al-Malik [Ibn al-Zayyāt] needed the caliphal seal, in order to seal documents and other items, he would call for it. When his eye fell upon it, it being in a golden receptacle specially fashioned for it and wrapped in silk, he would rise in its honour and advance towards it with a few steps; then he would remove it from its wrapping and kiss it. He would use it to seal whatever he wished, and then he would return it to its place and surrender it to the treasurer

[110] Abū l-Walīd was a son of Abū 'Abdallāh Aḥmad Ibn Abī Du'ād (160–240/776 or 777–854), who had advised al-Ma'mūn and was appointed Chief Judge by al-Mu'taṣim. Ibn Abī Du'ād, a prominent Mu'tazilite, was closely identified with the prosecution of the *miḥna* (the ninth-century caliphal initiative to impose upon religious specialists the doctrine of the created Qur'an), and he played a major role in shaping aspects of the ninth-century Abbasid state until his dismissal in 237/851–2 (Turner, 'Aḥmad b. Abī Du'ād'). Abū l-Walīd, a prolific author in the field of jurisprudence, was appointed to the judgeship during his father's lifetime and predeceased his father by less than a month (Ibn al-Nadīm, *al-Fihrist*, I: ii: 590; al-Khaṭīb al-Baghdādī, *Ta'rīkh Baghdād*, II: 129–33, no. 113; al-Ṣafadī, *al-Wāfī bi-l-wafayāt*, II: 25–6, no. 293).

[111] This section of al-Jahshiyārī's work has been lost (see above, n. 104). On the involvements of Ibn al-Zayyāt and Ibn Abī Du'ād in the political life of their times, as well as their interactions with one another, see Kennedy, *When Baghdad Ruled the Muslim World*, 200–42.

[112] 'Ubayd Allāh b. Sulaymān b. Wahb was the last vizier under al-Mu'tamid (r. 256–79/870–92) and vizier under al-Mu'taḍid (r. 279–89/892–902) until his own death in 288/901. See Kennedy, *The Prophet and the Age of the Caliphates*, 181–2, 185, 191; Bosworth, 'Wahb'; al-Ziriklī, *al-A'yān*, IV: 194.

responsible for it. He would escort it for a few steps until it disappeared from his vision; and he behaved in this manner out of reverence and high esteem for the caliphal seal.

It is related that ʿUthmān b. ʿAffān used to say, 'I have not touched my private parts with my right hand since I paid allegiance with that hand to the Prophet.'[113]

I heard from my grandfather, Abū ʿAlī l-Thaʿālibī, that Naṣr b. Ṭ. al-Sharābī used to say:[114]

> I have not touched any fatty substance since the Commander of the Faithful appointed me to oversee his wine cellar. He demanded my complete attention in this matter and singled me out for his particular service, until he departed to join his Lord.

I asked him: 'How then did you manage to consume broth (*maraq*) and meats?' He said: 'With spoons and *bārijiyyāt*;[115] and sometimes I might be fed, if no spoon were available.'

I heard Abū Naṣr b. Abī Zayd say that at the tables of the Samanid kings, when rice pudding (rice with *laban*) was brought, it was the custom that everyone would partake of it with a golden spoon. On one occasion, various provincial kings (*mulūk al-aṭrāf*) were present at the table of al-Amīr al-Saʿīd [Naṣr b. Aḥmad, r. 301–31/914–43] (or perhaps he said it was the table of al-Amīr al-Ḥamīd [Nūḥ b. Naṣr, r. 331–43/943–54]). One of these vassal kings was Abū Saʿīd Aḥmad b. Muḥammad b. ʿIrāq. When the rice dish was brought, everyone was given a golden spoon as usual. All the guests took their spoons and began using them, except for Abū Saʿīd. He picked up his spoon and put it down in front of him. When the assembly rose from the table, the king ordered that Abū Saʿīd be asked the cause of his abstention from using the spoon in the manner of his peers. He said, 'I did not wish to place a spoon in my mouth, and then place it in the bowl at the king's table.' This much-admired example

[113] Al-Thaʿālibī, *Khāṣṣ al-khāṣṣ*, 75.

[114] Al-ʿAṭiyya's printed text reads Ṭ.zz; Topuzoğlu suggests Ṭurā (Topuzoğlu, 'Kitāb Ādāb al-Mulūk' (1974), 20, 255; Topuzoğlu, *Kitāb Ādāb al-Mulūk* (2015), 22). The individual to whom al-Thaʿālibī refers is probably the Naṣr-i Sharāb-dār who, at the behest of the Samanid al-Amīr al-Ḥamīd, conducted the mourning ceremonies for Abū l-Muẓaffar b. Abī ʿAlī Aḥmad Chaghānī (Gardīzī, *Zayn al-akhbār*, 230 = Bosworth, *Ornament of Histories*, 64).

[115] The meaning of the word reproduced in transliteration is uncertain; in the context, 'scoops' is a possible conjecture.

points to Abū Saʿīd's excellent manners; and the custom of using spoons at table was suspended on his account.[116]

Text 3
Al-Māwardī, *Tashīl al-naẓar wa-taʿjīl al-ẓafar*. Opening to Part II[117]

Translator's Introduction

This extract comprises the opening section of part II of al-Māwardī's mirror. While part I dealt with the ethical qualities necessary in the ruler (*akhlāq al-malik*) (see below, Text 7), part II is dedicated to 'the governance of the kingdom' (*siyāsat al-mulk*). In it, al-Māwardī examines theoretical treatments of the foundations of the state and details the ruler's practical responsibilities. The section opens with a discussion of religion, which al-Māwardī presents as an essential precondition for governance. More than any other factor, religion, in al-Māwardī's presentation, promotes consensus and trust; it is essential to the creation and maintenance of social cohesion and political stability. Throughout this section, al-Māwardī stresses the interdependence of religion and sovereignty, with the former taking priority over the latter. Like Pseudo-Māwardī, he emphasises the ruler's moral obligations – his responsibility for his moral burden – and the standard against which he will be judged. He begins with the example of David, prophet and king, divinely appointed and called upon to enact justice. The theme of reciprocity is more marked than in al-Thaʿālibī's presentation of the royal office in the preceding extract (Text 2).

Translation

The Chief Judge [al-Māwardī], may God have mercy upon him, has said:

The person whom God Almighty has placed in power over His earth and in His lands, and to whom He has entrusted His creatures and His

[116] This Abū Naṣr b. Abī Zayd is probably the individual to whom Abū l-Faḍl al-Hamadhānī addressed a composition, cited in al-Thaʿālibī, *Yatīmat al-dahr*, IV: 299–300.

[117] Translation prepared from al-Māwardī, *Tashīl al-naẓar wa-taʿjīl al-ẓafar*, ed. Riḍwān al-Sayyid (Beirut: Dār al-ʿUlūm al-ʿArabiyya, 1987), 197–202. For the corresponding section in Abbès's translation into French, see Makram Abbès, *Al-Māwardī. De l'Éthique du prince et du gouvernement de l'état* (Paris: Les Belles Lettres, 2015), 355–65.

servants, is under an obligation to respond to this bounty with goodness of heart and, among the subjects, good conduct. God Almighty has said:

> O David: We have made you a deputy (*khalīfa*) on the earth. Judge fairly, then, among the people; and do not follow your passion (Q 38: 26).

He has also said:

> Do not forget your share (*naṣīb*) in this world. Do good, as God has done good to you (Q 28: 77).

It is reported from the Prophet, may peace be upon him, that he said:

> He who conducts himself well among his companions will reap the reward for his own good behaviour, as well as for the good conduct of the people who follow his example, until the Day of Judgement, without any of his recompense being diminished. He whose conduct among his companions is bad will carry the burden of this conduct and the burdens of those who behave likewise, until the Day of the Last Judgement, without any decrease in these burdens.[118]

It is narrated from ʿUmar [b. al-Khaṭṭāb] (r. 13–23/634–44), may God be pleased with him, that he said:

> If a single lamb goes astray along the banks of the Euphrates, I fear that God will interrogate me over it.[119]

It is related that ʿUthmān b. ʿAbdallāh appeared before the judge [Abū ʿAbdallāh] Muḥammad Ibn Samāʿa (d. 233/847–8); the latter was in his court, where he was adjudicating the cases that the people brought before him. ʿUthmān said: 'Listen well, Ibn Samāʿa – for you have not listened!' Then he recited:

> Miserable wretch, you are charged with an authority
> That causes the hearts of the fearful to tremble.
> Remember that the Lord of the Throne is a Judge,
> As you judge among the creatures of the world.

[118] Muslim, *Ṣaḥīḥ*, VII: 142–5, *Kitāb al-Zakāt*, ch. 20, no. 69; al-Tirmidhī, *al-Jāmiʿ al-kabīr*, IV: 407–8, *Abwāb al-ʿilm*, ch. 15, no. 2675; al-Nasāʾī, *Sunan*, 347, *Kitāb al-Zakāt*, ch. 64, no. 2554. See also above, n. 91.

[119] Abū Nuʿaym al-Iṣfahānī, *Ḥilyat al-awliyāʾ*, I: 52–3. Cf. Ghazālī, *Naṣīḥat al-mulūk*, part I, 24 = Bagley, *Ghazālī's Book of Counsel for Kings*, 18; Niẓām al-Mulk, *Siyar al-mulūk*, 16 = Darke, *Book of Government*, 12–13.

Ibn Samāʿa rose from his court with tears streaming down his cheeks.[120]

There is no one for whom caution, solicitude, effort and exertion (*ijtihād*) are more appropriate and more fitting than the person charged with responsibility for the affairs of the subjects.[121] The subjects are a trust, responsibility for whom God has consigned to this individual; they are His flock, and He has established this person, the ruler, as their shepherd. God has appointed the ruler over the subjects' affairs, and it is God Almighty who will question him concerning them. For He, may He be praised, has deprived the subjects of the means to resist the ruler's actions. He has obstructed their tongues from rejection of whatever by his individual reasoning (*ijtihād*) the ruler sees fit to do. God has compelled the subjects to obey this person; He has obligated them to follow the ruler's decrees and commanded them to proceed in accordance with his orders and prohibitions. For God has said, 'O you who believe: Obey God, obey the Messenger and those in authority among you' (Q 4: 59).

God has made the welfare (*ṣalāḥ*) of the subjects in their entirety contingent upon the ruler's well-being, and the corruption (*fasād*) of their affairs a corollary of his corruption. He is the heart, and they are the limbs; he is the pole and they the flanks. An intelligent person said: 'The integrity of the ruler (*rashād al-wālī*) is better than a time of plenty (*khiṣb al-zamān*).'[122]

The ruler of greatest integrity (*arshad al-wulāt*) is he through whose authority religion is well protected and through whose attention the well-being of the Muslims is regulated. Religion ensures the goodness of our

[120] Ibn Samāʿa was a prominent judge in Baghdad. He composed a number of books on judicial matters; see Ibn al-Nadīm, *Fihrist*, II: i: 26; al-Dhahabī, *Siyar aʿlām al-nubalāʾ*, X: 646–7 (no. 228); al-Ṣafadī, *al-Wāfī bi-l-wafayāt*, III: 116, no. 1086.

[121] The term *ijtihād* denotes effort in a general sense, but in the field of jurisprudence it also carries the technical meaning of independent reasoning or judgement, that is, individual legal interpretation. It is consistent with his respect for the resources of human reason that al-Māwardī appears to have endorsed the qualified exercise of independent reasoning; see Schneider, 'Vernunft oder Tradition?', esp. 72–3.

[122] Ascribed to Ardashīr in *ʿAhd Ardashīr*, 53; al-Thaʿālibī, *al-Iʿjāz wa-l-ījāz*, 62, no. 34; al-Thaʿālibī, *Ghurar al-siyar*, 483. For variants, see al-Masʿūdī, *Murūj al-dhahab*, I: 298 (*ṣalāḥ amr al-raʿiyya anṣar min kathrat al-junūd wa-ʿadl al-malik anfaʿ min khiṣb al-zamān*, attributed to Anūshīrvān); Ibn al-Ḥaddād, *al-Jawhar al-nafīs*, 67 (*ʿadl al-sulṭān anfaʿ lil-raʿiyya min khiṣb al-zamān*, inscribed on Anūshīrvān's seal); Ibn Qutayba, *ʿUyūn al-akhbār*, I: 5 (*ʿadl al-sulṭān anfaʿ lil-raʿiyya min khiṣb al-zamān*, attributed to 'the ancient philosophers' (*al-ḥukamāʾ*)); *Sirr al-asrār*, in *al-Uṣūl al-yūnāniyya*, 125; al-Tawḥīdī, *al-Imtāʿ*, II: 259; al-Rāghib al-Iṣfahānī, *Muḥāḍarāt al-udabāʾ*, I: 169 (attributed to ʿAmr b. al-ʿĀṣ) and I: 163 (without attribution); al-Ibshīhī, *al-Mustaṭraf*, I: 228 (unattributed).

hearts' secrets; it prevents the commission of sins, induces godliness and equal sharing, and promotes concord and mutual affection. These things constitute foundations without which the world cannot prosper; nor can humanity attain the right path without them. Power is merely a device[123] for the maintaining of these foundations, and it provides an incentive to act in accordance with them. If the people were to be neglected – given the attraction of the promptings of appetite and the appeal of differences in opinion – then they would produce disorder and strife, since truth could not be known from falsehood, and the correct would not be distinguishable from the corrupt. Reason lacks the capacity to unite people within an order in which the strong and the weak, and the noble and the ordinary, are equal. For this reason, the people's best interests (*maṣāliḥ*) lie in a religion that leads them towards communal unity and agreement in their points of view. With religion, the strife among the people will cease, the grounds for their different objectives and disagreements will be removed, their innermost hearts will be restored to well-being and their trust will be protected.

It has happened that kings have neglected religion and relied in their affairs on their ability to use force and the sheer numbers of their troops. This kind of king does not realise that if his troops are not convinced, on religious grounds, of their duty of obedience to him, they can become more harmful to him than any other adversary, since they may demand of him things that he does not support, and they may induce him to take steps that undermine his position. If they hear of a credible contender against him, their desire to despoil him of his possessions will grow stronger, and the task of maintaining his position will hold no satisfaction for them. The ruler will find himself, in relation to his troops, on the edge of a fragile precipice, with no security against their assault. It has been said:

> The ruler who makes his sovereignty a servant to his religion will find that all power yields to him; whereas the ruler who makes his religion a servant to his sovereignty will find that every human being will desire it.[124]

[123] Literally a rein or bridle (*zimām*); the implied metaphor of control of an animal for reason's control of the passions or the ruler's control of an unruly populace features frequently (see above, n. 6).

[124] The phrase echoes a frequently cited passage in *Sirr al-asrār* (see *al-Uṣūl al-yūnāniyya*, 77); cf. below, n. 126. Pseudo-Māwardī reports having read in Aristotle's epistle to Alexander, 'The king who puts his sovereignty in the service of his religion is deserving

Section

It befits the king to reject the possibility that his subjects might include any person more excellent in religion than he is, just as he would reject the notion that there should be anyone whose command might be more effective than his. Ardashīr b. Bābak said in his Testament to the kings of Persia:

> Religion and sovereignty are twins; neither one of them endures without the other. Religion is the foundation, and sovereignty is the guardian. Sovereignty cannot dispense with its foundation, and the foundation cannot survive without its guardian; for whatever lacks a guardian falls into ruin, and whatever lacks a foundation inevitably collapses.[125]

The Greek philosopher (*ḥakīm al-rūm*) wrote to Alexander:

> Defend your religion with your sovereignty; do not defend your sovereignty with your religion. Make your life in this world your protection for the hereafter; do not make the hereafter your protection for your life in this world.[126]

How can the king who manifestly neglects religion hope for stability in his sovereignty and for a state of well-being? The supporters of his turn

of leadership; as for the king who puts his religion in the service of his sovereignty, in his case, sovereignty is a calamity' (*Naṣīḥat al-mulūk al-mansūb ilā . . . al-Māwardī*, 109). The same version appears amongst the *ḥikam* and *ādāb* of Aristotle in al-Mubashshir b. Fātik, *Mukhtār al-ḥikam*, 192. See also, without definite attribution, Usāma b. Munqidh, *Lubāb al-ādāb*, 54.

125 A celebrated formula: *'Ahd Ardashīr*, 53, 97; Ibn 'Abd Rabbihi, *al-'Iqd al-farīd*, I: 23; Ibn Qutayba, *'Uyūn al-akhbār*, I: 5, 13; *Kitāb al-Tāj*, 3; al-'Āmirī, *al-I'lām bi-manāqib al-Islām*, 153; al-Rāghib al-Iṣfahānī, *Muḥāḍarāt al-udabā'*, I: 167; Ibn Ḥamdūn, *al-Tadhkira al-Ḥamdūniyya*, I: 286; Fakhr al-Dīn al-Rāzī, *Jāmi' al-'ulūm*, 489 (the first maxim only); Ghazālī, *Naṣīḥat al-mulūk*, part II: 106 = Bagley, *Ghazālī's Book of Counsel for Kings*, 59; Niẓām al-Mulk, *Siyar al-mulūk*, 80 = Darke, *Book of Government*, 60; al-Ṭurṭūshī, *Sirāj al-mulūk*, I: 252; Usāma b. Munqidh, *Lubāb al-ādāb*, 18; al-Nuwayrī, *Nihāyat al-arab*, VI: 34. Compare the maxim 'sovereignty endures through religion; religion gains strength through sovereignty' (*al-mulk bi-l-dīn yabqā wa-l-dīn bi-l-mulk yaqwā*), al-Tha'ālibī, *al-Tamthīl wa-l-muḥāḍara*, 96, al-Tha'ālibī, *al-Ẓarā'if wa-l-laṭā'if*, 74 (ascribed to Ibn al-Mu'tazz); al-Māwardī, *Adab al-dunyā wa-l-dīn*, 138 (ascribed to Ibn al-Mu'tazz); Ibn Abī l-Ḥadīd, *Sharḥ Nahj al-balāgha*, XX: 439, no. 759 (among the maxims of 'Alī) (on this pairing of attributions, see above, n. 58); al-'Āmirī, *al-I'lām bi-manāqib al-Islām*, 189 (without attribution); al-Tha'ālibī, *Ghurar al-siyar*, 483 (Ardashīr).

126 Cf. *Sirr al-asrār*, 77, see above, n. 124. The second element appears, ascribed to Aristotle, in al-Mubashshir b. Fātik, *Mukhtār al-ḥikam*, 193.

in power (*a'wān dawlatihi*) will become his opponents, and the rest of his subjects will turn into his enemies – in addition to the ugly impact of his rule and the extreme harm that he will have wrought. In this vein the Prophet, upon him be peace, said:

> You will covet command, yet it will become an affliction and a regret on the Day of Resurrection; the wet-nurse [the life of this world] may be bountiful, but the weaned infant [the hereafter] is miserable.[127]

It has also been said:

> The king is God's deputy (*khalīfat Allāh*) in His lands; his deputyship will never attain stability if he opposes Him.[128]

The fortunate ruler is he who safeguards his religion with his sovereignty, rather than seeking to protect his sovereignty with his religion. This ruler enlivens established practices with his justice; he does not abolish a sound custom with his injustice. He guards the subjects through his beneficial administration; he does not suppress them by ruination. In this fashion, the pillars of his sovereignty profit from a ruler who maintains their solidity, the foundation of his state benefits from a person who keeps it standing firm and the divine command flourishes in his lands by virtue of an individual who follows it in complete obedience. God will never separate the upholding of religion from the governance of the realm and the careful management of the subjects.

[127] Al-Bukhārī, *Ṣaḥīḥ*, IV: 529, *Kitāb al-Aḥkām*, ch. 7, no. 7148; al-Nasā'ī, *Sunan*, 574, *Kitāb al-Bay'a*, ch. 39, no. 4211; *Kitāb Ādāb al-quḍāt*, 715, no. 5385.

[128] This statement involves a play on the various connotations of the root *kh-l-f*: certain words derived from *kh-l-f* denote deputyship and succession; other words connote opposition. On the concept and title *khalīfat Allāh*, with principal reference to the Umayyad and early Abbasid periods, see Crone and Hinds, *God's Caliph*; for responses to and refinements of their arguments, see Rubin, 'Prophets and Caliphs', and Alajmi, 'Ascribed vs. Popular Legitimacy'. The term became an established element in political discourse; for example, the caliph al-Manṣūr, preaching in Mecca, announced himself 'God's *sulṭān* on His earth' (*sulṭān Allāh fī arḍihi*, al-Ābī, *Nathr al-durr*, II: 64). The axiomatic status that the formula had attained by the period in which al-Māwardī, as suggested by his use of the passive voice, wrote is confirmed by Usāma b. Munqidh, who relates, on the authority of *al-ḥakīm* and *al-ḥukamā'*, the formula *al-sulṭān khalīfat Allāh fī arḍihi* (*Lubāb al-ādāb*, 58, 72). Writing in the first half of the eleventh century, al-Māwardī presents the formula less as an assertion of the ruler's divine mandate than as an injunction upon him to govern in accordance with the demands of religion. See further Abbès, *De l'Éthique du prince*, 359, n. 12.

Text 4
Ghazālī, Pseudo-Ghazālī, *Naṣīḥat al-mulūk*. Part II, Chapter One[129]

Translator's Introduction

This selection constitutes the opening section of the work traditionally received as part II of the Persian *Naṣīḥat al-mulūk* of or attributed to Abū Ḥāmid Ghazālī. The premise of this section, as its author makes plain in his opening sentences, is the unparalleled stature of kings among human beings and their exceptional place in the divine plan; kings enjoy divine favour and represent a manifestation of divine wisdom (*ḥikmat*). The section offers an unqualified statement of the unique cosmic position of kings, and their qualitative otherness from other human beings (the notion of *farr-i īzadī*, the 'divine aura', evokes a divine marking of kings, a sign of their divine mandate).[130] Recalling the treatment of al-Thaʿālibī, Pseudo-Ghazālī's portrayal of the royal office is also reminiscent, to a degree, of the representation of Pseudo-Māwardī in the opening passages of Text 1; both authors, to convey the exceptional status of kings, employ the concept of *faḍl* (Persian *faẓl*).[131] But whereas Pseudo-Māwardī rapidly turns his focus to the moral obligation that this divinely awarded status imposes upon kings, and the consequences to kings and to their subjects if they fail to meet it, Pseudo-Ghazālī, in a manner more reminiscent of al-Thaʿālibī, asserts the subjects' unqualified duty not only to obey kings but to love them. Pseudo-Ghazālī cites Qurʾanic verses and Prophetic materials (as he understood them), and in addition, he turns to the copious Iranian cultural repertoire for his exemplars of royal justice; an exposition of Iran's pre-Islamic kings, according to this tradition, follows the section presented in this extract. (Pseudo-)Ghazālī locates the principal duty of kings in the maintenance of justice, but he leaves

[129] Translation prepared from Ghazālī, *Naṣīḥat al-mulūk*, ed. Jalāl al-Dīn Humāʾī (Tehran: Kitābkhānah-yi Millī, 1972), 81–4. For the corresponding section in Bagley's translation, see F. R. C. Bagley, *Ghazālī's Book of Counsel for Kings* (London: Oxford University Press, 1964), 45–7; and for the corresponding section in the Arabic translation, see *al-Tibr al-masbūk fī naṣīḥat al-mulūk*, ed. Muḥammad Aḥmad Damaj (Beirut: Muʾassasat ʿIzz al-Dīn lil-Ṭibāʿa wa-l-Nashr, 1996), 147–50.

[130] See section 3.4, at n. 42, section 3.7, at n. 65, and below, n. 133.

[131] Compare the discussion of *tafḍīl* in Pseudo-Māwardī, *Naṣīḥat al-mulūk*, in the opening section of Text 1.

no room for the implication that the subjects' duty of obedience lapses in the case of royal injustice.

Translation

Chapter One: On the Justice, Governance and Conduct of Kings

Know and remain mindful of the fact that God Almighty has chosen two groups from among humankind, and that He has preferred (*fażl nihād*) these two groups over others: one of these groups is prophets, the other kings. As for prophets, He sent them to His bondsmen, so that they might show them the path to Him. He chose kings so that they would preserve human beings from one another, and, in His wisdom (*ḥikmat*), He bound humanity's well-being (*maṣlaḥat*) in life to kings. He has awarded kings a great station: as you will hear in the traditional reports, 'The *sulṭān* is the shadow of God on earth' (Ar.), that is, the *sulṭān* is the shadow of God's majesty (*haybat*) on the face of the earth.[132] This means that the king's position is grand; he is appointed by God over His creation. Accordingly, it should be understood that the person to whom God has given kingship and divine charisma (*farr-i īzadī*) must be held dear, and that kings must be followed.[133] There should be no dispute with kings, nor hostility towards them. For God Almighty has said: 'Obey God, obey the Messenger and those in authority among you' (Q4: 59). The interpretation (*tafsīr*) of this verse is, 'Be obedient to God, to the prophets and to your rulers (*amīrān-i khᵛīsh*)'. Accordingly, everyone to whom God has given religion should hold kings in affection and obey them, in the knowledge that it is God who has given them this kingship, and that He gives it as He wishes; for He has said, 'Say, O God, Owner of Sovereignty, You bestow kingship on whom You will, and You take kingship away from whom You will; You raise up whom You will and cast down whom You will, by Your good hand; for You are capable of all things' (Q3: 26); that is, He said that God Almighty is the King of all kings, and that He gives kingship to

[132] This last sequence consists of the author's quotation of the Arabic formula with his Persian paraphrase. The phrase *dar akhbār* connotes derivation from a corpus of transmitted accounts, without reference to a specific source; see the discussion of the connotations of *khabar* (pl. *akhbār*) in Bagley, 'Introduction', lvii.

[133] The term *farr-i īzadī* appears again at Ghazālī, *Naṣīḥat al-mulūk*, 127 = Bagley, *Ghazālī's Book of Counsel for Kings*, 74; in this second instance, the author lists sixteen signs that indicate the presence of the divine charisma (127–8). The *farr*, a development of an ancient Iranian concept, signifies possession of the divine mandate (see Gnoli, 'Farr(ah)'); see also section 3.4 and its n. 42.

whomever He wishes; He makes one person great through His favour (*fażl*); another person He humbles through His justice (*ʿadl*).[134] The *sulṭān*, in truth, is he who performs justice among God's bondsmen and does not enact injustice and corruption; for an unjust *sulṭān* is inauspicious, and he will not endure: as the Prophet, God's peace be upon him, said, 'Sovereignty endures with unbelief, but it does not endure with tyranny' (Ar.).[135]

In the chronicles it is recorded that for four thousand years the Magians held this world, and the kingdom (*mamlakat*) was held in their familial house.[136] The reason that their sovereignty lasted was that they upheld justice among the subjects and looked after them. In their religion (*kīsh*) they did not permit injustice or oppression, and they made the world prosperous through justice and equity. It is reported that God Almighty inspired (*vaḥy kard*) the prophet David to instruct his people not to speak ill of the Persians (*ʿajam*), 'since they were the people who made the world prosperous so that My bondsmen might live in it'.[137]

It must also be known that the prosperity and ruin of the world stem from kings, for if the king is just, the world becomes prosperous and the subjects are secure – as was the case in the time of Ardashīr, Farīdūn, Bahrām-i Gūr and Khusraw Anūshīrvān. Conversely, when the king is oppressive, the world falls into ruin – as was the case in the time of Żaḥḥāk, Afrāsiyāb, Yazdagird the Sinner and other kings like them.[138]

[134] These clauses represent the author's Persian paraphrase of the preceding Qurʾanic verse.

[135] The author provides neither translation nor paraphrase of this Arabic maxim, which he presents as Prophetic. The saying appears without attribution in al-Thaʿālibī, *al-Tamthīl wa-l-muḥāḍara*, 95, and it is adduced on the authority of 'the great men of religion' (*buzurgān-i dīn*) in Niẓām al-Mulk, *Siyar al-mulūk*, 15. The maxim articulates the common association of select rulers of the *jāhiliyya* with exemplary justice (most notably, the name of Anūshīrvān became inseparable from justice (see above, n. 86)).

[136] Magians (*mughān*) (Ar. *majūs*) or Zoroastrians, an allusion to the pre-Islamic rulers of Iran; the mention of four thousand years and the familial house (*khāndān*) (in the singular) implies a continuity from the primordial (legendary) Pīshdādiyān, through the legendary Kayāniyān, the Ashkāniyān (Arsacids or Parthians), to the fully historical Sasanian dynasty (see further below, n. 139).

[137] The introductory formula again reads *dar khabar āmadeh ast* (82); see above, n. 132. In this context, the term *ʿajam*, in other cases denoting non-Arabs in general, refers specifically to Persians. The report recalls a similar account in the *Thimār al-qulūb* of al-Thaʿālibī, according to which one of the prophets (unidentified) appealed to God, asking 'O Lord! Why have You given [this gift of kingship] to the Khusraws (*akāsira*)?' God, by way of inspiration (*waḥy*), responded, 'Because they have made My lands prosperous (*ʿammarū bilādī*) so that My servants can live in them' (*Thimār al-qulūb*, 179, no. 255).

[138] The adage expounded in this passage appears in Ibn Abī Dharr, *al-Saʿāda wa-l-isʿād*, 207 (ascribed to Anūshīrvān); al-Ibshīhī, *al-Mustaṭraf*, I: 231 (ascribed to al-Walīd b. Hishām). Ardashīr (= Ardashīr I, r. *c.* 224–40 or 242) was the founder of the Sasanian dynasty, and the

Lest anyone should find it difficult to accept this proposition, and should say, 'It can't be true that in the four thousand years that the Magians possessed the world, every one of them governed with justice, and that they never countenanced injustice or oppression' – we shall make plain the condition of these kings, the length of their reigns, the nature of their lives and conduct, every king separately. We shall describe how each king lived and how he treated his subjects, so that whenever anyone reads this account, he will be relieved of his doubts.[139]

Text 5
Al-Ṭurṭūshī, *Sirāj al-mulūk*. Chapter Nine[140]

Translator's Introduction

The final extract in this chapter sums up many of the themes introduced in the previous selections. As the latest author among the mirror-writers presented in this volume, al-Ṭurṭūshī inherited the thinking of his predecessors and was able to integrate and synthesise a remarkably wide-ranging repertoire of ideas and texts. For example, in the opening section of his ninth chapter, presented in Text 5, al-Ṭurṭūshī integrates the metaphor of kingdom and body, the body politic, with the medieval

putative 'author' of the 'Testament of Ardashīr'; Farīdūn is a legendary king of the primordial period in Iranian tradition; Bahrām-i Gūr is Bahrām V (r. 420–38) of the Sasanian dynasty; Anūshīrvān is Khusraw I ('The Immortal Souled', r. 531–79). Żaḥḥāk, who reportedly ruled for a thousand years, is the legendary wicked king of the primordial era. Afrāsiyāb is the legendary ruler of Turan, and figures in the Iranian epic tradition as the enemy and rival of Iran. (Although the adversary of Iranian kings, Afrāsiyāb is not an irredeemably negative figure; in *Kutadgu bilig*, he appears as the glorious ancestor of the Karakhanids (*Kutadgu bilig*, 48).) Yazdagird 'the Sinner' is the Sasanian king Yazdagird I (r. 399–420); his derogatory epithet probably derives from his execution of members of the nobility and his policy of tolerance towards religious minorities (Daryaee, *Sasanian Persia*, 21–2).

[139] The author concludes this section with the statement that he will proceed with a chronological account of the kings, one by one, and he embarks on this narrative in the section that follows (for a translation of this section, see Bagley, *Ghazālī's Book of Counsel for Kings*, 47–53). The account follows the traditional depiction of Iran's experience from the world's creation to the beginnings of the Islamic period, and it offers an abbreviated version of the narrative expounded in its most celebrated form in the *Shāhnāmeh* of Firdawsī.

[140] Translation prepared from al-Ṭurṭūshī, *Sirāj al-mulūk*, ed. Muḥammad Fatḥī Abū Bakr (Cairo: al-Dār al-Miṣriyya al-Lubnāniyya, 1994), ch. 9, I: 205–7. For the corresponding section in Alarcón's translation into Spanish, see Maximiliano Alarcón, *Lámpara de los Príncipes por Abubéquer de Tortosa*, 2 vols. (Madrid: Instituto de Valencia de Don Juan, 1930), I: 183–5.

medical theory of the body's humours. Al-Ṭurṭūshī begins this ninth chapter with a series of analogies for the ruler and the subjects. Each of his similitudes is drawn from the natural world: the ruler controls his subjects as fire controls the fuel it consumes; the just ruler is a life-giving rainfall or spring; the corrupt or unjust ruler poisons the water supply, and thereby the vegetation and animal life that depend on it.[141] Al-Ṭurṭūshī's likenesses assume his audience's full grasp of the interdependence among the elements of the natural world and the dangers of environmental pollution.

Translation

*Chapter Nine: Explication of the Position of the Ruler (*Sulṭān*) in Relation to the Subjects*

Know that the position of the *sulṭān* in relation to the subjects is the same as the position of the spirit (*rūḥ*) in relation to the body. If the spirit is pure of pollution, it will flow healthily to the limbs and throughout all the parts of the body. The body will be protected against injury, the limbs and senses will be sound and the body's condition will be properly ordered. If, on the other hand, the spirit is spoilt and its temperament (*mizāj*) impaired, then alas for the body! For the spirit will spread pollution into the senses and the limbs, and it will unsettle the equilibrium among them.[142] Every limb and sense will succumb to its portion of

[141] The likening of the king to rainfall and to fire is ancient and ubiquitous; see, for example, *Sirr al-asrar*, 81 = 188; al-Thaʿālibī, *Ādāb al-mulūk*, 55–6; al-Thaʿālibī, *al-Tamthīl wa-l-muḥāḍara*, 95–6. See also below, Text 6.

[142] This passage evokes the medical philosophy, primarily associated with Galen and diffused across ancient western Asia, of the humours (*akhlāṭ*) and temperaments (*amzija*, sing. *mizāj*). According to this philosophy, the human body consists of an intermixture of four elemental humours, blood, phlegm, yellow bile and black bile, each of which possesses two natures or qualities, hot or cold and dry or moist. Each humour was associated with one of the four seasons, and with a 'temperament'. In a healthy body, the four humours co-exist in equilibrium, and sustain the distinctive temperament (*mizāj* or *ṭabʿ*) of each individual; illness occurs as a result of an imbalance among the humours and, by extension, in the temperament. A feature also of the Byzantine mirror literature (see the 'Letter of Themistius', 25–7), by the end of the ninth century, this system formed the basic principle of almost all learned Arabic medical discourses (see Pormann and Savage-Smith, *Medieval Islamic Medicine*, 41–79, esp. 43–5; Conrad, 'The Arab-Islamic Medical Tradition', 93–138, esp. 99–104). By no means limited to medical contexts, the theory permeated virtually all branches of intellectual life and, as the texts in this anthology illustrate, literary culture. It figures conspicuously in the *Sirr al-asrār* (for example, 76–92 and *passim*), and in the *Qābūsnāmeh*, where it directly informs Kaykāʾūs's thirty-third chapter dedicated to

the spirit's corruption: the limbs will weaken and collapse, the body's good order will become damaged, and it will pass towards decay and perdition.[143]

In another analogy, the *sulṭān* resembles fire and the people resemble wood. As long as the wood is straight, it does not require fire; if, however, the wood is crooked, it needs fire to straighten its crookedness and to rectify its curvature. If the fire is excessive, the wood will burn up before its crookedness can be corrected; if the fire is insufficient, the wood will remain impervious to straightening, and it will remain crooked. Only if the fire is properly modulated will the wood become straight. The states of the *sulṭān*'s power resemble the states of the fire: if in his exercise of power the ruler is excessive, he will cause the people to perish; if his power is deficient, they will not become straight; if his exercise of power is balanced, the people too will perdure in equilibrium.

In another similitude, the ruler is like a gushing spring in the midst of dry ground. If the spring's water is fit to drink, its taste agreeable and its properties free of contamination and decay, it will animate the earth, which will absorb its purity and itself become purified. In this way the roots of the trees will consume it and find nourishment in it. Their trunks will grow sturdy, their branches will ramify and their twigs will spread. They will produce leaves, bring forth flowers and drop their fruits, which will display the perfect forms of their nature in size, taste, colour and smell. God's servants (human beings) will find nourishment in them, the animals and insects will eat their share of them, birds will alight upon them, and each of these creatures will obtain his sustenance from them. Order will be maintained. If in the peripheral areas of the earth there is anywhere too constrained to produce vegetation or to yield a profit, anywhere that furnishes little *zakāt* and little revenue of any kind, or anywhere scarcely fit to sustain trees that in any case provide virtually no income, the spring will give of itself; it will bring assistance to the full extent of its capacity and leave no possible channel untried.

If, however, the spring contains pollution, decay or salination, the trees will absorb its water in that condition. Their natures will lose their equilibrium; the corrupt part will harm the good, their trunks will

medicine (175–84, esp. 175–7 = Levy, *Mirror for Princes*, 166–75, esp. 166–7), and also shapes the comprehensive conceptual system laid out in his forty-fourth and final chapter, dedicated to *javānmardī* (244–6 = Levy, *Mirror for Princes*, 240–5).

143 The analogy evokes a passage cited in Text 1; see above, at n. 12.

separate, their branches will weaken, their leaves will turn, their flowers and fruits will become meagre. Corruption will settle into all these parts. The trees' yield will decrease to a negligible amount, their fruits will taste unpleasant, and their colour will be dull. This deficiency will spread among all the animals, just as in the former case the fruit's beneficial properties reached them. On this matter, the Prophet, God's peace be upon him, said: 'The insects will die in their holes, wasting away because of the sins of the Sons of Adam.' That means, if humankind's acts of disobedience multiply in the earth, the sky will hold back its rain, the earth will restrict its vegetation, and reptiles, insects and beasts of burden will perish.

6

The King's Person and Character

It is a common feature of the mirror literature that power and sovereignty are identified with the king's person. The king's conduct established a model, which his subjects would follow; as a result, the ruler's actions and behaviour, for better or worse, determined the nature of the polity.[1] His righteous conduct would curb abuses on the part of his officials, whereas corruption in the ruler would lead to corruption among his subjects, a condition which would inevitably result, sooner or later, in his defeat or overthrow. That the ruler should cultivate virtue was, therefore, a pragmatic as well as a moral imperative. The mirror-writers insist on the importance of self-discipline as a prerequisite for governance: if the king is unable to govern himself, by controlling his immediate impulses and acting only after reasoned reflection, he will be unable to govern anyone else. The idea that until he has demonstrated mastery of himself the king is both unfit and incapable of governing other people is an ancient one, common also in the Byzantine and Carolingian mirror literatures.[2] The injunction to pursue moral excellence applies to all human beings, but specific qualities are especially necessary in individuals who occupy specific social positions; for kings in particular, certain virtues are conspicuously

[1] For examples of this idea in the Carolingian mirror literature, see Falkowski, 'The Carolingian *Speculum Principis*'; Eberhardt, *Via regia*, 444–8, 606–7; and in the seventeenth-century German mirror literature, Müller, 'Die deutschen Fürstenspiegel des 17. Jahrhunderts', 576–7.

[2] See 'Letter of Themistius', 36; cf. Dvornik, *Early Christian and Byzantine Political Philosophy*, II: 540, 543, 668, 713, cited in Crone, *Medieval Islamic Political Thought*, 161, n. 80; for Carolingian examples, see Stone, 'Kings are Different', esp. 76, 81–2; Nelson, 'Kingship and Empire in the Carolingian World', esp. 60; see also Hellerstedt, 'Cracks in the Mirror'.

essential.[3] Although the mirror-writers vary in their presentations of the necessary royal qualities, they emphasise reason, intellect, wisdom, justice, generosity, courage, vigilance, forbearance, patience and clemency. Some authors, such as Yūsuf Khāṣṣ Ḥājib, insist on the quality of royal or noble birth. Some mirror-writers situate their moral instruction in a philosophical presentation of human nature; the king, in this portrayal, is a human being, no different from the subjects over whom he rules; like them, he possesses the potential to develop virtues, some of which are innate or instinctive and some of which must be acquired through discipline and determined practice. Several strands of discourse – scriptural, philosophical, ethical – contributed to the shaping of these discussions.[4] Yet the singular responsibilities of the royal office render the king's duty to develop virtues and suppress vices more urgent than the general human imperative to pursue moral improvement.

The three extracts in this chapter describe the virtuous and effective king. They treat the ethical and philosophical problems of human nature, virtues and vices, how to strengthen, acquire and practise the former and how to overcome and eradicate the latter. They evoke overlapping but also contrasting conceptual frameworks for these problems.

Text 6
Yūsuf Khāṣṣ Ḥājib, *Kutadgu bilig*. The Qualifications of a Prince[5]

Introduction

In contrast to the other mirrors discussed in this volume, *Kutadgu bilig* (written in Kashghar in 462/1069–70) is composed in verse.

[3] Cf. Vasalou, *Virtues of Greatness*, 68.

[4] Notable contributions to the formation of the Arabic discipline of moral philosophy, *'ilm al-akhlāq*, include Plato's *Republic* and Aristotle's *Nicomachean Ethics*, the contents of which were well known among philosophers writing in Arabic from the ninth century. The earliest ethical treatises in Arabic, such as the *Tahdhīb al-akhlāq* of Miskawayh (d. 421/1030), address the cultivation of virtue in the individual; later philosophers, notably Fakhr al-Dīn al-Rāzī (543–606/1149–1209) (*Jāmi' al-'ulūm*, chapters 55, 56, 57, pp. 458–75) and Naṣīr al-Dīn Ṭūsī (597–672/1201–74), added treatments of household management and governance, to make up the three branches of practical philosophy (*al-ḥikma al-'amaliyya*) of ethics, politics and economics (see further Vasalou, *Virtues of Greatness*; and above, Chapter 1).

[5] From Robert Dankoff, *Wisdom of Royal Glory (Kutadgu bilig)* (Chicago: Chicago University Press, 1983), 103–11, ll. 1921–2180. Republished with permission of the

Furthermore, unique among the mirrors represented here, the poem's central text constitutes an allegory, in which qualities, principles, functions and occupations appear in personified forms. The extract offered in Text 6 consists of a dialogue, a session of instruction, between the king Rising Sun (a personification of justice) and the sage Highly Praised (a personification of intellect or wisdom). Although adduced anonymously, the quatrains and verses that appear are almost certainly Yūsuf's own compositions.[6] Affirming the principle of the divine mandate, the section offers a description of the qualifications and qualities necessary for the royal office. Yūsuf emphasises a combination of, on the one hand, innate and hereditary qualities and, on the other hand, virtues that the prince should cultivate through training, discipline and will. He draws a sharp distinction between the military and the common people, the latter comprising the productive groups who generate the revenue on which the ruler depends to maintain his army. This binary, in keeping with the model of governance articulated in the ubiquitous 'circle of justice', underlies Yūsuf's treatment of kingship.[7] The king's relationships with the two sections of the population are different, his need for the former immediate and direct, his need for the latter indirect but fundamental.[8] The two constituencies are interrelated in their relevance to royal power, and it is the ruler's responsibility, also the necessary underpinning of his rule, to acknowledge the respective claims of each.

Translation

The Qualifications of a Prince

The king said:

> "Now this is what I had to ask. God created mankind, some great, some small, some with a bad name, some a good; there are wise and foolish, poor and rich, intelligent and ignorant, wicked and virtuous.

University of Chicago Press from Robert Dankoff, *Wisdom of Royal Glory (Kutadgu bilig)*, © 1983 by The University of Chicago; permission conveyed through Copyright Clearance Center, Inc. The section corresponds to chapter XXVIII in Arat's edition, *Kutadgu Bilig*, I: 210–33. The footnotes that appear in Text 6 are the present author's additions.

6 Dankoff, *Wisdom of Royal Glory*, 10. In contrast, Kaykāʾūs, who also incorporates his own verses, in many instances explicitly identifies himself as their author (see below, Text 8).

7 See further below, Text 9.

8 See Chapter 1, n. 6, and section 2.1, n. 10.

"Of what sort should be the prince, who is at the head of all these? How should he conduct his affairs so that his realm will prosper, his people grow rich, and his name be glorified when he passes on; so that he will lay up treasure of silver and precious stuffs; that he may crush the neck of the foe, and remove civil strife; so that he can muster troops effectively, and dispense justice equitably; so that his name will spread abroad, and his Glory [*ḳut*] daily increase; that he may live contented and enjoy a long reign, and, when his life is cut off, enjoy the next world too?"

Highly Praised replied:

"This is a difficult question indeed. Only princes know what it is to be a prince. Law and custom and protocol derive from them. They are born for princely rule, and they study how to do it well. When God gives someone princely rule He gives him the mind and heart corresponding to the task. When God wishes to create a prince, He first gives him the proper character and mentality, wing and feather both. Rule is the business of princes, and only royal persons know how to perform it. The king knows this business better than I: his father was a prince, and so is he."

The king said:

"Your words are true, and fragrant as musk. Still, the man who performs a task simply performs it, while one who observes knows its virtues and defects. I am the performer, you the observer; and the performer can learn something from the observer. Now God has given you a good mind, and you have grown intelligent and sage. Also you have served me since you were very young, and have learned by observation what good government is. You understand the essence of every matter. And you have been loyal to me, both in word and deed. A man can ask advice of one who is loyal to him, for the loyal one will ransom his soul for that man. I can trust in your answer because of your loyalty. Speak then out of your loyalty, for loyalty is the head of humanity; as the poet says:

> Praise the man who is true to you,
> Keep him close to your heart;
> If you find a loyal man,
> Never let him part."

Highly Praised answered:

"May the king live long in health and power!

"The first requirement for being a prince is noble birth; (then he will be) a marksman brave, hardy and strong, with a solid heart. If the father is a prince, then the son is born a prince, just like his father before him.

"Then he must be intelligent and wise, generous and virtuous. With wisdom the prince must rule the people, and with intellect govern the realm. In fact the words for 'wisdom' (*bilig*) and 'prince' (*beg*) are connected: take away the *l* from *bilig* and this leaves *beg*. He needs to have a good mind because he will have many foes. A sage experienced in this regard has said:

Wise and wakeful a prince must be
To ward off all calamity;
Of myriad virtues, of vices few,
To hold his name and keep his hue.

"All of Adam's sons are of noble parentage, but the choicest of all are the wise. One who comes from good seed will be wellborn, and so will rise to the place of honor. Favored of heaven is princely rule: it wants purity and along with purity it wants vigilance in the realm. The choicest of the people must be a marksman, brave; he must be bold to deal with mighty matters. Hear the mature words spoken by the Prince of Ötüken on this subject: The prince of the people must be the choicest among them, his heart and tongue upright, his character outstanding; wise and generous, with full eye and heart; his heart extended toward every good; modest, graceful, and even tempered. Such a one is fit to be prince, and from him will come good seed in turn.[9]

"A man must undertake a task with wisdom, and apply intellect as well, if that task is to succeed. It is only by means of wisdom that princes keep the people in check. Where wisdom is lacking, their minds are unsuited to the task. When a prince errs, O glorious king, his rule becomes sick and requires treatment. But the only medicine is knowledge and wisdom. So use intellect to treat the sickness, O virtuous one! Only a prince who is intelligent and sage can cure this illness. Such a ruler has a good place in both the worlds. And the person who gains both worlds is the very epitome of Fortune. As the poet says:

The man endowed with brains will have
The Luck of both worlds as his share;

[9] Dankoff suggests Ötüken is perhaps the Tannu-Ola mountain range: *Wisdom of Royal Glory*, 9. He notes that Yūsuf Khāṣṣ Ḥājib's appeals to authority are invariably drawn from the Turkish Inner Asian background. The Beg of Ötüken appears again at p. 128, l. 2682, where the figure is credited with the composition of a testament.

He'll live a happy life down here
And have a place of honor There.

"The prince must be straight-dealing and upright; then his day will pass in joy. When God gives a man good character and good conduct, the world pours its favors upon him. He can enjoy them himself, or share them with others. It is God who favors His slave with Fortune so that his character is good and his conduct sound. Thus endowed, with virtues by the thousand, he disperses the fog and grasps the realm. What a fine thing is good character: it is a man's food and dress. But when God gives a man an unruly character, then Time's arrow harasses him. And if a prince is so endowed, then all his actions are contrary, and his joy turns to care.

"The prince must be God-fearing and devout. The one of pure seed must needs practice purity. The pious man has a fearful heart, and the prince with a fearful heart governs equitably, while if the prince is not pious and pure his deeds are all unclean and uneven.

"A quiet temper is the prince's ornament. Calm dignity is the tether by which his rule is bound.

"The prince requires a good mind if he is to undertake affairs and bring them to a successful end. But mindless men must be kept away from affairs of state. Just as the eye is useless without the heart, so the heart is helpless without the mind. Hear the words of one whose heart is tried and true:

While a man possesses intellect
Let praise for him endure;
What seems bad in him is good,
What seems unripe, mature.

"What a fine thing a good mind is. The man with a good mind (*ög*) is rightly called 'Counselor' (*öge*).

"Know that haste is evil in anyone; and when it appears in a prince, his face turns grey with shame. Rashness and quick temper are sure signs of folly. Things done in haste are undercooked; food and drink consumed in haste cause sickness. Prefer to be slow and steady in every action. The only exception is serving God: for that you may rush!

"He should be full-eyed, modest, and forbearing, also open and frank in word and deed. A greedy-eyed man is insatiable: the food of this world is not enough for him. Greed is a sickness for which there is no remedy; the diviner of this world cannot cure it. When a hungry man eats and drinks, he is satisfied; but the greedy man stops being hungry only when he dies. The greedy-eyed person never gets rich: he is still greedy and needy, though he has gained the entire world.

"The prince should also be modest, for a modest character never wanes, but is full. When a man has modesty and purity, his hand never reaches out for what is improper. To whomever God gives modesty and water-of-eye (tears), He also gives Fortune and water-of-face (honor). It is modesty that holds one back from all that is improper, and joins one to all that is good. What a fine thing is modesty, an adornment to a man! It is the tether which binds him to all good things.

"He should have a truthful tongue and an honest heart, if he is to be beneficial to the people, and his sun of good fortune is to rise. There is no hope for the prince who has a treacherous heart, and no benefit from him for the people. If he is not straightforward in his heart, his tongue, and his deeds, then Fortune has no way to him and will flee that realm. Despair for a prince who breaks his word: his life is vanity and regret.

"The prince should be wakeful and alert; if he is negligent, he will suffer the consequences. There are two bonds which hold the state together. One is wakefulness; the other is justice, the root of government. If the prince is wakeful, he keeps guard over his realm and crushes the foe's neck and tramples upon him. And if the prince dispenses justice, he keeps the realm in good order and causes its sun to shine. These are the two bonds of rulership: as long as they are perfect, princely state endures. And a stalwart champion said: With wakefulness the prince defeats his enemy and increases his territory, with neglectfulness the foundation of princely rule is undermined. Be wakeful then, O prince, watch over all your realm, wrench the neck of your foe and deal justly with your subjects. Then you will live in peace.

"There are two things which undermine princely rule, and cause the ruler to stray from the straight path. One is injustice, the other is negligence. With these two the prince may ruin his realm. For if you wish to crush your foe, you must keep your ears and eyes alert. With wakefulness the prince pierces his enemy, with negligence he breaks the bond of rule. The careless prince cannot carry out his affairs or enjoy his rule securely. The careful man is always ready, lying in ambush for the neglectful. And if the enemy were not neglectful, who could defeat him? As long as the prince is wakeful, no hand can touch his realm without being thwarted with wise devices. As for the one who is unjust, he cannot enjoy his rule, nor can the people bear his injustice. A wise man has said that unjust rulers never rule for long. Injustice is a blazing fire which burns whatever it comes near. And justice is water that brings forth blessing wherever it flows. The prince who desires to enjoy a long rule must promote justice and protect his people. With justice the territory will increase and the realm will thrive; with injustice the territory will diminish and the realm will fall to ruin. Many a royal court has been ruined by an unjust ruler, who himself grew weak and died of hunger in the end. As long as a prince keeps a steadfast heart and promotes justice, his rule will not collapse but long stand upright.

"Worst of all, glorious king, is for the prince to get a name for dishonesty. He should be truthful in word and sincere in deed. Then the people will trust in him and share in his Fortune. A dishonest man is treacherous, committing acts unsuited to the people in his charge. Here is how a trusty man has put it:

The man with a lying tongue
Is a treacherous-hearted brute.
'Trust not the liar' – this advice
Is of bitter years the fruit.

"The prince should be brave and bold and steadfast against the foe. As army commander he must be courageous so that cowardly troops take heart from him. For when a brave man commands the cowardly, they all become brave. Witness the following verse:

A dog is leonine
If he gets a lion's head;
Give the dog's head to a lion,
He becomes canine instead.

"The prince should be generous, yet keep a humble heart and quiet demeanor. It is through generosity that the prince acquires a good name, and it is through his name and fame that the world becomes secure. He then attracts troops who crowd about his standard, and with these he attains his goal. Hear how a successful warrior has put it: O brave one! strike, take, and give to your men. Be generous, give gifts, entertain with food and drink. And when you lack, then strike, take, and give again. The valiant man never lacks for wealth. The swooping falcon never lacks for prey. As long as a man has sword and battleaxe, bow and arrow – and a strong heart! – he has nothing to fear.

"What need for a prince to hoard up treasure? Wherever he has ready troops, there treasure is at hand. Troops are needed to maintain the state, and wealth is needed to pay the troops; a prosperous people is needed to attain this wealth, and for the people to be prosperous, you must maintain justice. If any one of these is lacking, all four are left behind; and when this occurs, princely rule disintegrates.[10]

"In order to maintain his good repute, the prince should keep these five things far from him: haste, stinginess, quick temper, an unruly character, and a lying tongue. If he stays far from these his name will not go bad and his command will be effective. Worst of all is an unruly disposition. As the poet says:

The unruly man
Gives himself much woe;
The stubborn man's a captive,
Foe to friend and friend to foe.

"One who would rule over many lands should do these three: with his right hand wield a ready sword; with his left hand give out his gathered goods; and with his tongue speak sugar-sweet. Then prince and slave, great and small alike, will offer him their necks.

"These things, O king, are what a prince requires in order to be loved by the people and raised in their esteem: a smiling face, a sweet tongue, a pure soul, and deeds befitting these; a humble heart and an open hand, and compassion befitting these. Such as he will know every virtue and keep far from every vice. He is the choicest of the people, flawless and complete. The world's people are all his slaves, and their prince attains all his desire of the world.

"But a frowning face, a rough tongue, and a haughty mien: these make him incorrigible and despised. Immodesty, haste, and frivolity: these are the manners of commoners. The prince should keep such manners far from himself, for if they come near he will be sullied. White is the color of nobles, black of commoners and slaves. Distinguish well between these! He who would be a noble prince must hold to noble virtues. He may have the name of 'prince,' but if his character is black, he will be called 'ignoble' among the common people.

"The prince should be handsome and trim, and of middle stature. A fine appearance makes him loved and trusted by the people when they see him. His manliness then will be a hard blow to the enemy; while his beauty will bring tears of love to the eye. As for stature, if he is too tall, wisdom will not praise him, while if too short, he will

[10] A version of the 'circle of justice'; see below, Chapter 7, nn. 2, 13, 58.

not be graceful and refined. It were best for him to be of middle height. An aged and experienced man has said:

The man short of stature
Is short-tempered and mean;
The middling man is moderate
And seeks the mean.

"The prince should not drink or fornicate. Fortune flees from these two activities. While princes of the world enjoy sweet wine, their lands and subjects suffer bitter ills. When the ruler of the world gives himself up to sport, he ruins his land, and turns himself into a beggar. If he dissipates his rule during his reign, then he cannot recover it, though he hunt it down with hawks. Hear what a wise and abstemious man has said on this: Do not drink, for the wine-bibber is a slave to his throat, and by drinking opens the way to poverty. When a commoner drinks, his wealth turns to wind. When the prince drinks, how can the state endure?

"Wine is an enemy, the tavern-keeper a highway-robber, the drinker a brawler. When a man gets drunk he goes mad, and a madman's deeds cannot go right. Hear what a chaste-tongued man has said, and apply his words, you who are slave to your throat! How many a deed that should be done is left undone when wine is drunk. How many a deed that should not be done comes to pass when a man is drunk.

"If a prince indulges in wine and sport, when will he set his mind on the business of state? Fornication spells the ruin of princely rule: wherever it is found, Fortune flees. For Fortune is pure, it seeks out purity and supports the pure. When the prince becomes a drinker, vile and corrupt, then all his subjects follow him to drink. It is up to princes to set aright their subjects' improper acts: if the prince himself does what is improper, who is to guide *him*? Only water can clean out filth; if water itself is filthy, what can make *it* clean? When a person is sick, it is the physician who gives the medicine; but who can treat the physician's sickness? Therefore princes must keep their actions pure and straight, for the prince's way makes straight the way of the people. Whatever customs the prince adopts, the people follow his example. Witness this charming verse:

Whatever way the master walks,
The slave walks with a similar gait;
If the master's way is straight and good,
The slave's is good and straight.

"He should not be haughty and proud-hearted, for pride leads astray from the straight way. Princes become great by virtue of Fortune, and must keep their hearts humble if they are to maintain this lot. A virtuous sage has expressed this as follows: When a prince puffs himself up he is bound to be humbled, my son. Pride has never raised a man to heaven, though humility has kept him from ruin. Pride does not benefit a man, but only makes his heart cold; while a humble heart in fact raises a man's estate. Despair then of the prince who is haughty and proud. While the prince's heart should be lowly, it should also be open, and ready to forgive those who have sinned. Then his troops will love him, and his followers will be loyal and obedient.

"The prince requires both moral purpose and fitting manliness. Thus he will get a good name, gain his desire, and be successful in the hunt. A man who lacks moral purpose is as good as dead: his lot in either world is lost. Along with moral purpose the prince needs authority as well as the quality of leadership necessary to enforce it. For it is by means of authority that he sets his realm in order, and puts aright the actions of his subjects. Witness this verse which proves the point:

> Authority is an adornment
> Of the governor's gate;
> With it he cleanses civil strife
> And sets his province straight.

"The cement of the state, that which holds its foundation firm, consists of two fundamental things. One is justice, which is the share of all the subjects; the other is silver, which is the share of the military. With justice the subjects will live happily, and with silver the military will obey cheerfully. As long as these two classes are happy with their prince, he will be content, and his realm and court will prosper. When the prince stops administering justice and no longer guarantees his subjects security, then he has set a fire among them, and has undermined the foundation of his rule. And when the prince no longer inspires the love of his troops, from that moment on the sword stays in the scabbard. A prince maintains his power only by the sword; without the sword he cannot keep down his own realm. Sword and battleaxe are guardians of the land. It is by the sword that a ruler gains control of his land in the first place. Hear the words of this warlike emperor: A careless eater can eat poison, so take care, O noble one, and keep sword and battleaxe your guardians. The prince with a sword as guardian will enjoy contentment. While he brandishes the sword, the enemy will not move; but when the sword stays in the scabbard, his contentment will vanish. Therefore, O prince, keep happy the one who wields your sword. Then you shall ever live happy and carefree."

Highly Praised continued:

"O glorious king! The business of state is great and difficult. It is a weighty thing to rule, full of hardship and headache. There is little joy in it, and much care. Few are those who praise it, and many who curse. Wherever you look, there is fear; and if you look for happiness from it, there is little to be found. Few are its lovers, many those who despise it; for there is too much strife in it, and too little pleasure. Everywhere it inspires lack of confidence, and where there is no confidence, there is distress. Everything it undertakes is full of risk, and when there is risk in a thing, the taste goes out of it. Listen to these words of wisdom, strung like pearls:

> The king's head is like a tower,
> His neck is like a thread,
> His rule is risky, like a sword
> Suspended over his head.

"This is the way of princely rule. Some find satisfaction in it, others disillusionment. If you wish to enjoy both this world and the next, then pay attention to these things: Keep heart and tongue upright. Take refuge in God and obey His command. Be satisfied with whatever comes from the Lord, for servitude to Him is the basis of contentment. Have compassion for all creatures. Always do what is right and what benefits the people, and put down what is wrong and what does them harm. Then this world is yours, you may eat and sleep without anxiety as long as you live; and when your life is cut off, you may be of good hope that God will requite your goodness with a good road.

"The virtues that pertain to princes are these, as I have explained to the king. Any man who possesses these virtues deserves the name of 'prince' and a high position in the state. The perfect prince is the head of his people, and from him every virtue is expected. A clever man summed it up this way: The prince should be intelligent, wise, and just; also cunning and courageous to gain good repute. He must be generous and forbearing, modest and pure; kindly and protective, full-eyed, patient, and humble; sparing and forgiving, and quiet-mannered. He must be a paragon of virtue among men, and deal justly with the people. Whatever realm has a prince such as this, its people's ills are gone, for Fortune's sun has risen on that land. Alas that men such as this must die!

"This that I have offered you, O king, is the extent of what I know."

The king said:

"You have spoken well and true."

Text 7
Al-Māwardī, *Tashīl al-naẓar wa-taʿjīl al-ẓafar*. Part I, Chapter One[11]

Translator's Introduction

This section comprises the first chapter in part I of *Tashīl al-naẓar*; it follows al-Māwardī's preface. This opening chapter, in which al-Māwardī sets forth a theory of virtue and its acquisition, provides an important conceptual underpinning to part II of *Tashīl al-naẓar*, which deals with the principles and practices of good governance (see above, Text 3, and Texts 10 and 13, below). Al-Māwardī begins his exposition with the moral formation of the ruler. He asserts that while our characters and dispositions are innate, our actions are matters of choice. He deals with both of these aspects of the human psyche: essential moral characteristics (*akhlāq*) grounded in nature, and actions driven by human volition.[12] He proceeds to make the striking point that moral characteristics are the principal instruments of the ruler's

[11] Translation prepared from al-Māwardī, *Tashīl al-naẓar wa-taʿjīl al-ẓafar*, ed. Riḍwān al-Sayyid (Beirut: Dār al-ʿUlūm al-ʿArabiyya, 1987), 101–16. For the corresponding section in Abbès's translation into French, see Makram Abbès, *Al-Māwardī. De l'Éthique du prince et du gouvernement de l'état* (Paris: Les Belles Lettres, 2015), 245–57.

[12] The emphasis in al-Māwardī's ethical thought on the ability of human beings to choose their actions and shape their destinies, in contradistinction to a predestinarian focus, provides an example of al-Māwardī's frequent endorsement of Muʿtazilī points of view. Whether al-Māwardī's rationalist orientation, which emerges strongly in his ethical writings, implies an alignment with the Muʿtazilī movement is less clear, although al-Māwardī's relationship to Muʿtazilism has been a matter of speculation since the

authority (*imra*) and power (*sulṭān*). Incorporating and synthesising several philosophical concepts, al-Māwardī introduces the ideas, central in ethical theory, of scale and balance, with the human virtues situated at the point of equipoise between countervailing poles. His fluency in the philosophical tradition permits him to move readily from rational ethical theory to its practical application in governance. In this respect, al-Māwardī's reasoning coincides with the exposition of the philosopher al-Fārābī (d. 339/950), whose treatment of ethics similarly precedes his discussion of politics.[13] The text presented in Text 7 differs from most of the previous selections in its rationally and logically based framework of argument and presentation. It resembles the distinct ethical discourse of the science of *akhlāq*, which, as noted in Chapter 1, is, especially for the later periods, often contrasted with the mirror literature. It was not unusual, however, for mirror-writers to avail themselves of the *akhlāq* tradition, and to draw on a great variety of concepts and materials, as the polymath al-Māwardī demonstrates in his discussion of human nature and its potential.

Translation

Moral characteristics (*akhlāq*) are hidden instincts that manifest themselves in the course of experience and can be overridden only by force. The soul's (*nafs*) moral characteristics arise from its nature, and its actions issue from it by will. The soul cannot be separated from these two things: essential moral characteristics, and wilful actions.[14]

medieval period (Yāqūt, *Mu'jam al-udabā'*, V: 1955, no. 822; al-Subkī, *Ṭabaqāt al-Shāfi'iyya al-kubrā*, III: 304–5; al-Dhahabī, *Siyar a'lām al-nubalā'*, XVIII: 67, no. 29; see further Schneider, 'Vernunft oder Tradition?'; Mikhail, *Politics and Revelation*, xxxi, 11, 17; Melchert, 'Māwardī, Abū Ya'lá, and the Sunni Revival', 46; Cook, *Commanding Right and Forbidding Wrong*, 344, n. 401).

[13] See, for example, al-Fārābī's *Mabādi' ārā' ahl al-madīna al-fāḍila* (Walzer, *Al-Farabi on the Perfect State*).

[14] Riḍwān al-Sayyid notes the importance in this discourse of Galen's thought (*Tashīl al-naẓar*, 101, n. 1; cf. Kraus, *Kitāb al-Akhlāq li-Jālīnūs*, 25–55). Important well beyond the circles of medical practitioners, Galen was 'present in the minds of the whole erudite class of Muslim society as a natural scientist of paradigmatic stature' (Strohmaier, 'Uses of Galen in Arabic Literature', 114), a point illustrated well in the writings of al-Māwardī, who invokes Galen explicitly later in the current text (see below, at n. 29). Cf. Miskawayh, *Tahdhīb al-akhlāq*, 31–73 (Second Discourse) = Zurayk, *Refinement of Character*, 29–31.

Essential moral characteristics are the results of our innate natures (*fiṭra*).[15] They are called 'moral characteristics' (*akhlāq*) because, like our physical beings (*khilqa*), they assume forms.

The human being is imprinted by nature with moral characteristics that are rarely entirely praiseworthy or entirely blameworthy; in most cases, some of our characteristics are praiseworthy and others blameworthy, the difference lying in the mixture of instincts and resistance to anything that conflicts with its natural tendencies. It is therefore impossible for a person, by nature and by instinct, to be perfect in his moral characteristics in terms of the virtues; the vices necessarily, by nature and instinct, mingle with them. In our natural temperaments and innate dispositions, then, our moral characteristics combine praiseworthy virtues and blameworthy vices, which cannot be detached from one another.[16] As the poet said:

> These moral characteristics are nothing but products of nature:
> Among them are the praiseworthy and the blameworthy.[17]

A philosopher said:

> For every virtuous characteristic there is a base one keeping watch; only the person who makes a priority of moral excellence over everything else can avoid this [liability].

Since these moral characteristics are settled on this foundation, it follows that the excellent person is he whose virtues prevail over his vices, who by the abundance of his virtues is capable of overcoming his vices, and who is therefore free of disgrace and fortunate in the virtue of distinction. For this reason, ʿAlī, upon him be peace, said:

> The place to start in your *jihād* is with the *jihād* of your souls.[18]

This is clear; for the well-being (*ṣalāḥ*) of the soul puts everything else to rights as well. It is therefore most fitting to give this process of correction precedence and priority.

[15] The term *fiṭra* is Qurʾanic (see Q 30: 30); see further Hoover, 'Fiṭra'.

[16] Cf. al-Māwardī, *Adab al-dunyā wa-l-dīn*, 226.

[17] See also al-Rāghib al-Iṣfahānī, *al-Dharīʿa ilā makārim al-sharīʿa*, 50, where the couplet appears as the second line in a verse cited without attribution.

[18] Ibn Abī l-Ḥadīd, *Sharḥ Nahj al-balāgha*, X: 395 = part 20, no. 49 (*al-ḥikam wa-l-mawāʿiẓ*). On the greater challenge and superiority of the internal *jihād*, specified as the controlling of passion and anger, to the external kind, see the Prophetic report recorded in al-ʿAjlūnī, *Kashf al-khafāʾ*, I: 375, no. 1360; see also al-Thaʿālibī, *al-Tamthīl wa-l-muḥāḍara*, 262 (Ibn al-Muʿtazz); Fakhr al-Dīn al-Rāzī, *Jāmiʿ al-ʿulūm*, 488.

There is a difference of opinion concerning the roots of moral characteristics: are they to be traced back to virtues and vices, or to the soul – from which virtues and vices arise in order to appear in our moral characteristics? Some have proposed that moral characteristics revert to an [essence] from which the individual soul originates.[19]

Opinions also differ over the essential virtues: are they to be desired in themselves, for their own sake, or for the happiness that originates from them? Some philosophers have taken the view that it is the virtues themselves that constitute the desired purpose, since they produce happiness. Other philosophers have regarded the object of desire as the happiness that the virtues produce, because it is happiness that constitutes the virtues' goal and objective.

There is also a difference of opinion regarding happiness. Does it lie in the praiseworthy virtues themselves? Or in the praise that these virtues generate? Some philosophers take the position that happiness lies in the praiseworthy virtues, since it is the result of a person's actions. Others claim that happiness lies in the praise that the virtues generate, because it is the fruit of a person's virtues.

It is therefore fitting for a person invested with authority and power (*dhū l-imra wa-l-sulṭān*) to attend to the cultivation of his moral characteristics and the correction of his faults. His moral characteristics are the instrument of his power and the foundation of his authority (*ālat sulṭānihi wa-uss imratihi*). It is not possible for the ruler to rectify all his moral characteristics merely by submitting to his natural disposition and acquiescing to the promptings of his innate instinct. Instead, he must practise virtue, and rectify and discipline his moral characteristics; he should pursue this process of self-reformation and self-education in stages, until he has rectified his moral characteristics altogether. Some of his characteristics represent innate dispositions; others are manufactured dispositions, for an (innate) characteristic (*khuluq*) stems from nature and instinct, and an (acquired)

[19] As Abbès points out, al-Māwardī refers in this passage to the disagreement between Plato and Aristotle regarding the virtues; al-Māwardī, with Aristotle, rejects the notion that the virtues and vices exist independently outside the human soul (Abbès, *De l'Éthique du prince*, 247, n. 4; see further Aristotle, *Nicomachean Ethics*, Book I: 4 (pp. 5–6)).

characteristic (*takhalluq*) arises from naturalisation (*taṭabbuʿ*) and exertion.[20] As the poet said:

O you who seek the adornment of characteristics that you do not possess, and
whose natural disposition is towards exaggeration and adulation:
You must devote your full attention to the actions that you perform, for
behind acquired characteristics lies natural character.[21]

A philosopher said:

> There is nothing that, even if it is harmful, does not become beneficial when it receives proper attention; and nothing that, even if it is beneficial, does not become harmful when neglected.

Characteristics are of two kinds: they are either instinctive and determined by nature, or they are acquired and established through naturalisation (*taṭabbaʿa lahā*). Kings are distinguished by their instinctive virtues to a greater degree than the common people, because in kings, their instinctive virtues are both more abundant and more apparent, since they are distinguished by their noble origins and their high aspirations.[22] The common people, meanwhile, are distinguished to a greater degree than kings by their acquired virtues, since they are quicker to seek them and more tolerant of weariness; moreover, their general inactivity permits them to devote great attention to their pursuit – whether out of desire for the advantages that the virtues bring, or out of fear of the hostility that might arise from (not having) them. For kings, these two factors do not apply, except in the case of a ruler whose soul is noble and who inclines towards the

[20] On the acquisition of virtue, cf. *Nicomachean Ethics*, Book II, 1–4 (pp. 23–8). The distinction between the innate and the acquired underlies much of al-Māwardī's ethical thought; elsewhere, he distinguishes between two parts or types of reason (*ʿaql*), namely, *gharīzī*, instinctive, and *muktasab*, acquired (*Adab al-dunyā wa-l-dīn*, 20–3).

[21] Variously attributed; attributions to Sālim Ibn Wābiṣa (al-Asadī) appear in al-Jāḥiẓ, *al-Bayān wa-l-tabyīn*, I: 233, and al-Mubarrad, *al-Kāmil*, I: 17, n. 8 (but at p. 18, the first hemistich of the first line appears with the second hemistich of the second line, related from Abū Zayd [al-Anṣārī]); attributions to ʿAbdallāh b. ʿUmar al-ʿArjī appear in al-Jāḥiẓ, *al-Ḥayawān*, III: 128; Ibn Qutayba, *al-Shiʿr wa-l-shuʿarāʾ*, 575; and al-Ḥuṣrī, *Zahr al-ādāb*, I: 84 (with slightly different wording).

[22] The virtue of high aspiration, *ʿiẓam al-himma*, also *buʿd al-himma*, *ʿuluww al-himma*, is a recurrent feature of the discourse relating to royal virtue, and indeed to human virtue altogether; see Vasalou, *Virtues of Greatness*, 4–5, 23, esp. 84–130. Vasalou translates the virtue as 'greatness of spirit', distinguished from 'greatness of soul' (*kibar al-nafs*) (4–5, 22–23, 84); for her discussion of the virtue's prominence in the mirrors of Pseudo-Māwardī, al-Māwardī and Ghazālī, see 86–97.

virtues out of the elevated nature of his aspirations, and who dedicates himself to them out of the nobility of his nature; such a ruler is not without acquired excellence, and no stranger to acclaimed action. He is, in fact, singular in his attainment of virtues of the soul, just as he is singular in his possession of vast power and firm command. Through his cultivation of the virtues, he gains greater experience in the exercise of his power, and he becomes more capable in his governance over his subjects. Praise is merited in the case of acquired virtues, since they are gained through action; it is not merited in the case of innate virtues – even though these virtues themselves receive praise – owing to their existence without any action on the part of the individual.

There is also a difference of opinion about the better of the two types of characteristic in terms of their essence. Some philosophers give preference to characteristics that are innate and instinctual over characteristics that are naturalised and acquired, on account of the strength of the instinctive and the weakness of the acquired. Others favour characteristics that are naturalised and acquired over characteristics that are innate and instinctive, because they have triumphed over adversity and transmuted opposing characteristics. Yet others have said: each of the two stands in need of the other, since characteristics cannot be separated from one another. They resemble the situation of the soul and the body: just as the deeds of the soul only become apparent by means of the body, and the body does not stir other than by the movement of the soul, so the instinctive and the acquired come face to face in action, and participate jointly in the formation of excellence. Accordingly, the two kinds of characteristic are equal in nature and instinct. As the poet al-Buḥturī (d. 284/897) said:

> I do not deem a young man meritorious
> Unless his merit is visible in his actions.[23]

A certain lexicographer has developed a linguistic distinction between the two kinds of characteristic: he has described nature as the seal, and naturalisation as character.[24]

[23] Abū ʿUbayda al-Buḥturī (206–84/821–97), famous poet of the Abbasid period. For the poem from which these lines are taken, see his *Dīwān*, I: 279 (line 23). The term *ḥasab* refers particularly to an acquired form of merit; it is often paired with *nasab*, which denotes inherited merit (this second term appears later in the poem).

[24] The metaphor draws an analogy between acquired characteristics and the impression made by the seal. See the discussion in Abbès, *De l'Éthique du prince*, 249–50, n. 11.

Section

Virtues rest on principles, which may be anterior or posterior. The first of the virtues is reason, and the last is justice. Reason is the first of the virtues because the other virtues arise from it and are governed by it; it is therefore the first of them. Justice, by contrast, is the result of the virtues: because the other virtues are measured by it, it is the last of them. These two virtues are well-attuned companions; no two things persist in harmony without one being in full need of the other. All the other virtues are intermediaries between reason and justice, reason being distinguished by its control of them, and justice being distinguished by its estimation of them. Reason, then, is a manager; justice is an assessor. The remaining virtues cannot be detached from either one of these two. Nor can the soul be detached from either one of them; rather, it encompasses them both. If the soul is pure, clear and readily disposed for the virtues, then it will act in accordance with them. If, on the other hand, the soul is base and disposed towards the vices, then it will deviate towards them. Whichever of these two – virtue or vice – corresponds to the soul, it will come easily to it; because of its affinity with it, it will assimilate it quickly. Likewise, whatever is contrary to the soul's disposition comes only with difficulty; on account of its incompatibility, the soul will require a long time to assimilate it. This correspondence of forms is rooted in the natural. As it has been said:

> Love is a natural formation in personal types that find affinities with one another, in ways that can be known and in ways that cannot be known.[25]

A philosopher said:

> The foundations of virtuous characteristics are four, from which all other virtues branch off. These four foundations are discrimination, courage, temperance and justice.[26]

[25] *Nicomachean Ethics* VIII, 1 (15–20) (pp. 142–3).

[26] This theory, rooted in Plato's theory of the soul's three faculties and the characteristics that issue from them (also a feature of Byzantine mirrors; see the 'Letter of Themistius', 21–4; Dvornik, *Early Christian and Byzantine Political Philosophy*, II: 668), permeated learned discourse far beyond the circles of philosophers; see, for example, *Kalīla wa-Dimna*, in *Āthār Ibn al-Muqaffaʿ*, 44; Miskawayh, *Tahdhīb al-akhlāq*, 15–18 = *Refinement of Character*, 14–17; al-Rāghib al-Iṣfahānī, *al-Dharīʿa ilā makārim al-sharīʿa*, 72–5. These four cardinal virtues are sometimes designated 'moral' or 'ethical' (*khulqiyya*) virtues, distinguished from a second set of intellectual or rational virtues. In a classical formulation of this theory, al-Fārābī lists in the former category the virtues of temperance, courage, generosity and justice, and in the latter category, which he terms

The remaining vices branch off from the opposites of these four virtues. The vices too have foundations that are their beginnings and ends that are their points of termination. The first of the vices is foolishness (*ḥumq*), and the last of them is ignorance (*jahl*). There are two points to be made about the difference between them. Firstly, the foolish person imagines the impossible in the form of the possible, while the ignorant person does not know the impossible from the possible. Secondly, the foolish person knows what is correct but does not act accordingly, while the ignorant person does not know what is correct; were he to know it, however, he would act in accordance with it. It is transmitted from the Prophet, God's peace be upon him, that he said:

> The foolish person is the most loathsome of God's creatures in His sight, since He has forbidden to him the things dearest to him.[27]

The Arabs say:

> The epithet *aḥmaq* (fool) derives from the phrase 'the market is void' (*ḥamuqat al-sūq*) when its supplies have become deficient, as if it were a reference to the loss of the foolish person's reason.[28]

The ignorant person has two states. The first state is that he is ignorant, and he knows that he is ignorant. This state permits the possibility that, if supported by a strong incentive and an accepting soul, he might be amenable to guidance, and might thereby come to know that of which he is ignorant. As it has been said: were it not for error, the light of the correct would never dawn. And the poet said:

> When a man's senses are sound, his analogical reasoning is sound.
> The intellect of the person whose senses are corrupt is not sound.

nuṭqiyya, the virtues of wisdom, intellect, astuteness, cleverness and sound understanding (*Fuṣūl al-madanī*, 108 (text) = 31 (translation) (§7)). Ibn Abī Dharr lists in the former category the virtues of purity, temperance and courage, and he includes in the latter category, for which he employs the term *naẓariyya*, the virtues of knowledge, intellect and wisdom (*al-Saʿāda wa-l-isʿād*, 70).

[27] Al-Māwardī, *al-Amthāl wa-l-ḥikam*, 90, no. 227/646; al-Māwardī, *Adab al-dunyā wa-l-dīn*, 30.

[28] Cf. al-Ibshīhī, *al-Mustaṭraf*, I: 40 (from the philologist Muḥammad b. Ziyād Ibn al-Aʿrābī (150–231/767–846)).

The second state is that he is ignorant, and ignorant of his ignorance. This is the worse of the two states and, as a quality, the uglier of the two, since if this person is ignorant of his ignorance, this state produces two types of ignorance, similar in form but different in their effects: one of them deprives him of guidance, while the other attracts misguidance. As a result, the first induces him to go astray in the pursuit of his intoxications, while the second causes him to rejoice in his faults. In this case, the ignorant person's awakening is not an option, and his recovery is not to be hoped for. Galen said:

> Ignorance of ignorance is ignorance compounded; to be ignorant and know that I was ignorant would be preferable to me than to be ignorant and ignorant of my ignorance.[29]

Solomon, son of David, upon him be peace, said:

> Lamentation over the dead lasts for seven days; but for the ignorant person, it is fitting every day of his life. Death is preferable to a wretched life.[30]

It is reported in the 'Circulating Proverbs':[31]

[29] Al-Sayyid (*Tashīl al-naẓar*, 110, n. 1) notes the affinity of this formulation with a frequently repeated fourfold division of humankind according to knowledge and ignorance; attributed to al-Khalīl b. Aḥmad (al-Farāhidī, d. 160/776, 170/786 or 175/791), this formula appears in Ibn Qutayba, *'Uyūn al-akhbār*, II: 126; al-Māwardī, *Adab al-dunyā wa-l-dīn*, 84; Ibn al-Ḥaddād, *al-Jawhar al-nafīs*, 111.

[30] David and Solomon, in the Islamic tradition prophets as well as kings, are frequently invoked as exemplars of righteous rule; cf. the extensive use of these examples in the Byzantine and Carolingian mirror literature (Hunger, *Die hochsprachliche profane Literatur der Byzantiner*, 159–60; Nelson, 'Kingship and Empire', 214–19; Anton, *Fürstenspiegel und Herrscherethos*, 419–32 and *passim*; Eberhardt, *Via regia*, 225–6, 230–1, 603–5 and *passim*; Hellerstedt, 'Cracks in the Mirror', 303–5).

[31] Al-Māwardī draws frequently on a source to which he refers as *manthūr al-ḥikam*. This term is quite likely to refer to a specific, written collection of maxims, possibly the compilation *al-Farā'id wa-l-qalā'id* of Abū l-Ḥusayn Muḥammad b. al-Ḥusayn al-Ahwāzī (fl. 330/941) (see Abbès, *De l'Éthique du prince*, 254, n. 7). It is also possible, however, that al-Māwardī is referring in a general sense to the repertoire of well-known maxims that circulated among men of learning in various oral and written forms. It is perhaps in this general sense that Ibn Abī Dharr cites 'transmitted maxims' or 'the transmitted speech of the wise philosophers' (*ḥikam manthūra*, *manthūr kalām ahl al-ḥikma* and *al-kalām al-manthūr*, in *al-Sa'āda wa-l-is'ād*, 102, 130, 159). The term *manthūr* might also imply a set of maxims in prose (*nathr*) as opposed to verse (*naẓm*). Al-Ṭurṭūshī employs the same phrase in numerous locations. On the sources and transmission of the vast Arabic repertoire of wise maxims, see Gutas, 'Classical Arabic Wisdom Literature'; 'Abbās, *Malāmiḥ yūnāniyya fī l-adab al-'arabī*, 15–20.

> Even if the days of his life are many in number, the ignorant person is as if he had been born yesterday, his hour of birth barely begun.

An Arab said:

> If reason were to be depicted, the sun would appear darkened next to it, and if ignorance were to be depicted, the night would appear lit up next to it.[32]

A poet said:

> The human being is created for intellect (*lil-ʿaql*), so seek
> Your fortune by intellect, not by ignorance or rank.
> Ignorance reaps for its possessor continual shame
> And causes the joy of merit to depart from him.

Virtues form a praiseworthy mean between two reprehensible vices: in cases of deficiency, they become shortcomings, and in cases of excess, they become exaggerations. The corruption of every virtue lies on the axis that runs in these two directions. Reason is the point of balance between cunning and stupidity; wisdom is the mid-point between malice and ignorance; generosity is the mid-point between avarice and profligacy; courage is the mid-point between cowardice and recklessness. Modesty is the mid-point between shamelessness and shyness; dignity is the mid-point between contempt and folly; tranquillity is the mid-point between rage and insipidity. Forbearance is the point of balance between excessive anger and humiliation of the soul. Temperance is the mid-point between avidity and weakness of appetite. Self-esteem lies between envy and disaffection, refinement between dissipation and clumsiness, love between pretensions to affection and soundness of character (*ḥusn al-khuluq*), humility between arrogance and lack of self-esteem.[33]

[32] Ibn Qutayba, *ʿUyūn al-akhbār*, I: 280; Miskawayh, *Jāvīdān khirad*, 151 (in his section devoted to *ḥikam al-ʿarab*); al-Rāghib al-Iṣfahānī, *Muḥāḍarāt al-udabāʾ*, I: 13.

[33] Cf. *Nicomachean Ethics*, II, 6–9 (pp. 28–37); Pseudo-Māwardī, *Naṣīḥat al-mulūk al-mansūb ilā ... al-Māwardī*, 191; al-Fārābī, *Fuṣūl al-madanī*, 113–14 = 34–5 (§16); al-Māwardī, *Adab al-dunyā wa-l-dīn*, 143–4; Ibn Abī Dharr, *al-Saʿāda wa-l-isʿād*, 70; Miskawayh, *Tahdhīb al-akhlāq*, 24–9 = *Refinement of Character*, 22–5. See further Chapter 1.

Combining virtues with other virtues gives rise to yet further virtues. The combination of reason with courage produces endurance in adversity and loyalty in the fulfilling of commitments. From the combination of reason with generosity stem the fulfilling of promises and aid proffered by virtue of rank. From the combination of reason with temperance stem integrity and aversion to excessive questioning. From the combination of courage with generosity arise concord and a disposition to think the best of other people. From the combination of courage with temperance come the rejection of obscenities and zeal in the protection of women. From the combination of generosity with temperance come the generous provision of food for other people and the consideration of other people before oneself.

Many characteristics produce results that sometimes develop into vices. It is related from ʿAlī, peace be upon him, that he said:

> The most remarkable aspect of the human being is the soul (*nafs*), in which lie patterns of opposites. When hope arises in the soul, avidity abases it. When avidity excites it, avarice destroys it. When despair overcomes the soul, remorse kills it. When anger stirs in it, rage gathers strength in it. When contentment gives it happiness, it becomes forgetful of caution. When fear assails the soul, wariness preoccupies it. When security surrounds it, heedlessness snatches it away; when it enjoys the renewal of a benefit, it creates new aspirations for satisfaction. When an affliction befalls it, anxiety compromises it. If the soul acquires property, temptation leads it to recklessness. If it experiences satiety, gluttony burdens it. For every shortcoming is injurious to it, and every excess is destructive to it.[34]

[34] A slightly different version appears in the *Dustūr maʿālim al-ḥikam* of al-Qāḍī Muḥammad b. Salāma al-Quḍāʿī (d. 454/1062): in the translation of Tahera Qutbuddin, 'The most wondrous part of the human being is the heart (*qalb*). It has elements of wisdom, and others that are quite the opposite. If the heart is lifted by hope, ambition debases it; if ambition boils over, greed destroys it; and if disappointment takes hold, regret kills it. If aggravated, its rage runs rampant; and if made happy, it forgets to be circumspect. If fear takes hold, caution preoccupies it; and if safety is secured, heedlessness strips it away. If it gains property, wealth makes it a tyrant; and if poverty touches it, it panics. If hunger emaciates it, weakness ensconces it; and if satiety is excessive, the surfeit oppresses it. Every deficiency harms it, and every excess injures it' (Qutbuddin, *A Treasury of Virtues*, 149). See also al-Thaʿālibī, *al-Iʿjāz wa-l-ījāz*, 40.

Another person said:

> Excessive humility constitutes humiliation; excessive pride results in hatred. Excessive caution leads to the deception of the people; excessive affability earns malicious companions. Excessive oppression repels the sincere counsellor.[35]

Ibn al-Muʿtazz said:

> Were things to be distinguished from one another, then falsehood would be grouped with cowardice, honesty with courage, repose with resignation, abjection with cupidity, deprivation with craving.[36]

Virtues are divided into two sorts: one division consists of virtues that compel the praise of God's creatures, and that is the kind of virtue that conveys benefits to them; the second division consists of virtues that earn the praise of the Creator, and that is the kind of virtue by which the face of God the Exalted is contemplated.

It is related from Jaʿfar b. Muḥammad [al-Ṣādiq, d. 148/765] that he said:

> One of God's prophets turned to his Lord in private supplication. He said: 'O Lord, which of Your creations is dearest to You?' The Lord said: 'Those who remember Me most.' He said, 'O Lord, which of Your creatures is most patient?' He said, 'Those who control their anger.' He said, 'O Lord, which of Your creatures is most just?' He said, 'He who subdues his lower self.' He said, 'O Lord, which of Your creatures is richest?' He said, 'He who is most content with his sustenance.' He said, 'O Lord, which of Your creatures is happiest?' He said, 'He who gives preference to My command over his fleeting desires.' He said, 'O Lord, which of Your creatures is most abject?' He said, 'He for whom admonition is useless.'[37]

What I have written completes the treatment of things connected with the essential characteristics.

[35] Al-Jāḥiẓ, *Rasāʾil*, I: 111 (*al-Maʿāsh wa-l-maʿād*); cf. al-Thaʿālibī, *al-Tamthīl wa-l-muḥāḍara*, 260; al-Mubashshir b. Fātik, *Mukhtār al-ḥikam*, 211 (Aristotle); al-Murādī, *al-Ishāra*, 181; al-Maydānī, *Majmaʿ al-amthāl*, II: 108; Zakeri, *Persian Wisdom in Arabic Garb*, II: 440–1, no. 865.

[36] Al-Tawḥīdī, *Akhlāq al-wazīrayn*, 390; Ibn Abī l-Ḥadīd, *Sharḥ Nahj al-balāgha*, X: 438 = part 20, no. 739 (on the reattribution of the aphorisms of Ibn al-Muʿtazz to ʿAlī, see Bray, 'Ibn al-Muʿtazz and Politics', 125–6, 132, and Chapter 5, nn. 58, 125 above). Al-Nuwayrī attributes the saying to Porphyry (Furfūriyūs) (*Nihāyat al-arab*, VIII: 183).

[37] On Jaʿfar al-Ṣādiq, Sixth Imam of the Shiʿa and highly regarded among Sunni and Shiʿi Muslims alike, see Gleave, 'Jaʿfar al-Ṣādeq', and above, section 2.1, at n. 21.

Text 8
Kaykāʾūs b. Iskandar, *Qābūsnāmeh*. Chapters Twenty-Eight and Twenty-Nine[38]

Translator's Introduction

The two chapters reproduced in this section, though addressed by the Ziyarid amir Kaykāʾūs to his son, Prince Gīlānshāh, offer counsel for the benefit of not only a royal and courtly audience but also a general readership. They demonstrate the pervasiveness in Kaykāʾūs's counsel of the theme of *mardumī*, which corresponds loosely to the idea of 'humanity'. This quality appears in association with, and sometimes as a synonym for, the concept of *javānmardī*, a notion that underlies, frames and informs the entirety of Kaykāʾūs's encyclopaedic mirror.

The term *javānmardī* conveys an all-encompassing view of the world, as well as a set of values, a group of virtues and a code of conduct. In his final and longest chapter, on the regulations for the way of life of the *javānmard* (*dar āyīn-i javānmard pīshagī*), Kaykāʾūs enumerates three primary principles of *javānmardī*: wisdom (*khirad*), honesty (*rāstī*) and *mardumī*.[39] In the same chapter he ascribes to the 'wise philosophers' (*ḥakīmān*) the drawing of a metaphorical likeness of *mardumī* and wisdom: in this image, the human body corresponds to a *javānmard*, whose soul corresponds to truth (*rāstī*), whose senses correspond to knowledge (*dānish*) and whose ideas (*maʿānī*) correspond to attributes (*ṣifā[t]*). Developing this image, Kaykāʾūs describes a four-part hierarchy, in which each of four categories of people is distinguished according to the qualities of body, soul, sense and ideas that it possesses; these combinations determine the form that the group's *mardumī* assumes.[40] This typology illustrates the system of correspondences through which Kaykāʾūs understands the universe and the place of humanity within it. Kaykāʾūs also links *javānmardī* with *ʿayyārī*, that is, the way of life of the *ʿayyār*, the chivalric code that governed the conduct of the

[38] Translation prepared from ʿUnṣur al-Maʿālī Kaykāʾūs b. Iskandar, *Qābūsnāmeh*, ed. Ghulām-Ḥusayn Yūsufī (Tehran: Shirkat-i Intishārāt-i ʿIlmī va-Farhangī, 1989), 139–43, 144–51. For the corresponding section in Levy's translation, see Reuben Levy, *A Mirror for Princes: The* Qābūs Nāma *of Kai Kāʾūs ibn Iskandar, Prince of Gurgān* (London: The Cresset Press, 1951), 127–31, 132–39.

[39] *Qābūsnāmeh*, 243. In their Arabic translation, Nashʾat and Badawī translate the Persian *javānmardī* as *muruwwa* (*Kitāb al-Naṣīḥa al-maʿrūf bi-sm Qābūsnāma*, 230 and *passim*).

[40] *Qābūsnāmeh*, 245–6 = Levy, *A Mirror for Princes*, 242.

fraternal paramilitary groups of *ʿayyārān*.[41] In evoking the compound category *javānmardī-yi ʿayyārī*, he describes a man possessed of various virtues (sing. *hunar*): he must be brave, manly (*mardāneh*), patient in all undertakings, true to his word, chaste in his sexual behaviour, pure of heart, never considering another man's loss to be his profit, willing to accept a loss to himself if it is for the sake of his friends; he must reject extortion from prisoners, support prisoners and the helpless, prevent the wrongs of oppressors from harming the good, listen to the truth as well as speak truthfully, dispense justice in person, never cause harm at a table at which he has eaten bread, never repay a good action with a bad one, display modesty in the presence of women and regard adversity with tranquillity.[42]

As these examples of meritorious behaviour suggest, Kaykāʾūs placed emphasis on the enactment of virtue in the context of personal relationships and social transactions. The paired chapters reproduced in this section, on the subjects of friends and enemies, illustrate several of Kaykāʾūs's most valued attributes.

Translation

Chapter Twenty-Eight: On Making Friends

Know, O son, that for as long as people live, they must have friends; it is better for a man to have no brother than for him to have no friend. When a wise philosopher was asked whether it was preferable to have a friend or a brother, he answered, 'Best of all is the brother who is at the same time a friend'. Pay close attention, then, to the matter of your friends, by keeping ever fresh the custom of sending presents and performing acts of courtesy (*mardumī*). Whoever fails to concern himself with his friends will find that his friends will not concern themselves with him, and that man shall be forever friendless. Accordingly, it has been said, 'The friend builds his own prison.'

[41] The term *ʿayyār* carries several meanings and a varied set of connotations. Kaykāʾūs uses the term to denote a member of a local band of voluntary militiamen bound together in common observance of a code of chivalric conduct (see Tor, 'ʿAyyār'; and below, n. 44).

[42] *Qābūsnāmeh*, 247 = Levy, *A Mirror for Princes*, 243. Shortly after this description, Kaykāʾūs recounts an episode in which an envoy from the *ʿayyārān* of Marv arrived in Kuhistan to convey a set of three questions to a local gathering of *ʿayyārān*. The three questions concern the *ʿayyārī* code of conduct, and the challenge of its application in situations in which two *ʿayyārī* principles would appear to conflict (247–9 = 243–4).

Make a habit of cultivating friends at all times, because when people have many friends, their faults are concealed and their virtues (*hunarhā*) revealed. When you make a new friend, do not turn your back on old friends; rather pursue your new friend and continue to maintain your old friendships. In this way, you will always have many friends. It has been said that a good friend is a precious treasure. Consider also the people who travel the path of friendship with you but are only half friends: treat them with kindness (*nīkū'ī*) and amenability (*sāzkārī*), agree with them in all matters good and bad; when they see nothing but humane courtesy (*mardumī*) from you, they will become single-heartedly your friends. Alexander was asked which quality had enabled him, in such a short amount of time, to acquire such a vast kingdom (*mulk*). He replied: 'Kind consideration (*talaṭṭuf*), by which I conciliated my enemies; and loyal support (*ta'ahhud*), by which I rallied my friends.'

Give a thought to your friends' friends, for they too are your friends. Be wary, however, of any friend who is also a friend of your enemy: his friendship with your enemy may exceed his friendship with you, and in that case he will not hesitate to cause you harm for your enemy's sake. Refrain from friendship with a person who displays hostility towards your friend; and do not desire friendship with a friend who reproaches you with neither pretext nor proof.

Do not consider any person in the world to be without fault. But be virtuous yourself (*hunarmand*), for the virtuous person possesses fewer faults. Do not take as a friend any person lacking in virtue, for no prosperity (*falāḥ*) arises from a friend without virtue.

Consider friends of the cup (*dūstān-i qadaḥ*) as your boon-companions (*nadīmān*) rather than as friends; for they are friends of the moment and of the cup rather than friends in times of sorrow and joy alike. Cast your regard among the good (*nīkān*) and the bad (*badān*); and make friends in both groups. With the good, be a friend in your heart; with the bad, make a show of friendship with your tongue, so that you will gradually acquire friends among both groups. Not every need can be satisfied by the good; it may happen, on occasion, that a situation requires the friendship of the bad, and that a good friend may not be able to achieve a given aim. Although your consorting with the bad may diminish your standing among the good, just as your consorting with the good may increase your reputation with the bad, you should maintain the way of the good, so that you may obtain the friendship of both groups.

Never befriend a person who lacks wisdom, for a friend lacking in wisdom is worse than an enemy who possesses wisdom. A friend without wisdom may, out of wickedness, do to a friend what a hundred enemies endowed with wisdom could not do to an enemy. Cultivate your friendships with people of virtue, loyalty (*nīk-ʿahd*) and pleasing appearance, so that you too may attain renown and praise for the very virtues that have earned your friends their reputation and commendation.

> Prefer solitude to bad company. As I have said:
> O heart, you have gone, just like a wild animal into the desert –
> You suffer neither my grief nor your own.
> You were a wicked companion; it is for the better that you have left.
> Solitude is better by far than a wicked companion.[43]

Never overlook the rightful claims of people and friends, so that you never give cause for blame. It has been said that two sorts of people deserve blame: the first is the person who neglects the rightful claims of his friends; the other is the person who fails to acknowledge acts of goodness (from which he has benefited). Know that there are two criteria by which you may learn whether a person is suitable or not to become your friend: the first is whether, when a friend is in straitened circumstances, he does not, as far as he is able, withhold his own things from that friend, and does not abandon him in times of duress; the second is whether, when a friend departs from this world, he enquires after that friend's children, relatives and friends and treats them well. Whenever he visits his friend's grave, he should grieve, even though it is nothing more than his grave. I have heard it said of Socrates that as, under duress to confess idolatry, he was being borne off to execution, he said, 'May God be my refuge, should I worship the Creator's creature!' – and they led him on to be executed. A group of his followers were walking with him and lamenting according to their custom. They asked him: 'O philosopher, now that you have prepared your heart for death, tell us where we should bury you.' Socrates smiled and said, 'If you should find me again,

[43] Here in its Persian form, the maxim *al-wiḥda khayr min jalīs al-sūʾ* (Ar., 'solitude is better than a wicked companion') appears in Arabic in Kaykāʾūs's Chapter Eleven, 67 = Levy, *A Mirror for Princes*, 58. Often considered a Prophetic proverb (al-Thaʿālibī, *al-Iʿjāz wa-l-ījāz*, 29, no. 26 (see also 75, no. 6); al-Ibshīhī, *al-Mustaṭraf*, I: 68, al-Nuwayrī, *Nihāyat al-arab*, VIII: 182), the maxim also forms part of an exchange that took place in Medina between al-Aḥnaf b. Qays and Abū Dharr (al-ʿAskarī, *Jamharat al-amthāl*, II: 261–2, no. 2075).

bury me anywhere you must!' – by which he meant that it would not be him, but rather his body, that they would bury.

Keep your friendship with people at a middling level. Do not bind yourself to friends out of some expectation, or for the sake of having many friends. Be your own special friend; look behind you and in front of you. In your reliance on your friends, do not be careless of yourself; for even if you were to have a thousand friends, none of them would be a better friend to you than you are to yourself. Test your friend in times of plenty and adversity: times of plenty invariably bring deference (*ḥurmat*); times of adversity bring benefit and loss. In the case of a friend who does not consider your enemy to be his own enemy, consider him to be no more than an acquaintance; such a person is an acquaintance only, and not a true friend. With your friends, be the same in times of displeasure as in times of satisfaction. In sum, recognise as your true friend the person who holds you in affection.

Do not, in friendship, impart to your friend anything that that person, were he to become your enemy, could use to harm you; once that happens, regret is to no avail. If you are poor, do not seek out a rich friend; no one, least of all the rich, befriends a poor man. Seek friends of your own degree; it is acceptable, however, if you are wealthy and you have a friend who is poor. Be constant in your friendships with people, so that your affairs will remain constant. If, however, a person, despite your faultless affection, withdraws his friendship from you, do not become preoccupied with winning him back. In addition, keep your distance from any friend who is covetous, for his friendship with you is not true: it stems only from his desires. Never take as friends any persons who are mean-spirited; mean-spirited people are unfit for friendship, for their hearts are never free of spitefulness. Since such a person is always disposed to inflict injury and to seek revenge, friendship for you can never become firmly established in his heart, and he cannot be relied upon.

Now that you have mastered the subject of making friends, consider the subject of enemies and their doings; direct your attention to this next topic.

Chapter Twenty-Nine: Regarding Enemies

Make every effort, O son, not to make enemies. If you have an enemy, however, do not fear, nor become anxious; for a person without enemies may yet suffer from ill will. Never neglect an enemy's doings whether hidden or overt, and do not relax your guard against his bad actions; be continually alert to his tactics, cunning and malice, and at no time feel secure against his strategy. Enquire constantly into your enemy's condition and design; otherwise, you court tribulation, calamity and negligence.

Until you are ready to confront your enemy, do not display your hostility towards him openly; then, once you are prepared, show him your strength. If you should suffer defeat, employ some stratagem; do not let him see you among the fallen. Do not allow yourself to be persuaded by an enemy's seemingly kind actions or fine words; if an enemy offers you sugar, take it, without any doubt, to be colocynth (*sharangī*). Always fear a powerful enemy, for it has been said that there are two people who should be feared: one is a powerful enemy; the other is a treacherous friend. Do not despise a humble enemy, either. Behave with a weak enemy in exactly the same way as you would with a strong enemy; never say that he is of no importance.

A Story

I have heard that there was an *ʿayyār* in Khurasan who was extremely powerful (*muḥtasham*), a fine, highly esteemed and well-known man.[44] His name was Muhallab.[45] They say that one day, as he was walking in the village, he trod on a piece of watermelon-rind, which was lying in the road. His foot slipped and he fell. He drew his knife and struck the watermelon-rind. His servants said to him, 'O

[44] The term *ʿayyār* (Pers. pl. *ʿayyārān*) refers to a member (or in this case a leader) of an organised paramilitary chivalric band (see Tor, '*ʿ*Ayyār'). Groups of *ʿayyārān* were active along the eastern frontier in the ninth century. Used in many sources in a negative sense, the term *ʿayyār* carries strongly positive connotations in the *Qābūsnāmeh*. Indeed, for Kaykāʾūs the *ʿayyār*s are practitioners of the code of *javānmardī*, the quality that in his conception embraced the sum of the humane virtues. In different sections of the *Qābūsnāmeh*, Kaykāʾūs suggests affinities and overlapping interests among individuals committed to the *javānmardī* and *ʿayyārī* ways of life, non-specific military personnel and merchants. For instance, he links 'military people and people who follow the code of the *ʿayyār*' (*qawmī sipāhī va-ʿayyār-pīshagān*) (195–6), and advises merchants to associate with 'people who follow the code of the *javānmard* and *ʿayyār*; powerful people endowed with the manly virtues; and people who know the routes and are familiar with the region' (*mardum-i javānmard-pīsheh va-ʿayyār va-bā mardum-i tavāngar va-bā muruvvat va-bā mardum-i rāh-dān va-būm-shinās*, 170).

[45] I am unable to identify the individual in question (Levy reads 'Mudhahhab'; *A Mirror for Princes*, 133). It is conceivable that the person intended is connected in some way to the Muhallabid family, descendants of the Arab general al-Muhallab b. Abī Ṣufra (*c.* 10–82/632–702), who campaigned in Khurasan and was eventually rewarded with the governorship of the province (see below, Chapter 8, n. 60).

commander, a man of such chivalry (*'ayyārī*) and importance (*muḥtashamī*) as you – are you not ashamed to strike a melon-rind with a knife?' Muhallab answered, 'It was the melon-rind that cast me down; whom else should I strike with my knife? Whoever assaults me I strike, for that person is my enemy.' Never belittle an enemy, no matter how contemptible he might be; for whoever treats an enemy as contemptible soon becomes contemptible himself.

Plan, then, for the ruination of your enemy before he has a chance to enact his plans for your perdition. When you triumph over an enemy, do not then constantly denigrate him, nor insult him to people with charges of weakness, because in that event, your victory over him will bring you no glory, since you will have triumphed only over the powerless and contemptible. And if, may God be my refuge against such an eventuality, this enemy should prevail over you, your disgrace and weakness will become vastly magnified, since you will have fallen at the hands of the powerless and despised. Take note: whenever a king makes a conquest, even if his adversaries were few in number, once the poets compose their verses in commemoration of his victory and the secretaries write their proclamations of conquest (*fatḥnāmeh*), they refer first to the adversary's consummate power; then they praise his army, liken his cavalry and foot soldiers to lions and dragons, and heap the utmost praise upon the various ranks of his army, its centre and wings, and on the generals. Finally they declare that it was a force of these colossal proportions that General So-and-so put to flight and forced to retreat when he advanced with his troops, whose victory was divinely assured (*manṣūr*) – and they exaggerate in this way in order to proclaim the greatness of their patron and to evoke the strength of his army. If they had denigrated that vanquished lot and portrayed their king as powerless, the victorious king would have garnered scant acclaim; about having defeated an enemy so weak and powerless, the authors of his charter of victory and the poets commemorating his triumph would find little reason to boast.

A Story

Once upon a time, in Rayy, the ruler was a woman; they called her by the title Sayyideh ('Lady').[46] She was the daughter of a king. Chaste, austere

[46] Shīrīn, the daughter (or possibly granddaughter) of Rustam II (r. *c.* 353–69/964–79) of the Bāvandī dynastic family (Āl-i Bāvand) of Isfahbadhs in Tabaristan and wife of the Buyid Fakhr al-Dawla (r. 366–87/977–97), was the mother of Rustam Majd al-Dawla (r.

and thoroughly competent, this princess was the daughter of my maternal great-uncle and the wife of Fakhr al-Dawla (ʿAlī b. Rukn al-Dawla, r. 366–87/977–97).[47] When Fakhr al-Dawla died, he had a young son, who received the title Majd al-Dawla (d. 420/1029). In name, it was Majd al-Dawla who became king, but in fact it was the wife of Fakhr al-Dawla who continued to rule for thirty-odd years.

When Majd al-Dawla grew up, he turned out to be degenerate and unsuited for kingship. Although it was he who bore the name of king, he remained in his private quarters, indolent and in constant congress with his slave-girls, while his mother continued to rule in Rayy, Isfahan and Quhistan for some thirty-odd years. My point in relating this story is that your forebear Sultan Maḥmūd, may God have mercy upon him, once sent an envoy to Rayy. The envoy conveyed Maḥmūd's command that the Sayyideh have the *khuṭba* read in his name, that she order his name to be imprinted on her coinage and that she surrender the land-tax to him.[48] If she did not agree to these conditions, he would advance, take possession of Rayy and reduce her to nothing; and he made many other threats as well. When the envoy arrived, he delivered the letter and conveyed Maḥmūd's message. The Sayyideh said, 'Tell Sultan Maḥmūd that as long as my husband, Fakhr al-Dawla, was alive, I was constantly apprehensive that the

387–420/997–1029) and Abū Ṭāhir Shams al-Dawla. When Fakhr al-Dawla died in 387/997, Majd al-Dawla and Shams al-Dawla were, officially, installed as the rulers of Rayy and Hamadhan respectively. Majd al-Dawla, however, was still a minor at this time: according to Ibn al-Athīr, he was only four years old (Ibn al-Athīr, *al-Kāmil*, VII: 489), or, according to Mustawfī, eleven (*Tārīkh-i guzīdeh*, 419). The princes' mother, known as Sayyideh, assumed the functions of government and remained the actual ruler in Rayy until her death in 405/1014. During these years, Sayyideh withstood the resistance of her grown sons and their efforts to unseat her (Majd al-Dīn attempted to wrest control from her in 397/1006–7), as well as the threats of the Ghaznavid sultan Maḥmūd, who, as Kaykāʾūs recounts, refrained from attacking Rayy during her lifetime (see nn. 48, 49). Mustawfī describes Sayyideh as 'a highly intelligent woman, highly skilled in her administration' (*zanī ʿāqileh va-ṣāḥib tadbīr*) and remarks that she executed the affairs of state with *éclat* (*kār-i mulk bi-rawnaq mīdāsht*) (*Tārīkh-i guzīdeh*, 420).

[47] Both based in the Caspian regions, the Ziyarids and Bāvandids interacted frequently; they intermarried, and competed over territory (Mazandaran was conquered by Kaykāʾūs's grandfather Qābūs b. Vushmgīr in 397/1007). See further Madelung, 'Āl-e Bāvand'; 'Minor Dynasties', 216–19.

[48] The appearance of the ruler's name in the Friday oration on the occasion of the weekly congregational prayer and in the coinage were the traditional markers of authority; receipt of the taxes collected in a territory was another marker of rule. A vassal ruler was called upon to include his (or, as in this case, her) overlord's name in the oration and coinage and to submit the taxes collected in his territories to his (or her) suzerain (see above, section 2.2, n. 35).

idea might occur to him to advance towards Rayy. But once my husband died and the duties of the royal office passed to me, the worry departed from me. I thought to myself, Maḥmūd is an intelligent king; he knows that a king like him should never go to war against a woman. Now, if you advance, God, may He be exalted and glorified, knows that I shall not take to flight; I shall stand ready for battle, because there are only two possible outcomes: of the two armies, one will be defeated. If I defeat you, I shall immediately write a proclamation to the whole world; I shall declare that I have triumphed over a sultan who has vanquished a hundred kings. If, on the other hand, you defeat me, what can you write? If you say that you have defeated a woman, you shall win for yourself neither a declaration of victory nor poems of triumph, since the defeat of a woman is not really much of a victory.' On account of these words, for as long as she lived Sultan Maḥmūd never advanced towards Rayy.[49]

For this reason, I say that you should never go too far in belittling an enemy. In no circumstances should you feel secure against an enemy, especially in the case of an enemy inside your household. An enemy inside the household is to be feared more than a stranger, since the latter is not as well positioned to observe your affairs as the former. If an enemy inside your household becomes apprehensive of you, his heart will never be free of malevolence towards you; he will watch your circumstances with the utmost attention, while the enemy outside your household can never obtain the same kind of information about you.

You should never, therefore, enter whole-heartedly into friendship with any enemy. Instead, keep up a semblance of friendship; it is possible that the facsimile will become truth, for it often happens that out of enmity a friendship may arise, just as friendship may turn into enmity. Friendships and hostilities that arise in this way tend to be fraught (*sakhttar*).[50]

Know that the proximity of enemies is a great misfortune. If you cause injury to the enemy, do so in such a way that no trouble accrues to you from your injurious action. Make every effort to ensure that your friends

[49] In 420/1029, after Sayyideh's death and during the reign of her son Majd al-Dawla, Maḥmūd occupied Rayy; the Ghaznavid troops sacked the city, and Majd al-Dawla was taken prisoner. See further Nagel, 'Buyids'; Madelung, 'Āl-e Bāvand'; and above, section 2.2, n. 47.

[50] Literally 'harder'. I take Kaykāʾūs to mean that such friendships and hostilities are harder in the sense that they are more difficult to manage and maintain; it is also possible, however, that he means they are firmer and more resilient; *sakht* carries both possible senses.

are double the number of your enemies. Seek to have many friends and few enemies. Yet even if you have a hundred thousand friends, you should avoid making a single enemy, because those thousands of friends may be negligent in their solicitude on your behalf, while that one enemy will never relent in his malevolence towards you.

Regard it as a disgrace when people blow hot and cold; for he who does not know his own worth is lacking in human dignity (*mardumī*). Never initiate hostilities with an enemy who is more powerful than you are; and never cease to pursue your advantage against an enemy who is weaker than you are. But if an enemy seeks refuge with you, even if his hostility has been bitter and his behaviour towards you hostile, grant him asylum and consider it a great boon (*ghanīmat*).[51] For people have said, what does it matter if an enemy is dead, has fled or seeks asylum? But even when you find your enemy at his weakest, do not relax your guard completely.

If an enemy should perish at your hands, it is permissible for you to celebrate; but if he dies a natural death, you should not rejoice much at all, and only if you know for a certainty that you shall not die. As the philosophers have said: 'Whoever lives on by a single breath after the death of his enemy should count that death a boon (*ghanīmat*).' But since we know that we all shall die, it is not appropriate to be particularly happy. As I have said in a quatrain (*dūbayt*):

> If death overtakes a person who wishes you ill
> Why be so quick to celebrate his demise?
> Since death will strike you too
> Why rejoice at the death of someone else?

We are all preparing for a journey, and we shall carry with us as provisions nothing but our good conduct.

I have heard that Dhū l-Qarnayn, may God have mercy upon him, having travelled through the world and subjected the entire world to his command, turned back and began his return.[52] When he arrived in Damghan he died. In his Testament, he left instructions that his body should be placed in a coffin, cut with holes on each side, and that through these holes, his hands,

[51] Literally a spoil of war, appropriate to the context; more generally an unlooked-for benefit or advantage.

[52] Dhū l-Qarnayn ("The Two-Horned') is the Qur'anic figure (Q 18: 83, 86, 94) usually identified with Alexander the Great (d. 323 BCE); see Renard, 'Alexander'; Doufikar-Aerts, *Alexander Magnus Arabicus*, 93–133. The ancient city of Damghan lies to the south-east of the Caspian (see Map 1).

with palms open, should be drawn. 'Carry the coffin in this fashion, so that the people shall all see that even if we seize the whole world we leave it empty-handed.' He also instructed that his mother should receive this message: 'If you wish my spirit (*ravān*) to be pleased with you, lament my loss to a person who has never lost someone dear to them, or to someone who shall never die.'[53]

Any person whom you cast down with your hand, lift him back up onto his feet; for if you twist a rope to a certain limit and extent, its strands will link together, yet if you twist it too much, you will exceed this limit and the strands will break apart. So maintain the appropriate measure in all matters, whether in friendship or enmity; for moderation is a part of the universal intellect (*iʿtidāl juzʾ-īst az ʿaql-i kullī*).[54] With persons who envy you, do your utmost to avoid revealing to them things that will arouse their anger, in the hope that they might perhaps concede. With those who wish you ill, you should wish them ill too. With those who seek increase from you, do not quarrel; feign negligence in their affairs, for their seeking of advantage shall be their undoing, because the ewer never comes straight from the water. With fools and those who clamour for war, be forbearing; but with the arrogant, be arrogant. At all times and in every matter in which you are involved, do not deviate from the path of humane courtesy (*mardumī*). In times of anger, consider it your obligation to swallow your anger. Speak gently with friend and foe; be agreeable in your speech, because courteous speech is a kind of magic (*jādūʾī*). Whatever you say, good or bad, do not lose sight of the likely answer, and whatever you would not wish to hear, do not force others to hear. Whatever you cannot say in front of people, do not say behind their backs. Do not threaten people when you have no grounds to do so, nor boast of things that you have not done. Rather than saying that you intend to do something, speak only when you have accomplished it. As I have said:

> Idol, I have cast my love for you out of my heart;
> I have made that mountain of sorrows into a plain.

53 Cf. Pseudo-Callisthenes, *The Greek Alexander Romance*, 156. According to Pseudo-Callisthenes, Alexander died in Babylon (*The Greek Alexander Romance*, 150–1).

54 In several systems of philosophical and metaphysical thought, the Universal Intellect or Intelligence (also the First, Active or Actual Intellect) is the first emanation issuing from the Necessary Being (*wājib al-wujūd*); the concept became particularly prominent and well developed in certain Shiʿi and Sufi discourses. The theory underlies and shapes Kaykāʾūs's understanding of the cosmos and the place of humanity within it; cf. *Qābūsnāmeh*, 244–5.

> I shall not tell you today what I shall do
> But tomorrow you shall know, when I tell you what I have done.

Know that action is worth more than words. But keep your mouth shut with a person who, if he wished to speak ill of you, would be able to do so. Never be two-faced and keep away from two-faced people. A slanderer is more to be feared than a seven-headed dragon; the damage that a slanderer can inflict in an hour cannot be repaired in a year. However great and powerful (*muḥtasham*) you might be, do not quarrel with a person stronger than you are. As the philosopher, in his wise counsel, has said:

> If you wish to be spared from tribulation, practise ten qualities. Do not contend with someone stronger than you are. Do not argue with someone who is quick tempered. Do not spend your time with someone who is jealous. Do not dispute with ignorant people. Do not befriend dissemblers. Do not engage with liars. Do not associate with misers. Do not drink wine with anyone who is bad-tempered and jealous. Do not consort too frequently with women. Do not reveal your secrets to anyone, lest you detract from the lustre of your stature and dignity; yet if someone finds fault with you, strive to banish that fault.

Do not conduct yourself with such ostentation that if you were deprived of such ceremony your standing would diminish. Do not praise anyone so excessively that if one day you should need to disparage him you could not do so. Do not disparage anyone to the extent that if one day you should need to praise that person you could not do so. Never attempt, by your anger and reproach, to intimidate someone who has accomplished a task without your support – because someone who is independent of you has no reason to fear your blame and anger, and by seeking to intimidate him you will have exposed yourself to his derision. Do not regard the person who is unable to accomplish any task without your support as altogether helpless, and do not treat him in an overbearing manner. Do not arouse the anger of others against a person, and even if he commits a major offense, overlook it. Do not without cause bring charges against those who are subservient to you; it is through them that you prosper, and it is in your interests that they should not flee from you. Keep your subordinates (*kihtarān*) prosperous, because they are your estates; if you maintain your estates in a flourishing condition, you shall be well set up; but if you ruin your estates, you shall be left with neither provisions nor profit. Retain a servant who carries out your commands.

When you issue a command, do not instruct two people to execute it, in order to avoid mistakes in the matter. As it has been said, a pot with two people in charge never comes to the boil. As Farrukhī (*c.* 390–431/1000–40) said in a hemistich (*miṣrāʿ*):

> A house with two mistresses remains unswept.[55]

There is an Arabic proverb:

> Too many sailors cause the ship to sink.[56]

If you are charged to execute a command (*farmān*), do not wish for a partner or companion, lest you introduce error and deficiency into the task at hand, and in order to retain your lord's continuing satisfaction. Be generous (*karīm*) with friend and foe alike. Do not be severe over people's misdeeds; do not overreact to the slightest slip of the tongue; do not insist on punishment, whether a person's claim is valid or invalid. Keep fast to the path of generosity (*karam*), so that every tongue shall sing your praises.

[55] Abū l-Ḥasan ʿAlī Farrukhī Sīstānī, an eminent poet in Persian; he served at several courts in the eastern regions, including the Ghaznavid court, where he composed panegyrics for Sultan Maḥmūd and his son Masʿūd (r. 421–32/1031–40) as well as for various princes and ministers (Meneghini, 'Farrukhī Sīstānī'). Niẓām al-Mulk also cites this maxim, which he regards as a proverb (*mathal*) (*Siyar al-mulūk*, 213–14 = Darke, *Book of Government*, 158).

[56] Al-Maydānī, *Majmaʿ al-amthāl*, II: 329; al-Thaʿālibī, *Khāṣṣ al-khāṣṣ*, 35.

7

Foundations of Royal Authority and Principles of Governance

If divine selection and personal merit constituted important elements in the rhetoric of royal legitimacy, they required demonstration in the ruler's measured but effective exercise of his power. Several rulers held up their military triumphs, especially against external enemies, as evidence of their fitness to rule,[1] but for mirror-writers, it was usually the condition of the realm, particularly its stability and prosperity, that reflected most distinctly the king's disposition, qualifications and divinely mandated success (or the lack thereof). Foremost among the principles of governance was justice, understood partly in legal terms – the ruler was responsible for upholding the law – and partly in terms of the king's judicious management of the multiple constituencies who made up his realm.[2] The ruler's duty to the law reflected his power but also imposed limits upon it; it obliged him to consult and heed the leading jurists.[3] In cases of injustice, particularly cases that involved extortion and abuse perpetrated by royal agents against the subject population, it was the ruler who constituted the recourse of last resort.[4]

[1] Once again, Carolingian history provides instructive parallels; see Fouracre, 'Conflict, Power and Legitimation in Francia', 19–21, 23.

[2] Both conceptions are ancient (Darling, *History of Social Justice*). The 'circle of justice', in many variants, depicted the interconnections and interdependence of the various indispensable elements of the polity (Sadan, 'A "Closed-Circuit" Saying'; Darling, 'Circle of Justice'; and see below, Text 9). For the well-being of the individual as well as the collectivity, it fell to the ruler to ensure that each person practised the profession appropriate to his or her station (see also the 'Letter of Themistius', 40).

[3] This theme appears also in the ninth-century writings of Hincmar of Rheims (806–82) (see Nelson, 'Kingship, Law and Liturgy', esp. 275–7, 279).

[4] Cf. Arjomand, 'Religion, Political Action and Legitimate Domination', 71.

The four texts that comprise this chapter address the underlying supports of royal authority and the principles that rulers should adopt in their governance. Justice, central to the theory of virtue treated in Chapter 6, here appears as central to the theory of governance. The compelling injunction to rule with justice was taken seriously by many Muslim rulers of the period. The Samanid amir Ismāʿīl b. Aḥmad, for example, held regular sessions for the redress of grievances; the Seljuk sultan Tughril held a *maẓālim* court in Nishapur in 429/1038; Sultan Malikshāh dispatched heralds throughout the Seljuk Empire, and ordered the proclamation in the mosques that he personally would hear and investigate complaints of injustice.[5]

Text 9
Pseudo-Aristotle, *Sirr al-asrār*. Third Discourse[6]

Translator's Introduction

This widely disseminated pseudo-Aristotelian text constitutes a formative element in the development of political discourse in the Muslim and Christian spheres. The extract presented in Text 9 opens with an analogy between God's role in the cosmos and the king's role in human societies. The premise, alluded to in the penultimate paragraph of Text 9, is that Alexander had requested Aristotle's presence and counsel, a summons that the philosopher-teacher rejected, but for which he substituted his instruction in the written form of the correspondence. Among the text's distinguishing features is a 'circular' formulation, that is, a proposition that begins and ends with a single theme, and passes through a series of interlinked elements. This eight-pointed proposition, frequently depicted in graphic form, highlights the theme of justice; like similar formulations, often described as 'circles of justice', it constituted a staple of political writing,

[5] Marlow, *Counsel for Kings*, I: 49, 51; Lambton, 'Internal Structure of the Saljuq Empire', 227; Bosworth, 'Political and Dynastic History', 86.

[6] Translation prepared from *Sirr al-asrār*, in *al-Uṣūl al-yūnāniyya lil-naẓariyyāt al-siyāsiyya fī l-Islām*, ed. ʿAbd al-Raḥmān Badawī (Cairo: Dār al-Kutub al-Miṣriyya, 1954), 125–7. For the corresponding section in Ismail Ali's translation, see *Secretum secretorum* cum glossis et notulis, ed. Robert Steele; including the translation from the Arabic [by Ismail Ali], ed. A. S. Fulton, in *Opera hactenus inedita Rogeri Baconi*, Fasc. V (Oxford: Oxford University Press, 1920), 224–7 (Discourse III).

its association in this case with Aristotle lending it stature and prestige. The 'circle of justice' refers exclusively to the present world, but mirror-writers, including Pseudo-Aristotle, present justice as the linchpin of the divinely ordained cosmos, as a reflection of the wisdom and attributes of the Creator; without it, nothing can flourish. The veracity of Aristotle's words is often demonstrated in the mirror literature with reference to the paradigmatic emblems of Sasanian royal justice and Islamic justice, in the figures, respectively, of Ardashīr and Anūshīrvān, and the Prophet, ʿUmar and ʿAlī.

Translation

Third Discourse: On the Form of Justice

O Alexander, justice is a noble attribute; it is one of the attributes of the Creator, may His name be exalted. The king, to whom God has entrusted the care of His servants, whom He has appointed over their affairs and management, and to whom He has granted authority over their persons, properties, lives and all their affairs, is like a god. Since he resembles a god, it is imperative that he resemble Him in all his states: God is wise and merciful, and His names and attributes are many more than can be counted.

Wisdom, O Alexander, opposes injustice, and the opposite of injustice is justice. By justice the heavens rise above the earth, and by justice the holy prophets have been sent. Justice is the form of reason that God, great and glorious, has praised in the most beloved of His creation. By justice the earth is made prosperous, kingdoms rise and the people become obedient. By justice the disaffected become reconciled, the distant are brought close, souls are safeguarded against all harm and kings made secure from all corruption. In this vein, the people of India have said: 'The ruler's justice benefits the subjects more than a time of prosperity,'[7] and among the pronouncements of their philosophers is the maxim, 'A just ruler is more beneficial than a copious and continuous rainfall'.[8] Moreover, a certain stone bears a Syriac inscription that

[7] See above, Text 3 and n. 122, and the following note.

[8] The saying is variously attributed (for the present reading, see Manzalaoui, 'The Pseudo-Aristotelian *Kitāb Sirr al-asrār*', 241). In Ibn ʿAbd Rabbihi, *al-ʿIqd al-farīd*, I: 9, and al-Nuwayrī, *Nihāyat al-arab*, VI: 34, the maxim is ascribed to *al-ḥukamāʾ*. It also appears attributed to Ardashīr (*ʿAhd Ardashīr*, 99, 'Scattered Sayings', no. 18; al-Thaʿāliḅī, *Ādāb al-mulūk*, 54; al-Thaʿālibī, *al-Iʿjāz wa-l-ījāz*, 62, no. 34 (where al-Ṣāḥib b. ʿAbbād insists

reads, 'As for kingship and justice, neither one can dispense with the other'.[9]

All things derive from, in each case, an element that constitutes its ground (*sabab*), a cause that comprises the action that compels its existence, and an agent who is wise and powerful. The element's acceptance of the imprint of the action constitutes the effect. The ground that is the element is potential, and the effect is the existent that manifests the wisdom of the Wise Creator. The element's acceptance of the imprinting of the action, in accordance with its capacity to accept, is justice.[10]

Justice, then, falls into two divisions: the manifest and the hidden.[11] The manifest is that which is apparent in the acts of the disposing Creator, in the conditions of equality and balance in weight and measure, since 'justice' derives its name from these conditions.[12] The hidden kind of justice entails conviction in the Creator's wisdom, in the perfection of His creations and in the truth of His words. It is rightful that you should strive to arrange the kingdom in a manner that corresponds to the wisdom of the Creator. In a similar manner, the king's actions with regard to the people near him, both his inner circle and the common people, should rest on a foundation of justice, in perpetuation of the wisdom of the Creator and in accordance with His will for them. The king, too, must be convinced of this necessity, so that by his conviction the law (*nāmūs*) will reach perfection in the consummation of his rule, and by the apparent aspects of his actions he will win the hearts of the subjects. The privileged and the common

that the king should inscribe these words in his innermost heart); al-Thaʿālibī, *Ghurar al-siyar*, 483); among the maxims of ʿAlī (al-Qāḍī al-Quḍāʿī, *Dustūr maʿālim al-ḥikam*, in Qutbuddin, *Treasury of Virtues*, 16, 17; al-Ṭurṭūshī, *Sirāj al-mulūk*, I: 215; and see below, Text 12, n. 55); and among the pronouncements of ʿAmr b. al-ʿĀṣ (al-Ābī, *Nathr al-durr*, I: 256; al-Rāghib al-Iṣfahānī, *Muḥāḍarāt al-udabāʾ*, I: 169).

9 The present rendering follows Badawī, *al-Uṣūl al-yūnāniyya*, 125. Manzalaoui points out, however, that this wording departs from the frequent inclusion of the term *akhawān*, 'twin brothers' ('The Pseudo-Aristotelian *Kitāb Sirr al-asrār*', 240, and 216; cf. Steele, *Secretum secretorum*, 224–5, nn. 3, 4). Cf. Ibn ʿAbd Rabbihi, *al-ʿIqd al-farīd*, I: 23 (*inna al-mulk wa-l-ʿadl akhawān lā ghinā bi-aḥadihimā ʿan ṣāḥibihi*, from Ardashīr). Often encountered is the form in which the two concepts are kingship (or sovereignty) and religion; see above, Chapter 5, n. 125.

10 Cf. al-Māwardī, *Tashīl al-naẓar*; see above, Text 7, at n. 24.

11 The categories *ẓāhir* and *bāṭin*, manifest or visible and hidden or invisible, form a binary that runs throughout *Sirr al-asrār* (see Manzalaoui, 'The Pseudo-Aristotelian *Kitāb Sirr al-asrār*', 165, 211).

12 The root *ʿ-d-l*, from which the term *ʿadl*, 'justice', derives, connotes equality and balance.

people comprise different categories, and the spreading of justice among them differs accordingly. 'Justice' is a noun, and its meaning involves equity (*inṣāf*), the removal of injustice, the soundness of weights and the equivalence of measures; it is a term that encompasses the characteristics of manly virtue, the qualities of nobility and acts of kindness.

Justice is divisible into various kinds. One sort of justice is the kind necessary to rulers (*ḥukkām*) in their governance (*ḥukm*). Another sort of justice is the kind necessary to the human being in the responsibility that he bears for himself in relation to his Creator. Then there is the kind of justice required in your dealings with other people according to their conditions and the level of your connections with them.

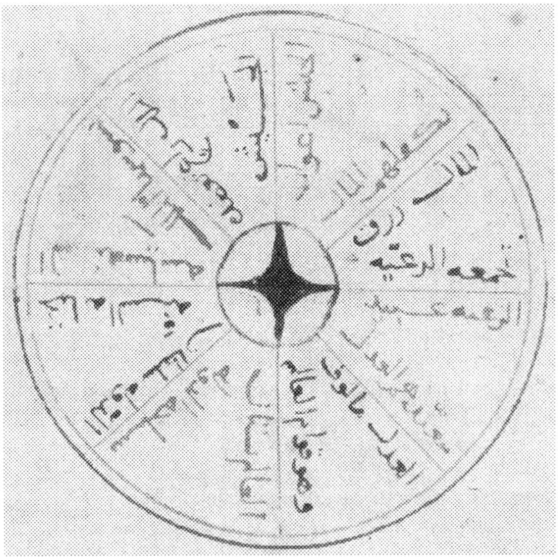

Figure 3 A 'circle of justice', depicting in decorative diagrammatic form the eight points of the formulation that appears at the end of the passage rendered in Text 9. This image appears in the top section of a page from an Arabic copy (possibly produced in the fourteenth century) of *Kitāb al-Siyāsa fī tadbīr al-riyāsa*.

Photograph: The Bodleian Libraries, University of Oxford, MS Laud Or. 210, f. 90r. Reproduced in accordance with Creative Commons Licence CC-BY-NC 4.0

I shall illustrate this principle for you in an octagonal figure [Fig. 3], incorporating wisdom, philosophy, law and divinity. This figure shall teach you about the world in its entirety: it comprehends the governance of the world, and it includes the world's categories and how to deliver the necessary justice to each category. I have divided the image according to the divisions of the celestial sphere; each of its divisions represents a category. Begin with whichever division you wish; it will lead you to the following division, like the continuous revolution of the firmament. Since all forms of administration, upper and lower, involve the world, I have seen fit to begin this guide with the world.

This figure, Alexander, captures the essence of this book, and it represents the most praiseworthy guide for you in the pursuit of your objective. Had I sent you nothing else in response to your request, this figure would have sufficed for you. If you reflect upon it with sincere consideration, it will assist you in your affairs, guide you towards your ambitions and bring you fulfilment in everything that you love, if God wills.

The world is a garden, and its fence is the state (*al-dawla*)
The state is power (*sulṭān*), constrained by law (*sunna*)
Law is governance (*siyāsa*), which is administered by the king
The king is a shepherd, supported by the army
The army are auxiliaries (*aʿwān*), whose provisions require revenue
Revenue provides sustenance, and it is produced by the subjects
The subjects are servants, and they are subject to justice
Justice is concord, and the foundation of the world.[13]

[13] See also al-Mubashshir b. Fātik, *Mukhtār al-ḥikam*, 222; Ibn al-Ḥaddād, *al-Jawhar al-nafīs*, 66–7 (ascribed to Anūshīrvān *al-ḥakīm*); Ibn Juljul, *Ṭabaqāt al-aṭibbāʾ wa-l-ḥukamāʾ*, 26; al-Murādī, *Kitāb al-Ishāra*, 145–6; and see further Subtelny, *Le monde est un jardin*, 58–65, esp. 62. This circular, eight-pointed formulation was reputedly inscribed on the eight sides of Aristotle's tomb; see Ibn Juljul, *Ṭabaqāt al-aṭibbāʾ wa-l-ḥukamāʾ*, 26; Ibn Abī Uṣaybiʿa, *ʿUyūn al-anbāʾ*, 102–3; al-Shayzarī, *al-Nahj al-maslūk*, 98. Manuscript copies of the *Kitāb al-Siyāsa* frequently include illustrations of this circular model of justice; for some examples, see Figs. 2 and 3. In the 'Long Form' of the *Sirr al-asrār*, the eight-pointed formulation is sometimes followed by a differently formulated 'circle' of justice (*lā . . . illā bi-*); see below, n. 58. Often identified as a Persian political concept, the 'circle of justice', as Linda Darling has pointed out, consists of interconnected ideas that, while they certainly flourished in Iran, were not exclusively or first attested in Persian contexts, but reach far back into antiquity (""The Vicegerent of God"').

Text 10
Al-Māwardī, *Tashīl al-naẓar wa-taʿjīl al-ẓafar*. Part II, Section[14]

Translator's Introduction

In the source text, al-Māwardī's *Tashīl al-naẓar wa-taʿjīl al-ẓafar*, Text 10 follows Text 3, and it in turn is followed by Text 13. These three texts, presented in different chapters of this anthology, represent the first sections of part II of al-Māwardī's mirror. The section offered in Text 10 details principles of sovereignty and governance, in two divisions: the three necessary foundations involved in the founding of sovereignty, whereby it is strongly built and enduring; and the four principles or foundations involved in the governance of the realm. Text 10 covers al-Māwardī's discussion of the first of these two areas. The three foundations of sovereignty, in his exposition, are religion, force and wealth. Al-Māwardī assesses the significance of these three foundations of sovereignty, which he treats in a hierarchical sequence, and the ways in which each one is liable to become compromised. The entire discussion reflects al-Māwardī's strongly ethical outlook. He sets great store by the subjects' voluntary and willing obedience to the king, an obedience that the king earns by merit, and which comprises an essential element in his legitimacy as well as a necessary practical condition for any lasting polity.

Translation

Section

The pillars of sovereignty, I propose, rest on two things: governance and a firm foundation. Constructing the foundation of sovereignty entails the establishment of beginnings and principles, and the laying down of sovereignty's bases and components. There are three parts to the foundation of sovereignty: religion, force, and property and wealth.

The first part, that is, the foundation of religion, is the firmest base of the three, the most enduring of them over time, and the most conducive

[14] Translation prepared from al-Māwardī, *Tashīl al-naẓar wa-taʿjīl al-ẓafar*, 203–6. For the corresponding section in Abbès's translation into French, see Abbès, *De l'Éthique du prince*, 361–5.

to garnering the subjects' sincerity in their obedience. Any transfer of sovereignty on religious grounds will occur only in one of three ways.

The first possibility is that the king may deviate from the established forms of religion to the point that he becomes unfit, and he may display a religious outlook that is contrary to established doctrine. In this case, the people will shun him as long as he remains mild, and they will oppose him if he becomes harsh. In their hearts, the people will disobey him, even if their bodies comply with his commands. They will seek a means of deliverance from him and open the gates to revolt against him. They will readily expend their lives and their possessions in order to protect their religion. Accordingly, the king's sovereignty will be exposed to whomever seeks it, his womenfolk potential booty to the marauder. As the Greek philosopher said:

> The people will tolerate an unjust king unless he disregards the pillars of prosperity and transgresses the foundations of the law; if he takes aim at those two things, the end of his term will rapidly approach.[15]

The second possibility is that the king may be a person who denigrates religion, despises its practitioners, neglects its ordinances and dispenses with its guiding fixtures, to the point that religious precepts remain unimplemented and religious duties cease to be observed – whether because of a lack of religious commitment on the king's part, or because of his surrender to the pursuit of pleasures. The people will consider religion the stronger obligation, and they will find its duties and precepts more compelling. As a result, the king's religion will suffer serious compromise and his sovereignty will dissolve. A philosopher has said:

> When the state is on the rise, passions are in the service of intellects; when the state is disintegrating, it is intellects that serve passions.[16]

The third possibility is that the king may originate a repugnant innovation in religion, and he may subscribe to offensive doctrines. If these practices and ideas spread and persist, the religion will suffer alteration, modification and impairment. People's souls will recoil from any religion other than the religion whose tenets ring true to them, and whose principles and foundations are established in their hearts.

[15] See also *Sirāj al-mulūk*, below, at n. 70.
[16] Al-Mubashshir b. Fātik, *Mukhtār al-ḥikam*, 138 (among the pronouncements of Plato).

Consequently, the king's religion will meet with rejection and his sovereignty will be abolished.

If these three conditions should beset the religion, and if there should appear an individual who rises in its support, rejects the alterations introduced by the innovators and follows the established practices, the people will willingly offer him their obedience and give him their strong support and assistance. They will regard the risk of their lives in support of him to be a divinely mandated duty, and assistance to him as one of God's binding commandments. This individual will therefore possess the people's hearts and their bodies, and he will be in a position to claim the loyalty of the ruler's officials (*aʿwān*) and his troops. If these groups, in transferring their support to this person, stand to gain a goodly portion in this world and to combine, through him, their interests in this world with their well-being in the next, the challenger will find himself impelled towards sovereignty without even seeking it, desired for it without evincing desire for it. He will find every difficulty made smooth for him, and every peril diminished. The foundation of the challenger's sovereignty will be so strong that it will obviate any possibility of resistance to his power, and his supporters will not waver in their assistance. These developments arise from the differences between the sovereignty of a person who seeks it and the sovereignty of a person who, rather than seeking it, is sought for it; between obedience shown to a person who demands it and obedience that is willingly given.

The second part of sovereignty's foundation is the foundation of force. With regard to this foundation, the good order of the realm is liable to dissolution either through the ruler's negligence and powerlessness, or through his tyranny and oppression. In these cases, the powerful will dedicate themselves to the pursuit of sovereignty, and the mighty will turn against the ruler, either out of their ambition for sovereignty in its time of weakness or in defence of the kingdom against unrelenting tyranny. An army is able to bring this course of action to completion only if it combines three qualities: large numbers, manifest bravery and the command of a leader whose appointment over his troops rests either on his lineage and paternal descent or on his excellent judgement and courage. If the soldiery, by dint of its large numbers, is able to seize power and to capture it by force, these actions will produce a sovereignty based on coercion. If they proceed to act justly towards the subjects and to display good conduct among them, their sovereignty will be rooted in an implicit delegation (of legitimate authority) and the obedience of the population, and it will grow stable and firm.[17] If, on the contrary, the soldiers are unjust and harsh, then the basis of their rule will consist of usurpation and the exercise of force; tyranny will destroy it and oppression will eliminate it – but only after they have already brought the subjects to perdition and the territories have fallen into ruin.

The third part of sovereignty's foundation is the foundation of property and wealth. When wealth becomes abundant among a people (*qawm*), it sometimes fosters among them the ambitious aspiration to attain sovereignty. In fact, this is a rare occurrence, except in the case of individuals who have already had dealings with power and have associated with the leading officials (*aʿwān*) of the realm. In a case of this kind, the ruler's supporters may seek to achieve their desires through obedience to the aspirant, and they may deliver the power of command to his leadership. This process is unlikely to proceed to its completion unless the king is weak and fragile, and his supporters and subordinate leaders corrupt. It is said in the 'Transmitted Wisdom':

> Wealth has the potential to make a lord out of a person who is not a lord, and to strengthen an individual who lacks strength.[18]

If sovereignty is transferred as a result of wealth, wealth is the weakest factor in the foundation of sovereignty and the shortest in duration; for wealth becomes depleted as a result of the objectives of those who seek it, and it disappears through the initiatives of those who desire it. It has been said:

> He who loves you on account of a particular thing will turn his back on you as soon as that thing has passed.[19]

Solomon, son of David, upon him be peace, said:

> The ruler who depends for his sovereignty upon his wealth will face an abrupt fall from power. If his wealth is accompanied by some other source of firmness for his sovereignty, [it will play a role in the

[17] Al-Māwardī's willingness to condone power attained through violence and usurpation as long as the new authorities rule with justice and clemency towards the subjects is a striking part of his political thinking; his notion of 'delegation' (*tafwīḍ*) is developed at greater length in his *al-Aḥkām al-sulṭāniyya* (23, 92–3). Al-Thaʿālibī and Niẓām al-Mulk portray the passing of power from one dynasty to another as part of the divine plan; al-Māwardī, more explicitly, makes the legitimacy of power gained by force conditional on the exercise of justice and virtuous behaviour.

[18] Al-Tawḥīdī, *al-Imtāʿ wa-l-muʾānasa*, II: 259. On *manthūr al-ḥikam*, see above, Chapter 6, n. 31.

[19] Al-Thaʿālibī, *al-Iʿjāz wa-l-ījāz*, 57, no. 18 (on the authority of B.l.h.z., an Indian king).

> maintenance of his rule]; if not, his sovereignty faces an imminent demise and will be transferred in short order [to someone else].[20]

You should know that at their inception, states begin with rough natures and severe violence; under these conditions, the people are quick to show their obedience. Over time, the state moderates, with the ruler's exercise of mildness and uprightness, which will uphold his sovereignty and ensure the subjects' equanimity. Eventually, it reaches its end, through the spread of injustice and extreme weakness, results of the disorder in affairs and a lack of constructive resolve.[21] Kings, in their opinions and natures, develop in accordance with these three conditions. Our forebears have likened the state to a piece of fruit: it begins fine to the touch, but bitter in taste; as it matures, it becomes softer in texture and agreeable in taste; finally, once fully ripe, it decays rapidly, and it changes in its form. Similarly, just as the state originates in force, it terminates in weakness; it begins with loyalty and ends with perfidy, since loyalty supports the realm whereas treachery engenders fear and abandonment.[22]

Text 11
Niẓām al-Mulk, *Siyar al-mulūk*. Chapter Three[23]

Translator's Introduction

The subject of Niẓām al-Mulk's third chapter in *Siyar al-mulūk* is the royal duty to hear and redress grievances (*maẓālim*). This activity was at once an

[20] Cf. Proverbs XI: 28: 'Those who trust in their riches will wither, but the righteous will flourish like green leaves' (*New Oxford Annotated Bible*, 816).

[21] Cf. Ibn Khaldūn, in Rosenthal, *The Muqaddimah*, II: 118–28.

[22] The components of this paragraph, including the metaphor of the fruit, appear as statements of Plato in al-Mubashshir b. Fātik, *Mukhtār al-ḥikam*, 163, 176, and Gutas, *Greek Wisdom Literature in Arabic Translation*, 146–7, no. 67. See further Gutas, *Greek Wisdom Literature in Arabic Translation*, 136–7, 148–9, nos. 45, 68, 69 (Plato), and Ibn Khaldūn, in Rosenthal, *The Muqaddimah*, I: 343–6.

[23] Translation prepared from Niẓām al-Mulk, *Siyar al-mulūk*, ed. Hubert Darke (Tehran: Bungāh-i Tarjameh va-Nashr-i Kitāb, 1962), 18–29. For the corresponding section in Darke's translation, see H. S. G. Darke, *The Book of Government or Rules for Kings*, Revised Edition (London: Routledge and Kegan Paul, 1978), 13–22; and for a German translation, see Karl Emil Schabinger, *Nizāmulmulk, Reichskanzler der Saldschuqen 1063–1092 n. Chr. – Siyāsatnāma, Gedanken und Geschichten* (Freiburg/Munich: Verlag Karl Alber, 1960), 106–15.

essential part of the king's royal responsibility and a symbolic ceremonial performance of his dedication to maintaining justice. Niẓām al-Mulk moves rapidly from asserting the necessity for the ruler to sit regularly for the redress of grievances to an extended narrative sequence which apparently takes him far away from his chapter's stated topic, but which underlined the imperative for the ruler's direct oversight in the governance of his realm. The story of the Saffarid amir Yaʿqūb b. al-Layth (Pers. Yaʿqūb-i Layth) provides an example, from Niẓām al-Mulk's point of view, of the issue of usurpation and legitimacy addressed in the preceding text of al-Māwardī. Moreover, the caliph, in Niẓām al-Mulk's telling, seeks to portray Yaʿqūb in the terms that al-Māwardī had designated as destructive to royal authority: innovation in religion, abandonment of established beliefs and practices, reliance on force, illicit seizures of wealth. The theme of heterodoxy addressed in direct terms later in Niẓām al-Mulk's mirror is anticipated in this chapter. The note on which Niẓām al-Mulk ends the narrative is a lament for the lapsed honesty among the appointed officials (*gumāshtagān*) of his time. Incompetent and self-interested officials, he argues, subvert the commitment to justice on which the population depends. Niẓām al-Mulk begins and ends his chapter with the admired Samanid amir Ismāʿīl, celebrated for the extreme lengths of physical hardship to which he was prepared to go in order to accommodate potential petitioners. Ismāʿīl, it seems, provided the associative link between the long story with no apparent connection to the topic of *maẓālim* and the brief account that brings Niẓām al-Mulk back to the stated subject of his chapter.

Translation

Chapter Three: On the King's Sitting for the Redress of Grievances and the Practice of Fine Conduct

It is incumbent upon the king that on two days a week, he should sit for the redress of grievances.[24] On those days, he should extract justice from the unjust, dispense equity and listen with his own ears, without an

[24] The ancient practice of sitting for the redress of grievances – hearing and adjudicating upon the petitions submitted by individual subjects – was an important component of the royal office. From the early centuries of the Islamic era onwards, a variety of personnel – governors, caliphs, viziers, deputies of viziers, judges, rulers and persons whom the ruler designated specifically for the task (such as the *ṣāḥib al-maẓālim* or *nāẓir al-maẓālim*) – took responsibility for the function. Very widespread, in provincial as well as central locations, the courts of complaint represented a parallel system of justice to the system

intermediary, to the words of his subjects. In addition, a certain number of the more important written petitions (*qiṣṣeh*) should be submitted, and the king should provide a ruling (*mathāl*) in each case.[25] The reason for these practices is that when the news spreads throughout the kingdom that on two days a week the Lord of the World summons into his presence persons who have been aggrieved and are seeking justice, and that he listens to their words, all oppressors will become afraid, and they will refrain from aggression. No one will dare to commit injustice or extortion out of fear of punishment.

A Story on This Theme

I have read in the books of the ancients that most of the Persian kings used to erect a high platform. They positioned themselves, mounted on horseback, on top of this platform, so that they could see all the petitioners who had gathered on the plain and deliver justice to each one of them. Their reason was that when the king sits in a place that has gates, doors, locks, halls, screens and chamberlains, self-interested persons and

represented by the court of the qadi; the two systems were not entirely separate, however, since judges quite often presided over *maẓālim* as well as *sharʿī* courts. It was al-Māwardī who first provided a comprehensive theoretical treatment of the topic (*al-Aḥkām al-sulṭāniyya*, 86–107 = Wahba, *Ordinances of Government*, 87–106), yet in practice the area of jurisdiction covered by the *maẓālim* system had been less clearly defined than al-Māwardī's portrayal would suggest (van Berkel, 'Abbasid *Maẓālim* between Theory and Practice'; see also Shahar, 'Legal Pluralism', 126–8). Its significance to al-Māwardī, and, as Text 11 indicates, Niẓām al-Mulk, reveals the importance of the court of complaints in the creation of political legitimacy; the high value of the public enactment of justice is further evidenced in the twelfth century, when three cities – Damascus, Aleppo and Cairo – in the eastern Mediterranean region saw the construction of purpose-built 'houses of justice' (sing. *dār al-ʿadl*). The theoretical appeal of *maẓālim* lay in its role as the mechanism whereby the lowliest of the subjects came face-to-face with the powerful sovereign (or his deputy) in expectation of a just resolution, often against the abuse of the sovereign's own officials; in practice, it sometimes provided a mask for state violence (see Tillier, 'Courts of Law'; Tillier, '*Qāḍīs* and the Political Use of the *Maẓālim* Jurisdiction'; Rabbat, 'Dār al-ʿadl'; Rabbat, 'Ideological Significance').

25 The *qiṣṣa* (Pers. *qiṣṣeh*) was a written petition (synonymous with Ar. *ruqʿa*); it might be submitted in the court of *maẓālim*, or, according to Ḥanafī legal procedures, in the context of the sharia system, which otherwise admitted oral complaints (see Tillier, 'Courts of Law'; Berkel, 'Abbasid *Maẓālim* between Theory and Practice', 237). For an example of a *qiṣṣa* submitted to Sitt al-Mulk, half-sister of the Fatimid caliph al-Ḥākim (r. 386–411/996–1021) and head of the Fatimid state between his death and her own in 414/1023, see Rustow, 'Petition to a Woman at the Fatimid Court'.

oppressors can impede the people's access and prevent them from going before the king.

A Story on This Theme

I have heard it told that a certain king was hard of hearing. He worried that the people who were interpreting for him and his chamberlains might not convey his petitioners' words to him correctly, and that he might, in ignorance of the true circumstances, pronounce a decree that did not accord with the matter in question. He issued a command that petitioners, and petitioners alone, should dress in red clothing, so that he would be able to recognise them. Mounted on an elephant, this king positioned himself on the plain. When he saw anyone dressed in red, he ordered that all such persons should be brought together in a group. Then he sat in a space that was otherwise empty. Each petitioner was brought forward, so that, in a loud voice, he could state his matter, and the king could deliver justice to each one.[26]

Kings have taken all these precautions so that, when they are called upon to answer in the next world, nothing will have escaped their knowledge.

The Story of the Just Amir

Among the Samanid kings there was one who was called Amir Ismāʿīl Ibn Aḥmad (r. 279–95/892–907). He was extremely just and followed many fine practices. He possessed a pure belief in God, may He be exalted and glorified, and he gave generously to the poor. People still talk about his excellent conduct. This Ismāʿīl was a ruler whose capital was in Bukhara; his forefathers had held Khurasan, Iraq and Transoxiana.

Yaʿqūb-i Layth [= the Saffarid amir Yaʿqūb b. al-Layth (r. 253–65/867–79)] raised a revolt in the town (*shahr*) of Zarang and seized all

[26] For versions of this frequently invoked story, see Pseudo-Māwardī, *Naṣīḥat al-mulūk al-mansūb ilā ... al-Māwardī*, 399; Ghazālī, *Naṣīḥat al-mulūk*, part I, 31–2 (= Bagley, *Ghazālī's Book of Counsel for Kings*, 21); al-Ṭurṭūshī, *Sirāj al-mulūk*, I: 223 (= Text 12, see below, at nn. 74–5). In several of these cases, the account, set in China, is embedded in a narrative in which a lone renunciant voices a complaint against a caliph (identified in Pseudo-Māwardī's version as al-Manṣūr) for the corruption and oppression that he has allowed to flourish; in Pseudo-Māwardī's much longer version, the attentiveness of the Chinese sovereign, an unbeliever (*mushrik*), is held up as an example to the Muslim (*Naṣīḥat al-mulūk al-mansūb ilā ... al-Māwardī*, 397–400).

of Sistan.[27] Next he entered Khurasan and seized that province; from Khurasan he went to Iraq and seized it in its entirety. Missionaries (*dāʿiyān*) deceived him, and he secretly pledged allegiance to the Ismailis.[28] In his heart he fostered hostility towards the caliph of Baghdad. Then he mustered the armies of Khurasan and Iraq and made for Baghdad in order to put the caliph to death and overthrow the House of the Abbasids.

The caliph received word that Yaʿqūb had set out for Baghdad. He sent an envoy to say, 'You have no business in Baghdad; it would be more appropriate for you to pay attention to Kuhistan in Iraq and Khurasan, in order to ensure that no confusion or cause for concern should arise. Turn back.' Yaʿqūb, however, did not obey the caliph's command. He said, 'My desire is to come without fail to the court, and to perform the customary pledge of service and to renew my covenant (*ʿahd*); until I have completed these actions I shall not turn back.' However many times the caliph sent envoys, Yaʿqūb sent back the same reply. He gathered his armies and made for Baghdad. The caliph was suspicious of him. He summoned the great men of the court (*buzurgān-i ḥaẓrat*) and said, 'I see that Yaʿqūb-i Layth has removed his head from the collar of obedience to us, and I surmise that he is heading here in an act of betrayal; for we did not summon him, yet he is coming, and even though we have commanded him to turn back, he has not turned back. In any event it seems that he is carrying treachery in his heart, and I think he may have pledged allegiance to the Batinis.[29] Until he arrives here he will not manifest that allegiance openly. We must not be negligent in taking precautions. What course of action is required in this situation (*tadbīr-i īn kār chīst*)?'

[27] Reading (with Darke) 'Zarang', chief town in the province of Sistan in the early Islamic period and capital of the Saffarids until the Ghaznavid occupation of 393/1002 (Bosworth, 'Zarang').

[28] Niẓām al-Mulk's imputing of Ismailism to Yaʿqūb is a projection, deployed in order to present, in the form of Yaʿqūb, a dramatic instance of the danger to which heterodoxy, unchecked, in Niẓām al-Mulk's view inevitably led – topics dealt with at length in the second part of *Siyar al-mulūk*. D. G. Tor has argued convincingly that Yaʿqūb followed, like his Samanid competitors, the model of the *mutaṭawwiʿ*, the voluntary religious warrior, and that he acted in a specifically Sunni framework; furthermore, the majority of his campaigns were conducted against groups considered, from a Sunni point of view, to be heterodox ('Historical Representations of Yaʿqūb b. al-Layth').

[29] Adherents of hidden, esoteric (*bāṭin*) interpretations of scripture; in this context, more or less a synonym for the Ismailis (see below, Chapter 9, at n. 42).

They decided that the caliph should not remain in the city but should go out into the plain and set up a military encampment there. His inner circle (*khāṣṣagiyyān*), the great men (*buzurgān*) of Baghdad and all his retinue should accompany him. When Yaʿqūb arrived, he would see the caliph and his encampment in the plain, and his purpose would soon go awry. His disobedience towards the Commander of the Faithful would emerge clearly, since people would go back and forth from one camp to the other. If Yaʿqūb were planning a rebellion, not all the leading men and captains (*sarān*) of Khurasan and Iraq would be in agreement with him or give their consent to his proposal. If Yaʿqūb were to display his revolt in an open manner, the caliph's camp would seek to divert the rebel army through one stratagem (*tadbīr*) or another; if they were unsuccessful in this attempt and unable to hold their own in battle against him, at least they would have an open path by which to retreat, so that they would not have to face capture, like prisoners within four walls, but could make their way to one place or another. This plan (*tadbīr*) met with the approval of the Commander of the Faithful, and so they acted accordingly. This Commander of the Faithful was al-Muʿtamid ʿalā llāh Aḥmad (r. 256–79/870–92).[30]

When Yaʿqūb-i Layth arrived, he dismounted parallel to the caliph's encampment and pitched his tents. The soldiers in both armies mixed with one another. That very day Yaʿqūb made open display of his rebellion: he sent to the caliph a person bearing the message, 'Abandon Baghdad, and go wherever you wish.' The caliph requested a stay of two months. Yaʿqūb refused to grant him this respite. When night fell, the caliph secretly sent someone to each of Yaʿqūb's captains with the message, 'He has openly rebelled, and made common cause with the [Ismaili] Shiʿis;[31] he has planned to overthrow our House and to install our enemy in our place. Are you in agreement with him in this venture or not?' One group responded, 'It is from him that we receive our subsistence, and from his fortune and our service to him that we have received our current status, prosperous circumstances and dignified position. Whatever he has done, we have done.' Most said, 'We have heard no report of the situation that the Commander of the Faithful has

[30] In 260 or 261/874 or 875, Caliph al-Muʿtamid (r. 256–79/870–92) had confirmed the governorship of Ismāʿīl's older brother and predecessor, Naṣr I b. Aḥmad (r. 250–79/864–92), over the entire province of Transoxiana. In 285/898, Caliph al-Muʿtaḍid (r. 279–89/892–902), successor to al-Muʿtamid, appointed ʿAmr b. al-Layth, brother of Yaʿqūb and his successor, to the governorship of Transoxiana.

[31] Cf. Darke's reading, *Book of Government*, 246, n. 3.

mentioned, and we do not think that Yaʿqūb would ever oppose the Commander of the Faithful. If, however, he makes open display of such opposition, we should not under any circumstances consent to it. On the day of battle, we shall be on your side, not his, and when the time comes to draw up the ranks, we shall come over to your side and support you.' This group consisted of the military commanders of Khurasan.

Once the caliph heard this kind of speech on the part of the captains in Yaʿqūb-i Layth's army, he was greatly cheered. The next day, with a stout heart, he sent word to Yaʿqūb-i Layth, saying, 'Now you have displayed your ingratitude for the benefits that we have bestowed (*kufrān-i niʿmat*); you have entered into agreement with my opponent and taken an adversarial position towards me. The sword now stands between us. Despite the fact that my army is small while yours is large, I have no fear. God, may He be exalted and glorified, who is the Supporter of the Right, is with me, and the army that you have is my army.' He ordered his troops to take up arms, to beat the drums of war and sound the trumpets, to leave the camp and draw up ranks in the plain.

When Yaʿqūb heard the caliph's message in these terms, he said, 'I have achieved my purpose.' He too ordered the drums to be struck. His entire army mounted; in formation they entered the plain, and they drew up ranks parallel to the caliph's army. On his side, the caliph came forward and took up a position in the centre; on the other side, Yaʿqūb-i Layth did likewise. Then the caliph ordered a man with a strong voice to advance into the middle ground between the two lines of battle, and to declare at the top of his voice, 'O Muslims, know that Yaʿqūb-i Layth has become a rebel. He has come to overthrow the House of ʿAbbās, and to bring the caliph's adversary and install him in the caliph's place. He intends to eliminate the customary religious practices (*sunnat*) and to spread innovation (*bidʿat*) openly. Whoever opposes the caliph has opposed the Messenger of God; and whenever a person removes his head from the collar of obedience to the Messenger (may the blessings and peace of God be upon him), it is as if he has removed his head from obedience to God, and thereby departed from the Muslim fold. As God, may He be exalted and glorified, has said, in the unambiguous parts (*muḥkam*) of His Book, "Obey God, obey the Messenger and those in authority among you" (Q4: 59).[32] Now, who among you will

[32] Uses of this verse have already been seen; see above, Texts 1, 2 and 4. The reference to the 'unambiguous' (*muḥkam*) parts of the Qur'an stems from the Qur'anic verse 3: 7,

choose Paradise over Hell, lend his support to the Right and turn away from the False? Let him join our side, not the side of our adversary.' When the army of Yaʿqūb-i Layth heard these words, the commanders of Khurasan turned as a single group, and came towards the caliph. They said, 'We thought that he had come here in response to your order and command, and in obedience and service to you. Now that he has revealed his opposition and disobedience, we shall join you, and we shall fight on your side for as long as we remain alive.'

The caliph, now increased in strength, ordered his entire army to charge. Yaʿqūb-i Layth was routed in the first assault and retreated in defeat towards Khuzistan. The caliph's forces plundered his treasury, storehouse and encampment, and by means of these riches grew still more powerful. Once Yaʿqūb reached Khuzistan, he sent people out in every direction. He began to call up troops and to summon agents, whom he ordered to bring supplies and funds from the treasuries of Khurasan and Iraq.

As soon as the caliph received the report that Yaʿqūb had settled in Khuzistan, he immediately sent him a representative, who brought with him a letter. The letter read, 'It has become known to us that you are a man of simple heart and that you have been deceived by the words of our adversaries. You did not foresee the outcome of this matter. As you now perceive, God Almighty has shown you His work; He has defeated you by means of your own army, and He has preserved our House. This was a simple mistake on your part. Now I know that you have become aware of your error and that you regret having acted in this fashion. No one is more suited than you for the governance of Iraq and Khurasan. We shall not increase our favour (*mazīd*) towards anyone other than you, nor place anyone above you; for we recognise that through your many services, you have accumulated many claims upon our favour. We regard this single error in the light of these several pleasing services.' The caliph surmised that since he was prepared to overlook Yaʿqūb's rebellion and to treat his action as if it had not taken place, Yaʿqūb would now also put the event aside. He assumed that he would set off for Iraq and Khurasan as soon as possible, and that he would occupy himself with overseeing that province. Closely behind his letter the caliph planned to send

which distinguishes between categories designated *muḥkam*, precise or clear, and *mutashābih*, 'ambiguous'. The verse, itself ambiguous, has been variously interpreted; see Chaumont, 'Ambiguity', and Kinberg, 'Ambiguous'.

a banner and a robe of honour as tokens of his consent to Yaʿqūb's rule of these provinces, so that no disorder should arise.

When Yaʿqūb read the letter, his heart did not soften in the slightest, nor did he regret his action. He ordered leeks, fish and some onions to be placed on a wooden tray and brought before him. Then he ordered the caliph's envoy to be brought in and seated. He turned towards the caliph's representative, and said, 'Go. Say to the caliph that I was born the son of a coppersmith, and that I learnt that trade from my father. My diet consisted of barley bread, fish, onions and leeks. It is by dint of principled initiative (*ʿayyārī*) and courage (*shīr-mardī*) that I have acquired this kingship, this treasure and these goods; I did not inherit them from my father, nor did I receive them from you.[33] I shall not rest until I have sent your head to Mahdiyya and eliminated your House.[34] Either I shall do as I say, or I shall return to my diet of barley bread, fish and onions. Here, I have opened up the doors to my treasuries and summoned my troops. I shall follow fast in the tracks of the courier bearing this message.' He dismissed the caliph's representative. However many representatives and letters the caliph sent, Yaʿqūb's words remained exactly the same. He assembled his troops, and he set out from Khuzistan towards Baghdad. When he had travelled three stages, however, he developed colic. His condition reached the point that he knew that there would be no escape from the pain. He appointed his brother ʿAmr-i Layth (= the Saffarid amir ʿAmr b. al-Layth [r. 265–88/879–901]) as his heir-apparent, gave him the records of his treasury and died.

ʿAmr-i Layth turned back. He proceeded to Kuhistan in Iraq, where he spent a certain amount of time, and from there he continued to Khurasan, where he exercised royal authority (*pādshāhī hamī-kard*). At the same time, he displayed obedience to the caliph. Both the army and the subjects liked ʿAmr better than Yaʿqūb, for this ʿAmr was exceedingly virtuous, generous, alert and effective in his governance.[35] His

[33] The term *ʿayyārī* (*Siyar al-mulūk*, 23) carries many connotations; see above, Chapter 6, nn. 41, 44. Darke translates the term in this instance as 'bold enterprise' (*Book of Government*, 18, also 246, n. 4); Schabinger renders the term as 'waghalsiges Herumziehen' (*Siyāsatnāma, Gedanken und Geschichten*, 111).

[34] Before their conquest of Egypt in 358/969 and their construction of Cairo in the following year, the Fatimids had founded the town of al-Mahdiyya, in Tunisia. Al-Mahdiyya was named after its founder, ʿUbayd Allāh al-Mahdī (297–322/909–34), who took it as his capital in 308/920 (see section 2.2).

[35] The text reads *īn ʿAmr bas buzurg-himmat va-buzurg-ʿaṭā va-bīdār va-bā-siyāsat* [*būd*] (24); Darke translates: 'ʿAmr was magnanimous, generous, enlightened and statesmanlike to a degree' (*Book of Government*, 18); Schabinger offers 'außerordentlich hochsinnig, freigebig, aufgeweckt und staatsmännisch' (*Siyāsatnāma, Gedanken und Geschichten*, 111);

manly virtue (*muruvvat*) and generosity of spirit (*himmat*) were so far-reaching that it took four hundred camels to transport his kitchen; and further examples might easily be adduced along these lines.

But the caliph felt apprehensive about him, lest ʿAmr too should embark on the path of his brother, and sooner or later exhibit the same propensities that his brother had displayed. Despite the fact that ʿAmr held absolutely no conviction of this kind, the caliph remained nervous about the matter. Secretly, the caliph dispatched a constant stream of people to Ismāʿīl b. Aḥmad in Bukhara. These envoys conveyed to Ismāʿīl the caliph's instruction: 'Muster an army and revolt against ʿAmr-i Layth; seize the kingdom (*mulk*) from his control. You possess a greater claim to govern Khurasan and Iraq, since for many years this kingdom belonged to your forefathers, whereas they (the Saffarids) simply took it by force.[36] Firstly, you possess a rightful claim to it (*khudāvand-i ḥaqq tu-ī*); secondly, your conduct is pleasing; thirdly, my prayers will support you. By virtue of these three factors, I have no doubt that God Almighty will grant you victory against ʿAmr. Do not let the paucity of your supplies and the small numbers of your troops deter you; consider instead the words of God, may He be exalted and glorified: "How many a band (*fiʾa*) of few people has triumphed over a band of many, by God's permission; and God is with those who endure patiently"' (Q 2: 249).[37]

The caliph's words wrought their effect in Ismāʿīl's heart, and he reached a firm determination to oppose ʿAmr-i Layth. He assembled all the troops that he had, and as they passed the near side of the Oxus, he counted them with the tip of his whip. He counted ten thousand cavalry, most of whom had only wooden stirrups; among every ten men, one had no shield; in every twenty, one man lacked a coat of mail; one man in every fifty had no lance; and there were some men who, lacking a mount, had bound their coats of mail onto saddle straps. Ismāʿīl departed from Amuy (Amul) and went to the city of Balkh.

News reached ʿAmr-i Layth that Ismāʿīl b. Aḥmad had crossed the Oxus and arrived in the city of Balkh, and furthermore that the governor (*shiḥna*) of Sarakhs and Marv had fled, as Ismāʿīl was intent

Pistoso renders the clause 'era persona di grande nobiltà morale, generoso, illuminato, e dotato di senso politico' (*L'arte della politica*, 67).

[36] A point that Niẓām al-Mulk had anticipated at the outset of his narrative, when he introduced the protagonists of Ismāʿīl and Yaʿqūb (see above, and n. 30).

[37] The verse appears in the context of David's contest with Goliath; see further Lindsay, 'Goliath'.

upon taking the kingdom. ʿAmr-i Layth was in Nishapur. He reviewed seventy thousand cavalrymen, all of them supplied with weapons and fully equipped, and all of whose mounts were clad in armour. Then ʿAmr set out for Balkh. When these two forces encountered one another, they drew up lines of battle. It so happened that ʿAmr-i Layth was captured at the gates of Balkh, and his cavalry, seventy thousand-strong, fled in defeat. Not a single horseman suffered injury, nor was anyone – among that entire army – taken prisoner, except for ʿAmr-i Layth. ʿAmr, once captured, was brought before Ismāʿīl, who ordered that he be placed in the custody of his guards. This singular victory is among the wonders of the world.[38]

At the time of the afternoon prayer, a servant (*farrāsh*) attached to ʿAmr-i Layth was moving about in the camp. His eye fell upon ʿAmr-i Layth. His heart burned with sympathy for him, and he approached him. ʿAmr said to him, 'This evening, stay with me, because I have been left very much alone.' Then he added, 'As long as people remain alive, they must have food. Devise a means (*tadbīr kun*) to obtain something for me to eat, for I am hungry.' The servant fetched a *mann*[39] of meat and borrowed a round pan, made of iron, from the troops. He hurried about in all directions, collected a piece of dry dung from the plain, put together two or three clods of dry earth and placed the pan on top of them, in order to fry the meat. Having put the meat in the pan, it occurred to him to go in search of a little salt. The day reached its end. A dog appeared. It put its head into the pan to retrieve a bone, and burnt its mouth; when it lifted its head, the pan's ring-shaped handle, hot from the fire, fell over its neck. The dog leapt up in a great rush and carried off the pan. Observing this episode, ʿAmr-i Layth turned towards the troops and guards and said, 'Take this as a cautionary example (*ʿibrat*): I am a man whose kitchen, in the morning, required four hundred camels to transport; in the evening, a single dog took it and carried it off.' He also said [in Arabic], 'In the morning I awoke as an amir; in the evening I became a prisoner (*asīr*).'[40] The meaning of this Arabic sentence is, 'At

38 The battle took place in 287/900. Having taken ʿAmr prisoner, Ismāʿīl sent him on to Baghdad, where the former was executed soon after the death of al-Muʿtaḍid in 289/902.

39 The *mann* was the most important measure of weight for goods in Iran until the beginning of modern times, though its equivalency varied from region to region and from period to period; see Hinz, *Islamische Masse und Gewichte*, 16–23, esp. 17–21.

40 An admired and frequently recounted example of wit and brevity; al-Thaʿālibī (*al-Iʿjāz wa-l-ījāz*, 90, no. 51; *Ādāb al-mulūk*, 76), ascribed it to Ismāʿīl b. Aḥmad, in his report (in the third person) to the caliph al-Muʿtaḍid.

dawn I was an amir, and in the evening I am a prisoner.' This situation too is among the wonders of the denizens of this world.

Even more remarkable, and still connected with Amir Ismāʿīl and ʿAmr-i Layth, is that once ʿAmr-i Layth had been taken captive, Amir Ismāʿīl turned towards the great men in his entourage, and said, 'God, may He be exalted and glorified, has granted me this victory. For this favour I have no obligation towards anyone except God, exalted be His name.' Then he said, 'Know that this ʿAmr-i Layth was a man of virtue and generosity.[41] He was well supplied with weapons and equipment, and in addition he possessed sound judgement and foresight (*tadbīr*). He was alert in affairs, liberal in his provisions and honoured the rightful claims of those to whom he was beholden (*ḥaqq-shinās*). In my view, I should make efforts to ensure that he suffers no mortal injury, and that he finds release from this bondage.' The leading men said, 'The amir's judgement is best. Let him command whatever he deems most beneficial (*maṣlaḥat*) in this situation.' Ismāʿīl sent someone to ʿAmr-i Layth to say, 'Do not suffer any anxiety; I shall contrive a plan (*tadbīr*) whereby I shall ask the caliph to spare your life. Even if I am obliged to expend my entire treasury to this end, I would consider it right, in order that you should be spared any mortal injury and able to spend the remainder of your life in safety.'

When ʿAmr-i Layth heard these words, he said, 'I know that I shall never find release from these bonds, and that no life is left to me; the caliph will be content with nothing less than my death. But you, who are Ismāʿīl – send me one of your trusted agents, because I have something to say; just as he hears these words from me, let him convey them to you.' Ismāʿīl's courier returned to the amir and disclosed to him ʿAmr's request. Immediately Ismāʿīl sent a trusted agent to ʿAmr. ʿAmr-i Layth said to this agent, 'Tell Ismāʿīl that it was not he who defeated me but rather his devotion to religion (*diyānat*), his faith, and his excellent conduct, as well as the displeasure of the Commander of the Faithful, that defeated me. God, may He be exalted and glorified, has recently taken this kingdom away from me and given it to you. You, by virtue of your beneficence and excellence, are worthy and deserving of this favour. I accept God's decree, and I wish you nothing but good. You, meanwhile, have acquired a new kingdom; yet you have no wealth and no reserves. My brother and I own many treasures and buried troves, and I have in my

[41] This list of attributes (*buzurg-himmat va-buzurg-ʿaṭā ... bīdār dar kār-hā*) echoes the language used previously in describing ʿAmr; see above, n. 35.

possession a list of all these items. I am placing all these riches at your disposal, in order to supply you with reserves; thereby you will increase in strength; you shall be in a position to amass equipment and supplies, and to replenish your treasury.' Then he took the list of treasures from his sleeve, gave it to the agent and sent it to Amir Ismāʿīl.

The agent returned, repeated what he had heard and placed the list of treasures before Amir Ismāʿīl. Amir Ismāʿīl turned towards the great men in his entourage and said, 'This ʿAmr-i Layth, with all his cleverness, wishes to evade the clever; indeed, he seeks to capture them in a snare of eternal torment.' He picked up the list of treasures and threw it in front of the agent who had delivered it. As he did so, he said to him, 'Take this list of treasures back to him. Tell him that in his audacity (*jaldī*) he wishes to escape from everything. From what source did this treasure fall into his hands and the hands of his brother? Their father was a coppersmith, and they too learnt that craft. Say to him, "By some celestial chance you usurped the power that you held by force, and by dint of your recklessness your efforts succeeded. These treasures are made up of dirhams and dinars, all of which you seized from people through oppression and by wrongful means. You attained this wealth at the price of thread spun by frail, elderly women and widows, from the provisions of strangers and travellers, and from the property belonging to orphans and the weak.[42] Soon you shall have to answer for every grain of it before God, may He be exalted and glorified, and you shall taste God's chastisement and retribution. Now, in your rash opportunism (*jaldī*), you wish to shift the burden of these injustices from your neck to mine, so that tomorrow, on the Day of Resurrection, when your adversaries take hold of you and demand that you restore to them the wealth that you wrongfully seized from them, you shall be able to say, 'Everything that we took from you, we entrusted to Ismāʿīl; ask him for it.' You wish to transfer all of it to me. I shall have no capacity to answer these adversaries, nor to answer to the wrath and questioning of God, may He be exalted and glorified."' Because of his fear of God and his intense piety, Ismāʿīl did not accept ʿAmr's list of treasures; instead, he sent it back to him, and he was not deceived by this world.[43]

[42] The list of the wrongfully divested coincides with categories singled out in the Qurʾan for kindness and benefaction; see, for example, Q 9: 60, 2: 177. The injustice constitutes a religious infraction and an offence against humane values.

[43] A version of this postlude to the story appears in Ghazālī, *Naṣīḥat al-mulūk*, part II, 123–4 = Bagley, *Ghazālī's Book of Counsel for Kings*, 71.

Does this amir resemble the appointed agents (*gumāshtagān*) of these times, who, for the sake of one illicit dinar, will, without the slightest trepidation and taking no heed for the consequences, declare ten illicit things lawful and ten lawful things illicit?[44]

Story

It was the custom of this same Ismāʿīl b. Aḥmad that on days of extreme cold and heavy snow, he would mount alone and come to the square, where he remained on horseback until the midday prayer. He used to say, 'It may be that an aggrieved person will come with a petition to the court, and that he may lack the money needed for his subsistence and accommodation. If, on the pretext of the cold and snow, we fail to take up our position, it will be difficult for him to reach us; whereas if he knows that we have been standing here he will come, settle his affairs and go away in safety.'[45]

There are many stories of this kind; we have related only a few. This care and attention have been taken in anticipation of the answer due in the next world.

Text 12
Al-Ṭurṭūshī, *Sirāj al-mulūk*. Chapter Eleven[46]

Translator's Introduction

In this eleventh chapter of *Sirāj al-mulūk*, al-Ṭurṭūshī discusses the pillars of stable rule. Like all mirror-writers, he emphasises the centrality of justice, to which he adds kindness, the mitigator of severity. Justice and pardon are both among the divine qualities, which the ruler, within

[44] Darke, following the stories' highlighting of the role of rulers, substitutes 'amirs' for the term *gumāshtagān*. Compare Ghazālī, *Naṣīḥat al-mulūk*, part I, 37 = Bagley, *Ghazālī's Book of Counsel for Kings*, 23: following the mention of the ruler's appointed officials (*ʿummāl*) and retainers (*chākirān, khādimān-i vālī*), Ghazālī asks, 'What greater enemy is there than one who promotes your utter destruction for the sake of a few unlawful dirhams that (he hopes) to grab?'

[45] Ismāʿīl's reputation for extraordinary efforts in order to ensure his accessibility to potential petitioners appears also in Ghazālī, *Naṣīḥat al-mulūk*, part II: 122 = Bagley, *Ghazālī's Book of Counsel for Kings*, 70–1; see further Marlow, *Counsel for Kings*, I: 49.

[46] Translation prepared from al-Ṭurṭūshī, *Sirāj al-mulūk*, I: 213–24. For the corresponding section in Alarcón's translation into Spanish, see Alarcón, *Lámpara de los Príncipes*, I: 193–205.

the limits of his humanity, should strive to emulate.[47] The ruler should be just, but at the same time benevolently disposed towards his subjects. Where justice allows for it, he should err on the side of clemency and forbearance, and never inflict punishment in haste, spite or retaliation. Al-Ṭurṭūshī supports this softening of justice's imperative with Qurʾanic speech. He also distinguishes between two kinds of justice, one based on scripture and revelation and the second based on human understanding: the former obtains in polities built on a prophetic foundation, the latter in polities based on a 'rectifying', 'improving' or 'reformist' foundation, their mode of governance geared towards the public good (*siyāsa iṣlāḥiyya*). The 'reformist' model carries the rich semantic resources of the root *ṣ-l-ḥ*, with its development in law.[48] This category accommodates and attaches value to the ancient, non-Muslim and humanistic contributions to political thought and political culture. Al-Ṭurṭūshī develops his exposition of these two political foundations in some detail and outlines the benefits of both the prophetic and the reformist systems, apparently acknowledging in both cases their potential for good. He makes extensive use of 'the tales of the prophets' (*qiṣaṣ al-anbiyāʾ*), especially the prophet-kings; these narratives play a prominent role in shaping his embracing vision of human welfare and the political arrangements necessary for it to flourish.

Translation

Chapter Eleven: On Knowing the Qualities That Constitute the Pillars of the Ruler's Power, without Which It Has No Stability

The first and most important quality for the subjects is justice. Justice is the mainstay of sovereignty. It is indispensable for the endurance of states and constitutes the foundation of every kingdom, whether that foundation be prophetic or reformist (*kānat nabawiyyatan aw iṣlāḥiyyatan*) (that is, whether it originated in a prophetic mission or in a human initiative to promote the well-being of humankind). Know, may God guide you aright,

[47] Cf. Mediano, 'L'amour, la justice et la crainte', 96–7. Fakhr al-Dīn al-Rāzī states that kings should emulate the prophets as far as possible in all situations, and he enumerates nine prophetic virtues that kings should seek to imitate (*Jāmiʿ al-ʿulūm*, 486).

[48] Notably, the principle of *maṣlaḥa*, the common good, regarded by some of al-Ṭurṭūshī's contemporaries as a fundamental purpose of the divine law; and the related principle of *istiṣlāḥ*, the public good, especially prominent in Mālikī jurisprudence, in which al-Ṭurṭūshī was the leading scholar of the period.

that God Almighty has commanded justice. In addition, He knows, let Him be praised, that not all souls are amenable to justice; rather they seek kindness (*iḥsān*), which is above justice. For He said: 'God has commanded justice, kindness and giving to relatives (*al-ʿadl wa-l-iḥsān wa-ītāʾ dhī l-qurbā*)' (Q 16: 90). If justice alone had sufficed for people, God would not have accompanied it with kindness. For those people who are amenable to justice only when it is amplified with kindness, how can they possibly thrive if justice alone fails to reach them?

Justice is God's scale in the earth, by which He takes from the strong for the sake of the weak and from the undeserving for the sake of the deserving.[49] This scale occupies a position not only among the subjects but also between the ruler and the subjects. Whoever removes the scale that God has established for the correction, through equity, of human affairs risks the wrath of God Almighty.

Know, O ruler, that the realm reflects the form of a man. You are the man's head; your vizier is his heart; his hands are your officials (*aʿwān*); his feet are your subjects; his spirit is your justice. The body cannot survive without spirit.[50] If you wish to achieve the summit of justice, know that the subjects comprise three types: great, small and middling. Consider the great among them a father, the middling among them a brother and the small among them a son. Treat your father with honour (*birra abāka*), your brother with generosity (*akrim akhāka*), and your son with compassion (*arḥam ibnaka*).[51] For by these means you will attain the honour (*birr*), generosity (*karāma*) and compassion (*raḥma*) of God.

[49] The identification of justice as God's scale or balance on the earth appears in numerous locations and with various attributions. It is often ascribed to Aristotle: see Maróth, *Correspondence*, 18; Miskawayh, *Jāvīdān khirad*, 224; al-Mubashshir b. Fātik, *Mukhtār al-ḥikam*, 190. Pseudo-Māwardī (*Naṣīḥat al-mulūk al-mansūb ilā … al-Māwardī*, 251–2) ascribes the formulation to an Indian Testament; Usāma b. Munqidh (*Lubāb al-ādāb*, 57) knew it as a saying of Buzurgmihr; Ghazālī (*Naṣīḥat al-mulūk*, part II: 104–5 = Bagley, *Ghazālī's Book of Counsel for Kings*, 58) and Ibn al-Ḥaddād (*al-Jawhar al-nafīs*, 65) knew the maxim as Prophetic; al-Thaʿālibī, *al-Tamthīl wa-l-muḥāḍara*, 99, ascribed the maxim *al-ḥukm mīzān Allāh fī arḍihi* to Bahrām-i Gūr. Cf. Proverbs 11: 1: 'A false balance is an abomination to the Lord, but an accurate weight is his delight' (*New Oxford Annotated Bible*, 814).

[50] See above, Text 1, at nn. 12–13; like the previous paragraph, this passage appears in Pseudo-Māwardī's *Naṣīḥat al-mulūk* as a citation from the 'Testament of an Indian King'.

[51] Ibn ʿAbd Rabbihi, *al-ʿIqd al-farīd*, I: 39 (the counsel of Sālim b. ʿAbdallāh and Muḥammad b. Kaʿb to ʿUmar b. ʿAbd al-ʿAzīz (r. 99–101/717–20) on his assumption of the caliphate); al-Rāghib al-Iṣfahānī, *Muḥāḍarāt al-udabāʾ*, I: 166 (ʿUmar b. ʿAbd al-ʿAzīz to his governor). The terms *kabīr*, *ṣaghīr* and *wasaṭ* suggest not only differences in

Know that the king's justice induces his subjects to unite in support of him, while oppression on his part inevitably causes their alienation from him. The king's justice is the life of his subjects. Among the wise sayings that have been passed down (*manthūr al-ḥikam*) is the maxim, 'Forty years of an unjust ruler are better than a single hour's neglect of the subjects.'[52] If the king exercises justice among the people closest to him, then the people furthest from him will feel goodwill towards him.

The excellence of kings lies in generosity, their nobility in forgiveness, their greatness in justice. The needful provisions of kings consist of three things: the consultation of sincere counsellors, ensuring the sound intentions of their officials (*thabāt niyyāt al-aʿwān*) and upholding the marketplace of justice. The best of times are the times of just leaders.

Justice is divisible into two kinds. The first kind is divine, sent from God Almighty through His messengers and prophets, upon them be peace. The second kind consists of something that resembles justice, namely reformist governance (*siyāsa iṣlāḥiyya*), which provides a framework of support for the elderly as they become frail and the young as they grow up. It is impossible for a ruler to endure or for a subject population to prosper, whether in a state of faith or unbelief, without the upholding of justice; nor will their affairs assume a state of

status but also, as al-Ṭurṭūshī's analogy implies, differences in age. The division of the king's subjects into three hierarchically structured groups, each requiring different treatments (*siyāsāt*), recurs in a number of forms. The groupings include the *khāṣṣa*, the *ʿāmma* and protégés (*ṣanāʾiʿ*), in a formulation ascribed to al-Walīd b. ʿAbd al-Malik (Ibn ʿAbd Rabbihi, *al-ʿIqd al-farīd*, I: 24; Usāma b. Munqidh, *Lubāb al-ādāb*, 35); the noble (*aḥrār*), common (*ʿāmma*) and lowly (*sifla*) categories, ascribed to Buzurgmihr (Usāma, *Lubāb al-ādāb*, 39); the *khāṣṣa*, subdivided into the righteous and the wicked (*abrār* and *ashrār*), and the *ʿāmma*, ascribed to Anūshīrvān (Usāma, *Lubāb al-ādāb*, 53; cf. al-Nuwayrī, *Nihāyat al-arab*, VI: 44; see Zakeri, 'Some Early Persian Apophthegmata', 291, n. 31, with further attestations and variants). A triad imputed to ʿAlī combines several of these elements: 'Treat the *aḥrār* with pure generosity (*karāma*), the middling (*awsāṭ*) with inducement and threat (*al-raghba wa-l-rahba*), and the *sifla* with contempt (*hawān*)'; Ibn Abī l-Ḥadīd, *Sharḥ Nahj al-balāgha*, XX: 428, no. 574.

[52] This formulation recalls the common Prophetic report, 'An hour of justice in government is better than sixty years of worship' (and variants) (Ibn ʿAbd Rabbihi, *al-ʿIqd al-farīd*, I: 10; Ghazālī, *Naṣīḥat al-mulūk*, part I: 15 = Bagley, *Ghazālī's Book of Counsel for Kings*, 14; part II: 124 = Bagley, *Ghazālī's Book of Counsel for Kings*, 71–2; Ibn al-Ḥaddād, *al-Jawhar al-nafīs*, 65; Usāma b. Munqidh, *Lubāb al-ādāb*, 34; al-Nuwayrī, *Nihāyat al-arab*, VI: 33; al-ʿAjlūnī, *Kashf al-khafāʾ*, II: 54, no. 1719); adduced also in al-Ṭurṭūshī, *Sirāj al-mulūk*, I: 184 (with the related hadith, 'A just ruler's single day of action among his subjects is better than a hundred years of a worshipper's observances among his people', or, in a variant, fifty years). Fakhr al-Dīn al-Rāzī adduces the Prophetic report 'An hour of justice is better than a year of worship' with the explanation that the former benefits the whole, while the latter benefits only a single individual (*Jāmiʿ al-ʿulūm*, 489).

proper order, since such an order will lie beyond the scope of the probable and even the possible.[53]

In the beginning of our book, we mentioned that Solomon, the son of David, peace be upon them both, was deprived of his sovereignty when two adversaries, one of whom held a special position in relation to him, appeared before him seeking his judgement.[54] Solomon said to himself, 'I hope that the person whom I hold in special regard is in the right', and he proceeded to judge in that person's favour. God Almighty deprived him of his sovereignty, and Satan occupied his throne. Make justice the head of your governance; then all calamities that are harmful to governance will depart from you, and all the conditions that support the kingdom will stand firm for you.

ʿAlī b. Abī Ṭālib, may God be pleased with him, said: 'A just leader (*imām ʿādil*) is better than abundant rain, a raging lion is better than a tyrannical ruler (*sulṭān ẓalūm*) and a tyrannical ruler is better than lasting sedition (*fitna*).'[55] [ʿAbdallāh] Ibn Masʿūd (d. *c.* 32–3/652–4) said: 'When a leader is just, he merits recompense, and you are obliged to show gratitude. When he is unjust, his is the burden of responsibility, and your obligation is patient endurance.'[56]

Solomon, the son of David, said: 'Mercy and justice preserve sovereignty.'

The wise philosophers among the Arabs and the non-Arabs[57] have agreed upon the following proposition: that sovereignty is a building, and its foundation is the army; if the foundation is strong, the building will

[53] See also Ibn ʿAbd Rabbihi, *al-ʿIqd al-farīd*, I: 23.

[54] The cross-reference is to *Sirāj al-mulūk*, I: 159–60, where al-Ṭurṭūshī relates an occasion upon which Solomon, in a dispute brought before him, favoured members of his wife's family over their adversaries. On Solomon's rule and occasional lapses, see Walker [Fenton], 'Sulaymān b. Dāwūd'; on his restoration after praying for forgiveness, Q 38: 34, 35, 40.

[55] Ibn ʿAbd Rabbihi, *al-ʿIqd al-farīd*, I: 9 (ascribed in generic fashion to *al-ḥukamāʾ*); and see above, nn. 7–8.

[56] Ibn Masʿūd, one of the very earliest Muslims, was an important transmitter of the Prophet's hadith and a major authority on the Qurʾan (Anthony, 'Ibn Masʿūd, ʿAbdallāh'). Ibn ʿAbd Rabbihi cites the report on the authority of ʿAbdallāh b. ʿUmar [b. al-Khaṭṭāb] (d. 73/693) (*al-ʿIqd al-farīd*, I: 10).

[57] The term *ʿajam* is commonly used as the antonym of *ʿarab*, and it therefore carries the general meaning of non-Arab. Very often, in its applied uses, the term refers to Persians, an inference possible in this instance, given the content of al-Ṭurṭūshī's passage. In al-Ṭurṭūshī's homeland of al-Andalus, however, the term was frequently applied to the local Romance-speaking population, whose language was sometimes described as *ʿajamiyya* (Safran, *Defining Boundaries in al-Andalus*, 57, 75).

last, but if the foundation is weak, the building will collapse. There is no power (*sulṭān*) without an army, no army without wealth, no wealth without raising revenue, no revenue without prosperity and no prosperity without justice. Justice provides the foundation for all these sources of authority.[58]

As for prophetic justice, it is universally agreed that the ruler should gather in his presence the carriers of religious knowledge. They are his guardians (*ḥuffāẓ*), protectors (*ruʿāt*) and instructors (*fuqahāʾ*).[59] They provide guidance in matters related to the Almighty God; they uphold God's command and preserve His statutory limits (*ḥudūd*), and they offer sincere counsel to God's bondsmen. Abū Hurayra (d. 57, 58 or 59/678, 679 or 680) related that the Prophet, may God's peace be upon him, said, 'Religion is counsel (*al-dīn al-naṣīḥa*), religion is counsel, religion is counsel!' He was asked, 'For whom, O Messenger of God? He replied, 'For God and His Book, for His Prophet, and for the leaders of the Muslims and the ordinary people among them (*li-aʾimmat al-muslimīn wa-ʿāmmatihim*).'[60]

58 Versions of this formulation, often described as a 'circle of justice', are ubiquitous in the classical Arabic and Persian literary repertoires; see above, nn. 2, 13; Sadan, 'A "Closed-Circuit" Saying on Practical Justice'; Darling, *History of Social Justice*. For examples, all ascribed to Ardashīr unless otherwise noted, see *ʿAhd Ardashīr*, 98, no. 16 (among the 'Scattered Sayings'); al-Thaʿālibī, *Ādāb al-mulūk*, 54; al-Thaʿālibī, *al-Tamthīl wa-l--muḥāḍara*, 98; al-Thaʿālibī, *al-Iʿjāz wa-l-ījāz*, 62, no. 34 (among the maxims that al-Ṣāḥib b. ʿAbbād urges kings to inscribe in their innermost hearts); al-Thaʿālibī, *Ghurar al-siyar*, 482; Ibn Qutayba, *ʿUyūn al-akhbār*, I: 9 (*kāna yuqālu*); Ibn ʿAbd Rabbihi, *al-ʿIqd al-farīd*, I: 33 (ascribed to ʿAmr b. al-ʿĀṣ); al-Nuwayrī, *Nihāyat al-arab*, VI: 35 (ʿAmr b. al-ʿĀṣ); Pseudo-Māwardī, *Naṣīḥat al-mulūk al-mansūb ilā ... al-Māwardī*, 243 (Anūshīrvān); Ghazālī, *Naṣīḥat al-mulūk*, part II: 100 = Bagley, *Ghazālī's Book of Counsel for Kings*, 56 (*ḥakīmān-i jahān*); cf. also Maróth, *Correspondence*, 80. When included in the 'Long Form' of the *Sirr al-asrār*, this 'circle' is often attributed to ʿAlī b. Abī Ṭālib (see Badawī, *al-Uṣūl al-yūnāniyya*, 128, n. 1; Steele/Ali, *Secretum secretorum*, 227; Manzalaoui, 'The Pseudo-Aristotelian *Kitāb Sirr al-asrār*', 187, 230; cf. 214). Variants appear in Ibn al-Muqaffaʿ, *al-Adab al-ṣaghīr*, 325, and Ibn ʿAbd Rabbihi, *al-ʿIqd al-farīd*, I: 32 (*qālat al-ḥukamāʾ*).

59 The root *ḥ-f-ẓ* connotes the concepts of preservation, conservation, guarding and protecting, and of committing to memory. The term *ḥuffāẓ* (sing. *ḥāfiẓ*) carries, in addition to these general senses, the specific meaning of persons who have committed the Qurʾan to memory. On the term *ruʿāt* (sing. *rāʿin*), see above, Chapter 5, n. 5. The term I have rendered in this instance as 'instructors' is *fuqahāʾ*, usually 'jurists', but suggesting in this case, given the quasi-metaphorical language of the passage, facilitators of religious or legal understanding.

60 Ibn ʿAbd Rabbihi, *al-ʿIqd al-farīd*, I: 11; Pseudo-Māwardī, *Naṣīḥat al-mulūk al-mansūb ilā ... al-Māwardī*, 43. Al-Ṭurṭūshī treats this Prophetic saying at length later in his mirror; see below, Chapter 8, n. 62. Abū Hurayra, a famous Companion of the Prophet, is

Take, O king, the religious scholars as a mantle (*shiʿār*) and the righteous as a cloak (*dithār*);[61] then the kingdom will orbit between the counsels of the learned scholars and the benevolent prayers of the righteous. Fashion a sovereignty that rotates between these two phenomena, so that its pillars will stand firm and its duration will grow long. How could it not be so, when God in His power has set these people apart and chosen them for true knowledge of Him? – As He, Most Glorious of Speakers, has said, 'God is witness that there is no god but He, and the angels and those who possess knowledge (*ūlū l-ʿilm*) (are witness as well); He maintains justice (*qāʾiman bi-l-qisṭ*)' (Q 3: 18). In this verse He began by mentioning Himself; secondly He mentioned His angels, and thirdly the possessors of knowledge, the last group of whom constitute the heirs of the prophets, upon them be peace. The heirs of the prophets represent the people to whom God has granted success, because the prophets' bequests consisted of neither dinar nor dirham, but only of knowledge.[62] Treating this group with honour and drawing them close constitute compliance with God Almighty's command, as well as honourable treatment of the people whom God has praised. It is incumbent upon the king that he should elevate the places assigned for them to sit, and that he should differentiate their positions from the places assigned to other groups. God Almighty said, 'God will raise those of you who believe, and those who have knowledge (*alladhīna ūtū l-ʿilm*), by degrees' (Q 58: 11).[63]

Honourable treatment of the men of learning and seeking association with them will incline the hearts of the subjects towards the ruler, purify their intentions towards him and unite them in love and respect for him. The ruler should never settle a matter nor reach a decision without consulting scholars, since he is required to exercise judgement within the framework of God's sovereignty and to adjudicate within the confines

notable for the very large number of Prophetic hadith transmitted in his name (Juynboll, 'Abū Hurayra').

61 The terms *shiʿār* and *dithār* denote an under and an upper garment respectively.

62 The phrase [*inna l-ʿulamāʾ*] *warathat al-anbiyāʾ lam yuwarrithū dīnāran wa-lā dirhaman wa-warrathū l-ʿilm* is itself part of a Prophetic hadith; see al-Bayhaqī, *Jāmiʿ shuʿab al-īmān*, III: 220–1, no. 1573; Ibn ʿAbd al-Barr, *Jāmiʿ bayān al-ʿilm*, 160, no. 169; al-ʿAjlūnī, *Kashf al-khafāʾ*, I: 156, no. 512; cf. Gilliot, 'ʿUlamāʾ', I. Al-Thaʿālibī includes it amongst his selected Prophetic metaphors (*istiʿārāt*) (al-Thaʿālibī, *al-Iʿjāz wa-l-ījāz*, 13, no. 11).

63 The preceding text in this Qurʾanic verse reads: 'O you who believe, when you are told to make room in the assemblies (*fī l-majālis*), then make room; God will make room for you. And if you are told to rise up higher, then rise'; this text finds an echo in the passage that precedes al-Ṭurṭūshī's scriptural citation.

of His religious law. The least of the obligations upon the ruler is that he should subordinate himself in his relationship to God in accordance with the position of his own governors (*wulāt*) in relation to himself. Is it not the case that if his governor should oppose his command and resist the ordinances that he has laid down for him, the ruler will dismiss and castigate him, and that the governor enjoys no security against his power? And conversely, that if the governor complies with his commands and observes the limits of the ruler's restrictions, he enjoys the ruler's pleasure? How extraordinary, then, would be the case of the ruler moved to rage in the face of the disobedience of his governor but fearless of the power of his Lord over him when he resists Him!

This is the way of establishing the justice of the religious law (*al-ʿadl al-sharʿī*) and Islamic governance (*al-siyāsa al-islāmiyya*), which unites various kinds of welfare (*wujūh al-maṣlaḥa*), takes up the reins of sound administration, is free of faults and facilitates the upholding of the world and religion. Just as the prudent king's resolve (*ḥazm*) cannot become perfect without consultation with viziers and men of integrity (*akhyār*), in the same way his justice (*ʿadl*) cannot become perfect without seeking the professional opinions of the upright religious scholars.[64]

In the story of a petitioner wronged by ʿAmr b. Masʿada, al-Maʾmūn interjected, 'O ʿAmr, perpetuate the divine favour that you enjoy through justice, for oppression will destroy it.'[65]

The diffusion of justice promotes strength of heart, the welfare of the soul, the confidence of certainty and security against enemies.

When al-Hurmuzān (d. 23/644) sought permission to present himself to ʿUmar b. al-Khaṭṭāb, may God be pleased with him, he found neither chamberlain nor gatekeeper at the caliph's residence. He was told that the caliph was in the mosque. So he went to the mosque and found ʿUmar lying down, his head resting on a pillow of pebbles, his whip in front of him. He said to him, 'You are just, and therefore safe; and so you are able to sleep.'[66]

64 The conjunction of *ḥazm* and *ʿadl* may suggest, in this case, combining humane, worldly knowledge and wisdom with specifically religious learning.

65 On ʿAmr, see above, Chapter 5, n. 78. The saying entails a play on the letters ʿ-*m*-*r*, which form the base of ʿAmr's name and at the same time connote life (*ʿumr*); the caliph's exhortation to ʿAmr (*iʿmar niʿmataka bi-l-ʿadl*) calls upon him to enliven or extend the life of the divine favour that he has received.

66 The Persian general al-Hurmuzān was a prominent figure in the early conquests of the Sasanian Empire. He led Sasanian armies at the Battle of al-Qādisiyya in 16/637, and he remained active until he was taken prisoner in 21/642 and brought to Medina. Several

Al-Ḥasan said:

> I saw ʿUthmān b. ʿAffān, may God be pleased with him, in the Mosque of the Prophet, may the blessings and peace of God be upon him. His head resting on a pile of pebbles, ʿUthmān, who was at that time Commander of the Faithful, had pulled part of his cloak over his body. No one was with him, and his whip lay in front of him.

The governor of Homs wrote to ʿUmar b. ʿAbd al-ʿAzīz to report that the city had been destroyed and stood in need of restoration. ʿUmar wrote back to him, 'Fortify it with justice, and expunge all traces of injustice from its streets. Farewell.'[67] The sages have said: 'Anyone who withholds justice has no good in him, and there is no good for the people in his possession of power.'

Yaḥyā b. Aktham (d. 242/857) related that on one occasion he was walking in a garden alongside al-Maʾmūn. The right side of the path was in full sun; al-Maʾmūn was walking in the shade. On their return, once again it was Yaḥyā who was in the sun. Al-Maʾmūn said to Yaḥyā:

> Change places with me. I'll take your place so that you'll be in the shade, just as I was; and you'll enjoy protection from the sun, just as I had protection from it when we set out. For the first component of justice is that a man should deal fairly with his closest companions (*biṭāna*), then with those next to them, and so on, until justice reaches the very lowest category.

Yaḥyā reported: 'He insisted upon this principle, and so I changed places with him.'[68]

It used to be said that nothing is more unlikely than the endurance of rule seized through usurpation.

reports suggest that he eventually became a Muslim and rose to a position of some importance in Medina before his murder at the hands of ʿUmar's son ʿUbayd Allāh b. ʿUmar in 23/644 (see Veccia Vaglieri, 'al-Hurmuzān'). In one version of the account, al-Hurmuzān contrasts ʿUmar with all four of the Sasanian kings whom he had served, none of whom, he avers – their crowns notwithstanding – had inspired the awe (*hayba*) that ʿUmar inspired (al-Thaʿālibī, *Thimār al-qulūb*, 86; al-Nuwayrī, *Nihāyat l-arab*, VI: 36). Ghazālī (*Naṣīḥat al-mulūk*, part I, 25–6 = Bagley, *Ghazālī's Book of Counsel for Kings*, 18) reports a version of the story in which it is envoys from Byzantium whose conversion is occasioned by the sight of ʿUmar in this vulnerable condition.

[67] Ibn Qutayba, *ʿUyūn al-akhbār*, I: 13; al-Thaʿālibī, *al-Iʿjāz wa-l-ījāz*, 79, no. 15.

[68] See also Ibn Qutayba, *ʿUyūn al-akhbār*, I: 23. Yaḥyā b. Aktham was a judge and counsellor to some of the Abbasid caliphs; he became Chief Judge of Baghdad in 202/817–18, as well as a member of al-Maʾmūn's court circle and his boon-companion (Bosworth, 'Yaḥyā b. Aktham').

It was suggested to Alexander that he consort with many women, so that he would produce numerous offspring and thereby perpetuate his memory. He said, 'Only good deeds and praiseworthy conduct perpetuate memory; and it is not becoming for a man who has overcome men to be defeated himself by women.'[69] The sage philosopher (*al-ḥakīm*) said: 'He who makes a habitual practice of justice has the best protection, and he who dons the dress of justice completes the adornment of excellence.'

Abū ʿUbayd b. ʿAbdallāh b. Masʿūd said: 'The just leader mutes the voices raised to God in distress, while the unjust ruler increases the complaints raised to Almighty God.'

The philosopher said: 'The ruler will enjoy continuing respite until he transgresses the pillars of prosperity and the foundations of the religious law; at that point, God will deliver the people from him.'[70]

It has been said: 'Do not act unjustly with the weak, lest you become one of the ignoble strong.' One of the sages said:

> A ruler (*amīr*) devoid of justice is like a cloud without rain; a learned man who lacks scrupulousness is like a land without plants; a young man deficient in repentance is like a tree without fruit; a rich man devoid of generosity is like a lock without a key; a poor man without patience is like a lamp without light; a woman lacking in modesty is like food without salt.

Khusraw said:

> The Persian kings have agreed on four principles: food should not be consumed in the absence of appetite; a woman should not be observed except in the context of marriage; the only rightful posture towards the king is obedience; and the only fitting approach towards the subjects is justice.

The persons who must, above all others, ensure that they act in accordance with justice are kings, who by their justice set other people to rights, and who, when they speak and act, are effective and do not meet with resistance. The sages have said, 'As long as your wish accords with equity, seek whatever you desire, and I shall lead the call for your success

[69] Al-Thaʿālibī, *Ādāb al-mulūk*, 64; al-Thaʿālibī, *al-Iʿjāz wa-l-ījāz*, 55, no. 15; cf. al-Mubashshir b. Fātik, *Mukhtār al-ḥikam*, 246, 248. The *Sirr al-asrār* expressly discourages Alexander from excessive copulation, and indeed from indulgence in all physical pleasures (*al-Uṣūl al-yūnāniyya*, 79 = Steele/Ali, *Secretum secretorum*, 186 and *passim*).

[70] Al-Māwardī, *Tashīl al-naẓar*; see above, Text 10, n. 15.

in achieving it. It is injustice that is most likely to prompt a reversal in the favour that you enjoy, and to hasten retribution.'

The sage philosopher (*al-ḥakīm*) said: 'The worst provision for the afterlife is continual sin; worse still is hostility to God's bondsmen.' When a ruler desires a good reputation and a fine remembrance, let him uphold the marketplace of justice; if he aspires to approach God and to attain a noble station in His sight, let him uphold the marketplace of justice; and if he wishes for both of these things, let him uphold the marketplace of justice. Two qualities have perpetuated the remembrance of kings from time immemorial: pure justice and shameful injustice. The former necessarily fosters people's compassion towards him, whereas the latter inevitably causes him to be cursed.

Section

As for the second division of justice, it comprises governance for the welfare of humankind (*al-siyāsa al-iṣlāḥiyya*). Even if the roots of such governance lie in oppression (*jawr*), as long as it provides firm support for the affairs of the world, it will reflect degrees of fairness (*inṣāf*), in the manner, for example, that pertained in the days of the Persian *mulūk al-ṭawāʾif* (regional rulers of the Parthian period before the rise of the Sasanians).[71] These kings were infidels (*kuffār*) who adored the sun, worshipped fires and followed the notions of Satan, yet they established customs, founded ordinances, instituted degrees of equity (*naṣafa*) among the subjects and regulated the exaction of the land-taxes and the imposition of levies on commercial transactions. They enacted all of these practices on the basis of their intellects, according to ways of reasoning that derived neither from the power nor the proof of divine revelation. When, however, God Almighty brought humankind the religious law (*sharīʿa*) on the tongue of His Prophet Muḥammad, bearer of the divine miracle, the divine law confirmed the establishment of certain parts of the

[71] The phrase *mulūk al-ṭawāʾif*, kings of territorial divisions or of groups of people, characteristically denotes either, with reference to Iran, the regional rulers of the Parthian or Arsacid period who ruled Iran for roughly half a millennium between the conquest of Alexander and the rise of the Sasanians, or the 'party kings' who ruled principalities that emerged in Iberia between the collapse of the Umayyad state in the wake of the deposition of Hishām II al-Muʾayyad (r. 366–99/976–1009; d. 403/1013) and the late eleventh-century invasions of the Almoravids. Al-Ṭurṭūshī explicitly links his use of the term to the pre-Islamic Persian context (his Andalusi predecessor, the judge and author Ṣāʿid al-Andalusī (420–62/1029–70), equated the two groups of *mulūk al-ṭawāʾif* (*Ṭabaqāt al-umam*, 84)).

earlier regulations, abrogated other parts and invalidated certain ordinances. The most effective wisdom (*al-ḥikma al-bāligha*) now rested on the foundation of the commandments of God Almighty, and the religious ordinances on the divine revelation; everything else became null and void.[72]

It was their attention to the prevailing customary laws (*al-qawānīn al-ma'lūfa baynahum*) that protected the sovereignty of the Persian kings and severed the rope of neglect. By these laws, the kings upheld the people's mandatory claims, and they attended to their rights and responsibilities. Given this experience, it used to be said that the infidel ruler who maintains the conditions of governance necessary for the welfare of the subjects (*sharā'iṭ al-siyāsa al-iṣlāḥiyya*) enjoys a longer reign and possesses greater strength than the believing ruler who, although just in himself, neglects the justice of prophetic governance (*al-siyāsa al-nabawiyya al-'adliyya*). Injustice that rests on the basis of an established order proves more enduring than (prophetically founded) justice, if the latter is neglected; for nothing improves the ruler's position more effectively than the sound arrangement of affairs, and nothing corrupts it more thoroughly than their neglect.

Know that a single dirham taken from the subjects in a careless manner contrary to custom, even if the grounds for its collection are just, causes them deeper distress than ten dirhams taken in accordance with well-known governmental practice and familiar custom, even if its basis is unjust. Power (*sulṭān*) remains firm neither for the people of faith nor for the people of unbelief without the establishment of either prophetic justice or a system that resembles justice in its arrangements for the public good (*al-tartīb al-iṣṭilāḥī*).

Ibn al-Muqaffa' said:

> There are three types of sovereignty: sovereignty rooted in religion, in prudent resolve (*ḥazm*) and in capricious desire. As for sovereignty rooted in religion: if it establishes the people's religion in the kingdom they will be content; anyone who is displeased will still align himself with the ranks of the contented. As for sovereignty rooted in prudent resolve: it will ensure the firm establishment of the kingdom's affairs; the king will not be immune from criticism and displeasure, but the criticism of the base will never threaten the

[72] On *ḥikma bāligha*, see above, Chapter 5, n. 55.

resolve of the strong. As for sovereignty based in whimsical appetite:
an hour's amusement will entail an aeon of ruin.[73]

We have heard the account of an Indian king who, afflicted by deafness, became withdrawn and anxious over the affairs of aggrieved petitioners, since he could no longer hear their appeals for help. He ordered his herald to proclaim that no one in his kingdom should wear red clothing unless he sought redress.[74] He said, 'My hearing may be impaired, but my sight remains intact.' Consequently, everyone who had suffered oppression dressed in red clothing and came to stand before his palace; in this way each petitioner revealed his grievance.[75]

Our shaykh reported that Abū l-ʿAbbās al-Ḥijāzī, who had travelled to China, had informed him of a strange yet remarkable practice particular to the governance of the Chinese kings. In the king's residential quarters, according to his report, is a gong, connected to a chain; the end of the chain is positioned outside in the street, where the ruler's stewards and guardians observe it. The person who has suffered a grievance arrives at the royal quarters and pulls the chain. The king hears the sound of the gong, and he orders the petitioner's admittance. Whenever anyone pulls the chain, the king's guardians take hold of him and bring him into the presence of the ruler.

[73] Ibn al-Muqaffaʿ, *al-Ādāb al-kabīr*, 284; Ibn Qutayba, *ʿUyūn al-akhbār*, I: 2 (I have followed the published text of *ʿUyūn al-akhbār* in reading *mulk* for *malik*). Cf. Kristó-Nagy, 'Marriage after Rape', 173, with reference to the translation of this passage in van Gelder, *Classical Arabic Literature*, 173: 'Know that there are three kinds of rules: one of religion, one of judiciousness, and one of personal inclination. As for the ruler who is religious, if he upholds the religion of his people, and if their religion is such that he gives them their due and metes out to them what they deserve, they will be pleased with him and he will turn the discontented among them into people who will gladly conform and submit. The reign of a ruler who is judicious is stable; he will not be free of criticism and discontent, but the criticism of a lowly person will not be harmful if the judicious ruler is strong. As for a ruler of arbitrariness, his reign is one hour of play and an eternity of ruin.' For a discussion of this passage, see also Yavari, *Advice for the Sultan*, 41–2.

[74] It was the responsibility of the herald (*munādī*) to call forward the litigants in the qadi's court and in the *maẓālim* court; Tillier, 'Courts of Law'.

[75] See above, n. 26. In the passage that follows this account, al-Ṭurṭūshī appears to move by way of association from a well-known example of justice in a remote context to a less well-known Chinese example, for which he supplies his source. It is interesting to note that the exemplary status accorded to non-Muslim rulers applied not only to monarchs of the distant (and pre-Islamic) past but also, occasionally, to contemporary examples, particularly to groups, like the Qara Khitai, located beyond the eastern borders (see Biran, 'True to Their Ways'; Lane, *The Phoenix Mosque and the Persians of Hangzhou*, 21–2).

8

The Practice of Good Governance

The selections in Chapter 8 discuss specific royal practices intended to enact the ethical and pragmatic principles of governance treated in Chapter 7. Prominent among these practices is constant royal oversight of the many officials and intermediaries employed to carry out the tasks of government, above all, the collection of taxes. These intermediaries represented not only a link between the ruling power and its subjects but also the visible 'face' of the ruler across the far-flung territories that made up his realm.[1] Strict and consistent oversight, accompanied by swift dismissal when cases of abuse came to light, were the only measures that would protect the revenue-producing categories on whose labour the entire edifice of government depended. In cases of injustice, it was the ruler's obligation to provide a means of redress, through the practice of listening to the petitions of his subjects and restoring to them any property that had been wrongfully seized.[2]

The selections highlight the royal responsibility for fairness, particularly in fiscal matters. It is the king's responsibility to ensure the prosperity of land and people, which, as the writers point out repeatedly, he neglects at his peril. The practices of good governance urged upon the wise and virtuous ruler reflect the principle of *maṣlaḥa*, the

[1] I adopt the term from Cristina Jular Pérez-Alfaro's study of royal officers in thirteenth- and fourteenth-century Castile ('The King's Face on the Territory', 108).

[2] See Crone, *Medieval Islamic Political Thought*, 159 and n. 63; Niẓām al-Mulk, *Siyar al-mulūk*, 18–29 (see above, Text 11), 57–8, 59–60 = Darke, *Book of Government*, 14–22, 44–5, 46–7; Ghazālī, *Naṣīḥat al-mulūk*, 47–8, 99–100, 122 = Bagley, *Ghazālī's Book of Counsel for Kings*, 29, 55–6, 70. See further above, Chapter 7, n. 24.

common good.[3] The mirror-writers link the well-being of the land with the well-being of the people who live in it, depend upon it and work it. There is, accordingly, a strong consciousness of environmental health, in an agrarian age in which people and land were directly interdependent, the people's control over the land and its resources limited and achieved only through intelligent management and hard labour. As the writers point out, the small proportion of people who were not directly dependent on the land were indirectly dependent on it, since wealth, necessary for their own maintenance, derived from two principal sources: the produce of the land and commerce. Contemporary readers may note in particular the pre-modern authors' sense of limits – the limits of the ruler's power, and the limits of humanity's exploitation of the land.

Text 13
Al-Māwardī, *Tashīl al-naẓar wa-taʿjīl al-ẓafar*. Part II, Section[4]

Translator's Introduction

This section, like the passages reproduced in Texts 3 and 10, appears in *Tashīl al-naẓar*'s part II, which is devoted to the practical aspects of governance. Text 13 follows directly from the section reproduced in Text 10. The section opens with al-Māwardī's identification of four principles of good governance. Interrelated and interdependent, these four principles mirror the constituent elements of the 'circle of justice'; unless each part thrives, the polity as a whole can never prosper. Most of Text 13 represents al-Māwardī's treatment of the first of his four principles: the cultivation of the lands. In his treatment of this topic, al-Māwardī emphasises the ruler's responsibility for the environmental health of the kingdom and the welfare of the peasantry. Also in this extract, al-Māwardī acknowledges the necessity of the religious law and non-religious legislation, *qānūn* (pl. *qawānīn*),[5]

[3] The flexibility of the concept, and its potential for bringing together scholars and specialists of all kinds, including men of letters, is explored in Hartung, 'Enacting the Rule of Islam'.

[4] Translation prepared from al-Māwardī, *Tashīl al-naẓar wa-taʿjīl al-ẓafar*, 207–23. For the corresponding section in Abbès's translation into French, see Abbès, *De l'Éthique du prince*, 367–82.

[5] The term initially applied especially to regulations for and registers pertaining to the assessment of the land-taxes; these regulations derived not from sacred texts but from local

a pairing that coincides in his presentation with the realms of sharia and *ʿadl*; his distinction in some respects recalls al-Ṭurṭūshī's categories of prophetic (*nabawī*) and reformist (*iṣlāḥī*) modes of governance (see Text 12), both of which provide for the welfare of the subjects. The eclecticism of al-Māwardī's citations is a characteristic feature of his mirrors. Notably, Text 13 also includes one of al-Māwardī's occasional references to his own experience, in this instance his service as an envoy between rulers.

Translation

After the foundation and establishment of the state have been achieved, its governance involves four principles: cultivation of the lands, protection of the subjects, management of the army and proper assessment of its revenues.[6]

Let us begin with the first principle, that is, cultivation of the lands. There are two kinds of land: agricultural and urban. The agricultural lands are the source of the material products on which the state depends for its subsistence and by which the subjects' circumstances are maintained in good order. Maintaining the good health of the lands results in their fertility and rich productivity; if they fall into poor condition, the results are barrenness and failure to produce. These lands constitute stored-up treasures and ready funds. Any country with abundant fruits and crops is, by virtue of its flourishing condition, independent; furthermore, its felicity overflows to the benefit of others. A prosperous country attracts revenues; its food products remain in high demand. The opposite conditions result if the agricultural lands suffer diminishment or degradation.

The administrator of the state (*mudabbir al-mulk*) must fulfil three obligations (*ḥuqūq*) in regard to the agricultural lands. First, he must take responsibility for maintaining the good condition of the water supplies over which he exercises authority. He possesses the power to ensure that

custom. As the term's meaning evolved, it came to connote legal prescriptions issued by rulers.

[6] Elsewhere, al-Māwardī lists seven things incumbent on the ruling authorities of the *umma* (*sulṭān al-umma*): the safeguarding of religion; protection of the territory and defence of the community; cultivation of the land; assessing the ruler's share in the revenues; undertaking the redress of grievances and the implementation of ordinances; maintaining the stipulated penalties; and the selection of deputies (*Adab al-dunyā wa-l-dīn*, 139). In his juridical treatise, he provides a list of the ten mandatory public responsibilities of the imam (al-Māwardī, *al-Aḥkām al-sulṭāniyya*, 12–14 = Wahba, *Ordinances of Government*, 16; see below, n. 15).

the water flows copiously without being cut off, and that it reaches the entire population without interruption, so that everybody, near and far alike, can share it, and the strong and the weak benefit equally from it. If the water supplies are neglected, they will diminish, and people will compete, by force and by violence, for access to water; the sound management of the water supply will become defective, and the repair necessary to maintain it will lapse. The person who is most able to exercise domination will take possession of it, and he will appropriate the funds and foodstuffs that depend on it. People will suffer shortages so that this one person can enjoy his plenty, and their lives will become disrupted for the sake of his well-being. This person's prosperity will bring barrenness, and the comfort of his situation will entail hardship for the rest of the population.[7]

The ruler's second responsibility is to protect the people from exploitation and avert harm from them, for they are vulnerable to the powerful and mighty, who regard them as morsels and crumbs available for their consumption. The ruler must ensure that the people are secure in their lands, so that they are relieved of the need to defend themselves, having no task other than cultivation. For each occupation, there is a suitable group of people who will devote themselves to it. If the ruler governs in this way, the cultivators will multiply as a result of their prosperity; they will live at ease through their agriculture, and they will bring aid and support to other groups. The Prophet said: 'Seek sustenance from that which is hidden in the earth', through cultivation.[8]

The third task incumbent upon the ruler is assessment of the levies due from the people. These sums should be reckoned according to the judgement of the religious law (*shar*ʿ) and the verdict of justice (*ʿadl*), so that the amounts due do not cause damage, nor does their collection involve oppression. For the peasantry depend on the ruler's justice to ensure their equitable treatment in the matter of taxation. If the ruler ensures this equity, they will render obediently the amounts due from them, and will enjoy the surplus left to them by the lightening of the burdens placed upon them. When the peasants live in ease, times will be

[7] Al-Māwardī includes an extensive discussion of water supplies in *al-Aḥkām al-sulṭāniyya*, 203–9 = Wahba, *Ordinances of Government*, 197–201.

[8] Al-ʿAjlūnī, *Kashf al-khafāʾ*, I: 161, no. 529; also cited in al-Māwardī, *Qawānīn al-wizāra*, 162; al-Māwardī, *Adab al-dunyā wa-l-dīn*, 210; al-Māwardī, *al-Amthāl wa-l-ḥikam*, p. 77, no. 194/551; al-Thaʿālibī, *Thimār al-qulūb*, 509; al-Thaʿālibī, *al-Tamthīl wa-l-muḥāḍara*, 158; al-Thaʿālibī, *Khāṣṣ al-khāṣṣ*, 120; al-Tawḥīdī, *al-Baṣāʾir wa-l-dhakhāʾir*, VII: 259, no. 748.

plentiful, and when their affairs are in good order, the kingdom will flourish. If, on the other hand, the amount of their taxes causes harm to the people, or if its collection involves oppressive means, this state of well-being will be turned into its opposite. The peasants will fall into debt, and they will be forced into penury. The ruler's governance will depend on force, and it will depart from the path of justice and equity. The injury and disruption that the people have suffered will lead them to disaffection from the ruler, and to abandon their lands.

Solomon, son of David, upon him be peace, said: 'Drink water from your own well, and let your water flow into your markets; your well will then be blessed.'[9] Buzurgmihr said, 'He who fills his treasury by means of injustice to his subjects is like he who patches his roof with bricks taken from the foundations of his house.'[10] Ziyād wrote to his officials in Iraq, 'Treat the agriculturalists well, for you will remain well-fed only as long as they are well-fed.'[11]

As for cities, they are places that bring many people together, for five purposes. Firstly, a city's inhabitants settle in it for the sake of peace and tranquillity. Secondly, cities are intended to facilitate the conservation of financial resources and to prevent their exhaustion and waste. Thirdly, cities are designed for the protection of women and the dependent members of the household from abuse and humiliation. Fourthly, cities offer the opportunity to find necessary commodities and occupations. Fifthly, they provide opportunities for earning a livelihood and obtaining materials. If a city lacks any one of these five things, not only will the settlement fail to endure; it will also become a place of desolation and ruin. Al-Zubayr b. al-ʿAwwām, God be pleased with him, said:

> I heard the Prophet of God say: 'The lands belong to God; wherever you find good (in them), praise God and take up residence.'[12]

9 Cf. Proverbs, V: 15: 'Drink water from your own cistern, flowing water from your own well' (*New Oxford Annotated Bible*, 808).

10 *Thimār al-qulūb*, 179 (Anūshīrvān); al-Thaʿālibī, *al-Tamthīl wa-l-muḥāḍara*, 99 (Anūshīrvān); al-Ṭurṭūshī, *Sirāj al-mulūk*, II: 497 (among the reports of Jaʿfar b. Yaḥyā the Barmakid).

11 Ibn Qutayba, *ʿUyun al-akhbār*, I: 10; Ibn Ḥamdūn, *al-Tadhkira al-Ḥamdūniyya*, I: 295; al-Rāghib al-Iṣfahānī, *Muḥāḍarāt al-udabāʾ*, I: 169; al-Ṭurṭūshī, *Sirāj al-mulūk*, II: 496. Ziyād b. Abīhi, also known as Ziyād b. Abī Sufyān (d. 53/673), held the post of governor of Iraq and the eastern provinces of the Umayyad caliphate during the reign of Muʿāwiya (r. 41–60/661–80) (see further Hasson, 'Ziyād b. Abīhi').

12 Al-Sakhāwī, *al-Maqāṣid al-ḥasana*, 240, no. 304. Al-Zubayr b. al-ʿAwwām, a Companion of the Prophet, was closely connected to the Prophet's family and to the family of Abū Bakr, the first caliph. He was also the father of ʿAbdallāh b. al-Zubayr, who would rule

The ruler's role in cultivating the lands and building cities is more extensive than that of his subjects, since he is the root and they are the branches, he the one followed and they his followers.

In founding cities, there are six conditions that must be taken into account. The first requirement is the availability of an abundant supply of fresh water; the second, the potential for constructive development; the third is the temperateness of the site, and the corresponding properties of healthful air and soil; fourthly, the site should offer proximity to two necessities, grazing lands and sources of wood; fifthly, its living quarters must be well fortified against enemies and brigands; sixthly, it should be surrounded by agricultural land, the products of which are ample enough to support its people. When these six conditions are fully met in the founding of a city, its enduring foundations will be exceedingly strong, and it will only disappear if subject to a divine judgement or when the time appointed for its end, known only to God, approaches.

In addition to these six necessary conditions for the siting of cities, there are eight conditions, incumbent upon the founder of the city, that concern the rights of the city's inhabitants. The founder's first charge is to ensure that running water reaches even its most distant areas, whether by means of flowing rivers or through well-stocked reservoirs, so that people will be able to break their journeys there without needing to divert their routes. Secondly, the ruler must calculate the measurements of the city's thoroughfares and streets, so that they are well proportioned in relation to one another, in order to avoid congestion and allow people to pass through them without risk of injury. The ruler's third responsibility is the construction of a Friday mosque for the congregational prayers. This mosque should be located in the middle of the city, so that it is equally close to all the inhabitants; he should then construct smaller mosques in the streets throughout the city. Fourthly, he must assess and determine its markets, ensuring that they suffice for the city's inhabitants and are located in the places where they are most needed. The fifth condition is that he should ensure the distinctness of each urban neighbourhood according to the composition of its residents and the backgrounds of its inhabitants; he should not group together rivalrous and conflicting groups or members of different ethnic communities (*ajnās*). Sixthly, if the king wishes to reside in the city, he should reside

from Mecca for almost a decade before Umayyad forces defeated his forces and killed him in 72–3/691–2.

in its most spacious area, and surround his residence with the houses of all his retainers and a sufficient number of military personnel; he should disperse the rest of his military forces in the remaining parts of the city, so that they are able to provide protection for the town from all directions. The ruler must treat the urban population with particular justice. He should settle the ordinary townspeople in the city centre, for two reasons: so that the people benefit from the protection of his troops, and so that the king will rarely find it necessary to ride in their midst, and he will therefore avoid appearing lenient in their eyes. The seventh condition is that if the city borders on hostile territory or its inhabitants fear seizure, he must surround the townspeople with sturdy walls, so that no one is able to enter unless it is in accordance with the townspeople's wish, and no one is able to leave without their knowledge; for the city should be a safe haven for its inhabitants and a refuge for its residents. The founding king's eighth responsibility is to move into the city a sufficient number of specialists in the various sciences and occupations, so that the urban population need not depend for the provision of their needs on persons living elsewhere.

If the city's founder satisfies these eight conditions, he will have fulfilled his obligations towards the townspeople; their only remaining claim against him is that he should act among them according to the finest conduct and that he should adopt in his relations with them an exemplary path. In these circumstances, the new city will belong among the most perfect places to live, and among the most equitable places to settle.

Cities are of two kinds: they are based either on pasturage and agricultural lands, or on economic opportunity and commerce. Of these two types, the first, that based on lands suitable for grazing and for agriculture, is the more firmly established in terms of its people. It is also preferable to the second type of city in terms of its conditions, and more desirable as a place to live, owing to its ready supply of provisions and the possibility of acquiring the sources for these provisions. Among the requirements of such a city is that it be located in the middle of its arable land, situated at the mid-point of all the surrounding land's extremities, so that the supplies of agricultural produce will be evenly accessible from one area to another, and the roads from these areas to the city equal to one another. A city sited in this fashion will be abundantly prosperous as long as its arable land remains under cultivation. If an injustice should afflict the city's people, the harm will cause them to disperse among their arable lands, where they will be able to achieve a fully satisfactory way of life and defend themselves against the prevailing injustice for a certain period of time. If, on the other hand, the [governor of the] arable land treats its inhabitants unjustly, they are in a position to seek the security and shelter available in the city. In other words, both places, the land and the city, provide places of refuge from one another.

The second type of city, the city of [economic] opportunity and commerce, is among the perfections of the region and the adornments of the realm. It is the destination for the rarities of many lands and the novelties of many regions; it lacks for no desirable commodity, nor is a single import excluded from it. For such cities, there are three conditions that must be considered. One consideration is that the city of opportunity and commerce should be situated in the midst of cities of the first kind, namely cities of the countryside; furthermore, it should lie in proximity to the lands traversed by merchants, so that it is not far away for anyone seeking it and not too distant for any person who directs his path towards it. The second condition is that it should lie on a route made up of easily passable roads that allow for the transport of heavy burdens, either by river or on the backs of animals. If the route consists of roads that are rough and deserts that are arid, people will abandon it, unless under duress. The third condition for this type of city is that its roads should be safe for people carrying rare commodities, and they should involve minimal discomfort and little burden. The main people who frequent this city are traders in transit, looking for the most profitable goods in the lands; in their case, if the route becomes too arduous, the city will be abandoned.

This latter type of city is the more sought-after one, the type that is more widely talked about throughout the region. It furthers the objectives of kings rather than supplying them with the resources that they need, for, if they resort to extreme measures or exercise injustice in it through the raising of illegal taxes and tithes, the city's population will flee. If the townspeople find an alternative city comparable to it, the first city will turn into a place to which people come only out of necessity and not out of choice, and, moreover, cities founded on the basis of coercion cannot last. It is not improbable that a city of this kind will become extinguished, as the person who lives there only because he has been coerced to do so may well join the person who has exercised choice [and left]. Since the city's wealth is derived from moveable trade, if the king does not redress his sovereignty by lightening the burden [of taxation] and establishing equity, it will not be onerous for the people to change [the city in which they conduct their trade]; they will settle in more equitable lands, and will aim for the easiest environment for trade and transactions, since even if a country is far away, to these people, all lands constitute their country. The poet said:

> Leave an evil place; do not take up residence in it.
> If there is a better place to live that lies far away, then depart.[13]

Section

The second of the four principles involved in the governance of the realm is the protection of the subjects. The subjects are like trusts that God has deposited with the king: God has charged the king with the duty of protection for the people over whom He has appointed him.[14] The subjects lack the capacity to defend themselves by any means other than through his power; nor are they capable of achieving justice and equity among themselves, other than through his kindness. In relation to the subjects, the king is in the position of the orphan's guardian, who is commissioned to protect the orphan and responsible for his welfare. The orphan's guardian must, according to the custody and trust with which he is charged, rectify his charge's slips, correct his errors, protect his possessions and augment his resources. Similarly, the king's position in relation to his subjects demands that he defend them, maintain his oversight of them and take responsibility for their interests. The benefit of their welfare on their conditions will redound to him, just as any harm that they may suffer will return to him. There will never exist a stable sovereignty in which the conditions of the subjects are corrupt.

With regard to his role as guardian of the subjects, ten things are necessary for the king.[15]

[13] Al-Mufaḍḍal al-Ḍabbī, *Dīwān al-Mufaḍḍaliyyāt*, 751, CXVI, line 8; al-Māwardī, *al-Amthāl wa-l-ḥikam*, 84, no. 187/607 (citing ʿAbd Qays b. Khufāf al-Burjumī).

[14] Cf. Pseudo-Māwardī, Text 1.

[15] There are some points here common to the ten general duties of the imam that al-Māwardī lists in *al-Aḥkām al-sulṭāniyya*: safeguarding the religion, as the community's forebears have agreed upon it; executing ordinances between disputants in order to further the spread of equity (*naṣafa*); protecting the territory and defending the subjects' households so that they can pursue their livelihoods and travel in safety; upholding the statutory penalties; fortifying the borders; struggling against the enemies of Islam; collecting the *fayʾ* and *ṣadaqāt* according to the religious law; assessing the stipends due from the treasury and ensuring their payment without delay; appointing reliable and sincere persons to delegated offices; personal oversight of matters and observing the

Firstly, he must ensure that the subjects are able to reside in their homes in tranquillity. Secondly, he must leave them unmolested and secure in their homes. Thirdly, he must avert injury from them and restrain the hands of the overbearing from them. Fourthly, he must treat them with justice and equity. Fifthly, he must settle the disputes that arise among them. Sixthly, he must induce them to heed the requirements of the religious law in their acts of worship and in their transactions with one another. Seventhly, he must uphold among them the statutory penalties of God Almighty and His rightful claims. Eighthly, he must ensure the security of their routes and roads. Ninthly, he must attend to their welfare by preserving their water supplies and viaducts. Tenthly, inasmuch as they differ in religion, occupation, means of livelihood and probity, he must assess their various qualities and order them according to their worth and their stations.[16]

If the king upholds these ten rights among his subjects, he will have manifested just governance and virtuous conduct, which will earn him the subjects' obedience and ensure the welfare of the kingdom. If he falls short in them, then these outcomes will be reversed. Ardashīr b. Bābak said:

> The happiness of the subjects lies in obedience to the king (*ṭāʿat al-malik*), and the happiness of the king lies in obedience to the Possessor [of Sovereignty] (*ṭāʿat al-mālik*).[17]

A man of wit and intelligence said:

> If the power of the king occasions no joy for his subjects, then his sovereignty is a kind of tyranny.[18]

conditions of the people (*al-Aḥkām al-sulṭāniyya*, 16–17 = Wahba, *Ordinances of Government*, 16). In the present context, it is the subjects' perspective that predominates, and the list reflects the subjects' rights to the ruler's fulfilment of the conditions necessary to their welfare; the absence of *jihād*, prerogative of the imam alone, from the list of duties in *Tashīl al-naẓar* supports the supposition that it was written for a Buyid ruler rather than a caliph. See further above, n. 6.

16 Assuring that each individual occupied the economic position and practised the professional function appropriate to his station and faculties constituted an important element in conceptions of royal justice. See al-Sayyid, 'Tamhīd', 8–21, 26–8; Marlow, *Hierarchy and Egalitarianism*, 143–55; above, Text 9; and below, Text 17.

17 Similarly attributed to Ardashīr in *Kitāb al-Tāj*, 2, and Pseudo-Māwardī, *Naṣīḥat al-mulūk al-mansūb ilā . . . al-Māwardī*, 146 (adduced from Ardashīr's Testament but, as al-Sayyid points out, the line does not appear in the published version of *ʿAhd Ardashīr*; nor does it appear in the appended 'Scattered Sayings' of Ardashīr). The linking and at the same time contrasting of *al-malik* and *al-mālik* recalls the Qurʾanic language discussed in Pseudo-Māwardī (see above, Text 1).

18 Al-Māwardī, *Qawānīn al-wizāra*, 144 (*baʿḍ al-ḥukamāʾ*).

It is related that Anūshīrvān dispatched an envoy to a king who was determined to wage war against him. Anūshīrvān ordered his envoy to acquaint himself with this king's behaviour, both his personal conduct and his behaviour in his dealings with his subjects. The envoy returned and said, 'In this king, I found that jesting was stronger than seriousness, falsehood more frequent than truthfulness, injustice prevalent over justice.' Anūshīrvān said, 'Then I am already blessed with victory over him. March against him! And in fighting him, arm yourself with whatever he deems weakest, least and most humble; in this way you will triumph over him and he will suffer defeat.' Accordingly, he set out against this enemy, was duly victorious against him and took possession of his kingdom.[19]

The third principle entailed in the governance of the realm is management of the army. It is by means of his army that the king achieves sovereignty and domination, and that he rises to rule and power. When the troops thrive, they will use their force to further his interests; if, however, they become dispirited, they may turn their force against him. It is extremely unlikely that an individual who was once on his side and has turned against him will later regard it as in keeping with his integrity to renew his support for him.

It is through his good management of the troops that the king is able to sustain their obedience and demand their support. This good management rests on four conditions. If these four criteria are met perfectly, the army will, by his efforts, thrive and remain stalwart in their support of him. If, on the other hand, the king fails to fulfil these conditions, the army will suffer damage on his account, and in turn they will cause damage to his sovereignty.

The first condition is the provision of training (*adab*) in order to strengthen the troops. Proper education will preserve the troops' strong support and their complete mobilisation on the king's behalf; through it, the troops will improve their condition – for their own benefit as well as for the benefit of the king and his subjects.

This improvement (*ṣalāḥ*) – which benefits the troops, the king and the subjects – consists of several facets. The improvement that benefits the troops themselves entails three things. The first comprises extensive practice for the king's troops in the necessary mounted exercises and military strategy, because the military arts combine knowledge and

[19] See also Pseudo-Māwardī, *Naṣīḥat al-mulūk al-mansūb ilā … al-Māwardī*, 172; al-Ṭurṭūshī, *Sirāj al-mulūk*, II: 728 = Alarcón, *Lámpara de los Príncipes*, II: 368–9.

action. Secondly, the troops benefit from their ability to specialise solely in the military profession; limiting themselves to this profession ensures that they are not obliged to interrupt their service in order to earn a livelihood by any other means, a diversion that would undermine them in their military service. Thirdly, the troops benefit by the restriction of their pleasures to the permitted level of moderation; this moderation ensures that they are neither overly preoccupied and distracted by their pleasures, nor denied them – which latter condition would only increase their desire for them.

Maintaining the good condition of the army also benefits the king, again in three ways. Firstly, it establishes and sustains his troops' love for him, and this love will prompt them to offer him their sincere counsel. Secondly, it will magnify the awe in which they hold him in their hearts, and their awe will ensure their obedience to him. Thirdly, it will convince them that the sound condition of the king's sovereignty will return benefits to them, and equally that damage to it will redound against them.

Finally, the army's well-being benefits the subjects, again in three ways. Firstly, it will restrain anyone who might seek to harm them; secondly, it will dispose the troops to repel anyone who seeks to exploit them; thirdly, it will induce the army to assist them in attaining that which is useful and valuable to them.

If the king succeeds in urging his troops to undertake this training, and if they remain committed to this discipline, his troops will form the very best army for the most fortunate of kings. Alexander sought guidance from his teacher, and the latter wrote to him in reply:

> Pay the closest attention to your soldiers: for they are enemies, through whom other enemies suffer revenge.

What he meant was that the soldiers become the king's enemies if they are left to corruption, whereas as long as they prosper, it is the king's enemies who suffer their revenge.

The second condition of good management of the army lies in ranking the troops according to their military skills, their defence of the realm and their quickness to obey. If the king bases the soldiers' ranks on these criteria, they will know that their effort is appreciated with gratitude, that their counsel is taken into account when they offer it and that they will be duly rewarded. This practice will, furthermore, produce three effects, all of which cause the troops' affairs to prosper and promote the good management of the army. Firstly, a soldier who performs well will increase his commitments to obedience and counsel, confident that his efforts will earn him advancement and hoping for a doubling of his salary. Secondly, out of desire for the same increases in status and compensation that the good soldier attains, the soldier who falls short or performs his duties poorly will emulate the former in manifesting his obedience and seek to resemble him in his offering of sincere counsel. Thirdly, the soldier who falls short will be deterred from seeking that which he does not deserve and will hesitate from [seeking] a position to which he is not entitled. Instead, given the limitations of his ambitions, he will content himself with obscurity, and given his lack of strength, he will be satisfied with less than his more highly motivated comrades. Nevertheless, if stirred by fervour, he will not hesitate to act, if not even to increase his efforts.

The third condition for the good management of the army is that the king must take responsibility for their sufficient supplies, so that they are never in need. Need will induce the soldiers to adopt one of three measures, none of which has anything good about it: the troops will either take possession of the subjects' property [by force]; or they will abandon the king to serve someone else, who is capable of providing for their sufficiency; or they will occupy themselves with some other means of earning a living, and their military skills will thereby decline. Furthermore, when he needs them, the king will find them of little help, since they will risk their lives for him only as long as he maintains them adequately. It has been said: 'He who trusts in your good treatment will show greatest solicitude for your power.'

When the troops become preoccupied with the search for alternative sources of income, their expectations of receiving it [from the king] will weaken in their souls, and the stipend that the king provides will appear diminished in their eyes. Therefore, the king should grant his troops generous stipends, lest they feel impelled through need to pursue alternative means; for the person seeking restitution becomes emboldened, and the boldness of the soldiery is likely to lead to breaches of deference and a weakening of the awe in which they hold the king. It is rare for the realm to suffer damaging disturbances other than in this kind of way, because as a rule, potential harms are averted through the soldiery. When, however, it is the soldiers who constitute the source of injury, who then will defend the subjects, and guarantee kindness and equity? Indeed, the soldiers call to mind the well-known proverb, expressed in the words of the poet:

> Salt makes good that in which change is to be feared.
> How, then, to proceed when changes have dissolved the salt itself?[20]

It is generally held that the purpose of the soldiers' salaries should be to match, in an adequate fashion, the extent of their needs, rather than to lavish increases upon them in excess of their needs. Such increases may steer the troops towards one of two reprehensible characteristics: either they may squander the funds in corrupt activities, by which they will become corrupt, or they may become fully independent, and withdraw from the king's service. Ibn Qutayba related that Abarwīz said to his son:

> You should neither bestow so lavishly on your troops that they no longer need you, nor constrain them to the point that they raise an outcry against you. Give them moderate stipends: withhold from them gently, and increase their hope; do not grant them overly abundant stipends.[21]

The fourth condition for the good maintenance of the army is that no report concerning the troops should be concealed from the king and none of their actions hidden from him, since they are the guardians of his state and the protectors of his subjects. If the sick among them pass unnoticed, or the good among them are overlooked for the sake of the bad, then the worse among them will prevail over the good, because wickedness is more apt to spread among the good: they will incline and cause others to incline with them. The troops will find themselves beset by three dangerous calamities, which will impair their well-being (*ṣalāḥ*) and hinder their thriving. One of these calamities is that they will come to dislike times of security and peacefulness and despise periods of calm, on account of the diminished functions of their profession and the reduced demand for their services. For these reasons they will fabricate causes for rupture and open the gates for hostile offensives, in order to further their own ambitions, which peace and tranquillity had curtailed. If their machinations are not forestalled, then the soldiers may become the most

[20] Al-Tawḥīdī, *al-Baṣā'ir wa-l-dhakhā'ir*, II: 168, no. 523 (in the context of a discourse concerning passionate love); al-Ṭurṭūshī, *Sirāj al-mulūk*, I: 211.

[21] Ibn Qutayba, *'Uyūn al-akhbār*, I: 11; Ibn 'Abd Rabbihi, *al-'Iqd al-farīd*, I: 26; Ibn Abī Dharr, *al-Sa'āda wa-l-is'ād*, 400; al-Tha'ālibī, *Ādāb al-mulūk*, 72; al-Tha'ālibī, *Ghurar al-siyar*, 690; Ibn Ḥamdūn, *al-Tadhkira al-Ḥamdūniyya*, I: 291; al-Ṭurṭūshī, *Sirāj al-mulūk*, II: 493 (modified); al-Nuwayrī, *Nihāyat al-arab*, VI: 17.

disastrous element in the realm and cause the most rampant oppression. The second risk is that, taking advantage of the king's negligence towards the soldiery, the king's enemy may succeed in winning the troops' positive inclination towards himself. When arrows take aim at objects of desire, they often meet their targets; and if not deterred by vigilance or restrained by caution, the enemy, by a stratagem, will triumph, the king will fall and the realm will fall into the possession of his enemy. Thirdly, the king's neglect may encourage the troops to use their force to take control, and his negligence may incite them to extend their control in a bid for power. In this case, the soldiery will not refrain from seizing whatever they desire; in so doing, they will deplete the wealth and undermine the conditions of the population, causing multiple disasters and ruining the subjects. In these circumstances, the troops cause far greater damage to the realm than any potential conqueror and far more injury to it than any aspiring usurper. If this situation continues, it can only be brought to an end by severe suppression.

The troops are the ruler's strength. He must seek the assistance of the upright among them, if he is able to retain their allegiance; if he does not succeed in securing this support, then the realm is bound for perdition and will continue its procession towards corruption. As long as the king's sovereignty is firmly established, it is unlikely that corruption among the soldiery will become general. If the king is fortunate enough to retain the soldiers' goodwill, he must use the opportunity to rectify his initial errors. He must conduct a thorough study of the troops' conditions, no matter how insignificant their affairs may seem to him. He must not neglect a trifling matter for a larger one, for great affairs begin small – like fire, a little of which, through inattention, becomes harmful, unless it is speedily corrected.

The governance of the troops is the most difficult task facing the administrator of the state. It is through them that he achieves the domination that allows him to rule. If as a result of their corruption he becomes powerless, he will become the object of their domination; if, on the other hand, he governs them in a resolute manner and they are willing to follow him, he, through strength, attains power over them, and they, in obedience, become his supporters. It has been said:

> Among the signs of the [flourishing] state is the absence of carelessness.[22]

[22] Al-Māwardī, *Qawānīn al-wizāra*, 146 (*fī manthūr al-ḥikam*).

Section

The fourth foundation of the realm's governance is the assessment of financial resources, for it is the abundance of these resources that maintains the stability of the realm, whereas their deficiency leads to its disorder. This task of assessing financial resources comes with difficulty to kings, since by virtue of their power they consider that they ought to be able to achieve every goal and attain any desired objective – whether by easy and gentle means, or by difficult and harsh means; whether by means that they deem permissible according to the religious law, or by adopting prohibited measures, and exercising coercive methods. If, through their virtuous resolve, they uphold the standards of just governance, and if, through their power over the assessment of financial resources, they consider the very best means to sustain their sources of revenue and to facilitate its collection, neither exacting levies from the needy nor occasioning hardship, then the balance of their kingdoms will be maintained, and their exigencies kept moderate. They will not lack the capacity to levy their due, nor will they transgress into the unsanctioned. The ruler who succeeds in this regard is the most fortunate of kings, and his subjects are, through him, the most fortunate of subjects; whereas for the ruler who falls short in these matters, the opposite is the case.

A certain king, who had abandoned himself to pleasure, yet cast aspersions on another king for the same reason, said to me, while I was an ambassador between the two of them:

> I measured my expenditures against my income, and I assigned to each expenditure a sufficient amount of revenue. I appointed in this matter trusted and competent people, and I gave permission to anyone whose income fell short of his expenditure to borrow from someone else whatever he required, in order to augment his revenue. Having established these ordinances in a precise manner, I have spent my time engaged in pleasure, my soul at peace over the arrangements that I have made. The purpose of sovereignty is the pursuit of pleasure. Had I not behaved as I did, I would have been blameworthy in my preoccupation with pleasure. If this king had, like me, instituted ordinances before dedicating himself entirely to his pleasure, then I would not blame him; but since he neglected to do so, he is the blameworthy one, and not I.

I said to him:

> You are blaming someone else for a sin that you once committed but have since relinquished. You have deemed it an excusable matter in your own case, yet an offence for someone else. By my life, the person who has triumphed over his weakness is indeed more excusable than the person who still lacks restraint.

As a concession to his dignity, I refrained from proceeding in this dispute with him, although in fact his argument was weak and his excuse defective. For even he who has few faults is not exempt from a little reproof.[23]

Since the assessment of financial resources is among the four foundations of the realm's governance, its calculation must be considered from two perspectives. The first perspective entails the assessment of incoming revenue. These revenues should be assessed by one of two approaches: either by the religious law, in the case of sacred texts that determine the assessment of specific items – and it is not permissible to alter assessments based on this approach; or by independent reasoning (*ijtihād*), in matters for which God has entrusted humanity, through reasoning, with the task of establishing and determining judgements – and it is not permitted to infringe these rules either. If the rules rest on established laws (*qawānīn*), then they will produce fruit in the form of justice, and they will be immune to efforts to weaken them through injustice.[24] The second perspective entails the assessment of expenditures. Expenses should likewise be assessed in two ways: firstly, according to need, for items that are mandatory or permissible; secondly, according to the capability necessary for their collection, so that no

[23] This report constitutes one of al-Māwardī's occasional illustrations of his points with reference to his own experience. It constitutes an example of a 'fragment of autobiography', of the kind that Hilary Kilpatrick has studied ('Autobiography and Classical Arabic Literature', 2). In this case, al-Māwardī alludes to his service as an envoy, although he tactfully refrains from identifying the rulers in question. As noted in section 3.6, he conducted embassies between the caliphal and Buyid courts; see al-Sayyid, 'al-Māwardī (364-450h/974-1058m): al-rajul wa-l-ʿaṣr', 76–9, 81–2.

[24] The term *qānūn* (pl. *qawānīn*) referred to financial regulations: both the assessment and the collection of taxes, as well as to the sum due from the taxpayer; the term, in the settings, such as Egypt and Syria, where it was used, denoted a kind of fiscal cadaster. In formerly Sasanian settings, it connoted registers and lists recording land-taxes, and the regulations laid down therein, and came to be regarded as the foundation of sound and just administration. The term also acquired the sense of 'code of regulations' or laws laid down by the political authorities (as opposed to the laws of the sharia, grounded in the sacred sources of Qurʾan and hadith). See Linant de Bellefonds *et al.*, 'Ḳānūn'.

legitimate source of income remains untapped, and so that its extraction does not involve injustice.

When income is placed side by side with expenditures, it will correspond to one of three possible conditions:[25]

Firstly, income may exceed expenditures. This situation indicates a robust realm with a steady method of assessment. The surplus in revenue will be ready for use in the course of the various vicissitudes and disturbances that may occur. The subjects will feel secure against the extraction of additional levies that may arise from the ruler's need; the army, in view of this evidence of the king's capability, will feel confident that they will receive their stipends; the king will possess the power to defend the realm against the perils that may befall it and the misfortunes that may occur. For sovereignty is vulnerable to numerous unanticipated occurrences, and time witnesses countless unexpected developments.

The second possible condition is that income may fall short of expenditures. In this case the realm will be weak and its administration defective, because the ruler, by virtue of his power, will seek to obtain the amount that he needs, regardless of the force required to collect it. He will interpret the mandatory dues according to his interests, and he will then demand additional sums that are not mandated (by the law). Need will induce him to abandon the requirements of the religious law and established governmental regulations (*qawānīn*), and to devise a means to attain the needed funds and to achieve his desired ends. By his actions, the subjects will perish, and the troops will disperse and oppose him; furthermore, need will drive the soldiery to the same sort of behaviour that it initiated in the king. It will not be possible to restrain them from using force, since the king himself resorted to it; nor will it be possible to prevent them from corruption, since the king also adopted corrupt means. Either the king must correct matters by accepting the smaller amount of revenue to which he is entitled, and, with the support of his troops, establish a balanced economy; or corruption will lead inexorably to ruin.

The third possible condition for revenues and expenditures is that they are equally balanced, with neither surplus nor deficit. Under these circumstances, in times of peace, the realm will be self-sufficient, but in times of rupture and unforeseen setbacks, it will fall into disorder. For each of these two sets of conditions, there is an appropriate ordinance. As

[25] Cf. Bryson, apud *Der Oikonomikos*, 154–8.

long as the divine decree favours the king with enduring peace, he may govern in tranquillity and stability. When disturbed by unanticipated troubles, however, he will quickly tire of the continuous exertion (*ijtihād*) demanded of him, and his supporters (*a 'wān*) may begin to threaten him. Therefore, against the vicissitudes entailed in these kinds of circumstances, the king should build for himself a store of reserves, on the basis of his kindness towards the subjects and his execution of justice in his governance. He will then enjoy the appreciation of his subjects and the productivity that stems from justice.

Text 14
Niẓām al-Mulk, *Siyar al-mulūk*, Chapter Four[26]

Translator's Introduction

Niẓām al-Mulk introduces his fourth chapter, which falls in the first part of *Siyar al-mulūk*, with a statement of his instructions regarding the proper collection of taxes. From this topic he moves quickly to the related subject of the vizier, and in particular, the calamity of the malevolent and perfidious vizier.[27] The larger part of this chapter, like Text 11, is taken up by a single narrative, preceded by shorter narratives. The narrative pays less attention to the collection of taxes than it does to the larger theme of malfeasance on the part of royal officials, and it emphasises the perils of royal inattentiveness. Niẓām al-Mulk's brief conclusion consists of the assertion that actions, rather than words or names, reveal a person's inner self, and that the king must be guided in his interactions by the evidence of people's behaviour. It illustrates dramatically the perils of rapacity, of the despoiling of the subjects and the neglect of the land, and the ruler's responsibility to pay personal attention to the condition of both; if he delegates responsibility for these matters, the king must then scrutinise the conduct of the individuals to whom he has delegated – a point that recapitulates al-Māwardī's criticism of the king to whom

[26] Translation prepared from Niẓām al-Mulk, *Siyar al-mulūk*, 30–42. For the corresponding section in Darke's translation, see Darke, *Book of Government*, 22–32; in Schabinger's translation into German, Schabinger, *Siyāsatnāma, Gedanken und Geschichten*, 116–27; and in Pistoso's translation into Italian, Pistoso, *L'arte della politica*, 71–83.

[27] On the seeming irony of the vizier's warnings against vizieral wickedness and the specific occasion that underlies the passage, see Yavari, *Advice for the Sultan*, 122–5.

he carried an embassy in the previous extract. Niẓām al-Mulk's narratives are intended as cautionary examples (*ʿibrat*), and frequently involve a protagonist's heeding or failing to heed such lessons.

Translation

Chapter Four: On the Conditions and the Continual Monitoring of Tax-Collectors and Viziers

Officials charged with the collection of taxes in a fiscal district must be advised to treat God's creatures kindly and to claim no more than the licit amount (*māl-i ḥaqq*), which, furthermore, they should seek with moderation and leniency. Tax-collectors should further be instructed against demanding payments in advance of when they fall due, since such demands cause great distress: to meet the demand, the subjects are compelled to sell their crops at half the usual price, and when reduced to desperation they resort to flight. If any of the subjects becomes destitute and needs oxen and seed, he should be given a loan and granted relief, so that he will be able to stay where he is and not be forced to abandon his home.

A Story on This Theme

I have heard that in the time of King Qubād, the world suffered a drought that lasted for seven years. During this time the heavens withheld their blessings. The king ordered his officials to sell such crops as they had collected, to make charitable donations (*ṣadaqeh*) of some of the proceeds and to give assistance to the poor from the royal treasury and reserve supplies. By these means, in those seven years not a single person died of hunger in his entire kingdom – on account of the king's admonishment of his agents.

It is essential to enquire continually into the affairs of officials. If an official behaves in the manner that we have described, his fiscal district can be confirmed upon him, but if not, he should be replaced with someone suitable. If the official seizes anything illicitly from the subjects, the amount seized should be reappropriated from him and restored to the subjects. If after this reappropriation the official still possesses any property, it should be removed from him and brought to the treasury. He should be dismissed and never reappointed to another district, so that his example will prove cautionary (*ʿibrat*) for other officials and they will refrain from extortion.

Section on Viziers

It is also necessary that the king enquire in secret into the affairs of his viziers and trusted agents (*muʿtamadān*), in order to ascertain whether they are conducting their tasks well or not; for the well-being (*ṣalāḥ*) or corruption (*fasād*) of the king and kingdom are dependent upon the vizier. When the vizier is of good conduct the kingdom prospers, the army and the subjects are content, satisfied and well provisioned, and the king is free of worry. When, however, the vizier is of bad conduct he generates in the kingdom the kind of harm that cannot be remedied, and as a result the king is constantly distressed and anxious, and the province falls into disorder.

Story[28]

It has been related that Bahrām-i Gūr had a vizier named Rāst-Ravishn.[29] Bahrām-i Gūr had placed the entire kingdom in the hands of this vizier, whom he trusted; he would listen to no one's word against him. The king meanwhile spent day and night engaged in entertainment, hunting and drinking. This Rāst-Ravishn said to a person who was Bahrām-i Gūr's deputy (*khalīfeh*), 'Our excessive justice has induced the subjects to become ill-disciplined (*bī-adab*) and presumptuous (*dalīr*). If they are not punished, I fear a calamity (*tabāhī*) will soon occur. The king is preoccupied in hunting and drinking, and he has become neglectful of the affairs of the subjects and the people (*mardumān*). Punish them, before disaster strikes. Now, you should know that punishment has two aspects: reducing the bad people and seizing the property of the good. Whomever I tell you to seize, seize him.'

Afterwards, from anyone whom the deputy seized and detained, Rāst-Ravishn extracted a bribe. He then ordered the deputy to release the person. This pattern continued until anyone in the kingdom who possessed wealth, horses, fine male and female slaves, property or a fine

28 A much shorter version of this narrative, in which the Iranian king is Gushtāsp, appears in Ghazālī, *Naṣīḥat al-mulūk*, part II, 154–7 = Bagley, *Ghazālī's Book of Counsel for Kings*, 93–4.

29 The word *rāst* corresponds to the English 'honest', 'true', 'straight' or 'upright'; *ravish* or *ravishn* corresponds to 'conduct'. Consequently, the name Rāst-Ravishn evokes upright, honest, true conduct. The irony of the malevolent vizier of the story bearing this name is spelt out in the version of Ghazālī, in which Gushtāsp appoints his vizier on the basis of his name; this error, in Ghazālī's text, becomes the central element in the narrative (*Naṣīḥat al-mulūk*, 154, 156–7). Niẓām al-Mulk also alludes to the incongruity of the vizier's name and his behaviour (see below, n. 32).

estate lost it all to seizure. The subjects became impoverished, the notables (*ma ʿrūfān*) emigrated and nothing came into the treasury.

Sometime after these events had taken place, an enemy appeared, and confronted Bahrām-i Gūr. The king wished to give monetary gifts to his army, to ensure that they were well supplied, and to send them against the enemy. He went to the treasury and saw that there was nothing in it. He questioned the notables, the municipal leaders and heads of districts (*mar ʿūfān va-ra ʾīsān-i shahr va-rustāq*).[30] They said, 'It has been several years since so-and-so abandoned his home and possessions (*khān va-mān*) and made for such-and-such a territory.' The king asked why these individuals had fled, and the notables and leaders replied that they did not know. No one dared to tell the king the truth, out of fear of the vizier. Bahrām-i Gūr spent that day and night pondering this situation. He could think of nothing that might account for the problem.

The next day, deeply troubled, he mounted and, alone, rode out into the wilderness. He remained in constant thought until the day grew long, and he had ridden some six or seven *farsang*s without being aware of it. The heat of the sun grew strong. Overcome by thirst, Bahrām badly needed a drink of water. Looking out into the distance, he saw a rising plume of smoke, and thought that whatever else, it must indicate the presence of people. He made his way in the direction of that smoke. As he drew near, he saw a flock of sheep, asleep; a pitched tent; and a dog suspended from a gibbet. Astonished, he advanced to approach the tent. A man came out of the tent and greeted him, helped him dismount and brought him some of whatever food he had. He did not recognise his visitor as Bahrām. Bahrām said to the man, 'Before I eat this bread, first tell me about this dog, so that I may know the cause of his condition.'

The honest man (*javānmard*)[31] said, 'This dog was the trusted guardian (*amīnī*) of my flock of sheep. I knew that in his resourcefulness (*hunar*)

[30] The background, status and duties of the urban office of *ra ʾīs* ('head' or 'chief') differed considerably from one city to another in the Seljuk period; see Paul, 'The Histories of Isfahan', 129–32; Paul, 'Where Did the Dihqāns Go?', 26–8; Havelmann, 'The Vizier and the Ra ʾīs'.

[31] The term *javānmard*, and the associated abstract noun *javānmardī*, carry various meanings according to the contexts in which they appear; see above, Chapter 6, n. 44. The protagonist in Niẓām al-Mulk's narrative appears as an isolated figure – the only other individual mentioned is his wife – in a remote mountainous location; apparently a pastoralist, he is referred to later as a 'Kurd' (see below, n. 36). I have opted for a translation that conveys the common ethical associations of the concept of *javānmardī* (cf. Zakeri, 'Javānmardi').

he could contend with ten men, and that for fear of this dog, no wolf would dare to approach the sheep. Many a time I would go to the town for some business matter, and I would return the next day. The dog used to take the sheep to graze and bring them back safely. Things continued in this fashion for some time. One day I counted the sheep, and I noted that there were fewer of them. I began to look in the same manner every few days, and I found the number of sheep continually decreasing. No one remembers a thief having ventured into these parts, and I could not in any way understand the reason for my sheep to be growing fewer in number by the day. The state of my sheep reached such a degree of depletion that when the collector of charitable donations (*ṣadaqāt*) arrived and requested from me, in accordance with past custom, the usual amount, which had been assessed upon the entire flock, I had to give up the remaining remnant of my flock in order to pay the *ṣadaqāt*; as a result I am now the shepherd of that official.

'It happened that this dog had developed an affection for a she-wolf and had mated with her; I, meanwhile, was unaware of and had no knowledge of his goings-on. One day, by chance, I went out into the plain in search of wood. As I returned, I came up from behind a hill, and I saw the sheep grazing. I also saw a wolf, running around looking at the flock. I sat down behind a thorn-bush and watched in secret. When the dog saw the wolf, he headed towards her and began to wag his tail. The wolf stood silent. The dog mounted her and mated with her, then made for a corner and slept. The wolf rushed into the midst of the flock, seized one of the sheep, tore it apart and ate it; the dog made no sound. Once I observed this commerce between dog and wolf, I realised and understood that the ruin of my affairs had arisen from the waywardness of the dog. I therefore took hold of the dog and, his treachery having come to light, hanged him on the gibbet.'

This account struck Bahrām-i Gūr as remarkable. During his return he pondered the matter the entire time, until the thought occurred to him, 'Our subjects are our flock, and our vizier is our trusted guardian. I see that my kingdom is impaired and that my subjects are greatly disturbed. No matter whom I ask, no one tells me the truth; rather, they keep it hidden from me. My strategy (*tadbīr*), therefore, shall be to examine the subjects' relations with Rāst-Ravishn.'

When he had returned to his residence, the first thing that Bahrām did was to request the daily listings of prisoners. From top to bottom the records revealed the slander of Rāst-Ravishn, and the king realised that his vizier had mistreated and oppressed the people. The king said, 'This is not correct behaviour (*rāst ravishn*) but rather falsehood and darkness.'[32] Then, observing that its wise originators had spoken correctly, he repeated the proverb, 'Whoever is deceived by a name forfeits his bread, and whoever practises deceit for the sake of his bread forfeits his life.'[33]

Bahrām continued to muse, 'I have strengthened the hand of this vizier. Seeing his high rank and dignified status, the people, for fear of him, do not dare to speak to me about him. To remedy this state of affairs, tomorrow, when the vizier comes to the court, I shall lower his dignified status in front of the magnates (*buzurgān*) in attendance; I shall detain him and command that heavy shackles be placed on his feet. Then I shall summon the prisoners to appear before me and I shall ask after their circumstances. I shall also command the issuing of a proclamation, in which I shall announce that I have dismissed Rāst-Ravishn from the vizierate, detained him and shall never again appoint him to office. I shall further proclaim that anyone who has suffered harm from Rāst-Ravishn and has a petition against him should come to the court and make his situation known to us, so that we may grant that person justice from him. Without fail, once the people hear this proclamation, they will make their experience, of whatever kind, known to us. If the vizier has treated the people well and has not seized their property wrongfully, and if they express gratitude towards him, then I shall treat him favourably and reinstate him in his duties. If he has behaved in the opposite manner, then I shall punish him (*siyāsat farmāyam*).'[34]

[32] In this passage, Bahrām alludes explicitly to the incongruity of the name Rāst-Ravishn and its unscrupulous bearer (see above, n. 29). The letters *r-v-sh-n* that make up the word *ravishn* are identical with the letters that make up the word *rawshan*, 'light', 'clear' or 'bright', and in the unvocalised Persian script the two words are indistinguishable; this overlap provides an added element of irony, as Darke suggests (*Book of Government*, 246, n. 2).

[33] Following the textual reconstruction proposed by Darke (*Book of Government*, 246–7, n. 3), on the basis of the passage in Ghazālī, *Naṣīḥat al-mulūk*, 157.

[34] In Persian, and in Niẓām al-Mulk's lexicon in particular, the term *siyāsat* not only evoked, in a general sense, governance and government, but also carried the specific meaning of royal punishment. This dimension of the term persisted, especially in Persianate contexts; for its development in the thirteenth- and fourteenth-century South Asian context of the Delhi Sultanates, see Auer, 'Concepts of Justice'; and see Matthee, 'Was Safavid Iran an Empire?', 251, where the author makes the important point for this much later period that the arbitrary infliction of punishment (*siyāsat*) was tempered by the equally strong imperatives of *musāmaḥa* and *mudārā*, leniency and accommodation.

The next day King Bahrām-i Gūr held court. The magnates came forward, and the vizier, having entered, sat in his appointed place. Bahrām-i Gūr turned to him and said, 'What is this disorder that you have stirred up in our kingdom? You have left our army ill-supplied and ruined our subjects. We ordered you to deliver the soldiers' stipends in a timely fashion. We instructed you not to neglect the cultivation of the province, nor to exact from the subjects anything other than the appropriate land-tax. We ordered you further to ensure the continued abundance of the resources in the treasury. Now I see that the treasury is empty, the army lacks supplies and the subjects have been forced to move. You perhaps imagined that in my preoccupation with drinking and hunting, I would neglect the affairs of the kingdom and the condition of the subjects.'

Bahrām then ordered the summary removal of the vizier and his transfer to a house, where heavy shackles were attached to his feet. At the door of the palace, he ordered the reading of a proclamation:

> The king has dismissed Rāst-Ravishn from the vizierate. He is angry with him, and he will not appoint him to another duty. Let anyone who has suffered harm from Rāst-Ravishn and has a grievance against him come to the court. Let him, without any fear or trepidation, set forth his circumstances, so that the king may give him justice.

Thereupon Bahrām ordered further that the door of the prison be opened, and the prisoners brought before him. He asked each of them in turn to relate the crime for which he had been detained.

One said, 'I had a wealthy brother who owned a great deal of property and many rich possessions. Rāst-Ravishn seized him, divested him of all his property and killed him under torture. When asked the reason for my brother's execution, Rāst-Ravishn averred that he had been in correspondence with the king's enemies. He put me in prison so that I could not bring a grievance against him and to ensure that the entire situation would remain hidden.'

Another said, 'I had a garden of great beauty; it was left to me by my father. Rāst-Ravishn established an estate on the land that lay next to it. One day he came into my garden. It pleased him greatly. He wished to buy it, but I refused to sell. He seized me and put me in prison, claiming that I had fallen in love with the daughter of such-and-such a person and must have committed a crime. He ordered me to relinquish my possession of this garden – to draw up a contract stating that I had renounced my rights to it, had no claim over it and that it was now the rightful claim and property of Rāst-Ravishn. I refused to issue such a statement, and today I have been in prison for five years.'

Another said, 'I am a merchant, and my business involves travel by sea and on land. I accumulate only a little capital. Whatever fine items I find in a city I buy; then I travel to the next city and sell them. I content myself with only a small amount of profit. It happened that I had a necklace made of pearls. When I came to this city, I offered it for sale at a certain price. News of this item reached the king's vizier. He sent someone and summoned me. He bought this string of pearls from me, but rather than paying me its price he sent the necklace directly to his treasury. For several days I went to pay my respects to him. He withheld all acknowledgement of the outstanding payment that he owed me for the pearl necklace. My endurance reached a limit, and I was in any event on the point of departure. I appeared before him one day and I said, "If this necklace is satisfactory, please oblige me by paying its price; if it is not satisfactory, then please return it to me, since I am on the point of departure." Rāst-Ravishn gave me no reply. But when I returned to my lodgings, I saw a captain (*sarhangī*) with four foot-soldiers. They entered my lodgings and demanded that I come with them, since the vizier had summoned me. I was pleased, thinking that the vizier was going to pay me the price for the pearls, so I stood up and went with these ruffians (*ʿavānān*). But they brought me to the prison for thieves. They told the gaoler that according to their orders I was to be imprisoned with heavy fetters fixed to my feet. It has now been a year and a half that I have been in prison.'

Another said, 'I am the headman (*raʾīs*) of such-and-such a district. My house was permanently open to receive guests, strangers and people of learning. I used to provide assistance for people, especially people in distress, and, observing the practice of my forefathers, I was constantly donating funds for charitable (*ṣadaqeh*) and benevolent (*khayrāt*) purposes and for the benefit of the deserving. The costs of maintaining my guests and ensuring their comfort accounted for any income that I received from the property and estates bequeathed to me. Claiming that I had found a treasure, the vizier seized me. He subjected me to torture and interrogation, and he detained me in prison. Of necessity I have been forced to sell for half its worth every property and estate that

I had, and to give the proceeds to him. It is now four years that I have been in prison and in fetters, and I do not have a single dirham at my disposal.'

Another said, 'I am the son of such-and-such a local leader (*za'īm*). The vizier mulcted the property of my father and killed him under torture and interrogation. He assigned me to prison, and it has now been seven years that I have suffered the trials of incarceration.'

Another said, 'I am a military man. I served the king's father for several years, and accompanied him in his campaigns; I have also spent a number of years in the service of the present king. I am allotted a small stipend through the military register (*dīvān*). Last year I received nothing. This year, therefore, I submitted a claim to the vizier. I informed him that I had a family, and that I had not received the stipend due to me for the previous year; I therefore requested that this year he release the funds so that I might use some of them to pay off my creditors and expend some of them for purposes of general maintenance. The vizier responded, "The king has no undertakings in view for which he would need an army. It does not matter whether you and your kind are or are not in service; if you need bread, go to work as a builder." I replied, "I should not have to work as a builder when I have a rightful claim, based on many years of service, to an allowance. But you, tasked with stewardship (*kadkhudāy kardan*) on behalf of the king, should learn something: I am more meritorious in swordsmanship than you are in penmanship, since in wielding the sword I risk my life for the king, and furthermore I do not discount his command; whereas you, when the time comes for dispensing stipends (*bi-gāh-i dīvān*), deprive us of bread and ignore the king's command. Do you not know even this much, that in relation to the king, you are a servant (*chākir*), just as I too am a servant? He has appointed you to one kind of task and me to another. The difference between the two of us is that I carry out the king's commands whereas you proceed as if you had no orders. If the king has little need for people like me, he has little need for people like you either. If you have received official notice that the king has expunged my name from the registry, then show it to me; otherwise, send us the allowance that the king has assigned to us." The vizier responded, "Go; I have charge over both you and the king. If it were not for me, the vultures would have eaten your brains long ago." A day later he sent me to prison, and it is now four months that I have remained in confinement.'

There were more than seven hundred prisoners. Fewer than twenty men turned out to be murderers, thieves or criminals. All the others were persons whom the vizier, out of sheer greed and oppression, had wrongfully put in prison. Once the people of the city and the region heard the news of the king's proclamation, the next day so many aggrieved persons came to the court that there was no limit or end to them.

As Bahrām-i Gūr came to perceive the state of the people and the scale of the vizier's irregularities, injustices and cruelty, he said to himself, 'The corruption that this man has caused in the kingdom seems to defy description. His insolence towards God, towards God's creatures and towards me exceeds anything that the mind might be able to comprehend. I must look more deeply into this matter . . .' He ordered a group of men to go to Rāst-Ravishn's residence, to bring all his files of paper and to seal all the doors of his houses. A group of the king's trusted stewards (*muʿtamadān*) went and did these things. When they had assembled all the vizier's papers, they set about examining them. Among these materials they found certain documents, full of flattering words, that a rebellious king intent on the overthrow of Bahrām-i Gūr's kingdom had sent to Rāst-Ravishn. They also found a document in the hand of Rāst-Ravishn; addressed to this rebel king, this letter was similarly replete with flattery. In it, Rāst-Ravishn asked the reason for the rebel king's delay, and continued, 'The wise have said that negligence is the undoing of the state. Out of my good wishes for your success and my servitude, I have made every possible arrangement. I have changed the minds of several people, such as so-and-so and so-and-so and so-and-so, all of them heads of the army, and I have brought them into allegiance; I have left most of the army with neither equipment nor supplies; I have appointed some of them to specific locations and deprived them of funds; I have kept the subjects without food, reduced them to weakness and forced them to flee. Everything that I have acquired over all this time I have placed at your disposal in your treasury, so that today no king possesses a treasury like it. I have had your crown, your belt and your golden seat[35] decorated with jewels, in a manner the like of which no one has ever seen. Yet my life is not secure against that man. The field lies vacant, and the adversary remains unaware. Make haste, and the sooner the better, before the man awakens from the sleep of negligence.'

[35] I have interpreted the term *majlis* in its literal meaning, 'a place to sit'. Darke understood the word to refer to a royal tray or salver, characteristically made of gold (as in this instance) or silver; Darke, *Book of Government*, 247, n. 4.

When Bahrām-i Gūr saw these writings, he said, 'I see! So it is he who, through his deceit, has incited this enemy against me. Of his bad faith and hostility there can be no further doubt.' He ordered that whatever possessions the vizier had be brought to the treasury; his slaves and his animals were to be taken away. The king also ordered the return of any goods that the vizier had seized from the people through bribery, injustice and other illicit means, as well as the sale of his properties and estates and their restoration to the people and to their rightful claimants. He had the vizier's residence, home and possessions (*khān-o mān*) levelled to the ground. Then Bahrām commanded the erection of a high gallows at the gate of the vizier's palace, and the setting up of thirty additional gibbets in front of that gallows. First, they hanged Rāst-Ravishn on the gallows, just as that Kurd[36] had hanged his dog on the gibbet. Then they hanged the vizier's accomplices, who had pledged allegiance to him. The king ordered that for seven days, it should be proclaimed:

> This is the reward of the person who harbours ill intent towards the king and enters into agreement with the king's enemies. It is the recompense of the person who chooses treachery over honesty, oppresses the people and displays insolence against God and God's creatures.

Once the king had carried out this punishment (*siyāsat*), every malefactor became fearful of King Bahrām-i Gūr. Everyone whom Rāst-Ravishn had appointed to office was dismissed, and never again entrusted with an official function; everyone whom Rāst-Ravishn had removed and dismissed from office was reinstated in an official position. The king replaced all the secretaries and officials. When this news reached the other king, who had set out against Bahrām-i Gūr, the former retreated immediately from the position that he had reached and regretted his action. He sent copious riches and priceless tokens of his subservience to Bahrām, begged his pardon and pledged his loyal servitude.[37] He said, 'It

[36] Possibly, as in pre-Islamic times (Grenet, *La geste d'Ardashir*, 32, and see chapter VI, 78–81), 'Kurd' in this instance serves as a general reference to any mountain-dwelling people. In earlier centuries, Kurdish groups had played a prominent political and military role over a wide terrain, including forming states in mountainous areas, but their ascendancy was threatened by the arrival of the Ghuzz Türkmen, who by 420/1029 had reached Maragha and competed with the Kurds for pasturage. From this time onwards the pressure against the Kurds from Turkish groups was more or less continuous (Kennedy, *The Prophet and the Age of the Caliphates*, 250–66, 259).

[37] The use of plurals conveys tangible tokens of servitude (*farāvān māl va-żarā'if bi-khidmat firistād va-'udhr-hā khvāst va-bandagī-hā namūd*).

would never have occurred to me to disobey the king, were it not for the king's vizier, who led me to this path by dint of his constant sending of letters and envoys. I suspected all along that he was a criminal in search of a refuge.' King Bahrām accepted his excuse and spared him. He gave the office of vizier to a God-fearing man whose beliefs were sound. The affairs of the army and the subjects all assumed their proper order; activities resumed their smooth course, the world turned in the direction of prosperity and the people were rescued from oppression and injustice.

As for the man who had hanged his dog from the gibbet: He was on the point of going back inside his tent when King Bahrām drew an arrow from his quiver and released it in front of him.[38] The king said to the man, 'I have eaten your bread and salt, and learnt about the trouble and loss that have afflicted you. I have sustained a mandatory obligation towards you. Know that I am one of King Bahrām-i Gūr's chamberlains. All the magnates and chamberlains of his court are on friendly terms with me and are well acquainted with me. You must rise and come to the court of King Bahrām. Bring this arrow with you; everyone who sees you with this arrow will direct you to me. I shall then discharge my responsibility towards you so that some of your losses may be repaired.' Then he left.

Some days later the man's wife said to him, 'Rise and go to the city; bring this arrow with you, for that horseman, so well apparelled, was without doubt powerful and wealthy. Although the amount of kindness that he shows you may be modest, for us, in our present circumstances, that little may be much. Do not delay, for the word of such a man is not empty.' The man got up and went to the city. He slept that night, and the next day he went to the court of King Bahrām. Bahrām-i Gūr had instructed his chamberlains and courtiers that when a man of such-and-such a description arrived at the court and they saw in his hand one of the king's arrows, they were to bring that man before the king.

When the chamberlains saw the man with that arrow in his hand, they called him, and said, 'O honourable man (*āzād mard*), where have you been? We have been expecting you for several days. Sit here, and we shall bring you to the owner of that arrow.' Some time passed. Bahrām-i Gūr came out, seated himself on the throne and held audience. The chamberlains took the man's hand and brought him to the court. The man's eye fell upon the king, and he recognised him. He said, 'Alas, that horseman was King Bahrām!

[38] The detail evokes Bahrām's proverbial prowess in archery; see al-Thaʿālibī, *Thimār al-qulūb*, 179–80, no. 657 (*ramy Bahrām*).

And I was unable to display the proper service to him; moreover, I spoke to him in an impudent manner. May it not be that he has taken against me!'

When the chamberlains brought him before the throne, the man supplicated the king. Bahrām-i Gūr turned towards the magnates and told them, 'This man is responsible for my having become aware of the conditions of the kingdom.' He related to the notables the story of the dog and the wolf, and added, 'Furthermore, I took this man to be an omen.' Then he ordered the man's investiture with a robe of honour, and he commanded that he receive seven hundred sheep from the royal flocks – ewes and rams according to his wishes. And for as long as Bahrām-i Gūr lived, the man was to be exempt from the payment of taxes (*ṣadaqāt*).

When Alexander killed Darius, it was because the latter's vizier had secretly made common cause, in heart and in mind, with Alexander. When Darius was killed, Alexander said, 'The negligence of the amir and the treachery of the vizier have made off with his kingship.'

The king should never neglect the conditions of his officials; he must always remain informed of their demeanour and conduct. An official who shows signs of dishonesty or betrayal should never be retained; rather he must be dismissed and punished in proportion to the measure of his crime. In this way others will draw a cautionary lesson (*ʿibrat*), and out of fear of punishment (*siyāsat*), no person will dare to plot harm against the king. Whenever anyone is appointed to an important post, the king should install someone to observe him secretly, in such a way that the appointee is unaware that he is being watched – so that the king is always informed of his doings and conditions.

Aristotle said to King Alexander, 'If you should rebuke any of the people who ply their pens in the service of your kingdom, never appoint that person to another official post, because it is probable that he will secretly make common cause with your enemies and strive for your perdition.'

King Parvīz said, 'There are four groups of people whose sins the king should not overlook: firstly, people who take aim at his kingdom; secondly, people with designs on his womenfolk; thirdly, people who instead of keeping his secrets disclose them; and fourthly, people who in their speech support the king, but in their hearts take the side of the king's enemies, and who secretly pursue the purposes of the latter.'[39]

[39] A list of three, rather than four, of these unpardonable faults appears in *Kitāb al-Tāj*, 94 = Pellat, *Livre de la couronne*, 119. See also al-Rāghib al-Iṣfahānī, *Muḥāḍarāt al-udabāʾ*, I: 226 (al-Maʾmūn).

The actions of a man reveal his secrets. When the king is aware of the affairs of his kingdom, nothing remains hidden from him.

Text 15
Al-Ṭurṭūshī, *Sirāj al-mulūk*, Chapter Twenty-Seven[40]

Translator's Introduction

This extract from *Sirāj al-mulūk* explores the principles and practices of the royal duty to solicit and heed consultation and advice. The mirror-writers' insistence on this duty constitutes a further element in the system of values designed to contain and limit the ruler's power. According to this value, the king, in conformity with his development of self-control, is admonished not to act on the basis of his instincts and desires. The assumption is that the advice the king receives, if it is genuine and not self-interested or the product of fear of royal retaliation, is likely to be unpopular, and to conflict with the king's desires and impulses. Authors of mirrors not only emphasise the royal duty of listening to advice, however unpalatable, but also to spare its purveyors, the more critical of whom have the king's genuine well-being and that of his state at heart. In presenting these points, al-Ṭurṭūshī appears throughout this section to have made extensive use of the writings of Ibn al-Muqaffaʿ and of Ibn Qutayba's *ʿUyūn al-akhbār*.

Translation

Chapter Twenty-Seven: On Consultation and Counsel

This chapter concerns matters that the wise have taken to belong among the foundations of the kingdom and the pillars of rulership, required by the ruler and the ruled alike. We have mentioned these issues in the chapter concerning the divinely enjoined qualities (*al-khiṣāl al-furqāniyya*).[41] In the present context, we shall mention their benefits and virtues.

[40] Prepared from al-Ṭurṭūshī, *Sirāj al-mulūk*, I: 319–31. For the corresponding section in Alarcón's translation into Spanish, see Alarcón, *Lámpara de los Príncipes*, I: 319–33.

[41] The cross-reference is to Chapter Ten, I: 208–12, where al-Ṭurṭūshī presents three qualities with scriptural mandate (*warada al-sharʿ bihā*), the second of which is consultation (*mushāwara*).

Know that a person who seeks counsel, even if he possesses better judgement than the counsellor, will find the clarity of his judgement increased through his seeking of another person's opinion, just as oil increases the light shed by the fire. Do not dwell on the idea that when you seek consultation, it demonstrates to people that you need the opinion of persons other than yourself, lest that notion should deter you from consultation; for the point of desiring someone else's opinion on a matter is not in order to boast about it but rather to benefit from it. If, however, you seek a good reputation in your governance, persons of intelligence will consider you worthier and more estimable if they are able to say of you that you did not limit yourself solely to your own opinion, to the exclusion of men of sound judgement among your brethren.[42]

Nor should your determination to enact your judgement, and your conviction of its rectitude, prevent you from seeking advice. Consider the case of Abraham, upon him be peace: when he received the divine command to sacrifice his son, the decision admitted no consultation; yet his habitual good conduct and his knowledge still disposed his soul to seek consultation. He said: 'O my son, I have seen in a dream that I should sacrifice you; consider: what do you think?' (Q 37: 102). This case is among the finest examples of meritorious practice in this regard.

ʿUmar b. al-Khaṭṭāb, may God be pleased with him, said: 'A single individual's judgement is like a very thin thread. Two converging opinions are like two threads, wound together. Three opinions are strong enough that the thread can scarcely be cut.'[43]

It has been related that a Greek and a Persian were vying with one another in boasting of their respective groups. The Persian said, 'We never appoint a person to rule over us if he consults other people.' The Greek said, 'We never appoint a man to rule over us if he does not consult other people.' Buzurgmihr said, 'If a prudent person fails to reach a conclusive judgement in a matter, he responds, as it were, as if he had dropped a pearl: he collects everything that he finds in the vicinity of the place where he lost it, searches for the pearl among these items and eventually finds it. Similarly, if a resolute person elicits various opinions concerning a difficult matter, he is able to weigh one against another until the correct course becomes clear to him.'

[42] Ibn al-Muqaffaʿ, *al-Ādāb al-kabīr*, 282 = van Gelder, *Classical Arabic Literature*, 171.
[43] Ibn Qutayba, *ʿUyūn al-akhbār*, I: 31.

It used to be said that whenever a king made a frequent practice of seeking consultation, his rule would be praised. It is reported, furthermore, among the wise sayings of the Indian people that a king once remarked: 'The judgement of prudent viziers augments the stature of the resolute king, just as the influx of the rivers augments the volume of the sea. Through resolve and judgement, the king achieves ends that he could not attain by force and military might.'[44]

Prudent men invariably find sweetness in the bitter talk of sincere counsellors, just as the ignorant person delights in words that encourage him towards his desire.[45] With reference to his brother al-Amīn, al-Maʾmūn asked Ṭāhir b. al-Ḥusayn (r. 205–7/821–2) to describe the moral characteristics of the deposed.[46] Ṭāhir replied, 'His chest is broad, but his moral discipline (*adab*) is narrow. He behaves in ways that the scruples of honourable men would render impossible for them. He neither listens to advice, nor accepts consultation; instead, he acts in an arbitrary fashion, in accordance with his opinion alone. Although he observes the negative consequences that result, this experience does not restrain him from the pursuit of his ends.' Al-Maʾmūn asked, 'How does he conduct himself in war?' Ṭāhir answered, 'He musters his forces through extravagance, then causes them to desert, through his poor management.' Al-Maʾmūn commented, 'These characteristics account for his current situation. Yet, by God, had he experienced the delicious taste of counsels, chosen to consult other people and succeeded in controlling his personal desire, then he would not have suffered defeat.'[47]

Another individual proposed that the king's discharging of his affairs without deliberation is akin to worship without intention.[48] The

[44] Ibn Qutayba, *ʿUyūn al-akhbār*, I: 27. [45] Ibn Qutayba, *ʿUyūn al-akhbār*, I: 28.

[46] The term *makhlūʿ* for al-Amīn (cf. *Kitāb al-Tāj*, 42; al-Jāḥiẓ, *al-Bayān wa-l-tabyīn*, I: 346; al-Zamakhsharī, *Rabīʿ al-abrār*, IV: 236) evokes his defeat and replacement in the caliphal office by his brother; but the term also connotes a person who is heedless and rejects restraint. On al-Amīn and Ṭāhir, see also the account of al-Thaʿālibī, below, Chapter 9, n. 18.

[47] Ṭāhir b. al-Ḥusayn, first ruler of the Ṭahirid dynasty in Nishapur, was also the author of a widely disseminated 'testament' or moral exhortation (*waṣiyya* or *ʿahd*), composed for his son ʿAbdallāh on the occasion of the latter's appointment to the governorship of Diyar Rabiʿa in 206/821 (see al-Ṭabarī, *Taʾrīkh al-rusul wa-l-mulūk*, VIII: 582–91 (*sub anno* 206) = Bosworth, 'Early Arabic Mirror for Princes' and Bosworth, *History of al-Ṭabarī*, XXXII: 110–28); see above, Chapter 1, n. 23.

[48] Intention (*niyya*) is a mandatory element in the proper fulfilment of the ritual prayer (*ṣalāt*); the declaration (whether audible or internal) of the intention to perform the prayer must immediately precede its performance in order for the prayer to be valid.

intelligent, notwithstanding their differences of opinion, continually seek the guidance of people willing to disclose to them their faults. They seek out the true opinion of each person, even the ignorant maidservant. In this spirit, ʿUmar b. al-Khaṭṭāb, God be pleased with him, said, 'May God have mercy upon the man who guides me to my faults.'[49]

It used to be said that whoever accomplished four things would not lack for four things. Whoever displays his gratitude shall not lack for an increase in favour; whoever demonstrates his repentance shall not lack for acceptance; whoever seeks the best shall not lack for the best; and whoever consults shall not fail to find the correct path.[50] Furthermore it has been observed that maturity of judgement is preferable to impulsivity, and that delay in acting on a judgement is preferable to excessive haste.[51]

The author of the *Kitāb al-Tāj* mentioned that when one of the Persian kings consulted his viziers, one of them remarked, 'It would be more fitting for the king to seek our advice individually and in private. Under those conditions, each vizier would be more likely to disclose his secret thoughts, more deliberate in formulating his judgement, more confident of his safety and more likely to avoid the ill-will of the others.'

When another Persian king consulted his lords of the borderlands (*marāziba*, sing. *marzbān*) and found them remiss in their judgement, he summoned the officials charged with issuing their stipends and punished them.[52] The officials said, 'It was your provincial lords who were at fault; why, then, are you punishing us?' The king replied, 'Indeed; they were at fault, but only because their hearts were intent upon their stipends, and in their preoccupation, they made an error.' Had the officials considered the conditions necessary for a man to be available for consultation, they would have sent him and his family a full year's worth of provisions, so that his mind would have been at rest. It used to be said that when the self (*nafs*) obtains its necessary provisions, it is at peace.[53]

[49] Al-Ṭurṭūshī cites this utterance again; see below, n. 71.

[50] Ibn Qutayba, *ʿUyūn al-akhbār*, I: 31; al-Ibshīhī, *al-Mustaṭraf*, I: 169.

[51] Ibn Qutayba, *ʿUyūn al-akhbār*, I: 30; al-Ibshīhī, *al-Mustaṭraf*, I: 169. The terms *khamīr* and *faṭīr* employ the metaphor of leavened and unleavened bread to evoke the relative qualities of maturity and freshness.

[52] The pre-Islamic Iranian title *marzbān*, used to denote the leader of a border province, continued in use, especially in Khurasan, in the early centuries of the Islamic era, and designated, sometimes as a synonym for *dihqān*, a regional commander or leader (see Paul, 'Dihqān'; Paul, 'Where Did the Dihqāns Go?').

[53] Ibn Qutayba, *ʿUyūn al-akhbār*, I: 31. An allusion to the Qurʾanic term *al-nafs al-muṭmaʾinna* (Q 89: 27), which denotes a state of inner tranquillity.

When you consult on a matter, be truthful in your report, so that the consultation will attest to your truthfulness. Do not conceal the truth from the person whom you consult, lest you undermine yourself.

A Persian king said, 'Do not allow the extremity of your self-regard, nor your high position, to prevent you from embracing the opinion of someone else. For in so doing, if you behave in a praiseworthy manner, you shall be loved for it, and if you err you shall be excused.'

There are various facets to this issue. If, for example, your judgement coincides with the judgement of someone else, the strength of your judgement will be increased. If, on the other hand, your judgement conflicts with someone else's opinion, you will devote full consideration to that opinion; if you find it superior to your earlier judgement, you are in a position to accept it, and if you consider it inferior, you can dispense with it. If you proceed in this manner, you shall enjoy the sincere advice of the person whom you consult, even if he errs, and you shall encounter the sincerity of his love for you, even if he falls short.

Not least among the virtues of consultation is that, even if in reaching your independent opinion you hit the mark, the envious cannot accuse you of rejecting the benefits of striving for accuracy in your judgement. Someone once said, 'What has occurred, has occurred; but were he to have acted in such-and-such a way, it would have been better.' If you consult people and hit the mark, they will praise your judgement, because in so doing they are praising themselves; if you err, they will release you from the responsibility, because in so doing they are defending themselves.[54] Know that harsh words should be heeded because of the excellence of the outcome to which they guide the listener, just as people will tolerate the bitterness of medicine for the excellence of its effects. A Bedouin once claimed that he had never slipped up unless his entire tribe (*qawm*) had stumbled in a matter. When he was asked to account for this claim, he said, 'I do nothing unless I have consulted them.'[55] Similarly, a man of the Banū ʿAbs was asked to explain the notable frequency of his people's accurate judgement. He said, 'We are a group of a thousand men. A single person among us is known for his prudence, so we obey him, and as a result, it is as if we were a thousand prudent

[54] Cf. Ibn al-Muʿtazz, 'He who makes a common practice of consultation shall not lack for praise in cases of rectitude, nor for forgiveness in cases of error' (*man akthara al-mashwara lam yaʿdam fī l-ṣawāb mādiḥan wa-fī l-khaṭāʾ ʿādhiran*) (al-Ḥuṣrī, *Zahr al-ādāb*, II: 824).

[55] Ibn Qutayba, *ʿUyūn al-akhbār*, I: 31.

people.'[56] A wise philosopher once said something similar: 'If you obey a rational person, his reason becomes yours.'

Ibn Hubayra, the amir of Basra, used to say: 'O God, I take refuge in You from the company of the person intent solely upon his personal objectives, and from succumbing to the desire to consult him.'[57] Among the wise sayings of the Indians is the maxim, 'He who seeks a dispensation (*rukhṣa*) [to do as he wishes] from his brethren in times of consultation, from his physicians in times of sickness and from the jurists in times of doubt, will surely err in his judgement, increase in his sickness and bear a burden of responsibility.'[58]

The sages have advised against consulting students, shepherds, men who spend excessive time in the company of women, petitioners seeking the settlement of their claims, persons who are fearful and people given to excessive eating and drinking. They have opined that the *ḥāqin*, *ḥāziq* and *ḥāqib* all lack judgement; nor should you consult anyone who lacks subtlety (*daqīq*). The *ḥāziq* is a person whose shoes are too tight, and the *ḥāqib* is a person with a rumbling belly.[59] They have also said that anyone who complains to a powerless person exposes his own powerlessness, and that in his anxiety he increases it.

A fine case of consultation occurred when Ziyād b. ʿUbayd Allāh al-Ḥārithī sought the advice of ʿUbayd Allāh b. ʿUmar as to whether he should appoint his brother Abū Bakr to the office of judge. When ʿUbayd Allāh responded in the affirmative, Ziyād sent word to Abū Bakr, who,

[56] Ibn Qutayba, *ʿUyūn al-akhbār*, I: 31; Ibn ʿAbd Rabbihi, *al-ʿIqd al-farīd*, I: 60.

[57] Ibn Qutayba, *ʿUyūn al-akhbār*, I: 31; Ibn ʿAbd Rabbihi, *al-ʿIqd al-farīd*, I: 59. The Ibn Hubayra in the account is presumably one of the two individuals, father and son, who bore this name; both men served as governors of Iraq under the Umayyads. The father, ʿUmar Ibn Hubayra (d. between 105/724 and 107/726), governed the province from 102/720 until the accession of Hishām in 105/724. His son Yazīd b. ʿUmar (d. 132/750) governed from 129/741 to 132/749. See Judd, 'ʿUmar b. Hubayra'; Judd, 'Yazīd b. ʿUmar b. Hubayra'.

[58] Ibn Qutayba, *ʿUyūn al-akhbār*, I: 30. Other sources (*Kalīla wa-Dimna*, in *Āthār Ibn al-Muqaffaʿ*, 120; Pseudo-Māwardī, *Naṣīḥat al-mulūk al-mansūb ilā . . . al-Māwardī*, 44; Ibn ʿAbd Rabbihi, *al-ʿIqd al-farīd*, I: 12; also al-Nuwayrī, *Nihāyat al-arab*, VI: 10) record a similar pronouncement, in which the verb is *katama*, to 'conceal' or 'withhold': 'He who withholds his counsel from the ruler, his illness from the doctors and his sorrow from his brothers betrays himself.'

[59] Ibn Qutayba, *ʿUyūn al-akhbār*, I: 31–2; Ibn ʿAbd Rabbihi, *al-ʿIqd al-farīd*, I: 61; al-Ibshīhī, *al-Mustaṭraf*, I: 169, with the reading *lā khāʾifan wa-lā ḥāqinan*. On the inadvisability of seeking consultation from persons who are hungry (*jāʾiʿ*) or famished (*ḥāqin*), see also Ibn al-Ḥaddād, *al-Jawhar al-nafīs*, 123–4. For these terms and their various associations (many of which entail physical discomforts or illnesses), see *Lisān al-ʿarab*, II: 857–9 (*ḥ-z-q*), II: 936–8 (*ḥ-q-b*), II: 947–8 (*ḥ-q-n*).

however, declined the invitation. Ziyād then sought ʿUbayd Allāh's assistance with Abū Bakr. Abū Bakr said to ʿUbayd Allāh, 'I beseech you, by God: do you really consider me suitable for the judgeship?' ʿUbayd Allāh replied that he did not. Ziyād then said to ʿUbayd Allāh, 'Praise God, I consulted you in this matter, and you responded positively to me. Yet now I hear you denying his suitability!' ʿUbayd Allāh replied, 'O amir, when you consulted me, I exercised my judgement on your behalf, and I offered you my sincere advice, on behalf of the Muslims. When Abū Bakr likewise sought my advice, I exercised my judgement for his sake, and advised him accordingly.'

It is related that al-Ḥajjāj [b. Yūsuf, d. 95/714] wrote to al-Muhallab [b. Abī Ṣufra, d. 82/702 or 83/703] in order to bid him make haste in going to war against the Azāriqa. Al-Muhallab wrote to him, 'It is a calamity that judgement lies with the person who possesses the power to implement it, and not with the person in a position to discern the optimal course of action.'[60]

Section: On Counsel

Know that offering counsel for the Muslims and for all human beings is one of the practices of God's messengers (*min sunan al-mursalīn*). Concerning Noah, upon him be peace, God Almighty reported his words: 'Even if I wish to counsel you, my counsel will be of no use to you if God intends that you should go astray' (Q 11: 34). Shuʿayb, upon him be peace said: '[O my people, I have delivered to you the messages of my Lord,] and I have counselled you. How, then, can I grieve for a people who do not believe?' (Q 7: 93), and '[I have delivered to you the message

[60] Ibn Qutayba, *ʿUyūn al-akhbār*, I: 31, where Ibn Qutayba also provides an alternative version of the exchange, in which two different interlocutors refer to the Khawārij rather than, more specifically, the Azāriqa. Al-Ḥajjāj b. Yūsuf al-Thaqafī was one of the most famous and able governors of the Umayyad period. Active under the caliphs ʿAbd al-Malik and his successor al-Walīd (r. 86–96/705–15), al-Ḥajjāj governed Iraq from 75/694, and, from 78/697–8, also Khurasan and Sistan; he left the former to be governed by al-Muhallab (Dietrich, 'al-Ḥadjdjādj b. Yūsuf'). Al-Muhallab (b. *c.* 10/632) was one of the most prominent generals of the first/seventh century. In active service in the Ahwaz during the caliphates of ʿUmar and ʿAlī, he also campaigned much further to the east, in Sistan, Khurasan and possibly Sind. On behalf of successive political authorities, al-Muhallab waged a long if intermittent war against the Azāriqa, a militant group among the Khawārij. For this service, al-Ḥajjāj rewarded him in 78/697–8 with the governorship of Khurasan (Crone, 'al-Muhallab b. Abī Ṣufra').

of my Lord,] and I have counselled you; but you have no love for sincere counsellors' (Q 7: 79).[61]

The Prophet, God's peace be upon him, said, 'When the slave counsels his master and surpasses him in his worship of God, his recompense is twofold.' Abū Hurayra related that the Prophet said, 'Religion is counsel, religion is counsel, religion is counsel.' He was asked, 'For whom, O Messenger of God?' The Prophet replied, 'For God and His Book, for His Prophet, and for the leaders of the Muslims and the ordinary people among them (*li-a'immat al-muslimīn wa-'āmmatihim*).'[62]

In sum, sincere counsel (*nuṣḥ*) is to act with a view to the promotion of welfare (*ṣalāḥ*) and the avoidance of blame (*malāma*).[63] The term is derived from *naṣāḥa*, which refers to the way in which an item has been sewn; its diminutive is *nuṣayyiḥa*. The Arabs say, 'This is a *manṣūḥ* shirt', that is, stitched. To say, 'I counselled him with my sincere counsel' (*naṣaḥtuhu nuṣḥan*) evokes the metaphor of stitching.[64]

The 'stitching' (*nuṣḥ*) of things differs according to the item to which the term is applied. *Nuṣḥ* for God means describing Him in terms that are worthy of Him, and divesting Him of any epithets that are not worthy of Him, whether in reason or in speech; constant exaltation of Him and submission to Him in the external and internal dimensions; desire for the things that He loves and distance from the things that displease Him; friendship with the people who obey Him and hostility towards the people who disobey Him; striving to induce the disobedient to obedience, in speech and in action; and aiming to disseminate all of the things that we have mentioned among His servants.

[61] The prophet whose speech is recorded in this last verse is Ṣāliḥ, the prophet sent, according to the Qur'anic narrative, to the people Thamūd (see Q 7: 73–9; 11: 61–8; 26: 141–59; 27: 45–53; and elsewhere); Rippin, 'Ṣāliḥ'; Tottoli, 'Ṣāliḥ'.

[62] With more than one chain of transmission, the hadith appears in several of the standard collections: al-Bukhārī, *Ṣaḥīḥ*, I: 46, *Kitāb al-Īmān*, ch. 43, no. 57 (Jarīr); Muslim, *Ṣaḥīḥ*, II: 48–51, *Kitāb al-Īmān*, ch. 23, nos. 95, 96 (Tamīm al-Dārī); al-Tirmidhī, *al-Jāmi' al-kabīr*, III: 485, *Kitāb al-Birr wa-l-ṣila*, ch. 17, no. 1926 (Abū Hurayra); al-'Ajlūnī, *Kashf al-khafā'*, I: 204, no. 698. It is also frequently cited; see Ibn 'Abd Rabbihi, *al-'Iqd al-farīd*, I: 11; Pseudo-Māwardī, *Naṣīḥat al-mulūk al-mansūb ilā … al-Māwardī*, 43; al-Ḥuṣrī, *Zahr al-ādāb*, I: 173–4; al-Nuwayrī, *Nihāyat al-arab*, VI: 9. See further Marlow, *Counsel for Kings*, II: 303; and see above, Chapter 7, n. 60.

[63] Cf. the Prophetic hadith, 'Consultation is a fortress against regret and a surety against blame' (al-Māwardī, *Adab al-dunyā wa-l-dīn*, 289).

[64] Ibn Manẓūr, *Lisān al-'arab*, VI: 4438–9. The meaning indicated in al-Ṭurṭūshī's discussion is adduced on p. 4439 (*al-niṣāḥ: al-silku yukhāṭu bihi*, 'the thread with which it is sewn'). Ibn Manẓūr also reports the association of *n-ṣ-ḥ* with purification (*Lisān al-'arab*, VI: 4438–9; see also Marlow, *Counsel for Kings*, II: 31–2).

As for the meaning of *naṣīḥa* when applied to His Book, it connotes the upholding of the Book through recitation, the appreciation of it through reading, striving to understand its contents, acting in accordance with it, deterring its interpretation by criminals and its criticism by sceptics, and teaching its contents to all of God's creatures. God said, 'We have sent down to you a Book, which is blessed; so that they might contemplate its signs, and so that persons of understanding [*ūlū l-albāb*] might reflect' (Q 38: 29).

Naṣīḥa for the Prophet, may God's blessings and peace be upon him, means assisting and supporting him; protecting him from everyone, alive and dead; maintaining the life of his normative practice through its performance and the life of his teaching through promoting the call to belief, spreading the word and behaving with pure moral characteristics.

Naṣīḥa for the leaders (*aʾimma*) means supporting them in the matters that they are charged to uphold, reminding them of their responsibilities in times of negligence, guiding them in cases of slips, instructing them in matters of which they are ignorant, warning them against persons who wish them ill, alerting them to the moral characteristics and conduct of their officials, supplying them in times of need, supporting them in times of dissent and seeking to restore to them the loyalty of disaffected hearts.

Nuṣḥ for the general population of the Muslims means the manifestation of compassion towards them: treating the elderly among them with dignity and the young with mercy, dispelling their cares, inviting them to pursue their happiness, showing vigilance when their minds become preoccupied and guarding them against detrimental insinuations. *Naṣīḥa* for the Muslims includes provision for them from the personal stores that an individual may have amassed in order to meet the needs of his body and soul. According to al-Aṣmaʿī (122–213 or 216/740–828 or 831), ʿUmar b. al-Khaṭṭāb, may God be content with him, once found the kernel of a date in the road. He picked it up and held it in his hand until he passed the house of a family. He then threw it into the courtyard of the house, and he remarked that the family's domestic animals would eat it.[65]

As for the meaning of *nuṣḥ* for all the communities, it means that an individual should desire that they embrace Islam. He should call them –

[65] Al-Aṣmaʿī, a prolific author, was a celebrated philologist, as well as an intellectual companion to Hārūn al-Rashīd (Weipert, 'al-Aṣmaʿī').

by word – to faith, and he should warn them against the bad consequences of unbelief. If they possess power, he should be ready to employ the sword, until they desist from fighting the Muslims, so that they are eligible to become a people protected by the pact of *dhimma*; if they will not desist, he should fight them, as part of his *nuṣḥ* towards God, in upholding His command among them.[66] Muʿādh related the Prophet's words, 'There are three things from which the Muslim heart should not hold back: acting for the sake of God, offering sincere counsel to the holders of command and vigilance on behalf of all the Muslims, for such attentiveness protects them, like a wall, from that which lies beyond them.'[67]

Jarīr b. ʿAbdallāh related that he had pledged allegiance to the Prophet 'to hear and obey'. The Prophet had suggested that he add to this formula, 'to the extent of your capacity, and *nuṣḥ* for every Muslim'.[68] Anas (b. Mālik, d. 93/712) related the Prophet's words, 'Not one of you truly believes unless he loves for his brother what he loves for himself.'[69] Abū l-Dardāʾ said, 'Knowledge is open to attainment for the pious and the profligate alike; wisdom is open to articulation by the pious and the debauched alike; but *naṣīḥa* for God Almighty is firm only

66 Al-Ṭurṭūshī's unusual addition of non-Muslim populations among the proper recipients of counsel, and his interpretation of what the duty of such counsel might entail, reflects his experience of the threat of Christian military campaigns against Muslim-held territories, in Iberia and in the eastern Mediterranean; on this element in his writings, see Mallett, 'Two Writings of al-Ṭurṭūshī', and above, section 3.9.

67 Recalls hadith recorded, on the authority of Anas, in Muslim, *Ṣaḥīḥ*, II: 17–19, *Kitāb al-Īmān*, ch. 15, nos. 67, 68; al-Tirmidhī, *al-Jāmiʿ al-kabīr*, IV: 367, *Kitāb al-ʿIlm*, ch. 10, no. 2624; Ibn Māja, *Sunan*, 1338–9, *Kitāb al-Fitan*, no. 4033; al-Nasāʾī, *Sunan*, 671, *Kitāb al-Īmān*, chs. 2–4, nos. 4987, 4988, 4989; Abū Nuʿaym al-Iṣfahānī, *Ḥilyat al-awliyāʾ*, I: 17, II: 288. On Anas, see below, n. 69.

68 Reading, with the specialists who recorded this hadith in their collections, Jarīr for Jābir. See al-Bukhārī, *Ṣaḥīḥ*, I: 46, *Kitāb al-Īmān*, ch. 43, nos. 57, 58; see also I: 257, *Kitāb Mawāqīt al-ṣalāt*, ch. 3, no. 524; I: 598, *Kitāb al-Zakāt*, ch. 2, no. 1401; II: 154, *Kitāb al-Buyūʿ*, ch. 68, no. 2157; II: 379, *Kitāb al-Shurūṭ*, ch. 1, nos. 2714, 2715; IV: 549, *Kitāb al-Aḥkām*, ch. 43, no. 7204; Muslim, *Ṣaḥīḥ*, II: 52–3, *Kitāb al-Īmān*, ch. 23, nos. 98, 99; al-Tirmidhī, *al-Jāmiʿ al-kabīr*, III: 484, *Kitāb al-Birr wa-l-ṣila*, ch. 17, no. 1925; Abū Dāʾūd, *Sunan*, VII: 397, *Kitāb al-Adab*, ch. 59, no. 4859; al-Nasāʾī, *Sunan*, 567–8, *Kitāb al-Bayʿa*, ch. 6, nos. 4156, 4157; al-Dārimī, *Sunan*, 359, *Kitāb al-Buyūʿ*, ch. 9, no. 2574; Ibn Ḥanbal, *Musnad al-Imām Aḥmad*, XXXI: 533, 535, 557, 572, nos. 19195, 19229, 19199, 19258; 500–1, 529, 556, 566–7, nos. 19162, 19163, 19191, 19228, 19245, 19248 (Jarīr b. ʿAbdallāh). See also Pseudo-Māwardī (*Naṣīḥat al-mulūk al-mansūb ilā ... al-Māwardī*, 44), also with reference to Jarīr b. ʿAbdallāh.

69 Al-Bukhārī, *Ṣaḥīḥ*, I: 23, *Kitāb al-Īmān*, ch. 7, no. 13; Muslim, *Ṣaḥīḥ*, II: 21–2, *Kitāb al-Īmān*, ch. 17, nos. 71, 72. Anas b. Mālik (d. 93/712), who died in Basra, was a prolific transmitter (Juynboll, 'Anas b. Mālik'); see above, n. 67.

in the hearts of the chosen, whose intellects are sound and whose intentions are true. Know that swallowing counsel is bitter, and only persons of determination can accept it.'[70]

ʿUmar b. al-Khaṭṭāb, may God have mercy upon him, used to say, 'May God have mercy upon the man who guides me to my faults.'[71] Maymūn b. Mihrān (d. 117/735–6) reported that ʿUmar b. ʿAbd al-ʿAzīz (r. 99–101/717–20), may God have mercy upon him, said to him, 'Tell me to my face whatever you find most objectionable. For a man does not truly counsel his brother unless he tells him face to face what he considers objectionable.'[72] Mālik said, 'Counsel for God on His earth is the purpose for which God sent it His prophets.'

Endeavour and counsel for the benefit of God's servants in their affairs are parts of Islam, even though people find counsel burdensome and feel disaffection towards persons who offer it, and even though people incline only to the parts of it that coincide with their desires. It is recorded in the transmitted wisdom (*manthūr al-ḥikam*), 'He who offers you sincere counsel loves you, whereas he who encourages you in your desire detests you.' It used to be said, 'Your brother is he who bears the burden of counselling you.'

A poet once said:

I gave Zayd a piece of my advice.
He said: 'You have disappointed me, and your counsel is bitter!'
Why should I counsel Zayd,
He being of flawless character and pious?
It had reached me that someone in his residence
Had spoken ill of Zayd.
I therefore counselled him to avoid everything
Ill that had been spoken against him, for the man free of fault is truly free.

Another said:

The duty to counsel me is a burden upon a person of sincerity;
If I reject a sincere person's counsel, the burden of responsibility is mine.

70 Abū l-Dardāʾ ʿUwaymir b. Zayd al-Anṣārī (d. early 30s/650s or later), a Companion of the Prophet, was a famous ascetic. Born in Medina, he moved after the conquest to Damascus, where he died (Melchert, 'Abū l-Dardāʾ').

71 Al-Ṭurṭūshī cited this utterance earlier; see above, n. 49.

72 Maymūn, an early Muslim jurist and administrator under the Umayyads, is also remembered for his religious and ethical maxims (Abū Nuʿaym al-Iṣfahānī, *Ḥilyat al-awliyāʾ*, IV: 82–97 (no. 251); Donner, 'Maymūn b. Mihrān').

Al-Quṭāmī (d. 101/719–20) said:

Hearing of disobedience in a person for whom you feel compassion
Adds to its bitterness.
The best thing to do is to confront him about it
And not to follow his example.[73]

Waraqa b. Nawfal said:

I have counselled people, and I have said to them:
I am here to warn you, so that no one should mislead you;
Nothing that you now behold and that currently gives you happiness will last
Except for the Divine; wealth and progeny alike will meet perdition.
Hurmuz was unable to survive without his treasuries even for a single day,
And while ʿĀd attempted to reach eternity, that people did not endure.[74]

[ʿAbdallāh] Ibn Wahb (125–97/743–813) said: 'Only he who chooses well for himself can choose well for other people. There is no good for anyone else in the person who possesses no good in himself.'[75]

The scholars have said: 'A man will never counsel you well if he does not counsel himself.'

Another person said, 'If you and I each form judgements concerning you, mine will reflect greater knowledge of you than yours, since my judgement of you will be free of your desire.'

Abū l-Dardāʾ said, 'If you wish, I shall counsel you: the most beloved of God's servants in His sight are those who instil love of God in His servants, and those who act in the world in accordance with good counsel.'

It is related that a man once struck Ibrāhīm b. Adham. Ibrāhīm raised his head to the heavens and said, 'My God, if by this action You were rewarding me and punishing him, then do not reward me and do not punish him.'[76]

[73] Al-Quṭāmī, a seventh-century poet, probably a Christian; see Ibn Qutayba, *al-Shiʿr wa-l-shuʿarāʾ*, 724, no. 1283 (ʿUmayr b. Shuyaym al-Quṭāmī, 723–6, no. 167); Ibn ʿAbd Rabbihi, *al-ʿIqd al-farīd*, I: 61.

[74] Al-Ibshīhī, *al-Mustaṭraf*, I: 174. A contemporary of the Prophet, Waraqa was an early Arabian monotheist, or *ḥanīf*, who may have converted to Christianity (Robinson, 'Waraḳa b. Nawfal'). Hurmuz(d) is the name of several Sasanian kings; the reference here is probably to Hurmuzd IV (r. 579–90), who succeeded Khusraw I, or to Hurmuzd V (r. 630–2), who succeeded Khusraw II. ʿĀd were an ancient Arabian tribe, mentioned in the Qurʾan as the people to whom the prophet Hūd was sent; associated with longevity, prosperity and monumental architecture, they suffered divine punishment for their refusal to accept the prophet's message (Rippin, 'ʿĀd').

[75] A Mālikī traditionist; he was born and died in Cairo, and reputedly studied in Medina.

[76] Ibrāhīm b. Adham (d. 161/777–8), born in Balkh, was a noted renunciant (Jones, 'Ibrāhīm b. Adham').

9

Problems in the Kingdom and Their Remedies

The final chapter of this anthology explores mirror-writers' diagnoses of political and social ills, and, usually in less detail, their proposed remedies for them. Collectively, the three texts presented in this chapter convey the precarious nature of royal power, and they remind their courtly audiences of its limits. The perils against which the mirror-writers warn their royal readerships range from kings' propensities to indulge to excess in food, drink and sex, to the dangers of heterodoxy, portrayed as an appealing yet deceptive mask for political dissent, to external enemies' seizing advantage at moments of internal weakness. The texts differ in tone and emphasis: al-Thaʿālibī's litany of royal misfortunes is less prescriptive than it is a further illustration of the exceptional nature of the royal lot; Niẓām al-Mulk's lament for a lapsed political order reflects the waning sway of *al-dawla al-Niẓāmiyya*; al-Ṭurṭūshī's concise depiction of the perils of the royal office carries a strongly exhortative message.[1]

Text 16
Al-Thaʿālibī, *Ādāb al-mulūk*, Chapter Seven[2]

Translator's Introduction

As Pseudo-Māwardī had also done, al-Thaʿālibī devoted one of his ten chapters to the misfortunes that afflict kings and imperil their tenures in

[1] On *al-dawla al-Niẓāmiyya*, see above, Chapter 2, n. 58.

[2] Translation prepared from al-Thaʿālibī, *Ādāb al-mulūk*, 155–72. For the corresponding section in Topuzoğlu's translation, see Topuzoğlu, 'Kitāb Ādāb al-Mulūk al-Khwārazm-shāhī' (1974), I: 122–41, and Topuzoğlu, *Kitāb Ādāb al-Mulūk al-Khwārazm-shāhī* (2015), I: 117–35.

power. He begins with kings' susceptibility to excess. A long exposition, presented in hierarchical order (caliphs before kings) as well as chronological order, of rulers who have fallen prey to certain failings or who have suffered acute misfortunes follows. These cases provide exemplars of admonition. They illustrate al-Thaʿālibī's previously noted observation that if kings enjoy virtually limitless status and splendour, they also endure the greatest burdens and hardships. Indeed, for al-Thaʿālibī, it might be said that kings cannot win; even if they rule well, people will eventually get fed up with them and desire a change. The chapter ends with a long narrative illustrating the dangers of heterodoxy. As Pseudo-Māwardī had done and as Niẓām al-Mulk would also do, al-Thaʿālibī portrays heterodoxy as one of the most destructive forces in the body politic; religious dissent, for these authors, was synonymous with political subversion. The heroic figure of the piece is Maḥmūd of Ghazna, a contemporary of al-Thaʿālibī and brother-in-law of his patron and addressee, the Khᵛārazmshāh Maʾmūn II (r. 399–407 or 408/1009–17). Al-Thaʿālibī presents a picture of powerless caliphs, often surrendering to a life of pleasure, but always outmatched by slaves, soldiers, commanding officers, rival potentates, viziers and members of their own families. He provides a commentary on the political culture of his time and locality, and a distinctive perspective on the history of the early Islamic period. His use of historical narrative to make his points is extensive and would be developed still further by Niẓām al-Mulk.

Translation

Chapter Seven: On the Calamities That Befall Kings

Section: On the Disturbance of the Humours (*Takhlīṭ*) in Kings

Three problems loom large among the greatest calamities to which kings are subject. They are, firstly, the sheer abundance of special foods and fancy dishes produced in their kitchens and brought to their tables; secondly, the frequency of their convivial assemblies, which entail excessive consumption of wine; and thirdly, the fact that their palaces are packed with inducements to the pursuit of the carnal appetites and over-indulgence in the physical pleasures. Kings are likely to overdo these three things, whereas the appropriate response in each case should entail infrequency and moderation. Too much of anything will attack a person's natural constitution (*ṭabīʿa*). Kings, however, indulge in one or all of these pleasures. Through constant disturbance of the humours (*takhlīṭ*), kings risk harming their temperaments (*mizāj*) and reducing the length of their lives.[3]

How many a king has been ruined as a result of his own doing, slain by his stomach and sexual organs! Sulaymān b. ʿAbd al-Malik b. Marwān (r. 96–9/715–17), for example, used to eat more voraciously than fire, which consumes whatever lies in its path; to drink more abundantly than sand, which absorbs water; and to copulate more frequently than a sparrow. One day he ate thirty roasted chickens and a hundred boiled eggs, drank several quarts (*arṭāl*, sing. *raṭl*)[4] of date wine and enjoyed four virgins. He was overtaken by surfeit; his strength declined, and his final destiny caught up with him.[5]

In this regard Sulaymān resembled al-Wāthiq billāh (r. 227–32/842–7), for he too used to eat an extreme amount, and furthermore, he used to eat without regard to the cleanliness of the food. This caused a disequilibrium in his temperament (*mizāj*), and he developed dropsy. A physician of the military district of Nishapur was brought to see him. This doctor ordered that a pit be heated for him, and the caliph sat in this pit until a great sweat ran from his body. Then he felt better. The physician said to him, 'If you make a habit of what you've been doing, the illness will return, just as it did before; but in the future, the kind of treatment by which I have just cured you will not be effective.' The caliph paid no attention to his words and resumed his habit of eating to excess. The illness returned and before long, it claimed his soul.[6]

Al-Ṣūlī mentioned that Muḥammad b. Yaḥyā b. Abī ʿAbbād reported hearing his father swear that had al-Mutawakkil (r. 232–47/847–61) not been killed, he would not have lived in any case, because his brain had become weak and his body dry from excessive

[3] On the broadly disseminated theory of the humours, see above, Chapter 5, n. 142. The term *mizāj*, literally 'mixture', connotes in this context the balance of elements within the body (Samangustin, 'Mizādj'). Accordingly, I have usually rendered *fasād al-mizāj* as 'disequilibrium'.

[4] One of the major and most widely distributed measures of weight; see Hinz, *Islamische Masse und Gewichte*, 27–33.

[5] Similar reports of the Umayyad caliph Sulaymān's voracious appetite appear in al-Ṣafadī, *al-Wāfī bi-l-wafayāt*, XV: 245–6 (no. 5133, on the authority of the caliph's son), and Ibn Khallikān, *Wafayāt al-aʿyān*, II: 420–7 (no. 279).

[6] On the Abbasid caliph al-Wāthiq and his treatment for dropsy, see Kennedy, *When Baghdad Ruled the Muslim World*, 231–3.

sexual activity. A small amount (*ūqiya*)[7] of oil of violet used to be poured into his ear, but this treatment made little difference, and he was afflicted by great insomnia. He used to say, 'Sex makes my limbs feel exhausted; I need to satisfy my desire without becoming tired.' Next, he was prescribed a treatment involving mercury. The mercury was put into containers made of skin; a pool was filled with these skins, and his bed was prepared on top of them. Through this treatment, the caliph attained his desire without the need for movement, since the movement of the mercury proved enough to satisfy him.[8]

In his youth, al-Muktafī (r. 289–95/902–8) was prone to frequent fainting, an illness that entailed the disequilibrium of his temperament and extreme dryness. The prescribed remedy required him to eat very little, to consume liquid little by little in order to moisten his body and to avoid fatigue. But he did the opposite of these things. The physicians would check to see that he was looking after himself, but as soon as they left, al-Muktafī called for cheese, olives and sardines – indeed, for everything that did not agree with him – and he ate a great deal of these things. He also devoted himself to sexual enjoyment, and he did not pause in these activities until his strength dissipated and his illness grew stronger. Finally, his fate overtook him.[9]

All of these examples involve caliphs; who could number the kings gripped by this calamity of sensual appetite? For instance, [ʿAlī b. Rukn al-Dawla] Fakhr al-Dawla (r. (in Rayy) 366–87/977–97) made no effort to rein in his appetite. One day he left the citadel in Rayy, where he had been staying, for the mountain of Ṭabarak.[10] He developed a craving for

[7] Usually one-twelfth of a *raṭl*; see Hinz, *Islamische Masse und Gewichte*, 34–5.

[8] On Caliph al-Mutawakkil and his assassination, see Kennedy, *The Prophet and the Age of the Caliphates*, 169–72, and Kennedy, *When Baghdad Ruled the Muslim World*, 232–42, 261–7. The al-Ṣūlī family enjoyed close association with the Abbasids for several generations. The unspecified reference is presumably to the prolific author and companion of several caliphs Abū Bakr Muḥammad b. Yaḥyā al-Ṣūlī, who died in 335/947 (see Leder, 'al-Ṣūlī'). Possibly al-Ṣūlī's source, Muḥammad b. Yaḥyā Ibn Abī ʿAbbād, was a relative of Abū l-Ḥasan Muḥammad b. ʿĪsā Ibn Abī ʿAbbād, known to Ibn al-Nadīm as the author of a composition entitled *al-ʿAmal bi-dhāt al-shuʿbatayn* (*Fihrist*, II: i: 248).

[9] On al-Muktafī, see Kennedy, *The Prophet and the Age of the Caliphates*, 183–7; Zetterstéen [Bosworth], 'al-Muktafī'.

[10] Yāqūt, *Muʿjam al-buldān*, IV: 16–17 (Ṭabarak). Construction of the later tenth-century Citadel of Ṭabarak, built to accommodate the garrison of Isfahan, has been ascribed to both Rukn al-Dawla (d. 366/977) and Fakhr al-Dawla (d. 387/997) (see further Durand-Guédy, *Iranian Elites and Turkish Rulers*, 32, n. 55). Fakhr al-Dawla was the husband of Sayyida (Persian Sayyideh), the main protagonist of a story narrated by Kaykāʾūs (see above, Chapter 6, n. 46).

some cuts of beef. So an extremely well-fattened cow was slaughtered right in front of him, and immediately his slaves began to roast it. In eating it, he answered the call of his appetite and his greed, while cups, filled to the brim, circulated all around him. He did not cease his eating and drinking even as the pain mounted – his belly began to complain, and soon he began to cry out, right up until death overtook him.

Section: On the Misfortunes That Befall Kings through Their Slaves

How truly ʿAlī b. al-Jahm (d. 249/863) spoke when, in his ode on the killing of Caliph al-Mutawakkil at the hands of his slaves, he noted the absence of the Tahirids:

Had there been in his presence a scion of the Tahirid family –
They whose fathers and grandfathers had all been received with honour –
Then the hands of fate would have found it difficult to grasp him
Even though their advent had been ordained.
But the Tahirids were far away, and his slaves conspired against him:
The greatest of calamities for kings are their slaves.[11]

The reason for this danger is that kings cannot do without slaves and servants under any circumstances, and yet not every king has succeeded in governing them with kindness, managing them with due exactitude and satisfying all of them. It is customary for the king to elevate one enslaved person over another in accordance with their relative merits, and to single out, firstly, the slaves best suited for royal service, and secondly, those whose pleasing appearance qualifies them for the king's personal intimacy. This practice engenders envy, hostility and aversion among the slaves, who eventually struggle against one another, or form alliances and co-operate with one another in the greatest of crimes. How many a noble person has met his fate at the hands of an ignoble person, and how many a king has perished at the hands of a slave!

[11] ʿAlī b. al-Jahm, *Dīwān ʿAlī b. al-Jahm*, 56–64, no. 18 (the lines appear at p. 61). On this Abbasid poet and his celebrated verses in praise of his patron al-Mutawakkil, see Ali, *Arabic Literary Salons*, 75–116. Initially as powerful in Baghdad as they were in Khurasan, the Tahirids were, by this time, ruling in the east; their authority in Baghdad weakened after the siege of the city in 251–2/865–6, and especially after the accession of Sulaymān b. ʿAbdallāh b. Ṭāhir to the military governorship of Baghdad in 255/869; see Kennedy, *The Prophet and the Age of the Caliphates*, 161–2, 173–4.

As [Abū l-Ṭayyib Aḥmad b. al-Ḥusayn] al-Mutanabbī (303–54/915–55), in his remarkable words, put it:

> May the nights (of fate) never reach you! For they use wisps of willow
> To break the strong wood of the *naba*ʿ tree.
> And may they never come to the aid of the enemy over whom you have triumphed!
> For they hunt the falcon with the bustard.[12]

Some kings are excessive in the training of their slaves; this excessive discipline turns a king's slaves into his enemies and disposes them to collaborate against him. There are other kings who bestow all manner of kindnesses upon their slaves; they tolerate bad manners on the part of their slaves and overlook their defects. Anūshīrvān was an example of the latter type of king. One day the mobad (a Zoroastrian priest) was in the royal presence, and he heard the king's slaves laughing outside the doors. The mobad said: 'Should not fear (*hayba*) of the king prevent this lot from this kind of behaviour?' Anūshīrvān replied, 'Only our enemies fear us.'

A certain king used to say of his slaves: 'We have entrusted them with our lives; if we make them fearful of us, how are we to feel secure against them?' Al-Maʾmūn used to say, 'Poor manners on the part of their slaves is a sign of the generosity of kings.'

Among the calamities that beset kings is their capricious appointment of beardless youths to tasks the execution of which might challenge the competence of even a mature person. As a result of this practice, two things compound against these kings: first, scorn stirs in the minds of the free; secondly, the negative effects of appointing the young men, who have gained neither prudence in handling important affairs nor experience in warfare, soon become apparent. On the subject of a beardless youth made into a commander over the army, Ibn al-Muʿtazz composed these highly regarded words:

> To assume command of the lands, he has been vested with a tunic
> Which weighs heavily on his slender waist.
> When he appears, the men of the lands see in their minds
> The cheeks of a girl or the eyes of an antelope.

[12] Both metaphors – the wood of the *naba*ʿ and the *kharab*, the male bustard (*hubārā*) (*Lisān al-ʿarab*, VI: 4327, II: 750) – evoke the undoing of the strong by means of the weak. The wood of the *naba*ʿ tree is strong, whereas the willow is weak; the falcon is used in hunting, whereas the bustard is a terrestrial bird (see *Ādāb al-mulūk*, 158, nn. 1–2). Al-Thaʿālibī cites these lines again in his *Thimār al-qulūb*, 484.

If he wishes, but fails, to accomplish a matter, he weeps over it,
His cry like that of a child, who, being weaned, is prevented
from suckling.
And when he advances towards his adversary, his hands
Suggest the cup, rather than spears brandished high above.

Muʿizz al-Dawla Abū l-Ḥusayn b. Buwayh (r. 334–56/945–67) had a young slave called Tigin al-Jāmdār (the Robe-Bearer).[13] This beardless youth had a face full of radiance, but he was addicted to drinking; he was never separated from entertainment and unaccustomed to sobriety. Out of the extremity of his inclination towards this slave, the king made Tigin head of a military detachment that he sent into a campaign against [the Hamdanid brothers] Abū l-Murajjā [Jābir] and [Abū l-Qāsim] Hibat Allāh, sons of Nāṣir al-Dawla Abū Muḥammad [Ḥasan b. ʿAbdallāh] b. Ḥamdān (d. 358/969).[14] The vizier Abū Muḥammad [al-Ḥasan b. Muḥammad] al-Muhallabī (291–352/903–63) indicated to the king that he should not send Tigin out for this kind of purpose, and that he should turn instead to one of the prudent, experienced, resolute and judicious senior commanders. The king did not heed the vizier's remarks and dispatched Tigin at the head of a thousand men. This force caught Abū l-Murajjā and Hibat Allāh by surprise, and the two leaders abandoned all the mounts, supplies and military equipment that they had. In their haste to plunder these supplies, Muʿizz al-Dawla's army

[13] The Buyid amir Abū l-Ḥusayn Aḥmad b. Buwayh (Būya) received the title of Muʿizz al-Dawla when he took Baghdad in 334/945 (al-Thaʿālibī adduces another account involving Muʿizz al-Dawla later in the same chapter; see below, at nn. 33–4). The Hamdanid brothers Abū Muḥammad Ḥasan and Abū l-Ḥasan ʿAlī, who feature in this account, received the titles Nāṣir al-Dawla and Sayf al-Dawla respectively in 330/942. The assumption of these titles – ending in *al-Dawla* – by the Hamdanids and shortly afterwards by the Buyids indicated the caliph's cession of substantial power to these figures (see Rosenthal, 'Dawla'). The use of these titles quickly proliferated, in a trend that Niẓām al-Mulk would deplore (see below, Text 17).

[14] On the Hamdanids, see Kennedy, *The Prophet and the Age of the Caliphates*, 221–2; Canard, 'Ḥamdānids'. Nāṣir al-Dawla (d. 358/969), Hamdanid ruler of Mosul (r. 317–58), was the brother of Sayf al-Dawla (303–56/916–67, r. 333–56/945–67), who ruled in Aleppo. After Muʿizz al-Dawla assumed control of Baghdad and Iraq, the Buyids' relations with the Hamdanids were frequently hostile. Muʿizz al-Dawla dealt only with Nāṣir al-Dawla's eldest son, Abū Taghlib Faḍl Allāh al-Ghaḍanfar, who eventually replaced his father; Nāṣir al-Dawla's sons deposed their father in 356/967. The episode perhaps concerns Nāṣir al-Dawla's sending two of his sons to occupy Baghdad in 345/956–8 at a time when Muʿizz al-Dawla was called away to deal with a revolt; in the ensuing confrontation, Muʿizz al-Dawla prevailed and the Hamdanids decamped (Bowen, 'Nāṣir al-Dawla'). Hibat Allāh was appointed to govern Harran under Sayf al-Dawla in 352/963. See Zambaur, *Manuel de généalogie*, 134.

scattered, and the soldiers fell upon the tents of the opposing force (*qawm*). They were still marauding when the other side rallied against them in a surprise counter-attack. The opposing forces killed many of Muʿizz al-Dawla's men, took others prisoner and more than avenged themselves against them. Tigin the Robe-Bearer escaped on his horse, but a certain Arab brigand (*ṣuʿlūq*), intending to rob and capture him, intercepted him. Tigin made himself known to his captor, and he pledged to give him whatever he wanted as long as he would bring him to Muʿizz al-Dawla. Other than Tigin, only the intensely fearful and a detachment of the very youngest troops escaped safely from that mob (*qawm*). The good sense of al-Muhallabī's cautionary words became clear to Muʿizz al-Dawla, yet he would not acknowledge it in an open fashion.[15]

According to Abū Isḥāq [Ibrāhīm] al-Ṣābiʾ (313–84/925–94), al-Muhallabī admired this slave and found his appearance pleasing, but he regarded him as more suited for enjoyment than for the clamour of war. He had reportedly recited to al-Ṣābiʾ a poem of his own:

> A child, whose tears flow down his cheeks;
> Whose body is so slender,
> He appears almost like a virgin
> Whose breasts are just beginning to appear:
> They have slung a sword over his hips
> And a belt so heavy that he buckles under its weight.
> They have made him commander of an army:
> And the troops, whom he leads, are as good as lost.[16]

[15] Celebrated chief minister and vizier from 339–52/950–63 to Muʿizz al-Dawla, al-Muhallabī was a member of the illustrious Muhallabī family that stemmed from the Umayyad commander and governor al-Muhallab b. Abī Ṣufra (see above, Chapter 8, n. 60). On al-Muhallabī, see al-Thaʿālibī, *Yatīmat al-dahr*, II: 265–85, no. 114; Ibn al-Nadīm, *Fihrist*, I: ii: 417–18; Ibn Khallikān, *Wafayāt al-aʿyān*, II: 124–7 (the poem is cited at p. 126); al-Ṣafadī, *al-Wāfī bi-l-wafayāt*, XII: 139–41, no. 3451; Kennedy, *The Prophet and the Age of the Caliphates*, 223.

[16] For this celebrated poem, see al-Zamakhsharī, *Rabīʿ al-abrār*, IV: 133; al-Thaʿālibī, *Yatīmat al-dahr*, II: 267–8, also citing al-Ṣābiʾ, *Kitāb al-Tājī*. On the Ṣābiʾ (Ṣābī) family, scholars originally from Harran and over several generations high-ranking members of the bureaucracy in Baghdad, see de Blois, 'Ṣābiʾ'. Abū Isḥāq al-Ṣābiʾ was a secretary, promoted to Chief Secretary or Director of the Chancery (*ṣāḥib dīwān al-inshāʾ*) in 349/960, in service to Muʿizz al-Dawla; after the death of Muʿizz al-Dawla, al-Ṣābiʾ fell from office and was imprisoned, but he returned to favour after the death of ʿAḍud al-Dawla in 372/983 (de Blois, 'Ṣābiʾ', no. 7). He was the author of the largely lost *Kitāb al-*

Section: On the Most Severe Adversities That Face Kings
Among the calamities that befall kings is that their tribulations, in greatness and severity, are in proportion to their exalted and elevated stations. The extreme difficulties that kings face are worse and more bitter than those that arise for other people. May Almighty God spare our Master, the King and Lord, from the vicissitudes of the time and the misfortunes of events! May He augment his portion of the happiness that attends kingship and kings, and of their bounties; and may He protect him from their misfortunes and afflictions! By His power and might, may He cast a lasting protection over his person and his realm!

It is well known that among the kings of this world, none bear comparison with the kings of the Abbasid family, for God has given them the keys of the earth and has made them rule over the furthest reaches of the created world. Their possessions have encompassed the realms of the Khusraws, the Caesars, the Pharaohs, the Tubbaʿs of Yemen, the Ṭarkhāns of the Turkish steppe, as well as other kings and tyrants.[17] The tribulations and adversities that have befallen and afflicted the Abbasids are commensurate with the numerous and magnificent bounties, and with the unparalleled share of this world's goods, that they have received.

If I were to mention all these rulers, I would reach the utmost extremities of prolixity and be obliged to abandon the structure of my book. I shall, however, produce some choice examples (*nukat*) that offer caution and admonition for anyone who ponders and reflects upon them.

The first example concerns Muḥammad al-Amīn (r. 189–93/809–13), at the time when he was besieged by the forces of Ṭāhir b. al-Ḥusayn. As the siege took hold and al-Amīn's circumstances became increasingly dire, his army rioted against him, demanding their wages. One morning al-Amīn was awakened by a stone; shot from a mangonel, it had fallen on to his bed. He could hear the din of the besiegers from one direction and the clamouring voices of his troops from the other. Choking with tears, he exclaimed, 'May God curse both parties! One lot seek my blood; the other lot want my wealth.' It was not long thereafter that he was defeated and killed.[18]

Tājī, also known, according to Ibn al-Nadīm, as *al-ʿAḍudī*, but properly titled *Dawlat banī buwayh wa-akhbār al-daylam wa-btidāʾ amrihim* (*Fihrist*, I: ii: 416–7).

17 A list that includes these and other royal titles appears in al-Rāghib al-Iṣfahānī, *Muḥāḍarāt al-udabāʾ*, I: 158.

18 Al-Zamakhsharī, *Rabīʿ al-abrār*, IV: 236. Compare al-Ṭurṭūshī's reference, above, Chapter 8, n. 46. On the events surrounding the siege of Baghdad by Ṭāhir and

The trials of al-Mutawakkil (r. 232–47/847–61) provide another example. One evening, surrounded by his boon-companions and musicians, he was presiding over his convivial assembly; cups were circulating and spirits merry. Suddenly, the party was assailed by a group of Turks, who were in collusion with al-Muntaṣir (r. 847–8/861–2). One of the Turks, Bāghir al-Turkī (d. 251/865), began striking the caliph and killed him. The party that had assembled for entertainment and enjoyment was upturned into an assembly of anguish and strife.[19]

The poets have made much of describing this caliph's assassination. Among the finest of these poets is Aḥmad b. Ibrāhīm al-Asadī, who wrote:

> Let the fate of the noble unfold in this fashion:
> In the midst of flutes, stringed instruments and wine –
> Between two cups, offered at the same time:
> The cup of pleasures, and the cup of death![20]

In a further example of the Abbasids' particular ordeals, al-Mustaʿīn billāh (r. 248–52/862–6) was compelled to relinquish the caliphate.[21] As he made the pledge of allegiance to al-Muʿtazz billāh (r. 252–5/866–9),

Harthama b. Aʿyan in 196/812 and al-Amīn's defeat, see Kennedy, *The Prophet and the Age of the Caliphates*, 148–52; Kennedy, *When Baghdad Ruled the Muslim World*, 85–110.

19 It had been the aim of al-Mutawakkil's vizier ʿUbayd Allāh b. Yaḥyā b. Khāqān to replace the caliph's choice for successor with another of his sons, al-Muʿtazz. Al-Mutawakkil's son Muḥammad, upon whom his father had bestowed the title al-Muntaṣir, was involved in the conspiracy of the Turkish soldiery that led to the caliph's death. Bāghir al-Turkī was among the Turkish military leaders involved in the assassination of al-Mutawakkil. Al-Muntaṣir received the *bayʿa* in 247/861 but died the following year at Samarra. In the civil conflicts that engulfed the Samarran caliphate, Bāghir was assassinated in 251/865 by the commanders Bughā al-Ṣaghīr (d. 254/868) and Waṣīf al-Turkī (Bosworth, 'al-Muntaṣir'; Kennedy, *When Baghdad Ruled the Muslim World*, 261–72, 275–6; Kennedy, *The Prophet and the Age of the Caliphates*, 170–3; Gordon, *Breaking of a Thousand Swords*, 88–90; Gordon, 'Bughā al-Ṣaghīr').

20 Al-Thaʿālibī, *Thimār al-qulūb*, 190–1, no. 270, where the events and the verse are recounted in explication of the expression 'the night of al-Mutawakkil' (*laylat al-Mutawakkil*).

21 Al-Mustaʿīn (r. 248–52/862–6), a grandson of Caliph al-Muʿtaṣim, had been picked for the caliphate by Turkish commanders in Samarra after the death of his cousin, al-Muntaṣir (see above, n. 19). Al-Mustaʿīn's caliphate was contested from the outset by supporters of his cousin al-Muʿtazz, whom the new caliph arrested once the resistance to his accession had been suppressed. But when al-Mustaʿīn left Samarra for Baghdad in 251/865, supporters of al-Muʿtazz released the latter from prison, and the ensuing conflict led to al-Mustaʿīn's abdication in 251/866. Although arrangements had been made for him to move to and settle in Medina, he was murdered in 252/866 in Samarra (see further Gordon, *Breaking of a Thousand Swords*, 132–5 and *passim*; Zetterstéen [Bosworth], 'al-Mustaʿīn').

the judge [al-Ḥasan b. Muḥammad b. ʿAbd al-Malik] Ibn Abī l-Shawārib was summoned, in order to read to al-Mustaʿīn the conditions of his deposition. Ibn Abī l-Shawārib said to him: 'O Commander of the Faithful, I call upon you to bear witness to the contents of this document.' Al-Mustaʿīn assented. The judge said, 'May God choose in your favour, O Abū l-ʿAbbās.' Al-Mustaʿīn wept, and cried, 'O God, if You have deposed me from Your caliphate, do not depose me from Your mercy.' Then he recited these verses:

> The fate of all sovereignty is to abscond
> Except for the Sovereignty of the Protector, the All-Bountiful.
> All that you behold will fade away and vanish;
> On the Day of Reckoning, all God's bondsmen shall receive
> their recompense.[22]

Upon hearing these words, the judge asked the deposed caliph to choose the town in which he wished to settle. Al-Mustaʿīn replied that he had already chosen to move to Basra. When told that the climate in Basra was excessively hot, al-Mustaʿīn responded, 'Can you imagine any heat more oppressive than the loss of the caliphate?'[23]

The tribulations of al-Muʿtazz billāh (r. 252–5/866–9) provide another example. The Turks not only deposed him and beat him, but also dragged him, barefoot and bare-headed, in the extreme heat of high summer and at the hour of the midday sun. Al-Muʿtazz begged for shoes to put on. When he did not receive them, he loosened his trousers and walked with them underfoot. Finally his tormentors humiliated him with the most wicked punishment, and deposited him, parched with thirst and exhausted, in a bath-house. One of his clients brought him water with ice in it, and once he had drunk it, he died.[24]

[22] Al-Zamakhsharī, *Rabīʿ al-abrār*, IV: 243.

[23] A member of the Banū Abī l-Shawārib, a family of prominent Iraqi jurists and judges, al-Ḥasan b. Muḥammad b. ʿAbd al-Malik Ibn Abī l-Shawārib held the post of qadi in 250–61/864–74. A loyal servant of al-Mutawakkil, he had fallen out of favour under al-Mustaʿīn, who deprived him of his office as official counsellor; Ibn Abī l-Shawārib returned to and retained his office under al-Muʿtazz, al-Muhtadī and al-Muʿtamid (Vadet, 'Ibn Abī 'l-Shawārib').

[24] Al-Muʿtazz, a son of al-Mutawakkil, attempted to curb the power of the Turkish commanders. He instigated the execution of Bughā al-Ṣaghīr in 254/868, but Turkish power in the state revived in 255/869, while that of the Tahirid governors and commanders of the guard in Baghdad decreased, notably upon the assumption of the governorship of Baghdad by Sulaymān b. ʿAbdallāh b. Ṭāhir (r. 255–66/869–79) (see above, n. 11). A combination of factors and constituencies, including the demands of the Turkish soldiery for their pay, contributed to the deposition of al-Muʿtazz in 255/869

Another example of the Abbasids' afflictions is the ordeal of al-Muhtadī billāh (r. 255–6/869–70).[25] Sufyān al-Thawrī (97–161/716–78) used to say that the true caliphs were five: the first four were the four Rightly Guided caliphs, and the fifth was (the Umayyad) ʿUmar b. ʿAbd al-ʿAzīz. It has been asserted that the sixth true caliph would be, without a doubt, al-Muhtadī, since he resembled the two ʿUmars in his conduct. He was fair and just, and he used his independent judgement (*ijtihād*) to adjudicate in religious matters. He enjoyed the highest respect among the people generally and the Turks especially, to the point that when he rode out and people saw him, they raised a great clamour of weeping and prayers on his behalf. Among his notable acts was his ordering the confiscation of musical instruments, his expulsion of singers and effeminate men from Samarra, his rejection of presents submitted at the festivals of Nawrūz and Mihrajān, and his sitting in person for the redress of grievances (*maẓālim*).[26] His conduct in these matters remained unchanged – until, that is, zealous partisans of al-Mutawakkil's offspring took to the stratagem of claiming to the Turks that the caliph was an infidel, and that he was considering using the sword against

(Bosworth, 'al-Muʿtazz'; Kennedy, *When Baghdad Ruled the Muslim World*, 261–2, 277–88; Gordon, *Breaking of a Thousand Swords*, 98–101).

[25] Al-Muhtadī, a son of al-Wāthiq, was widely esteemed for his piety and rectitude, and reputedly modelled himself upon ʿUmar b. ʿAbd al-ʿAzīz, as al-Thaʿālibī's invocation of Sufyān al-Thawrī's remark suggests. The caliphate's continuing economic strains and hostility between al-Muhtadī and the Turkish general Mūsā b. Bughā culminated in the caliph's execution of Mūsā's brother Muḥammad b. Bughā and Mūsā's advance against the caliph. Defeated, al-Muhtadī refused to abdicate, and he was murdered in 256/870 (Kennedy, *When Baghdad Ruled the Muslim World*, 174–5, 288–94; Gordon, *Breaking of a Thousand Swords*, 101–4). Sufyān al-Thawrī was a prominent figure in the development of early law, tradition and Qurʾanic interpretation; numerous examples of his pronouncements have been preserved (Abū Nuʿaym al-Iṣfahānī, *Ḥilyat al-awliyāʾ*, VI: 356–93, VII: 3–144 (no. 387)).

[26] On the practice of caliphal redress of grievances in the later ninth and early tenth centuries, before al-Māwardī's well-defined and systematised presentation in *al-Aḥkām al-sulṭāniyya*, see van Berkel, 'Abbasid *Maẓālim* between Theory and Practice'. The ancient Iranian festivals of Nawrūz, marking the vernal equinox and the first day of the new year according to the Iranian solar calendar, and Mihragān (Ar. Mihrajān), marking the autumnal equinox, continued to be widely celebrated, particularly in Muslim courtly settings, in and beyond Iran. These celebrations often featured the presentation of gifts, and sometimes the collection of exceptional taxes. Al-Thaʿālibī's reference to al-Muhtadī's scruples suggests the disapproval, among some religious authorities, of the continuing observance of these pre-Islamic festivals and the extra-*sharʿī* levies that sometimes accompanied them (see Shahbazi, 'Nowruz ii: In the Islamic Period'; Cristoforetti, 'Mehragān').

them. The Turks swore that they had never witnessed the slightest indication of infidelity in him. In response, the caliph's accusers insinuated, 'Is it not the case that (Christian) monks, having forsaken the world, are intent upon nothing but worship in their monasteries, yet, being infidels, they are nevertheless bound for the fire? The caliph is like them.' In this way, these individuals undermined al-Muhtadī's reputation for justice and scrupulousness (*waraʿ*). The Turks, no longer satisfied with his pleasing conduct, began to oppose him, and he in turn fought against them. Those whom he had relied upon deserted him. As he sought help from the common people, he said, 'Will you not fight against a people (*qawm*) who broke their oaths?' (Q 9: 13).[27] But no one came to his aid, and he was seized and killed.

Then there was the trial of al-Muʿtamid ʿalā llāh (r. 256–79/870–92).[28] Notwithstanding the length of his reign and his sustained personal safety, he was beset by the Turks' mastery over him and their belittling of him, and by al-Muwaffaq's appropriation of power and exclusion of him from the management of affairs. Al-Muʿtamid said:

> I have been deprived of any defence against the unjust treatment meted out to me. The people's affairs carry on without me, and I hear very little about them. When I desire something, they always find some reason for withholding it from me.

One evening, he asked for three hundred dinars, which he was unable to find. He said:

> Is it not remarkable that someone such as I
> Should find his access to revenue impeded?
> The whole world submits its levies in his name
> Yet none of that wealth reaches his hands.
> The revenues in their entirety are delivered to him
> Yet he is prevented from access to even a part of
> what is collected for him.[29]

[27] The caliph's calling upon the people for their support in his struggle with Mūsā and Muḥammad (see n. 25), whom he had accused of embezzlement, is a Qurʾanic citation.

[28] Al-Muʿtamid, a son of al-Mutawakkil, was never able to build up an independent power base. Largely a figurehead, he spent most of his caliphate in Samarra, while his brother Abū Aḥmad, who assumed the quasi-caliphal title al-Muwaffaq, exercised effective rule from Baghdad. Al-Muwaffaq held the allegiance of the Turkish military. See Kennedy, *The Prophet and the Age of the Caliphates*, 172–82; Gordon, *Breaking of a Thousand Swords*, 141–4; Kennedy, 'al-Muʿtamid ʿalā ʾllāh' and 'al-Muwaffaḳ'.

[29] Ibn Ḥamdūn, *al-Tadhkira al-Ḥamdūniyya*, I: 442.

Among the trials that he is reported to have suffered, and an example of the Turks' ascendancy over him, is that [Abū Ṣāliḥ] Mufliḥ once sent him a message asking him to give him, as a present, his slave-girl Hazār and his servant Badr al-Julnār. At this request al-Muʿtamid was moved to tear his tunic in frustration; 'Is this how slaves treat their masters (*mawālī*)?' he asked, 'by extorting their women and slaves?' But later he said, 'Someone like Abū Ṣāliḥ (Mufliḥ) cannot be refused,' and he ordered that Hazār be conveyed to him. She was the most beautiful woman of her time, and the most talented in music and singing. At the same time, al-Muʿtamid said: 'As for Badr al-Julnār, he has a special place in our affections, and he (Mufliḥ) must comply with our wishes by leaving him with us.' When the messenger relayed the report to Mufliḥ, the latter said, 'In the case of Hazār, I have already acquired her; as for Badr, I shall find a way to acquire him too, whether the caliph likes it or not.' Later, Mufliḥ set out on a campaign against the Zanj, in the course of which he was killed. May God keep him at a distance.

Another example of the Abbasids' tribulations is the ordeal of al-Muqtadir billāh (r. 295–6/908, 296–317/908–29, 317–20/929–32).[30] For he, notwithstanding the magnificence of his position, the display of his power and the profusion of worldly goods that he enjoyed for a period of twenty-four years, suffered affliction at the hands of Muʾnis al-Khādim, who eventually killed him as if he were a dog.[31] Muʾnis beheaded him and tossed aside his corpse, naked; the rabble stole his clothing, and left nothing but tufts of grass to cover his private parts. A woman came along and gleaned the perfume that was in his navel.

[30] Al-Muqtadir, who acceded at the age of thirteen, reigned from 295/908 to 320/932, with two temporary depositions: a matter of months into his reign, in 296/908, when Ibn al-Muʿtazz replaced him for a day; and in 317/929, when his brother Muḥammad, given the regnal title al-Qāhir, was raised to the throne for two days. From 296–21/908–33, the leading military commander Muʾnis al-Khādim exercised enormous power in the caliphate, especially since he defended al-Muqtadir against the supporters of Ibn al-Muʿtazz in 296/908 and restored him to the throne after his second deposition (see the following note).

[31] Muʾnis, who received the *laqab* al-Muẓaffar ('the Victor') for repelling the Fatimid al-Mahdī in 307/919–20, eventually turned against al-Muqtadir and overthrew him. See Kennedy, *When Baghdad Ruled the Muslim World*, 191–8; Kennedy, *The Prophet and the Age of the Caliphates*, 187–95; Zetterstéen [Bosworth], 'al-Muḳtadir'; Bowen, 'Muʾnis al-Muẓaffar'.

Other examples of the caliphs' misfortunes include the trials of al-Qāhir (r. 317/929, 320–2/932–4) and al-Muttaqī (r. 329–33/940–4), who suffered deposition and the gouging out of their eyes.[32]

The tribulations of al-Mustakfī (r. 333–4/944–6) involved Muʿizz al-Dawla Abū l-Ḥusayn (r. 334–56/945–67 (in Iraq)), who grew disaffected from the caliph and increasingly settled and firm in his intention and determination to depose him.[33] Resolved to adopt a tactical approach (*tadbīr*), Muʿizz al-Dawla hastened to make a display of friendship towards the caliph. On a Thursday, he rode at the head of an army to greet him. Al-Mustakfī, seated on his throne, was surrounded by his servants, who were admitted into the caliph's presence in the first group. Muʿizz al-Dawla kissed the ground in front of the caliph several times; then he kissed the caliph's hands and stood near him, talking to him and conversing with him. The caliph ordered him to be seated, so he sat on a stool (*kursī*), while other eminent and important persons (*al-ruʾasāʾ wa-l-wujūh*) remained standing in their places and ranks. The caliph gave permission to the high-ranking members of the Hashimite family, the secretaries and the judges to enter the court, followed by all of the army, including the Daylamites and the Turks; finally, he admitted the various categories of the general public. When the assembly was complete, two commanders of the Daylami corps came forward. One of them, Rūstākīm, was strong and rough. The two commanders spoke in Persian, in words that al-Mustakfī could not understand. The caliph was told that they wished to take their leave for the court of ʿImād al-Dawla (r. 322–38/934–49 (in Fars and Khuzistan)), and hoped that the Commander of the Faithful would grant the two of them the

[32] Al-Qāhir, brother of and successor to al-Muqtadir, was seized and imprisoned after an uprising in 322/934. When he refused to abdicate, he was blinded. He was released only under the next caliph, al-Mustakfī, and he died in 339/950 (Kennedy, *When Baghdad Ruled the Muslim World*, 156–9, 196–7; Kennedy, *The Prophet and the Age of the Caliphates*, 198; Sourdel, 'al-Ḳāhir biʾllāh'). Al-Muttaqī was a son of al-Muqtadir. During a tumultuous caliphal period, he sought the protection of the Hamdanids on more than one occasion. In 333/944, he was blinded and then deposed by the Turkish general Tuzun (d. 334/945); al-Muttaqī died in 357/968 (Zettersteen [Bosworth], 'al-Muttaḳī liʾllāh').

[33] Raised to the throne by Tuzun after the blinding of al-Muttaqī, one of the latter's cousins, al-Mustakfī occupied the caliphal office when the Buyid leader Aḥmad b. Būya arrived in Baghdad in 334/945. The caliph was obliged to grant Aḥmad the *laqab* Muʿizz al-Dawla, to place his name with his own on the coinage, and to recognise him as *amīr al-umarāʾ*. As al-Thaʿālibī relates, Muʿizz al-Dawla, the effective ruler of Iraq, soon deposed and blinded al-Mustakfī (334/946) and replaced him with al-Faḍl b. al-Muqtadir, who now received the title al-Muṭīʿ. Al-Mustakfī died in prison in 338/949 (Kennedy, *The Prophet and the Age of the Caliphates*, 218, 250; Bosworth, 'al-Mustakfī').

honour of allowing them to kiss his hand.[34] The caliph covered his hand with his sleeve and stretched it out to them. Rūstākīm took it, then dragged the caliph from his throne so that he fell to the ground. The caliph was wearing a turban made of cloth from Ruṣāfa, and it slipped off his head. The two men wrapped the turban round the caliph's throat and dragged him away. Muʿizz al-Dawla rose; horns were sounded, cries were raised and the palace was looted. Immediately al-Faḍl b. al-Muqtadir billāh was summoned; in fact, he was already present, since he had been prepared in advance and was waiting to be called. So al-Faḍl appeared, surrounded by supporters, and he sat upon the caliphal throne. The new caliph took the title (*laqab*) of al-Muṭīʿ lillāh (r. 334–63/946–74). Al-Mustakfī was brought forward and made to stand before him. Al-Mustakfī then greeted the new caliph with the caliphal greeting, and testified to his own deposition. During the coming night, his eyes were put out and he was detained in the palace.

The experience of al-Muṭīʿ likewise belongs among the tribulations of the Abbasids.[35] His ordeal began with the arrival of letters and reports bearing the news that the Byzantines had [in 362/972] raided Nasibin. They had occupied it, then set fire to it and left it in ruins, having killed many of its men and captured their children. A group of the city's inhabitants, as well as the people of Diyar Rabiʿa and Diyar Bakr, came to Baghdad, where they sought to rouse the Muslims in the mosques and markets. A large number of people gathered. They broke the pulpits in the mosques. Then they made for the palace of al-Muṭīʿ, which they tried to assault: they wrenched out some of the windows, but just as they were about to reach the caliph and attack him, the gates were bolted to keep them out. At this setback they subjected the caliph to repulsive language; they accused him of powerlessness and failure to fulfil the duties that God had made mandatory for imams, and they hurled every kind of repugnant and ignominious insult at him.[36]

[34] On the early Buyids' lack of familiarity with Arabic, see Kennedy, *The Prophet and the Age of the Caliphates*, 224. In the case described in al-Thaʿālibī's narrative, the Buyids' use of Persian prevented the caliph from gleaning their purpose.

[35] A son of al-Muqtadir and brother of al-Muttaqī, al-Muṭīʿ suffered a stroke which left him incapacitated. Turkish military leaders compelled him to abdicate in favour of a son who became al-Ṭāʾiʿ; he died in 364/974 (Kennedy, *The Prophet and the Age of the Caliphates*, 241; Zettersteen [Bosworth], 'al-Muṭīʿ liʾllāh').

[36] In 362/972–3, Byzantine forces, having already retaken a number of locations, made incursions deep into Muslim territory. The arrival of refugees in Baghdad prompted demands for action (Kennedy, *The Prophet and the Age of the Caliphates*, 225).

This episode coincided with [ʿIzz al-Dawla] Bakhtiyār's imposition of financial pressure upon al-Muṭīʿ and his vizier's resorting to reprehensible and disapproved methods of extracting funds.[37] In one of the demands that he sent to al-Muṭīʿ, Bakhtiyār insinuated that the caliph possessed vast riches. Changing his approach, Bakhtiyār then appeared before the caliph with an urgent request for funding for military action (*ghazw*), which was the imam's mandatory duty. Al-Muṭīʿ responded: 'I would be responsible for military campaigning only if I possessed any worldly goods; but all I have is the small amount of food allotted to me. It is you and the rulers of the provinces (*aṣḥāb al-aṭrāf*) who possess the world's wealth; under these conditions, neither warfare (*ghazw*) nor the pilgrimage (*ḥajj*), nor any other obligation of the imams, is incumbent upon me. All that you get from me is my name, which is recited in your pulpits (in the Friday sermon), and which maintains the quiescence of the masses of your subjects. If you wish me to step aside, then I shall step aside.' The correspondence on this matter continued, with the exchange of several messages and a mounting sense of threat. The caliph therefore pledged to contribute four hundred thousand dirhams, to raise which he was obliged to sell his clothing and equipment; this divestment eventually caused the collapse of his palace. Reports of the confiscation of the caliph's wealth spread throughout the City of Peace (Baghdad), among the élites and the common people, the pilgrims from Khurasan and the delegations representing the outer provinces and regions; the ugliness and ignominy doubled and multiplied.

The trial (*fitna*) of al-Ṭāʾiʿ lillāh (r. 363–81/974–91) constitutes another example of the Abbasids' tribulations.[38] At the hands of [Fīrūz b. ʿAḍud al-Dawla] Bahāʾ al-Dawla (r. 379–403/989–1012 (in Iraq)), al-Ṭāʾiʿ experienced something similar to what had befallen al-Mustakfī at the hands of Muʿizz al-Dawla.[39] Al-Ṭāʾiʿ was seized, interrogated and

[37] Bakhtiyār, the son of and successor to Muʿizz al-Dawla, took the title ʿIzz al-Dawla and attempted to rule Iraq from 356–67/967–78 (Kennedy, *The Prophet and the Age of the Caliphates*, 224–6).

[38] Following the deposition of al-Muṭīʿ in 363/974, his son, taking the title al-Ṭāʾiʿ li-Amr Allāh, was proclaimed caliph. He married a daughter of ʿAḍud al-Dawla (d. 372/983). After the latter's death, Bahāʾ al-Dawla, in financial difficulties, overthrew the caliph and seized his treasury in 381/991. Bahāʾ al-Dawla held al-Ṭāʾiʿ prisoner; the latter was succeeded by his cousin Abū l-ʿAbbās Aḥmad, who took the name al-Qādir. Allowed to come to al-Qādir's palace in 382/992, al-Ṭāʾiʿ died in 393/1003 (Kennedy, *The Prophet and the Age of the Caliphates*, 241; Hanne, *Putting the Caliph in His Place*, 55–65).

[39] On Bahāʾ al-Dawla, see Kennedy, *The Prophet and the Age of the Caliphates*, 237–9, 241–3; Hachmeier, 'Bahāʾ al-Dawla'; and the fuller account in Bosworth, 'Bahāʾ al-Dawla wa-Ḍiyāʾ al-Milla, Abū Naṣr Fīrūz'.

deposed, and delivered to al-Qādir billāh (r. 381–422/991–1031), who had him imprisoned and strictly constrained.[40] From prison, al-Ṭāʾiʿ billāh wrote to al-Qādir:

O, you who have imprisoned me – you who yourself were released from prison:
You have visited upon me the same treatment that you have suffered.
What an ugly thing it is when treachery afflicts a former ruler
For whose qualities it is justice that would be more fitting!
I have not betrayed my covenant with you, yet you have betrayed
Your covenant with me; and in this matter God is my witness.

All of these cases involve the sovereigns of Islam. As for kings of lesser status, such as subordinate and provincial kings, who could count the number of grievous tribulations and momentous misfortunes that they have experienced?

Section: Concise and Comprehensive Summations of the Calamities That Afflict Kings

One of these calamities is that if a king's reign grows long, even if he maintains justice, practises good governance and displays good conduct, his subjects will criticise him simply because of the length of his rule. How true are the words of the poet who said:

A man is never content with his condition.
He is content neither with youth nor with old age;
The most pleasurable time for him is his youth, yet
As it passes, it gives way to rebuke and discontent.

In another reference to this state of affairs, a poet said:

If a man has no stake or share in another man's turn in power (*dawla*)
He will wish for an end to it –
Not out of dislike for it, nor in anticipation of an alternative;
But simply because he wishes for change.[41]

[40] Al-Qādir, a grandson of al-Muqtadir and cousin of al-Ṭāʾiʿ, whom he succeeded after Bahāʾ al-Dawla's deposition of al-Ṭāʾiʿ in 381/991, received the name al-Qādir billāh. In opposition to the Buyids, the Samanids and Ghaznavids withheld their recognition of al-Qādir until about 390/1000. After Bahāʾ al-Dawla settled in Shiraz, the caliph gained greater freedom in Baghdad (Kennedy, *The Prophet and the Age of the Caliphates*, 241–3; Sourdel, 'al-Ḳādir Biʾllāh').

[41] Abū Aḥmad b. Abī Bakr al-Kātib, in *Yatīmat al-dahr*, IV: 76 (the verses constitute 'one of his circulating proverbs'). According to al-Thaʿālibī, Abū Aḥmad's father, Abū Bakr

Another misfortune of kings is the common people's enthusiasm for them and at the same time their predilection for speaking ill of them, seeking information about them and gossiping about their faults. These tendencies have always been part of people's natural dispositions, and only a person of superlative knowledge, the highest manly virtue, manifest authority and the strictest scrupulousness can hope to be spared from this treatment. Muʿāwiya used to say, 'Do you know which person is (truly) noble (*nabīl*)? Let me tell you who it is who is truly noble: the person whom, in his presence, you hold in high regard, and with whom, in his absence, you find fault. This is the lot of the mighty in the eyes of the common people, of kings in the eyes of their subjects and of masters (*sāda*) in the eyes of their slaves.'

Another misfortune of kings is that if, in accordance with sound governmental practice and as a necessary precaution and safeguard, an individual deemed to pose a threat to the realm is detained by the current king, and if, while in custody, this individual should die a natural death, the people will have no doubt that it was the king who ordered that he be killed. Even if this individual should die in his bed, the people will believe without doubt that it was the king who gave the command for the administration of a poison or the spilling of his blood. If the man dies at a far remove from the king, the people will still believe without doubt that the king resorted to a ruse against him and acted through the agency of a physician, a servant, a cook or a wine-bearer, notwithstanding the remoteness and distance of his place of residence and settlement. Even if he is held in an impregnable hiding place, and his custody and supervision are strictly controlled; even if he is killed in a storm or struck by lightning, someone will still come up with a different idea.

Another calamity is the great number of kings' enemies, enviers and opponents, among the rulers both above and below them, and among their peers, equals and relatives, for various reasons and under different circumstances. It is therefore necessary for the king that he remain alert and vigilant, day and night, whether he is in residence or on a campaign, at rest or moving from place to place. He must inspect every piece of information concerning these people; he must follow their locations, and guard against their scorpion-like infiltrations and their machinations. It is vital that he maintain extreme wariness regarding everything that he eats and drinks,

b. Ḥāmid, served in the Samanid administration, as chief secretary to Amir Ismāʿīl b. Aḥmad and vizier to Amir Aḥmad b. Ismāʿīl before the appointment to the vizierate of Abū ʿAbdallāh al-Jayhānī (*Yatīmat al-dahr*, IV: 73).

and that he guard himself against the dangers of poison. Poison is the greatest of the calamities of kings; the number of kings who have perished in this fashion cannot be counted. Poison is especially potent when infused into perfumes, for when it takes this form the poison flies into the brain and destroys it instantly; on the spot, it causes a lethal nosebleed. May God protect our Master the King with His eye which never sleeps; may He prolong his reign through the surety of His oversight and His care!

Also among kings' misfortunes are the deceitful, cunning, infidel proselytisers of free-thinking, innovating and atheistic sects such as the Batiniyya, the Qaramita and the Ismailis.[42] These sects include people who profess belief in the power of natural forces and the stars, and who, instead of affirming the truth of prophetic missions, consider the significance of prophets to be limited to the realms of law and human need. Such people have often succeeded in infiltrating the circles of kings who have neither listened to the teachings of theologians nor examined the science of theology. In their private meetings with such kings, these people deceive them with their vain incantations, their planting of doubts and their counterfeit doctrines. By means of their false claims, they extricate these kings from the yoke of the sharia and offer them the freedom (*ḥurriyya*) of atheism.[43] They liberate them from the bondage of religious observance; they permit them both to abandon the ritual prayers and the other acts of worship, and to follow their passions. In this fashion, kings become compliant and submissive in the hands of these people.[44] The latter then take advantage of their safety, latitude and security, and they use their ample opportunities to encourage the perpetration of criminal acts, the committing of sins, the spilling of blood, the seizure of properties, the violation of covenants and contracts, and the denigration of Islam.

Al-Amīr al-Saʿīd Naṣr b. Aḥmad (r. 301–31/914–43) fell into this trap at the hands of two prominent atheists, Abū l-Ṭayyib al-Muṣʿabī and

[42] This section of al-Thaʿālibī's mirror has been translated and discussed in Crone and Treadwell, 'A New Text on Ismailism'. The translation appears on pp. 37–41; the article also compares al-Thaʿālibī's account of the conversion of the Samanid amir Naṣr b. Aḥmad to Ismailism with the accounts of Ibn al-Nadīm and Niẓām al-Mulk. Julia Bray, drawing on the presentation of al-Shahrastānī, has proposed revisions to parts of this translation in her 'Al-Thaʿalibi's *Adab al-mulūk*', 41–4. I have benefited from the translations and the extensive commentaries that appear in both of these articles.

[43] The idea of freedom from the law, and the release from the religious obligations of worship and public morality for the pursuit of individual spiritual perfection, is discussed in Crone and Treadwell, 'A New Text on Ismailism', 60.

[44] Reading, with Bray, *yaslasu qiyāduhum* for *yusalsilu qiyāduhum* ('Al-Thaʿalibi's *Adab al-mulūk*', 46, n. 26).

Abū l-Ḥasan Ibn Sawāda al-Rāzī, who had dedicated their persistent attention to the amir.[45] It had been reported of al-Saʿīd that he had repented of his consumption of wine, was remorseful over his shedding of blood, had become fearful of standing before his Lord[46] and had knocked on the door of asceticism (*nusk*); he would withdraw in prayer and weeping, and had become intensely fearful of death. Al-Muṣʿabī and Ibn Sawāda made relentless efforts to deceive him with their honeyed words and to coax him by degrees towards their path (*madhhab*). They professed to him that care and sorrow provide no defence against adversity and trouble. Instead, they claimed, the most effective path entails the pursuit of pleasures, drinking without restraint and listening to beautiful singing girls. These activities relieve the rational soul (*al-nafs al-nāṭiqa*) of its distress in this corporeal world that is made up entirely of anxiety and pain; for only entertainment, enjoyment and music can repel these afflictions. They induced the king to imagine that the bitterness of death lay only in the fear of it, whereas in fact, they maintained, death represented the consummate pleasure and the ultimate release, because it was the gate to the spiritual world in which there is no pain, no sorrow and no terror. And they related other tales of this kind, until the king began to incline towards their doctrine and eventually joined their path.

Abū ʿAlī al-Jayhānī[47] adopted their path, and he went to even greater lengths than this pair, calling the people of jurisprudence the people of filth – by which he meant that they discussed such matters as the cleansing of the body of gross impurities and menstruation.[48] Then they (all three) prettified their chosen path, that is, the path of the Ismailiyya. This was also the path of Aḥmad b. Muḥammad al-Bazdahī (d. 333/944).[49] The

[45] Muḥammad b. Ḥātim al-Muṣʿabī, a secretary, became vizier in 330/941–2, or earlier. Ibn Sawāda, also mentioned in the account of Niẓām al-Mulk (*Siyar al-mulūk*, 228, 295 = Darke, *Book of Government*, 212, 218), was an Ismaili missionary.

[46] The phrase *khāfa maqāma rabbihi* echoes Qurʾanic language (Q 55: 46, 79: 40).

[47] Reading, with Crone and Treadwell ('A New Text on Ismailism', 39), al-Jayhānī for al-Jubbāʾī. The sources report three generations, a grandfather, father and son, all bearing the family name al-Jayhānī and all appointed to the Samanid vizierate. The Jayhānī intended in al-Thaʿālibī's text is taken to be the middle one of the three, Abū ʿAlī Muḥammad b. Muḥammad, who became vizier to Naṣr from 326/937–8 until he was succeeded, in 330/941–2 or earlier, by al-Muṣʿabī (Crone and Treadwell, 'A New Text on Ismailism', 54–5).

[48] See further Crone and Treadwell, 'A New Text on Ismailism', 60.

[49] The Ismaili missionary al-Nasafī, who came from the village of Bazda near Nasaf (Nakhshab) (Yāqūt, *Muʿjam al-buldān*, I: 409–10, noting the *nisba*s Bazdī or Bazdawī), and whose name is normally given as Muḥammad b. Aḥmad (Crone and

three men induced the king to summon al-Bazdahī and listen to his words. Al-Saʿīd duly ordered that al-Bazdahī be summoned. When the latter appeared, he was treated with honour and deference. Al-Saʿīd accepted his exposition in all its frivolity and assented to his accursed teaching.

Al-Saʿīd ordered the minting of seventy dinars, each containing a hundred *mithqāl* (of gold).[50] He then expedited the dispatch of these dinars to the ruler of *al-jazīra*,[51] whom they regarded as the imam of that persuasion. These dinars were struck accordingly.

God then favoured Islam with the demise of al-Muṣʿabī. The force of that rabble (*qawm*) grew weaker, and their choice position proved of no avail. Al-Bazdahī returned to his village, still cleaving to his error; he kept some of those dinars, while others were in the possession of Ibn Sawāda. When al-Saʿīd died and his son al-Ḥamīd (Nūḥ I b. Naṣr II, r. 331–43/943–54) replaced him on the throne, Ibn Sawāda resumed his embellishing talk of that path in the presence of the new amir. He wrote to al-Bazdahī, asking him to send to al-Ḥamīd's court the most cunning, the most adept in argument and the most articulate of his missionaries. Al-Bazdahī complied. Al-Ḥamīd was a perceptive man and well versed in religious matters; he had studied with Muḥammad, known as [Muḥammad b. Muḥammad al-Sulamī, d. 334 or 335/945 or 946] al-Ḥākim al-Jalīl (the Great Judge), the leader (*imām*) of the school of Abū Ḥanīfa.[52] When al-Bazdahī's messenger arrived, he conversed with al-Ḥamīd in private, and he disclosed his doctrine to him. Al-Ḥamīd said to him: 'If this teaching is contrary to Islam, then I take refuge in God from it. If it is in accordance with Islam, then Muḥammad who is the lord of all true missionaries, the Prophet Muḥammad, has already proclaimed it before you. The perfection of his religion admits of no increase, and his actions and ordinances, transmitted to us, admit of no improvement.

Treadwell, 'A New Text on Ismailism', 39, n. 7), was executed under the Samanid amir al-Ḥamīd in the year 333/944.

50 For the *mithqāl*, see Hinz, *Islamische Masse und Gewichte*, 2–8.

51 The copyist appears to have taken this name to refer to the province of al-Jazīra; cf. the reading of Crone and Treadwell, who take the reference to *al-jazīra* to refer not to the region of that name but to the 'diocese' ('A New Text on Ismailism', 39). The reading Jibāl, while orthographically more distant, would also fit the context quite well, since that region, in west-central and north-western Iran, emerged in the 260s/870s as a leading centre of Ismaili activity, and Ismaili *dāʿī*s succeeded in converting several of the region's rulers.

52 Al-Ḥākim al-Jalīl, Abū l-Faḍl Muḥammad b. Muḥammad al-Sulamī, a Hanafī scholar and qadi of Bukhara, was appointed vizier after the accession of Nūḥ (Crone and Treadwell, 'A New Text on Ismailism', 47–8, n. 48).

Suppose I were to accept this path: what would be the sense in concealing it from people?' In this regard, Zuhayr, despite his unbelief, said:

> Where there is covering up, there are indecencies;
> You never find the covering up of something good.[53]

The messenger replied that this stipulation was what the imam had promulgated. The amir responded, 'It must arise from fear of either the common people, or the élite (*khāṣṣa*), or the ruler (*sulṭān*). If it stems from fear of the common people, then they are my subjects; not one of them dares to oppose me. If it comes from fear of the élite [or of the ruler], then what ruler is superior to me, and in whose hands is greater power? No other reason remains for covering up this religion, nor for lying about it or requiring a covenant regarding it.' The unbelievers were confounded.[54] The missionary, struck dumb, was unable to answer. He returned to al-Bazdahī and told him what had happened; the latter sensed that evil lay in store.

It was not long before al-Ḥamīd demanded the previously mentioned dinars from Ibn Sawāda. The latter denied having them; he swore solemn oaths that he neither possessed the money nor had any knowledge of it; the dinars were not in his house nor in the possession of any of his companions. Later, the amir discovered most of those dinars hidden in a secret place in his house, and he had them removed. Al-Ḥamīd had Ibn Sawāda beaten so violently that he perished. Then al-Ḥamīd summoned al-Bazdahī, who, interrogated regarding the remaining dinars, did not release them. When addressed on the subject of his doctrine, he requested a disputation, and said, 'If a proof is brought against me, then I shall repent of my doctrine and shall renounce my belief.' But al-Ḥamīd would not engage in disputation with him. Instead, he requested a professional legal opinion (*fatwā*) from the jurists in his regard. The jurists expressed the opinion that he should be executed. He was duly executed and crucified.

Among the kings of the time who succumbed to the wickedness of this corrupt path were Bakr b. Mālik, Abū ʿAlī Ibn Ilyās, Abū Jaʿfar b. Bānū, the father of Khalaf, Ṭāhir b. Muḥammad al-Sijzī and Abū ʿAlī Ibn Sīmjūr.[55] This deplorable sect had been incubated and hatched in Khurasan. Had it not been for the resolve of the great sultan Yamīn al-Dawla Amīn al-Milla

[53] Zuhayr b. Abī Sulmā, *Dīwān*, 56.

[54] Following the emended reading of Crone and Treadwell, 'A New Text on Ismailism', 40, n. 14, noting the allusion to Q 2: 258 (*fa-buhita lladhī kafara*, 'he who disbelieved was confounded').

[55] On these figures, see Crone and Treadwell, 'A New Text on Ismailism', 55–8.

Abū l-Qāsim Maḥmūd Ibn Nāṣir al-Dīn (r. 388–421/998–1030) to devote his efforts to the victory of the faith and the upholding of the practices of Islam, severing the shoots of atheism from their stems and uprooting the seedlings of divesting God of His attributes (*ta ʿṭīl*), then these debauched free-thinkers would have rallied their supporters, the markers of the religion would have been eliminated, the signposts of Islam obliterated and the heads of the Muslims bowed low. But the sultan proceeded according to the determination of his perception and the excellence of his character in protecting the religion and in his severity against the atheists. His sword quenched its thirst with the blood of the people who followed fallacy and were committed to error. He weakened and brought down every sign and demolished every element of their futile teachings, until the affairs of religion returned to their optimal position, and every envier and antagonist of Islam had been suppressed.[56] May God Almighty shape his efforts, prolong his life and reward him well for his loyalty to his religion and his upholding of his certain beliefs; may He perpetuate his lucky star and his auspicious time, and may He not displace him from his right command and his praiseworthy position. May we begin in all of these matters with our Master the King and may we, in goodwill, devote to him the most abundant portion and the widest share of our prayers for good.

Text 17
Niẓām al-Mulk, *Siyar al-mulūk*, Chapter Forty[57]

Translator's Introduction

Chapter Forty opens part II of Niẓām al-Mulk's *Siyar al-mulūk*. As noted previously (see section 3.7), Niẓām al-Mulk added the eleven chapters that make up part II some years after he had completed the first thirty-nine, and

[56] See Bosworth, *Ghaznavids*, 52–4, 200. Maḥmūd defeated and eventually deposed the Ismaili ruler of Multan, Abū l-Fatḥ Dāwūd b. Naṣr, in the course of two campaigns (396/1006 and 401/1010); on his assault against Rayy in 420/1019, see above, section 2.2, n. 47, and Chapter 6, n. 49.

[57] Translation prepared from Niẓām al-Mulk, *Siyar al-mulūk*, 189–212. For the corresponding section in Darke's translation, see Darke, *Book of Government*, 139–57; in Schabinger's translation into German, see Schabinger, *Siyāsatnāma, Gedanken und Geschichten*, 236–43; and in Pistoso's translation into Italian, see Pistoso, *L'arte della politica*, 210–33.

by this time, Malikshāh appears to have withdrawn considerable support from his vizier. Perhaps never having received the later chapters, the sultan died a mere month after Niẓām al-Mulk's assassination in 485/1092. It has often been remarked that part II conveys a sense of foreboding. Niẓām al-Mulk begins with the warning that states and dynasties do not stay the same; they are vulnerable to change and inevitably come to an end. Power passes from one dynastic house to another, and the process whereby one state suffers dissolution and a new one rises and replaces it often involves violence and bloodshed. In these later chapters, Niẓām al-Mulk expatiates on the problems that he sees undermining the state and which represent hasteners or harbingers of the dynasty's fall. While his treatments of these problems are articulated in the form of general principles, each one evokes a particular contemporaneous situation and the cases and actions of specific individuals. In Chapter Forty, Niẓām al-Mulk's ostensible subject is royal pardon; the chapter also covers the restoration of abandoned practices that the vizier-author deems critical to the successful functioning of the polity. As in the previous extracts (Texts 11 and 14), Niẓām al-Mulk employs lengthy narratives. This strategy allows him to deflect attention from himself and the polity's immediate circumstances as he narrates the stories of earlier kings, their predicaments and how they overcame them or succumbed to them. Niẓām al-Mulk begins and ends his chapter with the social dislocation betokened by the indiscriminate proliferation of honorific titles. The positive roles of the female protagonists in several of the narratives are noteworthy, especially in the light of Niẓām al-Mulk's seemingly misogynistic statements elsewhere.[58]

Translation

Chapter Forty: On the King's Forgiveness of God's Creatures, May He Be Exalted and Glorified; and the Restoration to Their Proper Order of All Practices and Customs That Have Lost Their Order and Foundation

At any time, a celestial event may occur, and the evil eye (*chashm-i bad*) may gain access to the kingdom.[59] The state (*dawlat*) will either change and pass

[58] Foreshadowed here in the association of royal women's issuing of commands with disorder. As the narratives included in this chapter suggest, Niẓām al-Mulk's disapproval is not of women in general but of certain women in particular; see section 3.7 and its n. 69.

[59] Niẓām al-Mulk's reference to the evil eye evokes the fragility of good fortune; in this case, it suggests the difficulty of maintaining the conditions necessary to promote the security

from one dynastic house to another, or it will fall into disorder, as a result of sedition (*fitneh*), unrest (*āshūb*), the crossing of swords (*shamshīr-hā-yi mukhtalif*), killing, burning, plunder (*ghārat*) and tyranny. In such days of sedition (*fitneh*) and laxity (*futūr*), persons of noble descent (*sharīfān*) will be cast down and ignoble people will attain prominence. Whoever possesses strength will do whatever he pleases. The affairs of righteous persons (*muṣliḥān*) will weaken and their conditions will become poor; the wicked (*mufsidān*) will become powerful. The least of people will become a military commander (*amīr*); the basest of people will become a municipal governor (*ʿamīd*).[60] The noble (*aṣīlān*) and worthy (*fāżilān*) will suffer deprivation.[61] No person, however lacking in merit, will have the slightest trepidation in taking upon himself the title of king (*pādshāh*) or vizier. Turks will assume the titles of educated officials (*khᵛājagān*), and *khᵛājagān* will adopt for themselves the titles of Turks.[62] Turks and Tajiks alike will take upon themselves the titles of scholars and imams. The king's womenfolk will issue commands, the religious law (*sharīʿa*) will become weak, the subjects will be left in disorder, the soldiers will become oppressive, distinctions among people will disappear and no one will move to rectify matters. If a Turk has ten stewards (sing. *kadkhudāy*), it will be considered permissible; and if a Tajik is steward for ten Turkish amirs, it will not be counted a disgrace.[63] All the affairs of the kingdom will have lost, and will continue to lose, their foundation and proper order. The king, preoccupied with

and prosperity of the state and its people, since it is particularly the fine, fortunate, healthy and beautiful that attract the malign attention of the evil eye (see Šakūrzāda and Omidsalar, 'Čašm-zakm').

60 Although the terms *amīr* and *ʿamīd* might seem to imply, respectively, 'military' and 'civilian' functions, it should be noted that in the Seljuk period, the distinction held limited significance. Not only governors but also viziers played important military roles and had sizeable forces under their command; Niẓām al-Mulk commanded an especially large army, and he undertook military operations himself, as well as accompanying Alp Arslan and Malikshāh on many of their campaigns.

61 Although the term *aṣīlān* (sing. *aṣīl*) connotes nobility of descent (*aṣl*), it also carries the sense 'men of probity'; *fāżil* likewise connotes a status deriving from humane education and moral excellence.

62 The term *khᵛājeh* denotes an educated person, often a teacher. The word changed in meaning and status over time. Like *ṣāḥib*, *khᵛājeh* was used for viziers, including Niẓām al-Mulk, from the tenth century onwards; later the title extended to all high officials.

63 In the Ghaznavid and Seljuk periods, the term *kadkhudā* connoted a high-ranking official, a military or provincial administrator or steward appointed by the ruler or the vizier. The *kadkhudā* also functioned as a counsellor to the ruler and as an intermediary between the ruler and the vizier (see Floor, 'Kadkodā'). In a widespread usage, it designated a village headman.

campaigning, warfare and worry, will have no opportunity to attend to these kinds of matters or to devote much thought to this sort of topic.[64]

Later, when by celestial felicity the age of calamity passes and days of ease and security appear, God Almighty will bring forth a king who is just, possesses rational intelligence and is of royal descent. God Almighty will grant this king a turn in power so that he is able to triumph over all his enemies. He will endow him with reason (*ʿaql*) and knowledge (*dānish*), so that he is capable of astute discernment (*tamyīz*) in all matters. This king will make enquiries from everybody and seek to understand the ways and customs of (former) kings (*āʾīn-i pādshāhān*) in all matters. He will read accounts, so that he will soon be able to restore to their proper positions all the kingdom's structures (*tartīb*) and customs (*āʾīn*). He will manifest clearly the exact degree of each person: he will place the worthy in their rightful positions, constrain the unworthy and send them to the tasks and occupations that befit them. He will root out people who display ingratitude for benefits. He will be a friend to religion and an enemy to oppression. He will lend support to religion and expunge heresy (*havā*) and innovation (*bidʿat*), by God's permission and His granting of success.

We shall now mention a little more about this subject, in order to shed light on many issues and to provide guidance regarding matters that have fallen away from their proper arrangement, so that when the Lord of the World, may God perpetuate his rule, considers these matters, he may, if God wills, issue a prescription and a command concerning each one. Among the practices that kings of every age have maintained and to which they have paid attention is solicitude for the ancient families (*khānadān-hā-yi qadīm*)[65] and high regard for the sons of (former and vassal) kings (*abnā-yi mulūk*).[66] They have not allowed these members of formerly powerful families to be ruined, deprived and abandoned; during their turns in power, kings have appointed these individuals to office

64 For some thirty years, Niẓām al-Mulk had presided over an extensive network of individuals, placed in a variety of posts. His lament over the loss of social and professional boundaries is largely rhetorical; his implicit evocation of an idealised social order in which groups defined in terms of function, ethnicity and gender remained within firmly set confines reflects an anxiety concerning shifts in power.

65 For the addition of this clause, see *Siyar al-mulūk*, 190, n. 4.

66 The reference is to members of recently defeated or displaced dynastic families; such individuals were in a position to mobilise support and, given opportune circumstances, stage a revolt against the newly installed ruler. Niẓām al-Mulk advises the ruler to enlist the support of these individuals in order to stave off this potential threat.

according to the measure of their competency, so that their familial houses have remained firmly established. They have also awarded allowances from the treasury to other eminent and meritorious persons, including scholars, ʿAlids, righteous and honest people, warriors for the faith (*ghāziyān*), guardians of the frontiers and specialists in the Qurʾan. By these means, in the days when these rulers enjoyed their turns in power no person was left without an allowance, nor was he deprived; and the kings earned the people's prayers on their behalf and the rewards of both worlds.[67]

Story

They say that a group of deserving persons presented a written petition to Caliph Hārūn-i Rashīd. They stated:

> We are servants of God and children of the age.[68] Some of us specialise in the study of the Qurʾan and religious knowledge (*ahl-i Qurʾān va-ʿilm*); some of us possess noble status (*khudāvand-i sharaf*).[69] In some cases, our fathers held claims on this dynasty (*dawlat*) for the pleasing services that they performed; and we too have exerted ourselves in our toil. We are all Muslims of pure belief. Our allowance lies in the treasury, and the treasury is in your hands, since you are the Lord and Manager of the World (*kadkhudā-yi jahān*) and Commander of the Faithful. If that money belongs to the people, then spend it on us, for we are believers and we are entitled to it. You are for all intents and purposes the custodian of this wealth. Know that the king is due no more than one tenth, and that this amount is sufficient for you. Every day you expend several thousands in the satisfaction of your desires, and in outlays for stipends and daily rations, while we cannot even afford to buy bread.

The scholars reasoned, 'What is most surprising is that the king seems to suppose that whatever is in the treasury belongs to him. If he releases our portion, good. If not, we shall go to God's court and bring our grievance

[67] Niẓām al-Mulk's portrayal of an optimal reciprocity of king and subjects recalls the discourse of Pseudo-Māwardī (see Text 1).

[68] Following Darke in his equation of Niẓām al-Mulk's *farzandān-i rūzgār* with the Arabic *abnāʾ al-dawla*, a phrase that denoted the Khurasani troops who supported the early Abbasids and the descendants of these troops (as the text of the petition implies) (*Book of Government*, 252, n. 2).

[69] Although I have opted for a general phrasing in my rendering of *khudāvand-i sharaf*, it is possible that Niẓām al-Mulk, both in this instance and in his reference to *sharīfān* in the opening paragraph of this extract, intended descendants of the Prophet in particular.

there, with the request that the treasury be removed from the king's control and turned over to someone who will have compassion for the Muslims, and who shall employ gold and riches for the benefit of the people, rather than exploiting the people for the sake of gold.'

When Hārūn read this petition, he was distressed, and he did not answer it the same day. As, in a state of confusion, he was leaving his audience hall for his private palace, his wife Zubayda, who saw that he was not himself, asked, 'What has happened to the Commander of the Faithful?'[70] He replied to Zubayda, 'These people have written to me in such-and-such a manner; had they not invoked the fear of God against me I should order chastisement for them.' Zubayda said, 'You have done well not to molest them. Just as you received the caliphate as a bequest from your forefathers, you also inherited their conduct, disposition and practice. Look to what the caliphs before you have done with the servants of God, the Great and the Glorious. You too should do likewise, for greatness and kingship become finer still when accompanied with justice and liberality; the former goes with the latter. There is certainly no doubt that whatever is in the treasury belongs to the Muslims, and yet you make vast expenditures from it. You should display no more arrogance with regard to the wealth of the Muslims than the Muslims would do with your wealth. If they complain, you should pardon them.'

It so happened that that night both Hārūn and Zubayda dreamed that the Resurrection had arrived. In their visions they saw God's creatures called forth and brought forward one by one to the Place of Reckoning. The Chosen Prophet (Muḥammad) (may the blessings and peace of God be upon him and his family) was interceding for them, and they were on their way to Paradise. An angel took Hārūn and Zubayda by the hand, in order to bring them to the Place of Reckoning. Another angel took the hand of the first angel, and asked, 'Where are you bringing them?' He reported that the Chosen Prophet (may the blessings and peace of God be upon him and his family) had sent him with these instructions: 'As long as I [the Prophet] am present, do not allow them to be brought forward, for I should be ashamed; in their case I should not be able to say anything, for they considered the Muslims' wealth to be their own and they deprived the deserving of their rights, even though they were sitting in my place.' They both awakened in alarm. Hārūn said to Zubayda, 'What

[70] On the marriage of Zubayda to Hārūn, see Kennedy, *When Baghdad Ruled the Muslim World*, 61, 186–9 and *passim*.

happened to you?' She said, 'I saw such and such in my dream and I grew afraid.' Hārūn said, 'I had the same dream.' Then they gave thanks that it was not the Resurrection, and that what had happened had been only a dream.

The next day they opened the door to the treasury and issued a proclamation:

> All entitled persons are required to present themselves so that we may give them their allowances from the treasury and fulfil their needs and desires.

In response, countless people set out for the court,[71] and the charges to Hārūn al-Rashīd of the various stipends and gifts that he ordered to be awarded to the people amounted to three million dinars. Then Zubayda said: 'The treasury lies in your hands; it is you, not I, who must answer for it at the Resurrection. Through your recent accomplishments, you have discharged a part of your obligation: whatever you have just bestowed consisted of the Muslims' wealth, which you have now given back to them. What I shall do, I shall do with my own money, for the sake of God's contentment and for salvation at the Resurrection – for I know that I must depart from this world and that I must leave behind all these goods and riches. Through my own action, I can at least send something in advance by way of provision for the Resurrection.'

Zubayda then withdrew several million dinars' worth of jewellery, silver and clothing from her own treasury. 'All of this wealth', she said, 'must be spent on good works, so that the effects of these works, and the people's favourable prayers on my behalf, will last uninterrupted until the Resurrection.' Then she ordered the construction of wells at every stage along the route from Kufa to Mecca and Medina.[72] Each well was to be built open at the top, and it was to be lined from the bottom to the top with stone, baked brick, plaster and lime. Zubayda likewise ordered the construction of reservoirs and cisterns, so that pilgrims in the desert should no longer suffer hardship and restriction on account of water, since every year several thousand pilgrims used to die in the desert for lack of water. Once all these wells had been dug and all these reservoirs

[71] Following the sense of Darke's reading of *bī ḥaṣr* (*Book of Government*, 252, n. 3) and Qazvīnī and Chahārdahī's reading of *bī andāzeh* (*Siyāsatnāmeh*, 165).

[72] On Zubayda's extensive public works along the route from Iraq to the holy cities of the Hijaz, which in her honour became known as Darb Zubayda, see al-Rashid and Young, 'Darb Zubayda'; Kennedy, *When Baghdad Ruled the Muslim World*, 65.

constructed, a large amount of money still remained. Zubayda ordered the erection of fortified castles along the frontier. She ordered the purchase of weapons and horses, both mares and stallions, for the benefit of the ghazis; and the acquisition of sufficient land and property in conjunction with each fort so that, year after year, in times of need, it could supply food and fodder for one or two thousand ghazi warriors and allow for the breeding of horses.

After this, the remaining money was used at the borders of Kashghar, Bulur and Shuknan to build a city with four strong walls; called Badakhshan, this city still exists and prospers today. Another fortress, named Vayshgird, was constructed opposite Rasht, Famir and Kumiji,[73] on the border of Khuttalan; it too remains in existence and continues to flourish. Its arsenal and its herd of horses are likewise still in existence. In Isfijab, Zubayda ordered the construction of a fortified post (*ribāṭ*) so large it resembled a city; it too is extant and prosperous. On the road to Khᵛarazm, she had built a fortress called Faraveh; she had further fortresses built at Darband and at Alexandria. All in all, she commanded the construction of ten fortresses, each one as big as a city. There was still money left over. She ordered that the money remaining after all this construction be taken and distributed among the poor and the people who had taken up residence in the holy places of Mecca, Medina and Jerusalem.

Story

Zayd b. Aslam said:

> One evening the Commander of the Faithful ʿUmar b. al-Khaṭṭāb, may God be pleased with him, was patrolling in person, and I was with him.[74] We left Medina, and in the desert, we descried a ruined wall, and a fire burning in the vicinity. ʿUmar said to me, 'Come, Zayd, let us make for this place so that we can see who has lit a fire in the middle of the night.' We set off. As we drew near, we saw a woman who had placed a small pot on the fire. Two small children

[73] Localities in the Upper Oxus region traced, following Darke, with reference to the anonymous tenth-century Persian geography *Ḥudūd al-ʿālam*, 361–3 (commentary to § 26, pp. 119–22, section treating the region of the Transoxanian borderlands (*nāḥiyat-i ḥudūd-i mā warāʾ al-nahr*)).

[74] Zayd b. Aslam was a transmitter of hadith and an early jurist. A version of this account appears in Ghazālī, *Naṣīḥat al-mulūk*, part II: 115–18 = Bagley, *Ghazālī's Book of Counsel for Kings*, 66–7.

were asleep on the ground in front of her. She was pleading, 'Almighty God, grant me justice from 'Umar, for he has eaten his fill while we are hungry.'

When 'Umar heard these words, he said to me, 'Listen, Zayd; it turns out that this woman is invoking God against me, of all people. You stay here, so that I can approach the woman and find out about her situation.' He went up to the woman and asked, 'What are you cooking at this midnight hour in this desert?' She replied, 'I am a poor woman. I do not own a home in Medina, and I have no means at my disposal. I felt such shame that my two children were weeping and crying with hunger while I had nothing to fill their stomachs, and that my neighbours all knew that my children's cries were from hunger and that I was powerless to help them, that I came here yesterday, and we have been here since then. Every time my children cry from hunger and ask for food, I place this pot on the fire and say to them, 'You go to sleep; by the time you wake up this little pot will be ready.' In this way I lift their spirits, and with this hope they fall asleep. But when they awaken, they see nothing, and again they begin to cry. This very hour I have managed through some contrivance to induce them to sleep. For two days now I have eaten nothing, and they too have eaten nothing. There is nothing in this pot but water.' 'Umar's heart bled for her, and he said, 'It is with justice that you reproach 'Umar and invoke God Almighty against him.' The woman did not recognise 'Umar, who continued, 'Be patient a short while, and stay here until I return.' Then 'Umar left the woman.

When he reached me, 'Umar said to me, 'Come on, Zayd, we're off to our house.' Once he had reached the threshold, I sat down by the door of the house while he went inside. A while passed. Then he emerged with two leather bags on his back. He said to me, 'Come, let us return to that woman.' I said, 'O Commander of the Faithful, if we must go back there, at least place these bags on my back so that I can carry the load.' 'Umar said, 'Consider, Zayd; if you take up this load, who will lift the burden of sins from 'Umar's neck?'

'Umar kept going until he drew near to the woman. Then he put down the bags that he had been carrying on his back and placed them before her. One contained flour, another rice, pulses, a sheep's tail and fat. He said to me, 'Set off into this desert, Zayd; gather up whatever thorns and wormwood you can find, and return quickly.' I went off in search of wood. 'Umar took up a cup and fetched some water; then he washed the rice and pulses and put them in the pot. He added some of the sheep's tail and fat, and with the flour he made a large round of bread. I returned with the wood. With his own hand

ʿUmar cooked the contents of the pot, and he placed the round of bread beneath the fire.

When both the bread and the pot were ready, ʿUmar filled a cup with broth. Once it had cooled, he asked the woman to wake up her children, so that they could eat. The woman woke the little ones and ʿUmar placed the food in front of them. He, meanwhile, withdrew, spread out his prayer rug and occupied himself in prayer. After an hour had passed, he looked up: the woman and her children had finished eating, and the children were playing with their mother. ʿUmar rose and said, 'Now, woman; pick up your children. I shall carry the bags and Zayd can bring the pot and cup, so that we can bring you home.' And this they did. With her children the woman entered the house designated for her use, and ʿUmar put down the bags. When he was on the point of leaving, he said to the woman, 'Be humane; and from now on do not invoke God against ʿUmar – because ʿUmar does not have the capacity to withstand the punishment and retribution of God, may He be exalted and glorified, and, since he cannot know what's hidden (*ghayb*), he cannot know the condition of every person. Eat what I have brought you. When it has all gone, let me know so that I can give you more.'

Story

They say that one day, while Moses, upon him be peace, was still the shepherd of the prophet Shuʿayb, upon him be peace, and had not yet received divine inspiration, he had led a flock of sheep to graze.[75] By chance a sheep became separated from the rest of the flock. Moses sought to return the sheep to the flock. The little sheep hurtled off into the desert. When she could no longer see the other sheep, the errant sheep became fearful and kept running ahead. For some two or three *farsang*s Moses chased after the sheep, until the creature ran out of strength, fell down in exhaustion and could not get up. Moses caught up with the sheep and was moved to compassion for her. 'O unfortunate one', he said, 'Why are you fleeing, and of whom are you afraid?' When

[75] According to Qurʾanic narratives, the Arabian prophet Shuʿayb was sent to Madyan (Midian) (Q7: 85; 11: 84; 29: 36). Moses reached Midian, where he helped two women to water their flocks; the women's father, an elderly man, married Moses to one of his daughters and hired him to tend his flocks (Q28: 22–8). The elderly man, unnamed in the Qurʾanic narrative, is identified in later exegetical tradition as either Yathrā (Jethro, father-in-law of Moses, who, according to biblical narrative, tends his father-in-law's flock; see Exodus 3: 1, 4: 18, 18: 1) or as Shuʿayb (see Schöck, 'Moses', 421).

he saw that the sheep had no strength left to walk, he picked her up and carried her on his shoulders, all the way back to the flock. When the sheep caught sight of the flock, her heart quickened and began to throb with joy. Moses promptly let her down from his shoulders, and she rushed into the midst of the flock. God Almighty summoned the angels of the heavens, and said to them, 'Did you see the human kindness (*khuluq*) that My servant displayed towards that dumb sheep, and how, because of the trouble that he took on her behalf, he did her no harm, but rather treated her with mercy? By My glory, I shall raise him up, make him the recipient of My speech (*kalīm*), grant him prophethood and send him a Book; in this manner, he shall be remembered and talked about for as long as the world endures.' Then He conferred all these miracles (*karāmat-hā*) upon him.[76]

A Story on This Theme

In the city of Marv al-Rūdh lived a man called Raʾīs-i Ḥājjī.[77] He was a respected municipal leader (*raʾīs*) and he possessed great wealth, including many estates and farms. During his time there was no one more esteemed or more powerful in the whole of Khurasan. He had served Sultan Maḥmūd and Sultan Masʿūd, and indeed, I myself encountered him. In the beginning, when he was young, he was extremely oppressive: he practised torture and interrogation, he overturned families and there was no one more ruthless or more filled with contempt than he. Later, however, he woke up (*bīdārī yāft*).[78] He desisted from oppression and harming people, and began to busy himself with good works, caring for the poor and constructing bridges and *ribāṭ*s.[79] He

[76] The reference to Moses as God's *kalīm* alludes to Qurʾanic descriptions of God's speaking to Moses (*kallamahu rabbuhu*, 7: 143; *qāla yā Mūsā innī ṣṭafaytuka ʿalā l-nās bi-risālatī wa-bi-kalāmī fa-khudh mā ātaytuka wa-kun min al-shākirīn*, 7: 144); on the basis of these passages and other Qurʾanic texts (Q 4: 164; see also 20: 12; 79: 16), Moses is known by the epithet *kalīm Allāh*, 'the one to whom God spoke'. The Qurʾan also refers to Moses's receipt of divine revelation in the form of the Book (*kitāb*), as well as the 'criterion' (*furqān*) and 'pages' (*ṣuḥuf*); see Schöck, 'Moses'.

[77] Marv al-Rūdh ('Marv on the River') lay on the Murghāb River in Khurasan, five days' journey above the larger city of Marv (al-Shāhijān) (Yāqūt, *Muʿjam al-buldān*, V: 112).

[78] I have provided a literal translation of Niẓām al-Mulk's evocative phrase in this instance of its first usage. In subsequent passages, I have employed various phrases, including (following Darke) variants of the term 'enlightenment' to evoke Raʾīs-i Ḥājjī's transformation.

[79] A term used in a great many different senses according to context; in this case, probably a caravanserai, also known as a *khān*, an institution that provided accommodation and services for travellers, especially merchants, and their animals; see Chabbi and Rabbat, 'Ribāṭ'.

set many of his slaves free, paid the debts of the destitute, clothed the orphans and provided funds for pilgrims and ghazis. He constructed a Friday mosque in his own city and another fine Friday mosque in Nishapur.

In the reign of Amir Chaghri (r. 431–52/1040–60, in Khurasan), may God have mercy on him, after he had completed numerous good works, Raʾīs-i Ḥājjī went on the pilgrimage. When he reached Baghdad, he stayed there for nearly a month. During this time, one day he left the house and went to the market. In a passageway he saw a small dog covered in scabs; the dog's limbs had lost all their fur and the wretched animal was plainly in great distress. Raʾīs-i Ḥājjī's heart melted when he saw the dog. He said, 'This animal too is a living being created by God, may He be exalted and glorified.' He then instructed a servant to bring two *mann* of bread and a rope; he himself stayed right there until the servant returned. He broke the bread into pieces with his own hand, and he threw it piece by piece in front of the dog until the little animal felt well fed and secure. Next Raʾīs-i Ḥājjī threw the rope round the dog's neck and handed it to the servant, whom he instructed to bring the dog to the house where he had taken up his lodging. Then he too left the market immediately.

When he got home, he ordered his servant to purchase three *mann* of tail-fat, to melt it straight away, and to bring the clarified fat to him. He took a piece of wood and twisted a piece of cloth and wool round the top of it. Then he got up and approached the dog. With his own hand he dipped the rag and wool into the dish of clarified fat and rubbed it over the dog's limbs until his body was fully covered. Then he said to the servant: 'You are no more respectable than I am, and I feel no sense of shortcoming or shame at what I have done. You, who are my servant, should likewise feel no shame. I wish you to attach a nail to the wall and tie the dog to it. Give him a *mann* of bread in the morning and another *mann* in the evening, every day. Twice each day, rub the dog's body with clarified fat, and also give him scraps and bones left over from the table, until he gets better.' The servant did these things for two weeks, after which time that little dog threw off the mange and began to grow new fur, and he became nicely corpulent. He became so accustomed to the house that he could not have been turned out of it even if threatened with a stick. Raʾīs-i Ḥājjī duly proceeded with the caravan and performed the pilgrimage. He dispensed a great deal of money on the way. He returned to Marv al-Rūdh and some years later he died. Some time passed.

One night, a renunciant (*zāhidī*) saw him in a dream. In the dream, Ra'īs-i Ḥājjī was seated on a Burāq, surrounded to the front, back and on both sides by houris and young men, who smiled as they led him gently to one of the gardens of Paradise.[80] The renunciant ran towards him and greeted him. Ra'īs-i Ḥājjī drew up his reins and returned the greeting. The renunciant said to him: 'O so-and-so, you used to be cruel, ruthless and oppressive in your treatment of people. Then you became enlightened, and you not only desisted from cruelty towards people, but also performed more good works, and gave more charitable donations (*ṣadaqāt*) and wealth to the deserving, than anyone else. Moreover, you performed the pilgrimage of Islam. Tell me, by which specific deeds and acts of obedience did you attain your present elevated degree?' He said: 'O renunciant, I have been astonished at the workings of God. It is fitting that you too should draw a lesson (*'ibrat*), and not take your spiritual refuge (*takya*) to constitute obedience, nor allow yourself to be deceived by much worship.[81] Know that as a result of all those acts of disobedience that I committed in my youth, my place had been prepared in Hell; all the acts of obedience and all the good works that I performed subsequently were to no avail. As I faced the agonies of death, all my prayers and my fasting were rejected; all my acts of obedience, my charitable donations and good works, the mosques, *ribāṭ*s and bridges that I had built, and my pilgrimage were rendered worthless and useless. I fell into despair; I gave up hope of Paradise and resigned my heart to the punishment of Hell. Then I heard a voice, which said in my ear, "You were one of the dogs of the world, so we have considered you in relation to dogs. Accordingly, we regard all your acts of disobedience as cancelled; we consign you to Paradise and preserve you from Hell because you threw off the cloak of arrogance from your neck and showed mercy to that mangy dog." I beheld the arrival, like lightning, of the angels of mercy; they rescued me from the hands of the angels of punishment and they brought me to

80 Burāq is the name of the flying steed that, having carried previous prophets, bore the Prophet Muḥammad on his nocturnal journey (*isrā'*) from Mecca to Jerusalem, from which the Prophet ascended to the heavens (his *mi'rāj*) (see Gruber, 'al-Burāq'). Niẓām al-Mulk's phrasing implies that the term *burāq* designated not only a specific animal but a genus of such celestial creatures, here associated with Paradise and its denizens.

81 The term *takya* here probably designates a *khānaqāh*, a communal residential institution affiliated with a Sufi order; these institutions flourished in Niẓām al-Mulk's lifetime and often benefited from royal or powerful patronage, including the generous support of the vizier (al-Ṣafadī, *al-Wāfī bi-l-wafayāt*, II: 78).

Paradise. Of all my acts of obedience, this one act alone brought me relief in that time of hopelessness.'

I (your servant) have related this story so that the Lord of the World, may God perpetuate his sovereignty, should know how fine a quality it is to be merciful. Know that these individuals, the protagonists of the previous stories, showed mercy to a sheep and a dog respectively, and they attained a high degree and lofty station in both worlds. How fine a reward, it must therefore be inferred, will God Almighty grant to a person who shows mercy to a Muslim who has fallen into distress, and who extends his hand to him! If the King of the Age is God-fearing and mindful of the lasting consequences of his actions, he will manage to be just in every case, and the just person always succeeds in being merciful and kind. When the king is of this sort, his agents and his troops will resemble him, and they will imitate his conduct. In consequence, God's creatures will rest in ease, and the rulers and their officials shall enjoy the fruits of this state in both worlds, if God wills.

Section on This Topic

Enlightened kings (*pādshāhān-i bīdār*) have always made it their custom to respect the elderly and experienced, and to retain individuals who are skilled in affairs and tested in battle by placing each one in a suitable position and station. Whenever an important matter – concerning the welfare and prosperity of the kingdom, a person's promotion or dismissal, the construction of monumental buildings, the conclusion of an alliance, the seeking of intelligence regarding a foreign king, investigating matters of religion and the like – required urgent attention, the enlightened kings of the past formulated procedures (*tadbīr-hā*) in consultation with individuals who were knowledgeable and experienced. Similarly, when an enemy or a battle loomed, they always deliberated with men who had seen battle and were knowledgeable in military matters, so that the situation would reach the desired conclusion. If fighting broke out, they would send into battle a commander who had fought in many wars, broken enemy lines and seized fortresses, and who possessed a wide reputation for courage. To ensure that no error should occur, the kings of the past used to send with this individual – notwithstanding the latter's military competence – a senior man of worldly experience who had accomplished many things. In these times, it seems to be the case that whenever an important matter arises, it is inexperienced persons – children and youths – who are appointed, and errors occur regularly. In this regard, if at any point due caution were to be exercised in these matters, the course adopted would be more prudent and less dangerous.[82]

Section on the Topic of Titles (*Alqāb*)

Moreover, titles have proliferated; and whenever anything becomes abundant, it diminishes in value and its significance does not endure.[83] Regarding titles, kings and caliphs have always exercised restraint in awarding them, because one of the principles of the kingdom (*nāmūs-hā-yi mamlakat*) is to preserve the correspondence among each person's title, rank and degree. When the merchant (*mardī bāzārī*) and the local landowner (*dihqān*) bear the same titles as the appointed governor (*ʿamīdī*) and the notable (*maʿrūfī*), there is no difference between the two; and the position of the prominent and the obscure might as well be the same.[84] An imam, a scholar or a qadi might quite properly carry the title Muʿīn al-Dīn.[85] But if the title Muʿīn al-Dīn also belongs to a member of the Turkish military corps, whether a trainee or a ranking officer (*shāgird-i turkī yā kadkhudā-yi turkī*) – a person without the slightest idea of religious learning or legal knowledge, and perhaps one unable even to read and write – then what difference in rank is there between the learned and the ignorant, between judges and Turkish military trainees? In both cases the title is the same, and this situation is far from appropriate.

Similarly, the Turkish amirs have always borne titles such as Ḥusām al-Dawla, Sayf al-Dawla, Yamīn al-Dawla, Shams al-Dawla and the like, while statesmen, governors and officials (*kh^{v}ājagān va-ʿamīdān va-mutaṣarrifān*) have always borne titles of the kind ʿAmīd al-Mulk, Ẓahīr al-Mulk, Qiwām al-Mulk, Niẓām al-Mulk, Kamāl al-Mulk and suchlike.

[82] Niẓām al-Mulk recapitulates a theme that al-Thaʿālibī had explored in his litany of royal calamities (see above, Text 16).

[83] On titles and the history of their use in Iran, see Ašraf, 'Alqāb va ʿAnāwīn'.

[84] The meaning of the term *dihqān* changed very considerably over the centuries and varied according to region. In Sasanian times a station among the lesser nobility, the title retained its significance considerably longer in eastern than in western Iran; Niẓām al-Mulk's father was described as a *dihqān*. In the present context, Niẓām al-Mulk seems to ascribe, at most, a middling status to the *dihqān*. On the changing meanings of *dihqān* and the transfer of the *dihqān*'s functions to groups bearing other names, see Paul, 'Dihqān', and Paul, 'Where Did the Dihqāns Go?'.

[85] Among its several referents, the word *imām* probably appears here, as at the beginning of the chapter, as an honorific title for a respected religious authority.

Now the distinction has disappeared: Turks assume the titles of Tajiks and Tajiks assume the titles of Turks, and none considers it wrong. Titles, however, have always been held dear.

Story

When he acceded to the sultanate, Sultan Maḥmūd requested a title from the Commander of the Faithful al-Qādir billāh. He was duly awarded the title Yamīn al-Dawla. Subsequently Maḥmūd went on to seize the provinces of Nimruz and Khurasan, countless cities and provinces in Hindustan (for he went as far as Somnat and made off with its idol),[86] as well as Samarqand and Khᵛarazm. Furthermore, when he reached Kuhistan of Iraq, he took possession of Rayy, Isfahan, Hamadan and Tabaristan. Having achieved these conquests, Maḥmūd sent an envoy to the Commander of the Faithful. Laden with an abundance of presents and tokens of Maḥmūd's loyal service (*hadiyyeh va-khidmat-i bisyār*), the envoy conveyed to Caliph al-Qādir the sultan's request for more titles. His request was not answered. It is said that Maḥmūd sent envoys, each bearing tokens of his service, more than ten times, but to no avail.

The khaqan of Samarqand, meanwhile, had been given three titles: Ẓahīr al-Dawla, Muʿīn Khalīfat Allāh and Malik al-Sharq va-l-Ṣīn. This situation had aroused Maḥmūd's envy. Once again, the sultan sent to the caliph an envoy with the following message, 'I have made numerous conquests in the lands of unbelief; the glory of Islam in Hindustan, Khurasan and Iraq has been entrusted to me; I have seized Transoxiana; and I wield the sword in your name. The khaqan, who is now one of my vassals and subordinates, has been granted three titles, whereas I, having performed so many acts of service and benevolence, have received only one.'[87]

[86] In fact, Niẓām al-Mulk mentions a specific female divinity, Manāt, an ancient deity whose cult was established in pre-Islamic Arabia and who is mentioned in the Qurʾan (with al-Lāt and al-ʿUzzā, Q 53: 19–20).

[87] The title *khaqan* (from *khagan*, first meaning 'supreme ruler') is used in Persian sources of the period and earlier in a variety of applications. Applied in a specific sense to the rulers who bore the title when Muslim forces encountered them in the conquest of Central Asia, and to the rulers of Turkic confederations and states, including the Karakhanids (see *Kutadgu bilig*), the term also denoted, in the Seljuk period, certain local rulers (as in Niẓām al-Mulk's narrative). The term was sometimes used in a looser sense to designate a Chinese or a Tibetan ruler. The wives and female relatives of the *khaqan* carried the title *khatun* (see below); the Seljuks and Mongols used the title *khatun* for the women of the royal court (de la Vaissière, 'Khagan').

The caliph replied, 'A title represents a bestowal of honour (*tashrīf*) upon a man. By its bestowal, that person's noble standing (*sharaf*) is increased, and henceforth the denizens of the world know the individual by this title. Bear in mind that people possess the names that their mothers and fathers give them, as well as the patronymics (sing. *kunyat*) that they adopt for themselves; in some cases, an individual might also possess a title (*laqab*) that the king has awarded to him. Anything in addition to these three names is superfluous (*ḥashw*) and false (*makhraqat*), and no man of wisdom exposes himself to the false and preposterous (*muḥāl*). A small boy is called by his (first) name (*nām*), which brings pleasure to his father, because his parents chose that name for him. When the boy becomes a man, able to distinguish between good and bad, through his rational intellect and knowledge he chooses a patronymic for himself; as people have said, "Patronymics accord with aspirations (*al-kunā bi-l-munā*)." Then, on account of his maturity, people begin to call him by that *kunyat*, and this practice makes him glad. Later, if he displays aptitude and skill (*hunar*) in matters pertaining to the kingdom and the community (*millat*), the king will grant him a commensurate title as a mark of honour; this title distinguishes him among his peers and favours him over them. So the title that the king or caliph gives to a man is superior to the name that his mother and father have given him, and to the patronymic that he has chosen for himself. On account of his stature, dignity and high rank, then, people will call this person by the name that the king has given him, namely, his title. Any conceivable title in addition to these three names is pointless.'

The caliph continued, 'Now the khaqan knows very little. He is a Turk, the ruler of a remote province (*ṣāḥib-ṭaraf*).[88] Taking into account his lack of knowledge and negligible reputation (*nāmūs*), I granted his request. You, by contrast, are well versed in all branches of knowledge, and, furthermore, you are in close proximity to us. In your case, the superiority of our intention towards you and of our faith in you,

[88] The term *ṭaraf* (pl. *aṭrāf*) designated a province or region on the margins of the imperial domain, often under the governance of a vassal or virtually independent ruler. The belittling use of the term 'Turk', here and elsewhere in the chapter, suggests a person lacking in education. The protagonist of the story, Maḥmūd, was of Turkish ethnicity, and the recipient of *Siyar al-mulūk*, Malikshāh, was Turkish as well; in addition, Niẓām al-Mulk identifies the 'literate and well-read' female protagonist as Turkish. The vizier's disparagement of the khaqan was linked to the figure's distant location and his proximity to the steppe; Niẓām al-Mulk's use of the label 'Turk' linked these factors to the khaqan's lack of education and cultivated manners.

and the clarity of our confidence in you and in your religion are evident; there is no need for you to request from us something that people would use in speaking and record in writing, or for you to entertain the same desires that people of little knowledge expect.' When Maḥmūd heard these words, he was taken aback.

There was a woman who used to come constantly to the women's quarters of Maḥmūd's palace. Of Turkish parentage, literate and well read, proficient in several languages and highly articulate, this woman used to converse with Maḥmūd. She would amuse and entertain him, and she read him Persian books and stories; she was, indeed, on the most familiar terms with him. One day, she was sitting in Maḥmūd's presence and engaged in pleasantries with him. Maḥmūd declared: 'However much I strive to persuade the caliph to increase the number of my titles, he does not increase them. The khaqan, who is subordinate to me, has received numerous titles from the caliph, yet I have been given only one. I need someone to gain access to the khaqan's treasury and to steal – or to acquire in some way or other – the document of titular appointment (*ʿahdnāmeh*) that the caliph sent to the khaqan, and to bring that document to me. Whatever the person who brought me this document should demand of me I should readily give to him.'

The woman replied, 'O lord, I shall go and procure that document; but you shall have to give me whatever I ask for.' Maḥmūd agreed. She said, 'I do not have enough money of my own to fulfil and accomplish the lord's desire. If I, your servant, am granted assistance from the treasury, I shall accomplish the lord's desire or die in the attempt.' Maḥmūd asked her to state her demands. She then received whatever she requested, including money, goods, jewels, fine clothing, mounts, articles of exquisite manufacture, wealth and provisions for the journey. This woman had a fourteen-year-old son. She had entrusted the boy to a tutor for his education (*adab*). Taking her son with her, the woman left Ghazna for Kashghar. She bought some male slaves, who were Turkish, and some female slaves, as well as large quantities of every commodity – fine goods, musk, silk, cotton, *ṭarqūb*[89] and the like – that had been imported from Cathay (Khutay) and the province of China. In the company of a group of merchants, the woman and her son arrived in Uzgand [Özkent, in Farghana], and from there journeyed on to the city of Samarqand.

[89] Following Darke's well-supported reading, *Book of Government*, 151 and 252, n. 6.

After three days in Samarqand she stirred, and went to offer her greetings to the khatun. She presented the khatun with a young Turkish girl of exquisite beauty, as well as many pieces of the choice merchandise imported from China and Cathay. The woman told the khatun:[90] 'My husband was a merchant. He travelled all over the world and often used to take me with him. We were heading for Cathay. When he got to Khotan he died. I returned. Upon my arrival in Kashghar, I presented a token of my willing service (*khidmatī*) to the Khan of Kashghar. I visited his khatun and told her that my husband had been a servant of the Glorious Khaqan (*khāqān-i ajall*), and that I was a devoted attendant (*parastār*) upon the khatun of the khaqan. I told the khatun that I had been released and given to my late merchant husband as his wife; that this young boy of mine was his child. Now, I told her, my husband had died in Khotan, and I had been left with only the small remaining portion of the capital given to him by the khatun and the Glorious Khaqan. I told the khatun further that it was now my hope that out of his justice and greatness, the Glorious Khaqan might extend his hand in assistance to me, his khatun's servant, and to this young orphan, and that he might send us, in good company, on our way towards Uzgand and Samarqand, so that we should speak well of him and praise him, and pray on his behalf for as long as we remained alive.

'The khatun [of Kashghar] spoke most graciously to us, and the Khan did the same; both of them complimented us. They presented us with a guide (*daraqeh*), and they wrote a letter to the Khan of Uzgand, asking him to treat us well, and to send us on in good company towards Samarqand. Now, having arrived in Samarqand, I surrender myself to your dominion and dignity (*dawlat va-ḥashmat-i shumā*). Today, nowhere else in the entire world enjoys the justice and equity found in this city. My husband always used to say, "If by some way or another I manage to get to Samarqand, I shall never leave that city." I have been drawn here by your name and reputation. If you consider it expedient to accept me and to extend the hand of assistance and lordship over me, so

[90] What follows is a micro-story embedded in a secondary story. The protagonist, an unnamed Turkish woman, narrates an account that resembles the events in which she takes part. There are two khatuns and two khaqans, one of each in Kashghar and one of each in Samarqand. The protagonist-narrator relates an account of her experience with the khatun and khaqan of Kashghar to the khatun and khan of Samarqand. This narrative technique, involving multiple layers of narration, creates a multiply distancing effect for the narrator.

that I can settle here, sell such trinkets as I have, and purchase a residence and estate sufficient in size to suffice for my subsistence, then I shall continue to offer you my loyal service, and I shall continue to educate this young boy, in the hope that by your blessings God, may He be exalted and glorified, might grant him good fortune.'

The khatun [of Samarqand] said, 'Do not worry in the slightest. I shall refuse you nothing in terms of any possible kindness and attention. I myself shall provide you with a residence and a piece of land, in accordance with your wishes. And I shall not permit that you should be absent from my presence for even a short amount of time. I shall tell the khaqan to grant you whatever you should find needful and whatever you desire.' The woman pledged her service to the khatun, and said, 'Now you are my lord; I shall not recognise anyone else. You should now intercede for me before the Glorious Khaqan, present me to him and explain my situation to him, so that I, your servant, may hear also the words of the lord khaqan.' The khatun replied, 'I shall bring you before him any time you wish.' The woman said, 'I shall come tomorrow to pledge my service.' The khatun replied to confirm her extreme satisfaction with this proposal.

The next day the woman came to the khatun's residence. When the khaqan had left his audience hall and met the khatun in the palace, the khatun mentioned the woman's circumstances to him. He ordered that the woman should be summoned to his presence. The woman duly appeared and pledged her service to the khaqan. She brought with her a Turkish slave-boy, a fine horse and all kinds of items selected from her collection of choice gifts, and she said, 'I, your servant, have related a little of my condition to the khatun. In sum, when my husband died – may my lord live forever! – his trading associate said that I should not bring back any of the items bound for Cathay; instead, he took them on towards Cathay. Of whatever goods remained, the Khan of China [Khotan] took some, and I gave some to the Khan of Kashghar; I expended some during our travels, and finally I am left with a few trinkets, a certain number of animals and this orphan. If the Glorious Khaqan will accept me as a devoted attendant, as the magnanimous khatun has accepted me, I should hope to spend the rest of my life in your esteemed service.'

The khaqan responded with an abundance of favourable words and granted his acceptance. After that, every two or three days when the woman attended upon the khatun, she would present her with a pair of ruby rings, or a turquoise, or a veil of gold and silver thread, or some other costly item from her supply of choice articles, and she would relate pleasing stories and tales. She continued to treat the khaqan's khatun in this manner, and the latter soon could not be content without the woman's presence even for a single day.

At the same time, the khatun and khaqan began to feel abashed and embarrassed, since whenever they presented the woman with a village or an estate that belonged to the royal domains (*khāṣṣ*), she refused to accept it. Every few days she would leave the residence in which they had accommodated her and set out to visit a number of villages, three, four or five *farsangs* away from the city, and on each occasion she would announce her intention to purchase an estate. She would spend three or four days in each place; then she would find some fault, offer an excuse, refuse to buy it, and return to the city. When, missing her presence, the khatun and khaqan sent someone to summon her, and to ask what had prevented her from attending upon them, they received the reply, 'She is buying a property in such-and-such a village; she left some two or three days ago.' This report delighted the khatun and khaqan, who inferred that the woman had settled in the location in question. For a period of six months, the woman, in her service to the khatun and khaqan, continued to behave in this manner. Several times the khatun reported to the woman the khaqan's constant expressions of embarrassment over the woman's many services to them and the many days on which she presented them with precious items, while she refused to accept anything that they presented to her. 'I have never seen a woman with such graciousness (*nīkū'ī*),' he would say; 'What, in the end, should we do for her?' The khatun would add that she herself felt a thousand times more ashamed than the khaqan. The woman replied, 'For me, there is no greater favour than an audience with my lords; since it is through them that God, may He be exalted and glorified, has appointed my daily sustenance. When a need befalls me I shall ask; I shall not hesitate to presume upon your magnanimity.' All the while, she was tending her horses, and secretly giving whatever gold, jewels, carpets and robes she had to a merchant whose commerce entailed his regular travel between Samarqand and Ghazna. On each occasion she dispatched five riders and five fine horses towards the road to Balkh and Tirmidh, and she instructed each rider to take up lodging, with his horse, at a given stopping place, and to wait there until her arrival.

One day, she appeared before the khatun while the khaqan was sitting with her. She praised and extolled them both in fulsome terms. Then she said, 'Today I have come to you with a petition. Yet I do not know if I should pronounce it and ask for it, or not.' The khatun said, 'I am surprised to hear this question from you. By rights, by this point we ought to have fulfilled a hundred requests of yours; so speak: what is your request?' The woman replied: 'You know that in all the world I have only a young son, and that my heart is wholly devoted to him. I am seeing to his education. He has learnt the entire Qur'an, and I have entrusted him to a man learned in the literary arts (*adīb*), so that my son will acquire a literary education (*adab*), and be able to read treatises (*risāleh*) in Arabic and Persian. My hope is that by virtue of your favour (*dawlat*), my lords, he should find good fortune. After the Book of God and the Prophet, no written text on the face of the earth is superior to the correspondence that the Commander of the Faithful sends to kings. The secretary who writes these documents is more skilled than any other secretary, and the phrases and meanings (*lafẓ va-ma'nā*) that he employs in this correspondence are the very finest of words. If it comports with the judgement of my lords, might they allow me, for three or four days, to borrow the document known as the caliph's charter of titular appointment (*'ahd*), so that this child of mine might read it a few times with his teacher? If he remembers only five expressions out of the whole document, it will be of great value, and perhaps by its blessings he will become fortunate.'

The khaqan and khatun said, 'What is this request that you are asking of us? Why do you not request a city or district so that we can grant it to you? Up until this moment you have requested nothing at all, and now that you are finally asking for something, you have requested something of which we have fifty of its kind, all rotting away beneath the earth and dust in our treasury. What value can there be in a piece of paper? We shall give you all of these documents, if you wish.' The woman replied, 'Just this one letter that the caliph sent to you will be perfect.' They ordered a servant to go with her to the treasury and to give her whichever letter she requested.

The woman duly went to the treasury, took the charter (*'ahdnāmeh*) and went home. The next day she called for her horses to be saddled and her mules loaded, and she announced that she was going to such-and-such a village to buy property and that she would be there for a week. They set off straight away and arrived in the village. Before her departure, the woman had procured a letter of safe-conduct (*gushādeh-nāmeh-ī*).

This document stipulated that throughout every province of Samarqand and Bukhara, wherever this woman and her party should arrive for purposes of purchasing a property, acquiring an estate or taking up residence, their dignity was to be guaranteed. Governmental agents, officials and municipal authorities were required to treat them well, and not to withhold any possible assistance from them; they were to supply the woman and her party generously with whatever they might request and to grant them accommodation.

Then, in the middle of the night, she set off (*kūch kard*) from that village. She passed within three *farsang*s of the city of Kish [also Kishsh, a town on the route between Samarqand and Tirmidh], then in five days' time she arrived in Tirmidh. Wherever she arrived, when she needed anything she presented the letter of safe-conduct, and she was provided regularly with fresh horses. The khaqan remained unaware of the woman's departure until she had crossed the Oxus and arrived in Balkh, and he suffered not a moment's anxiety regarding that charter. The woman, meanwhile, proceeded from Balkh to Ghazna, where she placed the charter before Sultan Maḥmūd.

Maḥmūd dispatched a man who was learned and skilled in debate to deliver the document, as well as many tokens of his service, to the Commander of the Faithful al-Qādir billāh. Maḥmūd also sent a letter pledging his service. In this letter he related: 'A servant of mine was walking through the market of Samarqand. He arrived at a mosque where a teacher (*mu'addib*) was running an elementary school (*kuttab*) and teaching something to the children. My servant saw the Commander of the Faithful's letter in the hands of these young children. Counting it of little value or significance, the children were tossing it back and forth and rolling it along the ground. The servant recognised the document and was moved to rescue it from such mistreatment. He produced a quantity of raisins and gave them to the children, from whom he attained and bought the document, at a price fit for a tattered piece of paper. He returned to Ghazna with the document and placed it before me, your servant; and I have now sent it forward to the Lord of the World. If you were to look favourably upon your servant, with all his acts of benevolence and service, and to award titles to him, he would hold those documents more dearly than his own eyesight; he would deem them as precious as the crown on his head, and place them in the most exalted position in his treasury. Despite his amply attested servitude and his expectation of titles, you withhold them from your servant; yet you award titles to persons who do not acknowledge the worth of the caliph's decrees (*farmān-hā*), nor the honour that their bestowal represents; instead, these persons display the kind of contempt that we have just described, and they consider the titles granted to them to be worth next to nothing.'

When this scholar reached Baghdad, he delivered Maḥmūd's presents and presented his letters to the caliph. The caliph was deeply astonished, and he ordered a letter of rebuke to be written to the khaqan. Maḥmūd's envoy then remained at the caliph's door for six months. Continually he sent petitions, seeking titles of behalf of Maḥmūd, into the interior of the palace. He obtained no definitive answer, until one day he composed a request for a legal opinion (*fatvā*). In this request, he posited: 'If a king were to appear in the remote regions of the world, and if this king were to wield the sword for the sake of the glory of Islam, to make war against the infidels and idolators who are the enemies of God and His Prophet, to turn idol-temples into mosques, and to convert the abode of unbelief into the abode of Islam; and if this king were a great distance away from the Commander of the Faithful, separated from him by vast bodies of water, high mountains and fearsome deserts; and if the king were sometimes unable to report events and occurrences to the caliph in every instance; and if the king's requests to the caliph went unfulfilled – would it be permissible for this king to install a descendant of the Prophet (*sharīf*) as the caliph's deputy, and to follow him, or not?' Maḥmūd's envoy entrusted this *fatvā* to someone who conveyed it and delivered it to the Chief Judge of Baghdad. The judge read it, and determined that it would indeed be permissible. The scholar took a copy of this legal opinion and placed it inside a petition, addressed to the caliph, in which he had written, 'Your servant's stay has grown too long. Maḥmūd, with a hundred thousand emblems of servitude and service, requests a few titles; the Lord of the World has withheld them. He has not countenanced the fulfilment of the ghazi king's hopes, and the latter, on this account, suffers distress. If, in the future, Maḥmūd were to implement this legal opinion and dispensation, obtained through the religious law and in the hand of the Chief Judge of Baghdad, would he be excused?'

The caliph, upon reading the petition and *fatvā*, immediately sent his Chief Chamberlain to the vizier. Instructing the chamberlain, the caliph said to him, 'Summon Maḥmūd's envoy this instant. Reassure him; prepare the robes of honour, banners and titles that we shall command; and send him away satisfied.'

(a) (b)

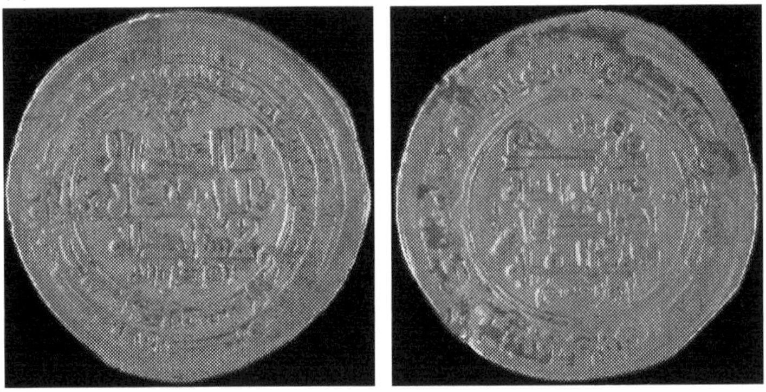

Figure 4 The obverse and reverse sides of a Ghaznavid dinar, struck at Ghazna and dated 414/1023–4. Fig. 4a: The name of the caliph al-Qādir appears on the obverse. Fig. 4b: The titles Yamīn al-Dawla wa-Amīn al-Milla and Sultan Maḥmūd's patronymic, Abū l-Qāsim, appear on the reverse.
Image: Ashmolean Museum, Islamic Coin HCR14556.

For all of Maḥmūd's goodwill, for all of his pleasing services and all of his efforts, and notwithstanding the scholar's quick-wittedness, he received only one additional title – Amīn al-Milla; and for as long as Maḥmūd lived, his titles remained Yamīn al-Dawla and Amīn al-Milla (Fig. 4).[91]

Today, if the least of persons is assigned fewer than seven or ten titles, he is roused to anger and resentment.

The Samanids, who for countless years were the greatest kings of the age and who ruled over the entirety of Transoxiana, as well as over Khurasan, Iraq, Khᵛarazm, Nimruz and Ghazna, each held only a single title. Nūḥ (= Nūḥ II b. Manṣūr I, r. 365–87/976–97) was called Shāhānshāh [al-Amīr al-Razī]; Nūḥ's father, Manṣūr (= Manṣūr I b. Nūḥ I, r. 350–65/961–76), was called Amīr-i Sadīd; Manṣūr's father, Nūḥ (= Nūḥ I b. Naṣr II, r. 331–43/943–54), held the title Amīr-i Ḥamīd; Nūḥ's father, Naṣr (= Naṣr II

[91] In fact, Maḥmūd received several titles, on different occasions, from the caliph; but only these two appear in his coinage (see Fig. 4). The sultan's preoccupation with titles is attested elsewhere (Bosworth, *Ghaznavids*, 44, 46, 52–3).

b. Aḥmad II, r. 301–31/914–43), was called Amīr-i Saʿīd; Ismāʿīl b. Aḥmad (= Ismāʿīl b. Aḥmad I, r. 279–95/892–907) was called Amīr-i ʿĀdil, and in the historical accounts he is known as Amīr-i Māẓī; Aḥmad (= Aḥmad II b. Ismāʿīl, r. 295–301/907–14) acquired the title Amīr-i Shahīd, and so on.[92]

Titles must suit the persons who hold them. The titles of judges, leading authorities (*aʾimmeh*) and scholars, learned in the religion of the Chosen Prophet, upon him be peace, should be of this kind: Majd al-Dīn, Sharaf al-Islām, Sayf al-Sunna, Zayn al-Sharīʿa, Fakhr al-ʿUlamāʾ and the like, since the domains of religion, Islam, law, authenticated Prophetic example (*sunnat*) and knowledge are closely linked with the religious scholars and the leading religious authorities (*aʾimmeh*). If anyone who is not a scholar should adopt one of these titles for himself, the king and indeed all persons of discernment and insight should not permit it; they should, in fact, punish that person, so that everybody will become mindful of his own rank (*andāzeh*) and station (*martabat*). According to the same principle, the titles of military generals (*sipahsālārān*), military commanders, holders of land-grants (*muqṭaʿān*, holders of *iqṭāʿ*) and governmental agents have been linked with the state (*dawlat*); for example, Sayf al-Dawla, Ḥusām al-Dawla, Ẓahīr al-Dawla, Jamāl al-Dawla, Shams al-Dawla and the like.[93] Similarly, the titles of local governors (*ʿamīd*), tax-officials (*ʿāmilān*) and worthy fiscal agents (*mutaṣarrifān*) have been linked with the realm (*mulk*); examples include

92 In the MS and in Darke's published text of 1962, this list of Samanid titles contains a few errors, probably due to a copyist. I have emended the translated version of the text to reflect the correct titles, as follows: Naṣr II b. Aḥmad (r. 301–31/914–43), who appears in the text with the title Amīr-i Rashīd, in fact bore the title al-Amīr al-Saʿīd (see above, Text 16); and I take the reference to Aḥmad, who appears in the text with the title Amīr-i Saʿīd, to apply properly to Aḥmad II b. Ismāʿīl (r. 295–301/907–14); it was Aḥmad's son Naṣr II who acquired the title supplied in the text, while Aḥmad II became known posthumously (after his assassination) as al-Amīr al-Shahīd.

93 The *iqṭāʿ*, properly the assignment to an individual holder (*muqṭaʿ*) of the revenues produced within a given village or district, was a major feature of the social and economic life of the Seljuk period (see above, section 2.1). Niẓām al-Mulk devoted an entire chapter of part I of *Siyar al-mulūk* to the topic of the holders of *iqṭāʿ* (chapter V, 43–55 = Darke, *Book of Government*, 32–42); his discussion makes clear that these *muqṭaʿān* not infrequently treated these lands as if they owned them outright and had full authority over their inhabitants. The position of the category in the present context indicates the high status some *muqṭaʿān* clearly possessed in Niẓām al-Mulk's later years. The institution of the *iqṭāʿ*, widespread within and beyond Iran, varied very considerably; a single individual might hold more than one *iqṭāʿ* under different arrangements. See Lambton, 'Eqṭāʿ'; the article includes a lengthy discussion of Niẓām al-Mulk's treatment of the topic.

ʿAmīd al-Mulk, Niẓām al-Mulk, Kamāl al-Mulk, Sharaf al-Mulk, Shams al-Mulk and the like. It has never been the custom that Turkish amirs should take upon themselves the titles of educated men in government service (*kh^{v}ājagān*).[94] Titles that invoke religion (*dīn*) and Islam should be reserved for scholars, titles involving the state (*dawlat*) should be used only for the amirs and titles entailing *mulk* should be awarded only to the *kh^{v}ājagān*. If anyone else should assume a title involving religion or Islam, it should not be permitted. Moreover, the person should be punished, so that other people will take warning (*ʿibrat*).

The main purpose of titles is to provide a means of identifying individuals. For example, a hundred people might be seated in an assembly or a gathering, and of that number there might be ten persons named Muḥammad. If someone were to call, 'Muḥammad!', all ten Muḥammads would be required to answer 'Yes, here I am!' (*labbayk*), for each one of them would suppose that it was he who was being called.[95] If, however, one Muḥammad were given the title Mukhtaṣṣ, and another Muwaffaq, another Kāmil, another Kāfī, another Rashīd and so on, then if in that gathering someone were to call, 'Kāmil!' or 'Muwaffaq!', the Muḥammad in question would know immediately that it was he who was being addressed.

Apart from the vizier, the chief of the chancery (*ṭughrāʾī*), the chief fiscal officer (*mustawfī*), the chief of the sultan's military department (*ʿarīż*) and the leading administrators (sing. *ʿamīd*) of Baghdad, Khurasan and Kh^{v}ārazm, no person in the kingdom should bear the title 'So-and-so al-Mulk'; they should carry only titles that lack the term *mulk*, such as Kh^{v}ājeh-yi Sadīd, Kh^{v}ājeh-yi Rashīd, Kh^{v}ājeh-yi Mukhtaṣṣ, or Ustād-i Amīn, Ustād-i Khaṭīr, Ustād-i Makīn and the like, so that the respective degrees and stations of the lower and the higher, the humble and the great, the distinguished and the commoner will be readily apparent, and the lustre of the administration will remain bright. When the stability of the kingdom is evident; when the king is just and alert, pursues the diligent performance of affairs and enquires into the practices and customs of his predecessors (*āyīn va-rasm-i gudhashtagān*); and when the king has a fortunate and successful vizier, who is knowledgeable in matters of established practice (*rasm-dān*) and skilful (*hunarvar*) – then the king will ensure that all matters proceed in

[94] On the title *kh^{v}ājeh*, see above, n. 62.

[95] The invocation *labbayk* is the expression used by pilgrims as they present themselves at the House of God in Mecca as part of the pilgrimage rituals.

good order (*tartībī nīkū*); he will revise all titles in the light of their proper foundations, and he will eliminate newly contrived principles and customs in accordance with his sound judgement, his strong command and his sharp sword.

Text 18
Al-Ṭurṭūshī, *Sirāj al-mulūk*, Chapter Six[96]

Translator's Introduction

The brief final selection in this anthology is an early chapter from al-Ṭurṭūshī's *Sirāj al-mulūk*. It too emphasises the ruler's risk of numerous perils and their unfortunate consequences. In this chapter, al-Ṭurṭūshī adopts an exhortative tone, admonishing the ruler to accept his lot and remain mindful of the severe testing that awaits him in the world to come.

Translation

Chapter Six: The Sultan Is a Debtor, Not a Creditor, in Relation to His Subjects, and He Stands to Lose, Not to Profit

Know that the sultan faces momentous risks and general tribulations. The misfortunes that afflict him and the vicissitudes that befall him would compel any intelligent person to take refuge in God in the face of the burdens that he bears, and to thank Him for His protection. The sultan's mind is never at rest, his thoughts never find repose, his conscience is never clear and his intelligence (*lubb*) can never settle.[97] The people are disaffected from him, yet he must preoccupy himself with them. A single man fears a single enemy, whereas he must fear a thousand enemies; a single man is constrained to manage the members of his household, oversee his estate and determine his livelihood, whereas the sultan is obliged to govern all the people of his kingdom. As soon as he repairs one rupture in the peripheries of his kingdom, another rupture appears; as soon as he rectifies one disorder, another division promptly

[96] Translation prepared from al-Ṭurṭūshī, *Sirāj al-mulūk*, I: 193–7. For the corresponding section in Alarcón's translation into Spanish, see Alarcón, *Lámpara de los Príncipes*, I: 169–74.

[97] The term that I have rendered here, and further down, as 'conscience' is *qalb* (lit. 'heart').

arises; whenever he succeeds in eliminating one enemy, other enemies are already preparing to move against him. The same pattern recurs in connection with every one of his subjects' circumstances that concerns him. The ruler contends with difficulty in settling his subjects' disputes, appointing governors and judges, dispatching armies, defending the frontiers, raising revenues and redressing grievances. In addition, astonishingly, the ruler possesses but a single corporeal self (*nafs*), yet he can deprive the world of its food, and cause the subjects to suffer deprivation; he will, one day, face questions about every one of them, while they will not be asked about him. By God, what a remarkable thing it is, that a man who should be content to take a single loaf from this world will be held responsible for a million loaves; that he who eats to fill a single belly will be held accountable for a million bellies; that he who enjoys the pleasures of a single physical self will be held accountable for a million selves and so on, in all aspects of his life: the sultan bears their burdens, safeguards their secrets, combats their enemies, defends their frontiers and constrains those who seek to prevail against them or to oppose them, as well as anyone amongst them who disobeys His Lord, opposes His command and violates His prohibitions. On condition of his vigilance on their behalf, the ruler confronts the depths of Hell; yet still he finds them loathing him and discontented with him.

Had God Almighty not intervened between the man and his conscience, no intelligent person would be content with this (the royal) station, and no mindful person would choose this station as his rank. Everything that I have mentioned in this chapter is encapsulated in the Prophet's saying: 'What is due to you, and what is due to my commanders (*umarāʾī*)? You are due the absolute best (*ṣifwa*) of their command, and they are due the worry (*kadar*) that the duty to command entails.'[98]

The sultan's relationship with his subjects resembles the relationship of the cook with his diners: his is the toil, theirs the wholesome enjoyment; his is the heat involved in the food's preparation, theirs the refreshing satisfaction of its consumption. Similarly, the sultan strives for the repose of his people (*qawm*) and in so doing endures fatigue; he seeks their felicity and himself falls short of the straight path. On this matter, people have said: 'The lord of the people (*sayyid al-qawm*) is the

[98] Reading *ṣifwa*, 'the best', 'the choicest part', for *ṣafw*; Muslim, *Ṣaḥīḥ*, XII: 95–6, *Kitāb al-Jihād wa-l-siyar*, ch. 13, no. 43 (1753); Abū Dāʾūd, *Sunan*, IV: 520–1, *Kitāb al-Jihād*, ch. 137, no. 2708.

most wretched person among them.' According to the hadith: 'The cup-bearer is the last person in the group to drink.'[99]

One of the kings of the Maghrib was travelling one day with his viziers when he saw a group of merchants. The king said to his vizier: 'Shall I show you three groups of people – one group who possess this world and the next; one group who possess neither this world nor the next; and one group who possess this world to the exclusion of the next?' The vizier replied, 'How is that so, O king?' The king said, 'Those who possess both this world and the next world are these merchants: they earn their sustenance and perform their prayers, and they harm no one. As for those who possess neither this world nor the next, they are the police and the servants in our employ; and as for those who possess this world to the exclusion of the next, that group consists of me, you, and all holders of power.'

It is fitting that all members of humankind should extend themselves in sincere counsel to the ruler. They should single him out in their prayers on his behalf and support him in all his endeavours. They should be his sharp eyes, his strong hands, his staunch heart and his articulate tongue; they should be the legs that lift him up and the feet that carry him. For the king is far from safety (*salāma*) – how else is he to attain it?[100] On this point, a king said one day to his companions: 'Know that power (*al-sulṭān*) and Paradise (*al-janna*) are mutually incompatible.'

Our shaykh, may God have mercy upon him, related having heard the following report from a man of substance. The ruler had contacted the man with the request that he divorce his wife, since the former wanted her for one of his companions. The man refused to do so, and he returned the sultan's messengers more than once. Eventually a counsellor offered him this advice: 'Accept the sultan's command. You have no stratagem to avoid it, since the ruler fears no mortal being in this world, and he does not fear the Fire in the next.' The man duly separated from his wife.

It is related that when ʿAbd al-Malik b. Marwān rose to the caliphate, he took a copy of the Qurʾan and placed it in an inaccessible location, saying, 'This moment marks the separation between you and me.'[101]

99 Abū Dāʾūd, *Sunan*, VI: 58, *Awwal Kitāb al-Ashriba*, ch. 19, no. 3677; al-Sakhāwī, *al-Maqāṣid al-ḥasana*, 382, no. 551.

100 Like several of the lexical choices in this section (such as *naʿīm*, above), the term *salāma* carries connotations of eternal salvation as well as physical security and good health in the present world.

101 The language is Qurʾanic; see Q 18: 78 (Moses).

Once, when Hārūn al-Rashīd was performing the pilgrimage, ʿUbayd Allāh al-ʿUmarī[102] came upon him circumambulating the Kaʿba. He said to him: 'O Hārūn!' The caliph said, 'Labbayka, uncle.' ʿUbayd Allāh asked him, 'How many people do you see here?' Hārūn said, 'So many that only God can count them.' His interlocutor said, 'Know, O man, that every one of these people will one day be asked to account for himself. You alone shall face questioning concerning all of them; consider, therefore, how you shall fare.' Hārūn wept, and as he sat down, his attendants hastened to bring him a handkerchief for his tears. ʿUbayd Allāh responded, 'By God, the man in a hurry for access to his own wealth deserves to be debarred from it; what, then, of the person who rushes to attain the property of the Muslims?' It has been reported that Hārūn used to say, 'By God, I should like to perform the pilgrimage every year. The only impediment to my doing so is a certain man, a member of ʿUmar's family, who makes me listen to words that I find painful.'

Mālik b. Dīnār (d. 130/747–8) reported having read in an ancient book that God Almighty said, 'Who is more foolish than the ruler? Who is more ignorant than the person who disobeys Me? Who is more glorious than the person who seeks glory through Me? O wicked shepherd: I have provided you with a healthy, fattened sheep, so that you may consume her meat, drink her milk, moisten your bread with her fat and dress in her wool. You have reduced her to nothing but clattering bones, you have neither sheltered the straying, nor cared for the sick. A day will come when this sheep is avenged against you.'[103]

[102] Alarcón reads ʿAbdallāh (I: 197). The individual in question is a descendant of ʿUmar b. al-Khaṭṭāb and a deputy of the governor of Medina.

[103] Mālik b. Dīnār, of Basra, was a renunciant, a preacher and a moralist; he made his living by copying the Qurʾan. Abū Nuʿaym al-Iṣfahānī notes that he was well versed in Christian scriptures, a point that fits well with the present citation's ascription to 'an ancient book' (*Ḥilyat al-awliyāʾ*, II: 357–88, no. 200; see 358 (the Torah), 359 (the Torah), 369 (citing Jesus), 370 (citing Jesus), 376 (the Psalms, the Torah), 380 (the Psalms), 382 (God's inspiration to Jesus; Jesus' entry into the temple and condemning the conduct of sale inside), 385 (Jesus' stopping at a house whose owner had died)). The latter portion of this report appears in *Ḥilyat al-awliyāʾ*, II: 370 (*qaraʾtu fī baʿḍ al-kutub*).

Appendix

Index of Qur'anic References and Quotations

Numbers in parentheses refer to the Texts in which the references appear.

1: 4 (1)

2: 247 (1)
2: 249 (11)
2: 251 (1)
2: 258 (2; 16, n. 54)

3: 7 (11, n. 32)
3: 18 (12)
3: 26 (1, 2, 4)
3: 92 (1)

4: 49 (3)
4: 54 (1)
4: 59 (1, 2, 4, 11)
4: 164 (17, n. 76)

5: 20 (2)
5: 54 (2, n. 82)

6: 166 (2)

7: 79 (15)
7: 85 (17, n. 75)
7: 93 (15)
7: 143, 144 (17, n. 76)

9: 13 (16)
9: 111 (1)

11: 34 (15)
11: 84 (17, n. 75)

13: 11 (1)

14: 7 (1)
14: 33, 34 (1)

16: 90 (12)

17: 71 (1)

18: 49 (1)
18: 78 (18, n. 101)
18: 83, 86, 94 (8, n. 52)

20: 12 (17, n. 76)
20: 43–4 (2)
20: 114 (1)

22: 11 (2, n. 62)

23: 116 (1)

24: 54 (2, n. 91)

26: 227 (1)

27: 21 (1)
27: 23 (1)

28: 22–8 (17, n. 75)
28: 77 (3)

29: 36 (17, n. 75)

30: 30 (7, n. 15)

31: 20 (2, n. 55)

34: 16, 17 (1)

35: 43 (2, n. 75)

37: 102 (15)
37: 156, 157 (1)

38: 26 (3)
38: 29 (15)
38: 34 (12, n. 54)

38: 35 (12, n. 54)
38: 40 (12, n. 54)

39: 15 (2, n. 62)

40: 16 (1)

43: 32 (1)

45: 12 (1, n. 3)
45: 13 (1)

49: 2 (2)

53: 19–20 (17, n. 86)

54: 5 (2, n. 55)

55: 46 (16, n. 46)

57: 21 (2, n. 82)

58: 11 (12)
58: 12 (2)

62: 4 (2, n. 82)

79: 16 (17, n. 76)
79: 24 (2)
79: 40 (16, n. 46)

89: 27 (15, n. 53)

Glossary

Unless indicated otherwise, the terms in this list appear in their Arabic forms. Where a term is Persian or Turkish rather than Arabic, it appears in its Persian or Turkish form.

adab (pl. *ādāb*) humane culture; moral and cultural education; a literary corpus composed of texts offering moral instruction, aesthetic pleasure and entertainment; in the plural, maxims, instructive examples, rules

ʿadl justice

ʿahd a contract or covenant; in literary terms, a 'testament' or 'charge' (see also *waṣiyya*)

ʿajam collective term for speakers of a language other than Arabic (in contrast to *ʿarab*, the collective term for speakers of Arabic); often used to denote speakers of Persian

ʿamīd a high-ranking administrator; a vizier or a provincial governor

ʿāmil (pl. *ʿummāl*) a provincial governor or government official tasked with the collection of taxes

amīn (pl. *umanāʾ*) trustee, steward; a trusted person

amīr (pl. *umarāʾ*) commander; governor; used as a title for military leaders, rulers and members of dynastic families

amīr al-muʾminīn 'Commander of the Faithful'; a title adopted by the caliph ʿUmar b. al-Khaṭṭāb on his accession to the caliphate, retained by subsequent caliphs, and connoting claims to the caliphal office

ʿāmm(ī) common, general

ʿāmma the collective term for the general, tax-paying population, made up of groups only in indirect relationship to the ruling power

ʿāqil (pl. *ʿuqalāʾ*) a person of rational intelligence

ʿaql intellect, reason, rational intelligence

***atabeg* (Turk.)** tutor, guardian or regent to a Turkish prince; usually a high-ranking *amīr*; in the twelfth century, *atabeg*s became powerful independently and the title became hereditary
***aʿwān* (pl.)** auxiliaries, high-ranking officials, functionaries; supporters, pillars of the state
***aʿyān* (sing. *ʿayn*)** notables; especially in urban contexts, persons of status in a position to mediate between the townspeople and the ruling authorities or other external parties
ʿayyār member of a militia, often adhering to a code of chivalrous conduct
bidʿa an 'innovation' in the religious sphere, whether in belief or practice; a development unattested in the time of the Prophet (the term usually carries negative connotations)
dāʿī a missionary (see also *daʿwa*)
***dargāh* (Pers.)** royal court
daʿwa call to adherence and commitment to a religious group; in the period covered in the anthology, used especially in the context of Ismaili missionary activity
dawla a 'turn in power'; political fortune; a dynasty or 'state'
***dīwān* (Pers. *dīvān*)** a division or ministry of the government; the collected compositions of a poet
***faḍīla* (pl. *faḍāʾil*)** a virtue
faḍl excellence; virtue; superior status (see also *tafḍīl*)
***farr* (Pers.)** glory, splendour; a sign of royal charisma and good fortune; in iconography, often depicted as an aura or nimbus of fire
***fatḥnāmeh* (Pers.)** proclamation of victory
fiqh religious understanding, jurisprudence
***ghulām* (pl. *ghilmān*)** a male youth; a servant or attendant; a soldier or bodyguard, frequently of slave status or formerly of slave status, bound by personal ties
hadith (pl. *aḥādīth*) an authenticated report that transmits the Prophet's speech or action
***ḥakīm* (pl. *ḥukamāʾ*)** a sage (a person possessed of *ḥikma*), philosopher, physician; an honorific title for a revered scholar or religious figure
***ḥaqq* (pl. *ḥuqūq*)** truth, right; in the definite singular, a name of God (*al-Ḥaqq*); a rightful claim
***ḥikma* (pl. *ḥikam*)** wisdom; philosophy; a wise saying or maxim
ʿibra a cautionary example, warning
iqṭāʿ the right to collect revenue in a given district (in lieu of salary); a land-grant (see section 2.1)
istiḥsān technical term for a method of legal reasoning in which *maṣlaḥa* (see below) provides a basis for legal decision-making

***javānmardī* (Pers.)** code of chivalrous conduct, practised by groups of *ʿayyārān*
khalīfa deputy, successor; caliph (name of the office held by leaders of the Muslim community after the death of the Prophet Muḥammad)
khānaqāh a communal residential, teaching and ritual institution affiliated with a Sufi order
***khāqān* (Turk., Pers.)** title designating the senior royal figure in Turkic contexts
khāṣṣ(ī) special, privileged
khāṣṣa collective term for the individuals in proximity, physical or political, to the ruler and in a direct relationship with him; privileged and exempt from taxation
khidma literally 'service'; a term to describe the bond of obligations and loyalties that tied protégés and vassals to their overlords
***khuluq* (pl. *akhlāq*)** a characteristic, moral quality, disposition
khuṭba oration delivered in mosques at the time of the weekly congregational prayer on Fridays
khᵛājeh an educated person, often a teacher; in the period covered in this anthology, used as a title for viziers and other high-ranking officials
laqab title, awarded by the caliph or sultan
***madhhab* (pl. *madhāhib*)** school of law
madrasa educational institution, often with residential facilities, for the teaching of the religious sciences (and sometimes a broader curriculum); especially associated with the teaching of law, with *madrasa*s often affiliated with one or more of the *madhahib*
***majlis* (pl. *majālis*)** a gathering, especially a regular convivial gathering held at the royal court or at the premises of a vizier
***malik* (pl. *mulūk*)** king; widely used as a royal title, often in combination with qualifying adjectives (e.g. al-Malik al-Ḥamīd, 'the Praiseworthy King'; al-Malik al-Kāmil, 'the Consummate King'); in Seljuk contexts, often a prince, subordinate to the sultan
mamlaka kingdom
***mamlūk* (pl. *mamālīk*)** literally 'a possession'; an enslaved person, especially persons imported and trained for military service
***maṣlaḥa* (pl. *maṣāliḥ*)** welfare, benefit; the common good, the public interest; used in general contexts and, in a specific sense, as a purpose of the divine law, in legal contexts
maẓālim acts of injustice, grievances; by extension, a public audience convened by the ruler or his deputy for the redress of grievances and the delivery of justice
milk property, possessions
mulk sovereignty, kingship; in some contexts, the term is contrasted in a negative sense with *khilāfa*, the caliphal office

muqṭaʿ holder of an *iqṭāʿ* (see above); sometimes, effectively, a governor
mustawfī chief fiscal officer
***naṣīḥa* (pl. *naṣāʾiḥ*)** counsel, advice, often of an exhortative or homiletic character
***niʿma* (pl. *niʿam*)** bounty, favour
***pādshāh* (Pers.)** king
***pādshāhī* (Pers.)** kingship, sovereignty
***pand* (Pers.)** advice, counsel
qadi (*qāḍī*) judge in the sharia system of law; appointed by the ruler to preside over the judicial court
***qānūn* (pl. *qawānīn*)** a term applied to various financial regulations: the assessment and collection of taxes, the sum due from the taxpayer; in Egypt and Syria, a kind of fiscal cadaster; in formerly Sasanian settings, registers and lists recording land-taxes, and tax-related regulations; the term also acquired the sense of 'a code of regulations', or laws laid down by the political authorities (as opposed to the laws of the sharia)
***raʾīs* (pl. *ruʾasāʾ*)** chief; title applied to a variety of municipal leaders or notables, leaders of urban constituencies or neighbourhoods; these figures often acted as intermediaries between the urban populations and the ruling authorities
raʿiyya subject (tax-paying) population
riyāsa leadership, rulership
rushd rectitude, right conduct
sāʾis literally 'a trainer or driver of animals'; applied to the ruler who governs his flock with a combination of hopeful expectation and fear of punishment
ṣalāḥ well-being, soundness, righteousness
***shāhānshāh* (Pers.)** 'King of Kings'; an ancient Iranian title applied to and adopted by several Muslim rulers in the period covered in this anthology
sharia (*sharīʿa*) the sacred law of Islam, made up of the rules and regulations governing the lives of Muslims
shukr gratitude; the appropriate response to *niʿma* (see above)
siyāsa governance; discipline; especially in Persian, punishment; a term derived from the training of animals (see also *sāʾis*)
sulṭān power, authority; adopted to describe ruling figures and eventually as a royal title, often conveying claims to broad, superior levels of sovereignty
tadbīr arrangement, order; strategy; especially in Persian, an expedient or remedy devised to address a specific situation
tafḍīl favour, preferment, precedence, privilege
taskhīr subjugation, subordination
***wālī* (pl. *wulāt*)** governor, ruler
waṣiyya a will, testament or bequest; advice, admonition; name of a literary genre

Bibliography

Abbreviations

EI^2	*Encyclopaedia of Islam, Second Edition*, ed. P. Bearman, Th. Bianquis, C. E. Bosworth, E. van Donzel, W. P. Heinrichs (Leiden: Brill, 1960–2007) (https://referenceworks-brillonline-com.ezproxy.wellesley.edu/entries/encyclopaedia-of-islam-2).
EI Three	*Encyclopaedia of Islam, Three*, ed. Kate Fleet, Gudrun Krämer, Denis Matringe, John Nawas, Everett Rowson (Leiden: Brill, 2007–) (https://referenceworks-brillonline-com.ezproxy.wellesley.edu/entries/encyclopaedia-of-islam-3).
EIr	*Encyclopaedia Iranica*, ed. E. Yarshater, Elton Daniel (London and Boston: Routledge and Kegan Paul, 1985–). *Encyclopaedia Iranica Online* © Trustees of Columbia University in the City of New York (https://referenceworks.brillonline.com/entries/encyclopaedia-iranica-online/).
EQ	*Encyclopaedia of the Qur'ān*, ed. Jane Dammen McAuliffe, 6 vols. (Leiden and Boston: E. J. Brill, 2001–6).
GAL	Carl Brockelmann, *Geschichte der arabischen Litteratur*, 2 vols. (first edition, Weimar: E. Felber, 1898–1902; second edition, Leiden: E. J. Brill, 1943–9).
GAL SI, SII, SIII	Carl Brockelmann, *Geschichte der arabischen Litteratur [Supplementbände]*, 3 vols. (Leiden: E. J. Brill, 1937–42).
PEIPT	*The Princeton Encyclopedia of Islamic Political Thought*, ed. Gerhard Böwering (Princeton and Oxford: Princeton University Press, 2013).

ʿAbbās, Iḥsān, *Malāmiḥ yūnāniyya fī l-adab al-ʿarabī* (Beirut: al-Muʾassasa al-ʿArabiyya lil-Dirāsāt wa-l-Nashr, 1977).
Abbès, Makram, *Al-Māwardī. De l'Éthique du prince et du gouvernement de l'état.* Traduit de l'arabe et précédé d'un *Essai sur les arts de gouverner en Islam* (Paris: Les Belles Lettres, 2015).
Al-Ābī, Manṣūr b. al-Ḥusayn, *Nathr al-durr* (Cairo: al-Hayʾa al-Miṣriyya al-ʿĀmma lil-Kitāb, 1980).
Abū l-ʿAtāhiya, *Dīwān Abī l-ʿAtāhiya* (Beirut: Dār Bayrūt lil-Ṭibāʿa wa-l-Nashr, 1986).
Abū Dāʾūd, *al-Sunan*, ed. Abū Turāb ʿĀdil b. Muḥammad and Abū ʿAmr ʿImād al-Dīn b. ʿAbbās (Beirut: Dār al-Taʾṣīl, 2010).
Adamson, Peter, 'The Kindian Tradition: The Structure of Philosophy in Arabic Neoplatonism', in *The Libraries of the Neoplatonists: Proceedings of the European Science Foundation Network 'Late Antiquity and Arabic Thought. Patterns in the Constitution of European Culture', held in Strasbourg, March 12–14, 2004*, ed. Cristina d'Ancona (Leiden and Boston, MA: Brill, 2007), 351–70.
Al-Afwah al-Awdī, *Dīwān al-Afwah al-Awdī*, ed. Muḥammad al-Tūnjī (Beirut: Dār Ṣādir, 1998).
ʿAhd Ardashīr, ed. Iḥsān ʿAbbās (Beirut: Dār Ṣādir, 1967).
Aḥmad, Fuʾād ʿAbd al-Munʿim, *Abū l-Ḥasan al-Māwardī wa-Kitāb Naṣīḥat al-mulūk* (Alexandria: Muʾassasat Shabāb al-Jāmiʿa, n.d.).
Aḥmad, Fuʾād ʿAbd al-Munʿim, 'Muqaddimat al-dirāsa wa-l-taḥqīq', in *Naṣīḥat al-mulūk al-mansūb ilā ... al-Māwardī* (Alexandria: Muʾassasat Shabāb al-Jāmiʿa, 1988), 5–33.
Al-ʿAjlūnī, Ismāʿīl b. Muḥammad, *Kashf al-khafāʾ wa-muzīl al-ilbās ʿammā shtahara min al-aḥādīth ʿalā alsinat al-nās*, 2 vols. in 1, ed. Al-Shaykh Muḥammad ʿAbd al-ʿAzīz al-Khālidī (Beirut: Dār al-Kutub al-ʿIlmiyya, 2018).
Aksan, Virginia H., 'Ottoman Political Writing, 1768-1808', *International Journal of Middle East Studies* 25 (1993), 53–69.
Alajmi, Abdulhadi, 'Ascribed vs. Popular Legitimacy: The Case of al-Walīd II and Umayyad *ʿahd*', *Journal of Near Eastern Studies* 72 (2013), 25–33.
Alam, Muzaffar, *The Languages of Political Islam: India, 1200–1800* (Chicago, IL: University of Chicago Press, 2004).
Alam, Muzaffar and Sanjay Subrahmanyam, *Writing the Mughal World: Studies on Culture and Politics* (New York: Columbia University Press, 2012).
Alarcón, Maximiliano, *Lámpara de los Príncipes por Abubéquer de Tortosa*, 2 vols. (Madrid: Instituto de Valencia de Don Juan, 1930).
Algar, Hamid, 'Introduction', in *The Path of God's Bondsmen from Origin to Return (Merṣād al-ʿebād men al-mabdaʾ elāʾl-maʿād): A Sufi Compendium by Najm al-Dīn Rāzī, Known as Dāya* (Delmar, NY: Caravan Books, 1982), 1–22.
Algar, Hamid, *The Path of God's Bondsmen from Origin to Return (Merṣād al-ʿebād men al-mabdaʾ elāʾl-maʿād): A Sufi Compendium by Najm al-Dīn Rāzī, Known as Dāya* (Delmar, NY: Caravan Books, 1982).
Ali, Samer M., *Arabic Literary Salons in the Islamic Middle Ages: Poetry, Public Performance, and the Presentation of the Past* (Notre Dame, IN: University of Notre Dame Press, 2010).

Alvi, Sajida, *Advice on the Art of Governance: An Indo-Islamic Mirror for Princes: Mau'izah-i Jahāngīrī of Muḥammad Bāqir Najm-i Sānī* (Albany, NY: State University of New York Press, 1989).

Al-ʿĀmirī, Abū l-Ḥasan, *Kitāb al-Iʿlām bi-manāqib al-Islām*, ed. Aḥmad ʿAbd al-Ḥamīd Ghurāb (Cairo: Dār al-Kitāb al-ʿArabī lil-Ṭibāʿa wa-l-Nashr, 1967).

Amirsoleimani, Soheila, 'Of This World and the Next: Metaphors and Meanings in the *Qābūs-nāmah*', *Iranian Studies* 35 (2002), 1–22.

Amitai, Reuven, 'Armies and Their Economic Basis in Iran and the Surrounding Lands, *c*. 1000-1500', in *The New Cambridge History of Islam, Vol. III: The Eastern Islamic World, Eleventh to Eighteenth Centuries*, ed. David O. Morgan and Anthony Reid (Cambridge: Cambridge University Press, 2010), 539–60.

Al-Andalusī, Ṣāʿid b. Aḥmad, *Ṭabaqāt al-umam*, ed. Ḥusayn Muʾnis (Cairo: Dār al-Maʿārif, 1993).

Aneer, Gudmar, 'Kingship Ideology and Muslim Identity in the 11th Century as Reflected in the *Siyāsatnāma* by Niẓām al-Mulk and in the *Kutadgu Bilig* by Yūsuf Khāṣṣ Ḥājib', in *The Middle East Viewed from the North: Papers from the First Nordic Conference on Middle Eastern Studies, Uppsala 26–29 January 1989*, ed. Bo Utas and Knut S. Vikør (Bergen: Nordic Society for Middle Eastern Studies, 1992), 38–48.

Ansari, Hasan, *see* Anṣārī, Ḥasan

Anṣārī, Ḥasan, 'Yek andīsheh-nāmeh-yi siyāsī-yi arzeshmand-i muʿtazilī az Khurāsān dawrān-i Sāmāyīyān', *Bar-rasī-hā-yi tārīkhī* (http://ansari.kateban.com/entryprint1951.html).

Anthony, Sean W., 'Ibn Masʿūd, ʿAbdallāh', *EI Three*. First print edition: 2018. First published online: 2018.

Anton, Hans Hubert, *Fürstenspiegel und Herrscherethos in der Karolingerzeit* (Bonn: Ludwig Röhrscheid, 1967).

Arabatzis, George, 'Nicephoros Blemmydes's *Imperial Statue*: Aristotelian Politics as Kingship Morality in Byzantium', *Mediaevistik* 27 (2014), 99–118.

Arazi, A., 'al-Nābigha al-Dhubyānī', EI^2. First print edition: 1960–2007. First published online: 2012.

Arazi, A. and H. Ben-Shammay, 'Risāla', 1. 'In Arabic', EI^2. First print edition: 1960–2007. First published online: 2012.

Aristotle, *The Nicomachean Ethics*, trans. David Ross, revised with introduction and notes by Lesley Brown (Oxford: Oxford University Press, 2009).

Arjomand, Said Amir, 'Religion, Political Action and Legitimate Domination in Shiʿite Iran: Fourteenth to Eighteenth Centuries AD', *Archives européennes de sociologie* 20 (1979), 59–109.

Arkoun, M. 'L'éthique musulmane d'après Māwardī', in *Essais sur la pensée islamique*, third edition (Paris: Éditions Maisonneuve et Larose, 1984), 251–81.

Al-ʿAskarī, Abū Hilāl al-Ḥasan b. ʿAbdallāh, *Kitāb Jamharat al-amthāl*, ed. Aḥmad ʿAbd al-Salām and Abū Hājir Muḥammad Saʿīd b. Basyūnī Zaghlūl (Beirut: Dār al-Kutub al-ʿIlmiyya, 1988).

Askari, Nasrin, *The Medieval Reception of the* Shāhnāma *as a Mirror for Princes* (Leiden and Boston, MA: Brill, 2016).

Asmussen, J. P. 'Barlaam and Iosaph', *EIr* III (1988), 801. In *Encyclopaedia Iranica Online* © Trustees of Columbia University in the City of New York. First print edition: 1988. First published online: 2020.

Ašraf, A., 'Alqāb va ʿAnāwīn', *EIr* I (1989), 898–906. In *Encyclopaedia Iranica Online* © Trustees of Columbia University in the City of New York. First print edition: 1989. First published online: 2020.

Auer, Blain, 'Concepts of Justice and the Catalogue of Punishments under the Sultans of Delhi (7th-8th/13th-14th Centuries)', in *Public Violence in Islamic Societies: Power, Discipline, and the Construction of the Public Sphere, 7th to 19th Centuries CE*, ed. Christian Lange and Maribel Fierro (Edinburgh: Edinburgh University Press, 2009), 238–55.

Al-Azmeh, Aziz, *Muslim Kingship: Power and the Sacred in Muslim, Christian, and Pagan Polities* (London and New York: I. B. Tauris, 1997).

Al-Azmeh, Aziz, *Secularism in the Arab World: Contexts, Ideas and Consequences* (Edinburgh: Edinburgh University Press, 2019).

Al-Azmeh, Aziz, *Times of History: Universal Topics in Islamic Historiography* (Budapest and New York: Central European University Press, 2007).

Badavī, Amīn ʿAbd al-Majīd, *Baḥth dar-bāreh-yi Qābūsnāmeh* (Tehran: Ibn Sīnā, 1956).

Badawī, ʿAbd al-Raḥmān, *al-Uṣūl al-yūnāniyya lil-naẓariyyāt al-siyāsiyya fī l-Islām* (Cairo: Dār al-Kutub al-Miṣriyya, 1954).

Badawī, Amīn ʿAbd al-Majīd, 'Tamhīd', in Muḥammad Ṣādiq Nashʾat and Amīn ʿAbd al-Majīd Badawī, *Kitāb al-Naṣīḥa al-maʿrūf bi-sm Qābūsnāmeh* (Cairo: Maktabat al-Anjalū al-Miṣriyya, 1958), 3–44.

Al-Baghdādī, Aḥmad b. ʿAlī al-Khaṭīb, *Taʾrīkh Baghdād aw Madīnat al-Salām* (Beirut: Dār al-Kitāb al-ʿArabī, 1966).

Bagley, F. R. C., *Ghazālī's Book of Counsel for Kings* (London: Oxford University Press, 1964).

Bagley, F. R. C. , 'Introduction', in *Ghazālī's Book of Counsel for Kings* (London: Oxford University Press, 1964), ix–lxxiv.

Barrau, Julie, 'Ceci n'est pas un miroir, ou le *Policraticus* de Jean de Salisbury', in *Le Prince au miroir de la littérature politique de l'Antiquité aux Lumières*, ed. Frédérique Laghaud and Lydwine Scordia (Mont-Saint-Aignan: Universités de Rouen et du Havre, 2007), 87–111.

Bauden, Frédéric and Antonella Ghersetti, 'L'art de servir son monarque: Le *Kitāb Waṣāyā Aflāṭūn al-ḥakīm fī ḫidmat al-mulūk*: Édition critique et traduction précédées d'une introduction', *Arabica* 54 (2007), 295–316.

Bauden, Frédéric and Antonella Ghersetti, '"Comment servir le souverain". À propos d'un traité pseudo-platonicien inédit', *Quaderni di Studi Arabi* 20–21 (2002–3), 245–50.

Al-Bayhaqī, *Jāmiʿ shuʿab al-īmān*, ed. ʿAbd al-ʿAlī ʿAbd al-Ḥamīd Ḥāmid (Riyadh: Maktabat al-Rushd, 2003).

Al-Bayhaqī, Ibrāhīm b. Muḥammad, *al-Maḥāsin wa-l-masāwī* (Beirut: Dār Ṣādir, 1970).

Ben Azzouna, Nourane, *Aux origines du classicisme. Calligraphes et bibliophiles au temps des dynasties mongoles (Les Ilkhanides et les Djalayirides, 656–814/1258–1411)* (Leiden and Boston, MA: Brill, 2018).

Ben Shemesh, A., *Abū Yūsuf's Kitāb al-Kharāj, Taxation in Islām*, Vol. III (Leiden: E. J. Brill and London: Luzac, 1969).

Van Berkel, Maaike, 'Abbasid *Maẓālim* between Theory and Practice', *Bulletin d'études orientales* 63 (2014), 229–42.

Van Berkel, Maaike, 'The People of the Pen: Self-perceptions of Status and Role in the Administration of Empires and Polities', in *Prince, Pen, and Sword: Eurasian Perspectives*, ed. Maaike van Berkel and Jeroen Duindam (Leiden: Brill, 2018), 384–451.

Van Berkel, Maaike, 'Politics of Access at the Court of the Caliph', in *New Perspectives on Power and Political Representation from Ancient History to the Present Day: Repertoires of Representation*, ed. Harm Kaal and Daniëlle Slootjes (Leiden and Boston, MA: Brill, 2019), 26–36.

Berkey, Jonathan Porter, *The Formation of Islam: Religion and Society in the Near East, 600–1800* (New York: Cambridge University Press, 2003).

Berkey, Jonathan Porter, *The Transmission of Knowledge in Medieval Cairo: A Social History of Islamic Education* (Princeton, NJ: Princeton University Press, 1992).

Biran, Michal, 'True to Their Ways: Why the Qara Khitai Did Not Convert to Islam', in *Mongols, Turks, and Others: Eurasian Nomads and the Sedentary World*, ed. Reuven Amitai and Michal Biran (Leiden and Boston, MA: Brill, 2004), 175–99.

Birnbaum, Eleazar, *The 'Book of Advice' by King Kay-Kā'ūs ibn Iskander: The Earliest Old Ottoman Turkish Version of His Ḳābūsnāme* (Duxbury, MA: Tekin, 1981).

Bizzarri, Hugo O., 'Le *Secretum secretorum* en Espagne: de traité médical à miroir du prince', *Trajectoires européennes du* Secretum secretorum *du Pseudo-Aristote (XIIIe-XVIe siècle)*, ed. Catherine Gaullier-Bougassas, Margaret Bridges and Jean-Yves Tilliette (Turnhout: Brepols, 2015), 187–213.

De Blois, François, *Burzoy's Voyage to India and the Origin of the Book* Kalīlah wa Dimnah (London: Royal Asiatic Society, 1990).

De Blois, François, 'Ṣābi'', No. 7, *EI²*. First print edition: 1960–2007. First published online: 2012.

Blum, Wilhelm, *Byzantinische Fürstenspiegel: Agapetos, Theophylakt von Ochrid, Thomas Magister* (Stuttgart: Anton Hiersemann, 1981).

Bonebakker, S. A., 'al-Ḥātimī', *EI²*. First print edition: 1960–2007. First published online: 2012.

Bonner, Michael, 'The Waning of Empire, 861-945', in *The New Cambridge History of Islam, Vol. I: The Formation of the Islamic World: Sixth to Eleventh Centuries*, ed. Chase F. Robinson (Cambridge: Cambridge University Press, 2010), 305–59.

Bosworth, C. E., 'Āl-e Moḥtāj', *EIr* I (1984), 764–6. In *Encyclopaedia Iranica Online* © Trustees of Columbia University in the City of New York. First print edition: 1984. First published online: 2020.

Bosworth, C. E., 'Amīr', *EIr* I (1984), 956–8. In *Encyclopaedia Iranica Online* © Trustees of Columbia University in the City of New York. First print edition: 1989. First published online: 2020.

Bosworth, C. E., 'Bahā' al-Dawla wa-Ḍiyā' al-Milla, Abū Naṣr Fīrūz', *EI²*. First print edition: 1960–2007. First published online: 2012.

Bosworth, C. E., 'On the Chronology of the Ziyārids of Gurgān and Ṭabaristān', *Der Islam* 40 (1965), 25–34.

Bosworth, C. E., 'An Early Arabic Mirror for Princes: Ṭāhir Dhū l-Yamīnain's Epistle to His Son 'Abdallāh (206/821)', *Journal of Near Eastern Studies* 29 (1970), 25–41.

Bosworth, C. E., *The Ghaznavids: Their Empire in Afghanistan and Eastern Iran 994–1040* (Edinburgh: Edinburgh University Press, 1963).

Bosworth, C. E., *The History of the Saffarids of Sistan and the Maliks of Nimruz (247/861 to 949/1542–3)* (Costa Mesa, CA, and New York: Mazda, 1994).

Bosworth, C. E., *The History of al-Ṭabarī, Vol. 32: The Reunification of the 'Abbasid Caliphate* (Albany, NY: State University of New York Press, 1987), 110–28.

Bosworth, C. E., 'Ilek-khāns or Ḳarakhānids', *EI²*. First print edition: 1960–2007. First published online: 2012.

Bosworth, C. E., 'Kay Kā'ūs b. Iskandar', *EI²*. First print edition: 1960–2007. First published online: 2012.

Bosworth, C. E., *The Later Ghaznavids: Splendour and Decay: The Dynasty in Afghanistan and Northern India 1040–1186* (Edinburgh: Edinburgh University Press, 1977).

Bosworth, C. E., 'al-Muntaṣir', *EI²*. First print edition: 1960–2007. First published online: 2012.

Bosworth, C. E., 'al-Mustakfī', *EI²*. First print edition: 1960–2007. First published online: 2012.

Bosworth, C. E., 'al-Mu'tazz', *EI²*. First print edition: 1960–2007. First published online: 2012.

Bosworth, C. E., 'Naṣīḥat al-mulūk', *EI²*. First print edition: 1960–2007. First published online: 2012.

Bosworth, C. E., 'The Political and Dynastic History of the Iranian World (A.D. 1000–1217)', in *The Cambridge History of Iran, Vol. V: The Saljuq and Mongol Periods*, ed. J. A. Boyle (Cambridge: Cambridge University Press, 1968), 1–202.

Bosworth, C. E., 'Wahb', *EI²*. First print edition: 1960–2007. First published online: 2012.

Bosworth, C. E., 'Yabghu', *EI²*. First print edition: 1960–2007. First published online: 2012.

Bosworth, C. E., 'Yaḥyā b. Aktham', *EI²*. First print edition: 1960–2007. First published online: 2012.

Bosworth, C. E., 'Zarang', *EI²*. First print edition: 1960–2007. First published online: 2012.

Bosworth, Edmund, 'The Steppe Peoples in the Islamic World', in *The New Cambridge History of Islam, Vol. III: The Eastern Islamic World, Eleventh to*

Eighteenth Centuries, ed. David O. Morgan and Anthony Reid (Cambridge: Cambridge University Press, 2010), 21–77.

Boutaleb, Hassan, *Le miroir du prince et le conseil aux rois (Kitâb al-tibr al-masbûk fî nasîhat al-mulûk)* (Beirut: Dar Albouraq, 2014).

Bowen, H., 'Mu'nis al-Muẓaffar', *EI*². First print edition: 1960–2007. First published online: 2012.

Bowen, H., 'Nāṣir al-Dawla', *EI*². First print edition: 1960–2007. First published online: 2012.

Boyce, Mary, *The Letter of Tansar* (Rome: Istituto Italiano per il Medio ed Estremo Oriente, 1968).

Bradley, Sister Ritamary, 'Backgrounds of the Title *Speculum* in Mediaeval Literature', *Speculum* 29 (1954), 100–15.

Bray, Julia, 'Ibn al-Muʿtazz and Politics: The Question of the *Fuṣūl Qiṣār*', *Oriens* 38 (2010), 107–43.

Bray, Julia, 'Al-Muʿtaṣim's "Bridge of Toil" and Abū Tammām's Amorium *qaṣīda*', in *Studies in Islamic and Middle Eastern Texts and Traditions in Memory of Norman Calder*, ed. G. R. Hawting, J. A. Mojaddedi and A. Samely (Oxford: Oxford University Press, 2000), 31–73.

Bray, Julia, 'Al-Thaʿalibi's *Adab al-muluk*, a Local Mirror for Princes', in *Living Islamic History: Studies in Honour of Professor Carole Hillenbrand*, ed. Yasir Suleiman (Edinburgh: Edinburgh University Press, 2010), 32–46.

Brett, Michael, 'Egypt', in *The New Cambridge History of Islam, Vol. I: The Formation of the Islamic World: Sixth to Eleventh Centuries*, ed. Chase F. Robinson (Cambridge: Cambridge University Press, 2010), 541–80.

De Bruijn, J. T. P., 'Kaykāvus b. Eskandar', *EIr* XVI, 180–2. In *Encyclopaedia Iranica Online* © Trustees of Columbia University in the City of New York. First published online: 2020.

Al-Buḥturī, Abū ʿUbayda, *Dīwān*, ed. Ḥasan Kāmil al-Ṣayrafī (Cairo: Dār al-Maʿārif, 1963–4).

Al-Bukhārī, Muḥammad b. Ismāʿīl, *Ṣaḥīḥ al-Bukhārī maʿa Kashf al-mushkil lil-Imām Ibn al-Jawzī*, ed. Muṣṭafā al-Dhahabī (Cairo: Dār al-Ḥadīth, 2000).

Bulliet, Richard W., 'Conversion to Islam and the Emergence of a Muslim Society in Iran', in *Conversion to Islam*, ed. Nehemia Levtzion (New York and London: Holmes and Meier, 1979), 29–51.

Bulliet, Richard W., *Islam: The View from the Edge* (New York: Columbia University Press, 1994).

Bulliet, Richard W., 'Local Politics in Eastern Iran under the Ghaznavids and Seljuks', *Iranian Studies* 11 (1978), 35–56.

Bulliet, Richard W., *The Patricians of Nishapur: A Study in Medieval Islamic Social History* (Cambridge, MA: Harvard University Press, 1972).

Busse, Heribert, *Chalif und Grosskönig. Die Buyiden im Iraq (945–1055)* (Beirut: In Kommission bei Franz Steiner Verlag, Wiesbaden, 1969).

Cahen, Claude, 'L'évolution de l'iqtâʿ du IXe au XIIIe siècle. Contribution à une histoire comparée des sociétés médiévales', *Annales. Histoire, Sciences Sociales*, 8ᵉ Année, 1 (1953), 25–52.

Campanini, Massimo, 'In Defence of Sunnism: al-Ghazālī and the Seljuqs', in *The Seljuqs: Politics, Society and Culture*, ed. Christian Lange and Songül Mecit (Edinburgh: Edinburgh University Press, 2011), 228–39.

Canard, M., 'Ḥamdānids', *EI²*. First print edition: 1960–2007. First published online: 2012.

Chabbi, J. and N. Rabbat, 'Ribāṭ', *EI²*. First print edition: 1960–2007. First published online: 2012.

Chamberlain, Michael, *Knowledge and Social Practice in Medieval Damascus, 1190–1350* (Cambridge: Cambridge University Press, 1994).

Chamberlain, Michael, 'Military Patronage States and the Political Economy of the Frontier, 1000-1250', in *A Companion to the History of the Middle East*, ed. Y. M. Choueiri (Malden, MA: Blackwell, 2005), 135–53.

Chaumont, Eric, 'Ambiguity', *EI Three*. First print edition: 2013. First published online: 2013.

Cheikh-Moussa, Abdallah, 'De la "communauté de salut" à la "populace": La représentation du "peuple" dans quatre *Miroirs arabes des Princes* (VIIIe-XIIIe s.)', in *Les non-dits du nom. Onomastiques et documents en terres d'Islam. Mélanges offerts à Jacqueline Sublet*, ed. Christian Müller and Muriel Roiland-Rouabah (Beirut: Presses d'Ifpo, 2014), 497–524.

Cheikh-Moussa, Abdallah, 'Du discours autorisé ou comment s'adresser au tyran?', *Arabica* 46 (1999), 139–75.

Chraïbi, Aboubakr, 'L'homme qui ne travaille qu'un seul jour par semaine', *Oriente Moderno*, Nuova Serie 89/2 (2009), 287–304.

Chraïbi, Aboubakr, 'Île flottante et oeuf de *ruḫḫ*', *Quaderno di Studi Arabi*, Nuova Serie 3 (2008), 83–95.

Conrad, Lawrence I., 'The Arab-Islamic Medical Tradition', in *The Western Medical Tradition 800 BC to AD 1800*, ed. Lawrence I. Conrad, Michael Neve, Vivian Nutton, Roy Porter and Andrew Wear (Cambridge: Cambridge University Press, 1995), 93–138.

Cook, Michael, *Commanding Right and Forbidding Wrong in Islamic Thought* (Cambridge: Cambridge University Press, 2000).

Cooperson, Michael, 'Abd Allah Ibn al-Muqaffa', in *Dictionary of Literary Biography, Vol. 311: Arabic Literary Culture, 500–925*, ed. Michael Cooperson and Shawkat M. Toorawa (Detroit: Thomson Gale, 2005), 150–63.

Cooperson, Michael, *Classical Arabic Biography: The Heirs of the Prophets in the Age of al-Ma'mūn* (Cambridge: Cambridge University Press, 2000).

Cottrell, Emily, 'An Early Mirror for Princes and Manual for Secretaries: The Epistolary Novel of Aristotle and Alexander', in *Alexander the Great and the East: History, Art, Tradition*, ed. Krzysztof Nawotka and Agnieszka Wojciechowska (Wiesbaden: Harrassowitz Verlag, 2016), 303–28.

Coulon, Jean-Charles, 'Magie et politique: événements historiques et pensée politique dans le *Šams al-ma'ārif* attribué à al-Būnī (mort en 622/1225)', *Arabica* 64 (2017), 442–86.

Cristoforetti, Simone, 'Mehragān', in *Encyclopaedia Iranica Online* © Trustees of Columbia University in the City of New York. First published online: 2020.

Crone, Patricia, 'Did al-Ghazālī Write a Mirror for Princes? On the Authorship of *Naṣīḥat al-mulūk*', *Jerusalem Studies in Arabic and Islam* 10 (1987), 167–91.

Crone, Patricia, '"Even an Ethiopian Slave": The Transformation of a Sunnī Tradition', *Bulletin of the School of Oriental and African Studies* 57 (1994), 59–67.

Crone, Patricia, *Medieval Islamic Political Thought* (Edinburgh: Edinburgh University Press, 2004).

Crone, Patricia, 'al-Muhallab b. Abī Ṣufra', *EI²*. First print edition: 1960–2007. First published online: 2012.

Crone, Patricia, *The Nativist Prophets of Early Islamic Iran: Rural Revolt and Local Zoroastrianism* (Cambridge: Cambridge University Press, 2012).

Crone, Patricia, *Slaves on Horses: The Evolution of the Islamic Polity* (Cambridge: Cambridge University Press, 1980).

Crone, Patricia and Martin Hinds, *God's Caliph: Religious Authority in the First Centuries of Islam* (Cambridge: Cambridge University Press, 1986).

Crone, Patricia and Luke Treadwell, 'A New Text on Ismailism at the Samanid Court', in *Texts, Documents and Artefacts: Islamic Studies in Honour of D. S. Richards*, ed. C. F. Robinson (Leiden and Boston, MA: Brill, 2003), 37–67.

Dadoyan, Seta B., 'Badr al-Jamālī', *EI Three*. First print edition: 2010. First published online: 2010.

Daftary, Farhad, *The Ismāʿīlīs: Their History and Doctrines*, second edition (Cambridge: Cambridge University Press, 2007; first published 1990).

Dahlén, Ashk P., 'Kingship and Religion in a Mediaeval *Fürstenspiegel*: The Case of the *Chahār Maqāla* of Niẓāmī ʿArūẓī', *Orientalia Suecana* LVIII (2009), 9–24.

Daiber, Hans, 'Das *Kitāb al-Ādāb al-kabīr* des Ibn al-Muqaffaʿ als Ausdruck griechischer Ethik, islamischer Ideologie und iranisch-sassanidischer Hofetikette', *Oriens* 43 (2015), 273–92.

Dakhlia, Jocelyne, 'Les miroirs des princes islamiques: une modernité sourde?', *Annales: Histoire, Sciences Sociales*, 57ᵉ année, 5 (2002), 1191–1206.

Damaj, Muḥammad Aḥmad, 'al-Muqaddima', in Abū Ḥāmid al-Ghazālī, *al-Tibr al-masbūk fī naṣīḥat al-mulūk*, ed. Muḥammad Aḥmad Damaj (Beirut: Muʾassasat ʿIzz al-Dīn lil-Ṭibāʿa wa-l-Nashr, 1996), 7–71.

Daniel, Elton L., 'The Islamic East', in *The New Cambridge History of Islam, Vol. I: The Formation of the Islamic World: Sixth to Eleventh Centuries*, ed. Chase F. Robinson (Cambridge: Cambridge University Press, 2010), 448–505.

Dānishpazhūh, M. T., 'Chand athar-i fārsī dar akhlāq', *Farhang-i Īrān-Zamīn* 19 (1973), 261–84.

Dānishpazhūh, M. T., *Tuḥfeh (dar akhlāq va-siyāsat)* (Tehran: Bungāh-i Tarjumeh va-Nashr-i Kitāb, 1962).

Dankoff, Robert, *Wisdom of Royal Glory (Kutadgu bilig): A Turko-Islamic Mirror for Princes* (Chicago, IL: Chicago University Press, 1983).

Al-Dārimī, ʿAbdallāh b. ʿAbd al-Raḥmān, *Musnad al-Dārimī al-maʿrūf bi-Sunan al-Dārimī* (Beirut: Dār Ibn Ḥazm, 2002).

Darke, H. S. G., *The Book of Government or Rules for Kings* (London: Routledge and Kegan Paul, 1960; revised edition, 1978).

Darling, Linda T., 'Circle of Justice', *EI Three*. First print edition: 2012. First published online: 2012.

Darling, Linda T., *A History of Social Justice and Political Power in the Middle East: The Circle of Justice from Mesopotamia to Globalization* (London and New York: Routledge, 2013).

Darling, Linda T., 'Mirrors for Princes in Europe and the Middle East: A Case of Historiographical Incommensurability', in *East Meets West in the Middle Ages and Early Modern Times: Transcultural Experiences in the Premodern World*, ed. Albrecht Classen (Berlin and Boston, MA: Walter de Gruyter, 2013), 223–42.

Darling, Linda T., '"The Vicegerent of God, from Him We Expect Rain": The Incorporation of the Pre-Islamic State in Early Islamic Political Culture', *Journal of the American Oriental Society* 134 (2014), 407–29.

Daryaee, Touraj, *Sasanian Persia: The Rise and Fall of an Empire* (London: I.B. Tauris, 2009).

Al-Dhahabī, Muḥammad b. Aḥmad, *Siyar aʿlām al-nubalāʾ*, ed. Shuʿayb al-Arnaʾūṭ (Beirut: Muʾassasat al-Risāla, 2001).

Al-Dhahabī, Muḥammad b. Aḥmad, *Taʾrīkh al-Islām wa-wafayāt al-mashāhīr wa-l-aʿlām*, ed. Bashshār ʿAwwād Maʿrūf (Beirut: Dār al-Gharb al-Islāmī, 2003).

Dietrich, A., 'al-Ḥadjdjādj b. Yūsuf', *EI²*. First print edition: 1960–2007. First published online: 2012.

Diez, Heinrich Friedrich von, *Buch des Kabus, oder, Lehren des persischen Königs Kjekjawus für seinen Sohn Ghilan Schach: ein Werk für alle Zeitalter aus dem Türkisch-Persisch-Arabischen übersetzt und durch Abhandlungen und Anmerkungen erläutert* (Berlin: In Commission der Nicolaischen Buchhandlung, 1811).

Donner, F. M., 'Maymūn b. Mihrān', *EI²*. First print edition: 1960–2007. First published online: 2012.

Donohue, John J., *The Buwayhid Dynasty in Iraq 334 H./945 to 403 H./1012* (Leiden and Boston, MA: Brill, 2003).

Doufikar-Aerts, Faustina, *Alexander Magnus Arabicus. A Survey of the Alexander Tradition through Seven Centuries: from Pseudo-Callisthenes to Ṣūrī*, trans. from the Dutch by Ania Lentz-Michaelis (Paris, Leuven and Walpole, MA: Peeters, 2010).

Drory, Rina, 'The Abbasid Construction of the Jahiliyya: Cultural Authority in the Making', *Studia Islamica* 83 (1996), 33–49.

Durand-Guédy, David, 'An Emblematic Family of Seljuq Iran: The Khujandīs of Isfahan', in *The Seljuqs: Politics, Society and Culture*, ed. Christian Lange and Songül Mecit (Edinburgh: Edinburgh University Press, 2011), 182–202.

Durand-Guédy, David, *Iranian Elites and Turkish Rulers: A History of Iṣfahān in the Saljūq Period* (London and New York: Routledge, 2010).

Durand-Guédy, David, 'Location of Rule in a Context of Turko-Mongol Domination', in *Turko-Mongol Rulers, Cities and City Life*, ed. David Durand-Guédy (Leiden: Brill, 2014), 1–20.

Durand-Guédy, David, 'New Trends in the Political History of Iran under the Great Saljuqs (11th–12th Centuries)', *History Compass* 13 (2015), 321–37.

Durand-Guédy, David, 'Ruling from the Outside: A New Perspective on Early Turkish Kingship in Iran', *in Every Inch a King: Comparative Studies in Kings and Kingship in the Ancient and Mediaeval Worlds*, ed. L. Mitchell and Charles Melville (Leiden: Brill, 2012), 325–42.

Durand-Guédy, David, 'Where Did the Saljūqs Live? A Case Study Based on the Reign of Sultan Mas'ūd b. Muḥammad (1134–1152)', *Studia Iranica* 40 (2011), 211–58.

Dvornik, Francis, *Early Christian and Byzantine Political Philosophy: Origins and Background*, 2 vols. (Washington, DC: The Dumbarton Oaks Center for Byzantine Studies, 1966).

Eberhardt, Otto, *Via Regia. Der Fürstenspiegel Smaragds von St. Mihiel und seine literarische Gattung* (Munich: Wilhelm Fink Verlag, 1977).

Ed. and J. Burton-Page, 'Nithār', *EI²*. First print edition: 1960–2007. First published online: 2012.

EIr, 'Gift Giving', (i) Introduction. In *Encyclopaedia Iranica Online* © Trustees of Columbia University in the City of New York. First print edition: 2016. First published online: 2020.

El-Azhari, Tael, *Queens, Eunuchs and Concubines in Islamic History, 661–1257* (Edinburgh: Edinburgh University Press, 2019).

El-Hibri, Tayeb, *Parable and Politics in Early Islamic History: The Rashidun Caliphs* (New York: Columbia University Press, 2010).

El Tayib, Abdulla, 'Pre-Islamic Poetry', in *Arabic Literature to the End of the Umayyad Period*, ed. A. F. L. Beeston, T. M. Johnstone, R. B. Serjeant and G. R. Smith, The Cambridge History of Arabic Literature (Cambridge: Cambridge University Press, 1983), 27–113.

Enderwitz, S., 'Adab (b) and Islamic Scholarship in the 'Abbāsid Period', *EI Three*. First print edition: 2013. First published online: 2013.

Ephrat, Daphna, *A Learned Society in a Period of Transition: The Sunni "Ulama" of Eleventh-Century Baghdad* (Albany, NY: State University of New York Press, 2000).

Ephrat, Daphna, 'The Seljuqs and the Public Sphere in the Period of Sunni Revivalism: The View from Baghdad', in *The Seljuqs: Politics, Society and Culture*, ed. Christian Lange and Songül Mecit (Edinburgh: Edinburgh University Press, 2011), 139–56.

Falkowski, Wojciech, 'The Carolingian *Speculum Principis*: The Birth of a Genre', *Acta Poloniae Historica* 98 (2008), 5–27.

Al-Fārābī, Abū Naṣr Muḥammad, *Fuṣūl al-madanī: Aphorisms of the Statesman*, ed. and trans. D. M. Dunlop (Cambridge: Cambridge University Press, 1961).

Al-Fārābī, Abū Naṣr Muḥammad, *Mabādi' ārā' ahl al-madīna al-fāḍila, see* Walzer, *Al-Farabi on the Perfect State*

De Felipe, Helena, 'Berber Leadership and Genealogical Legitimacy: The Almoravid Case', in *Genealogy and Knowledge in Muslim Societies: Understanding the Past*, ed. Sarah Bowen Savant and Helena de Felipe (Edinburgh: Edinburgh University Press, 2014), 55–69.

Ferguson, Heather L., *The Proper Order of Things: Language, Power, and Law in Ottoman Administrative Discourses* (Stanford, CA: Stanford University Press, 2018).

Ferster, Judith, *Fictions of Advice: The Literature and Politics of Counsel in Late Medieval England* (Philadelphia, PA: University of Pennsylvania Press, 1996).

Fierro, Maribel, *Abū Bakr al-Ṭurṭūšī (m. 520/1126): Kitāb al-Ḥawādith wa-l-Bidaʿ (El Libro de las novedades y las innovaciones)* (Madrid: Consejo Superior de Investigaciones Científicas, Instituto de Cooperación con el Mundo Árabe, 1993).

Fierro, Maribel, 'Al-Ṭurṭūshī', in *Christian-Muslim Relations: A Bibliographical History*, Vol. III (1050–1200), ed. David Thomas and Alex Mallett with Juan Pedro Monferrer Sala, Johannes Pahlitzsch, Mark Swanson, Herman Teule and John Tolan (Leiden and Boston, MA: Brill, 2011), 387–96.

Figueiras, Jesús Pensado, 'La traduction castillane de l'*Epistola Aristotelis ad Alexandrum de dieta servanda* de Jean de Séville', in *Trajectoires européennes du* Secretum secretorum *du Pseudo-Aristote (XIIIe-XVIe siècle)*, ed. Catherine Gaullier-Bougassas, Margaret Bridges and Jean-Yves Tilliette (Turnhout: Brepols, 2015), 215–42.

Figueroa, Manuel Ruiz, 'Algunos aspectos del pensamiento político de Al-Ghazālī sobre el gobierno islámico', *Estudios de Asia y Africa* 12/2 (34) (1977), 169–85.

Fleischer, Cornell H., *Bureaucrat and Intellectual in the Ottoman Empire: The Historian Mustafa Âli (1541–1600)* (Princeton, NJ: Princeton University Press, 1986).

Fletcher, Madeleine, 'Ibn Tūmart's Teachers: The Relationship with al-Ghazālī', *al-Qantara* 18 (1997), 305–30.

Floor, Willem, 'Kadkodā', *EIr* XV (2009), 328–31. In *Encyclopaedia Iranica Online* © Trustees of Columbia University in the City of New York. First print edition: 2009. First published online: 2020.

Forster, Regula, 'Buddha in Disguise: Problems in the Transmission of "Barlaam and Josaphat"', in *Acteurs des transferts culturels en Méditerranée médiévale*, ed. Rania Abdellatif, Yassir Benhima, Daniel König and Elisabeth Ruchaud (Munich: Oldenbourg Verlag, 2012), 180–91.

Forster, Regula, *Das Geheimnis der Geheimnisse. Die arabischen und deutschen Fassungen des pseudo-aristotelischen* Sirr al-asrār/Secretum secretorum (Wiesbaden: Reichert Verlag, 2006).

De Fouchécour, Charles-Henri, 'Ḥadāyeq al-siyar, un Miroir des Princes de la cour de Qonya au VIIe-XIIIe siècle', *Studia Iranica* 1 (1972), 219–28.

De Fouchécour, Charles-Henri, *Moralia. Les notions morales dans la littérature persane du 3ᵉ/9ᵉ au 7ᵉ/13ᵉ siècle* (Paris: Editions Recherche sur les civilisations, 1986).

Fouracre, Paul, 'Conflict, Power and Legitimation in Francia in the Late Seventh and Eighth Centuries', in *Building Legitimacy: Political Discourses and Forms of Legitimacy in Medieval Societies*, ed. Isabel Alfonso, Hugh Kennedy and Julio Escalona (Leiden and Boston, MA: Brill, 2004), 3–26.

Garden, Kenneth. *The First Islamic Reviver: Abū Ḥāmid al-Ghazālī and His Revival of the Religious Sciences* (Oxford and New York: Oxford University Press, 2014).

Gardīzī, ʿAbd al-Ḥayy, *Zayn al-akhbār*, ed. Raḥīm Riżā-Zādeh Malik (Tehran: Anjuman-i Āthār va-Mafākhir-i Farhangī, 2005) = C. Edmund Bosworth, *The Ornament of Histories: A History of the Eastern Islamic Lands AD 650–1041: The Original Text of Abū Saʿīd ʿAbd al-Ḥayy Gardīzī* (London: I.B. Tauris, 2011).

Van Gelder, Geert Jan, 'Apology', *EI Three*. First print edition: 2007. First published online: 2007.

Van Gelder, Geert Jan, *Classical Arabic Literature: A Library of Arabic Literature Anthology* (New York: New York University Press, 2013).

Van Gelder, Geert Jan, 'Mirror for Princes or Vizor for Viziers: The Twelfth-Century Arabic Popular Encyclopedia *Mufīd al-ʿulūm* and Its Relationship with the Anonymous Persian *Baḥr al-fawāʾid*', *Bulletin of the School of Oriental and African Studies* 64 (2001), 313–38.

Al-Ghazālī, Abū Ḥāmid Muḥammad, *Faḍāʾiḥ al-bāṭiniyya* (= *Kitāb al-Mustaẓhirī*), ed. ʿAbd al-Raḥmān Badawī (Cairo: al-Dār al-Qawmiyya lil-Ṭibāʿa wa-l-Nashr, 1964).

[Al-]Ghazālī, Abū Ḥāmid Muḥammad, *Naṣīḥat al-mulūk*, ed. Jalāl al-Dīn Humāʾī (Tehran: Kitābkhāneh-yi Millī, 1972) = F. R. C. Bagley, *Ghazālī's Book of Counsel for Kings* (London: Oxford University Press, 1964).

Al-Ghazālī, Abū Ḥāmid Muḥammad, *al-Tibr al-masbūk fī naṣīḥat al-mulūk*, ed. Muḥammad Aḥmad Damaj (Beirut: Muʾassasat ʿIzz al-Dīn lil-Ṭibāʿa wa-l-Nashr, 1996).

'Gift Giving', *EIr*, Josef Wiesehöfer, Rudi P. Matthee and Willem Floor, 'Gift Giving', *EIr* X (2016), 604–17. In *Encyclopaedia Iranica Online* © Trustees of Columbia University in the City of New York. First print edition: 2016. First published online: 2020.

Gilbert, Claire M., *In Good Faith: Arabic Translation and Translators in Early Modern Spain* (Philadelphia, PA: University of Pennsylvania Press, 2020).

Gilliot, Claude, '*In consilium tuum deduces me*: Le genre du "conseil", *naṣīḥa, waṣiyya* dans la littérature arabo-musulmane', *Arabica* 54 (2007), 466–99.

Gilliot, Claude, '`Ulamāʾ', I: 'In the Arab World', *EI²*. First print edition: 1960–2007. First published online: 2012.

Gleave, Robert, 'Jaʿfar al-Ṣādeq', (i) 'Life', *EIr* XIV (2008), 349–51. In *Encyclopaedia Iranica Online* © Trustees of Columbia University in the City of New York. First print edition: 2008. First published online: 2020.

Gleave, Robert, 'Jaʿfar al-Ṣādeq', (ii) 'Teachings', *EIr* XIV (2008), 351–6. In *Encyclopaedia Iranica Online* © Trustees of Columbia University in the City of New York. First print edition: 2008. First published online: 2020.

Gnoli, Gherardo, 'Farr(ah)', *EIr* IX (1999), 312–19. In *Encyclopaedia Iranica Online* © Trustees of Columbia University in the City of New York. First print edition: 1999. First published online: 2020.

Goethe, Johann Wolfgang von, *Goethes Westöstlicher Divan mit den Auszügen aus dem Buch des Kabus*, ed. Karl Simrock (Heilbronn: Henninger, 1875).

Golden, Peter B., 'Turks and Iranians: An Historical Sketch', in *Turkic-Iranian Contact Areas: Historical and Linguistic Aspects*, ed. Lars Johanson and Christiane Bulut with the editorial assistance of Sevgi Ağcagül and Vanessa Karam (Wiesbaden: Harrassowitz Verlag, 2006), 17–38.

Goldziher, Ignaz, *Streitschrift des Ġazālī gegen die Bāṭinijja-Sekte* (Leiden: E. J. Brill, 1916).

Gonzalez, Valerie, 'Sheba', *EQ* IV (2004), 585–7.

Gordon, Matthew S., *The Breaking of a Thousand Swords: A History of the Turkish Military of Samarra (A. H 200–275/815–889 C. E.)* (Albany, NY: State University of New York Press, 2001).

Gordon, Matthew S., 'Bughā al-Kabīr', *EI Three*. First print edition: 2010. First published online: 2010.

Gordon, Matthew S., 'Bughā al-Ṣaghīr', *EI Three*. First print edition: 2010. First published online: 2010.

Gordon, Matthew S., 'The Turkish Officers of Samarra: Revenue and the Exercise of Authority', *Journal of the Economic and Social History of the Orient* 42 (1999), 466–93.

Gottheil, Richard, 'A Supposed Work of al-Ghazālī', *Journal of the American Oriental Society* 43 (1923), 85–91.

Grenet, Frantz, *La geste d'Ardashir fils de Pâbag. Kārnāmag ī Ardaxšēr ī Pābagān*, traduit du pehlevi par Frantz Grenet (Die: Éditions A Die, 2003).

Griffel, Frank, *Al-Ghazālī's Philosophical Theology* (Oxford and New York: Oxford University Press, 2009).

Grignaschi, Mario, 'La diffusion du "Secretum secretorum" (*Sirr-al-ʾasrār*) dans l'Europe occidentale', *Archives d'histoire doctrinale et littéraire du Moyen Âge* 47 (1980), 7–70.

Grignaschi, Mario, 'L'origine et les métamorphoses du *Sirr al'asrār*', *Archives d'histoire doctrinale et littéraire du Moyen Âge* 43 (1976), 7–112.

Grignaschi, Mario, 'Les "Rasāʾil ʾArisṭāṭālīsa ʾilā-l-Iskandar" de Sālim Abū-l-ʿAlāʾ et l'activité culturelle à l'époque omayyade', *Bulletin d'études orientales* 19 (1967), 7–83.

Grignaschi, Mario, 'Remarques sur la formation et l'interprétation du *Sirr al-ʾasrār*', in *Pseudo-Aristotle,* The Secret of Secrets*: Sources and Influences*, ed. W. F. Ryan and Charles B. Schmitt (London: The Warburg Institute, 1982), 3–33.

Grignaschi, Mario, 'Le roman épistolaire classique conservé dans la version arabe de Sālim Abū 'l-ʿAlāʾ', *Le Muséon* 80 (1967), 211–54.

Grignaschi, Mario, 'La "Siyâsatu-l-ʿâmmiyya" et l'influence iranienne sur la pensée politique islamique', *Acta Iranica* VI, Deuxième Série, *Hommages et Opera Minora, Vol. III: Monumentum H. S. Nyberg* (Leiden: E. J. Brill, 1975), 33–286.

Gruber, Christiane, 'al-Burāq', *EI Three*. First print edition: 2012. First published online: 2012.

Gutas, Dimitri, 'Classical Arabic Wisdom Literature: Nature and Scope', *Journal of the American Oriental Society* 101 (1981), 49–86.

Gutas, Dimitri, *Greek Thought, Arabic Culture: The Graeco-Arabic Translation Movement in Baghdad and Early ʿAbbasid Society (Second/Fourth–Eighth/Tenth Centuries)* (London and New York: Routledge, 1998).

Gutas, Dimitri, *Greek Wisdom Literature in Arabic Translation: A Study of the Graeco-Arabic Gnomologia* (New Haven, CT: American Oriental Society, 1975).

Gutas, Dimitri, 'The Spurious and the Authentic in the Arabic Lives of Aristotle', in *Pseudo-Aristotle in the Middle Ages: The* Theology *and Other Texts*, ed. Jill Kraye, W. F. Ryan and C. B. Schmitt (London: Warburg Institute, 1986), 15–36.

Haarmann, Ulrich, 'The Library of a Fourteenth-Century Jerusalem Scholar', *Der Islam* 61 (1984), 327–33.

Hachmeier, Klaus, 'Bahāʾ al-Dawla', *EI Three*. First print edition: 2015. First published online: 2015.

Hadot, Pierre, 'Fürstenspiegel', *Reallexikon für Antike und Christentum* VIII (1972), 555–631.

Ḥājjī Khalīfa, Muṣṭafā b. ʿAbdallāh Kātib Chalabī, *Kitāb Kashf al-ẓunūn ʿan asāmī al-kutub wa-l-funūn*, ed. Muḥammad Sharaf al-Dīn Yāltaqāyā and Rifʿat Bīlgah al-Kilīsī = *Keşf-el-zunun*, ed. Şerefettin Yaltkaya and Kilisli Rifat Bilge (Istanbul: Wakālat al-Maʿārif = Maarif Matbaası, 1941–3).

Halm, Heinz, 'Fatimids', *EI Three*. First print edition: 2014. First published online: 2014.

Halm, Heinz, 'Ḡolāt', *EIr* XI (2001), 62–4. In *Encyclopaedia Iranica Online* © Trustees of Columbia University in the City of New York. First print edition: 2001. First published online: 2020.

Hamadhānī, Mīr Sayyid ʿAlī, *Dhakhīrat al-mulūk*, ed. Sayyid Maḥmūd Anvārī (Tabriz: Muʾassaseh-yi Tārīkh va-Farhang-i Īrān, 1979).

Al-Hamadhānī, Muḥammad b. ʿAbd al-Malik, *Takmilat Taʾrīkh al-Ṭabarī*, in *Dhuyūl Taʾrīkh al-Ṭabarī*, ed. Muḥammad Abū l-Faḍl Ibrāhīm (Cairo: Dār al-Maʿārif, 1977).

Hämeen-Anttila, Jaakko, 'Adab (a) Arabic, Early Developments', *EI Three*. First print edition: 2014. First published online: 2014.

Hämeen-Anttila, Jaakko, 'Jesus and His Disciples in Islamic Texts', in *Christsein in der islamischen Welt. Festschrift für Martin Tamcke zum 60. Geburtstag*, ed. Sidney H. Griffith and Sven Grebenstein (Wiesbaden: Harrassowitz Verlag, 2015), 107–22.

Hamori, Andras, 'Prudence, Virtue and Self-respect in Ibn al-Muqaffaʿ', in *Reflections on Reflections: Near Eastern Writers Reading Literature: Dedicated to Renate Jacobi*, ed. Angelika Neuwirth and Andreas Christian Islebe (Wiesbaden: Reichert Verlag, 2006), 161–79.

Hanne, Eric J., *Putting the Caliph in His Place: Power, Authority, and the Late Abbasid Caliphate* (Madison, NJ: Fairleigh Dickinson University Press, 2010).

Harmsen, Nils, *Die Wasiya als literarisches Genre bis ins 14. Jahrhundert*. Magisterarbeit an der Universität Hamburg, Fachbereich Orientalistik, Oktober 1979 Angabe (Hamburg: Diplomarbeiten Agentur, 1999).

Hartung, Jan-Peter, 'Enacting the Rule of Islam: On Courtly Patronage of Religious Scholars in Pre- and Early Modern Times', in *Court Cultures in the Muslim World: Seventh to Nineteenth Centuries*, ed. Albrecht Fuess and Jan-Peter Hartung (London and New York: Routledge, 2011), 295–325.

Hasson, I., 'Ziyād b. Abīhi', *EI*[2]. First print edition: 1960–2007. First published online: 2012.

Havelmann, Axel, 'The Vizier and the Raʾīs in Saljuq Syria: The Struggle for Urban Self-representation', *International Journal of Middle East Studies* 21 (1989), 233–42.

Heck, Paul L., 'The Crisis of Knowledge in Islam (I): The Case of al-ʿĀmirī', *Philosophy East and West* 56 (2006), 106–35.

Heck, Paul L., '*Jihad* Revisited', *Journal of Religious Ethics* 32 (2004), 95–128.

Heidemann, Stefan, 'Numismatics', in *The New Cambridge History of Islam, Vol. I: The Formation of the Islamic World: Sixth to Eleventh Centuries*, ed. Chase F. Robinson (Cambridge: Cambridge University Press, 2010), 648–63.

Hellerstedt, Andreas, 'Cracks in the Mirror: Changing Conceptions of Political Virtue in Mirrors for Princes in Scandinavia from the Middle Ages to c. 1700', in *Virtue Ethics and Education from Late Antiquity to the Eighteenth Century*, ed. Andreas Hellerstedt (Amsterdam: Amsterdam University Press, 2018), 281–328.

Hillenbrand, Carole, 'Aspects of the Court of the Great Seljuqs', in *The Seljuqs: Politics, Society and Culture*, ed. Christian Lange and Songül Mecit (Edinburgh: Edinburgh University Press, 2011), 22–38.

Hillenbrand, Carole, 'Islamic Orthodoxy or Realpolitik? Al-Ghazālī's Views on Government', *Iran* 26 (1988), 81–94.

Hillenbrand, Carole, 'A Little-Known Mirror for Princes by al-Ghazālī', in *Words, Texts and Concepts Cruising the Mediterranean Sea: Studies on the Sources, Contents and Influences of Islamic Civilization and Arabic Philosophy and Science, Dedicated to Gerhard Endress on His Sixty-Fifth Birthday*, ed. R. Arnzen and J. Thielmann (Leuven: Peeters, 2004), 593–601.

Hillenbrand, Carole, 'The Power Struggle between the Saljuqs and the Ismaʿilis of Alamūt, 487–518/1094–1124: The Saljuq Perspective', in *Mediaeval Ismaʿili History and Thought*, ed. F. Daftary (Cambridge and New York: Cambridge University Press, 1996), 205–20.

Hillenbrand, Carole, *Turkish Myth and Muslim Symbol: The Battle of Manzikert* (Edinburgh: Edinburgh University Press, 2007).

Hinz, Walter, *Islamische Masse und Gewichte umgerechnet ins metrische System* (Leiden: E. J. Brill, 1955).

Hirschler, Konrad, *Medieval Damascus: Plurality and Diversity in an Arabic Library: The Ashrafīya Library Catalogue* (Edinburgh: Edinburgh University Press, 2016).

Hitti, Philip K., Nabih Amin Faris and Buṭrus ʿAbd-al-Malik, *Descriptive Catalog of the Garrett Collection of Arabic Manuscripts in the Princeton University Library* (Princeton, NJ: Princeton University Press, 1938).

Hodgson, Marshall G. S., *The Venture of Islam: Conscience and History in a World Civilization*, 3 vols. (Chicago, IL: University of Chicago Press, 1974).

Von der Höh, Marc, Nikolas Jaspert and Jenny Oesterle, 'Courts, Brokerage and Brokers', in *Cultural Brokers at Mediterranean Courts in the Middle Ages*, ed. Marc von der Höh, Nikolas Jaspert and Jenny Rahel Oesterle (Bern: Wilhelm Fink/Ferdinand Schöningh, 2013), 9–31.

Hoover, Jon, 'Fiṭra', *EI Three*. First print edition: 2016. First published online: 2016.

Howard, Douglas A., 'Ottoman Historiography and the Literature of "Decline" in the Sixteenth and Seventeenth Centuries', *Journal of Asian History* 22 (1988), 52–77.

Ḥudūd al-ʿālam, trans. V. Minorsky, *The Regions of the World: A Persian Geography, 372 A. H. (982 A. D.)*, second edition (London: E. J. W. Gibb Memorial, 1970).

Hunger, Herbert, *Die hochsprachliche profane Literatur der Byzantiner* (Munich: Beck, 1978–).

Al-Ḥuṣrī, Ibrāhīm b. ʿAlī, *Zahr al-ādāb wa-thamar al-albāb*, ed. ʿAlī Muḥammad al-Bajāwī (Cairo: ʿĪsā al-Bābī al-Ḥalabī, 1953).

Ibn ʿAbd al-Barr, Yūsuf b. ʿAbdallāh, *Jāmiʿ bayān al-ʿilm wa-faḍlihi*, ed. Abū l-Ashbāl al-Zuhayrī (al-Dammām: Dār Ibn al-Jawzī, 1994).

Ibn ʿAbd Rabbihi, *al-ʿIqd al-farīd*, ed. Karam al-Bustānī (Beirut: Maktabat Ṣādir, 1951–5) = *The Unique Necklace*, trans. Professor Issa J. Boullata (Reading: Garnet Publishing, 2006).

Ibn ʿAbd al-Rabīʿ, Shihāb al-Dīn, *Sulūk al-mālik fī tadbīr al-mamālik*, ed. Nājī al-Takrītī (Beirut: Turāth ʿUwadāt, 1978).

Ibn Abī Dharr = al-ʿĀmirī, *al-Saʿāda wa-l-isʿād*, facsimile of the copy prepared by Mujtabā Mīnuvī (Wiesbaden: Franz Steiner Verlag, 1957–8).

Ibn Abī l-Ḥadīd, ʿAbd al-Ḥamīd, *Sharḥ Nahj al-balāgha*, ed. Muḥammad Ibrāhīm (Baghdad: Dār al-Kitāb al-ʿArabī, 2007).

Ibn Abī Uṣaybiʿa, Aḥmad b. al-Qāsim, *ʿUyūn al-anbāʾ fī ṭabaqāt al-aṭibbāʾ*, ed. Nizār Riḍā (Beirut: Dār Maktabat al-Ḥayāt, 1965).

Ibn al-Athīr, ʿIzz al-Dīn, *al-Kāmil fī l-taʾrīkh*, ed. Muḥammad Yūsuf Duqāq (Beirut: Dār al-Kutub al-ʿIlmiyya, 1987).

Ibn Farīghūn, *Jawāmiʿ al-ʿulūm = Compendium of Sciences: Jamāmiʿ al-ʿulūm by Ibn Farīʿūn (Tenth Century A.D.)*, ed. F. Sezgin (Frankfurt: Maʿhad Taʾrīkh al-ʿUlūm al-ʿArabiyya wa-l-Islāmiyya, 1985).

Ibn al-Ḥaddād, Muḥammad b. Manṣūr, *al-Jawhar al-nafīs fī siyāsat al-raʾīs*, ed. Riḍwān al-Sayyid (Beirut: Dār al-Ṭalīʿa lil-Ṭibāʿa wa-l-Nashr, 1983).

Ibn Ḥamdūn, Muḥammad b. al-Ḥasan, *al-Tadhkira al-Ḥamdūniyya*, 2 vols., ed. Iḥsān ʿAbbās (Beirut: Maʿhad al-Inmāʾ al-ʿArabī, 1983; first published 1958).

Ibn Ḥanbal, Aḥmad, *Musnad al-Imām Aḥmad b. Ḥanbal*, ed. Shuʿayb al-Arnaʾūṭ and ʿĀdil Murshid (Beirut: Muʾassasat al-Risāla, 1993–2008).

Ibn al-Jahm, ʿAlī, *Dīwān ʿAlī b. al-Jahm*, ed. Khalīl Mardam Bay (Beirut: Dār Ṣādir, 1996).

Ibn al-Jawzī, Abū l-Faraj ʿAbd al-Raḥmān, *al-Muntaẓam fī taʾrīkh al-mulūk wa-l-umam*, ed. Muḥammad ʿAbd al-Qādir ʿAṭā and Muṣṭafā ʿAbd al-Qādir ʿAṭā (Beirut: Dār al-Kutub al-ʿIlmiyya, 1992–3).

Ibn Juljul, Sulaymān b. Ḥassān, *Ṭabaqāt al-aṭibbāʾ wa-l-ḥukamāʾ*, ed. Fuʾād Sayyid (Cairo: Maṭbaʿat al-Maʿhad al-ʿIlmī al-Faransī lil-Āthār al-Sharqiyya [Imprimerie de l'Institut français d'archéologie orientale], 1955).

Ibn Khaldūn, ʿAbd al-Raḥmān, *The Muqaddimah: An Introduction to History*, trans. from the Arabic by Franz Rosenthal (New York: Pantheon Books, Bollingen Foundation, 1958).

Ibn Khallikān, Aḥmad b. Muḥammad, *Wafayāt al-aʿyān wa-anbāʾ abnāʾ al-zamān*, ed. Iḥsān ʿAbbās (Beirut: Dār Ṣādir, 1977).
Ibn Māja, Muḥammad b. Yazīd, *Sunan*, ed. Muḥammad Fuʾād ʿAbd al-Bāqī ([Cairo]: Dār Iḥyāʾ al-Kutub al-ʿArabiyya, 1952–3).
Ibn Manẓūr, Muḥammad b. Mukarram, *Lisān al-ʿarab* (Cairo: Dār al-Maʿārif, 1981).
Ibn Munqidh, Usāma, *Lubāb al-ādāb*, ed. Aḥmad Muḥammad Shākir (Cairo: Maktabat al-Sunna, 1987).
Ibn al-Muqaffaʿ, *Āthār Ibn al-Muqaffaʿ*, ed. ʿUmar Abū l-Naṣr (Beirut: Dār Maktabat al-Ḥayāt, 1966).
Ibn al-Nadīm, Muḥammad b. Isḥāq, *Kitāb al-Fihrist*, ed. Ayman Fuʾād Sayyid, 2 vols. (London: Al-Furqan Islamic Heritage Foundation, 2009).
Ibn Qutayba, ʿAbdallāh b. Muslim, *Kitāb ʿUyūn al-akhbār*, 4 vols. (Cairo: Maṭbaʿat Dār al-Kutub al-Miṣriyya, 1925).
Ibn Qutayba, ʿAbdallāh b. Muslim, *al-Shiʿr wa-l-shuʿarāʾ*, ed. Aḥmad Muḥammad Shākir (Cairo: Dār al-Maʿārif, 1966).
Al-Ibshīhī, Muḥammad b. Aḥmad, *al-Mustaṭraf fī kull fann mustaẓraf*, ed. Mufīd Muḥammad Qumayḥa (Beirut: Dār al-Kutub al-ʿIlmiyya, 1986).
Inaba, Minoru, 'Ghaznavids', *EI Three*. First print edition: 2016. First published online: 2016.
Irwin, Robert, *Ibn Khaldun: An Intellectual Biography* (Princeton, NJ: Princeton University Press, 2018).
Al-Iṣfahānī, Abū l-Faraj, *Kitāb al-Aghānī* (Cairo: al-Hayʾa al-Miṣriyya al-ʿĀmma lil-Kitāb, 1992).
Al-Iṣfahānī, Abū Nuʿaym, *Ḥilyat al-awliyāʾ wa-ṭabaqāt al-aṣfiyāʾ* (Beirut: Dār al-Fikr lil-Ṭibāʿa wa-l-Nashr wa-l-Tawzīʿ, 1996).
Al-Iṣfahānī, Maḥmūd b. Muḥammad b. al-Ḥusayn, *Dustūr al-vizāra*, ed. R. Anzābī-Nizhād (Tehran: Amīr-i Kabīr, 1985).
Al-Iṣfahānī, al-Rāghib, *al-Dharīʿa ilā makārim al-sharīʿa* (Beirut: Dār al-Kutub al-ʿIlmiyya, 1980).
Al-Iṣfahānī, al-Rāghib, *Muḥāḍarāt al-udabāʾ wa-muḥāwarāt al-shuʿarāʾ wa-l-bulaghāʾ* (Beirut: Dār Maktabat al-Ḥayāt, 1961).
Islamic Calligraphy (Catalogue, Sam Fogg Rare Books and Manuscripts; Text by Ramsey Fendall) (London: Sam Fogg, 2003).
Al-Jāḥiẓ, ʿAmr b. Baḥr, *al-Bayān wa-l-tabyīn*, ed. ʿAbd al-Salām Muḥammad Hārūn (Cairo: Khānjī, 1998).
Al-Jāḥiẓ, ʿAmr b. Baḥr, *Kitāb al-Ḥayawān*, ed. ʿAbd al-Salām Muḥammad Hārūn (Cairo: Maṭbaʿat Muṣṭafā al-Bābī al-Ḥalabī, 1966).
Al-Jāḥiẓ, ʿAmr b. Baḥr, *Rasāʾil al-Jāḥiẓ*, ed. ʿAbd al-Salām Muḥammad Hārūn (Cairo: Maktabat al-Khānjī, 1964–79).
Al-Jahshiyārī, Muḥammad b. ʿAbdūs, *Kitāb al-Wuzarāʾ wa-l-kuttāb*, ed. Muṣṭafa al-Saqqā, Ibrāhīm al-Ibyārī and ʿAbd al-Ḥafīẓ Shalabī (Cairo: Muṣṭafā al-Bābī al-Ḥalabī, 1980).
John of Salisbury, *Policraticus: On the Frivolities of Courtiers and the Footprints of Philosophers*, ed. and trans. Cary J. Nederman (Cambridge: Cambridge University Press, 1990).

Jones, Russell, 'Ibrāhīm b. Adham', *EI²*. First print edition: 1960–2007. First published online: 2012.
Jónsson, Einar Már, *Le miroir. Naissance d'un genre littéraire* (Paris: Les Belles Lettres, 1995).
Jónsson, Einar Már, 'La situation du *Speculum regale* dans la littérature occidentale', *Études Germaniques* 4 (1987), 391–408.
Judd, Steven C., 'ʿUmar b. Hubayra', *EI Three*. First print edition: 2019. First published online: 2019.
Judd, Steven C., 'Yazīd b. ʿUmar b. Hubayra', *EI Three*. First print edition: 2019. First published online: 2019.
Juynboll, G. H. A., 'Abū Hurayra', *EI Three*. First print edition: 2007. First published online: 2007.
Juynboll, G. H. A., 'al-Aʿmash', *EI Three*. First print edition: 2009. First published online: 2009.
Juynboll, G. H. A., 'Anas b. Mālik', *EI Three*. First print edition: 2011. First published online: 2011.
Kaabi, Mongi, *Les Ṭāhirides: étude historico-littéraire de la dynastie des Banū Ṭāhir b. al-Ḥusayn au Hurāsān et en Iraq au IIIème s. de l'hégire/IXème s. J.-C.*, Thèse de doctorat d'état ès lettres et sciences humaines (Paris: Université de Paris-Sorbonne, Faculté des Lettres et Sciences Humaines, 1971).
Kāshifī, Ḥusayn-i Vāʿiẓ, *Akhlāq-i Muḥsinī* (India, 1895).
Kaya, Veysel, '*Kalām* and *Falsafa* Integrated for Divine Unity: Saʿīd b. Dādhurmuz's (5th/11th Century) *Risāla fī l-tawḥīd*', *Studia Graeco-Arabica: The Journal for the Project Greek into Arabic: Philosophical Concepts and Linguistic Bridges* 4 (2014), 65–123.
Kaykāʾūs b. Iskandar, ʿUnṣur al-Maʿālī, *Qābūsnāmeh*, ed. Ghulām-Ḥusayn Yūsufī (Tehran: Shirkat-i Intishārāt-i ʿIlmī va-Farhangī, 1989) = *A Mirror for Princes: The* Qābūs Nāma *of Kai Kāʾūs ibn Iskandar, Prince of Gurgān*, trans. Reuben Levy (London: The Cresset Press, 1951).
Kempshall, Matthew S., 'The Rhetoric of Giles of Rome's *De regimine principum*', in *Le Prince au miroir de la littérature politique de l'Antiquité aux Lumières*, ed. Frédérique Lachaud and Lydwine Scordia (Rouen: Publications des Universités de Rouen et du Havre, 2007), 161–90.
Kennedy, Hugh, *When Baghdad Ruled the Muslim World: The Rise and Fall of Islam's Greatest Dynasty* (Cambridge, MA: Da Capo, 2004). Originally published as *The Court of the Caliphs* (London: Weidenfeld and Nicolson, 2004).
Kennedy, Hugh, 'The Late ʿAbbāsid Pattern, 945-1050', in *The New Cambridge History of Islam, Vol. I: The Formation of the Islamic World: Sixth to Eleventh Centuries*, ed. Chase F. Robinson (Cambridge: Cambridge University Press, 2010), 360–93.
Kennedy, Hugh, 'al-Muʿtamid ʿalā ʾllāh', *EI²*. First print edition: 1960–2007. First published online: 2012.
Kennedy, Hugh, 'al-Muwaffaḳ', *EI²*. First print edition: 1960–2007. First published online: 2012.

Kennedy, Hugh, *The Prophet and the Age of the Caliphates: The Islamic Near East from the Sixth to the Eleventh Century* (London and New York: Longman, 1986).

Khaleghi-Motlagh, Djalal, 'Bozorgmehr-e Boktagān', *EIr* IV (1990), 427–9. In *Encyclopaedia Iranica Online* © Trustees of Columbia University in the City of New York. First print edition: 1989. First published online: 2020.

Khalidi, Tarif, *Arabic Historical Thought in the Classical Period* (Cambridge: Cambridge University Press, 1994).

Al-Khaṭīb al-Baghdādī, *see* al-Baghdādī, Aḥmad b. ʿAlī al-Khaṭīb

Khismatulin, A., 'The Art of Medieval Counterfeiting: The *Siyar al-mulūk* (the *Siyāsat-nāma*) by Niẓām al-Mulk and the "Full" Version of the *Naṣīḥat al-mulūk* by al-Ghazālī', *Manuscripta Orientalia: International Journal for Oriental Manuscript Research* 14 (2008), 3–31.

Khismatulin, A., 'To Forge a Book in the Medieval Ages: Nezām al-Molk's *Siyar al-molūk* (*Siyāsat-nāma*)', *Journal of Persianate Studies* 1 (2008), 30–66.

Khoury, R. G., 'Al-ʿArim', *EQ* I (2001), 60–1.

Kilpatrick, Hilary, 'Autobiography and Classical Arabic Literature', *Journal of Arabic Literature* 22 (1991), 1–20.

Kınalızade Ali Efendi, *Ahlâk-î Alâ'î*, ed. Hüseyin Algül (Istanbul: Tercüman, n. d.).

Kinberg, Leah, 'Ambiguous', *EQ* I (2001), 70–7.

Kitâb-i Müstetâb, ed. Yaşar Yücel (Ankara: Ankara Üniversitesi Basımevi, 1974).

Kitāb al-Siyāsa fī tadbīr al-riʾāsa al-maʿrūf bi-Sirr al-asrār, in *al-Uṣūl al-yūnāniyya lil-naẓariyyāt al-siyāsiyya fī l-Islām*, ed. ʿAbd al-Raḥmān Badawī (Cairo: Dār al-Kutub al-Miṣriyya, 1954), 67–171.

Kitāb al-Tāj fī akhlāq al-mulūk, ed. Aḥmad Zaki Pasha (Cairo: Imprimerie Nationale, 1914) = Charles Pellat, *Le livre de la couronne attribué à Ǧāḥiẓ* (Paris: Les Belles Lettres, 1954).

Kraus, Paul, 'Kitāb al-Akhlāq li-Jālīnūs', *Majallat Kulliyyat al-Ādāb* 5 (1937), 1–55.

Kristó-Nagy, István, *La pensée d'Ibn al-Muqaffaʿ: un "agent double" dans le monde persan et arabe* (Versailles: Éditions de Paris, 2013).

Kristó-Nagy, István, 'Marriage after Rape: The Ambiguous Relationship between Arab Lords and Iranian Intellectuals as Reflected in Ibn al-Muqaffaʿ's Oeuvre', in *Tradition and Reception in Arabic Literature: Essays Dedicated to Andras Hamori*, ed. Margaret Larkin and Jocelyn Sharlet (Wiesbaden: Harrassowitz Verlag, 2019), 161–88.

Kristó-Nagy, István, 'On the Authenticity of *al-Adab al-Ṣagīr* Attributed to Ibn al-Muqaffaʿ and Problems concerning Some of His Titles', *Acta Orientalia Academiae Scientiarum Hungaricae* 62 (2009), 199–218.

Kristó-Nagy, István, 'Reason, Religion and Power in Ibn al-Muqaffaʿ', *Acta Orientalia Academiae Scientiarum Hungaricae* 62 (2009), 285–301.

Al-Kulaynī, Abū Jaʿfar Muḥammad b. Yaʿqūb, al-Uṣūl min al-Kāfī, in *al-Kutub al-arbaʿa* (Qum: Muʾassasat Anṣāriyān lil-Ṭibāʿa wa-l-Nashr, 2003), I: 1–353.

Lambton, A. K. S., 'The Dilemma of Government in Islamic Persia: The *Siyāsat-nāma* of Niẓām al-Mulk', *Iran* 22 (1984), 55–66.

Lambton, A. K. S., 'Eqṭāʿ', *EIr* VIII (1998), 520–33. In *Encyclopaedia Iranica Online* © Trustees of Columbia University in the City of New York. First print edition: 1998. First published online: 2020.

Lambton, A. K. S., 'The Internal Structure of the Saljuq Empire', in *The Cambridge History of Iran, Vol. V: The Saljuq and Mongol Periods*, ed. J. A. Boyle (Cambridge: Cambridge University Press, 1968), 203–82.

Lambton, A. K. S., 'Islamic Mirrors for Princes', in *La Persia nel Medioevo, Quaderno dell'Accademia Nazionale dei Lincei* (Rome: Accademia Nazionale dei Lincei, 1971), 419–42.

Lambton, A. K. S., *State and Government in Medieval Islam* (Oxford: Oxford University Pres, 1981).

Lane, George A., *The Phoenix Mosque and the Persians of Medieval Hangzhou* (Chicago, IL: The Gingko Library, 2018).

Laoust, Henri, 'La pensée et l'action politiques d'al-Māwardī (364–450/974–1058)', *Revue des études islamiques* 36 (1968), 11–92.

Laoust, Henri, 'La suivie de Ġazālī d'après Subkī', *Bulletin d'études orientales* 25 (1972), 153–72.

Latham, J. D., 'The Beginnings of Arabic Prose: The Epistolary Genre', in *Arabic Literature to the End of the Umayyad Period*, ed. A. F. L. Beeston, T. M. Johnstone, R. B. Serjeant and G. R. Smith, The Cambridge History of Arabic Literature (Cambridge: Cambridge University Press, 1983), 154–79.

Latham, J. D., 'Ibn al-Muqaffaʿ and Early Abbasid Prose', in *ʿAbbasid Belles-Lettres*, ed. Julia Ashtiany, T. M. Johnstone, J. D. Latham, R. B. Serjeant and G. Rex Smith, The Cambridge History of Arabic Literature (Cambridge: Cambridge University Press, 1990), 48–77.

Leder, Stefan, 'Aspekte arabischer und persischer Fürstenspiegel. Legitimation, Fürstenethik, politische Vernunft', in *Specula principum*, ed. Angela de Benedictis (Frankfurt: Vittorio Klostermann, 1999), 21–50.

Leder, Stefan, 'al-Ṣūlī', *EI²*. First print edition: 1960–2007. First published online: 2012.

'Letter of Themistius', *see* Themistius

Lev, Yaacov, *The Administration of Justice in Medieval Egypt: From the 7th to the 12th Century* (Edinburgh: Edinburgh University Press, 2020).

Lev, Yaacov, 'The Fāṭimid Caliphate (358–567/969–1171) and the Ayyūbids in Egypt (567–648/1171–1250)', in *The New Cambridge History of Islam, Vol. II: The Western Islamic World, Eleventh to Eighteenth Centuries*, ed. Maribel Fierro (Cambridge: Cambridge University Press, 2010), 201–36.

Levy, Reuben, *A Mirror for Princes: The* Qābūs Nāma *of Kai Kāʾūs ibn Iskandar, Prince of Gurgān* (London: The Cresset Press, 1951).

Lewin, B., 'Ibn al-Muʿtazz', *EI²*. First print edition: 1960–2007. First published online: 2012.

Lewis, G. L., *The Balance of Truth by Katib Chelebi* (= *Mizan ul-hakk fi ihtiyar ul-ahakk*) (London: Allen and Unwin, 1957).

Linant de Bellefonds, Y., Cl. Cahen, H. Inalcık and Ed., 'Ḳānūn', *EI²*. First print edition: 1960–2007. First published online: 2012.

Lindsay, James E., 'Goliath', *EQ* II (2002), 334–5.

Lowry, Joseph E., 'The First Islamic Legal Theory: Ibn al-Muqaffaʿ on Authority, Interpretation, and the Structure of the Law', *Journal of the American Oriental Society* 128 (2008), 25–40.

Luyster, Amanda, 'Kalīla wa-Dimna Illustrations', *EI Three*. First print edition: 2021. First published online: 2021.

Mach-Yahuda, *Catalogue of Arabic Manuscripts* = Rudolf Mach, *Catalogue of Arabic Manuscripts (Yahuda Section) in the Garrett Collection, Princeton University Library* (Princeton, NJ: Princeton University Press, 1977).

Madelung, Wilferd, 'Āl-e Bāvand', *EIr* I (1984), 747–53. In *Encyclopaedia Iranica Online* © Trustees of Columbia University in the City of New York. First print edition: 1984. First published online: 2020.

Madelung, Wilferd, 'The Assumption of the Title Shāhānshāh by the Būyids and "The Reign of the Daylam (*Dawlat al-Daylam*)"', Part I, *Journal of Near Eastern Studies* 28/2 (1969), 84–108, and Part II, *Journal of Near Eastern Studies* 28/3 (1969), 168–83.

Madelung, Wilferd, 'The Minor Dynasties of Northern Iran', in *The Cambridge History of Iran, Vol. IV: From the Arab Invasion to the Saljuqs*, ed. Richard N. Frye (Cambridge: Cambridge University Press, 1975), 198–249.

Makdisi, George, *Ibn ʿAqil: Religion and Culture in Classical Islam* (Edinburgh: Edinburgh University Press, 1997).

Malaṭyavī, Muḥammad-i Ghāzī, *Barīd al-saʿāda*, ed. M. Shīrvānī (Tehran: Dānishgāh-i Tihrān, 1972).

Mallett, Alex, 'Alp Arslan', *EI Three*. First print edition: 2013. First published online: 2013.

Mallett, Alex, 'Two Writings of al-Ṭurṭūshī as Evidence for Early Muslim Reactions to the Frankish Crusader Presence in the Levant', *Wiener Zeitschrift für die Kunde des Morgenlandes* 107 (2017), 153–78.

Manzalaoui, Mahmoud, 'The Pseudo-Aristotelian *Kitāb Sirr al-asrār*: Facts and Problems', *Oriens* 23–24 (1974), 147–257.

Marlow, Louise, 'Abū Zayd al-Balkhī and the *Naṣīḥat al-mulūk* of Pseudo-Māwardī', *Der Islam* 93 (2016), 35–64.

Marlow, Louise, 'Advice and Advice Literature', *EI Three*. First print edition: 2007. First published online: 2007.

Marlow, Louise, 'Among Kings and Sages: Greek and Indian Wisdom in an Arabic Mirror for Princes', *Arabica* 60 (2013), 1–57.

Marlow, Louise, *Counsel for Kings: Wisdom and Politics in Tenth-Century Iran: The* Naṣīḥat al-mulūk *of Pseudo-Māwardī*, 2 vols. (Edinburgh: Edinburgh University Press, 2016).

Marlow, Louise, *Hierarchy and Egalitarianism in Islamic Thought* (Cambridge: Cambridge University Press, 1997).

Marlow, Louise, 'Teaching Wisdom: A Persian Work of Advice for Atabeg Ahmad of Luristan', in *Mirror for the Muslim Prince: Islam and the Theory of Statecraft*, ed. Mehrzad Boroujerdi (Syracuse, NY: Syracuse University Press, 2013), 122–59.

Marlow, Louise, 'The Way of Viziers and the Lamp of Commanders (*Minhāj al-wuzarāʾ wa-sirāj al-umarāʾ*) of Aḥmad al-Iṣfahbadhī and the Literary and

Political Culture of Early Fourteenth-Century Iran', in *Writers and Rulers: Perspectives on Their Relationship from Abbasid to Safavid Times*, ed. Beatrice Gruendler and Louise Marlow (Wiesbaden: Reichert Verlag, 2004), 169–93.

Maróth, Miklós, *The Correspondence between Aristotle and Alexander the Great: An Anonymous Greek Novel in Letters in Arabic Translation* (Piliscaba: The Avicenna Institute of Middle Eastern Studies, 2006).

Marsham, Andrew, *Rituals of Islamic Monarchy: Accession and Succession in the First Muslim Empire* (Edinburgh: Edinburgh University Press, 2009).

Al-Masʿūdī, Abū l-Ḥasan ʿAlī b. al-Ḥusayn, *Murūj al-dhahab wa-maʿādin al-jawhar*, ed. Yūsuf Asʿad Dāghir (Beirut: Dār al-Andalus, 1984).

Matthee, Rudi P., 'Gift Giving', (iv) 'In the Safavid Period', *EIr* X (2001), 609–14. In *Encyclopaedia Iranica Online* © Trustees of Columbia University in the City of New York. First print edition: 2016. First published online: 2020.

Matthee, Rudi P., 'Was Safavid Iran an Empire?', *Journal of the Economic and Social History of the Orient* 53 (2010), 233–65.

Al-Māwardī, Abū l-Ḥasan, *Adab al-dunyā wa-l-dīn*, ed. Muṣṭafā Saqqā (Cairo: Muṣṭafā al-Bābī al-Ḥalabī, 1973).

Al-Māwardī, Abū l-Ḥasan ʿAlī b. Muḥammad, *al-Aḥkām al-sulṭāniyya wa-l-wilāyāt al-dīniyya* (Cairo: Shirkat Maktaba wa-Maṭbaʿat Muṣṭafā al-Bābī al-Ḥalabī wa-Awlādihi, 1966) = Wafaa H. Wahba, *Al-Mawardi: The Ordinances of Government* (Reading: Garnet Publishing, 1996).

Al-Māwardī, Abū l-Ḥasan ʿAlī b. Muḥammad, *al-Amthāl wa-l-ḥikam*, ed. Muḥammad Ḥasan Muḥammad Ḥasan Ismāʿīl (Beirut: Dār al-Kutub al-ʿIlmiyya, 2003).

Al-Māwardī, Abū l-Ḥasan ʿAlī b. Muḥammad, *Durar al-sulūk fī siyāsat al-mulūk*, ed. Fuʾād ʿAbd al-Munʿim Aḥmad (Riyadh: Dār al-Waṭan lil-Nashr, 1997).

Al-Māwardī, Abū l-Ḥasan ʿAlī b. Muḥammad, *Kitāb Naṣīḥat al-mulūk*, ed. Muḥammad Jāsim al-Ḥadīthī (Baghdad: Dār al-Shuʾūn al-Thaqāfiyya al-ʿĀmma, 1986).

Al-Māwardī, Abū l-Ḥasan ʿAlī b. Muḥammad, *Naṣīḥat al-mulūk*, ed. Khiḍr Muḥammad Khiḍr (Kuwait: Maktabat al-Falāḥ, 1983).

Al-Māwardī, Abū l-Ḥasan ʿAlī b. Muḥammad, *Naṣīḥat al-mulūk al-mansūb ilā Abī l-Ḥasan al-Māwardī*, ed. Fuʾād ʿAbd al-Munʿim Aḥmad (Alexandria: Muʾassasat Shabāb al-Jāmiʿa, 1988).

Al-Māwardī, Abū l-Ḥasan ʿAlī b. Muḥammad, *Qawānīn al-wizāra wa-siyāsat al-mulk*, ed. Riḍwān al-Sayyid (Beirut: Dār al-Ṭalīʿa lil-Ṭibāʿa wa-l-Nashr, 1979).

Al-Māwardī, Abū l-Ḥasan ʿAlī b. Muḥammad, *Tashīl al-naẓar wa-taʿjīl al-ẓafar fī akhlāq al-malik wa-siyāsat al-mulk*, ed. Riḍwān al-Sayyid (Beirut: Dār al-ʿUlūm al-ʿArabiyya, 1987) = Makram Abbès, *Al-Māwardī. De l'Éthique du prince et du gouvernement de l'état* (Paris: Les Belles Lettres, 2015), 237–477.

Al-Maydānī, Aḥmad b. Muḥammad, *Majmaʿ al-amthāl*, ed. Muḥammad Muḥyī l-Dīn ʿAbd al-Ḥamīd, 2 vols. (Miṣr: al-Saʿāda, 1959).

Mediano, Fernando R., 'L'amour, la justice et la crainte dans les récits hagiographiques marocains', *Studia Islamica* 90 (2000), 85–104.

Meier, Fritz, 'al-Ġazzālī, Abū Ḥāmid Muḥammad. *Naṣīḥatu 'l-mulūk*. Herausgeg. v. Ǧalāl-i Humā'ī' [Review], *Zeitschrift der Deutschen Morgenländischen Gesellschaft* 93 (1939), 395–408.

Meisami, Julie Scott, 'Exemplary Lives, Exemplary Deaths: The Execution of Ḥasanak', in *Actas XVI Congreso UEAI* (Salamanca: Agencia Española de Cooperación Internacional, 1995), 357–64.

Meisami, Julie Scott, 'History as Literature', *Iranian Studies* 33 (2000), 15–30.

Meisami, Julie Scott, *Persian Historiography to the End of the Twelfth Century* (Edinburgh: Edinburgh University Press, 1999).

Meisami, Julie Scott, 'Places in the Past: The Poetics/Politics of Nostalgia', *Edebiyat* VIII (1998), 63–106.

Meisami, Julie Scott, The Sea of Precious Virtues (Baḥr al-favā'id)*: A Medieval Islamic Mirror for Princes* (Salt Lake City, UT: University of Utah Press, 1991).

Melchert, Christopher, 'Abū l-Dardā'', *EI Three*. First print edition: 2009. First published online: 2009.

Melchert, Christopher, 'Māwardī, Abū Ya'lá, and the Sunni Revival', in *Prosperity and Stagnation: Some Cultural and Social Aspects of the Abbasid Period (750–1258)*, ed. Krzystof Kościelniak (Cracow: UNUM, 2010), 37–61.

Meneghini, Daniela, 'Farrukhī Sīstānī', *EI Three*. First print edition: 2012. First published online: 2012.

Mikhail, Hanna, *Politics and Revelation. Māwardī and After* (Edinburgh: Edinburgh University Press, 1995).

Minorsky, V., Ḥudūd al-'ālam 'The Regions of the World'*: A Persian Geography 372 A.H.-982 A.D.*, second edition (Cambridge: E. J. W. Memorial Trust, 1970).

Miskawayh, Abū 'Alī, *al-Ḥikma al-khālida (Jāvīdān khirad)*, ed. 'Abd al-Raḥmān Badawī (Cairo: Maktabat al-Nahḍa al-Miṣriyya, 1952).

Miskawayh, Abū 'Alī, *Tahdhīb al-akhlāq*, ed. Qusṭanṭīn Zurayk (Beirut: American University of Beirut Press, 1966) = *The Refinement of Character*, trans. Constantine K. Zurayk (Beirut: American University of Beirut Press, 2002).

Mottahedeh, Roy P., *Loyalty and Leadership in an Early Islamic Society*, second edition (London: I.B. Tauris, 2001).

Mottahedeh, Roy P., 'A Note on the "*Tasbīb*"', in *Studia Arabica et Islamica: Festschrift for Iḥsān 'Abbās on His Sixtieth Birthday*, ed. Wadād al-Qāḍī (Beirut: American University of Beirut Press, 1981), 347–51.

Mottahedeh, Roy, 'The Transmission of Learning: The Role of the Islamic Northeast', in *Madrasa: la transmission du savoir dans le monde musulman*, ed. Nicole Grandin and Marc Gaborieau (Paris: AP Éditions Arguments, 1997), 63–72.

Mourad, Suleiman A., ''Amr b. 'Ubayd', *EI Three*. First print edition: 2008. First published online: 2008.

Mourad, Suleiman A., 'al-Ḥasan al-Baṣrī', *EI Three*. First print edition: 2017. First published online: 2017.

Al-Mubarrad, Muḥammad b. Yazīd, *al-Kāmil fī l-lugha wa-l-adab*, ed. Muḥammad Abū l-Faḍl Ibrāhīm (Cairo: Dār al-Fikr al-ʿArabī, 1997).

Al-Mubashshir b. Fātik, *Mukhtār al-ḥikam wa-maḥāsin al-kalim* (*Los bocados de oro)*, ed. ʿAbd al-Raḥmān Badawī (Madrid: Maṭbaʿat al-Maʿhad al-Miṣrī lil-Dirāsāt al-Islāmiyya, 1958).

Al-Mufaḍḍal b. Muḥammad al-Ḍabbī, *Dīwān al-Mufaḍḍaliyyāt* [recension of Abū Muḥammad al-Qāsim b. Muḥammad b. Bashshār al-Anbārī] (Cairo: Maktabat al-Thaqāfa al-Dīniyya, 2000).

Mulder, Stephennie, 'The Mausoleum of Imam al-Shafiʿi', *Muqarnas* 23 (2006), 15–46.

Müller, Rainer A., 'Die deutschen Fürstenspiegel des 17. Jahrhunderts. Regierungslehren und politische Pädagogik', *Historische Zeitschrift* 240 (1985), 571–97.

Al-Murādī, Muḥammad b. al-Ḥasan, *Kitāb al-Ishāra ilā adab al-imāra*, ed. Riḍwān al-Sayyid (Beirut: Dār al-Ṭalīʿa lil-Ṭibāʿa wa-l-Nashr, 1981).

Murphey, Rhoads, 'The Veliyyuddin Telhis: Notes on the Sources and Interrelations between Koçi Bey and Contemporary Writers of Advice to Kings', *Belleten* 43 (1979), 547–71.

Muslim b. al-Ḥajjāj, *Ṣaḥīḥ Muslim bi-sharḥ al-Nawawī* (Cairo: Muʾassasat Qurṭuba, 1994).

Mustawfī, Abū l-Fażl Yūsuf b. ʿAlī, *Khiradnamā-yi jān-afrūz*, ed. Maḥmūd ʿĀbidī (Tehran: Markaz-i Nashr-i Farhangī-yi Rajāʾ, 1989).

Mustawfī, Ḥamd Allāh Qazvīnī, *Tārīkh-i guzīdeh*, ed. ʿAbd al-Ḥusayn Navāʾī (Tehran: Amīr Kabīr, 1983).

Al-Nābigha al-Dhubyānī, *Dīwān*, ed. Muḥammad Abū l-Faḍl Ibrāhīm (Cairo: Dār al-Maʿārif, 1977).

Nagel, Tilman, 'Buyids', *EIr* IV (1990), 578–86. In *Encyclopaedia Iranica Online* © Trustees of Columbia University in the City of New York. First print edition: 1990. First published online: 2020.

Al-Nasāʾī, Aḥmad b. Shuʿayb, *Sunan al-Nasāʾī*, ed. Rāʾid b. Ṣabrī Ibn Abī ʿAlfa (Riyadh: Dār al-Ḥaḍāra lil-Nashr wa-l-Tawzīʿ, 2010).

Nelson, Janet L., 'Kingship and Empire', in *The Cambridge History of Medieval Political Thought, c. 350-c. 1450* (Cambridge: Cambridge University Press, 1988), 211–51.

Nelson, Janet L., 'Kingship and Empire in the Carolingian World', in *Carolingian Culture: Emulation and Innovation*, ed. Rosamond McKitterick (Cambridge and New York: Cambridge University Press, 1994), 52–87.

Nelson, Janet L., 'Kingship, Law and Liturgy in the Political Thought of Hincmar of Rheims', *The English Historical Review* 92 (1977), 241–79.

The New Oxford Annotated Bible, ed. B. M. Metzger and R. E. Murphy (New York: Oxford University Press, 1991).

Nielsen, J. S., 'Maẓālim', *EI²*. First print edition: 1960–2007. First published online: 2012.

'Nithār', *see* Ed. and J. Burton-Page.

Niẓām al-Dīn Yaḥyā b. Ṣāʿid, *Ḥadāyiq al-siyar*, ed. Muḥammad Pārsā-Nasab with Maʿṣūmeh Asadniyā and Maryam Sayyidān (Tehran: Farhangistān-i Zabān va-Adab-i Fārsī, 2015).

Niẓām al-Mulk, *Siyar al-mulūk*, ed. Hubert Darke (Tehran: Bungāh-i Tarjameh va-Nashr-i Kitāb, 1962) = H. S. G. Darke, *The Book of Government or Rules for Kings* (London: Routledge and Kegan Paul, 1960; revised edition, 1978).

Niẓām al-Mulk, *Siyāsatnāmeh: Az rū-yi nuskheh-yi Shifir chāp-i Pārīs 1891 mīlādī*, ed. Muḥammad Qazvīnī, revised ed. Murtażā Mudarrisī Chahārdahī (Tehran: Kitābfurūshī Ṭahūrī, 1955).

Al-Nuwayrī, Shihāb al-Dīn Aḥmad, *Nihāyat al-arab fī funūn al-adab* (Cairo: Maṭbaʿat Dār al-Kutub wa-l-Wathāʾiq al-Qawmiyya, 2007).

Der Oikonomikos des Neupythagoreers 'Bryson' und sein Einfluß auf die islamische Wissenschaft, Edition und Übersetzung . . . von Martin Plessner (Heidelberg: Carl Winter, 1928).

O'Kane, Bernard, *Early Persian Painting:* Kalila and Dimna *Manuscripts of the Late Fourteenth Century* (London and New York: I.B. Tauris, 2003).

Orfali, Bilal, *The Anthologist's Art: Abū Manṣūr al-Thaʿālibī and His* Yatīmat al-dahr (Leiden and Boston, MA: Brill, 2016).

Orfali, Bilal, 'The Works of Abū Manṣūr al-Thaʿālibī (350–429/961–1039)', *Journal of Arabic Literature* 40 (2009), 273–318.

Paul, Jürgen, 'Dihqān', *EI Three*. First print edition: 2015. First published online: 2015.

Paul, Jürgen, *Herrscher, Gemeinwesen, Vermittler: Ostiran und Transoxanien in vormongolischer Zeit* (Beirut: In Kommission bei Franz Steiner Verlag Stuttgart, 1996).

Paul, Jürgen, 'The Histories of Isfahan: Mafarrukhi's *Kitāb maḥāsin Iṣfahān*', *Iranian Studies* 33 (2000), 117–32.

Paul, Jürgen, 'Karakhanids', *EI Three*. First print edition: 2021. First published online: 2021.

Paul, Jürgen, '*Khidma* in the Social History of Pre-Mongol Iran', *Journal of the Economic and Social History of the Orient* 57 (2014), 392–422.

Paul, Jürgen, 'Where Did the Dihqāns Go?', *Eurasian Studies* XI (2013), 1–34.

Peacock, A. C. S., 'Advice for the Sultans of Rum: The "Mirrors for Princes" of Early Thirteenth-Century Anatolia', in *Turkish Language, Literature, and History: Travelers' Tales, Sultans, and Scholars since the Eighth Century*, ed. Bill Hickman and Gary Leiser (London and New York: Routledge, 2016), 276–307.

Peacock, A. C. S., *Early Seljūq History: A New Interpretation* (London and New York: Routledge, 2010).

Peacock, A. C. S., *The Great Seljuk Empire* (Edinburgh: Edinburgh University Press, 2015).

Peacock, A. C. S., 'Politics, Religion and the Occult in the Works of Kamal al-Din Ibn Talha, a Vizier, *ʿAlim* and Author in Thirteenth-Century Syria', in *Syria in Crusader Times: Conflict and Co-existence*, ed. Carole Hillenbrand (Edinburgh: Edinburgh University Press, 2020), 34–60.

Peacock, Andrew, 'Shaddadids', *EIr*. First published online: 2020.

Pellat, Charles, *Ibn al-Muqaffaʿ (mort vers 140/757), 'conseilleur' du calife* (Paris: Maisonneuve et Larose, 1976).

Pellat, *Le livre de la couronne*, *see Kitāb al-Tāj*

Pérez-Alfaro, Cristina Jular, 'The King's Face on the Territory: Royal Officers, Discourse and Legitimating Practices in Thirteenth- and Fourteenth-Century Castile', in *Building Legitimacy: Political Discourses and Forms of Legitimacy in Medieval Societies*, ed. Isabel Alfonso, Hugh Kennedy and Julio Escalona (Leiden and Boston, MA: Brill, 2004), 107–37.

Pistoso, Maurizio, *L'arte della politica (lo specchio del principe nella Persia dell'XI secolo) (Siyāsatnāma)* (Milan: Luni, 1999).

Pomerantz, Maurice A., 'A Political Biography of al-Ṣāḥib Ismāʿīl b. ʿAbbād (d. 385/995)', *Journal of the American Oriental Society* 134 (2014), 1–23.

Pormann, Peter E. and Emilie Savage-Smith, *Medieval Islamic Medicine* (Washington, DC: Georgetown University Press, 2007).

[Pseudo-Aristotle], Kitāb al-Siyāsa fī tadbīr al-riyāsa al-maʿrūf bi-Sirr al-asrār, in *al-Uṣūl al-yūnāniyya lil-naẓariyyāt al-siyāsiyya fī l-Islām*, ed. ʿAbd al-Raḥmān Badawī (Cairo: Dār al-Kutub al-Miṣriyya, 1954), 67–171.

Pseudo-Callisthenes, *The Greek Alexander Romance*, trans. with an introduction and notes by Richard Stoneman (London: Penguin, 1991).

Al-Qāḍī, Wadād, 'Early Islamic State Letters: The Question of Authenticity', in *The Byzantine and Early Islamic Near East, Vol. I: Problems in the Literary Source Material*, ed. Averil Cameron and Lawrence I. Conrad (Princeton, NJ: Darwin Press, 1992), 215–75.

Al-Qāḍī, Wadād, 'The Myriad Sources of the Vocabulary of ʿAbd al-Ḥamīd al-Kātib (d. 132/750)', *Arabica* 66 (2019), 207–302.

Al-Qadi, W., '‘Abd al-Hamid al-Katib', in *Dictionary of Literary Biography, Vol. 311: Arabic Literary Culture, 500–925*, ed. Michael Cooperson and Shawkat M. Toorawa (Detroit: Thomson Gale, 2005), 3–11.

Qazvīnī, Ḥamd Allāh Mustawfī, *Tārīkh-i guzīdeh*, ed. ʿAbd al-Ḥusayn Navāʾī (Tehran: Amīr Kabīr, 1984).

Al-Qushayrī, ʿAbd al-Karīm, *al-Risāla al-Qushayriyya*, ed. ʿAbd al-Ḥalīm Maḥmūd and Maḥmūd b. al-Sharīf (Cairo: Dār al-Kutub al-Ḥadītha, n.d.).

Qutbuddin, Tahera, '*Khuṭba*: The Evolution of Early Arabic Oration', in *Classical Arabic Humanities in Their Own Terms: Festschrift for Wolfhart Heinrichs on His 65th Birthday Presented by His Students and Colleagues*, ed. Beatrice Gruendler and Michael Cooperson (Leiden: Brill, 2008), 176–273.

Qutbuddin, Tahera, *A Treasury of Virtues: Sayings, Sermons and Teachings of ʿAlī with the One Hundred Proverbs* (New York: New York University Press, 2013).

Rabbat, Nasser, 'Dār al-ʿadl (premodern)', *EI Three*. First print edition: 2012. First published online: 2012.

Rabbat, Nasser, 'The Ideological Significance of the *Dār al-ʿAdl* in the Medieval Islamic Orient', *International Journal of Middle East Studies* 27 (1995), 3–28.

Al-Rashid, Saad A. and M. L. J. Young, 'Darb Zubayda', *EI^2*. First print edition: 1960–2007. First published online: 2012.

Rāzī, Fakhr al-Dīn, *Jāmiʿ al-ʿulūm (Sittīnī)*, ed. Sayyid ʿAlī Āl-i Dāʾūd (Tehran: Bunyād-i Mawqūfāt-i Duktūr Maḥmūd Afshār, 2003).

Rāzī, Najm al-Dīn, *Mirṣād al-ʿibād min al-mabdaʾ ilā l-maʿād*, ed. Ḥusayn al-Ḥusaynī al-Niʿmatullāhī (Tehran: Sanāʾī, 1984) = Hamid Algar, The Path of God's Bondsmen from Origin to Return (Merṣād al-ʿebād men al-mabdaʾ elā'l-maʿād)*: A Sufi Compendium by Najm al-Dīn Rāzī, Known as Dāya* (Delmar, NY: Caravan Books, 1982).

Renard, John, 'Alexander', *EQ* I (2001), 61–2.

Richter, Gustav, *Studien zur Geschichte der älteren arabischen Fürstenspiegel* (Leipzig: Hinrichs'sche Buchhandlung, 1932).

Richter-Bernburg, Lutz, '*Amīr-Malik-Shāhānshāh*: ʿAḍud ad-Daula's Titulature Re-examined', *Iran* 18 (1980), 83–102.

Rippin, A., 'ʿĀd', *EI Three*. First print edition: 2008. First published online: 2008.

Rippin, A., 'Ṣāliḥ', *EI²*. First print edition: 1960–2007. First published online: 2012.

Robinson, C. F., 'Waraḳa b. Nawfal', *EI²*. First print edition: 1960–2007. First published online: 2012.

Rosenthal, F., 'Dawla', *EI²*. First print edition: 1960–2007. First published online: 2012.

Rosenthal, F., *Ibn Khaldûn: The Muqaddimah: An Introduction to History*, trans. from the Arabic by Franz Rosenthal (New York: Pantheon Books, Bollingen Foundation, 1958).

Rowson, Everett K., *A Muslim Philosopher on the Soul and Its Fate: Al-ʿĀmirī's* Kitāb al-Amad ʿalā l-abad (New Haven, CT: American Oriental Society, 1988).

Rowson, Everett K., 'The Philosopher as Littérateur: al-Tawḥīdī and His Predecessors', *Zeitschrift der Deutschen Morgenländischen Gesellschaft* 6 (1990), 50–92.

Rowson, Everett K., 'al-Thaʿālibī', *EI²*. First print edition: 1960–2007. First published online: 2012.

Rubin, Uri, 'Prophets and Caliphs: The Biblical Foundations of the Umayyad Authority', in *Method and Theory in the Study of Islamic Origins*, ed. H. Berg (Leiden: Brill, 2003), 74–99.

Rustow, Marina, 'A Petition to a Woman at the Fatimid Court (413–414 A. H./1022–23 C.E.)', *Bulletin of the School of Oriental and African Studies* 73 (2010), 1–27.

Ryan, W. F. and Charles B. Schmitt, eds., *Pseudo-Aristotle,* The Secret of Secrets*: Sources and Influences* (London: The Warburg Institute, 1982).

Sadan, Joseph, '*Ādāb* – règles de conduite et *ādāb* – dictons, maximes, dans quelques ouvrages inédits d'al-Ṯaʿālibī', *Mélanges offerts au Professeur Dominique Sourdel = Revue des études islamiques* 54 (1986), 283–300.

Sadan, Joseph, 'A "Closed-Circuit" Saying on Practical Justice', *Jerusalem Studies in Arabic and Islam* 10 (1987), 325–41.

Sadan, Joseph, 'A New Source of the Būyid Period', *Israel Oriental Studies* 9 (1979), 355–76.

Sadan, Joseph, 'Une nouvelle source sur l'époque būyide', in *Ḥaḍāra: Texts and Studies in the Civilization of Islam* (Tel Aviv: Tel Aviv University, n.d.).

Sadan, J. and A. Silverstein, 'Ornate Manuals or Practical *Adab*? Some Reflections on a Unique Work by an Anonymous Author of the 10th Century CE', *Al-Qanṭara* 25 (2004), 339–55.

Safa, Z., 'Andarz Literature in New Persian', *EIr* I (1985), 16–22. In *Encyclopaedia Iranica Online* © Trustees of Columbia University in the City of New York. First print edition: 1985. First published online: 2020.

Al-Ṣafadī, Khalīl b. Aybak, *Kitāb al-Wāfī bi-l-wafayāt*, ed. Aḥmad al-Arnaʾūṭ and Turkī Muṣṭafā (Beirut: Dār Iḥyāʾ al-Turāth al-ʿArabī, 2000).

Safi, Omid, *The Politics of Knowledge in Premodern Islam* (Chapel Hill, NC: University of North Carolina Press, 2006).

Safran, Janina M., *Defining Boundaries in al-Andalus: Muslims, Christians, and Jews in Islamic Iberia* (Ithaca, NY: Cornell University Press, 2013).

Al-Sakhāwī, Muḥammad b. ʿAbd al-Raḥmān, *al-Maqāṣid al-ḥasana fī bayān kathīr min al-aḥādīth al-mushtahara ʿalā l-alsina*, ed. Muḥammad ʿUthmān al-Khisht (Beirut: Dār al-Kitāb al-ʿArabī, 1985).

Šakūrzāda, Ebrāhīm and Mahmoud Omidsalar, 'Čašm-zaḵm', *EIr* V (1990), 44–7. In *Encyclopaedia Iranica Online* © Trustees of Columbia University in the City of New York. First print edition: 1990. First published online: 2020.

Samangustin, F., 'Mizādj', *EI*². First print edition: 1960–2007. First published online: 2012.

Sarıbıyık, Mustafa, *Siyaset Senati* (Istanbul: Sosyal Bilimler Enstitüsü, 1996).

Sattarzade, Malihe, 'Persian Institutions under the Saljuqs: As Reflected in the "Mirror for Princes" Literature', PhD diss., Columbia University, 1971 (University Microfilms, Ann Arbor, Michigan, © 1974).

Savant, Sarah Bowen, *The New Muslims of Post-conquest Iran: Tradition, Memory, and Conversion* (Cambridge: Cambridge University Press, 2013).

Al-Sayyid, Riḍwān, 'al-Māwardī (364-450 h/974-1058 m): al-rajul wa-l-ʿaṣr', in al-Māwardī, *Qawānīn al-wizāra wa-siyāsat al-mulk*, ed. Riḍwān al-Sayyid (Beirut: Dār al-Ṭalīʿa lil-Ṭibāʿa wa-l-Nashr, 1979), 5–114.

Al-Sayyid, Riḍwān, 'Tamhīd', in al-Māwardī, *Tashīl al-naẓar wa-taʿjīl al-ẓafar fī akhlāq al-malik wa-siyāsat al-mulk*, ed. Riḍwān al-Sayyid (Beirut: Dār al-ʿUlūm al-ʿArabiyya, 1987), 7–98.

Schabinger, Karl Emil, *Nizāmulmulk, Reichskanzler der Saldschuqen 1063–1092 n. Chr. – Siyāsatnāma, Gedanken und Geschichten* (Freiburg/Munich: Verlag Karl Alber, 1960).

Schmitt, Charles B., 'Francesco Storella and the Last Printed Edition of the Latin *Secretum Secretorum* (1555)', in *Pseudo-Aristotle,* The Secret of Secrets*: Sources and Influences*, ed. W. F. Ryan and Charles B. Schmitt (London: The Warburg Institute, 1982), 124–31.

Schmitt, Charles B., 'Pseudo-Aristotle in the Latin Middle Ages', in *Pseudo-Aristotle in the Middle Ages: The* Theology *and Other Texts*, ed. Jill Kraye, W. F. Ryan and C. B. Schmitt (London: Warburg Institute, 1986), 3–14.

Schneider, Irene, 'Vernunft oder Tradition? Abū l-Ḥasan ʿAlī al-Māwardīs (st. 449/1058) Hermeneutik des Korans im Spiegel seiner Zeit', *Zeitschrift der Deutschen Morgenländischen Gesellschaft* 156 (2006), 57–80.

Schöck, Cornelia, 'Moses', *EQ* III (2003), 419–26.

Schoeler, Gregor, *The Genesis of Literature in Islam: From the Aural to the Read*, revised edition in collaboration with and trans. Shawkat M. Toorawa (Edinburgh: Edinburgh University Press, 2009).

Schoeler, Gregor, 'The Relationship of Literacy and Memory in the Second/Eighth Century', in *Proceedings of the Seminar for Arabian Studies 40, Supplement: The Development of Arabic as a Written Language. Papers from the Special Session of the Seminar for Arabian Studies Held on 24 July, 2009* (2010), 121–9.

Schoeler, Gregor, 'Verfasser und Titel des dem Ǧāḥiẓ zugeschriebenen sog. *Kitāb at-Tāǧ*', *Zeitschrift der Deutschen Morgenländischen Gesellschaft* 130 (1980), 217–25.

Schönig, Hannelore, *Das Sendschreiben des ʿAbdalḥamīd b. Yaḥyā (gest. 132/750) an den Kronprinzen ʿAbdallāh b. Marwān II* (Stuttgart: Franz Steiner Verlag Wiesbaden, 1985).

Secretum secretorum cum glossis et notulis, ed. Robert Steele; including the translation from the Arabic [by Ismail Ali], ed. A. S. Fulton, in *Opera hactenus inedita Rogeri Baconi*, Fasc. V (Oxford: Oxford University Press, 1920), 176–266.

Seidensticker, Tilman, "Adī b. Zayd', *EI Three*. First print edition: 2009. First published online: 2009.

Shahar, Ido, 'Legal Pluralism and the Study of Shariʿa Courts', *Islamic Law and Society* 15 (2008), 112–41.

Shahbazi, A. Shapur, 'Nowruz ii: In the Islamic Period', in *Encyclopaedia Iranica Online* © Trustees of Columbia University in the City of New York. First published online: 2020.

Shaked, Shaul, 'Andarz and Andarz Literature in Pre-Islamic Iran', *EIr* I (1985), 11–16. In *Encyclopaedia Iranica Online* © Trustees of Columbia University in the City of New York. First print edition: 1985. First published online: 2020.

Shaked, Shaul, 'From Iran to Islam: Notes on Some Themes in Transmission', *Jerusalem Studies in Arabic and Islam* 4 (1984), 31–67.

Al-Shayzarī, ʿAbd al-Raḥmān b. Naṣr, *al-Nahj al-maslūk fī siyāsat al-mulūk*, ed. Muḥammad Aḥmad Damaj (Beirut: Dār al-Manāl, 1994).

Simidchieva, Marta, 'Kingship and Legitimacy in Niẓām al-Mulk's *Siyāsatnāma*, Fifth/Eleventh Century', in *Writers and Rulers: Perspectives on Their Relationship from Abbasid to Safavid Times*, ed. Beatrice Gruendler and Louise Marlow (Wiesbaden: Reichert Verlag, 2004), 97–131.

Simidchieva, Marta, '*Siyāsat-nāme* Revisited: The Question of Authenticity', in *Proceedings of the Second European Conference of Iranian Studies*, ed. B. Fragner, C. Fragner, G. Gnoli, R. Haag-Higuchi, M. Maggi, and P. Orsatti (Rome, 1995), 657–74.

Soravia, Bruna, '`Abbādids', *EI Three*. First print edition: 2011. First published online: 2011.

Sourdel, D., '`Amr b. Mas`ada', *EI²*. First print edition: 1960–2007. First published online: 2012.

Sourdel, D., 'Ibn al-Zayyāt', *EI²*. First print edition: 1960–2007. First published online: 2012.

Sourdel, D., 'al-Ḳādir Bi'llāh', *EI²*. First print edition: 1960–2007. First published online: 2012.

Sourdel, D., 'al-Ḳāhir bi'llāh', *EI²*. First print edition: 1960–2007. First published online: 2012.

Sourdel-Thomine, Janine, 'Les conseils du Šayḫ al-Harawī à un prince ayyūbide', *Bulletin d'études orientales* 17 (1961–2), 205–68.

Sperl, Stefan, 'Islamic Kingship and Arabic Panegyric Poetry in the Early Ninth Century', *Journal of Arabic Literature* 8 (1977), 20–35.

Spooner, Brian and William L. Hanaway, 'Introduction: Persian as Koine: Written Persian in World-Historical Perspective', in *Literacy in the Persianate World: Writing and the Social Order*, ed. William L. Hanaway and Brian Spooner (Philadelphia, PA: University of Pennsylvania Press, 2012), 1–68.

Steele, Robert, 'Introduction', in *Secretum secretorum* cum glossis et notulis, ed. Robert Steele; including the translation from the Arabic [by Ismail Ali], ed. A. S. Fulton, in *Opera hactenus inedita Rogeri Baconi*, Fasc. V (Oxford: Oxford University Press, 1920), vii–lxv.

Stetkevych, Suzanne Pinckney, 'The `Abbasid Poet Interprets History: Three Qaṣīdahs by Abū Tammām', *Journal of Arabic Literature* 10 (1979), 49–64

Stetkevych, Suzanne Pinckney, *The Poetics of Islamic Legitimacy: Myth, Gender, and Ceremony in the Classical Arabic Ode* (Bloomington, IN: Indiana University Press, 2002).

Stone, Rachel, 'Kings Are Different: Carolingian Mirrors for Princes and Lay Morality', in *Le Prince au miroir de la littérature politique de l'Antiquité aux Lumières*, ed. Frédérique Lachaud and Lydwine Scordia (Mont-Saint-Aignon: Publications des Universités de Rouen at du Havre, 2007), 69–86.

Strohmaier, Gotthard, 'The Uses of Galen in Arabic Literature', *Bulletin of the Institute of Classical Studies*, Supplement No. 77, *The Unknown Galen* (2002), 113–20.

Al-Subkī, Tāj al-Dīn, *Ṭabaqāt al-Shāfi`iyya al-kubrā* (Miṣr: al-Maṭba`a al-Ḥusayniyya al-Miṣriyya, 1906).

Subtelny, Maria Eva, 'A Late Medieval Persian Summa on Ethics: Kashifi's *Akhlāq-i Muḥsinī*', *Iranian Studies* 36 (2003), 601–14

Subtelny, Maria Eva, *Le monde est un jardin. Aspects de l'histoire culturelle de l'Iran médiéval* (Paris: Association pour l'avancement des études iraniennes, 2002).

Al-Ṭabarī, Muḥammad b. Jarīr, *Ta'rīkh al-rusul wa-l-mulūk = Ta'rīkh al-Ṭabarī*, ed. Muḥammad Faḍl Ibrāhīm (Cairo: Dār al-Ma`ārif, 1960–77) = *The History of al-Ṭabarī* (Albany, NY: State University of New York Press, 1985).

Al-Tabrīzī, al-Khaṭīb, *Sharḥ Dīwān Abī Tammām*, ed. Rājī al-Asmar (Beirut: Dār al-Turāth al-ʿArabī, 1994).

Talmon-Heller, Daniella, *Islamic Piety in Medieval Syria: Mosques, Cemeteries and Sermons under the Zangids and Ayyūbids (1146–1260)* (Leiden: Brill, 2007).

Al-Tawḥīdī, Abū Ḥayyān, *Akhlāq al-wazīrayn*, ed. Muḥammad b. Tāwīt al-Ṭanjī (Beirut: Dār Ṣādir, 1992).

Al-Tawḥīdī, Abū Ḥayyān, *al-Baṣāʾir wa-l-dhakhāʾir*, ed. Wadād al-Qāḍī (Beirut: Dār Ṣādir, 1988).

Al-Tawḥīdī, Abū Ḥayyān, *Kitāb al-Imtāʿ wa-l-muʾānasa*, ed. Haytham Khalīfa al-Ṭaʿimī (Beirut: al-Maktabat al-ʿAṣriyya, 2011).

Al-Thaʿālibī, Abū Manṣūr, *Ādāb al-mulūk*, ed. Jalīl al-ʿAṭiyya (Beirut: Dār al-Gharb al-Islāmī, 1990) = T. R. Topuzoğlu, 'Kitāb Ādāb al-Mulūk al-Khwārazm-shāhī of Abū Manṣūr ʿAbd al-Malik b. Muḥammad b. Ismāʿīl ath-Thaʿālibī', PhD diss., University of Manchester, 1974; *Kitāb Ādāb al-Mulūk al-Khwārazm-shāhī*, 2 vols. (Ankara: Türk Tarih Kurumu, 2015).

Al-Thaʿālibī, Abū Manṣūr, *Ghurar akhbār mulūk al-furs wa-siyarihim = Histoire des rois des Perses*, Texte arabe publié et traduit par H. Zotenberg (Paris: Imprimerie Nationale, 1900).

Al-Thaʿālibī, Abū Manṣūr, *al-Iʿjāz wa-l-ījāz*, ed. Muḥammad Ibrāhīm Salīm (Cairo: Maktabat al-Qurʾān, 1999).

Al-Thaʿālibī, Abū Manṣūr, *Khāṣṣ al-khāṣṣ*, ed. Maʾmūn b. Muḥyī l-Dīn al-Janān (Beirut: Dār al-Kutub al-ʿIlmiyya, 1994).

Al-Thaʿālibī, Abū Manṣūr, *Kitāb al-Mubhij*, ed. Ibrāhīm Ṣāliḥ (Damascus: Dār al-Bashāʾir lil-Ṭibāʿa wa-l-Nashr wa-l-Tawzīʿ, 1999).

Al-Thaʿālibī, Abū Manṣūr, *Laṭāʾif al-maʿārif*, ed. Ibrāhīm al-Ibyārī and Ḥasan Kāmil al-Ṣayrafī (Cairo: ʿĪsā al-Bābī al-Ḥalabī, 1960) = C. E. Bosworth, *The Book of Curious and Entertaining Information: The* Laṭāʾif al-maʿārif *of Thaʿālibī* (Edinburgh: Edinburgh University Press, 1968).

Al-Thaʿālibī, Abū Manṣūr, *al-Tamthīl wa-l-muḥāḍara*, ed. Qaṣī al-Ḥusayn (Beirut: Dār wa-Maktabat al-Hilāl, 2003).

Al-Thaʿālibī, Abū Manṣūr, *Thimār al-qulūb fī l-muḍāf wa-l-mansūb*, ed. Muḥammad Abū l-Faḍl Ibrāhīm (Cairo: Dār al-Maʿārif, 1985).

Al-Thaʿālibī, Abū Manṣūr, *Yatīmat al-dahr fī maḥāsin ahl al-ʿaṣr*, ed. Mufīd Muḥammad Qumayḥa (Beirut: Dār al-Maktaba al-ʿIlmiyya, 1983).

Al-Thaʿālibī, Abū Manṣūr, *al-Ẓarāʾif wa-l-laṭāʾif wa-l-yawāqīt fī baʿḍ al-mawāqīt*, ed. Nāṣir Muḥammadī Muḥammad Jād (Cairo: Dār al-Kutub wa-l-Wathāʾiq al-Qawmiyya, 2006).

Themistius, *Risālat Thāmisṭiyūs ilā Yūliyān al-malik fī l-siyāsa wa-tadbīr al-mamlaka*, ed. Muḥammad Salīm Sālim ([Cairo]: Maṭbaʿat Dār al-Kutub, 1970).

Tietze, Andreas, *Mustafā ʿĀlī's* Counsel for Sultans *of 1581, Edition, Translation, Notes*, 2 vols. (Vienna: Verlag der Österreichischen Akademie der Wissenschaften, 1978–82).

Tillier, Mathieu, 'Courts of Law, Historical', *EI Three*. First print edition: 2017. First published online: 2017.

Tillier, Mathieu, '*Qāḍīs* and the Political Use of the *Maẓālim* Jurisdiction under the ʿAbbāsids', in *Public Violence in Islamic Societies: Power, Discipline, and the Construction of the Public Sphere, 7th–19th Centuries CE*, ed. Christian Lange and Maribel Fierro (Edinburgh: Edinburgh University Press, 2009), 43–66.

Al-Tirmidhī, Muḥammad b. ʿĪsā, *al-Jāmiʿ al-kabīr*, ed. Bashshār ʿAwwād Maʿrūf (Beirut: Dār al-Gharb al-Islāmī, 1996).

Toelle, Heidi and Katia Zakharia, *À la découverte de la littérature arabe du VIe siècle à nos jours* (Paris: Flammarion, 2003).

Toorawa, Shawkat M., 'Defining *Adab* by (Re)defining the *Adīb*: Ibn Abī Ṭāhir Ṭayfūr and Storytelling', in *On Fiction and* Adab *in Medieval Arabic Literature*, ed. Philip F. Kennedy (Wiesbaden: Harrassowitz Verlag, 2005), 286–308.

Toorawa, Shawkat M., *Ibn Abī Ṭāhir Ṭayfūr and Arabic Writerly Culture: A Ninth-Century Bookman in Baghdad* (London: Routledge Curzon, 2005).

Topuzoğlu, T. R., 'Kitāb Ādāb al-Mulūk al-Khwārazm-shāhī of Abū Manṣūr ʿAbd al-Malik b. Muḥammad b. Ismāʿīl ath-Thaʿālibī', PhD diss., University of Manchester, 1974.

Topuzoğlu, T. R., *Kitāb Ādāb al-Mulūk al-Khwārazm-shāhī*, 2 vols. (Ankara: Türk Tarih Kurumu, 2015).

Tor, D. G., 'ʿAyyār', *EI Three*. First print edition: 2014. First published online: 2014.

Tor, D. G., 'al-Fuḍayl b. ʿIyāḍ', *EI Three*. First print edition: 2013. First published online: 2013.

Tor, D. G., 'Historical Representations of Yaʿqūb b. al-Layth: A Reappraisal', *Journal of the Royal Asiatic Society*, Series 3, 12 (2002), 247–75.

Tor, D. G., 'The Mamluks in the Military of the Pre-Seljuq Persianate Dynasties', *Iran* 46 (2008), 213–25.

Tor, D. G., 'The Political Revival of the Abbasid Caliphate: Al-Muqtafī and the Seljuks', *Journal of the American Oriental Society* 137 (2017), 301–14.

Tor, D. G., 'Sultan', *PEIPT*, 523–4.

Tor, D. G., 'A Tale of Two Murders: Power Relations between Caliph and Sultan in the Saljūq Era', *Zeitschrift der Deutschen Morgenländischen Gesellschaft* 159 (2009), 279–97.

Tottoli, Roberto, 'Ṣāliḥ', *EQ* IV (2004), 521–2.

Treadwell, Luke, '*Shāhānshāh* and *al-Malik al-Muʾayyad*: The Legitimation of Power in Sāmānid and Būyid Iran', in *Culture and Memory in Medieval Islam: Essays in Honour of Wilferd Madelung*, ed. Farhad Daftary and Josef W. Meri (London: I.B. Tauris, 2003), 318–37.

Treadwell, W. L., 'The Political History of the Sāmānid State', PhD diss., University of Oxford, 1991.

Tschudi, Rudolf, *Das Âṣafnâme des Luṭfî Pascha* (Berlin: Mayer & Müller, 1910).

Tuḥfeh dar akhlāq va-siyāsat, ed. M. T. Dānishpazhūh (Tehran: Bungāh-i Tarjumeh va-Nashr-i Kitāb, 1962).

Turner, John P., 'Aḥmad b. Abī Duʾād', *EI Three*. First print edition: 2007. First published online: 2007.

Al-Ṭurṭūshī, Abū Bakr, Muḥammad b. al-Walīd, *Sirāj al-mulūk*, ed. Muḥammad Fatḥī Abū Bakr, 2 vols. (Cairo: al-Dār al-Miṣriyya al-Lubnāniyya, 1994) =

Maximiliano Alarcón, *Lámpara de los Príncipes por Abubéquer de Tortosa*. 2 vols. (Madrid: Instituto de Valencia de Don Juan, 1930).

Ṭūsī, Naṣīr al-Dīn, *Akhlāq-i Nāṣirī*, ed. Mujtabā Mīnuvī and ʿAlī-Riżā Ḥaydarī (Tehran: Intishārāt-i Khaᵛārazmī, 1982) = G. M. Wickens, *The Nasirean Ethics* (London: Allen & Unwin, 1964).

Urmavī, Sirāj al-Dīn Maḥmūd b. Abī Bakr, *Laṭāʾif al-ḥikma*, ed. Ghulām-Ḥusayn Yūsufī (Tehran: Intishārāt-i Bunyād-i Farhang-i Īrān, 1972).

Usāma b. Munqidh, *see* Ibn Munqidh, Usāma

Vadet, J.-C., 'Ibn Abī ʾl-Shawārib', *EI*². First print edition: 1960–2007. First published online: 2012.

Vajda, Georges and B. M. Scarcia Amoretti, 'De la condemnation de la géophagie dans la tradition musulmane: ʿAbd al-Raḥmān b. Muḥammad Ibn Manda, *Taḥrīm ʾakl al-ṭīn waḥāl ʾākilih fī l-dunyā wal-āḫira*', *Rivista degli studi orientali* 55 (1981), 5–38.

De la Vaissière, Étienne, 'Khagan', *EIr* XVI (2017), 383–4. In *Encyclopaedia Iranica Online* © Trustees of Columbia University in the City of New York. First print edition: 2017. First published online: 2020.

Van Bladel, Kevin, 'Barmakids', *EI Three*. First print edition: 2012. First published online: 2012.

Van Bladel, Kevin, 'The Iranian Characteristics and Forged Greek Attributions in the Arabic *Sirr al-asrār* (*Secret of Secrets*)', *Mélanges de l'Université Saint-Joseph* 57 (2004), 151–72.

Van Ess, Josef, 'Political Ideas in Early Islamic Religious Thought', *British Journal of Middle Eastern Studies* 28 (2001), 151–64.

Van Ess, J., 'Thumāma b. Ashras', *EI*² 10 (2000), 449–50. First print edition: 1960–2007. First published online: 2012.

Van Renterghem, Vanessa, 'Controlling and Developing Baghdad: Caliphs, Sultans and the Balance of Power in the Abbasid Capital (Mid-5th/11th to Late 6th/12th Centuries)', in *The Seljuqs: Politics, Society and Culture*, ed. Christian Lange and Songül Mecit (Edinburgh: Edinburgh University Press, 2011), 117–38.

Van Steenbergen, Jo, *A History of the Islamic World, 600–1800: Empire, Dynastic Formations, and Heterogeneities in Pre-modern Islamic West-Asia* (Abingdon and New York: Routledge, 2021).

Vasalou, Sophia, *Moral Agents and Their Deserts: The Character of Muʿtazilite Ethics* (Princeton, NJ, and Oxford: Princeton University Press, 2008).

Vasalou, Sophia, *Virtues of Greatness in the Arabic Tradition* (Oxford: Oxford University Press, 2019).

Veccia Vaglieri, L., 'al-Hurmuzān', *EI*². First print edition: 1960–2007. First published online: 2012.

Viguera, María J. , 'Las cartas de al-Gazali y al-Turtuši al soberano almorávid Yusuf b. Tašufin', *al-Andalus* 42 (1977), 341–74.

Viguera-Molins, María Jesús, 'Al-Andalus and the Maghrib (from the Fifth/Eleventh Century to the Fall of the Almoravids)', in *The New Cambridge History of Islam, Vol. II: The Western Islamic World, Eleventh to Eighteenth Centuries*, ed. Maribel Fierro (Cambridge: Cambridge University Press, 2010), 21–47.

Waldman, Marilyn Robinson, *Toward a Theory of Historical Narrative: A Case Study in Perso-Islamicate Historiography* (Columbus, OH: Ohio State University Press, 1980).

Walker, J. [P. Fenton], 'Sulaymān b. Dāwūd', *EI²*. First print edition: 1960–2007. First published online: 2012.

Walker, Paul E., 'The Ismaili Daʿwa in the Reign of the Fatimid Caliph Al-Ḥākim', *Journal of the American Research Center in Egypt* 30 (1993), 161–82.

Walzer, Richard, *Al-Farabi on the Perfect State. Abū Naṣr al-Fārābī's* Mabādiʾ ārāʾ ahl al-madīna al-fāḍila. *A Revised Text with Introduction, Translation, and Commentary* (Oxford: Clarendon Press, 1985).

Al-Warrāq, Maḥmūd, *Dīwān Maḥmūd al-Warrāq shāʿir al-ḥikma wa-l-mawʿiẓa*, ed. Walīd Qaṣṣāb (ʿAjmān [UAE]: Muʾassasat al-Funūn, 1991).

Webb, Peter, '*Al-Jāhiliyya*: Uncertain Times of Uncertain Meanings', *Der Islam* 91 (2014), 69–94.

De Weese, Devin, 'Persian and Turkic from Kazan to Tobolsk: Literary Frontiers in Muslim Inner Asia', in *The Persianate World: The Frontiers of a Eurasian Lingua Franca*, ed. Nile Green (Oakland, CA: University of California Press, 2019), 131–55.

Weipert, Reinhard, 'al-ʿAkawwak, ʿAlī b. Jabala', *EI Three*. First print edition: 2008. First published online: 2008.

Weipert, Reinhard, 'al-Aṣmaʿī', *EI Three*. First print edition: 2009. First published online: 2009.

Wensinck, A. J. and P. Crone, 'Mawlā', *EI²*. First print edition: 1960–2007. First published online: 2012.

Williams, Steven J., *The* Secret of Secrets*: The Scholarly Career of a Pseudo-Aristotelian Text in the Latin Middle Ages* (Ann Arbor, MI: University of Michigan Press, 2003).

Woods, John E., *The Aqquyunlu: Clan, Confederation, Empire*, revised and expanded (Salt Lake City, UT: University of Utah Press, 1999).

Yāqūt al-Ḥamawī, Ibn ʿAbdallāh, *Muʿjam al-buldān* (Beirut: Dār Ṣādir, 1977).

Yāqūt al-Ḥamawī, Ibn ʿAbdallāh, *Muʿjam al-udabāʾ: Irshād al-arīb ilā maʿrifat al-adīb*, ed. Iḥsān ʿAbbās (Beirut: Dār al-Gharb al-Islāmī, 1993).

Yavari, Neguin, *Advice for the Sultan: Prophetic Voices and Secular Politics in Medieval Islam* (Oxford and New York: Oxford University Press, 2014).

Yavari, Neguin, *The Future of Iran's Past: Niẓām al-Mulk Remembered* (Oxford: Oxford University Press, 2018).

Yavari, Neguin, 'Mirrors for Princes or a Hall of Mirrors? Niẓām al-Mulk's *Siyar al-mulūk* Reconsidered', *Al-Masāq: Islam and the Medieval Mediterranean* 20 (2008), 47–69.

Yavari, Neguin, 'Neẓām-al-Molk', *EIr*. In *Encyclopaedia Iranica Online* © Trustees of Columbia University in the City of New York. First print edition: 2015. First published online: 2020.

Yavari, Neguin, 'The Political Regard in Medieval Islamic Thought', *Historical Social Research (Historische Sozialforschung)*, Special Issue: *Islamicate Secularities in Past and Present* 44 (2019), 52–73.

Yavari, Neguin, 'Polysemous Texts and Reductionist Readings: Women and Heresy in the Siyar al-Mulūk', in *Views from the Edge: Essays in Honor of Richard W. Bulliet*, ed. Neguin Yavari, Lawrence G. Potter and Jean-Marc Ran Oppenheimer (New York: Columbia University Press, 2004), 322–46.

Yavari, Neguin, 'Siar al-molūk', *EIr*. In *Encyclopaedia Iranica Online* © Trustees of Columbia University in the City of New York. First print edition: 2015. First published online: 2020.

Yılmaz, Hüseyin, *Caliphate Redefined: The Mystical Turn in Ottoman Political Thought* (Princeton, NJ: Princeton University Press, 2018).

Yousefi, Najm al-Din, 'Islam without Fuqahā': Ibn al-Muqaffaʿ and His Perso-Islamic Solution to the Caliphate's Crisis of Legitimacy (70-142 AH/690–760 CE)', *Iranian Studies* 50 (2017), 9–44.

Yücesoy, Hayrettin, 'al-Faḍl b. Sahl', *EI Three*. First print edition: 2013. First published online: 2013.

Yūsuf Khāṣṣ Ḥājib, *Kutadgu Bilig*, ed. Reşid Rahmeti Arat (Istanbul: Millî Eğitim Basımevi, 1947) = Robert Dankoff, Wisdom of Royal Glory (Kutadgu bilig)*: A Turko-Islamic Mirror for Princes* (Chicago, IL: Chicago University Press, 1983).

Yūsufī, Ghulām-Ḥusayn, 'Muqaddimeh-yi muṣaḥḥiḥ', in Kaykāʾūs b. Iskandar, *Qābūsnāmeh*, ed. Ghulām-Ḥusayn Yūsufī (Tehran: Shirkat-i Intishārāt-i ʿIlmī va-Farhangī, 1989), 13–51.

Zadeh, Travis, *The Vernacular Qurʾan: Translation and the Rise of Persian Exegesis* (Oxford: Oxford University Press; London: The Institute of Ismaili Studies, 2012).

Zakeri, Mohsen, 'Ādāb al-falāsifa: The Persian Content of an Arabic Collection of Aphorisms', *Mélanges de l'Université Saint-Joseph* 57 (2004), 173–90.

Zakeri, Mohsen, ''Alī ibn ʿUbaida al-Raiḥānī: A Forgotten Belletrist (*adīb*) and Pahlavi Translator', *Oriens* 34 (1994), 75–102.

Zakeri, Mohsen, 'Javānmardi', *EIr* XIV (2008), 594–601. In *Encyclopaedia Iranica Online* © Trustees of Columbia University in the City of New York. First print edition: 2008. First published online: 2020.

Zakeri, Mohsen, 'Muḥammad b. Khalaf b. al-Marzbān (d. 309/921) and His Role in Translations from the Middle Persian', in *The Place to Go: Contexts of Learning in Baghdad, 750–1000 C. E.*, ed. Jens Scheiner and Damien Janos (Berlin: Gerlach Press, 2021), 343–61.

Zakeri, Mohsen, *Persian Wisdom in Arabic Garb: ʿAlī b. ʿUbayda al-Rayḥānī (d. 219/834) and His* Jawāhir al-kilam wa-farāʾid al-ḥikam (Leiden: Brill, 2007).

Zakeri, Mohsen, 'Some Early Persian Apophthegmata: *Tawqīʿāt* in Arabic Transmission', *Jerusalem Studies in Arabic and Islam* 27 (2002), 283–304.

Zakharia, Katia, 'Al-Ghazâlî, conseilleur du prince', in *Savoirs et pouvoirs: Genèse des traditions, traditions réinventées*, ed. Katia Zakharia and Ali Cheiban (Paris: Maisonneuve et Larose, 2008), 209–34.

Zakharia, Katia and Ali Sheiban, eds., *Savoirs et pouvoirs. Genèse des traditions, traditions réinventées* (Paris: Maisonneuve et Larose; Lyon: Maison de l'Orient et de la Méditerranée, 2008).

Al-Zamakhsharī, Maḥmūd b. ʿUmar, *Rabīʿ al-abrār wa-nuṣūṣ al-akhbār*, ed. Salīm al-Nuʿaymī (Baghdad: Wizārat al-Awqāf wa-l-Shuʾūn al-Dīniyya, 1976).

Zaman, Muhammad Qasim, *Religion and Politics under the Early ʿAbbāsids: The Emergence of the Proto-Sunnī Elite* (Leiden and New York: Brill, 1997).

Zambaur, Edouard de, *Manuel de généalogie et de chronologie pour l'histoire de l'Islam* (Hannover: H. Lafaire, 1927; reprinted Bad Pyrmont: Orientbuchhandlung Heinz Lafaire, 1955).

Zetterstéen, K. V. [C. E. Bosworth], 'al-Muḳtadir', *EI*². First print edition: 1960–2007. First published online: 2012.

Zetterstéen, K. V. [C. E. Bosworth], 'al-Mustaʿīn', *EI*². First print edition: 1960–2007. First published online: 2012.

Zetterstéen, K. V. [C. E. Bosworth], 'al-Muṭīʿ liʾllāh', *EI*². First print edition: 1960–2007. First published online: 2012.

Zetterstéen, K. V. [C. E. Bosworth], 'al-Muttaḳī liʾllāh', *EI*². First print edition: 1960–2007. First published online: 2012.

Al-Ziriklī, Khayr al-Dīn, *al-Aʿlām* (Beirut: Dār al-ʿIlm lil-Malāyīn, 2007).

Zuhayr b. Abī Sulmā, *Dīwān*, ed. ʿAlī Ḥasan Fāʿūr (Beirut: Dār al-Kutub al-ʿIlmiyya, 1988).

Index

Abarwīz *see* Khusraw II Parvīz
ʿAbbādids *see* Banū ʿAbbād
Abbasids, 25, 26, 27, 31, 40n, 43, 116n, 117n, 194, 262n, 267, 268, 270, 272, 274, 275, 286n *see also* caliphate
Abbès, Makram, 62n, 79, 130, 158n, 160n
ʿAbdallāh b. Ṭāhir, 107n, 249n
ʿAbdallāh b. ʿUmar, 122n
ʿAbdallāh b. al-Zubayr, 102n, 107n, 220n
ʿAbd al-Ḥamīd al-Kātib, 9
ʿAbd al-Malik b. Marwān, Umayyad caliph, 102, 125n, 253n, 311
abnāʾ al-dawla, 286n
Abraham, 115, 248
Abū l-ʿAtāhiya, 101n
Abū Bakr, first caliph, 220n
Abū Bakr b. ʿAyyāsh, 123
Abū Bakr b. Ḥāmid, 276n
Abū Bakr b. Saʿd-i Zangī, Muẓaffar al-Dīn, 14n
Abū l-Dardāʾ ʿUwaymir b. Zayd al-Anṣārī, 256, 257n, 258
Abū Dharr, 170n
Abū Dulaf al-Ijlī, 91n
Abū l-Fażl Yūsuf b. ʿAlī Mustawfī, 13n
Abū Hurayra, 208, 254
Abū l-Murajjā Jābir, Hamdanid, 265
Abū Muslim, 116
Abū Naṣr b. Abī Zayd, 129, 130n
Abū l-Qāsim Hibat Allāh, Hamdanid, 265
Abū Tammām, 100
Abū ʿUbayd b. ʿAbdallāh b. Masʿūd, 212
Abū Yūsuf, Yaʿqūb b. Ibrāhīm al-Kūfī, 9
Acre, 43
adab, *ādāb*, 5–6, 10, 12–13, 14n, 62, 92n, 97, 101, 106, 118, 126, 127, 226, 236, 249, 299, 303
Adab al-dunyā wa-l-dīn, 62, 63n, 120n, 159n, 218n, 254n
al-Ādāb al-kabīr, 9
adab al-mulūk (genre), 13
Ādāb al-mulūk, 38, 55, 60, 64
Adam, 88, 116, 142, 147
ʿAdī b. Zayd, 91
al-ʿĀḍid, Fatimid caliph-imam, 43
ʿadl, 20, 92n, 132n, 138, 183n, 192n, 205, 210, 214, 218, 219 *see also* justice
admonition, 13, 166, 260, 267 *see also* exhortation, *mawʿiẓa*
ʿAḍud al-Dawla, Buyid ruler, 30n, 36, 266n, 275n
advice literature, 3, 4, 5, 6, 9, 10, 13, 14n, 16, 17, 18, 19, 24, 41, 47, 60, 61, 64, 67, 70, 72, 74, 103, 123, 146, 150, 247, 248, 249, 250, 251, 252, 253, 257, 311 *see also andarz*, counsel, mirror(s) for princes, *naṣīḥa*
al-Afḍal b. Badr al-Jamālī, 43, 72
Afghanistan, 26, 37, 38n
Afrāsiyāb, 138, 139n
agent, 201, 236
agriculture, 28, 29, 41, 60, 218, 219, 220, 221, 222

Index

ʿahd
  charge or testament, 9, 92, 249n
  covenant, 170, 194, 303
  see also testament, *waṣiyya*
ʿAhd Ardashīr, 7, 62, 106, 139, 208n, 225n
ʿahdnāmeh, 299, 303
aḥkām, 6 *see also* ordinances
al-Aḥkām al-sulṭāniyya, 61, 62, 189n, 192n, 218n, 219n, 224n, 225n, 270n
Ahlak-i Alaʾi, 16
Aḥmad, Fuʾād ʿAbd al-Munʿim, 51n, 77
Aḥmad b. Būya, Muʿizz al-Dawla *see* Muʿizz al-Dawla
Aḥmad Ibn Ṭūlūn, 25
Aḥmad II b. Ismāʿīl, Samanid amir, 277n, 307
al-Aḥnaf b. Qays, 170n
al-Ahwāzī, Abū l-Ḥusayn Muḥammad b. al-Ḥusayn, 163n
āʾīn, 7, 285, 308
ʿajam, 12, 138, 207n
ʿajamiyya, 207n
al-ʿAkawwak, ʿAlī b. Jabala, 91n
Akhbār al-wuzarāʾ see Kitāb al-Wuzarāʾ wa-l-kuttāb
akhlāq, 6, 13, 14, 17, 97, 144n, 155, 156, 157
akhlāq al-mulūk, 5, 10, 16n, 53, 62–3, 130
al-Akhlāq al-mushajjara, 19n
Akhlāq-i Ḥakīmī, 17
Akhlāq-i Jahāngīrī, 17
Akhlāq-i Jalālī (= *Lavāmiʿ al-ishrāq fī makārim al-akhlāq*), 14, 15n, 16n
Akhlāq-i Muḥsinī, 15
Akhlāq-i Nāṣirī, 14
akhlāṭ, 140n
Aktham b. Ṣayfī, 101n
ʿAlāʾ al-Dīn Kayqubād, Seljuk of Rum, 13n, 14n, 18, 19
Alamut, 14n
Alarcón, M. A., 81, 312n
Aleppo, 11n, 43, 44n, 116n, 192n, 265n
Alexander, 8, 12, 21, 47, 48, 49, 50, 51, 104n, 107, 119, 133n, 134, 169, 176n, 177n, 181, 182, 185, 212, 213n, 227, 246 *see also* Dhū l-Qarnayn
Alexandria, 70n, 71, 72, 73, 289
Alfonso VI, 73
ʿAlī b. Abī Ṭālib, 13, 30, 104, 108n, 111n, 117, 121n, 134n, 157, 165, 166n, 182, 183n, 206n, 207, 253n
ʿAlī b. Būya, ʿImād al-Dawla, Buyid ruler, 36
ʿAlī b. al-Jahm, 263
ʿAlī al-Hamadānī, 14, 14n
Ali, Ismail, 77
allegory, 56, 58, 145
Almohads, 72
Almoravids, 71, 72, 213n
almsgiving *see* charity, *ṣadaqa*, *zakāt*
Alp Arslan, 40, 41–2, 44, 63, 284
Alptigin, 37
al-Aʿmash, Sulaymān b. Mihrān, 108
ambassador(s), 11, 49, 231 *see also* envoy
al-Amīn, Muḥammad, Abbasid caliph, 249, 267
Amīn al-Milla, *laqab* of Sultan Maḥmūd, 281, 306
al-Āmir, Fatimid caliph-imam, 72
al-ʿĀmirī, Abū l-Ḥasan, 53–4
ʿāmm(a), 5, 52, 110, 206n, 208, 254 *see also* common people, ordinary people
Amorium, 100
ʿAmr b. al-ʿĀṣ, 132n, 183n, 208n
ʿAmr b. al-Layth, 195, 198–202
ʿAmr b. Masada, 118, 210
ʿAmr b. ʿUbayd, 98, 105
al-Amthāl wa-l-ḥikam, 62, 224n
Anas b. Mālik, 256
Anatolia, 14, 26, 28, 40n, 41, 42, 44
al-Andalus, 71, 72, 73, 207n, 213n
andarz, 5, 8n
andarznāmeh, 5, 59
Ansari, Hassan, 52, 54n
Antioch, 48
Anūshirvān (= Khusraw I), 12, 21, 60, 92n, 121, 123, 126, 132n, 138, 139n, 182, 185n, 206n, 208n, 220n, 226, 264 *see also* Khusraw I
aphorism, 5, 7, 49, 111, 112n, 166n *see also* *ḥikma*, maxim
Aqquyunlu, 15n
ʿarab, 12, 207n
Arabia(n), 9, 42, 90n, 107n, 108n, 258n, 291n, 297n
Arabic, 3, 4, 5, 6, 7, 8, 9, 10, 11, 12, 13, 14n, 16, 17, 18, 19n, 22, 24, 26, 27n, 34, 36, 37n, 38, 45, 47, 48, 49, 51, 52, 53, 54, 55, 56, 58, 59n, 61, 62, 63, 67, 68, 69, 70, 73, 76, 77–81, 83, 85, 87, 100n, 103n, 111n, 136n, 137n, 138n, 140n, 144n, 163n, 170n, 179, 200, 208n, 274n, 286n, 303
arbāb al-arḍ, 90, 91, 115, 118

Ardashīr, 7, 12, 45, 97, 106, 108n, 121n, 132n, 134, 138, 182, 183n, 208n, 225
Aristotle, 7, 8, 12, 47, 51, 62, 87, 92n, 104n, 107, 133n, 134n, 144n, 158n, 182, 185n, 205n
~ as counsellor to Alexander, 8, 47, 48, 51, 104n, 107, 133n, 181, 246
~ on virtue, 15, 158n
~ practical philosophy, 5
see also Pseudo-Aristotle
ʿArjī, ʿAbdallāh b. ʿUmar, 159n
Armenia(n), 41, 43, 59, 74
army, armies, 26, 27, 28, 37, 41, 42, 55, 60, 63, 145, 150, 173, 175, 185, 188, 194, 195, 196, 197, 198, 199, 200, 207, 208, 210n, 218, 226, 227, 228, 229, 233, 236, 237, 240, 242, 243, 245, 264, 265, 266, 267, 273, 284n, 310
Arrān, 59
al-Asadī, ʿAbdallāh b. al-Zubayr, 102n
al-Asadī, Aḥmad b. Ibrāhīm, 268
al-Asadī, Sālim Ibn Wābisa, 159n
Asaf, 16n
Asafname, 16
Ascalon, 43, 73
Askari, Nasrin, 57n
al-Aṣmaʿī, Abū Saʿīd ʿAbd al-Malik, 255
aspiration, 70, 97, 119, 121n, 159, 160, 165, 189, 298 *see also himma*
Asqaf of Najrān, 107
astrology, 6, 57
astronomy, 60, 119
atabeg, 14, 44, 63
al-ʿAṭawī (al-ʿAṭwī), Muḥammad b. ʿAbd al-Raḥmān, 100, 101n
al-ʿAttābī, Abū ʿAmr Kulthūm b. ʿAmr, 99n
ʿAṭṭār, Farīd al-Dīn, 59
attribution, 12, 45, 51, 62n, 92n, 111, 112n, 134n, 138n, 159n, 166n, 205n
authorship, disputed, 11, 12, 52, 61, 62, 63, 68–9
Avicenna *see* Ibn Sīnā
aʿwān, 92, 135, 185, 188, 189, 205, 206, 234
ʿayyār(ī), 167, 168, 172, 173, 198
Ayyubid(s), 11, 18n, 44
Azāriqa, 253
Azerbaijan, 28, 41, 59

Bacon, Roger, 49
Badakhshan, 289
Badawī, ʿAbd al-Raḥmān, 77
Badr al-Jamālī, 43
Baghdad, 11, 25, 29, 31, 32, 36, 37, 39, 41, 43, 52, 66, 71, 116n, 132n, 194, 195, 198, 200n, 211n, 263n, 265n, 266n, 267n, 268n, 269n, 271n, 273n, 274, 275, 276n, 293, 305, 308
Bāghir al-Turkī, 268
Bagley, F. R. C., 80, 137n
Bahāʾ al-Dawla, Fīrūz b. ʿAḍud al-Dawla, ʿIzz al-Dīn, Buyid ruler, 62, 275, 276n
Baḥr al-favāʾid, 14n
Bahrām-i Gūr (Bahram V), Sasanian monarch, 91n, 138, 139n, 205n, 236–46
al-Baḥrayn, 42
Bakhtiyār, ʿIzz al-Dawla, Buyid ruler, 275
Bakr b. Mālik, 281
balance, 86, 141, 156, 183, 231, 233
justice as ~, 183, 205n
between opposing virtues and vices, 15, 164
in the body, 49, 261
Balkh, 33, 100n, 114n, 117n, 199, 200, 258n, 302, 304
Banū ʿAbbād, 72n
Banū ʿAbs, 251
Banū Hūd, 70
Barcelona, 73
Barīd al-saʿāda, 13n
Barmakids, 100, 220n
Basra, 122n, 252, 256n, 269, 312n
al-Baṭāʾiḥī, Abū ʿAbdallāh *see* Ibn al-Baṭāʾiḥī
bāṭin, 54, 111n, 183n, 194n
Batiniyya, 194, 278
Bāvandid(s), 173n, 174n
al-Bazdahī, Aḥmad b. Muḥammad al-Nasafī, 279–81
Berkey, Jonathan P., 31
Bilawhar wa-Būdhāsaf, 7, 58
bilig, 147
al-Bīrūnī, Abū Rayḥān, 38, 55
biṭāna, 123
boon-companion(s), 59, 60, 169, 211n, 268
Bray, Julia, 55, 100n, 110n, 111n, 112n, 115n, 127n, 278n
Bryson, 7 *see also Oikonomicos*
Buddha, 52, 87, 104
Buddhism, 58
Bughā al-Ṣaghīr, 268n, 269n
al-Buḥturī, Abū ʿUbayda, 160

Bukhara, 33, 34, 193, 199, 280n, 304
Burāq, 294
al-Burjumī, ʿAbd Qays b. Khufāf, 224n
al-Burrī, Muḥammad b. Muḥammad al-Mālikī, 23n
Būstān, 14n
Buyids, 11, 27, 28n, 29, 30n, 31, 34, 35–7, 39, 40, 60, 61, 62, 173n, 225n, 232n, 265n, 273n, 274n, 276n
Buzurgmihr, 101n, 123, 205n, 206n, 220, 248
Byzantine, Byzantine Empire, 41, 42, 53n, 90n, 100, 140n, 143, 161n, 163n, 211n, 274

Cairo, 42, 43, 71, 72, 192n, 198n, 258n
caliphate, 8, 25, 30, 45, 61, 67, 98, 107n, 126n, 205n, 220n, 253n, 268, 269, 270n, 271n, 287, 311
Carolingian mirrors, 5n, 10n, 53n, 85n, 143, 163n, 180
Caspian, 34, 35, 36, 39, 54, 174n, 176n
Castile, 73
Caucasus, 28, 41
Chaghri Bey, 39–40, 44, 293
Chahārdahī, M. M., 80, 288n
chamberlain(s), 56, 57, 126n, 192, 193, 210, 245, 246, 305
charisma, royal, 55, 58n, 137 *see also farr*
charity, charitable donation(s), 19, 127, 235, 238, 241, 294 *see also ṣadaqa*
chess, 60
China, 215, 299, 300, 301
chivalry, 60, 173
Christian, Christianity
~ communities, 43, 49, 74
~ courts, 3, 5, 45, 49, 181
~ in Arabia, 91n, 107n, 258n
~ militarism, 41, 73, 74, 256n
circle of justice, 49, 50 (Fig. 2), 145, 151n, 180n, 181, 182, 184 (Fig. 3), 185n, 208n, 217
cities, conditions of, 220–4
clemency, 144, 189n, 204 *see also* forgiveness
coinage, 33, 35, 174, 273n, 306 *see also sikka*
commerce, 60, 217, 222, 302 *see also* trade
common good, 204n, 217 *see also maṣlaḥa*, public good
common people, 112, 128, 145, 151, 159, 183, 271, 275, 277, 281 see also *ʿāmm(a)*, ordinary people
conscience, 86, 309n
consultation, 68, 83, 206, 210, 247, 248–52, 254n, 295
corruption, 52, 97, 100, 132, 138, 141, 142, 143, 164, 182, 193n, 227, 230, 233, 243
counsel, 4n, 5, 9, 11, 13, 19, 22, 23, 49, 51, 52, 55, 56, 57, 83, 98n, 103, 104n, 107, 167, 178, 181, 205n, 208, 209, 227, 228, 247, 248, 249, 252n, 253–8, 311 *see also naṣīḥa*
counsellor, 56, 85, 123, 126, 148, 166, 206, 211, 248, 249, 269n, 284n, 311
courage, 15, 45n, 102, 144, 150, 155, 161n, 162n, 164, 165, 166, 188, 198, 295
court(s)
royal, 3, 4, 7, 9, 16, 17, 18, 19, 22, 38, 41, 54, 55, 56, 57, 59, 64, 65, 85, 116n, 127n, 131, 132, 150, 153, 167, 179n, 194, 203, 211n, 232n, 239, 240, 243, 245, 259, 270n, 273, 280, 286, 288, 297n
of law, 191, 192n, 215n
see also maẓālim
Crusades, Crusaders, 43, 73

Damascus, 14n, 22, 192n, 257n
Damghan, 176
Dandanqan, 39
Daniel, 122
Dankoff, Robert, 58, 78, 145n, 147n
dār al-ʿadl, 192n
Darband, 289
Darb Zubayda, 288n
dargāh, 65 *see also* court(s)
al-Dārī, Tamīm, 254n
Darke, H. S. G., 9n, 79–80, 194n, 198n, 203n, 239n, 243n, 286n, 289n, 292n, 299n, 307n
Darius, 246
Dāʾūd b. Bahrāmshāh, Mengücekid ruler, 14n
Davānī (Dawwānī), Muḥammad b. Asad, 15, 16n
David, 88, 130, 131, 138, 163, 189, 199n, 207, 220
daʿwa, 31, 33, 68, 194, 280n
dawla, 97, 135, 185, 267n, 276, 283, 286, 300, 303, 308
used in titles, 30n, 265n, 296, 297, 307
see also state
al-dawla al-Niẓāmiyya, 40, 259

Dāwūd b. Naṣr, Abū l-Fatḥ, 282n
Daylam(i), 27, 35, 273
De regimine principum, 53
Dhakhīrat al-mulūk, 14n
dhimma, 256 *see also* non-Muslims
Dhū l-Qarnayn, 176 *see also* Alexander
Diez, Heinrich Friedrich von, 61
dihqān, 250n, 296
disobedience, 95, 96, 142, 195, 197, 210, 258, 294
Diyar Bakr, 274
Diyar Rabiʿa, 249n, 274
doctor(s), 55, 252n, 261 *see also* physician(s)
Doctrina phísica y moral de príncipes, 17–18
dreams, 57, 248, 287, 288, 294
Durand-Guédy, David, 41, 65
Durar al-sulūk fī siyāsat al-mulūk, 62
Dustūr al-vizāra, 22n
Dvin, 59

economics, 4, 7, 14, 25, 28, 29, 52, 144n, 222, 223, 225n, 270n, 307n
education, 4, 71, 101n, 158, 226, 284n, 298n, 299, 303
Egypt, 24, 25, 31, 42, 43, 71, 73, 198n, 232n
élite(s), 16, 66, 110n, 275, 281
encyclopaedism, 57, 167
enemy, enemies, 52, 60, 105, 106, 112, 135, 139n, 149, 151, 152, 154, 168, 169, 170, 171–9, 180, 195, 203n, 210, 221, 224n, 226, 227, 230, 237, 240, 244, 246, 259, 264, 277, 285, 295, 305, 309, 310
enmity, 175, 177
envoy(s), 51, 57, 168n, 174, 194, 198, 199, 211n, 218, 226, 232n, 245, 297, 305
epistle, 6, 7, 9, 48, 133n
equity, 138, 184, 191, 205, 212, 213, 219, 220, 223, 224, 225, 229, 300 *see also naṣafa*
Erzincan, 14n
ethics, 4, 7, 14, 15n, 52, 144n, 156, 159n, 161n
evil, 117n, 148, 224, 281
evil eye, 283, 284n
exhortation, 6, 13, 52, 72, 102, 103, 210n, 249n, 259, 309 *see also mawʿiẓa*

faḍīla see virtue
faḍl, 97n, 88, 89, 111n, 120, 136
Faḍl Allāh al-Ghaḍanfar, Abū Taghlib, 265n
al-Faḍl b. al-Muqtadir *see* al-Muṭīʿ
al-Faḍl b. Sahl, 126
Fakhr al-Dawla, ʿAlī b. Rukn al-Dawla, Buyid ruler, 173n, 174, 262–3
Fakhr al-Dīn al-Rāzī, 120n, 134n, 144n, 157n, 204n, 206
Fakhr al-Mulk, son of Niẓām al-Mulk, 67
al-Fārābī, Abū Naṣr, 156, 161n
farāʾiḍ, 90, 94, 111 *see also* precept(s)
al-Farāʾid wa-l-qalāʾid, 163n
Farghana, 33, 35, 299
Farīdūn, 138, 139n
farr, *farr-i īzadī*, 58n, 64, 70, 136, 137 *see also* charisma, royal
Farrukhī, Abū l-Ḥasan ʿAlī Sīstānī, 179
Fars, 31, 36, 273
fasting, 294
al-Fatḥ b. Khāqān, 10
fatḥnāmeh, 173
Fatimids, 27, 29, 30, 31, 42–4, 72, 73, 74, 192n, 198n, 272n
fatwā, 72, 281, 305
favour, 86, 87, 94, 95, 96, 108, 111, 113, 120, 136, 138, 160, 197, 201, 207, 210, 213, 234, 250, 266n, 269, 280, 288, 298, 302, 303 *see also niʿma*
fiqh, 62, 71 *see also* jurisprudence
Firdawsī, 13n, 38, 57n, 58, 139
Fire (Hell), 113
fire, 140, 141
fitna, 207, 284
fiṭra, 157
forbearance, 52, 99, 102, 108, 121n, 144, 148, 155, 164, 177, 204
forgiveness, 60, 99, 206, 207n, 251n, 283 *see also* clemency
Francisco de Gurmendi, 17
Francisco de Sandoval y Rojas, 18
Franks, 43, 73
friend(s), friendship, 56n, 60, 151, 168–71, 172, 175, 176, 177, 178, 179, 254, 273, 285
al-Fuḍayl (Fuḍayl) b. ʿIyāḍ, 122, 123n
Full Moon, 56

Galen, 140n, 156n, 163
Ganja, 59
Georgia, 41
Ghassanids, 90n

Ghazālī, Abū Ḥāmid, 10, 11, 12, 13, 14, 17, 22, 41, 45, 66–9, 71, 72, 80, 136, 159n, 203n, 211n, 236n, 239n
ghazi(s), 286, 289, 293, 305
Ghazna, 37, 38, 55, 260, 299, 302, 304, 306 (Fig. 4)
Ghaznavids, 27, 28, 31, 32n, 33n, 34, 35, 36, 37–8, 39, 40, 57, 59, 60, 61, 64, 125n, 127n, 174n, 175n, 179n, 194n, 276n, 282n, 284n, 306 (Fig. 4)
ghazw, 275
ghulām, *ghilmān*, 27, 28
Ghuzz, 27n, 244n *see also* Oghuz
gift(s), gift-giving, 13, 14n, 18, 19, 23, 27, 69, 95, 127, 138n, 150, 168, 237, 270n, 272, 288, 297, 301 *see also* present(s)
Gīlānshāh, Ziyarid, 59, 60, 167
Giles of Rome, 53
Goethe, Johann von, 61
Goliath, 88, 199n
Gospels (New Testament), 107
governance, 4, 5n, 6n, 8, 11, 23, 26, 27, 40, 52, 53, 55, 58, 62, 63, 64, 69, 83, 86, 89, 90, 96, 110, 130, 135, 137, 143, 145, 155, 156, 160, 180, 181, 184, 185, 186, 191, 197, 189, 204, 206, 207, 210, 213, 214, 215, 216, 217, 218, 220, 224, 225, 226, 230, 231, 232, 234, 239n, 248, 276, 298n
  self- ~, 4, 52, 83, 97–8, 143, 247
  'three governances', 5n, 52, 205–6n
gratitude, 60, 87n, 94, 95–6, 102, 105, 122n, 127, 207, 227, 239, 250, 288, 309 *see also* *shukr*
Greek, 3, 7, 9n, 47, 62, 134, 187, 248
grievance(s), redress of, 27n, 181, 190, 191, 192, 215, 218n, 240, 270, 286, 310 *see also* *maẓālim*
Gulistān, 14n
Gurgan, 34, 38, 54
Gurganj, 38, 55
Gushtāsp, Iranian monarch, 236n

habit, 4, 87, 98, 100, 101, 169, 212, 261
Ḥadāʾiq al-siyar, 13n
hadiyya see gift(s)
ḥājib see chamberlain(s)
ḥajj see pilgrimage
al-Ḥajjāj b. Yūsuf al-Thaqafī, 120n, 125n, 253
Ḥājjī Khalīfa, 75
al-Ḥākim bi-Amr Allāh, Fatimid caliph-imam, 43n
Halm, Heinz, 43
Hamadhan, 174n, 297
al-Hamadhānī, Abū l-Faḍl, 125n, 130n
Ḥamd Allāh Qazvīnī Mustawfī, 174n
Ḥamdanids, 265, 273n
Ḥamdūn Qarmaṭ, 42
al-Ḥamīd, Samanid amir *see* Nūḥ I b. Naṣr II
Ḥanafī school of law, 32, 52, 192n, 280n
Ḥanbalī school of law, 32
ḥaqq, *ḥuqūq*, 199, 201, 218, 235 *see also* rightful claim(s)
al-Harawī, Taqī al-Dīn Abū l-Ḥasan ʿAlī b. Abī Bakr, 11
al-Ḥārithī, Ziyād b. ʿUbayd Allāh, 252–3
Harran, 265n, 266n
Hārūn al-Rashīd, Abbasid caliph, 9, 69, 100n, 112, 113n, 255n, 286–9, 312
ḥasab, 100, 160n
Ḥasan ʿAlī Munshī Khāqānī, 17
al-Ḥasan al-Baṣrī, 98n, 120n, 122, 211
Ḥasan Bughra Khan, 34
Ḥasan, Rukn al-Dawla *see* Rukn al-Dawla
Ḥasan b. Sulaymān, Tavghach Bughra Khan, Karakhanid ruler, 35, 56
al-Ḥashshāʾī, Abū l-Ḥasan ʿAlī b. Muḥammad al-Balkhī, 52
al-Ḥātimī, Abū ʿAlī Muḥammad b. al-Ḥasan, 116
Hebrew, 17, 48, 49
Heck, Paul, 54
Hell, 98, 197, 294, 310 *see also* Fire
Herat, 32, 33
heterodox, heterodoxy, 46, 54, 64, 65, 66, 73, 110, 191, 194n, 259, 260
Highly Praised, 56, 145, 146, 154
Hijaz, 288n
al-Ḥijāzī, Abū l-ʿAbbās, 215
ḥikma
  maxim, 12n, 17, 62, 119n, 134n, 157n, 163n, 164n, 165n, 189, 206, 257
  philosophy, wisdom, medicine, 12n, 15n, 17, 88, 110, 111n, 119, 136, 137, 144n, 214
ḥikmat-i ʿamalī, 15n
ḥikmat-i naẓarī, 15n
al-Ḥikma al-khālida see Jāvīdān khirad
Hillenbrand, Carole, 67n
ḥilm see forbearance

himma, 159n, 198n, 199, 201n
Hincmar of Rheims, 180n
Hindustan, 37, 38n, 59, 297
al-Ḥīra, 91n
Hishām, Umayyad caliph, 48, 252n
Hishām II al-Mu'ayyad, 213n
historiography, 6
Hodgson, Marshall G. S., 7n, 24
homiletic, 6, 11n, 13, 14n, 18, 67
Homs, 211
Hūd, 258n
al-Hudhalī, [Abū] Bakr, 124, 125n
Ḥudhayfa b. al-Yamān, 121
Hudids *see* Banū Hūd
Hülegü, 14n
Ḥumayd b. 'Abd al-Ḥamīd al-Ṭūsī, 91
humours, theory of, 140n
hunar, 168, 169, 237, 298, 308
al-Hurmuzān, 210
Hurmuz(d) IV, Sasanian monarch, 258n
ḥurriyya, 112n, 278
Ḥusayn Bayqara, 15n

Iberia, 48, 70, 71, 73, 213n, 256n
Ibn 'Abbād, al-Ṣāḥib, 36, 182n, 208n
Ibn 'Abbās, 120n
Ibn 'Abd Rabbihi, 10n, 183n, 205n
Ibn Abī 'Abbād, Muḥammad b. 'Īsā, 262n
Ibn Abī 'Abbād, Muḥammad b. Yaḥyā, 261, 262n
Ibn Abī Du'ād, Abū 'Abdallāh Aḥmad, 127n, 128n
Ibn Abī Du'ād, Abū l-Walīd Muḥammad b. Aḥmad, 128
Ibn Abī l-Ḥadīd, 111n
Ibn Abī l-Rabī', 19n
Ibn Abī l-Shawārib, al-Ḥasan b. Muḥammad b. 'Abd al-Malik, 269
Ibn al-'Arabī, Abū Bakr Muḥammad b. 'Abdallāh, 72
Ibn al-'Arabī, Abū Muḥammad 'Abdallāh b. 'Umar, 72n
Ibn al-Athīr, 'Izz al-Dīn, 40
Ibn Bānū, Abū Ja'far, 281
(Ibn) al-Baṭā'iḥī, Abū 'Abdallāh Muḥammad b. Abī Shujā' Fātik, 43, 72
Ibn Farīghūn, 19n
Ibn Hubayra, 252
Ibn Ilyās, Abū 'Alī, 281
Ibn al-Jawzī, Abū l-Faraj 'Abd al-Raḥmān, 11, 13, 30n, 39n
Ibn Khālawayh, Ḥusayn, 108n
Ibn Khaldūn, 'Abd al-Raḥmān, 74, 190n
Ibn Khallikān, Aḥmad b. Muḥammad, 69n, 101n
Ibn Mas'ūd, 'Abdallāh, 121, 207
Ibn Munqidh, Usāma, 120n, 123n, 135n, 205n
Ibn al-Muqaffa', 8, 9, 68n, 92n, 112n, 214, 215n, 247
Ibn al-Mustawfī, Sharaf al-Dīn, 69n
Ibn al-Mu'tazz, 'Abdallāh, 110n, 111, 134n, 166, 251n, 264, 272n
Ibn Nubāta al-Sa'dī, 116
Ibn Qutayba, 10, 91n, 229, 247, 253n
Ibn Samā'a, Abū 'Abdallāh Muḥammad, 131
Ibn Sawāda, Abū l-Ḥasan al-Rāzī, 279, 280, 281
Ibn al-Sikkīt, 90n
Ibn Sīmjūr, Abū 'Alī, 281
Ibn Sīnā, Abū 'Alī, 55
Ibn Tūmart, Muḥammad b. 'Abdallāh, 72
Ibn Wahb, 'Abdallāh, 258
Ibn al-Zayyāt, Muḥammad b. 'Abd al-Malik, 127, 128
Ibn al-Zubayr, 'Abdallāh, 102n, 107n, 220n
'ibra, 200, 235, 246, 294, 308
Ibrāhīm b. Adham, 258
Ibrāhīm b. al-Mahdī, Abbasid, 91n
ifrāṭ, 15
Iḥyā' 'ulūm al-dīn, 67
ijtihād, 92n, 132, 232, 234, 270
'Imād al-Dawla, 'Alī b. Būya, Buyid ruler, 36, 273
imām al-hudā, 91n
imamate, 30, 42, 45, 67
Imamiyya (Twelver) Shi'ism, 29, 37, 93
imārat al-istikfā', 45
imārat al-istīlā', 45
imra, 156, 158
indwelling (*ḥulūl*), 15–16
ingratitude, 95–6, 102, 196, 285
injustice, 68, 135, 137, 138, 139, 149, 150, 180, 181, 182, 184, 190, 192, 202, 211, 213, 214, 216, 220, 222, 223, 226, 232, 233, 243, 245
inner circle, inner public, 4, 5n, 14n, 52, 110, 123, 183, 195
innovation, 115, 191, 196, 285

instruments
  military, 119
  musical, 119, 268, 270
intermediaries, 5n, 37, 161, 192, 216, 284n
al-Iqnāʿ, 30n
iqṭāʿ, 28, 29, 307
iqtibās, 110n
Iran, 8, 28, 31, 33, 34, 35, 36, 39, 40, 41, 51, 57, 125n, 136, 138n, 139n, 185n, 200n, 213n, 270n, 280n, 296n, 307n
Iraq, 25, 28, 31, 35, 36, 40, 41, 42, 44, 107n, 122n, 193, 194, 195, 197, 198, 199, 220, 252n, 253n, 265n, 273, 275, 288n, 297, 306
Isfahan, 41, 54n, 65, 66, 174, 262n, 297
al-Iṣfahbadhī, Aḥmad, 22n
Ismāʿīl b. Aḥmad, Samanid amir, 33, 181, 191, 193, 195n, 199, 200, 201, 202, 203, 277n, 307
Ismāʿīl b. Jaʿfar al-Ṣādiq, 30
Ismaili(sm), 14n, 30, 31, 33, 42, 43, 54, 65, 66, 67, 68, 69n, 73, 194, 195, 278, 279n, 280n, 282n
iʿtidhāriyyāt, 90n
ʿIzz al-Dīn Kaykāʾūs I b. Kaykhusraw, Seljuk of Rum, 13n
ʿIzz al-Dīn Kaykāʾūs II, Seljuk of Rum, 15n

Jaʿfar al-Ṣādiq, 30, 166
Jaʿfar b. Yaḥyā al-Barmakī, 220n
Jahāngīr, Mughal emperor, 17
jāhiliyya, 108, 114, 123n, 138n
al-Jāḥiẓ, ʿAmr b. Baḥr, 10n, 159n
al-Jahshiyārī, ʿAbdallāh b. ʿAbdūs, 125, 126n, 127 *see also Kitāb al-Wuzarāʾ wa-l-kuttāb*
Jalāl al-Dawla, Buyid ruler, 39n, 62
al-Jalīs al-ṣāliḥ wa-l-anīs al-nāṣiḥ, 14n
Jarīr b. ʿAbdallāh, 256
javānmard(ī), 60, 141n, 167–8, 172n, 237 *see also* chivalry
Jāvīdān khirad, 12n, 17
Jawāmiʿ al-ʿulūm, 19n
al-Jayhānī, Abū ʿAbdallāh, 277n
al-Jayhānī, Abū ʿAlī Muḥammad, 279
Jerusalem, 43, 71, 73, 289, 294n
Jesus, 107, 312n
Jewish communities, 43, 74
Jibal, 36
jihād, 43, 54, 72, 157, 225n
Johannes Hispalensis *see* John of Seville
John of Salisbury, 6n
John of Seville, 48
judge(s), 9, 10, 15, 22, 37, 39n, 51, 55, 127n, 128n, 130, 131, 132n, 191n, 192n, 211n, 213n, 252, 269, 273, 280, 296, 305, 307, 310
  Chief Judge, 9, 10, 15, 37, 39n, 127n, 128n, 130, 211n, 305
Julian, the Apostate, 7
jurisconsult, 11, 71
jurisprudence, 71, 128n, 132n, 204n, 279 *see also fiqh*
justice, 4, 15, 20, 21, 23, 27n, 29, 46, 49n, 50, 56, 63, 64, 68, 69, 72, 83, 92, 102, 103, 104, 105, 107, 112, 114n, 117, 122, 130, 135, 136, 137, 138, 139, 144, 145, 146, 149, 150, 151, 153, 161, 168, 180, 181, 182, 183, 184, 185, 189n, 191, 192, 193, 203, 204, 205, 206, 207, 208, 209, 210, 211, 212, 213, 214, 215n, 217, 219, 220, 222, 224, 225, 232, 234, 236, 239, 240, 271, 276, 287, 290, 300 *see also* circle of justice

Kaʿba, 312
al-Kaʿbī, Abū l-Qāsim ʿAbdallāh al-Balkhī, 31, 125n
Kabul, 17n
kadkhudāy, 242, 284, 286, 296 *see also* steward, stewardship
Kalīla wa-Dimna, 7, 19
Kanz al-mulūk fī kayfiyyat al-sulūk, 14n
Karakhanids, 27, 34–5, 39, 56, 57, 58, 139n, 297n
Karrāmiyya, 114n
Kashghar, 35, 56, 144, 289, 299, 300, 301
Kāshifī, Ḥusayn-i Vāʿiẓ, 15
Kashmir, 14
al-Kātib, Aḥmad b. Abī Bakr, 276n
Katib Çelebi, 16n
Kayāniyān, 138n
Kaykāʾūs b. Iskandar, ʿUnṣur al-Maʿālī, Ziyarid ruler, 10, 17, 34, 35n, 55, 56n, 57, 59–61, 65, 78, 140n, 145n, 167–8, 170n, 172n, 174n, 175n, 177n, 262n
Kayseri, 14n
Kennedy, Hugh, 31

khalīfa, *khulafā'*, *khalā'if*, 89, 113, 131, 135, 236
khānaqāh, 32, 41, 294n
khaqan, 297–305
kharāj, 9 *see also* taxes
Khārijī, Khawārij, 253n
khāṣṣ(a), 5, 52, 110, 183, 195, 206n, 302 *see also* élites
khatun, 297n, 298–303
Khawarnaq, 91
khidma, 89, 244n, 297, 300
Khiradnamā-yi jān-afrūz, 13n
Khurasan, 11, 25, 31, 33, 37, 38n, 39, 40, 41, 44, 52, 53, 54, 66, 68, 73, 107n, 166n, 117n, 122n, 125n, 172, 193, 194, 195, 196, 197, 198, 199, 250n, 253n, 263n, 275, 281, 292, 293, 297, 306, 308
Khusraw I, Sasanian ruler, 12, 121, 123n, 138, 139n, 258n *see also* Anūshīrvān
Khusraw II Parvīz, 123, 229, 246, 252n
Khusraw Fīrūz, al-Malik al-Raḥīm, Buyid ruler, 39
Khusraws, 118, 138n, 267 *see also* Sasanian
khuṭba, 33, 39, 43, 102, 174 *see also* oration
Khuzistan, 36, 197, 198, 273
khᵛājeh, *khᵛājagān*, 284, 296, 308
Khᵛarazm, 38, 40, 55, 289, 297, 306, 308
khᵛārazmshāh (title), 38
Kīmiyā-yi sa'ādat, 67, 69
Kınalızade 'Alī Çelebi, 16
al-Kindī, Abū Yūsuf Ya'qūb, 53
kindness, 20, 21, 95, 96, 114, 169, 184, 202n, 203, 205, 224, 228, 234, 245, 263, 264, 292, 301
Kirman, 36, 40n, 44
Kish(sh), 304
kitāb, 9, 292n
Kitāb al-Adab wa-l-sulwān fī naṣā'iḥ al-salāṭīn, 22
Kitāb al-'Ibar, 74
Kitāb al-Kharāj, 9
Kitāb al-Mubhij, 124
Kitāb al-Mustaẓhirī (*Kitāb Faḍā'iḥ al-Bāṭiniyya wa-faḍā'il al-Mustaẓhiriyya*), 67n
Kitāb-ı Müstetab, 16n
Kitāb (*Risāla fī*) *al-Ṣaḥāba*, 9
Kitāb al-Siyāsa al-'āmmiyya, 48
Kitāb al-Siyāsa fī tadbīr al-riyāsa, 7–8, 22n, 47–51, 77, 104n, 185n *see also Sirr al-asrār*
Kitāb al-Sulṭān, 10
Kitāb al-Tāj fī akhlāq al-mulūk, 10, 16n, 53, 250
Kitāb al-Tājī, 266n
Kitāb al-Wuzarā' wa-l-kuttāb, 125, 126n, 127
Koçi Beg, 16n
Konya, 15n
Kubraviyya, 14n
Kufa, 108n, 288
kufr see unbelief
kufrān, 95, 196 *see also* ingratitude
kut, 58n, 146
kutadgu bilig (genre), 57
Kutadgu bilig, 35, 56–9, 78, 139n, 144–55, 297n

Lahore, 37n
Lakhmids, 90, 91
Lambton, A. K. S., 6n, 64n
laqab, 272n, 273n, 274, 296–309 *see also* titles
Laṭā'if al-ḥikmeh, 15, 18n
Latin, 3, 17
law, 4, 30n, 32, 44, 53, 83, 105, 146, 180, 183, 185, 187, 203, 204, 210, 212, 213, 214, 217, 219, 224n, 225, 231, 232, 233, 270n, 278, 284, 305, 307 *see also nāmūs*, *qānūn*, religious law, sharia
Lebanon, 71
legitimacy, legitimation, 4, 18, 25, 30n, 34, 45, 67, 70, 180, 186, 188, 189n, 191, 192n, 233
letters, Arabic, 36, 52 *see also adab*
letters, men of, 4, 32, 55, 111n, 125n, 127n, 217n
Levy, Reuben, 78–9, 172n
librarian, library, 18, 22, 36n, 37n, 64, 66, 74n
Libro de las calidades del rey, 18
literacy, 22
littérateur(s), 37, 54, 59n, 105n, 127n *see also* letters, men of
love, 60, 83, 90n, 98, 99, 114n, 116, 136, 151, 153, 161, 164, 177, 185, 189, 209, 227, 240, 251, 254, 256, 257, 258 *see also* passionate love
loyalty, 5n, 124, 146, 165, 170, 188, 190, 255, 282
lubb, 309
Lutfi Paşa, 16

madhhab, 30n, 32, 115, 279
madrasa, 32, 41, 66, 71n
maghrib, 44, 71, 119n, 311
Magians, 138, 139
al-Mahdī, Abbasid caliph, 105n, 117
al-Mahdī, ʿAbdallāh (ʿUbayd Allāh), Fatimid caliph-imam, 42, 198n, 272n
Mahdiyya, 42, 198
Maḥmūd, Ghaznavid sultan, 35, 37, 38, 174, 175, 179n, 260, 282, 292, 297–306, 306
Maḥmūd b. Muḥammad b. al-Ḥusayn al-Iṣfahānī, 22n
Majd al-Dawla, Rustam, Buyid ruler, 173n, 174, 175n
majlis, assembly or gathering, 18, 108, 124, 129, 209n, 243n, 260, 268, 273, 308
Malaṭyavī, Muḥammad-i Ghāzī, 13n
malik, 30, 36n, 39n, 44, 62, 63, 68n, 88, 93, 121n, 130, 132n, 215, 225, 297
Mālik b. Anas, 257
al-Malik al-Ashraf Muẓaffar al-Dīn, 14n
Mālik b. Dīnār, 312
Mālikī school of law, 70, 71, 74, 204n, 158n
al-Malik al-Kāmil, Ayyubid ruler, 18n
mālik al-mulk, 88
Malikshāh, Seljuk sultan, 40, 41, 44, 63, 64, 65, 66, 68, 181, 283, 284n, 298n
al-Malik al-Ẓāhir Ghāzī, Ayyubid ruler, 11n
mamlūk, *mamālīk*, 27, 43, 93 *see also ghulām*, military enslavement
al-Maʾmūn, Abbasid caliph, 33, 91n, 98, 118, 125, 126, 128n, 210, 211, 249, 264
Maʾmūnid Khʷārazmshāhs, 38, 55
al-Maʾmūn II b. Maʾmūn I, Khʷārazmshāh, 38, 55, 260
mandate, 55, 64, 85, 135n, 136, 137n, 145, 180, 188, 247
al-Manṣūr, Abbasid caliph, 35n, 98n, 105, 116n, 117, 126, 135n, 193n
Manṣūr I b. Nūḥ I, Samanid amir, 306
manthūr al-ḥikam, 163n, 189n, 206, 230n, 257
Manṭiq al-ṭayr, 59
Manzalaoui, M., 48n, 77n, 182n, 183n
Manzikert, 42, 74n
Mardāvīj b. Ziyār, 34, 36
mardumī, 167, 168, 169, 176, 177
Mārib, 96n
marriage, 39, 43, 60, 65, 212, 287n
Marv, 39, 40, 44, 168n, 199, 292n
Marv al-Rūdh, 292, 293
marzbān, 250
mashriq, 44, 68n
maṣlaḥa, *maṣāliḥ*, 90, 114, 133, 137, 201, 204n, 210, 216 *see also* common good, public good
Masʿūd b. Maḥmūd, Ghaznavid sultan, 38, 39, 179n, 292
al-Māwardī, Abū l-Ḥasan ʿAlī b. Muḥammad, 10, 11, 12, 22n, 30n, 37, 39n, 45, 51n, 52, 53, 58, 61–3, 67, 79, 97n, 130, 132n, 135n, 155–6, 158n, 159n, 163n, 186, 189, 191, 192n, 217, 218, 219n, 224n, 232n, 234, 270 *see also* Pseudo-Māwardī
Mawdūd b. Masʿūd, Ghaznavid ruler, 59
mawʿiẓa, *mawāʿiẓ*, 6, 13, 17, 35, 157n *see also* admonition, exhortation, *naṣīḥa*
Mawʿiẓeh-yi Jahāngīrī, 17
mawlā, 35, 117, 118, 272
mawlā amīr al-muʾminīn, 35
maxim, 7, 13n, 45, 60, 61, 62, 73, 101n, 107n, 108n, 111n, 119n, 120n, 124n, 134n, 138n, 163n, 170n, 179n, 182, 183n, 205n, 206, 208n, 252, 257n *see also* aphorism, *ḥikma*
Maymūn b. Mihrān, 257
maẓālim, 27n, 181, 190, 191, 192n, 215n, 270 *see also* grievance(s), redress of
Mazandaran, 174n
mean, mid-point, 15, 63, 152, 164, 222
Mecca, 42, 102, 107n, 121n, 122n, 135n, 221n, 288, 289, 294n, 308n
medicine, 49, 51, 60, 119, 140n, 141n, 147, 152, 251
Medina, 42, 122n, 170n, 210n, 211n, 257n, 258n, 268n, 288, 289, 290, 312n
Meisami, Julie Scott, 14n, 91n
merchant(s), 32, 57, 127n, 172n, 223, 241, 292n, 296, 299, 300, 302, 311
metaphor, 3, 61, 85, 90n, 92n, 133n, 139, 160n, 167, 190n, 208n, 209n, 250n, 254, 264n
Middle Persian, 7, 47, 58, 103n
sources for mirrors, 8, 47
Midian, 291n
Mihrajān, 270
military commander(s), 22, 25, 43, 57, 60, 91n, 125n, 150, 173, 196, 197, 250n, 264, 265, 266, 268n, 269n, 272n, 273, 274n, 284, 295, 307

military enslavement, 26, 27, 28 *see also ghulām*, *mamlūk*
military force(s) and personnel, 25, 26, 28, 29, 45, 145, 153, 222, 242, 249
military service, 27, 39, 227
mindfulness, 14, 60, 95, 96, 137, 295, 307, 309, 310
Minhāj al-wuzarāʾ wa-sirāj al-umarāʾ, 22n
miʿrāj, 294n
mirror (metaphorical use of), 4
mirror(s) for princes
  appearance of ~, 19, 20–1 (Fig. 1)
  definitions of ~, 5
  diverse forms of ~, 3–23
  mirror-writers, 3n, 4, 5, 6, 8, 11, 12, 15, 16, 17, 24, 29, 30, 38, 41, 51, 73, 76, 85, 139, 143, 144, 156, 180, 182, 203, 217, 247, 259
  secularity of ~, 44–6
  term(s) for ~, 3, 5
Mirṣād al-ʿibād min al-mabdaʾ ilā l-maʿād, 14n, 17, 22n
al-Miṣbāḥ al-muḍīʾ fī khilāfat al-Mustaḍīʾ, 11n
Miskawayh, Abū ʿAlī, 12n, 17, 36, 104n, 144n, 161n
mizāj, 140, 261 *see also* temperament(s)
moderation, 177, 227, 235, 260
Moses, 113, 291–2, 311n
Mosul, 265n
Muʿāwiya, Umayyad caliph, 101n, 124, 220n, 277
al-Mubayyiḍa, 117
Mufliḥ, Abū Ṣāliḥ, 272
Mughal(s), 15, 16, 17
al-Muhallab b. Abī Ṣufra, 172n, 253, 266n
al-Muhallabī, Abū Muḥammad al-Ḥasan b. Muḥammad, 265–6
Muḥammad, Prophet, 13, 21, 23, 42, 57, 67, 69, 87, 89n, 93, 94, 98, 101n, 108n, 109, 113, 119n, 120, 121, 122n, 123n, 126, 127, 129, 131, 135, 136, 138, 142, 157n, 162, 170n, 182, 205n, 206n, 207n, 208, 209n, 211, 213, 219, 220, 254, 255, 256, 257n, 258n, 280, 286n, 287, 294n, 303, 305, 307, 310
Muḥammad Bāqir Najm al-Thānī, 17
Muḥammad b. Bughā, 270n
Muḥammad Ḥakīm Mīrzā, 17n
Muḥammad b. ʿĪsā b. ʿAlī al-Hāshimī, 126n
Muḥammad b. Kaʿb, 205n
Muḥammad b. Malikshāh, Seljuk sultan, 44, 66, 68
muḥkam, 196, 197n
al-Muhtadī, Abbasid caliph, 269n, 270, 271
Muʿizz al-Dawla, Abū l-Ḥusayn, Buyid ruler, 30n, 36, 265–6, 273–4, 275
al-Muʿizz li-Dīn Allāh, Fatimid caliph-imam, 42
al-Muktafī, Abbasid caliph, 262
mulk, 45, 62, 88, 94, 114, 115n, 130, 134n, 169, 174n, 183n, 199, 215n, 218, 307, 308
Multan, 282n
mulūk al-aṭrāf, 129, 298n
mulūk al-ṭawāʾif, 70n, 213
municipal governor(s), 120, 127, 237, 284, 292, 304 *see also raʾīs*
Muʾnis al-Khādim, 272
al-Muntaṣir, Abbasid caliph, 268
al-Muqaddima, 74
al-Muqannaʿ, 116, 117n
muqṭaʿ, 29, 307
al-Muqtadir, Abbasid caliph, 272, 273n, 274, 276n
Murad III, Ottoman sultan, 16n
Murghab River, 292n
muruvvat, 172n, 199
Mūsā b. Bughā, 270n
Mūsā b. Jaʿfar al-Ṣādiq, 30n
Mūsā Yabghu, 39
Muṣʿab b. al-Zubayr, 107
al-Muṣʿabī, Abū l-Ṭayyib, 278–80
muṣannaf, 9, 10, 24
al-Mūsawī, Abū Jaʿfar Muḥammad b. Mūsā al-ʿAlawī al-Ṭūsī, 127
music, 119, 272, 279
musician(s), 55, 60
al-Mustaḍīʾ, Abbasid caliph, 11, 43
Mustafa Âlī, 16
al-Mustaʿīn, Abbasid caliph, 268, 269
al-Mustakfī, Abbasid caliph, 273, 274, 275
al-Mustaʿṣim, Abbasid caliph, 19n
mustawfī, 308
al-Muʿtaḍid, Abbasid caliph, 33, 128, 195n, 200n
muʿtamad, 201, 236, 243

al-Mu'tamid, Abbasid caliph, 128n, 195, 269n, 271, 272
al-Mutanabbī, Abū l-Ṭayyib Aḥmad b. al-Ḥusayn, 264
mutaqārib, 58, 59
al-Mu'taṣim, Abbasid caliph, 100, 127, 268n
al-Mutawakkil, Abbasid caliph, 10, 127n, 261, 262n, 263, 268, 269n, 270, 271n
Mu'tazila, Mu'tazilī, 30n, 37, 52, 98n, 114n, 128n, 155n
al-Mu'tazz, Abbasid caliph, 268, 269
al-Muṭī', Abbasid caliph, 273n, 274, 275
al-Muttaqī, Abbasid caliph, 273, 274n
al-Muwaffaq, Abū Aḥmad, Abbasid, 271

al-Nābigha al-Dhubyānī, 90
nadīm see boon-companion(s)
nafs, *anfus*, 97, 98, 106, 116, 156, 159n, 165, 250, 279, 310
  al-nafs al-muṭma'inna, 250n
  al-nafs al-nāṭiqa, 279
  see also self, soul
al-Nahj [al-Manhaj] al-maslūk fī siyāsat al-mulūk, 19n, Fig. 1
Na'ima, 16n
Najm al-Dīn Dāya Rāzī, 14, 17
Najrān, 107
al-Namarī, Manṣūr, 91n
nāmūs, 183, 296, 298
narrative, 7, 13, 21, 23, 53, 57, 60, 61, 64, 65, 73, 98n, 102n, 112n, 122n, 139n, 191, 193n, 199n, 204, 234, 235, 236n, 237n, 254n, 260, 274n, 283, 291n, 297n, 300n
naṣafa, 213, 224n *see also* equity
Nasibin, 274
naṣīḥa, *naṣā'iḥ*, 6, 13, 208, 254–7
naṣīḥat al-mulūk (genre), 5, 57, 59n, 68
Naṣīḥat al-mulūk (Arabic), 12, 33, 51–4, 55, 64, 68, 77
Naṣīḥat al-mulūk (Persian), 12, 17, 66–70, 80, 136
  Arabic translation of ~, 22, 69, 80
nasihatname, 5, 16, 61
Nāṣir al-Dawla, Abū Muḥammad Ḥasan b. 'Abdallāh b. Ḥamdān, 265
Nāṣir al-Dīn 'Abd al-Raḥīm b. Abī Manṣūr, Ismaili *muḥtasham*, 14n
Naṣīr al-Dīn Ṭūsī, 14, 14n, 98n, 144n
Naṣr I b. Aḥmad, Samanid amir, 195n
Naṣr II b. Aḥmad, Samanid amir, 31, 33, 54, 125, 129, 278–80, 306–7
Naṣr b. 'Alī, Karakhanid Ilig, 34
Naṣr al-Sharābī, 129
Nawrūz, 270
al-Naẓẓām, Ibrāhīm b. al-Sayyār, 99n
networks, 5, 31, 40, 64, 285n
Nicomachean Ethics, 7, 144n, 159n
ni'ma, *ni'am*, 87, 88, 94, 95, 96, 111, 123, 210n
  see also favour
Nimruz, 297, 306
Nishapur, 39, 54, 55, 66, 114n, 181, 200, 249n, 261, 293
nithār, 127 *see also* gift(s)
Niẓām al-Dīn Yaḥyā b. Ṣā'id, 13n, 19
Niẓāmiyya, 41, 66, 71
Niẓām al-Mulk, 8, 10, 12, 28n, 38, 40, 41, 54, 58n, 63–6, 67, 68, 70, 71, 72, 79, 179n, 189n, 190, 191, 192n, 194n, 199n, 234, 235, 236n, 237n, 239n, 259, 260, 265n, 278n, 279n, 282, 283, 284n, 285n, 286n, 292n, 294n, 296n, 297n, 298n, 307n
Noah, 116, 253
noble, nobility of birth, 55, 57, 99, 100, 133, 147, 151, 154, 159, 206n, 263, 268, 277, 284, 286, 298
nomad(s), 27, 28, 38, 40, 41
non-Muslims, 34, 37, 70, 73, 204, 215n, 256n
North Africa, 26, 42, 72, 74
Nūḥ I b. Naṣr II, Samanid amir, 129, 280–1, 306
Nūḥ II b. Manṣūr, Samanid amir, 306
al-Nu'mān III b. al-Mundhir, 90, 91n
Nūr Allāh Khāqānī, Qadi, 17
Nūr al-Dīn Maḥmūd b. Zangī, 43, 44n
Nushat üs-selâtin, 16n

obedience, 4, 55, 60, 64, 86, 90n, 94, 95, 96, 103, 109, 111, 113, 123, 124, 133, 135, 137, 186, 187, 188, 190, 194, 196, 197, 198, 212, 225, 226, 227, 228, 230, 254, 294, 295
occult sciences, 49
Oghuz, 27, 28, 38 *see also* Ghuzz
Oikonomicos, 7
oration, 33, 102, 174n *see also* *khuṭba*
ordinance(s), 61, 89, 90, 105, 187, 210, 213, 214, 218n, 224n, 231, 233, 280 *see also* *aḥkām*

ordinary people, 208, 222, 254 *see also* ʿ*āmm(a)*, common people
Ottoman, Ottoman Empire, 15, 16
  political literature, 16, 17, 75
  readership, 16, 74
  translations into Ottoman Turkish, 61, 79, 80
  see also nasihatname
Oxus River, 33, 38, 39, 125n, 199, 289n, 304
Özkend, 34, 299

'Pact of ʿUmar', 74
pādshāh, pādshāhī, 45, 198, 284, 285, 295
Palestine, 42
pandnāmeh, 5, 59n
panegyric, 85, 91n, 179n
Paradise, 105, 121n, 197, 287, 294, 295, 311
Parthian(s), 58, 138n, 213
passionate love, 98, 99, 229n
past, source of instructive examples, 6, 7, 12, 18, 53, 64, 83, 87, 90, 119, 123n, 215n, 283, 295
pastoralism, 28, 237n
patience, 14, 102, 122n, 144, 212
patient endurance, 52–3, 101, 165, 199, 207
patronage, 4, 5, 7, 17, 22, 32, 55, 294n
penalty, penalties, 90, 117n, 122, 218n, 224n, 225
Persian, 3, 4, 5, 6, 7, 8, 9n, 10, 12, 13, 14, 15, 16, 17, 18, 24, 26, 27n, 34, 35, 36, 38, 41, 45, 47, 49, 50, 51, 56, 58, 59, 61, 63, 66, 67, 68, 71n, 75, 76, 80, 81, 83, 85, 90n, 98n, 100n, 103n, 121n, 136, 137n, 138, 167n, 170n, 179n, 185n, 192, 207n, 208n, 210n, 212, 213, 214, 239n, 248, 250, 251, 252n, 273, 289n, 297n, 299, 303
petition(er), 191n, 192, 193, 203, 210, 215, 216, 239, 252, 286, 287, 303, 305
Pharoah, 113, 115, 267
Philip, translator of *Sirr al-asrār*, 48
Philip IV, 18
philosopher(s), 23, 32, 36, 47, 49, 53, 55, 62, 63, 70, 74, 89, 90, 101, 107, 109, 115, 118, 119n, 120, 132n, 134, 144n, 156, 157, 158, 159, 160, 161, 163n, 167, 168, 176, 178, 181, 182, 187, 207, 212, 213, 252
philosophy, 7, 15, 52, 63, 70, 119n, 140n, 144n, 161n, 185 *see also ḥikma*
physician(s), 57, 98, 119n, 152, 252, 261, 262, 277 *see also* doctor(s)
physiognomy, 49, 51
pilgrimage, 26, 107n, 275, 293, 294, 308n, 312
Pīshdādiyān, 138n
Plato, 7, 15, 62, 97n, 144n, 158n, 161n, 187n, 190n
poet(s), 14, 32, 57, 58, 60, 85, 87, 90, 91, 99n, 100, 101n, 102, 107, 108, 111n, 113n, 116n, 118n, 120, 146, 147, 151, 157, 159, 160, 162, 164, 173, 179n, 224, 229, 257, 258n, 263n, 268, 276
poetry, 13, 38, 52, 53, 58, 61, 62, 90, 91n, 107n *see also* verse
Policraticus, 6n
politics, 4, 5, 10, 14, 52, 66, 71, 76, 111n, 144n, 156
polo, 60
poor (impoverished), 57, 145, 171, 193, 212, 235, 289, 290, 292
practical philosophy, 5, 14, 15n, 63, 144n
prayer, 33, 117, 119, 122, 174n, 199, 200, 203, 209, 221, 249n, 270, 278, 279, 282, 286, 288, 291, 294, 311
precept(s), 90, 94, 100, 105, 111, 187
present(s), 18–19, 27, 168, 272, 297, 305 *see also* gift(s)
privilege(s), 87, 88, 89, 93
prophets, 53, 60, 70, 88, 113, 116, 137, 138n, 163n, 166, 182, 204, 206, 209, 257, 278, 294n *see also* Daniel, David, Hūd, Jesus, Moses, Muḥammad, Ṣāliḥ, Shuʿayb, Solomon
proverb(s), 13, 58, 62, 127, 163, 170n, 179, 229, 239, 276n
Psalms, 312n
pseudepigraphy, 12, 47, 52
Pseudo-Aristotle, 7, 11, 19, 47–50, 52, 77, 181–2
Pseudo-Callisthenes, 177n
Pseudo-Ghazālī, 58n, 66, 69, 136
Pseudo-Māwardī, 30n, 33, 45n, 51–4, 64, 70, 77, 86–7, 88n, 89n, 90n, 91n, 93n, 98n, 103n, 104n, 109, 110, 115n, 120n, 130, 133n, 136, 159n, 193n, 205n, 225n, 259, 260, 286n
public good, 204, 214 *see also* common good, *maṣlaḥa*

Index

punishment, 53, 60, 68, 83, 90n, 95, 96, 105, 111, 179, 192, 204, 236, 239n, 244, 246, 258n, 269, 294

Qābūs b. Vushmgīr, Shams al-Ma'ālī, Ziyarid ruler, 34, 55, 59n, 174n
Qābūsnāmeh, 17, 34, 57, 59–61, 78–9, 140n, 167–79
qadi, 72, 192n, 215n, 269n, 280n, 296 *see also* judge
al-Qādir, Abbasid caliph, 26, 30, 31, 275n, 276, 297, 304, 306 (Fig. 4)
Qādisiyya, Battle of, 210n
al-Qāhir, Abbasid caliph, 272n, 273
al-Qā'im, Abbasid caliph, 30, 39
qalb, 165n, 309n
Qanbar b. Ḥamdān, 117
qānūn, *qawānīn*, 214, 217, 232, 233
Qarmaṭiyya, 42, 278
Qawānīn al-wizāra wa-siyāsat al-mulk, 22n, 62
qawm, 115, 117, 121, 122, 172n, 189, 251, 266, 271, 280, 310
qiṣaṣ al-anbiyā', 204
quatrain, 58, 61n, 145, 176
Qubād, Sasanian monarch, 235
al-Quḍā'ī, al-Qāḍī Muḥammad b. Salāma, 165n
Quhistan, 11n, 174
al-Quṭāmī, 'Umayr b. Shuyaym, 258
Qutbuddin, Tahera, 165n

al-Rabī' b. Yūnus, 126
ra'īs, *ru'asā'*, 91, 120, 127, 237, 241, 273, 292
Ra'īs-i Ḥājjī, 292–5
ra'iyya, 23, 89n, 106, 111, 132n *see also* subject(s)
Ramaḍān, 18
Ramon Berenguer IV, 73
Rāst Ravishn, 236–46
rationalism, 52, 53, 86, 87, 114n, 155n, 156, 298
rationalist(s), 109, 113, 252, 285
ravān, spirit, 177 *see also rūḥ*
al-Rāwandī, 'Abdallāh, 117n
Rāwandiyya, 117
Rayy, 37, 173, 174, 175, 262, 282n, 297
reform, 16, 72, 74, 122, 204, 206, 218
religious law, 111, 187, 210, 212, 213, 214, 217, 219, 224n, 225, 231, 232, 233, 284, 305
religious sciences, 30, 37, 67, 72, 119n
renunciation, renunciant, 14, 98n, 122n, 193n, 258n, 294, 312n
repentance, 14, 117, 212, 250, 279, 281
Republic, 7, 144n
reward, 60, 68, 90n, 92n, 96, 97, 100, 105, 111, 122n, 131, 227, 244, 258, 282, 286, 295
reyes de taifas see mulūk al-ṭawā'if
ribāṭ, 289, 292, 294
rich (wealthy), 22, 145, 146, 149, 166, 171, 190n, 197, 202, 212, 218, 240, 244, 275, 287, 288
rifq, 20, 21 (Fig. 1)
rightful claim(s), 89, 95, 113, 170, 199, 201, 225, 241, 242, 244 *see also ḥaqq*
risāla, 9, 303 *see also* epistle
Rising Sun, 56, 145
Romanus IV Diogenes, Byzantine emperor, 42
rūḥ, 92, 115, 116, 140–1, 205
Rukn al-Dawla, Buyid ruler, 36, 262n
Rum, 12, 13n, 14n, 15n, 18, 40, 59
Rūstākīm, 273–4

al-Ṣābi', Abū Isḥāq Ibrāhīm, 266
Sa'd II b. Abī Bakr b. Sa'd-i Zangī, 14n
ṣadaqa, 19, 127, 224n, 235, 238, 241, 246, 291 *see also* charity, *zakāt*
Sa'dī, 14
Safavid(s), 17
al-Saffāḥ, Abū l-'Abbās, Abbasid caliph, 124–5
Saffarid(s), 33, 191, 193, 194n, 198n, 199
al-Ṣaghānī (Chaghānī), Abū 'Alī Aḥmad, 125
al-Ṣaghānī (Chaghānī), Abū l-Muẓaffar b. Abī 'Alī, 129n
Sahl b. al-Marzubān, Abū Naṣr, 125
Ṣā'id al-Andalusī, 213n
sā'is, 89, 97, 106, 111
Ṣalāḥ al-Dīn Yūsuf b. Ayyūb (Saladin), 43, 44
Ṣāliḥ, 254
Sālim Abū l-'Alā', 48n
Sālim b. 'Abdallāh, 205n
Samanids, 27, 31, 33–4, 35, 36, 37, 38, 39, 54, 55, 57, 60, 61, 125n, 129, 181, 191, 193, 194n, 276n, 277n, 278n, 279n, 280n, 306, 307n
Samarqand, 33, 117n, 297, 299, 300, 301, 302, 304
Samarra, 268n, 270, 271n

Sanjar, 39n, 44, 68
Sanskrit, 7, 37n, 47, 103
Saragossa *see* Zaragoza
Sarakhs, 199
Sasanian, Sasanian Empire, 8, 12, 40, 45, 90n, 91n, 118, 121n, 138n, 139n, 182, 210n, 211n, 213, 232n, 258n, 296n
Saul, 88
Sayf al-Dawla, Abū l-Ḥasan ʿAlī, Hamdanid ruler, 116n, 265n
sayyid, 108, 310
al-Sayyid, Riḍwān, 156n, 163n, 225n
Sayyida (Sayyideh), 173, 174, 175n, 262n
Schefer, Ch., 79
scholar(s) (*ʿulamāʾ*), 10, 11, 22, 23, 32, 45, 57, 68, 69n, 72n, 109, 118, 119, 120, 204n, 209, 210, 217n, 258, 266n, 280n, 284, 286, 296, 305, 306, 307, 308
scientist, 32, 38, 55, 156n
Sebüktigin, 37
secretary, secretaries, 4, 9, 13n, 17, 36n, 45, 48n, 49, 55, 57, 60, 62, 69, 85, 118n, 126n, 127n, 173, 244, 266n, 273, 277n, 279n, 303
Secretum secretorum, 8, 17, 47, 48n, 49n, 77 *see also Sirr al-asrār*
self, 52, 97, 98, 100, 102, 166, 234, 250, 310
see also nafs, soul
Seljuk(s), 13n, 14n, 15n, 18, 19, 26n, 27, 28, 29, 31, 32, 35, 36, 37, 38–42, 43, 44, 45, 54n, 60, 62, 63, 64, 65, 66, 67, 68, 69, 181, 237n, 284n, 297n, 307n
Semirechye, 35
Seville, 48, 71, 72
Shabīb b. Shayba, 105n
Shaddādid(s), 59
'Shadow of God', 70, 85, 89, 113, 120, 137
Shāfiʿī school of law, 30n, 32, 45n, 51, 69n, 71
shāhānshāh, 30n, 36n, 306
shāhnāmeh (genre), 57
Shāhnāmeh, 13n, 38, 57n, 58, 139n *see also* Firdawsī
Shams al-Dawla, Abū Ṭāhir, 174n
Shāpūr b. Ardashīr, 104
Shaqīq b. Salama, 108
sharia (*sharīʿa, sharʿ*), 43n, 192n, 213, 218, 219, 232n, 278, 284, 307 *see also* religious law
al-Sharīf al-Murtaḍā, 37
al-Sharīf al-Raḍī, 37
Shash (Tashkent), 33
shawka, 45, 67, 117
Shāwur I b. Faḍl I, Abū l-Aswar, Shaddādid ruler, 59
al-Shayzarī, ʿAbd al-Raḥmān b. Naṣr, 19n, 20–1 (Fig. 1)
Sheba, 93, 96
shepherd, 89, 107, 111, 112, 132, 185, 238, 252, 291, 312
Shia, Shiʿi(sm), 13, 29, 30n, 36, 37, 93
see also Imamiyya, Ismaili(sm)
shiḥna, 199
Shiraz, 276n
Shuʿayb, 253, 291
shukr, shākir, 87, 292n *see also* gratitude
Sibṭ Ibn al-Jawzī, 13, 14n
Ṣiffīn, Battle of, 117n
al-Sijzī, Ṭāhir b. Muḥammad, 281
sikka, 33, 44n *see also* coinage
Sirāj al-mulūk, 17, 43–51, 70–5
sirr, 104
Sirr al-asrār, 8, 19, 33, 47–51, 77, 90n, 104n, 133n, 140n, 181, 183n, 185n, 208n, 212n
Sistan, 194, 253n
Sivas, 14n
siyar al-mulūk (genre), 5
Siyar al-mulūk (= *Siyāsatnāmeh*), 8, 12, 33n, 63–6, 79, 80, 190, 194n, 234, 282, 298n, 307n
siyāsa, 6n, 63, 90, 96, 97, 130, 185, 198n, 204, 206, 210, 213, 214, 239, 244, 246
~ *iṣlāḥiyya*, 204, 206, 213, 214, 218
~ *nabawiyya*, 204, 214, 218
see also governance, punishment
Siyāsat al-mulūk, 11
Smaragd, 10n
Socrates, 170
Solomon, 16n, 93, 163, 189, 207, 220
soul, 15, 56n, 98, 100, 106, 111, 116, 119, 121, 139n, 146, 151, 156, 157, 158, 159, 160, 161
carnal ~, 100, 106
faculties of ~, 15, 161n, 162, 164, 165, 167, 182, 187, 205, 210, 228, 231, 248, 255, 261, 278
rational ~, 279
see also nafs, *rūḥ*, self
Spain, 51, 71 *see also* Iberia

speculative (theoretical) philosophy, 15n
speculum, 3n *see also* mirror
speculum principis, 3
state, 26, 27, 28, 29, 30n, 37n, 40, 42, 44, 64, 74, 93, 128n, 130, 135, 148, 149, 151, 152, 153, 154, 185, 187, 190, 192n, 204, 213n, 218, 229, 230, 243, 244n, 269n, 283, 297n, 307, 308 *see also dawla*
Steele, Robert, 48n, 77, 181
steward, stewardship, 113, 215, 242, 243, 284 *see also kadkhudāy*, *mu'tamad*
story, 93, 113, 172, 173, 174, 191, 192, 193, 202n, 203, 210, 211n, 235, 236, 246n, 262n, 286, 289, 291, 292, 295, 297, 298n, 300n *see also* narrative
subject(s), 5, 23, 26n, 27n, 43, 53, 63, 64, 68, 83, 86, 89, 90, 91, 92, 93, 94, 97, 105, 106, 109, 111, 112, 114, 116, 122, 131, 132, 134, 135, 136, 137, 138, 139, 140, 143, 144, 149, 152, 153, 160, 180, 182, 183, 185, 186, 187, 188, 189, 190, 191n, 192, 198, 204, 205, 206, 209, 212, 213, 214, 216, 218, 220, 221, 224, 225, 226, 227, 228, 229, 230, 231, 233, 234, 235, 236, 237, 238, 240, 243, 245, 275, 276, 277, 281, 284, 286n, 309, 310 *see also ra'iyya*
Sufi(sm), 14, 32, 57, 177
Sufyān al-Thawrī, 270
al-Sulamī, Abū l-Faḍl Muḥammad b. Muḥammad, al-Ḥakīm al-Jalīl, 280
Sulaymān b. 'Abdallāh b. Ṭāhir, 263n, 269n
Sulaymān b. 'Abd al-Malik b. Marwān, 261
al-Ṣūlī, Abū Bakr Muḥammad b. Yaḥyā, 261, 262n
al-Ṣūlī, Ibrāhīm b. al-'Abbās, 99n, 118n
sulṭān, 4n, 10, 39n, 68n, 89, 93, 94, 95, 120, 121, 124, 132n, 135n, 137, 138, 140, 141, 156, 158, 185, 208, 214, 218n, 281, 311
sultanate, 43, 45, 67, 239n, 297
al-sulṭān al-mu'aẓẓam, 39, 44
Sulūk al-mālik fī tadbīr al-mamālik, 19n
sunna, *sunan*, 87, 90, 97, 109, 185, 196, 253, 307
Sunni(sm), 26, 30, 31, 32, 36, 37, 42n, 43, 44, 45, 66, 67, 70, 74, 120n, 166n, 194n
al-Suyūṭī, Jalāl al-Dīn, 23
Syria, 11n, 13, 14n, 31, 40n, 42, 44, 71, 74, 110n, 232n
Syriac, 7, 47, 182

Ṭabarak, 262
Tabaristan, 34, 173n, 297
tafrīṭ, 15
tafsīr, 62, 137
tafwīḍ, 189n
al-Taghlibī (al-Tha'labī), 10n, 53 *see also Kitāb al-Tāj*
Ṭāhir b. al-Ḥusayn Dhū l-Yamīnayn, 9, 25, 249, 267
  Testament of ~, 9
Tahirids, 25, 249, 263, 269n
al-Ṭā'i' li-Amr Allāh, Abbasid caliph, 274n, 275–6
takhlīṭ, 260, 261
takya, 294
talisman, 49
Tansar, Letter of, 7
Tashīl al-naẓar wa-ta'jīl al-ẓafar, 61–3, 79, 108n, 130, 155–6, 186, 217, 225n
tashjīr, 19
taṣnīf, 9
tax, taxation, 5n, 9, 26n, 27, 28, 29, 37, 117, 174, 213, 216, 217n, 219, 220, 223, 232n, 234, 235, 240, 246, 270n, 307
tax collectors, 235, 307
al-Taymī, Abū Muḥammad 'Abdallāh b. Ayyūb, 112
temperament, 140, 157, 261, 262 *see also mizāj*
temperance, 15, 161, 162n, 164, 165
testament, 7, 9, 25n, 92, 104, 105, 106, 123n, 134, 147n, 176, 205n, 249n
  ~ of an Indian king, 92, 104, 105, 205n
  see also waṣiyya
al-Tha'ālibī, Abū 'Alī, 129
al-Tha'ālibī, Abū Manṣūr, 22n, 38, 54–6, 60, 64, 78, 109–10, 111n, 114n, 115n, 117n, 120n, 121n, 124n, 125n, 126n, 127n, 129n, 130, 136, 138n, 182n, 189n, 205n, 208n, 209n, 245n, 259–60, 264n, 265n, 268n, 270n, 273n, 274n, 276n, 278n, 279n, 296n
Thamūd, 254n
Themistius, Letter to Julian, 7, 140n
Thumāma b. al-Ashras, 98
al-Tibr al-masbūk fī naṣīḥat al-mulūk, 69n, 80
Tigīn al-Jāmdār, 265–6
Tirmidh, 302, 304

titles
of books, 15, 19, 22, 47n, 49n, 68, 80n
of individuals, 30n, 36n, 39, 72, 265n, 267n, 283, 284, 296–309
titulature, 30n, 36n
Toledo, 73
Topuzoğlu, T. R., 78, 109n, 111n, 119n, 129n
Torah, 107n, 312n
Tortosa, 70, 71n, 72, 73
townspeople, city dwellers, 220, 221, 222, 223, 274
trade, 26, 34, 41, 198, 223, 224 *see also* commerce
translation
into Arabic, 7–8, 47, 58
into Persian, 34
of mirrors, 17
Transoxiana, 26, 33, 35, 116, 117, 122n, 193, 195n, 289n, 297, 306
treasurer, 57, 128
treasury, 197, 198, 201, 202, 220, 224n, 235, 237, 240, 241, 243, 244, 275n, 286, 287, 288, 299, 303, 304
trust, 19, 83, 94, 103, 104, 111, 113, 130, 133, 146, 150, 151, 182, 190n, 201, 202, 224, 228, 232, 236, 244, 264, 297, 299, 303, 305
in God, 14
-s, 60, 86, 95, 132, 224
trustee, a trusted person, 89, 201, 231, 236, 237, 238, 243
Tughril Bey, 38–40, 41, 44, 62, 181
Tuḥfa, 19 *see also* gift(s)
Tuḥfat al-saniyya fī siyāsat al-ra'iyya, 23
Tulunids, 25
Tunisia, 31, 42, 198n
Turan, 57, 139n
Turkish, 3, 4, 5, 6, 7, 8, 10, 16, 17, 24, 25, 27, 28, 34, 35, 37, 38, 39n, 42, 45, 49, 50, 51, 56, 57, 58, 61, 74, 77, 78, 79, 80, 81, 83, 85, 147n, 244n, 267, 268n, 269n, 270n, 271n, 273n, 274n, 284, 296, 298n, 299, 300, 301, 308
Türkmen, 27, 28, 41, 244n
al-Ṭurṭūshī, Abū Bakr Muḥammad b. al-Walīd, 10, 17, 43–51, 70–5, 81, 92n, 139–40, 163n, 203–4, 206n, 207n, 208n, 209n, 213n, 215n, 218, 247, 256n, 257n, 259, 267n, 309
Tus, 41
Tuzun, 273n
Tyre, 43, 73

'Ubayd Allāh b. 'Abdallāh b. Ṭāhir, 102n, 107n
'Ubayd Allāh b. Sulaymān Ibn Wahb, 128
'Ubayd Allāh b. 'Umar, 211n, 252–3
'Ubayd Allāh al-'Umarī, 312
'Ubayd Allāh b. Yaḥyā b. Khāqān, 268n
Uighur, 58
'Umar I b. al-Khaṭṭāb, second caliph, 69, 74, 113n, 131, 182, 207n, 210, 211n, 248, 250, 253n, 255, 257, 270, 289–91, 312
'Umar II b. 'Abd al-'Azīz, Umayyad caliph, 69, 205n, 211, 257, 270
'Umar b. Hubayra, 252n
Umayyad(s), 7, 48n, 103, 107n, 116n, 135n, 213n, 220n, 221n, 252n, 253n, 257n, 261n, 266n, 270
unbelief, 117, 138, 206, 214, 256, 281, 297, 305
Universal Intellect, 177
Urmavī, Sirāj al-Dīn Maḥmūd b. Abī Bakr, 15, 18n
'Uthmān b. 'Abdallāh, 131
'Uthmān b. 'Affān, third caliph, 121, 129, 211
'Uyūn al-akhbār, 10, 247, 253n

Vayshgird, 289
verse, 13, 61, 62, 91n, 99, 100, 101n, 107n, 116n, 118, 144, 145, 150, 152, 153, 157n, 163n, 173, 263n, 268n, 269, 276n
Qur'anic ~(s), 13, 62, 69, 87n, 96, 114, 115n, 136, 137, 138n, 196n, 199n, 209, 254n
Via Regia, 10n
vice(s), 15, 63, 87, 102, 144, 147, 151, 157, 158, 161, 162, 164, 165
virtue(s), 13, 14, 15, 58, 63, 83, 87, 96, 97, 98, 100, 102, 104, 107, 120n, 121n, 143, 144, 145, 146, 147, 148, 151, 154, 155, 156, 157, 158, 159, 160, 161, 162, 164, 165, 166, 167, 168, 169, 170, 172n, 181, 184, 199, 201, 204n, 247, 251, 277
cardinal ~, 15, 161n
rational ~, 161n

vizier(s), 4, 10, 13, 16, 17, 22, 36, 40, 42, 43, 49, 55, 56, 57, 60, 62, 63, 64, 65, 66, 69, 71, 72, 75, 92, 100n, 125, 126n, 127, 128n, 191n, 205, 210, 234, 235–47, 249, 250, 260, 265, 266n, 268n, 275, 277n, 279n, 280n, 283, 284, 294n, 298n, 305, 308, 311
Vushmgīr, Ziyarid ruler, 34

wālī, *wulāt* (Pers. *vālī*), 67, 68n, 92, 107, 132, 210
al-Walīd b. ʿAbd al-Malik, Umayyad caliph, 206n, 273n
al-Walīd b. Hishām, Umayyad, 138n
Waraqa b. Nawfal, 258
warfare, 34, 55, 60, 74, 119, 264, 275, 285 *see also ghazw*, *jihād*
Waṣīf al-Turkī, 268n
waṣiyya, 9, 92, 104n, 107n, 249n
see also testament
water, 98, 140, 141, 218, 219, 220, 221, 225, 237, 269, 288, 290, 291n, 205
~ used as metaphor, 69, 100, 149, 150, 152, 177, 261
al-Wāthiq, Abbasid caliph, 127, 128, 261, 270n
wealth, 29, 37, 52, 60, 63, 95, 103, 112, 150, 151, 152, 163n, 171, 180, 189, 191, 201, 202, 208, 217, 223, 230, 236, 240, 245, 258, 267, 271, 275, 286, 287, 288, 292, 294, 299, 312
welfare, well-being (*ṣalāḥ*), 4, 53, 92, 94, 104, 110, 112, 132, 133, 134, 137, 157, 180n, 188, 204, 210, 213, 214, 217, 218, 219, 220, 224, 225, 226, 227, 229, 236, 247, 254, 295
Westöstlicher Divan, 61
Wide Awake, 56, 57
wine, 55, 56n, 60, 129, 152, 178, 260, 261, 268, 279
wisdom, 15, 19, 35, 58, 70, 87, 88, 91n, 103, 110, 111n, 114, 119, 136, 137, 144, 145, 147, 151, 154, 162n, 164, 165n, 167, 170, 182, 183, 185, 189, 210, 214, 256, 257, 298
~ literature, 7, 17
women, 65, 70, 105, 112, 165, 168, 178, 187, 202, 212, 220, 246, 252, 272, 283n, 284, 291n, 297n, 299

Yaḥyā b. Aktham, 211
Yaḥyā b. Muʿādh al-Rāzī, 114
Yamīn al-Dawla, *laqab* of Maḥmūd of Ghazna, 281, 297, 306
Yaʿqūb Ibn Killis, 42–3
Yaʿqūb b. al-Layth, Saffarid ruler, 191, 193, 194, 195, 196, 197
Yavari, Neguin, 63n, 234n
Yazdagird 'the Sinner', Sasanian monarch, 138, 139n
Yazīd b. Shajara al-Rahāwī, 124
Yazīd b. ʿUmar Ibn Hubayra, 252n
Yemen, 42, 96n, 107n, 267
Yūsuf Ibn Tāshufīn, Abū Yaʿqūb, 72
Yūsuf Khāṣṣ Ḥājib, 35, 56–9, 78, 144–55, 147n

Zaḥḥāk, 138, 139n
ẓāhir, 54, 88, 111n, 183n
zakāt, 141 *see also ṣadaqa*
Zanj, 272
Zaragoza, 71
Zarang, 193, 194n
Zayd b. Aslam, 289–91
Ziyād b. Abīhi (Ziyād b. Abī Sufyān), 220
Ziyarids, 34, 36, 39, 55, 59, 167, 174n
Zubayda, 287–9
al-Zubayr b. al-ʿAwwām, 220
Zuhayr b. Abī Sulmā, 281

CAMBRIDGE TEXTS IN THE HISTORY OF POLITICAL THOUGHT

Titles published in the series thus far

Aquinas *Political Writings* (edited and translated by R. W. Dyson)
Aristotle *The Politics and The Constitution of Athens* (edited and translated by Stephen Everson)
Arnold *Culture and Anarchy and Other Writings* (edited by Stefan Collini)
Astell *Political Writings* (edited by Patricia Springborg)
Augustine *The City of God against the Pagans* (edited and translated by R. W. Dyson)
Augustine *Political Writings* (edited by E. M. Atkins and R. J. Dodaro)
Austin *The Province of Jurisprudence Determined* (edited by Wilfrid E. Rumble)
Bacon *The History of the Reign of King Henry VII* (edited by Brian Vickers)
Bagehot *The English Constitution* (edited by Paul Smith)
Bakunin *Statism and Anarchy* (edited and translated by Marshall Shatz)
Baxter *Holy Commonwealth* (edited by William Lamont)
Bayle *Political Writings* (edited by Sally L. Jenkinson)
Beccaria *On Crimes and Punishments and Other Writings* (edited by Richard Bellamy; translated by Richard Davies)
Bentham *A Fragment on Government* (edited by Ross Harrison)
Bernstein *The Preconditions of Socialism* (edited and translated by Henry Tudor)
Bodin *On Sovereignty* (edited and translated by Julian H. Franklin)
Bolingbroke *Political Writings* (edited by David Armitage)
Bossuet *Politics Drawn from the Very Words of Holy Scripture* (edited and translated by Patrick Riley)
Botero *The Reason of State* (edited and translated by Robert Bireley)
The British Idealists (edited by David Boucher)
Burke *Pre-Revolutionary Writings* (edited by Ian Harris)
Burke *Revolutionary Writings* (edited by Iain Hampsher-Monk)
Cavendish *Political Writings* (edited by Susan James)
Christine de Pizan *The Book of the Body Politic* (edited by Kate Langdon Forhan)
Cicero *On Duties* (edited by E. M. Atkins; edited and translated by M. T. Griffin)
Cicero *On the Commonwealth and On the Laws* (edited and translated by James E. G. Zetzel)
Comte *Early Political Writings* (edited and translated by H. S. Jones)
Comte *Conciliarism and Papalism* (edited by J. H. Burns and Thomas M. Izbicki)
Condorcet *Political Writings* (edited by Steven Lukes and Nadia Urbinati)
Constant *Political Writings* (edited and translated by Biancamaria Fontana)
Dante *Monarchy* (edited and translated by Prue Shaw)
Diderot *Political Writings* (edited and translated by John Hope Mason and Robert Wokler)
The Dutch Revolt (edited and translated by Martin van Gelderen)

Early Greek Political Thought from Homer to the Sophists (edited and translated by Michael Gagarin and Paul Woodruff)
The Early Political Writings of the German Romantics (edited and translated by Frederick C. Beiser)
Emerson *Political Writings* (edited by Kenneth S. Sacks)
The English Levellers (edited by Andrew Sharp)
Erasmus *The Education of a Christian Prince with the Panegyric for Archduke Philip of Austria* (edited and translated by Lisa Jardine; translated by Neil M. Cheshire and Michael J. Heath)
Fénelon *Telemachus* (edited and translated by Patrick Riley)
Ferguson *An Essay on the History of Civil Society* (edited by Fania Oz-Salzberger)
Fichte *Addresses to the German Nation* (edited by Gregory Moore)
Filmer *Patriarcha and Other Writings* (edited by Johann P. Sommerville)
Fletcher *Political Works* (edited by John Robertson)
Sir John Fortescue *On the Laws and Governance of England* (edited by Shelley Lockwood)
Fourier *The Theory of the Four Movements* (edited by Gareth Stedman Jones; edited and translated by Ian Patterson)
Franklin *The Autobiography and Other Writings on Politics, Economics, and Virtue* (edited by Alan Houston)
Gramsci *Pre-Prison Writings* (edited by Richard Bellamy; translated by Virginia Cox)
Guicciardini *Dialogue on the Government of Florence* (edited and translated by Alison Brown)
Hamilton, Madison, and Jay (writing as 'Publius') *The Federalist with Letters of 'Brutus'* (edited by Terence Ball)
Harrington *The Commonwealth of Oceana and A System of Politics* (edited by J. G. A. Pocock)
Hegel *Elements of the Philosophy of Right* (edited by Allen W. Wood; translated by H. B. Nisbet)
Hegel *Political Writings* (edited by Laurence Dickey and H. B. Nisbet)
Hess *The Holy History of Mankind and Other Writings* (edited and translated by Shlomo Avineri)
Hobbes *On the Citizen* (edited and translated by Michael Silverthorne and Richard Tuck)
Hobbes *Leviathan* (edited by Richard Tuck)
Hobhouse *Liberalism and Other Writings* (edited by James Meadowcroft)
Hooker *Of the Laws of Ecclesiastical Polity* (edited by A. S. McGrade)
Hume *Political Essays* (edited by Knud Haakonssen)
Jefferson *Political Writings* (edited by Joyce Appleby and Terence Ball)
John of Salisbury *Policraticus* (edited by Cary J. Nederman)
Kant *Political Writings* (edited by H. S. Reiss; translated by H. B. Nisbet)
King James VI and I *Political Writings* (edited by Johann P. Sommerville)
Knox *On Rebellion* (edited by Roger A. Mason)

Kropotkin *The Conquest of Bread and Other Writings* (edited by Marshall Shatz)
Kumazawa Banzan *Governing the Realm and bringing Peace to All below Heaven* (edited and translated by John A. Tucker)
Lawson *Politica Sacra et Civilis* (edited by Conal Condren)
Leibniz *Political Writings* (edited and translated by Patrick Riley)
Lincoln *Political Writings and Speeches* (edited by Terence Ball)
Locke *Political Essays* (edited by Mark Goldie)
Locke *Two Treatises of Government* (edited by Peter Laslett)
Loyseau *A Treatise of Orders and Plain Dignities* (edited and translated by Howell A. Lloyd)
Loyseau *Luther and Calvin on Secular Authority* (edited and translated by Harro Höpfl)
Machiavelli *The Prince, Second Edition* (edited by Quentin Skinner and Russell Price)
Joseph de Maistre *Considerations on France* (edited and translated by Richard A. Lebrun)
Maitland *State, Trust and Corporation* (edited by David Runciman and Magnus Ryan)
Malthus *An Essay on the Principle of Population* (edited by Donald Winch)
Marsiglio of Padua *Defensor minor and De translatione Imperii* (edited by Cary J. Nederman)
Marsilius of Padua *The Defender of the Peace* (edited and translated by Annabel Brett)
Marx *Early Political Writings* (edited and translated by Joseph O'Malley)
James Mill *Political Writings* (edited by Terence Ball)
J. S. Mill *On Liberty and Other Writings* (edited by Stefan Collini)
Milton *Political Writings* (edited by Martin Dzelzainis; translated by Claire Gruzelier)
Montesquieu *The Spirit of the Laws* (edited and translated by Anne M. Cohler, Basia Carolyn Miller, and Harold Samuel Stone)
More *Utopia* (edited by George M. Logan and Robert M. Adams)
Morris *News from Nowhere* (edited by Krishan Kumar)
Nicholas of Cusa *The Catholic Concordance* (edited and translated by Paul E. Sigmund)
Nietzsche *On the Genealogy of Morality* (edited by Keith Ansell-Pearson; translated by Carol Diethe)
Paine *Political Writings* (edited by Bruce Kuklick)
William Penn *Political Writings* (edited by Andrew R. Murphy)
Plato *Gorgias, Menexenus, Protagoras* (edited by Malcolm Schofield; translated by Tom Griffith)
Plato *Laws* (edited by Malcolm Schofield; translated by Tom Griffith)
Plato *The Republic* (edited by G. R. F. Ferrari; translated by Tom Griffith)
Plato *Statesman* (edited by Julia Annas; edited and translated by Robin Waterfield)

Political Thought in Portugal and its Empire, c.1500–1800 (edited by Pedro Cardim and Nuno Gonçalo Monteiro)
The Political Thought of the Irish Revolution (edited by Richard Bourke and Niamh Gallagher)
Price *Political Writings* (edited by D. O. Thomas)
Priestley *Political Writings* (edited by Peter Miller)
Proudhon *What Is Property?* (edited and translated by Donald R. Kelley and Bonnie G. Smith)
Pufendorf *On the Duty of Man and Citizen according to Natural Law* (edited by James Tully; translated by Michael Silverthorne)
The Radical Reformation (edited and translated by Michael G. Baylor)
Rousseau *The Discourses and Other Early Political Writings* (edited and translated by Victor Gourevitch)
Rousseau *The Social Contract and Other Later Political Writings* (edited and translated by Victor Gourevitch)
Seneca *Moral and Political Essays* (edited and translated by John M. Cooper; edited by J. F. Procopé)
Sidney *Court Maxims* (edited by Hans W. Blom, Eco Haitsma Mulier, and Ronald Janse)
Sorel *Reflections on Violence* (edited by Jeremy Jennings)
Spencer *Political Writings* (edited by John Offer)
Stirner *The Ego and Its Own* (edited by David Leopold)
Emperor Taizong and ministers *The Essentials of Governance* (compiled by Wu Jing; edited and translated by Hilde De Weerdt, Glen Dudbridge, and Gabe van Beijeren)
Thoreau *Political Writings* (edited by Nancy L. Rosenblum)
Tönnies *Community and Civil Society* (edited and translated by Jose Harris; translated by Margaret Hollis)
Utopias of the British Enlightenment (edited by Gregory Claeys)
Vico *The First New Science* (edited and translated by Leon Pompa)
Vitoria *Political Writings* (edited by Anthony Pagden and Jeremy Lawrance)
Voltaire *Political Writings* (edited and translated by David Williams)
Weber *Political Writings* (edited by Peter Lassman; edited and translated by Ronald Speirs)
William of Ockham *A Short Discourse on Tyrannical Government* (edited by Arthur Stephen McGrade; translated by John Kilcullen)
William of Ockham *A Letter to the Friars Minor and Other Writings* (edited by Arthur Stephen McGrade; edited and translated by John Kilcullen)
Wollstonecraft *A Vindication of the Rights of Men and A Vindication of the Rights of Woman* (edited by Sylvana Tomaselli)

Printed in the United States
by Baker & Taylor Publisher Services